◎ STEALING AMERICA ◎

STEALING AMERICA

*The Hidden Story of
Indigenous Slavery in
US History*

LINFORD D. FISHER

Liveright Publishing Corporation

*A Division of W. W. Norton & Company
Independent Publishers Since 1923*

For information about permission to reproduce selections from this book, write to
Permissions, Liveright Publishing Corporation, a division of
W. W. Norton & Company, Inc., 500 Fifth Avenue, New York, NY 10110

For information about special discounts for bulk purchases, please contact
W. W. Norton Special Sales at specialsales@wwnorton.com or 800-233-4830

Manufacturing by Lakeside Book Company
Book design by Lovedog Studio
Production manager: Anna Oler

Library of Congress Cataloging-in-Publication Data
Names: Fisher, Linford D. author
Title: Stealing America : the hidden story of
Indigenous slavery in US history / Linford D. Fisher.
Other titles: Hidden story of Indigenous slavery in US history
Description: First edition. | New York : Liveright Publishing Corporation, a division
of W. W. Norton & Company, [2026] | Includes bibliographical references and index.
Identifiers: LCCN 2025038099 | ISBN 9781324094951 hardcover
Subjects: LCSH: Enslaved Indians—North America—History | Enslaved Indians—
United States—History | Slavery—North America—History | Slavery—United
States—History | Indians, Treatment of—North America—History | Indians,
Treatment of—United States—History | Slave trade—North America—History |
Slave trade—United States—History
Classification: LCC E98.S6 F57 2026
LC record available at https://lccn.loc.gov/2025038099

Liveright Publishing Corporation, 500 Fifth Avenue, New York, NY 10110
www.wwnorton.com

W. W. Norton & Company Ltd., 15 Carlisle Street, London W1D 3BS

Authorized EU representative: EAS, Mustamäe tee 50, 10621 Tallinn, Estonia

10 9 8 7 6 5 4 3 2 1

For Tall Oak Weeden
(1936–2022)

TALL OAK WEEDEN, ST. DAVID'S ISLAND,
BERMUDA, 2018.

ARTIST'S STATEMENT

"Reclaiming our Relatives"
Silvermoon LaRose (Narragansett)
(cover, frontispiece, and inside sections)

The trauma of Indigenous enslavement has touched many families over centuries, spanning across the Americas. The stealing of our loved ones from our communities is a disturbing legacy of those who have survived colonization. That trauma of abduction didn't end with emancipation but continued in what is now known as the MMIP movement, Missing Murdered Indigenous People. That movement is swathed in red, a bold color that demands attention to an issue that has not been rectified, the unsolved disappearances of our relatives. The figures in this portrait are clothed in red, placing them among the many thousands stolen from our communities for generations, calling attention to their stories in an effort to claim justice. These relatives are as diverse in characteristics, as are their stories. Incidents of stolen Indigenous people of all ages have encompassed the Americas since first contact. The unique identities that connected them to their families were often erased in the records. In the portrait, we see glimpses of those identities in the shades of their skin, the textures of their hair, the adornments on their bodies, but no definite faces. In chronicling this history, their stories are reclaimed, restoring our relatives to us.

CONTENTS

Part Four: RESURGENCE *(1820–1880)*

Part Five: TRANSFORMATIONS *(1880–1978)*

PREFACE

THE REALITY THAT INDIGENOUS PEOPLE HAVE BEEN STOLEN and enslaved in large numbers throughout American history was new to me, and it might be to you as well. So, too, was the connection between stealing people and stealing land and the understanding that both practices were central to the growth and development of the United States. This will come as no surprise to Native peoples, of course, since they and their ancestors experienced this directly. They have retained knowledge of these realities in oral histories and continue to wrestle with such legacies today, even if those accounts have been mostly excluded from the main narrative of American history.

The scale of this particular hidden layer of history slowly emerged for me in graduate school while reading some new works in the field, including Allan Gallay's *The Indian Slave Trade* about Native American slavery in the Carolinas.[1] At the same time, I was delving into New England church records for my dissertation research, and I began noticing references to Native "servants" in documents from the 1740s. This surprised me because enslaved Native Americans were not part of the usual telling of the history of New England or slavery. I didn't have answers at the time, so I made a few notes and moved on. But the presence of these people and the questions they provoked haunted me even as I finished up the dissertation and, later, the book (published in 2012 as *The Indian Great Awakening*).[2]

It wasn't until June 2011 that I was able to return to these queries. As I began searching for more such archival instances in the United States, the Caribbean, and the United Kingdom, I was flabbergasted by how much evidence for Native enslavement exists in bits and pieces if we are willing to look for it. The information I found in every archive caused this book to grow in its geographical and chronological reach. Native American enslavement was everywhere, it seemed, and was intermingled with land theft in cyclical ways throughout English and American colonization in the Americas. I added chapters on the nineteenth century to account for westward colonization but soon discovered that even chronological extension was not enough because the labor focus of boarding schools and adoptions in the late nineteenth and twentieth centuries was central to the ongoing stealing of Native children and land. And thus a shorter book became a longer one.

Beyond the archives, tribal collaborations and insights were essential for this project. Many of these conversations took place as part of a tribally collaborative project at Brown University called *Stolen Relations: Recovering Stories of Indigenous Enslavement in the Americas* (stolenrelations.org). Our exchanges redirected my attention toward tribal-centered understandings of slavery, land loss, and the long legacies of historical trauma up to the present.

Many of these discussions were with the late Pequot and Wampanoag elder Tall Oak Weeden, whose insights were deeply formative. Our paths crossed dozens of times between our first meeting in 2005 and his passing in 2022—at conferences, on campus at Brown, in the archives in Bermuda, and even in his home, which was lined with precariously stacked photocopies and old crinkly papers gathered from archives and libraries. One of his most repeated lines was that Americans are taught a stunningly sanitized—"white-washed" was the phrase he always used—version of American history throughout their primary and secondary educations. White people prefer cleaned-up versions of the past, he affirmed, one that clears them of wrongdoing by ignoring their violence against Native peoples. His encouragement to me and others was always to "connect the dots" to see the larger picture.[3] Both this book—which is dedicated to him—and the Stolen Relations project are attempts to ensure that we have the resources to tell more honest, interconnected histories.

None of these perspectives were part of my upbringing in southeastern Pennsylvania among the Amish and Mennonites, on traditional homelands of the Lenape. Growing up I heard very little about them or any Native nations, frankly. Like some other immigrants to

Turtle Island (what many Indigenous people call North America), my family's own Anabaptist histories and narratives of displacement and migration left little room for the consideration of the original inhabitants who had been displaced by our arrival. While I have attempted to tell these histories in a way that I hope is honest in its narrations of violence and yet respectful of Native peoples, past and present, in the end I and all non-Natives who benefit from the ongoing settler occupation of this country continue to bear the responsibility of working toward a more just future.

A NOTE REGARDING TERMINOLOGY

THE TERMS WE USE TO REFER TO PEOPLE AND CONCEPTS IS AN intensely sensitive issue with ever-changing preferences, and I respect the varying views present and future readers may hold. I hope that my word choices, which are offered in good faith, will not prevent you from engaging with the content of this book.

Throughout this volume, I refer to tribal names when possible, but I also interchangeably use the terms *Indigenous, Native, Native American, American Indian,* and *Indian*.[1] In my experience and conversations with Native scholars and tribal members, there is no one universally agreed-upon designator preferred by Native peoples today (although tribal names are always best when possible). And despite *Indian* perhaps feeling like the most outdated term, it is also one of the most common and durable designations in the United States. Not only is *Indian* used in virtually all the sources up through the late twentieth century, it is also ensconced in US Federal Indian Law through treaties, Supreme Court cases, and laws (in addition to being used, officially and colloquially, by some Native nations today). But as my Caribbean friends remind me, using *Indian* creates immense confusion for scholars regarding laborers in the nineteenth-century Caribbean from the subcontinent of India, who are also called Indians.

While I intentionally use *nation* when referring to Native American polities as a way of recognizing their appropriate international stature, sovereignty, and self-governance, I also intermingle terms like *tribe, band, clan,* and *community* when applicable, in part to vary the language but also to recognize the complexity of Indigenous social organization.[2]

Similarly, although there is no perfect way to refer to people with multiple ethnic and racial family lines, I employ a variety of terms like *mixed-race Indigenous* and *multiracial Native*, usually to recover Indigenous identities that the records have obscured. I do so without meaning at all to negate or erase Black identity, which in many cases was also part of mixed-race Indigenous identities. By highlighting the Indigenous aspects of these individuals, I hope to restore what has been hidden by the archives in ways that honor the multiple identities that mixed-race Indigenous people claim and have felt historically.

Furthermore, I use a wide range of terms to refer to people caught up in various forms of captivity, servitude, and slavery. I mostly use the term *enslaved* rather than *slave* when possible to acknowledge that slavery was an imposed condition, not a permanent state of being or identity. But in other cases, *captive* and *servant* are more precise, especially where initial stealing or abduction could lead to a liminal phase that preceded enslavement or where actual servitude status was unclear. When appropriate, I use the word *enslaver* for people who claimed control over peoples' bodies and labor. I also follow recent scholarship in questioning the terms *master* and *owner*—both of which imply somewhat static states of total domination. And yet, since *owner* and *master* were legal designations that applied differently to the range of servitude types imposed on Indigenous people, I use *legal master* and *legal owner* to denaturalize such claims. In all of these cases, I at times intermingle newer and older terminology for ease of reading.

Scholars have long tried to define *slavery*, and many of them use the League of Nations definition from 1926 as a starting place, which states it to be "the status or condition of a person over whom any or all of the powers attaching to the right of ownership are exercised."[3] The experiences of stolen and captive Natives did not always fit such a rigid definition, and many people found themselves in myriad situations of indenture, limited-term slavery, debt peonage, and captivity in addition to chattel slavery. Native languages, too, contain various terms for these experiences of stealing and bondage, as well as freedom, including *we-hait-wat-sha*, the Haudenosaunee term for captive that means "a body cut into parts and scattered around," or the

Cherokee phrase *atsi nahsa'i*, or "one who is owned."[4] Throughout this history, Native people defined freedom and sovereignty as often as they did slavery, usually while protesting mistreatment. As Miskitu leaders stated to British officials in 1780, for them freedom meant to live "without Molestation," to labor if "they chuse themselves to be so employed," to be fairly compensated for the labor, and to be "at liberty" to come and go at will.[5]

In an effort to connect past histories of enslavement to modern forms, I have followed recent studies that use the language of *trafficking*.[6] While this might feel jarring to some readers, it helps us understand the continuities of experience across time and space, whether captives transported in the early modern period for the purposes of enslavement, children stolen and transported to plantations or schools, or girls and women—then and now—who were and are forcibly removed from their homes for the purposes of sexual exploitation.

Although the surviving documents largely use gender binaries for Indigenous people, I recognize that Two-Spirit individuals were present throughout this history, even if their gender identities were suppressed by colonizers and perhaps especially ignored by the English and Americans.[7] As Chickasaw tribal member and scholar Chase Bryer has noted, "Many tribes had traditional tribal language terms that included more than two genders. Two-Spirit people were revered as healers, mediators, and held special roles in ceremonies."[8]

Finally, I generally follow terminology in the field by using *English* and *England* for colonists and their home country prior to the Acts of Union in 1708, after which *British* and *Britain* is more appropriate. As with other terms, I often use *English* alongside of *British* in later periods for ease of reading.

◎ STEALING AMERICA ◎

Prologue

STEALING INDIGENOUS PEOPLE AND LAND

ON A SUN-DRENCHED DAY IN JUNE 2018, A WOMAN IN TRADITIONAL
Native regalia dropped a large wreath of flowers into the Atlantic
Ocean. The impact jostled loose a few petals before the circle of blossoms slowly drifted away on the luminescent blue Bermudian swells. All
of the one hundred or so people gathered were silent, each absorbed
by their own thoughts. In its departure, the wreath commemorated
the journey of enslaved New England Native Americans to the island
nearly four hundred years earlier.[1]

Within an hour, the somber commemoration by the sea turned into
a vibrant two-day intertribal powwow. Representatives from the Narragansett, Wampanoag, and other nations in New England mingled
with Bermuda Natives on St. David's Island as they participated in
dancing, feasting, and communing. Men and boys fulfilled traditional
roles around a large circular drum, beating it rhythmically. Dancers in
brightly colored moccasins, robes, and headdresses shifted from one
foot to the other in a line around the large grassy space encircled by
tents. The smell of fry bread and stew wafted through the air, and for
hours the singing and drumming drifted skyward as the flower wreath
slowly caught a current and slipped out of sight into the open sea.

Native American powwows are important cultural celebrations, but
this one in Bermuda memorializes events often hidden in American history: the large-scale enslavement of Indigenous people and the simultaneous taking of Native land. The ancestors of the Bermuda powwow
attendees were part of this buried and intertwined history.

Nearly four hundred years earlier, New England puritans hunted
down well over one thousand Pequots, Wampanoags, Narragansetts,

RECONNECTION POWWOW,
ST. DAVID'S ISLAND, BERMUDA, JUNE 2018.

Nipmucs, and individuals from other nations and shipped them to Bermuda, Barbados, Spain, Mexico, and other international destinations. This took place during and after two wars between the puritans and local Indigenous populations. The first was the Pequot War in the 1630s, in which puritans tried to completely exterminate the Pequot nation. The second was King Philip's War in the 1670s, which was a massive uprising in response to the harms of colonialism. During and after both wars, puritans used large-scale enslavement of Native peoples to bolster their labor force and help clear land for colonial settlement.[2]

Native peoples in New England and Bermuda kept alive their family histories and stories throughout the centuries, even when colonial documents suppressed or omitted these connections. In Bermuda, enslaved Native Americans from New England and other regions eventually intermarried with enslaved and free Africans. After British emancipation in 1834, many of their descendants settled on St. David's Island, in the northern part of the archipelago. There they continued to work, connect, and intermarry into the twenty-first century, and they remain to this day.[3]

When St. David's Islanders and New England Natives started exploring this shared history in the late 1990s, they realized a vital reunification was taking place. Starting in 2002, the reconnection powwows like

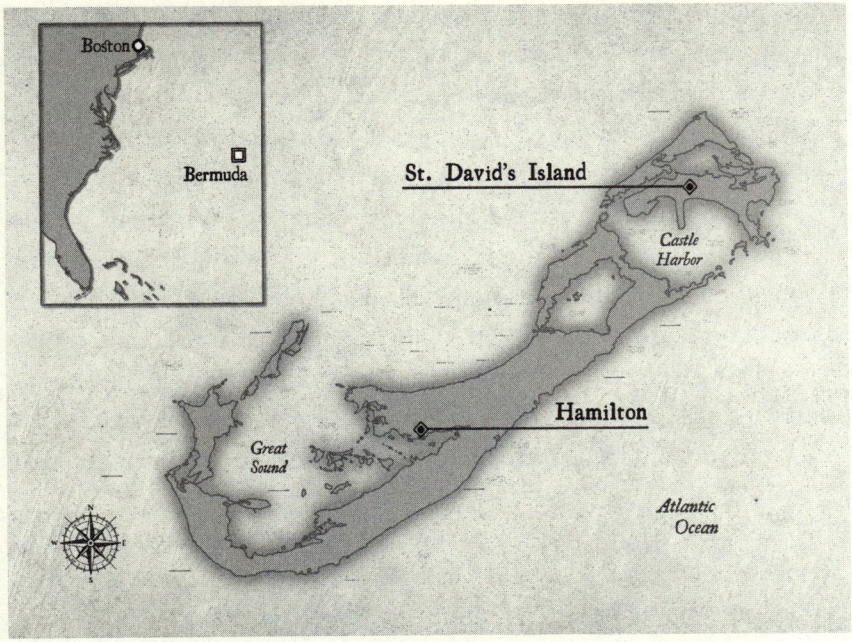

BERMUDA AND ST. DAVID'S ISLAND, CA. 1650.

the one I attended in June 2018 have served as a meaningful way for Natives in both New England and Bermuda to bring together what the violence of colonialism tore apart. As Nives Filice, whose ancestors were enslaved and sent to Bermuda, told me over lunch in the capital city of Hamilton, "Reconnecting with people in New England plugged a hole that I didn't even know existed. . . . When I first stepped foot on Mashpee Wampanoag tribal lands [in Massachusetts], I instantly felt a spiritual connection, like I was home."[4]

THIS BOOK USES THE CONCEPT OF *stealing* to understand Native Americans' experiences of losing kin and land—something I gleaned from many conversations with Native American collaborators and friends.[5] Scholarly writing about slavery in the Americas—which has mostly centered on Black enslavement—has emphasized its economic value in building plantations, wealth, and American capitalism.[6] But Native Americans experienced slavery as stealing of relatives, as a community loss, and it was always intermingled with the stealing of their land and disregard for their sovereignty. From their perspectives, stealing *people*, whether for enslavement or by forcing children into boarding schools, and seizing *land*, in wars or through removals, represented tangible community losses as part of a longer-term assault on their very existence.

Although largely erased from public consciousness, Indigenous enslavement was a colossal phenomenon that spanned the entire Americas, ensnaring an estimated 3 million to 6 million Indigenous people between 1492 and 1880 from Canada to Brazil.[7] In the area that later became the United States, as many as 600,000 Native Americans were enslaved during this period, with many more stolen from families into the twentieth century through boarding school, fostering, and adoption programs.[8] In comparison, approximately 530,000 enslaved Africans were forcibly transported to North America (excluding Mexico) through 1865.[9]

These numbers reveal a shocking truth: American forefathers and foremothers enslaved Native Americans in roughly the same numbers as they imported enslaved Africans. Enslaved African-descended people later came to officially outnumber enslaved Natives through reproduction as well as the erasure of Native Americans from the records when individuals from the two groups intermarried. Still, Native slavery was far more prominent and long lasting in American history than we have realized.

The enslavement of more than a half million Indigenous men, women, and children within the boundaries of what is now the United States is almost unthinkable because it defies what we have been taught about both American history and slavery. The conventional narrative of American slavery goes something like this: After Columbus "discovered" the Americas, the Spanish enslaved Native Americans in the Caribbean and South America until 1542, when it was outlawed and they instead started importing enslaved Africans. When the English landed in Jamestown in 1607, colonists first used white indentured servants but soon began importing enslaved Africans in 1619. This inaugurated the transatlantic African slave trade, which lasted until 1808, when it was banned by Congress. Black slavery expanded in the South until the American Civil War, when it was legally terminated by the Thirteenth Amendment in 1865.[10]

But that story is glaringly incomplete. *Stealing America* dramatically expands this history by tracing Indigenous enslavement and land dispossession throughout the full range of American history. This wider story spans five centuries from the first enslavement of the Caribbean Lucayan and Taíno in 1492 to the Indian Child Welfare Act in 1978, which slowly halted the stealing of tens of thousands of Native children through adoptions.[11] As Alexis Moreis (Chappaquiddick Wampanoag) has noted, "When we are talking about Native American slavery, it always involves dispossession."[12] There is not a time or place in American history when these intertwined stealings were not viscerally present. And yet this book is not a comprehensive Native American history of the continent, nor is it a detailed history of the United States. Rather, it tugs on the specific threads of Indigenous slavery and land loss, demonstrating their centrality to and ubiquity in every colony and state, in every era of American history.[13]

This centuries-long saga is one of both persistent colonialism *and* Indigenous resilience. A vast diversity of Indigenous peoples across the continent have found ways to negotiate and survive the waves of invading Europeans and Americans from 1492 to the present. This resilience has manifested in many forms. Powerful Native nations and smaller communities resisted and limited colonial aggression through diplomacy, alliances, petitions and court cases, and wars of resistance. Stolen and enslaved Indigenous people formed new networks of kinship;

DEMONSTRATION IN SUPPORT OF THE
INDIAN CHILD WELFARE ACT, 2022.

learned new skills and languages; retained memories of family, kin, and rituals; and, through it all, continually plotted to return home.

Colonization contained twists and turns. Native leaders and nations did not see themselves as universally on the same "side" as other Indigenous peoples and against all Europeans. Faced with foreign invasions, they made choices for survival and sovereignty that seem unexpected from a modern perspective. In some instances, Indigenous nations played surprising roles as collaborators with English merchants to conduct the large-scale slave trade of Native peoples, including in the Carolinas, Utah, and even Central America. As Narragansett scholar Mack Scott has noted, "Native Americans had their own histories, networks, goals, and purposes apart from European invaders."[14]

Although *Stealing America* focuses on the history of Indigenous slavery and land loss, this history also frequently intermingles with the story of African slavery. These are not competing histories since at times they connect and overlap. Nor does focusing on Native slavery minimize the weighty importance of Black slavery in US history. The damage and dislocation caused by Native enslavement and dispossession are part of a broader, layered, and "multidirectional" trauma in American history that involves Native Americans and African Americans, as well as Asian Americans, Mexican Americans, refugees, immigrants, and other historically marginalized populations. These injustices also coalesce with innumerable historical and contemporary global histories of genocide and displacement.[15] Such stories, along with the incredible resilience of populations harmed by colonialism, need to be told and understood to promote justice and healing. And yet this particular history of Indigenous enslavement and land theft in American history has been so obscured that it merits its own telling.

THE STEALING OF NATIVE AMERICANS and their homelands is not just a side story in the grand drama of American history. It is the central river that connects all other streams, coursing through the landscape of this country's past like the muddy, serpentine Mississippi, which bisects the continent and allows everything around it to flourish.[16] Native American enslavement was not just the "other" slavery, merely adding to the labor pool of the colonies and eventually the United States.[17] Instead, enslaving Native Americans furthered colonization in a more fundamental, two-pronged way. Stealing and enslaving Native Americans from coveted lands was stunningly effective since it provided colonists with labor *and* land at the same time. The loss of Native individuals led to the destabilization of Indigenous family units and entire communities. This diminished tribes' abilities to maintain demographic and vital community presence, making them easier to control, remove, or even legally terminate, or so colonists hoped.

This double theft was central to the origins, growth, and eventual success of the English colonies and the United States—not just initially but throughout all of American history. It is a powerful but overlooked process that has helped the United States become the superpower it is today.

How so? The financial strength and geographical spread of the American colonies and the United States emerged from stolen land and enslaved labor. Native Americans were forced to provide both. Fertile lands afforded the capacity to grow export crops that supported farmers and made plantation owners fabulously wealthy. Forests delivered lumber to build ships and barrels for transporting goods that allowed the United States to become a global trading power. A landscape teeming with deer, beaver, and buffalo provided boatloads of pelts and hides that sold for millions of dollars in Europe. Land itself was a commodity, representing wealth and financial stability; for centuries, owning it allowed white men to vote.

Without stolen Native lands, there would be no American capitalism and no nineteenth-century cotton kingdom; no homesteading rush and push for the individual home ownership so central to the American dream; no majestic national parks, which still are sacred to Native Americans; and no prime waterfront locations for twenty-first-century financial and cultural centers like New York City, Miami, Chicago, and Los Angeles.

In addition to land, enslaved human beings were also central to wealth creation. Enslaved Natives labored alongside Africans on plantations in Virginia, the Carolinas, Barbados, and elsewhere and provided the labor that allowed planters to export millions of tons of sugar, cotton, rice, corn, and potatoes, which bolstered the economy and created a new class of wealthy merchants. Even in smaller households and farms in the North, and well into the nineteenth century, enslaved Natives and Africans relieved Americans from the chores of daily labor, thereby opening up leisure and business time to pursue other ventures. Simply owning enslaved Native Americans and Africans vastly increased white Americans' wealth: the listings of personal possessions at the time of death (known as estate inventories) reveal that enslaved people were the single most valuable "possession" a person could claim. This was consistently true, from seventeenth-century Virginia to nineteenth-century New Mexico.

While this stealing of land and labor took many forms, Americans were particularly obsessed with capturing Indigenous women and children to keep as slaves and servants. The stealing of Indigenous women had especially devastating effects on Native nations: it was a double loss for tribes and a double gain for enslavers. Stealing Indigenous women and girls immediately contributed to the population decline of Native nations and stole away important community leaders in a matrilineal society. But it also undercut the future abilities of tribes like the Pequot, Diné, and many others to produce the next generation of leaders.[18] How many future shamans, artists, diplomats, and sachems (chiefs) were stolen away and kept from contributing to and strengthening their home communities? We will never fully know. Colonizers gained the productive labor of these women and girls as well as their reproductive capacity to provide additional people to enslave (often through rape, forced breeding, and marriage).[19]

This book's title, *Stealing America*, invokes "America" as a personified symbol of both Indigenous people and their land. In printed maps and pamphlets produced in the era of exploration, Native Americans, often women, were frequently depicted adorned with fruit or foliage to signify the abundance of the continents.[20] This Indigenous woman or person as "America" represented the people of these regions as well as their lands, and European arrival signaled the beginning of the theft of both. White colonists who eventually founded the United States and took the name "American" for themselves played a central role in these developments. It's not just that Americans have forgotten; it may be

AMÉRIQUE SEPTENTRIONALE, 1763.
THE MAP CARTOUCHE ON THE BOTTOM RIGHT SHOWS AN
INDIGENOUS WOMAN REPRESENTING "AMERICA."

that they have so successfully erased this history of stealing that they never knew it fully in the first place.

ONE OF THE REASONS Indigenous slavery is less known than African slavery is that Americans often tried to hide it. In many cases, this involved suppressing Native American identity in their record-keeping. Indigenous scholars have referred to this as "documentary genocide," by which they mean the erasure of Native identities in archival sources—and thus from national historical memory and narratives.[21] This can be seen most explicitly when colony censuses only reported enslaved Africans, even when hundreds and thousands of enslaved Natives labored in those same households and plantations. Such was the case in Bermuda in 1698, when the official census listed only "Blacks" enslaved in the colony, while at the same time up to 20 percent of Bermuda's enslaved population was Indigenous, including the ancestors of today's Bermuda Natives.[22] The same was true in New England, Pennsylvania, and across the South into the nineteenth century. This erasure has led to the misperception that Native American slavery was relatively insignificant. Scholars, in turn, have often repeated these archival silences, thereby omitting Native Americans from slavery history.[23]

Mixed-race Indigenous people were especially susceptible to having their Native identity erased. As the long history of racism in the United States illustrates, race is socially constructed and malleable; it is not rooted in fixed biological differences. Rather, it has been leveraged by individuals and groups to differentiate and subordinate peoples at various times.[24] As soon as Native Americans intermarried or produced mixed-race children, white Americans imposed racial designators like "mulatto" (a generic colonizer term for a Black mixed-race person) or "negro." Such actions erased their Indigeneity and associated them more clearly with Blackness and slavery. In the early eighteenth century, some colonies like Virginia and South Carolina required this suppression of Native identity by law.[25]

This racial erasure continued throughout American history, when enslavers in the early nineteenth century insisted in court proceedings that their enslaved people were "negroes" and not Indigenous. In the American South, I am estimating that this led to the invisibility of per-

Parrish/Tribes	Men	Women	Children	All persons capable of bearing arms			Women				
S.t Georges Parrish	190	239	351	180	34	27	37	102	155	82	12
Hamilton Tribe	70	78	173	65	7	.	54	72	129	52	1
Smith's Tribe	67	89	140	65	8	2	62	75	114	60	4
Devon Tribe	56	92	145	56	8	4	54	68	99	54	2
Pembrook Tribe	87	135	177	75	22	5	63	74	85	57	9
Pagitts Tribe	78	96	149	73	12	3	76	73	86	37	1
Warwick Tribe	93	87	246	91	9	1	41	54	120	38	5
Southton Tribe	101	115	216	97	19	3	64	73	144	62	3
Somersett or Sandys Tribe	61	119	165	62	13	2	67	58	97	67	1
Small	803	1050	1762	724	132	47	566	649	1032	529	-41

BERMUDA CENSUS, *A PERTICULAR ACCOUNT OF THE INHABITANTS MEN WOMEN AND CHILDREN ASWEL BLACKS AS WHITES PERSONS . . . FROM THE FIRST DAY OF JANUARY 1697 TO THE FIRST DAY OF JANUARY 1698.*

haps eighty thousand to two hundred thousand Native American and mixed-race Indigenous people who labored on southern plantations in the decades prior to the Civil War who were simply seen as "negro."[26]

Native people, however, did not forget their tribal origins or family lineages. This is especially evident in oral histories and court testimonies, despite repeated attempts at their erasure. As just one example, the Narragansett asserted their Native American identity in 1866 when the state of Rhode Island repeatedly told them they were "negroes" and not authentic Indians. Tribal leaders set the record straight: "We are not negroes: we are the heirs of Ninigret, and of the great chiefs and warriors of the Narragansetts. . . . We claim that while one drop of Indian blood remains in our veins, we are entitled to the rights and privileges guaranteed by your ancestors to ours by solemn treaty, which, without a breach of faith, you cannot violate."[27]

Hundreds of tribes that the United States tried to extinguish constantly fought back and took to the courts and even to the streets in the 1960s and 1970s during the Red Power protests, winning state and federal recognition, buying back lands, reconstituting community presence, and reclaiming language. The Narragansett today, for example, are one of 574 federally recognized tribes in the United States, with hundreds more recognized at the state level.[28]

Given this history of erasure, one of the central claims of *Stealing America* is that we need to expand our understanding of who "counts" as Indigenous. Once we resist the idea that "one drop of Black blood" erases all other identities, we can more clearly understand that mixed-race Indigenous people did not stop being Native just because of intermarriage and the racial terms imposed by whites.[29] Indigenous people retained knowledge of their identities through family stories, oral histories, and cultural practices in ways that neither racism nor the familial separation and cultural isolation of slavery could fully suppress.[30]

TO TELL THIS STORY, *Stealing America* is divided into five parts that narrate the origins, expansion, transitions, resurgence, and transformations of Indigenous enslavement in American history between the arrival of Columbus and 1978. The ruptures caused by stealing Natives and their land were not limited to territory that is now the United States. Following individuals and their experiences means that in this book you will encounter colonies and spaces in the Caribbean and Central and South America not usually associated with American history, though these were all connected regions. It was only in 1776 that "American" history became limited to a portion of the North American continent.

The story of Native American enslavement and dispossession begins with the Spanish invasion of the massive continents that were home to millions of Indigenous people. The English followed shortly thereafter and, despite condemning Spanish colonialism and enslavement of Natives, soon mimicked them in virtually every regard by exploiting natural resources and forcing Native Americans into coerced labor (Part One: Rise). From these beginnings, Indigenous slavery and land grabbing expanded in the late 1600s and early 1700s as the second and third generations of English colonists began enslaving Native Americans in much larger numbers. This took place in North America as well as in the Caribbean and parts of Central and South America through large-scale slave trades (Part Two: Expansion). In the eighteenth century, Indigenous enslavement in North America went through a series of changes between the 1720s and the early nineteenth century. This included a more mundane "everyday opportunism" used by colonists to enslave Natives, as well as a furious eruption of enslavement and land grabbing before, during, and after the American Revolution. The Revolutionary era was bookended by antislavery activism before the war and a slew of Indigenous freedom suits afterward (Part Three: Transitions).

Despite this push for freedom, Indigenous enslavement and land theft surprisingly surged in the nineteenth century with the colonization of the South and West as Americans revived older trends in new territories. This new American slavery became so entrenched that it required an act of Congress in 1867 to address it (Part Four: Resurgence). After the Civil War, Americans, as if embodying colonial shape-shifters, expanded and more aggressively imposed labor-based boarding schools, as well as fostering and adoption programs that lasted into the late twentieth century. In response to sustained tribal protest, the passage of the Indian Child Welfare Act in 1978 helped return more agency and sovereignty to Native nations and parents. Yet the ongoing challenges and after-effects have lingered for decades

(Part Five: Transformations). An epilogue queries how these histories became omitted from the narratives of American history.

Throughout, this book highlights the many nations and individuals who refused to be completely conquered or rendered invisible. Across the continent, and continuing to this day, Native Americans have fought to retain sovereignty in countless ways. Many who were enslaved or stolen attempted to reconnect with lost kin or build communities in new places. They waged wars of resistance, took white colonists and governments to court, and continued sacred practices and traditions, thereby passing along family histories to successive generations to retain the identities that whites attempted to erase.

A CENTRAL ISSUE THIS BOOK emphasizes is the repeated patterns of enslavement and land theft. English and American colonists arrived to stay in the early seventeenth century and expected to expand throughout the continent, pushing out Native Americans while using their land, resources, and labor. Scholars refer to this kind of takeover as *settler colonialism*, which, as Patrick Wolfe has noted, is a structure, a *process* of pushing out and eliminating Indigenous people, not a singular event.[31] It is driven by a quest for territory in which Native peoples are seen as obstacles. As Deborah Bird Rose has suggested, Indigenous people "got in the way just by staying at home."[32]

This mentality of elimination helps explain why colonists and Americans could not tolerate the presence of Native Americans. A deep current of anti-Indian sentiment courses through the circulatory system of American history. It drove Americans to pursue enslavement, removal, conversion, and education of Indigenous peoples in hopes of effecting complete assimilation or elimination. These efforts were cyclical and ongoing throughout US history. They did not end once the English arrived in Virginia in 1607; they repeated with each territory and state that was imposed southward and westward, and with every individual captured, locally enslaved, or sent overseas; with each Indigenous nation Americans encountered; with all the wars fought to wrest land from Native Americans; and with every removal of Indigenous people to reservations or boarding schools.

But these attempted colonizations took place not only in the realms of homelands, labor, and bodies. They also targeted Native rituals, languages, and ways of knowing and relating, what Marcelo Dascal has called the "colonization of the mind."[33] It's no wonder that Indigenous people in the United States and worldwide promote a "*de*colonization of the mind," which acknowledges "the psychological, mental, and spiritual aspects" of colonization, in the words of Indigenous scholars Waziyatawin (Dakota) and Michael Yellow Bird (Mandan, Hidatsa, and Arikara). This allows for intentional, positive steps of "meaningful and active resistance to the forces of colonialism that perpetuate the subjugation and/or exploitation of our minds, bodies, and lands."[34]

For many Native Americans today, the collective historical trauma of cyclical invasions, persistent theft, and attempted outright erasure weighs heavily. Historical trauma, as defined by Harvard anthropologist and Gros Ventre tribal member Joseph P. Gone, is "the collective, cumulative, and intergenerational psychosocial disability resulting from massive group-based oppression, such as forced relocation, political subjugation, cultural domination, and genocide."[35] This is especially true given that most Indigenous nations experience the United States as an actively colonizing power in the present, not just in the past.

However, as Narragansett museum director and educator Lorén Spears frequently observes, not all Native Americans were enslaved, nor were slavery and stealing the end of the story.[36] Despite these attempted thefts, "America"—meaning this continent's Indigenous people—survived and is still here. Through the long onslaught of colonization, Native Americans have constantly fought for their sovereignty, maintained community, retained sacred practices, and remembered, most of all, who they were and still are. The Native community on Bermuda's St. David's Island exemplifies this, as does every Native nation in the Americas today that continues to stand strong as Indigenous people while attempting to reckon with the long shadow of the past. This book, in illuminating a painful hidden history, recognizes every Indigenous person and nation who is still here today, and on whose lands all Americans reside.

Part One

RISE

1492–1650

AMERICAN HISTORY DID NOT SUDDENLY BEGIN WITH THE
founding of Jamestown in 1607, nor did slavery start in 1619.
The Spanish invasion in 1492 initiated a process that directly
influenced the English when they were finally able to explore and
attempt to establish their own colonies on Native lands a century
later. From the moment of arrival, Europeans viewed Native populations as potential laborers wherever they went, even if it was
not always possible to coerce powerful nations and confederacies
into slavery. The Spanish were perhaps the most famous initial
perpetrators of enslavement and dispossession, but they eventually were followed by French, English, and Dutch colonists who
hoped to found similarly lucrative colonies.

For a half century, the English persistently tried to establish
colonies in North America, South America, and the Caribbean.
English swashbuckling adventurers and would-be conquistadors
sailed throughout the Atlantic between the 1550s and the early
seventeenth century, kidnapping and abducting Natives for information and labor. When they finally established their first successful outposts in the Americas starting in 1607, English colonists
had to contend with large, powerful Native nations. Before long,
in virtually every location, the English turned to wars of extermination that involved large-scale enslavement of Native Americans
deemed to be enemies.

Within a few decades, these early American colonists worked
out policies regarding Native servitude and enslavement through
trial and error as they adjusted to the processes of colonization
itself. Ideas about race, about perceived cultural differences,

about who was enslavable and who was not—these were not set in stone or formalized by laws from the start. Instead, colonists drew upon a broad range of justifications and increasingly racialized ideas about Native Americans and Africans to affirm their own cultural superiority, including the right to enslave and steal people and take land.

One

COLONIAL
TEMPLATES

THE EMERALD-BLUE WATERS AND WHITE SAND BEACHES OF SAN
Salvador Island in the Bahamas are a deceivingly bucolic setting for the
origins of American slavery. Called Guanahani by the Lucayan Natives
who had lived there for centuries, the small landmass is just one of 181
tropical islands in the expansive archipelago they occupied. For generations, innovative and intrepid Lucayans—part of the larger group of
Taíno peoples of the Caribbean—thrived on plentiful fish, oysters, and
clams from the ocean and cultivated fruits and other crops. They tamed
parrots and dogs, manufactured cloth by growing cotton and spinning
thread, smelted and processed gold, and constructed wooden huts with
brick chimneys. Not secluded or isolated on individual islands, they
were part of a vibrant community that traveled among the numerous isles in large canoes capable of holding forty-five people. Spanish
sailors later noted with awe how Lucayans vigorously propelled their
watercraft far faster than any sailboat.[1]

On the morning of October 12, 1492, the Lucayan residents of Guanahani woke up to find three strange ships floating off their shores.
They immediately viewed these overdressed foreigners as trading partners and loaded up their canoes with small trade goods like glass,
pottery, parrots, and skeins of cotton thread. The swarthy Genoese
mariner who led the seaworn flotilla dismissed what he saw as trifling
trade goods and instead fixated on the gold rings in the Lucayans'
noses, along with their reports of spices on nearby islands. Columbus,
as he was later called, had badly miscalculated global geography and,
thinking he had arrived in India, called these Lucayans "Indians." This
misnomer stuck for centuries, in part because successive generations of

Europeans, too, thought that these lands might be part of or immediately adjacent to Asia.[2]

As it turned out, the emaciated and mutinous crew had stumbled upon a thriving world unknown to Europeans—an old world for Native Americans but a new one to the foreigners. Columbus and other early conquistadors dismissed these original inhabitants as savages and barbarians, but as Europeans would soon come to realize, the two massive continents of the Americas and the hundreds of islands between them were home to as many people as lived in all of Europe—perhaps around sixty million—with a breathtaking diversity of cultures and technologies that rivaled those of Europeans.[3]

From the moment of first contact, Columbus envisioned the Lucayan as valuable slaves. He brazenly reported to his royal sponsors, Isabella and Ferdinand of Spain, that Lucayans "should be good servants" and that "with fifty men they could all be subjugated and made to do what is required of them."[4] Columbus quickly tested his theory. During his third day on the flat, forested island of Guanahani, he captured seven Lucayans and forced them to serve as guides.[5] Obsessed with finding gold, Columbus plied them for directions as he sailed farther south, deeper into Taíno homelands, to Cuba and Hispaniola (present-day Haiti and the Dominican Republic). Before departing for Spain in 1493, he had taken at least two dozen Natives captive, stealing them from canoes and shorelines as he sailed from island to island.[6]

Such stealing was a terror-inducing act of violence that often tore apart families. One distraught Taíno man heard his wife and three children had been captured and were going to be taken away. He rushed to Columbus and begged to be taken too so he could remain with his family. Columbus complied. After a harrowing journey back across the Atlantic, these Taíno captives were paraded through the center of Seville, Spain, on Palm Sunday of 1493, in part to prove Columbus had reached "the Indies" but also to promote the labor potential of these Natives.[7] In fact, Columbus listed "*esclavos*" (slaves)—Indian slaves—as one of the many plentiful export commodities of the "Indies."[8]

The enslavement of these Taíno peoples by the Spanish set a devastating precedent for the entire hemisphere for the next four hundred years. Every European empire that explored and eventually colonized portions of the Americas stole and enslaved or otherwise coerced Indigenous people to provide information about navigation and natural resources or to labor on plantations or in households.

English and eventually American colonists also used Indigenous people in this way, even if they lagged behind the Spanish. In 1492, England was not powerful enough to claim new territories thousands of miles across the Atlantic Ocean, but it still tried. King Henry VII commissioned the Italian sailor Giovanni Caboto (known as John Cabot in English) to embark on a series of exploratory missions between 1498 and 1500. While sailing along the coast of Newfoundland, Cabot captured three Indigenous men, forced them onto his ship, and returned to London to present them as trophies to the king.[9] But England's initial overseas ambitions faltered; despite multiple attempts, permanent settlements did not succeed until the seventeenth century. For decades, the English could only aspire to the decadent wealth extracted from these vast and diverse lands by Spain and Portugal.

Still, for much of the sixteenth century, the English mimicked the Spanish by exploring the coastlines of the Americas. They searched for gold and quick profits while abducting Indigenous people in order to extort local and cartographic knowledge. English merchants dabbled in the transatlantic African slave trade, attempted to set up colonies in the Americas, and like Columbus, forced Natives back to Europe for display and servitude. All English colonization attempts—even the early ones in the sixteenth century that had failed—were driven by two primary motivations: to counter Spanish Catholic expansion with Protestant presence and to bring equal riches and glory to England. Both required the land and labor of Native Americans.

Natives who discovered Europeans on their shores actively shaped these events. Some resisted the invasion and slave raids through warfare; others relocated or escaped if captured. Certain Indigenous leaders used European presence to position themselves as intermediaries and allies. Mostly, though, Native Americans protested their treatment, registering their intense discontentment vocally and through their actions. Their remonstrations resonated with critics of colonization in Europe, setting off debates among the sharpest legal minds about the essential humanity of Native Americans and how they should be treated. But the die had been cast. Colonial invaders of the Americas viewed Native Americans as a key source of enslaved labor and would continue to do so in various forms for the next several hundred years.

EUROPEANS DID NOT INVENT SLAVERY, but they dramatically transformed it to serve capitalistic enterprises built on the forced labor of non-whites. Most Europeans understood slavery as a practice with a long history, extending back through the medieval period and the Roman empire to ancient Near Eastern civilizations. Even more important, the Hebrew and Christian Bibles provided justification, with stories of slaveholding Hebrew patriarchs and early Christian leaders.[10] Many Europeans—English men and women included—were increasingly accustomed to the idea of contractual labor. With the exception of wealthy patrons and landowners, the majority of lower-class English men and women experienced long periods of either servant or contract labor throughout most of the early modern period.[11]

Native nations in the vast continents of what was later called America were not inherently warlike, as Europeans believed, but they did have traditions of warfare and captivity. In many instances, Native wars and expansions prior to the coming of Europeans were attempts to control resources and create networks of tributaries or to keep rival enemy groups in subservient relationships.[12] For many Natives, raiding enemy tribes and taking captives played the important role of adoption and replacement. Some nations, like the Haudenosaunee (Iroquois Confederacy), had raiding and captivity practices often called "mourning wars" that were intended to replace lost loved ones.[13] The same was true in other parts of the hemisphere, where Native captives often became family members, with high levels of trust and incorporation and much less of the coercion and violence associated with European practices of slavery.[14]

Kingdoms in sub-Saharan Africa, too, had traditions of captivity and servitude that reached deep into that continent's long history.[15] African kings and rulers buttressed their power through harnessing the labor and resources of people under their jurisdiction, including enslaved individuals, but also wives and servants. Captives from neighboring kingdoms could be utilized in a variety of ways, from family and household inclusion to hard agricultural and commodity labor, as in the mining of gold on the so-called Gold Coast.[16] In particular, scholars have noted the practice of pawnship, in which a person would be assigned to a creditor as a guarantee for a loan.[17]

African kingdoms and Native nations saw themselves as distinct groups with their own interests, goals, and strategies of self-preservation. As Europeans began arriving, tribes and kingdoms tried to use European alliances and technology to their own advantage. This helps explain why one African kingdom might choose to attack and enslave members from another kingdom, or why one Native nation would take captives from another tribe, or in either case why they might cooperate with Europeans to capture rival tribes and kingdoms. Pan-African and pan-Indigenous solidarity developed much later. Europeans, too, did not initially see themselves as all one group. Exposure to non-whites rapidly created cultural and religious categories of difference that became based on race.[18]

Europeans exploited these preexisting practices of captivity and invented new ones to create the largest, most sustained slave trades and systems of enslavement in Western history. These new slave trades focused on enslaved labor almost exclusively from two sources: Africa and the Americas. This started in Africa in the 1440s, when the Spanish and Portuguese began trading for captives on the West African coast, using enslaved labor to help build new colonies on the Canary Islands and Madeira. Beginning in 1492, Europeans began regarding Indigenous people as having the same potential for enslaved labor. They quickly engaged in abduction and enslavement to successfully claim territories and more efficiently create wealth through capitalizing on natural resources and export commodities like sugar.[19]

AFTER HIS SECOND VOYAGE to the Americas in 1493–1494, Columbus brashly proposed a regularized Indian slave trade to fund colonization. Spanish conquistadors required cattle, horses, food provisions, swords, knives, and a whole host of manufactured goods in order to build towns, subdue Natives ("cannibals," he falsely called them), and coerce them to reveal and mine all available gold. But such endeavors required a mountain of financing, and the Spanish Crown was not in a position to bankroll it all. Columbus proposed a scheme in which

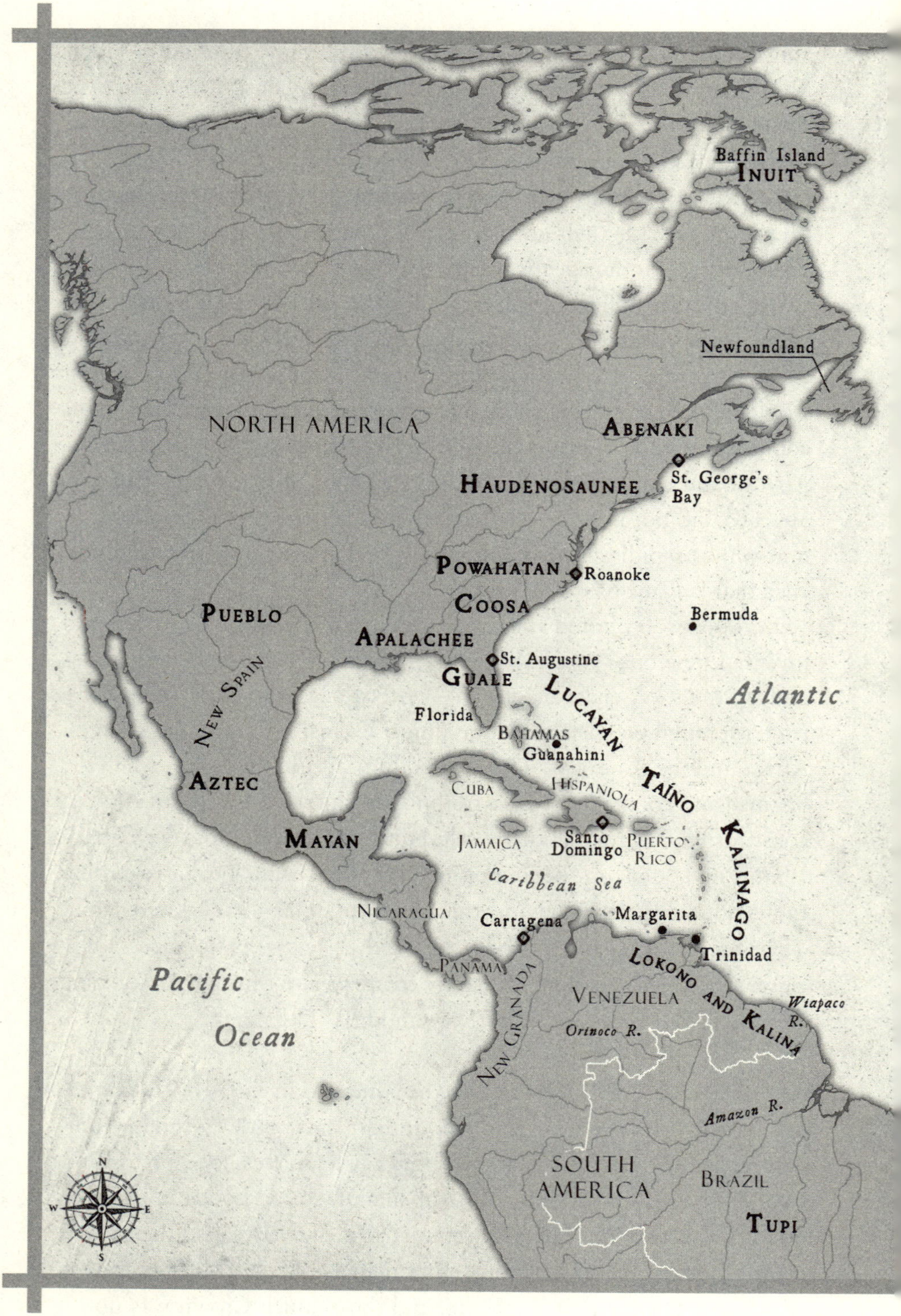

Baffin Island
INUIT

Newfoundland

NORTH AMERICA

ABENAKI

HAUDENOSAUNEE
St. George's
Bay

POWAHATAN
Roanoke

COOSA

PUEBLO

APALACHEE
St. Augustine

NEW SPAIN

GUALE
Florida

Atlantic

LUCAYAN

BAHAMAS
Guanahini

Bermuda

AZTEC

CUBA
HISPANIOLA

TAÍNO

MAYAN
JAMAICA
Santo
Domingo
PUERTO
RICO

KALINAGO

Caribbean Sea

NICARAGUA
Cartagena
Margarita

Trinidad

PANAMA

Pacific

Ocean

NEW GRANADA

LOKONO AND KALINA

VENEZUELA
Wiapaco R.

Orinoco R.

Amazon R.

SOUTH
AMERICA
BRAZIL

TUPI

N
W E
S

Sixteenth-Century Atlantic World

ENGLAND
London
Bristol

English Channel

FRANCE

NETHERLANDS

PORTUGAL
Lisbon
SPAIN
Seville

Mediterranean Sea

Azores

Madeira

Canary Islands

Ocean

WEST AFRICA

Cape Verde

Gold Coast

Guinea   Coast

a massive slave trade in Native Americans would keep the Spanish coffers full. Whole flotillas, he suggested, would leave the Caribbean packed with Native captives to either sell or barter as slaves in Spain in exchange for the much-needed provisions and supplies. These same ships would return to the Caribbean, offload the provisions, and raid local islands to fill the holds anew with captive Natives; then the process would start all over again.[20]

Columbus was likely modeling his plan after the Portuguese African slave trade that was at least fifty years old by the 1490s. Before sailing west and stumbling upon the Americas, Columbus had navigated down the coast of West Africa, where the Portuguese had initiated a regularized slave trade out of Africa to Cape Verde, Madeira, Europe, and the Mediterranean.[21] It was but a small conceptual step to modify the African slave trade to exploit Indigenous people in the Americas. After his voyage across the Atlantic, Columbus was convinced that Native Americans could not only be enslaved; he claimed they would prove to be "better than any other kind of slaves."[22]

The king and queen of Spain were skeptical about Columbus's plan and suspended the discussion for a time.[23] But Columbus was undeterred. In 1495, he rounded up 1,600 Taíno captives on the shores of Hispaniola and was disappointed to find he could only squeeze 550 of them into his four ships. The remaining Indigenous captives were distributed to local Spanish leaders or released. Conditions in the overly crowded vessels deteriorated during the Atlantic crossing, and Native captives began dying by the dozens—an early Indigenous Middle Passage, so to speak, that prefigured the later mass trafficking of enslaved Africans in the opposite direction. When Columbus's ships arrived in Spain, the 350 remaining Natives were forced out of the holds and sold into slavery in the bustling slave markets of southern Spain.[24] After his third voyage to the Americas in 1498, Columbus's violent colonization caught up with him, and in 1500 he was shipped back to Spain in chains for his scandalous treatment of Native Americans and misuse of his own men.[25]

Spanish slave raiding and enslaving grew rapidly in the decades following Columbus's death in 1506. Queen Isabella soon permitted conquistadors to enslave *indios caribes* (Kalinago, or island Caribs), justifying the decision by pointing to the Natives' supposed cannibalism.[26] And in 1508, the Spanish Crown expanded Native slavery even more by permitting the enslavement and trafficking of Indians living on "useless" islands of the Caribbean—useless to Spaniards only because they lacked gold or obvious export commodities. This permission was extended in 1518 to include the Kalina (mainland Caribs) on the South American coast.[27]

Official pronouncements by various Spanish kings and queens over the next fifty years ranged from prohibiting slavery under certain conditions (1530) and licensing Indian slavery when conducted during just wars (1534 and 1550) to allowing enslaving Natives through rescue (*rescate*). This last category was especially elastic, letting Spaniards buy, steal, or barter captive Natives from other Indigenous nations and take them as their own slaves.[28]

Despite its legality, Europeans still debated Native American slavery, especially as reports of its viciousness made their way back to Spain. Indigenous people vocalized protests that were rarely recorded, but their actions of resistance spoke volumes. When the brash conquistador Juan Ponce de León led a slaving raid against the Kalinago on the island of Guadeloupe, they mounted a fierce resistance, killing five Spanish soldiers and wounding twenty more.[29] Every Indigenous man, woman, and child who argued, fought, or killed their way to freedom testified to the injustice of kidnapping and enslavement.

Equally important were the actions of Natives who patiently plotted their revenge or used local and imperial courts to pursue justice. Such was the case with a Native woman named Catalina, who had been stolen as a young child by Sebastián de Benalcázar from her home in what is now El Salvador, branded on the face, and forced into slavery. After serving in various colonies, she was taken to Spain, where she protested her unjust enslavement before the Council of the Indies in Madrid in the 1540s.[30]

Spaniards who participated in the invasion of the Americas could see and hear the trauma of colonization and slavery. One early public rebuke came from the Dominican priest Antonio de Montesinos. Ascending to the pulpit of the large, thatched church building in Santo Domingo on the island of Hispaniola in December 1511, Montesinos preached a hair-raising, fiery sermon. "Tell me, by what right or by what interpretation of justice do you keep these Indians in such a cruel and horrible servitude?" Montesinos queried, to the shock of the Spanish conquistadors present. "By what authority have you waged such detestable wars against people who were once living so quietly and peacefully in their own land?"[31]

Perhaps the most important critique came from Bartolomé de las Casas, although this eventual "Defender of the Indians" started out as an ordinary conquistador. Las Casas arrived in the Americas in 1502 and quickly joined the masses of profit seekers who hoped to exploit Indigenous labor and natural resources. He was granted an *encomienda* by local authorities and forced his functionally enslaved Native workers who came with the land to profitably cultivate his estate. The *encomienda* system was at the heart of the first half century of Spanish colonization. Would-be colonists and adventurers were given a "donation" of Native Americans along with a large plot of land to cultivate with Native labor. Native Americans tied to the land would be under the direct control of the owner, the *encomendero*, in a form of coercive vassalage. But such subjugation was imposed and usually viewed by Spanish reformers as enslavement.[32]

Las Casas's investment in colonization deepened when he participated in the conquest of Cuba in 1512, where he saw firsthand the routine torture and physical dismemberment of Natives, along with widespread enslavement and dispossession at the hands of Spaniards like him. Over the course of several years, constant exposure to such humanitarian outrages changed his mind. He gave up his *encomienda* in 1515 and returned to Spain to eventually become a priest within the Franciscan order.[33]

For several decades, Las Casas documented the extreme mistreatment and enslavement of Lucayan, Taíno, and Kalinago peoples in the Caribbean. He recorded these stories in unpublished manuscript form—*Larguísima relación* (Very long account). Las Casas painted a grim picture of Spanish presence in the Americas, estimating that they had stolen, enslaved, or murdered four million Indigenous people in New Spain (Central America and southern North America) alone between 1518 and 1530. Spanish officials, *encomenderos*, and merchants continuously raided Native American homelands, transporting hundreds of thousands of individuals to labor in the gold and silver mines of the Caribbean and South America. On the island of Hispaniola, soldiers "violently forced away Women and Children to make them Slaves." When Natives began to resist, Spanish soldiers snatched Indian children from their mothers' arms and dashed their brains out on rocks. They slashed open the bellies of pregnant Indigenous women and slowly roasted Native nobles and commanders to death on gridirons.[34]

In 1542, Las Casas presented portions of his graphic account, along with other documentation and proposed reforms, to the pro-colonizing but deeply religious Spanish king Charles V. The effect was immediate. That same year, Charles V passed a series of regulations called the *Leyes nuevas* (New laws) that targeted the most egregious abuses against Native Americans. This included the *encomienda* system, which had institutionalized coerced Native labor and led to widespread exploitation. It was a significant victory for the cadre of reformers and priests who sought protections for Indigenous peoples. A decade later, in 1552, Las Casas published a shorter version of his catalog of Spanish abuses as *Brevísima relación de la destrucción de las Indias* (A brief account of the destruction of the Indies), which shaped how people viewed Spanish conquest for generations.[35]

The vast majority of Spanish colonists, leaders, and rulers remained unconvinced, however. As recent scholarship has suggested, these New Laws were imperfectly implemented, although they did create legal

ENSLAVED NATIVE AMERICANS IN SPANISH MINES, 1706.

opportunities for Native Americans to protest their enslavement, which they did by the thousands over the following century.[36] When it eventually became more difficult to legally enslave Natives outright within Spanish American territories during the second half of the sixteenth century, Spanish colonists more fully embraced African enslavement. Yet Spanish pilfering of the Americas continued.

THE ENSLAVEMENT OF NATIVE AMERICANS and the pillaging of their labor can be hard to grasp. The Catedral de Sevilla makes it more tangible. Often billed as the third largest cathedral in the world (after St. Peter's in Rome and St. Paul's in London), it is a stunning structure that sits prominently in the main central plaza of the quaint medieval city of Seville, Spain. Walking through the soaring stone naves of the cathedral, it is hard not to be awed by the scale and craftsmanship of this Gothic edifice that took more than a century to construct. The central feature of the cathedral is the altarpiece, the largest in the world, towering sixty-six feet above the floor and spanning fifty-nine feet. Depicting forty-four scenes from the life of Christ, the gold-gilt altarpiece was made by a Flemish craftsman named Pierre Dancart in 1482 and finally finished by other artists in 1564.[37]

Disconcertingly, the gold and silver that covers every square inch of the Christocentric altarpiece was imported directly from the mountains and rivers of Central and South America. It was mined by enslaved Indigenous people in the lands of the Náhuatl, Huastecos, and many other Indigenous nations. Breathing in the fine metallic dust in the mines led to the early deaths of tens of thousands of Indigenous laborers, who died of lung diseases such as pneumoconiosis or silicosis.[38] The cathedral in Seville is filled with an estimated 88,000 pounds, or 44 tons, of gold mined by enslaved Indigenous people, as are dozens of other cathedrals throughout Europe. The mass enslavement of Natives to work in gold and silver mines in the early sixteenth century not only led to the rapid global increase in gold and silver bullion trade from Spain to China but also allowed the Seville cathedral to receive its most famous and valuable finishing touches.

Perhaps fittingly, Columbus's remains rest in the same space as the altarpiece. Situated not far from the main altar, the four bronze and alabaster pallbearers carrying his ornately decorated coffin enable him

CATEDRAL
DE SEVILLA
ALTARPIECE,
2018.

to occupy, even in death, a space adorned with representations of the genocide and enslavement he initiated. Two million visitors tour this UNESCO World Heritage site annually, although few likely understand the murderous secrets contained in the gold and silver.

THE STEADY STREAM OF Spanish conquistadors into the Americas soon turned into a tidal wave of other European invaders. Most of these newcomers also had few qualms about kidnapping and enslaving Native Americans. For most of the sixteenth century, the Spanish and the Portuguese were the primary colonizing powers in the Americas. In 1494, the Treaty of Tordesillas had divided newly invaded lands in the Atlantic and the Pacific between the Spanish and the Portuguese. The Spanish claimed control over the Americas except for Brazil in eastern South America, which was carved out for the Portuguese. Brazilian planters, too, almost exclusively commandeered enslaved Indigenous labor for the first seventy years of colonization.[39] In the ensuing one

hundred years, most other European seafaring powers explored, kidnapped, and traded rather than investing time and materials in physical
settlements. Many exploratory trips were focused on finding the ever-
elusive Northwest Passage through or north of the Americas, which
would have provided a direct sailing route to the true Indies—Japan,
India, and China.

As always, stealing and kidnapping were part of this "exploration."
In 1500, a Portuguese explorer named Gaspar Corte-Real captured
fifty-seven Abenakis on the coastline of what is now Maine and loaded
them into two ships: fifty in his own and seven in another. Corte-Real's
ship sank in a storm on the way back to Europe, but the second ship
survived. Buyers in Lisbon remarked at the height and strength of the
Native captives, noting, "They are admirably calculated for labor, and
will make the best slaves I have ever seen."[40] Natives fought back when
they could. The Portuguese explorer Giovanni da Verrazzano, sailing
for France in 1524 off the coast of what later became New England,
tried to steal an old woman, two infants, an eight-year-old boy, and a
teenage girl. Verrazzano and his men grabbed the eight-year-old boy to
take back to France and would have also taken the young woman, but
she put up too much of a fight and they gave up.[41]

From their relative seclusion across the Channel, the English read
with both revulsion and envy about the Spanish and Portuguese conquest of the New World. They desperately wanted to mimic Spanish
commercial successes. English merchants sporadically explored the
American (and African) coasts, even if they were not yet able to claim
any lands for their country. Stealing Natives was almost always part
of these ventures. A thin-faced, sea-savvy English sailor named Martin Frobisher undertook three voyages between 1576 and 1578 to the
vast watery lands of what is now northern Canada.[42] On the arctic
coast of Baffin Island, Frobisher's men pulled a few Inuit men and a
leather kayak out of the water and took them to England. One stolen
Inuit man was so distraught that he gnawed his tongue in half during
the voyage. The fleet arrived at Bristol, where the three surviving
Inuits—Kalicho, Arnaq, and Nutaaq—were paraded around in 1577
and portrayed by the talented painter John White. As was common
with Indigenous people forcibly taken to Europe, the Inuits soon contracted diseases and passed away. Observers at his deathbed reported

that Kalicho sang the same "death song" that he had sung after being captured on Baffin Island.[43] In a way, Kalicho had died twice: spiritually, when he was stolen from his homeland, and bodily, when he perished in a foreign land.

During the 1570s, a rising generation of pro-colonization advocates pushed the newly crowned Queen Elizabeth not just to explore the New World but to firmly establish colonies there. English colonization represented a paradox. English monarchs and architects of colonization believed they could avoid the violence of the Spanish even as they desperately hoped to get rich.[44] Richard Hakluyt said as much in his *Inducements to the Liking of the Voyage Intended towards Virginia* in 1585, when he stated that the three purposes of the voyage were to plant "Christian religion," by which he meant Protestantism; to "trafficke," or trade with Native Americans and others; and "to conquer." Or, he added, "to do all three."[45]

Sir Walter Raleigh sprang at the chance to traffick and conquer. In 1585, Queen Elizabeth granted Raleigh a patent for colonizing North

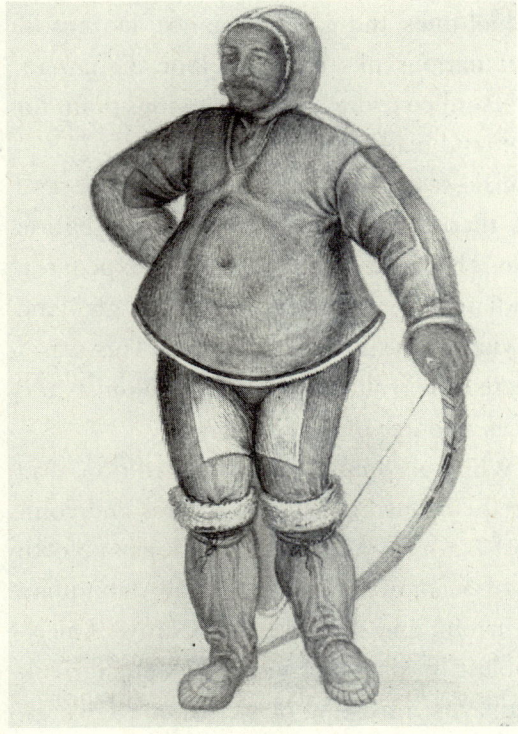

KALICHO, AN INUK FROM FROBISHER BAY; WEARING SEALSKIN SUIT, HOLDING A BOW, BY JOHN WHITE, 1585–1593.

America that was twofold. He was charged with setting up a permanent colony on the eastern seaboard just north of the Spanish settlement in Florida. But the queen also tasked him with raiding the Spanish treasure fleets that annually took gold and silver to Spain and sacking Spanish settlements in the Caribbean. In 1585, five ships carrying approximately six hundred English men and women landed on today's Outer Banks, in North Carolina, to establish a colony called Roanoke. They were led by Sir Richard Grenville, who had been appointed by Raleigh. Situated behind the string of barrier islands, Roanoke Island offered natural shelter from the ocean and a safe harbor, as well as an aqueous buffer from local Natives. The colony hoped to counter Spanish presence to the south in St. Augustine in Florida (founded in 1565) and exploit natural resources like gold and silver.[46]

Grenville and the English colonists arrived in the heart of a thriving network of Native nations and bands, which included the Roanoke. Their homelands—called Ossomocomuck—encompassed tributary towns of other nations in the region. The tributary system, which was common among Native nations, involved tribes or bands who were nominally under the head werowance, or chief, in this case, Wingina, to whom they also paid annual dues and gave allegiance. Dozens of towns occupied by powerful nations like the Pomeiooc, Croatoan, Weapemeoc, Chowanoc, and Pamlico drove home an obvious point for Grenville: this was not vacant land ready for the taking.[47]

Immediately, English officials feared colonists would enslave and mistreat Native Americans, thereby potentially inviting retribution and ruining the entire venture. The backers of the Roanoke expedition warned the men that "no Indian be forced to labor vnwillyngly" and that no colonist should "stryke or mysuse any Indian."[48] This was a strong admonition that reflected the reality that English colonists too looked to Indigenous people as a source of coerced labor.[49]

The colonial artist John White accompanied this expedition, and his colorful paintings provided curious English magistrates and commoners with their first view of Native American populations in North America. White's depictions of Secotan and other coastal Algonquian individuals and towns were irrefutable evidence that Native Americans were sophisticated peoples. In his paintings, they were agriculturalists who lived in small villages consisting of wetus, or wigwams, constructed with wooden poles and sheets of bark and woven mats. They planted gardens and skillfully fished with weirs and nets and in impressive canoes along the coastlines. White illustrated women and men working side by side, along with children who perhaps already knew enough to be afraid of being kidnapped by colonists. White's images were far from perfect, in that they confirmed European presumptions about Natives as more primitive and inferior people. Still, they conveyed a powerful message of Indigenous humanity to a wide audience. His paintings were fabulously popular and were copied by engravers and reused on maps and in books for decades.[50]

While Grenville was in charge at Roanoke, Sir Francis Drake was in the Caribbean, seizing Spanish holdings with his formidable entourage of several thousand men aboard twenty-seven ships.[51] By Drake's side was Pedro, a Native of the island of Margarita, just off the coast of present-day Venezuela. Pedro had been kidnapped by the French, but when Drake intercepted the French ship that held him, Drake kept Pedro, in part for his multilingual abilities and knowledge of the South American coast.[52] Drake sailed to and wreaked havoc on Santo

THE TOWNE OF SECOTA (SECOTAN VILLAGE), BY JOHN WHITE, ENGRAVING, CA. 1580S.

Domingo, on the south side of Hispaniola, pillaging the city and taking captives. Sailing southward, he invaded the major Spanish stronghold of Cartagena, on the northern coast of South America (modern-day Colombia), which he mostly burned after looting it.[53] When Drake's massive flotilla sailed out of Cartagena, they took with them what was likely England's largest human plunder in the Caribbean: three hundred captive Natives, along with two hundred additional Africans, Turks, and Moors.[54]

Drake's design was to supply the Roanoke settlement with this large influx of enslaved labor to bolster agricultural production. Sailing north, he stopped briefly to raid the Spanish outpost of St. Augustine in present-day Florida before continuing to Roanoke, where he arrived in June 1586 with his sizable fleet.[55] Drake found a feeble colony on the brink of disaster. Relationships with local Natives had soured (which included the grisly decapitation of the Secotan werowance Wingina), and colonists were desperate for a way out. Drake planned to provision the settlement and move on, but a massive three-day hurricane damaged Drake's ships, the Roanoke settlement, and settler enthusiasm. Most of the Roanoke colonists decided to pack up and sail with Drake back to England.[56]

Determined to install a functional colony at Roanoke, Sir Richard Grenville returned later that year with an additional four hundred colonists and more provisions. But what they found completely spooked them: the corpses of two murdered men hanging at the settlement site, one English and one Native. Grenville captured a local Indigenous youth to ply him for information and ended up keeping him as a personal servant, taking him back to England along with the would-be colonists who were too disturbed by what they had seen to remain.[57]

A year later, in 1587, another flotilla of ships loaded with colonists once again sailed to Roanoke, with John White as governor. However, they were left stranded there while Spain mounted an impressive invasion of England in July 1588. With the spectacle of 133 Spanish ships carrying 22,000 soldiers bearing down on England, the Crown refused to permit even one ship to travel to Roanoke to provision White and his crew. A combination of English ingenuity and a series of lucky turns in the weather resulted in a resounding defeat of the Spanish Armada, with a crippling loss of almost half the Spanish fleet and its soldiers.[58] This stunning victory marked the beginning of the slow rise of English naval, military, and commercial presence and eventual dominance in the wider Atlantic World. English adventurers and royal officials believed their time had finally arrived.

In the meantime, three thousand miles across the ocean, the Roanoke colonists waited three heart-wrenching years for supplies. When reinforcements finally arrived in 1590, it was too late. The settlement had been abandoned, with the cryptic word "Croatoan" carved into a nearby tree.[59] The only viable English settlement in North America had disappeared.

Scholars and lay enthusiasts have tried to parse the mysterious fate of the one hundred or so colonists. Some researchers claim to have found pottery shards fifty miles due west—led there by invisible ink on a map later housed in the British Museum—that suggests the place where Roanoke's colonists found refuge.[60] The general consensus, however, continues to be that after souring relations with local Indigenous leaders, the surviving Roanoke settlers went fifty miles south to Croatoan, what is now called Hatteras Island, home of the Croatoan Natives, where they eventually integrated into the Native community.[61]

NEWLY EMBOLDENED BY the crushing defeat of the Spanish Armada, English adventurers and merchants raced to establish new colonies. Ship after ship launched from English ports in the 1590s and early 1600s, their sailing routes reaching like fingers across the Atlantic Ocean to latch onto a small corner of the Americas. Sir Walter Raleigh once again led the way, with the full backing of the stately and victorious Queen Elizabeth. In 1595, Raleigh guided a fleet deep into the Spanish Caribbean, to the large island of Trinidad. His mission was straightforward: continue his quest for precious metals and a fast track for English colonists to share in Spain's perceived financial largesse.

Raleigh and other merchants were quickly attracted to the northern rim of South America that Kalina (mainland Caribs) and Lokono (Arawaks) called Paricora.[62] Bounded by the Amazon River to the south and the Orinoco River to the west (in present-day Venezuela) and encompassing the later colonies of French Guiana, Dutch Suriname, and English Guiana, some early mapmakers labeled the region Caribana, acknowledging that the whole coastal area was teeming with tens of thousands of powerful Kalina Natives who were independent and still free from European control.[63]

As they searched for gold and silver, Raleigh and his fellow merchants eagerly tapped into the burgeoning Indigenous slave trade in Caribana. They observed as Spanish merchants used canoes to follow riverways off the south bank of the Orinoco into the interior, where they purchased captives from the Kalina for what they considered a bargain: an offering of three or four hatchets was enough to exchange for a young Indigenous person.[64] Raleigh and his companions followed suit. A sailor named Francis Sperry purchased eight young, female Indian captives for one small knife. Although the sources are silent, we can be sure that sexual exploitation soon followed, as was so often the case with European men who preyed on women in virtually every Native town they encountered. In another instance, a ship that was traveling in Raleigh's larger flotilla came across a Spanish canoe full of Indigenous captives to be sold as slaves. The English ship chased it down and tried to abduct the Native people who were on board, but most of them escaped into the forest. Only a few captive Natives were brought back to Raleigh.[65]

Vivid published descriptions of the region by Raleigh invigorated the imaginations of an entire generation of English adventurers for the next one hundred years.[66] In 1604, an English captain named Charles Leigh set sail for Guiana's shores in yet another attempt to establish an English settlement.[67] Early English colonists to Guiana were clearly conflicted. Were Natives trading partners to be courted or groups to be exploited as potential laborers? The answer, as was so often the case, was both. When the *Olive Plant* first dropped anchor at the mouth of the Amazon River, Leigh's men attempted to capture a canoe full of Indians who had come to trade. Leigh came up empty except for one Native youth, who jumped off the ship the next day too far from shore to have survived.[68] Leigh had more success at the mouth of Oyapock (Wiapoco) River, which today serves as the natural boundary between French Guiana and Brazil. After landing, he found two Lokono men named Pluainma and William, who could speak English. And how?

They had been taken to England previously by explorers and eventually returned. Leigh and his men were invited by the coastal nation to stay, although only after Leigh agreed to help defend them from inland Kalina.[69] Leigh died a year later, and the English colony in Guiana slowly disbanded.

ALMOST THREE THOUSAND MILES due north, English merchants were testing possible sites for colonial settlement in coastal Abenaki territory, in what is now Maine. By 1600, seaside North American Natives had already experienced nearly a century of European predation and exploration, including kidnappings. Taking captives was a violent enterprise, even though English merchants did it routinely. Each Native stolen represented a lost child, spouse, or parent and an Indigenous family ripped apart. Natives whose lifeways intertwined with the rhythms of the ocean soon learned to deeply distrust European traders. Some Abenakis eventually refused to meet up close, instead insisting on passing trade items back and forth on long ropes from the shore to rowboats.[70] This strategy was perhaps due to fear of diseases but also likely used to avoid captivity.

English explorer George Weymouth gave the Abenaki yet another reason for distrust. In 1605, his crew arrived near the present-day Bay of St. George's in Maine.[71] As described by crew member James Rosier, they first tried to gain the confidence of the Abenaki.[72] Over the course of several weeks, Weymouth mostly stayed on his ship, the *Archangell*, and traded with the few Natives who dared row out in canoes. All the while, he was plotting which Abenaki youths they could kidnap and take back to England. But the Abenaki planned a preemptive attack, telling Weymouth they had plenty of furs upriver and inviting him to follow them. He became suspicious, however, and soon learned that nearly three hundred Indians were lying in wait around the riverbend with bows, arrows, and dogs. Weymouth retreated, and the attack failed.

Still, Weymouth was determined to abduct some of the Abenaki boys. The next morning, Weymouth's men laid a trap. Two canoes, each with three Abenakis, came to Weymouth's ship to trade as usual. Three of the Natives came on board, but the other three were more hesitant. To entice them, the sailors gave them a container of peas and bread, but the still-suspicious Abenakis took it back to the shore to eat it. Weymouth sent seven or eight men after them with a chest full of trade goods, along with more peas. Only two ventured to the water to trade, and, seeing that the third Native did not trust them, Weymouth's men seized the two Natives, who put up such a fight that it took six of Weymouth's men to physically overpower them, grabbing the long hair of the youths and forcing them into their rowboat and then onto the ship. Weymouth now had five Indians captive: Tahanedo, Amoret, Skicawaros, Maneddo, and Sassacomoit. Additionally, Weymouth carefully packed up their bows and arrows and stole their two canoes to take back to England.[73]

All five Abenakis survived the voyage. Three of them were presented to Sir Ferdinando Gorges, one of Weymouth's sponsors who held a royal patent for northeastern North America. Gorges exploited them for their knowledge of their homeland—information that he could use to colonize the region and profit by tapping into the vast resources of the region. Gorges twisted the violent affair into his own self-serving Christian worldview, suggesting that these Abenakis were "the means under God" to help spur further colonization.[74] Two of the Abenakis were given to John Popham, the chief justice of England. Eventually a few made their way back to their homeland with other English merchants.

Within a few decades, English adventurers and would-be colonists had stolen so many Natives and taken them to London that even Shakespeare joked about it. In *The Tempest*, written in approximately 1611, Trinculo, the shipwrecked jester, says he wishes he were in England so that he could paint up Caliban (an Indigenous-type character) and charge money to curious crowds, or perhaps at least tame him and present him as a gift for the emperor.[75]

Notably, Indigenous people were stolen not only for their physical labor. Before they had their own viable colonies in the Americas, English merchants like Raleigh, Greenville, and Sir Gorges colonized the knowledge of Natives by demanding intellectual labor: learning foreign languages, providing critical information about power dynamics, mapping the coastlines and waterways, pointing out familiar landmarks, and convincing their compatriots—unwisely, as it turned out—to trust the Europeans. The age of exploration and the colonization that soon followed would have been impossible without them.

BY THE END OF THE SIXTEENTH CENTURY, the invasion of Europeans had forever changed the homelands of millions of Indigenous Americans. In some regions, Native nations successfully withstood colonization, employing millennia-old strategies of adaptation and negotiation. In other areas, the relentless and lethal combination of slave raids, kidnapping, warfare, outright murder, and diseases had a staggering and compounded effect on Indigenous populations. Scholars used to blame "virgin soil" epidemics—diseases like smallpox for which Indigenous people in the Americas had no previous exposure or immunity—for precipitous population declines in some areas.[76] Diseases *were* devastating, but a singular focus on their impact obscures the direct violence of colonial invaders, something that later chroniclers of European conquest downplayed.[77] European arrival was catastrophic: they murdered, enslaved, and relocated millions of Native Americans over the course of one hundred years.[78]

The early genocide of Indigenous peoples in the Spanish Caribbean created a violent template for English colonization. For all European powers, exploitation of Native land and labor was built into the very framework of settler colonialism. It was neither incidental nor accidental. English colonists and later Americans would soon follow suit, with equal intentionality and vigor.

Two

AMERICAN
SLAVERY

WHEN THE *SUSAN CONSTANT, GODSPEED,* AND *DISCOVERY* HOISTED their sails in England and headed to North America in 1607, no one knew they would establish the first successful English colony in the Americas. But what is often called the start of "American" history, Indigenous nations like the Powhatan experienced as a perpetual invasion. Most Native communities in eastern North America already had decades of experience with Europeans who traded and raided on their shorelines. Virginia and other early English colonies were small and vulnerable and only survived because large, powerful Indigenous confederacies permitted them to do so.

Virginia's survival soon led to a flood of English colonization. Between 1607 and 1650, English merchants established outposts and colonies in South America (Guiana and the Amazon River basin), the Caribbean (Barbados, the Bahamas, Guiana, Providence Island, Nevis, Antigua, Saint Kitts, Barbuda, and Montserrat), North America (Newfoundland, Nova Scotia, New Hampshire, Plymouth, Massachusetts, Connecticut, Rhode Island, Maryland, and Virginia), and the North Atlantic (Bermuda). These colonies were not all the same nor were the explorers and colonists, who possessed different motivations and goals.

These invading newcomers and traders were not fully in control, as they quickly found out. Wherever English ships landed, they met Native nations and communities that had their own vibrant cultures and relationships with the land stretching back for generations. Indigenous communities often sought trade and diplomatic negotiations with the new English colonists in ways that helped strengthen their own nations in particular ways. Native presence and willingness, or unwillingness, to trade and enter into treaties with European intruders directly shaped when and where English colonists found success. And when the actions of invading colonizers became intolerable, Indigenous nations often resisted in important acts of refusal, asserting their own sovereignty and power through diplomacy and a vigorous defense of their lands.[1]

In all of these locations, English colonists fixated on land, commodities, and Indigenous labor in various forms. Although trade and uneasy alliance often marked the early years of colonization, when English colonists got the upper hand, they soon shifted from sporadic stealing and kidnapping of Natives along the coastlines to more systematic enslavement as an intentional tool of colonial domination and land theft. It is impossible to separate the founding of America from this hemispheric array of English colonial ventures, all of which were intensely driven by profits and exploitation.

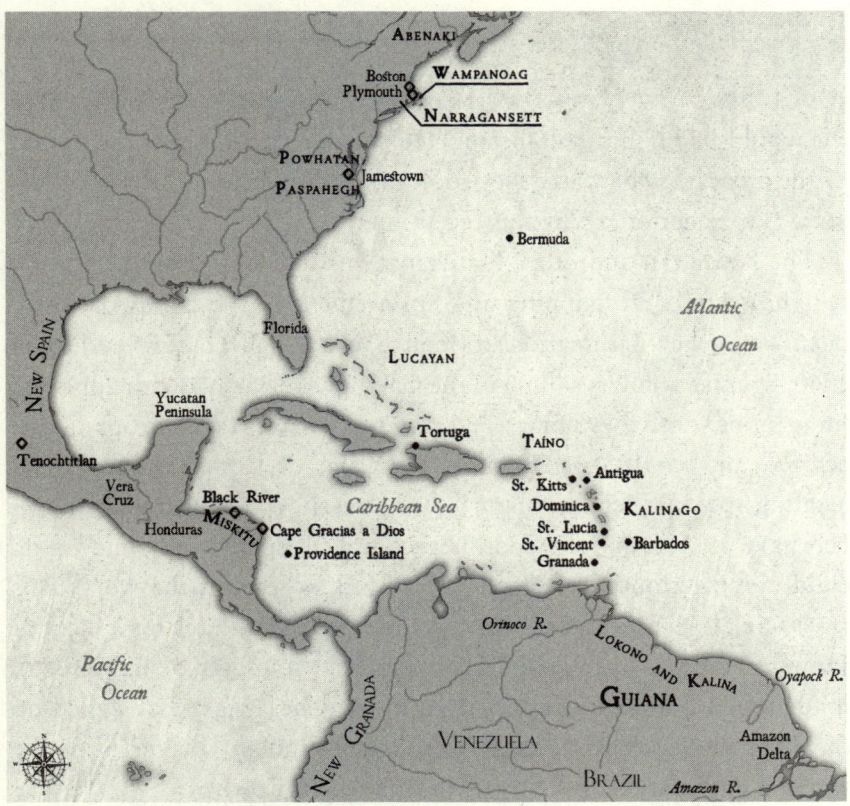

EARLY ENGLISH COLONIES.

Understanding the key role of Indigenous slavery in early colonization also helps expand our ideas about the origins of slavery in American history. In textbooks and wider American culture, the focus has been almost solely on African slavery, which scholars suggest started in 1619 when "20. And Odd Negroes" were transported to Virginia.[2] But that was only the start of *African* slavery in English North America; English colonists had been stealing and enslaving Native Americans from the time they first began exploring the lands that later became the United States. A narrow association of American slavery with Black slavery has resulted in the omission of the important role Indigenous enslavement played in US history, not only at the beginning but in every decade that followed, extending well into the late nineteenth century. The enslavement of Indigenous people was a core tactic of colonization that helped clear land for settlement and expansion, and it was employed from the moment English colonists set foot on American soil.

A VOLLEY OF ARROWS WAS the first greeting sent by the Powhatan to the would-be English colonists in 1607 as they landed near the mouth of the great body of water they soon called the Chesapeake Bay, after a local Native nation.[3] Why this reception?

The Powhatan and other Native nations in the region had already felt the sting of kidnapping and enslavement at the hands of Europeans, and they had learned to fight back. A half century earlier, in 1560, Spanish soldiers sailing in the Chesapeake Bay had kidnapped an Indigenous youth they named Paquiquineo. He was taken to Spain, catechized, and baptized as Don Luis, but he later returned and led a devastating attack of retaliation on a Jesuit mission town near his home in February 1571. Don Luis and his accomplices spared only one young child named Alonso de Olmos, who lived to recount the story. This massacre at Ajacán was not far from the site of the later settlement at Jamestown.[4] And in 1606, one year before the founding of Jamestown, unidentified European ships arrived in the Chesapeake Bay, sailed up the Rappahannock River to a Topahannock Indian village, killed the sachem, and carried off many of the Natives as captives.[5]

Arrows notwithstanding, the motley collection of profit-seeking Englishmen who arrived in 1607—and they were all men—cobbled together a settlement they called Jamestown, in honor of their king. It was situated along the Powhatan (Jamestown) River in the middle of a large territory known as Tsenacommacah, which covered a thirty-to-fifty-mile-wide swath of land stretching from present-day Virginia Beach one hundred miles northwest to Richmond. Tsenacommacah was home to perhaps as many as twenty thousand members of nations and bands confederated as the Powhatan, who lived in a thriving collection of towns, bands, and tribes as tributaries to the leader Wahunsonacock, also called Powhatan.[6]

Despite the deep mistrust of white invaders, the powerful Wahunsonacock decided to allow the English settlers to stay in hopes of incorporating the fledgling settlement as a tributary.[7] But as Wahunsonacock soon found out, the English would betray his trust on all fronts. When Jamestown colonists squandered their time hunting for gold instead of planting fields, their food stores dwindled in late summer, and they started eating literally everything, including vermin, snakes, dogs, and human excrement. During what became known as the "starving time" of 1609 to 1610, one colonist killed his wife and ate her; others dug up a recently interred Indigenous corpse to consume; still others devoured the bodies of those who had recently perished while scavenging in the woods.[8]

To stay alive, the Jamestown settlers needed more than rats and human flesh, so Smith captured the sachem of the Paspahegh tribe and forced some of the Paspaheghs to "worke in chaines" until they produced enough corn, meat, and other provisions for the rest of the Jamestown settlers.[9] And when the Paspaheghs resisted and war broke out in 1610, in what scholars call the First Powhatan War, the colonists soon tried to annihilate the entire nation.[10]

To destroy the Paspahegh, the English leaders captured a man from that tribe named Kempes—whom Governor George Percy called a "slave"—and forced him to lead seventy English soldiers to his home village.[11] On arrival, the small army surrounded the village and, with a pistol shot as a signal, chased the Paspahegh from their homes, murdered sixteen residents, and took the sunksqua (female sachem), her children, and one additional Paspahegh man as prisoners. After razing the village and torching the gardens and crops, Percy ordered the captured Paspahegh man to be beheaded on the spot and marched the sunksqua and her children three miles back to the boats. On the bank of the Powhatan River, Percy's men demanded that the Paspahegh children be put to death, so the soldiers forced the children from their mother, tossed them into the river, and took turns shooting them as they tried desperately to swim away. Thus the English deprived the Paspahegh of subsequent generations of hereditary leaders.

On the return to Jamestown, the army attacked and burned another town, with a total of sixty-five Paspaheghs killed in the day's raids.[12] Percy kept close watch over Kempes during the slaughter and forced him back to Jamestown, even though he ordered the Paspahegh sunksqua to be executed. Within a year, Kempes, still enslaved by the English, died from scurvy.[13]

After the brutal suppression of the Paspahegh, Thomas Dale, the new governor of Virginia, wrote to the Virginia Company in London in August 1611, laying out a plan to take over prime Powhatan territory

YEHAKINS, OR SINGLE-FAMILY HOMES, IN THE RECREATED
POWHATAN INDIAN VILLAGE AT THE JAMESTOWN
SETTLEMENT IN JAMESTOWN, VIRGINIA, 2019.

from the coast up the Jamestown River to the falls (near present-day Richmond). Wahunsonacock, Dale hoped, would have to either submit to the English presence or move his vast network of tributary and allied Native nations elsewhere.[14]

To force Wahunsonacock's hand, two years later Captain Samuel Argall turned the Patawomeck tribe against the Powhatan and had them kidnap Wahunsonacock's daughter, Amonute, and hold her hostage in Jamestown. Amonute, or Pocahontas, as she was later known, understood her role as an intermediary and diplomat when she married John Rolfe and traveled to London in 1616, where she quite likely crossed paths with a formerly enslaved Wampanoag man named Squanto and possibly other North American Native captives.[15]

TWO YEARS AFTER the founding of Virginia, a serendipitous shipwreck established another influential English colony. In 1609, the English ship *Sea Venture*, bound for Jamestown with much-needed supplies, was blown by a storm into the reefs of "the Bermudas." European seaborne empires had already dubbed the treacherous archipelago of Bermuda six hundred miles off the North American coast Devil's Island because, as one early inhabitant noted, the notorious "gusts, stormes, and foule weather" of the island made every captain steer clear of the place as they would the "Diuell himselfe."[16] More than three hundred battered hulls litter the reefs of the islands today, giving it the title of the shipwreck capital of the world.[17]

The *Sea Venture*'s misadventure led to an immediate rush to colonize the lush, unpopulated string of islands. Instead of an island of devils, Bermuda—or Somers Islands, as they were called, after Captain George Somers—was completely unpopulated, temperate, and fertile, making the archipelago ideal for English settlement.[18] Promoters of English colonization pounced on the islands as a third important colonial node, along with Virginia and Guiana (where the English established several short-lived colonies), to anchor English Atlantic colonialism and privateering.[19] Bermuda colonists quickly imported enslaved Native Americans and Africans to pilfer local resources. A privateering ship named the *Edwin* sailed into the port at St. George's from the Caribbean in 1616 with at least one enslaved Native and one enslaved African on board, brought to the islands in part because of their proven expertise in diving for pearl-bearing oysters.[20] These first enslaved pearl divers are memorialized in a large mural in the Bermuda National Museum to mark this important moment in Bermuda's early colonization.

Aspiring English privateers exulted at Bermuda's potential to become a slave-trading hub for Indigenous and African captives. An English privateer named John Powell captured at least three Portuguese ships in 1617 and deposited several dozen enslaved Africans in Bermuda.[21] In 1618, a determined merchant named Daniel Elfrith arrived on his ship the *Treasurer* and brought a load of African (and possibly Indigenous) captives to exchange for provisions.[22] Enslaved Natives and Africans arrived through other means, too, as when individual colonists moved to Bermuda and brought an enslaved person or two with them.[23] By 1620, Bermuda had more than one hundred enslaved Africans and Natives on the island, all brought by English privateers or newly arrived planters.[24] English colonists quickly learned the value of enslaved men and women for their knowledge and skills in planting and curing tobacco.[25] Bermuda governor Nathaniel Butler reflected

"PEARL DIVERS," DETAIL FROM *THE HALL OF HISTORY: BERMUDA'S STORY IN ART*, MURAL ILLUSTRATING 500 YEARS OF BERMUDA HISTORY, BY GRAHAM FOSTER, 2009.

a growing consensus when he confided to a friend in early 1621 that "slaves are the most proper and cheape instruments for this plantation that can be."[26]

ENGLISH COLONISTS HAD BEEN enslaving Native Americans for a half century by the time Virginia first received enslaved Africans in 1619. These captives arrived in Virginia in partnership with Daniel Elfrith, the English privateer who had previously trafficked enslaved Native Americans and Africans to Bermuda. Earlier that year, he had teamed up with the *White Lion*, an English-owned ship that operated out of Flushing (Vlissingen), Netherlands, and was commanded by the Dutch captain John Jope. They sailed to the Caribbean in search of Spanish and Portuguese ships to raid.[27]

In Mexican waters somewhere off the Yucatán Peninsula, Elfrith and Jope captured the Portuguese slave ship *São João Bautista*, laden with more than one hundred enslaved Africans from Angola.[28] Elfrith and Jope agreed to set sail for Virginia, loaded with these captives. On the way, the two ships got separated and possibly stopped at other ports to offload some of the human cargo. Jope arrived first at Point Comfort, Virginia, in late August 1619 with twenty-nine or thirty of the African captives in the hold of the *White Lion*, whom he traded to Virginians for food and provisions.[29] Four days later, Elfrith's boat, the *Treasurer*, also sailed into Point Comfort with the remaining enslaved Africans in its hold.[30] Elfrith seemingly sold a few more African captives there, because several months later, in early 1620, a colony census recorded thirty-two Africans, with a gender divide of fifteen men and seventeen women.[31]

Elfrith refreshed his crew and soon sailed out again, this time heading for Bermuda. There he sold the remainder of his stolen human cargo of "25 negroes" to Bermuda planters, including Miles Kendall, the deputy governor of Bermuda, who purchased fourteen of them.[32] Privateers continued transporting captive Africans and Natives to Bermuda, Virginia, and other colonies over the following years and decades, steadily increasing the enslaved population of these early settlements.[33]

The August 1619 arrivals of the *White Lion* and *Treasurer* did indeed bring the first enslaved Africans to Virginia, so far as existing records indicate. But merchants and explorers there had already been enslaving Native Americans for decades, and they would continue to do so, even as they gradually imported enslaved Africans. Perhaps Virginia was slower than Bermuda to fully embrace enslaved Africans because the colonists had already commandeered a local supply of Indian servants and slaves. As early as 1609, Virginia leaders encouraged colonists to take Native children into their homes—not only for religious conversion but also for servitude.[34] The early colony records are spotty, but on August 2, 1619, the House of Burgesses in Virginia approved the plan of trying to entice additional local Native Americans "to live & labour" among them, "to doe service, in killing of Deere, Fishing, beating Corne, & other workes."[35] And within three years of the arrival of enslaved Africans, Virginians turned their attention toward enslaving Natives in larger numbers as war erupted in their midst.

INDIGENOUS ENSLAVEMENT also marked the early history of New England—that other iconic founding settlement in American history. A thriving population of approximately a hundred thousand Native peoples lived in the Dawnland, as Indigenous nations in the Northeast called their homelands since they were the first to see the sunrise. Large and powerful confederacies exerted great influence in the region, including the Wabanaki in what is now Maine, the Wampanoag in the Cape Cod region, and the Narragansett on the western shores of the Narragansett Bay. In addition, there were dozens of smaller bands and communities that stewarded the fertile forests, hills, mountains, and coastlines for hundreds of years before the arrival of Europeans in the sixteenth century and whose ancestors had done the same for ten thousand years before them. Dawnland nations were expert fishers of marine creatures as well as agriculturalists who grew corn, beans, and squash. All over the region, they cleared large swaths of forest underbrush with controlled burns in order to travel and hunt more easily.[36]

Dawnland residents, despite living in the less-traveled, colder northerly latitudes, had seen their fair share of enslavement and captivity at the hands of Europeans. This started with the Spanish in the 1520s, nearly a century before the arrival of the separatist-minded English puritans later called the "Pilgrims." English exploration brought more of the same. In 1611, Captain Edward Harlow went on a captive-taking spree along the New England coast, abducting six Native Americans on his journey from Maine to Capawe, or Noepe (Martha's Vineyard). A Native man named Pechmo escaped, but Harlow took Monopet, Pekenimne, Sakaweston, Coneconam, and Epenow back to England to ply them for information, parade around London, and give to sponsors.[37]

A few years later, in 1614, Captain Thomas Hunt, who was sailing with John Smith, landed on Cape Cod and lured twenty-four Wampanoags into trading on his ship. Hunt and his men turned on the Wampanoags and forced them all below deck. Hunt's men knew the value of and market for captive Native Americans, so they sailed directly to Málaga, Spain, where they tried to sell these New England Natives for "private gaine," as Smith later reported.[38] The gaping loss that such stealings created for families and communities lingered for a lifetime and beyond. Seven years later, a still-grieving Wampanoag mother, while "weeping and crying," told the Plymouth colonists that all three of her sons had been stolen by Hunt. She never saw them again.[39]

Some of these enslaved New England Natives found their freedom and plotted their return home. Squanto, one of the Indigenous men captured by Hunt in 1614, secured his freedom in Spain, made his way to England, and returned to his homeland in 1619, which had by then been wracked by disease. Squanto, or Tisquantum, leveraged his familiarity with the English language and culture to position himself as an important intermediary between the Pilgrims, when they arrived in 1620, and Ousamequin (Massasoit), the chief sachem of the Wampanoag.[40] Epenow, who had been captured by Harlow in 1611, also found his way back home to Noepe and orchestrated a retaliation against Captain Thomas Dermer in 1619, killing everyone except one sailor who had stayed with the dinghy.[41]

Despite overwhelming signs of Native American presence, English promoters of colonization generally disregarded Native sovereignty and land rights, as can be demonstrated in a curious map created by Captain John Smith in 1616. Informed by Native knowledge, Smith crafted a detailed drawing of the region he called—for the first time in writing—New England. No English person yet lived in this area, but by drawing English towns instead of Wampanoag or Abenaki villages and by giving the towns English names (suggested by the young Prince Charles), Smith produced an aggressively colonized map that imagined the region as already settled by the English. Smith's New England was a fictive place perhaps, but his map made the landscape more legible to prospective colonists. It stands as powerful evidence of English settler-colonial aspirations regarding the desired eradication and replacement of Native Americans.[42]

Into this chaotic world of kidnapping, enslavement, and retribution, yet another English ship arrived on the coast of Cape Cod in 1620. On board the *Mayflower* were 102 passengers, mostly families and some crew, with a copy of Captain John Smith's Indian-less map in hand. Unlike previous traders, they came to stay. They are often referred to as Pilgrims, but that moniker only became popularized as nineteenth-century Americans began devising pious origin stories for the United States.[43] These English men and women were puritans who wished to reform the Church of England along lines they viewed as more strictly

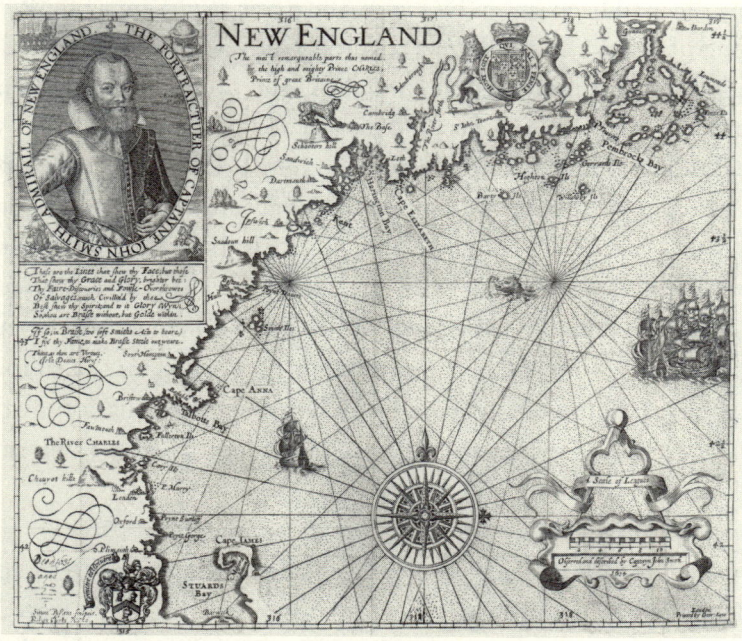

JOHN SMITH'S MAP, *NEW ENGLAND: THE MOST REMARQUABLE PARTS THUS NAMED BY THE HIGH AND MIGHTY PRINCE CHARLES, PRINCE OF GREAT BRITAINE,* ENGRAVED BY SIMON VAN DE PASSE, PRINTED BY HUMFREY LOWNES FOR ROBERT CLERKE, 1616.

biblical. Unlike the puritans who would found Boston a decade later, these earlier settlers believed in completely separating from the Church of England, which they believed was too Catholic.[44]

But even the godliest of all English colonists still dreamed of getting rich. They initially hoped to follow in the wake of Raleigh and Elfrith and settle in Guiana, on the South American coast, where prospects for wealth were greatest. Instead, they sailed to the Dawnland, where the *Mayflower* was greeted by the punishing icy winds of November. Travel weary and starving, the Pilgrims went ashore and pillaged a small Native village for buried corn and bean stores. When they finally found a place in the Cape Cod harbor to land and build a temporary shelter, they almost immediately experienced the same reception the English had in Jamestown: a flurry of arrows from a Native attack.[45]

That winter, these new English colonists watched while half of their party was whittled away through starvation, disease, and a suicide.[46] Even so, the Pilgrims likely only survived because they were eventually permitted to squat in an empty Patuxet village whose population had been decimated by diseases a few years earlier, between 1616 and 1618. These English colonists named this first town "Plimouth," and true to John Smith's map, erased the former name of the Patuxet Indian village.

The Plymouth settlement lasted because Squanto chose to aid it, despite his having been previously stolen and enslaved by the English. With Squanto translating, the Pilgrims were permitted to stay in Wampanoag territory, on Ousamequin's terms, as he hoped to use the English to bolster his own presence in the region.[47] Squanto could not have foreseen the devastating chaos and violence that successive waves of English immigration would eventually impose.

FARTHER SOUTH, the Powhatan grew weary of constant encroachment into their territory by Jamestown settlers. Opechancanough, the new Powhatan werowance who had come to power after his older brother Wahunsonacock passed away in 1618, grew increasingly impatient with the relentless arrival of colonists, cattle, and hogs and the never-ending clearing of Native land for lucrative tobacco plantations.[48] During the winter months of 1621–1622, Opechancanough concocted a plan of retaliation that secretly spread through the confederated Native towns surrounding Jamestown.

On the evening of March 21, 1622, unarmed members of Paspahegh, Pamunkey, and other Powhatan bands attacked colonists around Jamestown, using the Virginians' own knives, swords, clubs, and daggers to systematically slaughter as many residents as possible. Powhatan Natives also targeted other creatures that accompanied the detested invaders—the cows, horses, and pigs that ranged free and trampled Native gardens. Some warriors sent an additional message by stuffing bread into the mouths of colonists' corpses as a warning to not "eat up all of the land."[49]

Within a few hours, 347 colonists lay dead—roughly a quarter of the colony's English population.[50] The Powhatan avengers slipped off into the forest and continued an effective campaign of revenge, randomly targeting colonists along roadways and in their homes. "Since the massacre," Governor Argall reported, "they have killed us in our own doors, fields, and houses."[51] Virginians were stunned by this raw display of Indigenous power. As Ashley Atkins Spivey, an anthropologist and member of the Pamunkey tribe, has noted, "People forget that there was a powerful Indigenous nation negotiating its own situation with the English . . . and those descendants still continue to live today."[52]

In response, Virginians brashly pursued a policy of terror and enslavement, which led to a decade of sporadic fighting often called the Second Powhatan War. Militias traveled from town to town, on horseback, tracking fleeing Natives using bloodhounds and mastiffs to instill terror and "seaze them."[53] Edward Waterhouse, the secretary of the Virginia Company, stated publicly that Indians "who before were used as friends" could now "most justly be compelled to servitude and drudgery."[54]

Another Virginian named John Martin agreed. He argued in a December 1622 essay titled "The Manner Howe to Bringe the Indians into Subjection" that the Powhatan should be enslaved, not murdered, because they were more valuable as slaves. Martin believed that Indigenous captives could be commanded to perform the backbreaking labor demanded by the newly profitable tobacco fields. They could likewise be made to produce silk, hemp, and flax or serve as galley slaves endlessly rowing English ships around the Mediterranean.[55] Unsurprisingly, Natives began appearing more frequently in the colony papers as servants and slaves after this 1622 war and the sporadic conflicts that flared up during the following decade.

Colonists also shipped an unknown number of Powhatan captives to other colonies as slaves. Waterhouse suggested that some of these captives be sent to Bermuda to prevent further uprisings.[56] When London officials criticized these policies, Virginia governor Sir Francis Wyatt was unapologetic. "Our first worke," he thundered, "is expulsion of the Salvages to gaine the free range of the countrey for encrease of Cattle . . . for it is infinitely better to have no heathen among us, who at best were but as thornes in our sides, then to be at peace and league with them."[57] The English monarchy was unconvinced and in 1625 claimed direct control of Virginia and Bermuda as royal colonies. Royal presence did not halt the ongoing war against the Powhatan, nor would it stop additional Native land loss and enslavement, which were quickly becoming unstated English policy.

THE 1622 POWHATAN WAR was a warning that reverberated around the nascent English empire. Native nations had demonstrated that they were willing to defend themselves and their lands against encroachment and enslavement. Colonial governments used this resistance as rationale for launching full-scale "just wars" against Indigenous nations in order to take land and round up Natives for sale into slavery. These conflicts had obvious benefits for colonies in that they helped clear desired lands while providing a source of revenue through the sale of Native captives into slavery, whether locally or to other colonies. Rather than respect these displays of Native sovereignty, English colonists dug in, determined to act more preemptively in the future.

The same year the Powhatan rose up against Virginia colonists, a powerful Kalinago chief called Tegremond greeted Thomas Warner on the sandy shores of Liamuiga (today known as St. Kitts). Positioned at the northern edge of the Leeward Islands in the Caribbean, St. Kitts is one of many smaller islands where thousands of Kalinago and Taíno had fled during the Spanish invasion in the sixteenth century.

Tegremond's people had withstood 130 years of Spanish colonization through centuries-old strategies of adaptation and negotiation. They were expert agriculturalists, craftspeople, and sailors, with the ability to easily row between islands where European sailboats were at the mercy of relentlessly directional trade winds and currents.[58]

Tegremond seemed open to Warner's plan in 1622 to plant tobacco on the island since he likely saw Warner as a tributary and ally. When Warner returned in January 1624 with eager colonists, they stunned the island's Kalinago population by immediately building a military-style fort, replete with palisades and small openings from which to fire guns if need be. Perhaps with the Powhatan attack at Jamestown in mind, Warner joined with some recently arrived French colonists and led a preemptive raid in which he murdered Tegremond and hundreds of Kalinagos and enslaved as many of the survivors as possible. Warner forced the rest off the island in their great wooden canoes, thereby claiming their home as his own.[59]

Warner turned St. Kitts into his own lucrative fiefdom powered almost entirely by enslaved Native Americans. Colonists who later arrived from England noted that Warner had at least twenty-four enslaved Natives laboring on his estate, but no Africans. When Warner's enslaved Indigenous workforce decided to self-emancipate by rowing the arduous seventy miles eastward against the trade winds to Antigua, Warner hired a Scottish merchant named Captain Fletcher to hunt them down and force them back to his plantation on St. Kitts.[60] In 1636, the colony authorized the sale and purchase of enslaved Africans alongside Natives, with both being sold into slavery for life.[61]

English colonists also claimed the pear-shaped, forested island of Barbados as an early colony, but unlike St. Kitts, there were no Indigenous people there to enslave. Called Ich-rougan-aim by the region's Lokono (Arawak), it had been their home for centuries. The combination of early Spanish slave raiding and attacks by Kalinago drove the original inhabitants to flee to neighboring islands by the early seventeenth century.[62] Kalinago on nearby St. Vincent sailed to Barbados for a month at a time, building campgrounds and fire pits and bringing finely crafted clay pots in which to boil the pork, seafood, and birds that they captured.[63] Some colonists reported finding deity effigies made by the original Lokono or Kalinago inhabitants. The head of at least one weighed sixty pounds and was preserved into the mid-eighteenth century.[64]

English merchants quickly trafficked Natives and Africans to labor on Barbados, as they had done on Bermuda and St. Kitts. In 1627, Captain Henry Powell transported thirty-two Lokonos to the island from the Dutch colony of Suriname on the South American coast. These Lokonos also brought fruits and vegetables like cassava, yams, and pineapples to cultivate on the island, in addition to starters for tobacco, cotton, and annatto (a strong dye) for commodity production.[65] English merchants supposedly offered the Lokono a two-year agreement and payment of fifty pounds sterling in "axes, bills, hoes, knives, looking-glasses, and beads."[66] Whatever contract existed soon became null and void, for after Powell's departure, other Barbadian planters, perhaps following the examples of Virginia and St. Kitts, took the Lokono "by force and made them slaves."[67] Population estimates of the island from 1627 lump together the thirty or so Lokonos with the ten imported Africans for a total of between forty and fifty "slaves of Indyenes and blacks."[68]

With an early shortage of enslaved Native Americans and Africans, Barbados soon relied on indentured white servants, as did Virginia. To distinguish between white servants and enslaved Natives and Africans, Barbados passed the first race-based slavery law in all the English colonies. Enacted in July 1636, it stated, "*Negroes* and *Indians*, that came here to be sold, should serve for Life, unless a Contract was before made to the contrary," thereby establishing a clear racialized division of laborers.[69] Although enslaved Africans soon dominated Barbados plantations, enslaved Indigenous people continued to be listed in plantation records for the next two centuries.

THE METEORIC "SUCCESS" OF colonies like Barbados, Bermuda, St. Kitts, and Virginia soon inspired others. English merchants created two joint-stock companies in 1629 to finance separate colonies in the Americas: the Providence Island Company and the Massachusetts Bay Company. The first company sent a cluster of ships to Isla de Providencia, or Providence Island, a small land mass 120 miles off the eastern coast of Nicaragua, to try to set up successful plantations but also to rob, pilfer, and attack the Spanish. The colony lasted for just over a decade before the Spanish sacked it and dispersed the English planters. The second company sent a similar fleet of ships to New England, where they established the Massachusetts Bay Colony and founded Boston.[70] Although Massachusetts is better known now, from the perspective of financially motivated proprietors in London, it held less promise at the time.

The two colonies were related in that they shared many puritan investors in England. Unlike the puritans at Plymouth who espoused total separation from the Church of England, the Massachusetts and Providence Island puritans considered themselves to be a reformist subset of the Church of England. Both colonies had the twin goals of creating a "godly society" on the back of an economic program that would bring success to the ventures and wealth to the inhabitants and England.[71]

The initial wave of colonists that arrived in the Massachusetts Bay Colony in 1630 included the first governor, John Winthrop, on the *Arabella*. His famous vision for the colony as a "city on a hill" was distinctly bereft of Indigenous people, whom he did not even mention.[72] The group settled on a small neck of land the local Massachusett Natives called Shawmut, which was soon renamed Boston and chosen as the seat of their colony.

Following the precedents of other English colonies, these puritans sought to exploit the land and labor of Indigenous people. Early New England colonists refrained from enslaving Indians in large numbers at first, likely for practical reasons: they were outnumbered, and Native Americans were valuable trade partners. However, less than one year after the founding of Boston, so many colonists were either enticing or coercing Natives to labor for them that the colony's leadership had to pass a law in March 1631 stating that no one could keep an Indian in their family as a servant unless they were granted a "license from the Court." The law gave residents two months to comply.[73] Even leading magistrates and governors held Native servants, including John Winthrop and his son John Winthrop Jr., who each received a license in 1634.[74] Indigenous servants, along with white servants and workers, were an important source of labor in Massachusetts given that enslaved Africans had not yet been imported.

Within a half decade, Massachusetts puritans turned to mass

enslavement as a tool of colonial domination in a vicious war against the powerful Pequot nation. As English colonists spread deeply into the interior of the region, founding the trading posts and towns of Windsor, Hartford, and Wethersfield in what is now Connecticut, they inserted themselves farther into the territory of the powerful Pequot and close to Dutch trading posts. Two English traders were murdered in 1634 and 1636, and English authorities blamed the Pequot.[75]

Rumors soon swirled about an impending Pequot attack. New Englanders had been watching Virginia closely, and they believed, as English chronicler Philip Vincent later stated, that Virginians had been too lenient with the Powhatan, which had led to the 1622 surprise attack on the Jamestown settlements. To avoid a similar mistake, the colonists in Massachusetts and Plymouth launched a preemptive war against the Pequot, raising an army by promising soldiers the reward of Native captives and any other plunder they could find in exchange for their service.[76]

The results were devastating. Massachusetts magistrates sent their former governor John Endicott to Block Island in August 1636 with instructions to destroy the Manissean tribe, who they believed had murdered one of the traders. Endicott's men were authorized to burn villages, kill the men, and take the women and children as captives. On arrival, Endicott found all the Manisseans had fled into the woods, so he razed the towns and sailed to Connecticut. When negotiations with the Pequot broke down, Endicott decided to strike first, attacking a village and destroying Pequot food supplies. What started as a few raids soon turned into total war. In village after village, English troops burned towns, destroyed gardens, decimated food supplies, murdered Pequot men, and took women and children captive.[77]

The most significant mass murder of Pequots occurred in 1637. In the early morning stillness of Friday, May 26, English troops and their Mohegan and Narragansett allies invaded the large, circular Pequot fort at Mystic. After a fierce fight, Captain John Mason yelled to his men, "We must burn them!" So they set fire to as many dome-shaped bark wetus as they could and retreated through the two narrow entrances of the fort, shooting any Pequots who tried to escape. The rest burned to death inside, perhaps as many as four hundred to seven hundred in total.[78] Puritan leaders spun this horrifying massacre as a divine victory

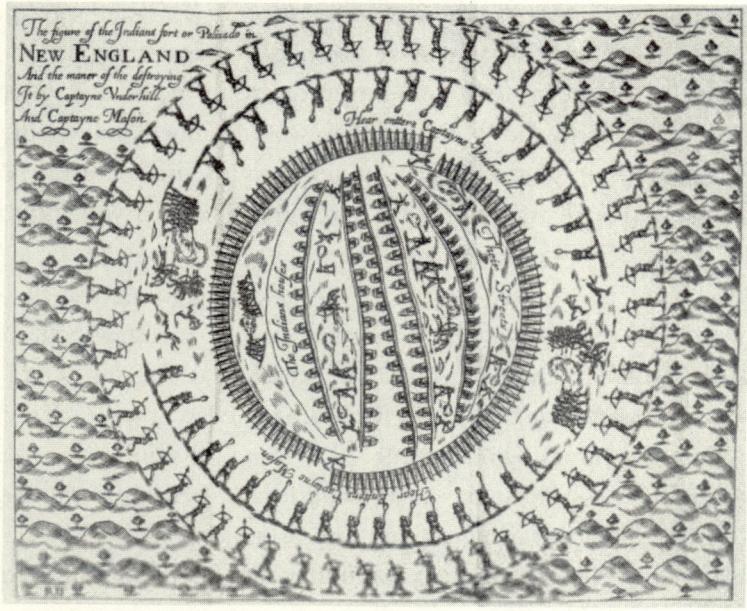

ENGLISH SOLDIERS AND NARRAGANSETT ALLIES
SURROUNDING MYSTIC FORT ARE DEPICTED IN *THE
FIGURE OF THE INDIANS' FORT OR PALIZADO IN NEW
ENGLAND AND THE MANER OF THE DESTROYING IT BY
CAPTYNE VANDERHILL AND CAPTAYNE MASON*, BY
JOHN AND DAVID HARRIS UNDERHILL, 1637.

with Old Testament overtones, noting that Pequots "frying in the fire"
were "a sweet sacrifice" to God.[79] The Mohegan and Narragansett allies
of the English were horrified by this indiscriminate killing of women,
children, and other noncombatants. "Mach it, mach it," they protested,
meaning it was too much and violated Indigenous codes of conduct
in warfare. After the Mystic Fort massacre, some of the Narragansett
withdrew their support for the English and returned to their homes.[80]

The Pequot War, as it was later called, quickly escalated into a land-
clearing, slave-raiding rampage against the Pequot and their allies.[81]
Fanning out from Mystic, English forces marauded through Pequot
lands, burning towns, destroying lush gardens and fields of beans and
squash, and stealing large supplies of corn. Mainly, however, they were
interested in taking women and children captive, while most captured
Pequot men were simply murdered. Puritan military commander Captain Israel Stoughton chased more than a hundred Pequots—roughly

seventy-five of whom were women and children—out of a large cedar swamp called Ohomowauke, between what is now called the Thames River and Ledyard, Connecticut. Stoughton quickly executed approximately twenty-three of the Pequot men, spared two sachems, and gathered eighty Pequot women and children on the shore of the Long Island Sound for shipment to Boston to be sold into slavery.[82] English commanders gave their coats to some of the Pequot women as a sign of their imposed ownership along with written instructions to back up their choices. When the *Giggles* arrived in Boston in late June, these women and other claimed captives were set aside; the rest were sold into slavery to local colonists.[83]

English troops spent an additional two months in the summer of 1637 chasing Pequot survivors and their allies down the Connecticut coast as far as present-day Fairfield, just south of what later became New Haven.[84] In the Fairfield Swamp Fight, troops captured at least two hundred surrendering Pequots who were immediately divvied up as slaves among the English soldiers from Massachusetts and Plymouth.[85] Wincumbone, the wife of the Pequot leader Mononotto, had two urgent requests after she was captured: "that the English would not abuse her body and that her children might not be taken from her."[86] In this profound statement, this strong Pequot woman gave voice to the concern of every Indigenous woman and mother who had been stolen. *Please don't rape me, and please don't take away my children.* Massachusetts governor John Winthrop disregarded her pleas. He claimed Wincumbone as his slave on her arrival in Boston and split up her family.

In the aftermath of the Pequot War, requests for Indian captives poured into Boston. The bumptious minister Hugh Peter of Salem, Massachusetts, wrote to John Winthrop in July 1637, asking for a few young, enslaved Pequots for himself and future Massachusetts governor John Endicott.[87] Even Roger Williams, the rogue puritan who founded Rhode Island in 1636 and was a relative admirer of Native cultures, requested and received a very specific Indian youth "with red about his neck"—likely a birthmark, tattoo, or sash—but also said he would settle for any Pequot captive.[88] Williams later thanked Winthrop for selecting a Pequot boy and asked him to rename him, which Winthrop did, calling him Will.[89]

Bermuda planters, too, demanded a share of enslaved Pequots. Winthrop attempted to comply, arranging for Captain William Pierce from Salem to take fifteen Pequot boys and two Pequot women onto his ship, the *Desire*, along with other provisions and trade items, and set sail for Bermuda. But Pierce sailed past the remote archipelago and instead continued another two thousand miles southward deep into Spanish Caribbean territory to Providence Island.[90] Once on the island, Pierce sold Pequot captives as slaves, which Providence Island records note as "Cannibal Negroes" from New England. In exchange, he purchased some cotton, tobacco, and enslaved Africans.[91] From there he set his course for Boston, where, in 1638, he unloaded the enslaved Africans and sold them to local colonists.[92]

Some enslaved Pequots resisted their captivity and ran away, attempting to reunite with kin. Roger Williams in Rhode Island functioned as a slave catcher, along with the Narragansett. Three Pequot women ran away from Boston in the late fall of 1637, after five months of enslavement. Two of them were tracked down and found starving in the woods by Narragansetts and taken to Williams's house in Providence. One of these women had been claimed by Samuel Cole, an innkeeper in Boston; she complained that she was harassed by white servants on Cole's property. One of the servants had tried to rape her; others had beaten her with branding irons. The younger Pequot woman had escaped from an unnamed family in Winisimmit, or what is now Chelsea, Massachusetts. The third enslaved Pequot ran away from the reclusive Anglican minister William Blackstone, but she eluded recapture.[93]

The stunning, genocidal Pequot War was a windfall for New England colonists. Pequot leaders were forced to sign the Treaty of Hartford in 1638, which completely exiled them from their homelands, distributed Pequot captives among Indigenous and English communities, and inserted the English as the arbiters in Indian politics.[94] Most visibly, enslaved Native Americans swelled the labor ranks of colonial households and farms across New England. In these spaces, they performed important household chores, cleared forests, planted fields, and in other ways performed the work of colony-building and wealth accrual for the English.

Of all the gains, the newly emptied lands were the most valuable, and puritans swarmed into Pequot homelands. Quinnipiac (New Haven) was founded in April 1638, and Milford, Guilford, Stratford, and Fairfield all followed in 1639. New London (formerly called Pequot) was founded in 1641, and the Pequot River was renamed the Thames River, after the primary waterway in London.[95] War veterans received payments in the form of Pequot land. Captain John Mason received five hundred acres in 1641, with another five hundred set aside for distribution to soldiers.[96] Slowly but surely, English colonists edged out Native names and Dawnland peoples themselves, just as John Smith's 1616 map had predicted.

The Pequot refused to be exterminated so easily, however. Within a few years some of them had moved back to their former lands, and even colonial records once again began to refer to them as Pequot, despite an official ban on their name.[97] Today two Pequot nations— the Mashantucket Pequot and the Eastern Pequot—remain on vastly reduced portions of their original homelands in Connecticut.

IN VIRGINIA, OPECHANCANOUGH, with his Powhatan warriors, made one final stand against English colonization. It too turned into a slave-raiding war. For nearly a century, the aged leader had watched the Powhatan confederacy grow and thrive through tributaries and trade networks.[98] English arrival and expansion threatened to destroy it all. So, from the portable bed carried by his men, Opechancanough— who had orchestrated the 1622 Powhatan attacks—masterminded yet another powerful blow to the Virginia Colony. Early in the morning of April 18, 1644, Powhatan warriors stormed through the doors of houses all along the north bank of the James River, killing colonists as they slept. By late morning, with farms burning and four hundred to five hundred colonists dead, the Powhatans disappeared again into the forest and up the river.[99]

The colony's response was slow but decisive. The royal governor, Sir William Berkeley, drafted an army and in late June launched a three-pronged attack on Powhatan homelands. Captain William Claiborne led three hundred soldiers and horse-mounted rangers up the York River, straight to the Pamunkey seat of power.[100] For more than a month they ranged through Pamunkey and other Powhatan homelands, burning villages and corn supplies. Two other English armies did the same farther south. Troops tracked down Opechancanough and put the centenarian in prison in Jamestown, where he languished until an English guard shot him in the back, ending a life that had begun decades before the English had ventured into the so-called New World.

During the long series of retaliatory raids, later called the Third Anglo-Powhatan War, Virginia militias again prioritized raiding for Native captives. As in New England, Indigenous children were seen as less dangerous servants and slaves, as well as more malleable for religious conversion or "civilization." Such was the case on July 10, 1645, when Virginia troops brought in "many prisoners." The children were retained locally, while all Natives over the age of eleven were placed in the hold of Governor William Berkeley's ship and sent to the "Western Islands," or the West Indies (as the Caribbean was called, in contrast to the East Indies in Asia).[101]

Some colonists positioned themselves as local Native slave traders, selling captives to other Virginians. Thomas Smallcombe of York County led a series of raids against the Pamunkey and later sold Native captives to colonists for considerable sums of money, including six Pamunkey individuals in 1646 to three different men. Governor Berkeley purchased two enslaved Pamunkeys, as did Captain Thomas Petters and Sir John Hammon, for between £250 and £300 per individual. When Smallcombe died later that year, his estate included six enslaved Natives.[102]

Virginia militias hunted the Powhatan and their tributaries for a year and a half before English officials and the new Powhatan chief, Necotowance, signed a treaty in October 1646 that represented massive gains for the English. The Powhatan were banned from the immense tract of land claimed by Virginians, on pain of death, unless on official business and wearing an appropriate badge. Colonists were legally allowed to kill any Indigenous trespassers. The Powhatan had to give up any Africans and Indians they had captured, but the English could keep their enslaved Natives. The treaty also allowed Virginians to take into their household any Native youths under the age of twelve—presumably as servants, but under the guise of civilizing and Christianizing them.[103]

As in New England, Virginia's wars against nearby Indigenous nations expanded the labor ranks of the colony and cleared valuable land for colonial expansion. Some Natives had been enslaved in the 1644 Powhatan war. Others were Native children who had been sent to English households for shorter terms of servitude and were sometimes later sold as lifelong slaves. Thomas Busby, as just one example, sold a five-year-old Indian boy to William Rollinson in 1660 "for ye term & time of his life."[104] Enslaved Natives and Indigenous servants were an important and often overlooked part of the early labor force in Virginia. By 1650, there were as many Native servants and slaves in the colony as Africans.[105]

BY MIDCENTURY, English colonists had embraced policies of Indigenous enslavement as a means of labor as well as land grabbing. In 1645, as Virginia militias were hunting and enslaving Powhatan tributaries, the Massachusetts puritan Emanuel Downing wrote to his brother-in-law John Winthrop that, if a "Just warre" could be fought against the large and powerful Narragansett nation, the English could sell them into slavery in the Caribbean in exchange for enslaved Africans, just as had already been done with some of the Pequot in 1637. If Winthrop wanted to create a permanent society in which their "Children's Children" would eventually take over "this great Continent," Downing suggested, they needed the land clear of Indians and the fields full of slaves.[106]

It was a breathtakingly genocidal vision that was never fully enacted. But even Winthrop knew that enslaving Native Americans could be financially profitable, as captives sold into slavery in Virginia and New England helped defray the costs of engaging in the war.[107] This self-funding aspect of land-clearing wars with Natives through enslavement was also noted by Virginia governor Berkeley two decades later in 1668, when he suggested waging war against the "Northern Indians" and selling Native women and children into slavery to pay for it.[108]

Within a few decades of English colonization, enslaved Native Americans had quickly become an essential part of colonial labor and production. Native servants and slaves joined enslaved Africans and white servants in performing thousands of vital tasks in houses and on farms, freeing up colonists for other ventures and pursuits. By focusing on enslaving Native women and children, colonists stifled the reproductive capacity of tribes while simultaneously harnessing both the labor and the reproductive labor of enslaved Indigenous women.[109] All of these processes enabled the stealing of Native land that was essential for colonial expansion, even if the English had not yet fully worked out how to justify their rapacity and plunder against Native Americans.

Three

THIN
JUSTIFICATIONS

THE ENSLAVEMENT OF NATIVE AMERICANS IN ENGLISH COLONIES
prompted moral and legal questions, just as it had for Las Casas and
legal scholars a century earlier. And like the Spanish, English leaders
struggled to answer them. Was it legal to enslave Native Americans?
The technical answer was no, at least not at first, considering there
were no specific laws in any English colonies before 1636 that legalized
slavery (what legal scholars call "positive" or "statutory" law).[1] More
questions soon followed. What were the differences between white servitude and Indigenous and African slavery? Was slavery always for life?
Could children of enslaved Native Americans and Africans also be
claimed as slaves?

Since English colonial leaders had no comprehensive answers, colonists acted on their own, enslaving Natives and Africans before explicit
laws permitted it. They justified their actions through implicit support
from the Crown, a combination of deeper cultural legal traditions (like
English Common Law), biblical precedents, just war theory, and a
vague emerging notion of the law of nations, which included the rights
of conquerors to enslave the conquered under certain circumstances.[2]
More practically, slavery was becoming commonplace by the seventeenth century, and little had been done to regulate it.

In the absence of laws, colonists improvised and innovated, as an
enslaved Indigenous couple named James and Frances experienced.
During the sweltering summer months of 1651, they were married in
Bermuda, but with some significant strings attached. The records are
silent about where James and Frances were originally from or how they

arrived in the rapidly growing colony, but they had been taken captive and sold as slaves to separate colonists. On August 2, 1651, their two owners, Philip Lea and William Williams, both of Bermuda, signed a contract mandating that the Indigenous couple's future children would not be their own. Lea and Williams would share Frances's offspring, with the first one going to Williams, the second one to Lea, the third to Williams, for as long as Frances should bear children.[3] Frances's first child went to Williams as per the contract. And when the second child was born and handed off to Lea, he promptly sold the infant to another planter named Lazarus Owen. In turn, Owen deeded the newborn to his daughter with a new contract that directed that this child's future children be split among Owen's daughters in a likewise alternating fashion, in perpetuity.[4]

Notably, there was no law in Bermuda that specifically permitted colonists to enslave Indigenous people and their children and grand-children. Regardless, Bermuda residents imposed heritable, chattel

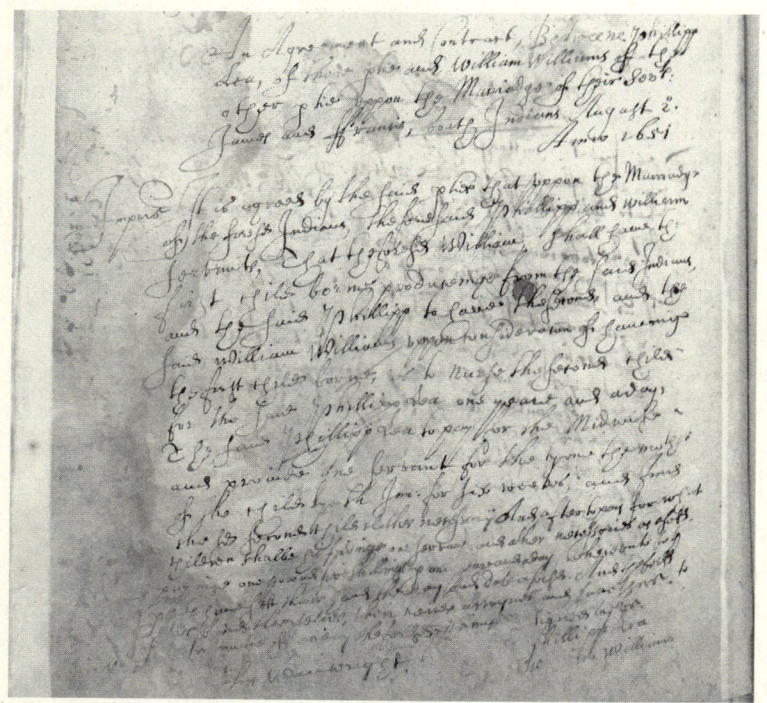

"AN AGREEMENT AND CONTRACT" REGARDING
JAMES AND FRANCES, BERMUDA, AUGUST 2, 1651.

enslavement on this Indigenous couple that was lifelong and multigenerational before any laws called it into being. And James and Frances were just one such example of hundreds, if not thousands, throughout the English colonies.

Scholars often cite Virginia laws in the 1660s as evidence of slavery's legal emergence in the English colonies. However, examining Indigenous slavery helps us understand that enslavement and racial prejudice did not wait for laws. In the decades after the Powhatan Wars and the Pequot War, English colonists and legislatures reactively experimented with laws that tried to justify and define slavery, largely prompted by the enslaved Native Americans in their midst and later by imported Africans as well. Colonial leaders either sanctioned Indigenous enslavement during times of war or implicitly licensed it when colonists, with impunity, claimed Natives as captives and slaves. Collectively, colonists carried with them deeper cultural assumptions of conquest and prejudiced notions of hierarchies of difference. These ideas provided a thin justification, with or without imperial or local laws, to give legal cover to their actions.

James's and Frances's multigenerational enslavement in Bermuda suggests that English colonists quickly developed racial prejudice based on skin color and cultural and religious differences beyond Black–white binaries. Surveying the wider landscape of Bermuda and other English colonies in 1651, James and Frances would likely have seen white servants, enslaved Africans, and enslaved Native Americans all laboring in households and on plantations. But there were important differences. Notably, white servants held contracts and received their freedom after five to seven years. The only people being sold as slaves for life were Africans and Indigenous people. And no white servants had their children and grandchildren claimed as lifelong slaves and divided between their masters. Perhaps most importantly, white servants were not being enslaved on their own land or shipped off to make room for English expansion.

The starting point for colonial stealing and forced labor of Indigenous people was the assumption that only non-whites could be enslaved for life and have the condition of slavery passed down to their children. These on-the-ground experiences were bolstered after the Restoration of the English Crown in 1660 by Charles II's full embrace of enslaved labor as the primary engine for powering plantations and farms in the colonies.[5] When colonists later crafted laws that made this racialized prejudice more explicit, they were not *creating* racialized slavery; they were merely legalizing a set of practices that were already in place.

ENSLAVE FIRST, JUSTIFY LATER. This seemed to be the reigning principle in most American colonies. Settlers in Virginia enslaved Powhatan peoples between 1610 and the 1640s, but they never passed any laws determining who could be enslaved, under what conditions, and for how long. In New England, the Pequot War prompted a bit more reflection about the legality of waging war and enslaving Native Americans, but puritan leaders could never bring themselves to clearly state what they had done and why. In October 1636, just two months after English troops first marched on the Pequot, the vocal and combative Boston minister John Cotton drafted proposed laws for New England, called *Moses His Judicialls*. In the section on warfare, Cotton was clear: women (especially virgins), children, and cattle were to be "spared and reserved for spoyle"—that is, captivity and slavery.[6]

Although Cotton's laws were never formally adopted, they influenced later laws and reflected a wider "just war" consensus, drawing on a long Christian tradition regarding the rules of warfare that dated back to the fourth-century theologian Augustine of Hippo.[7] If a war was justified (as defined by Europeans, of course), English jurists believed that capturing and potentially enslaving enemies, including Native women and children, was acceptable.

Four years after the Pequot War, Massachusetts published a legal code called the Body of Liberties, which delineated ninety-eight points of laws and rights for colonists. Only one of them—the ninety-first point—dealt with slavery. It prohibited "bond slaverie villinage or Captivitie" except for "lawfull Captives taken in just warres." But the law seems more like a justification of slavery than a prohibition against it considering it was drafted and signed into law while hundreds of recently enslaved Pequots labored all across New England. Rather than prohibit slavery entirely, this law allowed it in four broad instances, including in "just warres" and if slavery was judged appropriate "by Authoritie."[8]

The decree gave extraordinary powers to magistrates and courts to consign Native Americans to slavery for various infractions, something colony courts made full use of in the following years. The Massachusetts law was different from the Barbados law in that it did not specifically invoke race. But in the context of the taking of Pequot captives and importing Africans, there was little question as to whom this law was applied.

Indigenous nations also voiced strong opinions about the treatment of Native captives. The powerful Narragansett sachem Miantonomi had warily welcomed Roger Williams to the region in 1636 and had sided with the English in the Pequot War. He suggested to English magistrates that the Pequot captives "be not enslaved" but should be treated according to the "generall custome" of Native warfare: to be "used kindly, have howses and goods and fields given them."[9] Miantonomi envisioned Pequot captives more as tributaries and less as an enslaved workforce, which significantly differed from how English colonists viewed and treated captive Pequot women and children. For the Narragansett, treating captives as tributaries increased political prominence and provided a modest (and largely symbolic) annual payment in the form of wampum or hides. Instead, the English turned captives into slaves in order to clear land and bolster the labor base on which a colonizing society was built, both producing and making room for capitalistic activity.

England's Parliament did not pass laws either permitting or outlawing Indigenous enslavement; neither did most colonies. And yet every English colony implicitly authorized Indian slavery and servitude by offering captives (to be enslaved) as rewards for direct military campaigns; registering the sale of Native slaves and servants in colony records; enumerating Indigenous people in bondage for the purposes of taxation; defending the rights of enslavers and legal masters in courts of law; and eventually passing laws that specifically regulated the trade in enslaved Natives. Indigenous slavery became normalized through the actions of colonists and colonial governments.

SCHOLARS HAVE LONG DEBATED when slavery became based on race. Those who argue for a gradual and later linkage between slavery and race point to some instances of flexible servitude in the early years of colonization. This includes some of the Pequot captives in New England or the vaguely defined status of enslaved Africans and Natives in early Virginia and their ability to secure their freedom.[10]

Central to this view is the well-known journey of Anthony Johnson, who had been trafficked from Africa to Virginia's Eastern Shore and who later bought his freedom, secured a small farm, and eventually became an enslaver himself.[11] Johnson's case supposedly illustrates that colonists in Virginia and other places had a race-neutral approach to labor that incorporated forcibly transported Irish and Scottish prisoners, Africans, and Indians into an emerging plantation labor system. Laws that specified racial differentiation came later, these scholars argue, starting in the 1660s in Barbados and Virginia. The implication is that during the opening decades of English colonization, laboring conditions were similar for white servants and African slaves, race did not affect treatment of laborers, and there was no clear line of separation between indentured servitude and slavery.[12]

Enslaved Native and African men and women would have vehemently disagreed. On November 10, 1643, Joyne and Nangoe, "twoe women negroes," were sold as part of the estate of John Sawyer at Palmetto Hill in Barbados to Captain Edmund Read. The estate included two "Christian servants" (a term that only referred to Europeans) named John Roberts and Thomas Hudson and the two enslaved Africans, Joyne and Nangoe. But there was a huge difference between the pairs. Roberts and Hudson are marked in the deed of sale as having a set time left in their contract; Joyne and Nangoe are noted as slaves for "their naturall lives."[13] Even in 1643 in Barbados, before the third and devastating war against the Powhatan in Virginia, the distinction was clear: Christian servants had contracts with set times to serve; Africans served for life. Dozens of additional Barbados deeds and sales records show this to be the case for enslaved Natives, too. The deed of William Hillyard and George Standfast from March 20, 1653, contrasts the "Christian servants" and the "respective tymes they have to serve" with the "negroes indians & other slaves," who have no time listed—meaning they were enslaved for life.[14]

Practices varied by region, of course, but these colonies were all closely connected by family lines and trade. Barbados and St. Kitts had already racialized labor in 1636 by decreeing that Africans and Indians without a contract would be slaves for life.[15] Similarly, the Providence Island Company leaders referred to the hundreds of enslaved Africans and Native Americans on the island as "perpetually servants" in contrast to white servants who had contracts.[16] Maryland drew a slightly different dividing line—between slaves and Christians—in 1638, but the effect was still the same, the assumption being that only Europeans were Christians and that only non-Europeans (especially Native Americans and Africans) could be slaves.

The treatment of white servants in other places confirms this racial divide. Thousands of white servants from England, Ireland, and Scotland poured into the English colonies in the seventeenth century. Some came voluntarily, exchanging a set number of years of labor for their passage. Many others were brought against their will, whether as prisoners of uprisings against the English or as a result of a trade in white servants. English, Irish, and Scottish laborers were undoubtedly mistreated to the point that they felt like they were enslaved, but they all had contracts or soon had one assigned to them.[17] They also had a readier recourse to the law and even to powerful friends in London and on the expiration of their contract usually received clothing, money, and land.

Racialization of labor also meant that Blacks and Native Americans everywhere were potentially merchantable in ways that white servants were not. One particularly striking story involved a young Native woman named Yarico, who aided a Thomas Inkle, an English sailor shipwrecked on a Caribbean island. After supposedly falling in love with Yarico while shipwrecked, Inkle took her to Barbados where they planned to marry. Likely realizing the cultural difficulties of such a marriage and also acknowledging his own financial indebtedness, he decided to sell the visibly pregnant Yarico into slavery. Instead of married and free, Yarico (likely with her child) ended up enslaved in the 1650s on the plantation of Thomas Modyford, the eventual governor of Jamaica.[18] Later versions of Yarico's story reflected eighteenth-century assumptions about slavery on Barbados as involving only Africans. Even though Yarico was Indigenous, she was recast as an idealized "Negro virgin."[19]

Society was increasingly tilted against Native Americans and Africans in other powerful ways that are harder to trace. Such cultural

Un Anglais de la Barbade, vend sa Maitresse, by Jean-Michel Moreau and Nicolas Delaunay, 1780, shows Thomas Inkle selling Yarico, Barbados.

assumptions generally caused whites to view Natives and Africans as intellectual and cultural inferiors, with little place as equals in English society. Enslaved Indigenous or African people, even if they found their freedom, could not imagine a world in which they could participate as citizens in voting, serving on juries, holding public office, or being accepted as racial equals—all things to which white servants could aspire. Indeed, colonists quickly passed laws to suppress the activity of free people of color. In Virginia, some free Blacks and Natives were successful enough to purchase the contracts of white servants on their properties. This activity so bothered whites that they passed a law against it in 1670. Specifically, the law stated that "noe negro or Indian"—even if baptized and free—would be able to purchase indentured white Christian servants.[20]

SLAVERY WAS OFTEN LIFELONG for Native Americans, even if colonists used the words *servant* or *servitude*. George Carr, a carpenter from Salisbury, Massachusetts, was given a Native named James for life as partial payment for a boat in 1649. The terms were clear: William Hilton handed over James to be Carr's "servant forever or to whom ye said George Carr shall assigne."[21] On Barbados, when William Baldwin Sr. sold his plantation on May 20, 1654, it included four "Christian men servants for ye tyme they have to serve." The plantation also included twenty-two Africans and one Indian man, with no time listed, implying they were enslaved for life. The unnamed Native American was twice called "a slave."[22] Other Barbados estates were sold in the 1640s and 1650s that included Native Americans who were lifelong slaves in contrast to white servants who had specific numbers of years to serve.[23]

From a modern perspective, the imprecise language of the seventeenth century creates a legal miasma of sorts. Colonial administrators and colonists used *slave* and *servant*, *slavery* and *servitude* mostly interchangeably when it came to enslaved Africans and Indigenous peoples. *Servant* may have sounded more benign, but in many cases the word was used for Africans subjected to lifelong slavery via the transatlantic slave trade. Barbados deeds in the 1640s often referred to Africans enslaved for life as "servants," and this fluid terminology continued throughout the century.[24] In December 1674, a copy of a royal proclamation was sent to Massachusetts governor John Leverett asserting the monopoly of the Royal African Company over "Negro servants" carried from Africa.[25] But these "servants" were designated for lifelong slavery.

In rare cases, term-limited slavery (a set period of enslavement) was noted in bills of sale for Africans and Native Americans. When the privateer William Jackson sold his cargo of Indigenous and African slaves in Bermuda in 1643, there was a curious condition inserted in the bill of sale: a term of seven years of servitude. He also claimed the right, along with his sponsor, the Earl of Warwick, to be able to demand use of the Natives and Africans at any time, though he had to provide replacement servants.[26] But on an island colony where lifelong slavery for Africans and Natives was the norm, what would prevent seven years from turning into seventy?

Far more typical for Bermuda were sales receipts that indicated slavery for life, or effectively for life, as when the terms of service were "fourscore and nineteen years," or ninety-nine years. Such was the case with an enslaved Native woman named Nell, who was sold on

January 27, 1646, for ninety-nine years, with the taunting added phrase "if she shall so long live."[27] This mirrored documentation in other colonies, including a 1672 act regarding runaway slaves in Virginia, in which the colonial assembly referenced Africans and Natives as "servant for life."[28] Despite the ambiguous language of "servant" and "servitude," this often referenced lifelong slavery, and colonial authorities understood it as such.

ANOTHER PRESSING QUESTION soon emerged: could the children of enslaved women also be claimed as slaves? Colonists seemed to assume this was the case, although for the first half century of colonization, no statute authorized it. Drawing on older Roman and European precedents, colonists later used the Latin phrase *partus sequitur ventrem*: the offspring follows the mother. This meant that if a mother was enslaved, the child would be enslaved as well. Often referred to simply as *partus*, it was the functional law of the land in the wider European Atlantic world, although scholars have not fully acknowledged that it equally applied to enslaved Native Americans.[29] Some colonies eventually affirmed this in actual law; the rest seemingly believed *partus* to be self-evident and silently practiced it as a matter of course.

It was an extreme cruelty of slavery that rendered enslaved mothers the producers of legal property for their masters. Many enslaved Native (and African) women bore children, whether through rape, forced breeding, or marriage. And these Indigenous and African children, even if mixed race, were usually claimed as slaves and passed along to the next generation of legal owners.[30] Often, Indigenous and African women could only stand by and watch as their children—sometimes only days old—were taken away and sold or promised to some future owner. In this way, white enslavers coerced a double labor out of enslaved women, African as well as Indigenous: first through their productive labor in the household or field and then through their reproductive labor in producing children.[31]

Planters and later scholars called this enslaved reproduction "natural increase," but there was nothing natural about either the process, whether rape or forced breeding, or the imposed enslavement on the next generation. Claiming the children of enslaved women was a colonial strategy of domination and a major scheme for expanding both Indigenous and African enslavement.

An enslaved Indigenous woman on Barbados named Yow, for example, had her children enslaved through the unwritten logic of *partus* early in English colonization. It is likely that Yow was part of the Lokono group from Guiana that reportedly voluntarily went to Barbados in 1627 and were subsequently enslaved. But there was no law in Barbados that specified that the *children* of enslaved Native Americans or Africans should also be enslaved when Yow began having them in the 1630s. Planters made it the practice of the land by simply claiming her children as their slaves. Yow was fortunate in that she and her children found their freedom in the 1650s; others labored for their entire lives in anonymity on plantations and in households in every English colony.[32]

Virginia was the first English colony to pass legislation affirming *partus*, although the practice was already common. A 1662 law specifically stated that the status of children should follow the mother, largely in response to the case of Elizabeth Keye, a mixed-race woman with an African mother, who won her freedom.[33] Incensed, Virginians passed

INDIAN FAMILY OF THE
CARRIBEE NATION, BY
MICHELE BENEDETTI,
1792, DEPICTS A
KALINA FAMILY.

this law to ensure that mixed-race children of enslaved people (specifically those who had a white father and Black or Indian mother) could
be easily and legally enslaved. Although the law formally imposed a
fine for such interracial "fornication," it licensed and even incentivized planters to rape their enslaved women, knowing such an act could
result in enlarging their slaveholdings. Colonists applied the principle
equally to Indigenous women and their children.

Some colonies followed suit and passed similar laws making explicit
the principle of *partus sequitur ventrem*, but others did not. By the
1680s, Jamaica passed a law stating that "all such Negroa or Indian
slaves" that might be brought to the island from Africa, Asia, or America should be slaves for life, along with their children, legalizing what
was already being done on the island and elsewhere.[34] *Partus* was also
practiced in other colonies, like those in New England, which never
made it official but still organized slavery around this multigenerational principle.[35]

COLONIAL OFFICIALS DID RESTRICT Indigenous slavery at times,
especially when it posed a risk to the colonies or in other ways coun-
tered colonial goals. Stealing and enslaving Natives was thus tempered
by Native people themselves, by their presence, power, and importance
as trade partners.

One early example of this involved Powhatan children. In the wake
of the Third Anglo-Powhatan War in 1644, Virginia magistrates
allowed colonists to take Native children under the age of twelve into
their homes—a practice seemingly imposed on tribes as a requirement
of their loyalty to the English. Colonial families attempted to eradicate
Nativeness by suppressing Indigenous language and dress in the name
of Christianization and "civilization," a process that would continue
well into the twentieth century. Removing children from their communities also undercut the leadership and reproductive capacities of
tribes to sustain future presence and retain their land base. Unsurprisingly, some enterprising colonists viewed these Native children as their
personal slaves and treated them as such. This included selling them,
whether for profit or to be rid of them or both. Still others kept them
around as functional slaves well into adulthood.[36]

The outrage of Indigenous leaders forced Virginia's legislators to try to rein in the policy they had encouraged. The assembly passed a series of laws between 1649 and 1658 that, while trying to respond to Native demands, also continued to permit the ongoing servitude of Indigenous children. The 1658 law mandated that no Indian child could be kept in an English household after the age of twenty-five, but the actual impact was uncertain.[37]

Demand for Native children remained high, and colonists found ways to prey on Indigenous communities directly impacted by English expansion. The county of Accomack on Virginia's Eastern Shore hired an Indigenous man locals called Mr. John to go find Native orphans, promising a handsome reward for each child brought in.[38] Ann Toft, also of Accomack County, positioned herself as a local broker of Indigenous servants and slaves. Toft had arrived in Virginia in the 1660s and received a massive 3,800-acre land grant based on the transportation of sixty servants into the colony. Within a few years, four Indigenous boys were among her plantation's laborers, purchased in 1667 from the sachem of the Kickotank, farther north on the Eastern Shore. Toft repeatedly appeared before the county court to determine the ages of the Native children she held, which was required by law for the purposes of taxation.[39]

Throughout the colonies, the actions of colonists and Native leaders forced governments to figure out the permissibility of slavery. Rhode Island passed a law in 1652 acknowledging that colonists were enslaving "negars" for life (which likely included Native Americans) and tried to limit slaveholding to a ten-year period.[40] It is likely nobody listened. In March 1655, John Woodcocke and Adonijah Morris walked into the wetu of an unnamed Wampanoag Indian in Plymouth Colony, grabbed a child along with a few household items, and took them home. When the Wampanoag complained to the local magistrates, Woodcocke claimed the man owed him money and he had stolen the child in exchange for the debt. No doubt Woodcocke knew that he could either sell the child for profit or else commandeer a lifetime of enslaved labor.[41]

In 1670, the Virginia legislature addressed an ongoing controversy about whether Indigenous captives trafficked into the colony should be held "for life or terme of yeares." The legislature determined that enslaved Natives who were imported into Virginia by boat should be slaves for life, but if they came "by land," they should be considered servants for a set time: thirty years for children and twelve years for adults, both men and women.[42] This ruling perhaps came about because Natives trafficked by land had friends and relatives close enough to seek retribution. Indigenous captives who arrived by water were likely pilfered from Spanish and Caribbean areas, removing the fear of local blowback. Still, there is no evidence that colonists respected the restrictions placed on them by their government. Even those Indigenous people with set times of servitude were vulnerable to lifelong enslavement.[43]

CAPTIVE AND ENSLAVED Native Americans used murky legal situations to their advantage. Enslaved Indigenous people routinely ran away, petitioned the courts for their freedom, or sent word to relatives to help them escape. Native people were often their own greatest advocates, whether the enslaved themselves, their leaders, the parents of captive children, or all three.

Colonial governments were sometimes receptive to charges of unjust enslavement of Native Americans. Elizabeth Short purchased an enslaved Powhatan Indian named Metappin in Virginia "for life time," perhaps in the late 1640s. Metappin must have protested his enslavement, however, because the Virginia legislature heard about his case in the early 1660s. After investigating the details, they learned that Metappin had been sold as a slave to Short by the sachem of the Weyanoke. The legislature ruled in March 1662 that this sachem had no right to sell Metappin and so ordered him to be freed. But it is clear that Metappin was also playing into the sensibilities of the legislature. He could speak "perfectly" in English and expressed a desire to be baptized.[44] The Virginia legislature, in 1667, would explicitly reject the idea that baptism freed enslaved men and women, as would most other colonies.[45] But for Metappin, his desire for baptism seemed to play in his favor.

Sometimes Indigenous people self-emancipated by running away as a protest against their enslavement. In 1669, six Indian adult "servants" (likely slaves) ran away from Thomas Torrey on Block Island, off the coast of Rhode Island. At least two of them had been stolen out of the house of an elderly Niantic man in the late 1650s. They spent their childhood and adolescence enslaved but by 1669 had decided to run away. Torrey tried to blame the Niantic sachem Ninigret for inciting the men and helping them escape since Ninigret had recently visited Block Island. In response, Ninigret scolded colonists for stealing Native children in the first place.[46]

Indigenous people also protested when their servitude was extended in unjust ways. Over the course of a year in 1672–1673, five Native servants named Peter, Anthony, Will, Ned, and Besse petitioned for their freedom from Edmund Scarburgh of Accomack County in Virginia. In each case, the courts granted their freedom. In particular, Peter accused Scarburgh of illegally adding time to his indenture, which may have been the case for the other four as well.[47]

Other enslaved Natives protested more violently. In Virginia, a Native woman named Elizabeth tussled with her legal mistress, the wife of Captain John Wall, in their home, even biting her on the chest. Elizabeth later physically grabbed Mrs. Wall and tried to shove her head into a red-hot oven that had been prepped for baking bread.[48] Such actions surely brought personal retribution and punishments that were upheld by local authorities.

EVEN AS THEY TRIED TO RESTRICT Native enslavement in some instances, governments continued to brandish it as a method of colonial submission. English authorities threatened not just enslavement but shipping Indians out of the region, even during times of peace. After the Pequot War, the United Colonies (formed by Massachusetts, Plymouth, and Connecticut in 1643 to unify against Native nations) warned the Narragansett and Niantic that anyone among them who sheltered runaway Pequot slaves would either be enslaved themselves or shipped out of the country in exchange for "Negros." The United Colonies also decreed that Native individuals who sheltered other Natives accused of crimes would be subject to direct seizure and given to the aggrieved parties, who could, in turn, either enslave the Natives directly or sell them into the wider Atlantic slave market in exchange for African slaves.[49] Rhode Island passed its own version of this act in 1659.[50]

The same was true elsewhere. In 1660, Native Americans in Northumberland County, Virginia, were accused of raiding and damaging local estates. The colonial legislature empowered officials to demand payment and, if the Indians refused, to capture as many Natives as they deemed necessary and sell them "into a fforaigne country," which was promptly done.[51] The Virginia Court imposed the same punishment six years later against the Rappahannock River tribes accused of murdering some colonists over regional disputes. In 1666, the General Court ordered that war should be waged on the Rappahannock "for revenge" and the "prevention of future mischiefs" and their women and children should be taken and "disposed of" according to the will of Governor William Berkeley—which surely meant sale into slavery, either locally or out of the colony.[52]

EVENTUALLY, SOME COLONIES PASSED additional laws that more clearly specified the racial hierarchy that was already present. The most detailed early affirmation of racialized slavery in the English empire came in Barbados in 1661, with the passage of two separate acts: "An Act for the better ordering and governing of Negroes" and "An Act for the good Governing of Servants, and Ordering the Rights between Masters and Servants."[53]

The contrast was stark. The language in the act for "Negroes" demeaned enslaved men and women, as one scholar has noted, by "pointing out their dark complexions, by asserting offensive cultural characteristics, and by animalizing them as dangerous, exotic lions who needed to be caged."[54] This law severely curtailed the mobility of enslaved people, while also delineating harsh punishments for running away, theft, murder, and other forms of disobedience. No specific rights were granted to those who were enslaved. Notably, the law collapsed Native Americans and Africans into the category of "Negroes." This law might have erased them, but other colony records confirm enslaved Native American presence on the island.

The act regarding "servants," however, presumed servants to be white, not Native or African. The law discussed at length the shipments of servants from England and imposed contracts of set years as

SLAVES PROCESS SUGAR, PUBLISHED BY
PIETER VAN DER AA, 1707. THIS IMAGE IS BASED ON
AN EARLIER IMAGE PUBLISHED BY THEODOR DE BRY.

a protection against enslavement. The servant laws listed much lighter punishments for the same infractions and did not contain the dehumanizing language found in the slave code. Additionally, these white "Christian servants," as the law refers to them at one point, had protections and rights and could be heard in the local court of common law. Their previous marriages were to be honored, with spouses being assigned to the same master.

These Barbados slave codes did not *create* racialized distinctions as they were already in place, although they did give greater legal weight to them in important ways. They were also highly influential within the broader English world, serving as the model for Jamaica's slave and servant laws in 1664 and later for the Carolinas in 1691.[55] Even in colonies that did not pass comprehensive slave codes, like most New England colonies and Bermuda, additional indirect laws gave functional legal force to slavery by restricting the rights of enslaved people. The Bermuda legislature in 1660 limited the mobility and activity of Africans and Indians by prohibiting them from meeting together and by requiring a written pass from their owners.[56]

These local laws emerged from the actions of everyday colonial men and women and the legal silence of the wider English empire on the issue of slavery and, in particular, Indigenous slavery. Understanding the enslavement of Native Americans as an earlier and equally integral part of labor in the early English colonies helps reveal the ways slavery was racialized from the opening years of colonization. Only Native Americans and Africans and their children were enslaved for life, first in practice and then sometimes according to the law.

BY THE 1660s, Indigenous slavery had an important and enduring presence in English settlements even as it directly enabled colonization in multiple ways. In the sixteenth century, English merchants had stolen Natives from the shorelines to learn more about the Americas. The start of permanent colonies in 1607 ushered in a new era of enslaving Natives in larger numbers as a means of procuring labor but also stealing Indigenous land. These opening years of English invasion were formative and left a deep imprint on the American colonies and, eventually, the United States itself, placing Native American slavery at the center of a quickly growing and aggressive collection of English territories in the Americas.

But this was only the beginning. With the legal backing of the English empire, colonists soon turned to mass enslavement of Native Americans in even greater numbers.

Part Two

EXPANSION

1650–1750

THE ENSLAVEMENT OF NATIVE AMERICANS IN EARLY ENGLISH settlements exploded in scale between 1650 and 1750. With the success of colonies like Massachusetts, Virginia, and Barbados, English merchants fanned out in search of new territories in North America and the Caribbean whose Indigenous people might also yield labor and land. African slavery, too, experienced a significant expansion during this period, but North American colonies from Massachusetts to South Carolina still relied on a startlingly large number of Native Americans who were enslaved locally or imported into North America from the Caribbean. This was due to two factors: several important wars that resulted in large-scale enslavement and two major Indigenous slave-raiding nodes that somewhat mirrored the African slave trade in how they functioned (even if the volume was significantly less).

The rise of large-scale Native American enslavement by English colonists eventually coalesced in four places. The first was in the English Caribbean, where the Indigenous slave trade run by privateers flourished in the seventeenth century. The second was during and after two cataclysmic wars between Natives and colonists in the mid-1670s: King Philip's War in New England and Bacon's Indian War in Virginia. The third was the largest Indigenous slave trade in American history, the Carolina Indigenous slave trade, which unfolded between 1680 and 1720. The fourth was an overlooked but influential Native slave trade out of Central America, the Mosquito Shore Indigenous slave trade, which started in the seventeenth century, peaked around 1760, and finally sputtered to a halt in the 1780s. These centers of enslavement and slave trading were crucial to the growth and expansion of the English empire, both in terms of land taken (mostly in North America) as well as in the enslaved labor that these trades provided.

In many of these locales, Native Americans played complicated roles. Like kingdoms in West Africa, some Native nations chose self-preservation and served as intermediaries for an emerging Indigenous slave trade in that region. Other Native nations found themselves on the receiving end of English-sponsored slave raiding and chose to make brave military stands against colonialism. The end result was a precipitous rise in Native enslavement in all the English colonies in ways that reshaped labor practices, devastated Indigenous families, and ensured that the demand for enslaved Africans in some colonies initially remained low.

Four

THE ERASED CARIBBEAN TRADE

DURING THE SALEM WITCHCRAFT PANIC IN 1692, AN ENSLAVED Indigenous woman named Tituba was one of the first people to be accused. As skittish Massachusetts puritans frantically jailed and interrogated hundreds of women (and a few men) and finally executed nineteen of them, Tituba was one of those who confessed and was spared. Most of the court records identify her as an "Indian," although some simply call her a slave from the West Indies who was practicing voodoo.[1]

Tituba is mostly a side story in Salem's lamentable saga, but her presence points to the leviathan of an Indigenous slave trade lurking in the warm waters of the Caribbean whose tentacles spread outward in all directions, including to North America. We often think of Caribbean and oceanic slave trading in terms of African slavery. In many ways, this is not wrong since the Caribbean was one of the most significant sites of African slavery in the Americas, with approximately three million to five million Africans imported through the early nineteenth century—a close second behind Brazil.[2]

But the Caribbean was also the site of an Indigenous slave trade that completely altered the destinies and lives of approximately one million to two million Natives, starting with the arrival of Columbus and continuing into the nineteenth century. European merchant ships and privateering boats were constantly in motion on this vast body of water, a never-ending blur of aqueous activity from one island to the next, from the mainland to islands and back again. In addition to sugar, lumber, indigo, and numerous additional commodities, Indig-

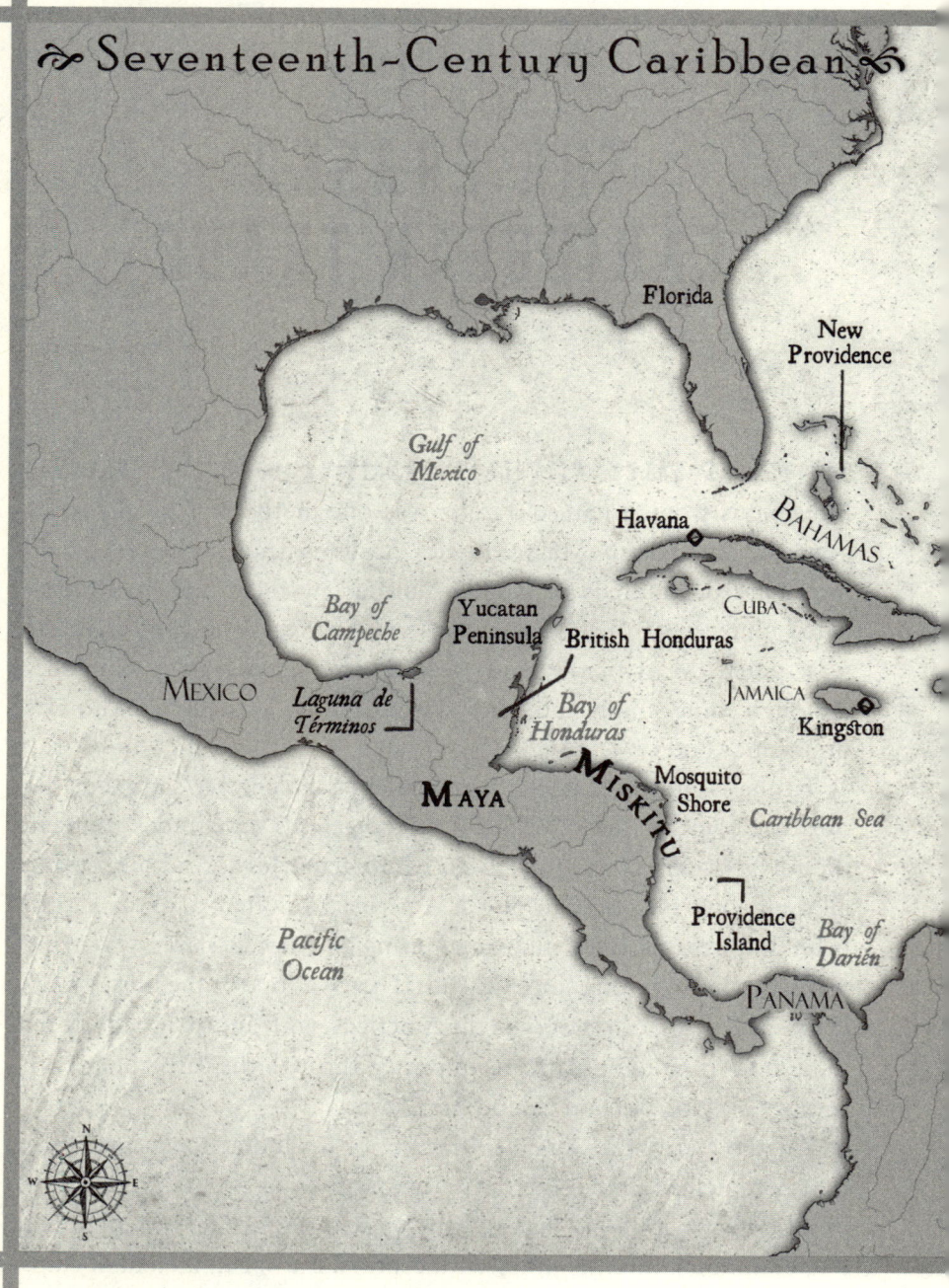

❧ Seventeenth-Century Caribbean ❧

Florida

New Providence

BAHAMAS

Gulf of Mexico

Havana

CUBA

Bay of Campeche

Yucatan Peninsula

British Honduras

JAMAICA

MEXICO

Laguna de Términos

Kingston

Bay of Honduras

MAYA

MISKITU

Mosquito Shore

Caribbean Sea

Pacific Ocean

Providence Island

Bay of Darién

PANAMA

N
W   E
S

BERMUDA

*Atlantic
Ocean*

TAÍNO

Tortuga

HISPANIOLA

St. KITTS AND NEVIS

KALINAGO

Santo
Domingo

ANTIGUA

MONTSERRAT   DOMINICA

St. VINCENT   BARBADOS

Demerara R.

Suriname R.

Berbice R.

Commewijne R.

LOKONO AND KALINA

VENEZUELA

Maroni R.

Orinoco R.

Oyapock R.

PARICORA
(GUIANAS)

Paramaribo
Surinam

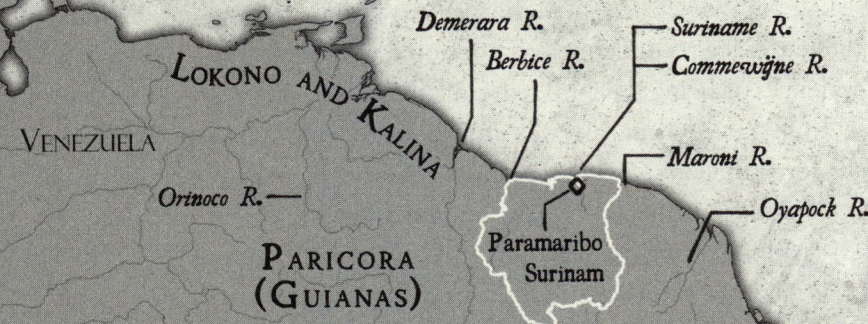

enous captives were a common and valuable part of the cargo, transported among the barrels and crates below the deck. Thousands of Indigenous captives were carried by sloops and brigantines flying the English flag.

It was this Caribbean Indigenous slave trade that trafficked Tituba to Massachusetts. She was most likely Lokono, from the Caribbean rim of South America, captured in one of any number of slave raids in the 1660s or 1670s by English merchants and taken to Barbados.[3] After a period of enslavement on that island, she was transported to Massachusetts by the puritan minister Samuel Parris, where she remained enslaved in anonymity until she was accused of sorcery in 1692.

This English Caribbean Indigenous slave trade was largely ad hoc, especially compared to the well-documented African slave trade. English privateers sacked Spanish ships and stole Native captives who were on board, slave-raided Indigenous people directly from the coasts, and traded with coastal Natives for Indian slaves from the interior. Although ship by ship the numbers were small, this informal network of privateers and pirates supplied English colonies with thousands of enslaved Native Americans in the seventeenth century alone.

Scholars have mostly overlooked this significant Indigenous slave trade in part because enslavers did not always record their captives as Native American once they were on plantations and in households, especially in the Caribbean. Tituba, for example, appears a few times in the Barbados records but was not noted to be Indigenous.[4] Tituba's experiences of being slave-raided, trafficked to a Caribbean island, and then anonymized as a slave was an experience multiplied by the thousands for Indigenous people. Natives resisted this racial recategorization, retaining connections to community practices and methods of hunting and working the land in ways that were often valued by enslavers. Despite her forced separation from kin, Tituba maintained firm connections with traditional practices and identities, including medicinal knowledge, which is what raised puritan suspicions about her in the first place.

This partially invisible Caribbean Indigenous slave trade delivered enslaved Native people to virtually every English Caribbean island and North American colony, making them a notable part of the local labor force. In the process, colonists also reinforced racial hierarchies and normalized Indigenous people as servants and slaves, not as rightful possessors of the land desired by colonists.

WILLIAM JACKSON WAS JUST ONE of scores of English captains circling the Caribbean and trading in enslaved Native Americans. His reputation as a privateer in the 1630s and 1640s stemmed from his repeated attacks on Spanish colonies. In early 1639, sailing under a Providence Island Company license, Jackson took a Spanish slave ship near the small outpost of Trujillo on the northern stretch of the Mosquito Shore, which was the five-hundred-mile-long Caribbean coastal region of what is now Honduras and Nicaragua.[5] In a published account of his exploits, Jackson proudly listed the various items of plunder taken from Spanish ships, towns, and forts over the course of a few years. His list included gold, silver—including the coveted Spanish pieces of eight—and pearls, as well as more mundane trade items, such as ammunition, sails, cables, and metal parts.[6]

Jackson's most valuable plunder, however, was human beings. He routinely purchased or pilfered Indigenous and African slaves as he made his journeys from Barbados to the Guianas to the Mosquito

SHIPS AT SHORE, PUBLISHED
BY PIETER VAN DER AA, 1705.

Shore and back again.[7] A few years after the 1639 attack on Trujillo, Jackson sailed into the burgeoning St. George's harbor, Bermuda, in January 1645. He unloaded his human cargo and tried to make them more presentable after the harrowing 1,200-mile voyage from the Caribbean. He quickly found buyers, and these trafficked Indigenous people disappeared into Bermuda's multiracial enslaved population.[8]

English merchants became well known for this Indigenous slave trade. Charles de Rochefort, a French Huguenot minister, called the English "the greatest enemies" of Native peoples in the Caribbean and South America.[9] From his station in Tortuga, a rogue multinational island off the coast of Hispaniola, he could easily observe English predatory activity. Enterprising English captains, Rochefort noted, had become experts at enticing Indians onto their ships under the guise of trade and free brandy, taking them captive, and transporting them to the closest English port to sell into slavery.[10] A band of marauding English privateers caught a small Mayan village by surprise in 1652 and took sixty families to Tortuga, where they were sold into slavery. Despite high rates of mortality among the captives, one traveler to the island a year later noted approximately 150 enslaved Indigenous men, women, and children.[11]

As a result, the early English Caribbean colonies contained hundreds, if not thousands, of enslaved Indigenous men and women who had been stolen from coastlines or from the Spanish.[12] When a sailor named Henry Whistler passed through Barbados in 1654, he described a multiethnic population containing English, French, Dutch, Scottish, Irish, and Spanish Jews, along with Native Americans and Africans who were "born to perpetuall slavery."[13]

As England's Caribbean ambitions expanded, so did its enslavement of Indigenous people. England only occupied a few small islands in the Caribbean and North Atlantic in 1650, including Bermuda, Barbados, Antigua, St. Kitts, St. Vincent, and Dominica. With its large enslaved population and rapidly growing, lucrative sugar exports, Barbados was quickly emerging as the most important colony in the entire English Atlantic World. As slaves and servants hacked down the few remaining trees to make room for more plantations on these small islands, prospective English planters began to look south to Guiana and west to the Mosquito Shore.

English merchants had already been slave raiding and trading on the Guiana coast and shipping captive Natives to Barbados, Bermuda, and other colonies. The governor general of Barbados and the Lesser Antilles, Francis Willoughby, wanted to make English presence in Guiana more official. He began actively promoting the South American coast six hundred miles to the southeast of Barbados in the late 1640s as an extension for large-scale sugar development. In 1650, Willoughby's vision became reality when three hundred English settlers landed along the Suriname and Commewijne Rivers.[14]

Barbados planters and magistrates alike saw in "Willoughby-Land" not just an addition of territory but a ready supply of labor: the South American coast was home to tens of thousands of Indigenous people.[15] Barbados planter and later Jamaican governor Thomas Modyford anticipated that colonists would be able to commandeer "an infinite number of naked Indians" to work the fields.[16] He had direct experience since his sprawling five-hundred-acre Barbados plantation included enslaved Native Americans, along with Africans and some white servants.[17]

English colonizers also looked to the western edge of the Caribbean, where much of the coastline of Central America was only loosely claimed by Spain. English privateers and colonists traded on the long, sandy Central American coast from the Yucatán Peninsula southward to Panama. Starting in the seventeenth century, the Mosquito Shore became a primary node of English settlement, as did several locations on the Yucatán Peninsula. In the case of the Mosquito Shore in particular, English desire for enslaved Natives coincided with the activity of a large coastal Native tribe known as the Miskitu, who had their own long practice of slave raiding other Indigenous nations.[18]

These coastal mainland areas vastly supplemented English resource extraction. Innumerable quantities of turtle shells, cotton, hammocks, fruit, planks of logwood (dyewood), and mahogany were carried out of these unofficially colonized spaces into the English Atlantic empire. Notably, Native captives were central to this trade. Richard Ligon, who lived in Barbados for a few years in the 1650s, stated that Indian slaves were "fetcht" from other countries, from neighboring islands, and from "the Maine"—that is, the American mainland, or Central and South America.[19]

The French colonial missionary Jean-Baptiste Du Tertre, too, reported that English, French, and Dutch traders purchased captive Natives from coastal Kalina tribes who had slave-raided their enemies in the interior.[20] In fact, these coastal mainland outposts were the single greatest source of Indigenous slaves for English colonists in the Caribbean and North Atlantic islands in the seventeenth century and beyond.

THE CARIBBEAN INDIGENOUS SLAVE TRADE received an unexpected boost with the English conquest of Jamaica in 1655. Out of the chaos of the English Civil War—which included the stunning beheading of King Charles I in 1649—the puritans and separatist groups in England were determined to expand their territorial holdings in the Americas. For the newly installed Lord Protector Oliver Cromwell and his puritan advisers, the Caribbean was vitally important because they still hoped to mimic the Spanish in their successful harnessing of the natural and human resources there. Conquering Spanish territory would also serve the equally important purpose of crippling Spanish hegemony in the region regarding trade, including the African slave trade.

To accomplish this, Cromwell and his advisers devised an aggressive ploy called the Western Design, which would allow the English to "strive with the Spaniard for the mastery of all those seas."[21] Throughout these schemes, the brief successes of Providence Island between 1630 and 1641 and its devastating sacking by the Spanish lurked in Cromwell's mind—as a taste of potential success, a warning, and motivation for revenge.[22]

After months of preparation, in April 1655, 9,500 soldiers in fifty ships set sail from England for Hispaniola.[23] After being resoundingly rebuffed by the Spanish in their attempt to capture Santo Domingo—the same Hispaniola port that Sir Francis Drake had successfully taken seventy years before, in 1586—Cromwell's fleet decided to invade nearby Spanish-held Jamaica. Lying approximately a hundred miles to the west of Hispaniola, Jamaica was far smaller, less populated, and minimally defended. It was a second-place prize, to be sure, but if taken, it would become the largest English island in the Caribbean, twenty-five times larger than Barbados and with seemingly endless wooded hills and mountains. Such an acquisition would be a lucrative outlet for English expansion in the region and a way to salvage Cromwell's Western Design.

In Jamaica, Cromwell's 1655 invasion found success, although it took a half decade to stifle Spanish counterattacks and ensure that most of the mountainous island remained in English hands.[24] As elsewhere, earlier Spanish colonization had taken a deadly toll on the island's original sixty thousand Taíno inhabitants. Yet they had persisted by creating independent communities along with self-emancipated Africans high in the mountains of central Jamaica.[25] As early as 1601, so many Taínos and Africans had disappeared into the iconic, towering Blue Mountains north and east of Kingston that the Spanish governor, Don Fernando Melgarejo de Córdoba, had sent a military unit to hunt them down.[26]

The Spanish demeaningly called these independent people *cimarróns*, which possibly also referred to feral livestock or other wild creatures. Over time the term *maroon* stuck as a reference to self-emancipated communities, and the English used it widely. The maroons of Jamaica—as in other places—exerted immense geopolitical influence. They frequently frustrated colonial attempts to maintain control over the island's extensive geography and growing slave population.

Modern archaeology of several maroon towns in the Jamaican mountains—Old Nanny Town and Old (Accompong) Town in particular—confirms that Taíno and other Natives were part of these communities from the beginning. Researchers found hand-manufactured stone tools, fragments of flint, shaped shell fragments, fired earthenware, and terracotta figurines that are all similar to artifacts from other regional Native archaeological sites. And in the western mountains of Jamaica, present-day descendants of the maroons in Accompong Town still claim Taíno ancestry drawn from oral histories, something that recent DNA testing has partially confirmed.[27]

During the English invasion in 1655, the departing Spanish carried away as many enslaved Africans and Native Americans as they could transport, but many others—perhaps thousands—either ran away or were left behind. As a result, Indigenous people, both free and enslaved, were a small but constant part of the wider population in

VIEW OF PORT ROYAL AND KINGSTON HARBOURS,
BY PETER MAZELL, 1774.

Jamaica.[28] The treatment of these former Spanish slaves was a source
of controversy and disagreement between Jamaica settlers and London officials. As had become standard for English wars of conquest,
English commanders allowed soldiers to keep any captured Spanish
"negroes and mulattoes"—which included Indigenous people. In this
instance, authorities only permitted personal enslavement for three
years, after which these enslaved people would be at the disposal of the
government.[29]

When he came to power in 1660, English king Charles II commanded Governor Edward D'Oyley and English colonists to give all
"Negros Natives and others" on the island "sure encouragements" so
that they might accept English rule and live peaceably on the island.[30]
Jamaica colonists were incensed, protesting and often refusing to give
up enslaved people they had claimed during the invasion.

But even Charles II understood the important role enslaved Indigenous people could play in Jamaica. The seal for the island given by
the king depicts, on one side, two Native Americans kneeling and pre-
senting fruits to the monarch. On the other side, two Natives stand
on either side of a shield, on which is emblazoned a cross. One Native
holds a bow, the other some fruit. Beneath is the Latin motto *indus
uterque serviet uni* ("Both Indians will serve one").[31] This seal told

an honest story of how most planters and magistrates saw Natives: as servants and slaves. This Native presence remains on the Jamaican national seal to this day, although the motto at the bottom has been changed to "Out of Many, One People."[32]

Despite orders from London, Jamaica magistrates knew that to be successful in growing export crops like sugar, they had to import enslaved men and women in large numbers. As one early law stated plainly, it was "utterly impossible to make and continue Plantations without such Slaves."[33] The Company of Royal Adventurers into Africa (precursor of the Royal African Company) was founded in 1660, in part to meet the increased enslaved-labor demands resulting from the takeover of Jamaica.[34] This Crown-approved slaving corporation was given exclusive rights for the lucrative privilege of keeping the English Caribbean islands well supplied with enslaved Africans. English merchants also kept up a steady importation of enslaved Native Americans.

Within a few years, enough African and Indigenous captives had been imported to require regulation. The Jamaica legislature adopted almost word for word Barbados's 1661 slave laws, which Jamaica implemented in 1664 as "An Act for the better ordering and governing of Negro Slaves."[35] Despite the reference to "Negro" in the title, the

DETAIL FROM THE MAP *NOVISSIMA ET ACCURATISSIMA INSULAE JAMAICAE DESCRIPTIO PER JOHANNEM SELLERUM*, BY JOHN SELLER, 1672, SHOWING THE SEAL OF JAMAICA.

actual text of the act references "slaves" in the generic sense, and planters applied the regulations to all enslaved people—Africans, Native
Americans, and mixed-race people.

THE CONQUEST OF JAMAICA emboldened English privateers but
turned the lives of some regional Native communities into a new living
hell. English merchants and buccaneers began using Jamaica as a base
for trade and piracy, which almost always involved a robust traffick in
Native American captives.

In 1667, a colonist in Suriname described the process by which
English traders purchased enslaved Indians. Coastal Kalinas slave-
raided their enemies in the interior, killed most of the men, and took
the women and children back to the coast, where they sold them for
"Trifles" as slaves to the traders.[36] Robert Searles was just one English
captain based in Jamaica who had a steady traffick in enslaved Natives
out of that island in the 1660s. Aboard his frigate *Port Royal*—named
after Jamaica's principal port in the 1660s—Searles traded widely
around the Caribbean basin in various items, including Indigenous
captives. Between 1665 and 1670, he routinely arrived in Bermuda,
almost always with enslaved Natives to distribute. He sold several in
September 1668, including a Native man named Whan Thomas.[37]

Even royal officials in London dreamed of a newly empowered
English empire based on an Indigenous slave trade and geographical
expansion. This included members of the London-based Board of
Trade, who were tasked with overseeing the English colonies. Benjamin
Worsley, who served in various government positions, watched in the
1650s and 1660s as English Caribbean colonies struggled to establish
themselves as legitimate Atlantic economic powerhouses. Other successful European empires used enslaved Native labor. The Portuguese
in Brazil, as Worsley well knew, had forced enslaved Indigenous populations there to build an empire of sugar, the products of which were
shipped all over Europe. In 1668, as a member of Charles II's Board
of Trade, Worsley proposed that if English merchants could tap into
existing Native slave-trading areas in Guiana, it could help make the
English the "sole masters of sugar for all the world," even edging out
the Portuguese in Brazil.[38]

Worsley's vision was naïve given the strength of both Brazil and

Indigenous nations, but English slave trading on the Guiana coast was real and received official sanction during time of war. The three periods of warfare that constituted the Anglo-Dutch Wars between 1652 and 1674 provided ample opportunity for directly raiding Dutch-allied coastal Kalina and taking captives.[39] These raids resulted in the sale of Native captives in colonies like Barbados, where on May 30, 1670, Captain Peter Wroth sold three slaves to Jonathan Kellicott: Semo, an Indian woman, and Cirus and Hannah, an African man and woman.[40] One of these raids likely ensnared Tituba and trafficked her to Barbados, along with hundreds of others whose experiences were not recorded.[41] When such raiding persisted after the war, Dutch officials complained, prompting a rebuke from King Charles II. The English king was seemingly indifferent about Native enslavement but in this instance was concerned with not disrupting diplomatic efforts in the region.[42]

During all of the raiding and slave trading, an untold number of Native Americans from the coastlands of the Caribbean were shipped to Barbados, Bermuda, Jamaica, and the North American colonies as slaves. Most of these enslaved Natives disappeared into the massive and growing plantation economies of the islands. But sometimes they elicited notice. An English merchant in Jamaica named James Davis was accused of holding free Indian men as slaves. An investigation revealed that these Native men, while technically free, stayed with Davis for an important reason: their wives were enslaved by Davis and served in his household. When placed under oath in court, these Native Americans—whose names, like so many others in the records, are missing—"confessed themselves to bee slaves" and made to work on Davis's plantation.[43]

This powerful statement by enslaved Natives themselves illuminates the tricky business of coerced Native labor in the Caribbean. Colonists could insist it was voluntary or hide from authorities what they were doing, but Native people knew their own circumstances and conditions better than anyone else.

ENGLISH PRIVATEERS AND MERCHANTS kept up a steady traffick in Indigenous captives in the wider Caribbean as they continued to exploit new locations. The powerful Kalinago of the Lesser Antilles in the Caribbean provided stout resistance to both colonization and enslavement. English merchants looked for opportunities to slave-raid these islands, usually with revenge attacks or war as a pretense.

In the late 1660s, the Kalinago from Dominica raided English settlements on Antigua and Montserrat as part of a longer series of antagonisms in the region prompted by English and French colonial presence. St. Vincent, Dominica, and Antigua, as part of the Leeward Islands, were officially under the command of Governor Willoughby of Barbados. In 1668, Willoughby ordered an expedition to Dominica to free English colonists captured by the Kalinago. But Willoughby also explicitly gave orders to James Walker to enslave as many Kalinago as possible, under certain conditions, and bring them back to Barbados.[44] An unknown number of captive Kalinago from Dominica—officially viewed as rebels—were accordingly enslaved in Barbados and Jamaica.[45]

English privateers and merchants also looked farther west, to the coast of Mexico, where they intertwined Indigenous slave raiding and trading with other commercial activities. In the 1660s, they established an outpost at Laguna de Términos on the Bay of Campeche. Edging out the Spanish, they brazenly elbowed their way into the lucrative logwood trade in the region, commandeering Indian and African slave labor to do so. The leafy, thirty-foot-tall logwood tree (*Haematoxylum campechianum*) hid a valuable surprise in its reddish-brown wood: the ability to produce highly desirable black, purple, gray, and red dyes.[46] In an era when reliable sources of dye were rare, European markets for logwood soon skyrocketed. Much of the logwood trade was conducted by New England captains and merchants, who routinely made the long, dangerous voyage from New England ports through the Caribbean to Mexico and then directly to the textile markets in Europe.[47]

While stationed in rudimentary towns on the coast, English logwood workers raided nearby Indigenous (likely Mayan) villages to boost their labor supply and for sport. As one traveler noted, the English kept the Mayan women as their forced sexual partners and sold their husbands to traders as slaves.[48] In July 1678, two English merchants named John Neville and George Spurre led a group of buccaneers in a raid of a village in Campeche, where they took captive approximately 250 Mayans and Africans. After forcing their captives to the coast, they sold them to Jamaican merchants and others at the port of Laguna de Términos.[49] Such enslaved Natives were often forcibly taken to nearby English colonies, such as Jamaica. But they also were shipped as far away as Bermuda and New York.

THE FLOW OF ENSLAVED NATIVES from the Caribbean into North American colonies sometimes alarmed magistrates. In the 1670s, the repeated arrival of enslaved Natives from Spanish territories caught the attention of New York authorities. New York City had grown from a small Dutch outpost on Munsee lands to a thriving English town after they wrested it from the Dutch in 1664. By 1680, the city was a bustling center of Atlantic trade, with deep harbors and a growing cluster of houses and shops perched on the tip of what is now southern Manhattan. Pirates and privateers routinely sailed into town, selling pilfered wares and swaggering through the streets loaded with gold and silver coins from around the world. The town housed three thousand English and Dutch residents and five hundred enslaved people.[50] Most of the enslaved population was African, but Indigenous people had been trafficked in and out of New York during both Dutch and English possession.[51]

At some point, New York officials learned of the presence of enslaved Mayans and other Indigenous people trafficked from Spanish territories, which prompted a strong response. In April 1680, the New York legislature passed an act prohibiting the importation of enslaved Indians from the Spanish Caribbean, particularly from the Bay of Campeche in the southern Gulf of Mexico and "other forraigne parts." Perhaps officials were afraid of an uprising if the Mayans had indeed been unjustly enslaved. In the act, the colony rewrote its own history, erasing previous Indigenous enslavement: "Resolved, That all Indyans here have Always been and are free, and not Slaves, nor forc't to bee servants." The law allowed for a six-month leniency period during which legal owners could sell their enslaved Natives outside of New York, whether to the Caribbean or to other parts of North America. And six months after the passing of the bill, all enslaved Indigenous people brought to New York were declared to be "Free Indyans."[52]

Like most laws regarding Native slavery, enforcement was rare and colonists indifferent. A logwood trader named James Barré arrived in New York City a few months after the 1680 decree with thirteen enslaved Mayans for sale. A colorful figure, Barré was a successful privateer who lived multiple lives, marauding for both the Spanish and English and marrying a supposed noblewoman in Cuba to great fanfare. In the 1670s, he sailed the Caribbean with a commission from William Stapleton of Barbados to "take Pirats," and his connections to New York City made it a logical destination to offload enslaved Natives, no matter the official laws of the colony.[53] These Mayans were eagerly purchased by well-to-do citizens who perhaps prized "exotic" Natives for domestic labor. Barré even gifted one to his wife and another to his mother-in-law.[54]

Despite New York's attempts to squelch this Caribbean slave trade, merchants found plenty of ready buyers in other colonies for Natives stolen from the Bay of Campeche and the Yucatán Peninsula.[55] In 1682, Captain Joseph Bannister sailed from New York to the coast of Spanish Florida, where he and his men took captive an unknown number of Natives who were paddling offshore in a large pirogue, or canoe. From Florida they sailed to Cuba, where he stole another seventeen Indians. From there they went to Jamaica, where Bannister sold these Indigenous captives into slavery, according to the governor.[56]

Only a few years later, in 1685, the longtime privateer Bartholomew Sharpe took part in a French raid on a Spanish town in the Bay of Campeche. As part of the plunder, he took several dozen "Spanish Indyans" to sell as slaves. When he reached Bermuda, he had more than thirty Natives to sell, which the colony's governor allowed him to do to ready buyers.[57] Sharpe's raid in the Bay of Campeche raised more than a few eyebrows. It wasn't the Indian slaves—they sold quickly enough—but rather the perception that he was unnecessarily provoking the Spanish in a time of relative peace. Sharpe was eventually arrested, deposed, placed on trial, and ultimately acquitted because he had been working under the commission of William Stapleton, governor of the Leeward Islands.[58]

ONE OF THE GREAT MYSTERIES regarding the Caribbean Indigenous slave trade is its partial invisibility. There are sporadic accounts of
Native individuals being enslaved, trafficked, and sold, but these Indigenous people are almost entirely absent from official colonial censuses.
In one such instance, in 1698, Bermuda took a survey of all its inhabitants. The official census showed 3,615 white people and 2,247 Black
men, women, and children.[59] Not a single Indigenous slave was noted in
the census, but we know from other records that enslaved Natives made
up almost 20 percent of the island's slave population at that time.[60] Two
years after Bermuda's 1698 census, the inventory of John Welsh Sr. of
St. George's listed five enslaved individuals, all of whom were Indians:
Philip, Jane, an elderly man named Tony, a girl named Plunkett, and a
breast-feeding infant named Jack.[61] The same was true of Boaz Sharpe,
a planter on Smith's Island, Bermuda, tucked in between St. George's
and St. David's Islands, who had nine enslaved people on his plantation
in 1707, all of them listed as Indigenous: two men, Phillip and Andrew;
two women, Dinah and Sue; four girls, Jude, Ruth, Dinah, and Rose;
and one unnamed two-day-old "Indian childe."[62]

Officials in London were suspicious of Bermuda's Indian-less census. On August 10, 1698, the Board of Trade in London noted that

BOAZ SHARPE INVENTORY, BERMUDA, 1707.

it was "commonly said there are many Americans at Bermuda kept as Slaves." A marginal summary clarified the terminology: "American Indian slaves." These Crown officials ordered the Bermuda governor to give an account of the number of enslaved Natives, where they had come from, and who brought them to the island.[63] Unsurprisingly, no separate tabulation or report survives, and it is unlikely that it was ever undertaken. Merchants and colonial officials had little incentive to reveal the full scale of their trade in Indigenous captives.

Other Caribbean colonies were no different. Throughout the seventeenth century, plantation deeds reported the presence of enslaved Indigenous people, even as they were omitted from official slave censuses. The 1680 census for Barbados only lists numbers for "Negroes" or "Slaves," depending on the parish reports, despite the sizable Indigenous slave trade into the colony.[64] Colonists in Antigua, too, held enslaved Natives, even if the censuses were silent about their presence. When the estate of Nathaniel Clarke of Antigua was sold in 1681 after his passing, it included "1 Indian woman" along with forty-six enslaved Africans.[65]

The same was true in Jamaica. In 1698, this crown jewel of the English empire reported 40,000 "slaves" and 7,365 whites, with no enslaved Indigenous people noted.[66] And yet, in one survey of 600 households and plantations in Jamaica between 1672 and 1701, a full 8.5 percent of them, or 1 in 12, included enslaved Native Americans.[67]

Most of the planters in Jamaica who enslaved Natives held between one and four of them on average. The estate inventory of James Banister in Jamaica, for example, lists thirteen slaves in 1675, including four Indigenous slaves: a man, a woman, and two children.[68] Others had slightly higher numbers. Andrew Knight had forty-nine enslaved people working on his Jamaican plantation when his estate was inventoried in 1677 or 1678, six of whom were Natives, both men and women, and valued at forty pounds.[69] And some enslaved many more Natives, like John Pollett, a planter in the parish of St. James. Out of the twenty-seven enslaved individuals working his plantation when Pollett died in 1733, seventeen were enslaved Indians.[70]

No wonder observers in Jamaica noted, in direct contrast to official censuses, that "the Indians are of Diverse nations brought hither as of

Seuranam [Suriname], Florida, New England &c. and are sold here for slaves."[71]

NO MATTER HOW THEY WERE FORCED into slavery, once in English colonies, Native Americans were integrated into a wider workforce that included enslaved Africans, white indentured servants, and wage laborers. On Caribbean plantations, enslaved Native Americans performed the wide range of tasks required for sugar, indigo, tobacco, and rice cultivation. But because of their smaller numbers and more specialized, regional skills, Native Americans were sometimes seen as exotic and were perhaps in slightly higher demand among wealthy planters and magistrates.[72] In some locations, Native men were prized for their abilities in fishing and hunting wild hogs, feral cattle, and birds, and so were forced to perform such activities for the planter and his family.[73] Native men were sometimes required to serve in roles less familiar to them, such as footmen in full English uniform.

Native knowledge of the local flora, fauna, and landscape was central to colonists' ability to survive on islands and in territories they found foreign and foreboding. Natives—even those brought from other locations—taught colonists how to prospect for gold and cure potentially fatal poisoning from dangerous plants. Enslaved Native sailors helped colonists make rafts, preserve ship bottoms with aloe plants, and navigate dangerous waterways and coastlines. Indigenous men and women played key roles in textile production, lending local knowledge about how to dye clothing with particular plants, make ropes from indigenous materials, spin cotton, and manufacture hammocks. They also provided other innumerable and often unrecorded important tidbits of local wisdom.[74]

English colonists admired and leaned on Native knowledge of foodways and the local environment, although they rarely admitted as much in writing. Enslaved Indigenous women were known for skillfully making bread from cassava, a New World tuber and relative of the potato. After drying the cassava, Native women pounded it into a powder and added water to make a mealy mixture. Using a rounded, flat, cast-iron pan, they then spread out the meal and baked it evenly on both sides, resulting in a loaf "as thick as a pancake." Spread differently, the same process could also be used to make a thinner wafer bread or a thicker cake and even pie crusts.[75] Skillful working of cassava by Natives also produced a popular drink called perino, that according to one observer was "farre beyond that of Beer, Wine, or Sider" in Europe.[76] Early colonists in Guiana noted Native women producing the cassava-based drink, and John Taylor in Jamaica remarked that Indigenous women in Florida, Suriname, Curaçao, and "most other parts of the Americas" were known for this.[77]

Colonists were also amazed by the deep Indigenous knowledge of nature and the ability to read and foretell weather patterns. This ability was especially crucial for fragile monocultural economies that experienced annually devastating hurricane seasons. One unnamed English resident boasted that while he was on the island of Dominica in the 1650s, his enslaved Native American had the notable skill of forecasting hurricanes fourteen days before they hit. This Englishman took the Dominica Indigenous person (who was unnamed in the records) to England, where eventually the Indian died in Southwark.[78]

Native knowledge in some areas outlasted visible Indigenous presence and was adopted by English colonists, with the cultural memory of Native ways of cultivating the local environment lasting for generations.[79] In these and other countless ways, English men and women continued to colonize Native knowledge and direct it toward their own self-serving ends, just as they had done with Natives kidnapped from the coastlines a generation earlier.

In Jamaica, owners sometimes catered to the demands and desires of their enslaved populations to keep their plantations functioning as smoothly as possible. John Taylor reported in the 1680s that planters tried to purchase enslaved men and women in roughly equal numbers so that each man would have a wife. Some couples were given a small plot of land to clear and plant a garden of maize, potatoes, and yams. In some cases, they even built rudimentary houses for themselves, which Taylor called wigwams, a term widely used for Native houses. Some enslavers, although surely not all, also gave some enslaved couples a pig, rooster, and hen, which with some luck and skill, could eventually produce a small supply of consumable and marketable meat.[80]

Planters gained the most out of this arrangement, of course. Not only did it appease enslaved populations, but they eagerly claimed and put to work any children that resulted from these unions. When Africans and Indigenous people married or had children, the already faint record of Indigenous presence grew fainter still. Multiracial enslaved children quickly lost any official remaining Indigenous identity, erased from the record by Europeans determined to keep both Indians and Africans enslaved and their own profits growing.

THIS DEVASTATING INDIGENOUS SLAVE TRADE has been all but forgotten in the Caribbean today. Just one example is Jamaica's only significant public monument to slavery: two larger-than-life, cast-iron figures situated at the corner of Emancipation Park in the capital city of Kingston. Rendered completely naked and thigh deep in a large circular fountain, the twelve-foot-high man and woman gaze not at each other but heavenward, reflecting the name of the monument, "Redemption Song," which takes its title from a track by Jamaica's most famous singer, Bob Marley. The figures are the primary way Jamaica has chosen to memorialize the hundreds of thousands of enslaved African men and women who labored on the island for over three centuries under

REDEMPTION SONG, BY LAURA FACEY,
KINGSTON, JAMAICA, 2003.

both Spanish and English rule. The monument is appropriately somber but distinctly hopeful.

Of course, while one history is remembered, another is forgotten. Taíno peoples had also been enslaved during the Spanish occupation of Jamaica and well before African captives were brought to the island. This continued long after the English takeover in 1655, when the number of enslaved Indigenous peoples swelled as Natives were trafficked to the island from other regions and forced to labor on plantations alongside enslaved Africans, even as they were relabeled "negro" in official censuses. Taíno peoples in Jamaica today continue to remind the world of their presence. Kasike Kalaan Nibonrix Kaiman, leader of the Yamaye Guani (Jamaica Hummingbird) Taíno people, points toward the "resilience, the strength, and the indomitable spirit that have allowed us to overcome adversity time and time again."[81]

Like the identities of enslaved people in Jamaica and elsewhere that are remembered as primarily African, so too Tituba's identity morphed in later generations. Henry Wadsworth Longfellow, in "Giles Corey of Salem Farms" (1868), suggested that Tituba was a multiracial girl from the island of San Salvador (in the Bahamas, where Columbus originally landed) with a "black and fierce" Obeah man as a father.[82] By the nineteenth century, Longfellow's identification of Tituba as a "mulatto" slave was more familiar and palatable than as an enslaved South American Lokono. Such erasures effectively hid her identity, as they did for thousands of other Native Americans stolen from coastlines and sold into slavery in the Caribbean and North America.

The Caribbean Indigenous slave trade and its violence, pillaging, and slavery cannot be isolated from the English colonies in North America—or the later history of the United States. Trafficking in Native slaves was an extension of a puritan and wider English impulse to subdue and rule and to extract human and natural resources from the Americas. It would continue with equal fervor in North American colonies.

Five

FORCED
DIASPORAS

THE SAME NETWORK OF CARIBBEAN ENGLISH MERCHANTS THAT
delivered enslaved Natives *to* North American colonies also trafficked
Native American captives *from* them. English colonists in New England
and Virginia had sporadically sold Native captives to Atlantic markets
in the first few decades of colonization. But there was an unprecedented spike in Natives trafficked out of North American English colonies to an unexpected number of Atlantic destinations in the second
half of the seventeenth century.

Initially, this increase in the outbound trafficking of Native captives
was due to English colonists in North America waging two major wars
against Indigenous peoples in the 1670s, in New England and Virginia.
Both were notable for the mass enslavement of Native Americans and
the shipment of them off the continent. English colonies grew rapidly
as settlers continually pushed away from the coastlines to claim more
arable land for farms and plantations until aggressive expansion triggered a blowback. These wars illustrated the growing willingness of the
colonies to leverage their expanding population and firepower against
Natives they deemed to be an impediment to colonial development.

As a result of this forced diaspora, Indigenous people found themselves enslaved far from home. This included a group of Wampanoag
who were torn from their homelands and forced to serve as galley
slaves in the Mediterranean. Their journey began in the summer of
1675, when English soldiers started rounding up Native people considered to be in rebellion, during what historians later called King Philip's
War. Plymouth Colony hired Captain Thomas Spragg to dispatch 178
captives overseas to be sold into slavery. Spragg sailed to Spain, where

30 of the Wampanoag captives were sold to another English merchant, John Matthews, who took them to the small English colony of Tangier (present-day Morocco) in hopes of selling them for a profit. Malnourished and sickly from the transatlantic voyage, 9 Indians died on the short sail from Cádiz to Tangier. Matthews sold the 21 remaining Natives to an English Royal Navy captain named Thomas Hamilton, who forced them to row on his naval galley ship, the *Margaret*, off the coast of North Africa.[1]

Hamilton was pleased with the enslaved New England rowers and wrote to the Board of Admiralty in London that "if there were every year a recruit from those parts . . . it might be very advantageous for his Majesty's service."[2] His suggestion highlights how commonplace Indian slavery had become in the wider Atlantic world, so much so that even a captain in the Royal Navy thought it unremarkable to suggest a regularized Indian slave trade out of New England into North Africa and the Mediterranean for Crown service.

These wars in the 1670s were decisive turning points in Indigenous–colonial relationships in New England and Virginia. In both regions,

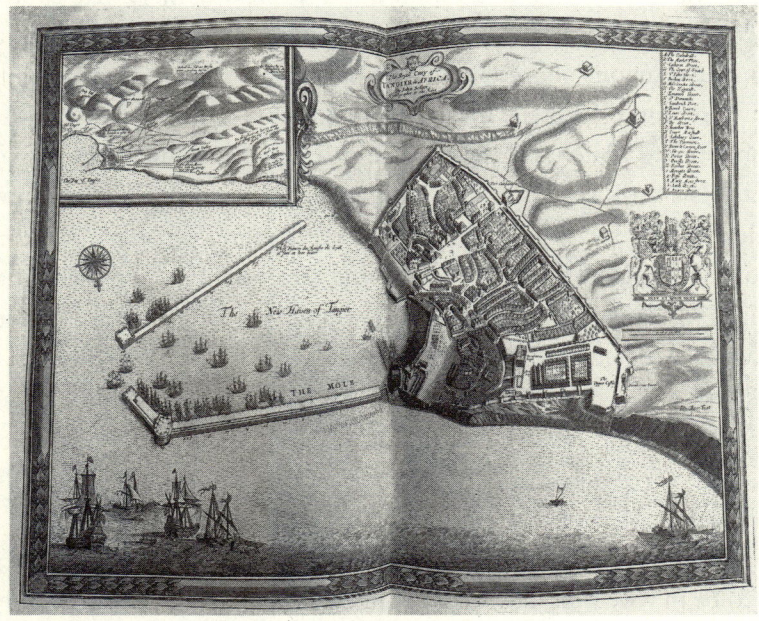

THE ROYAL CITY OF TANGIER IN AFRICA,
BY JOHN SELLER, CA. 1680.

English magistrates used Native resistance to assert power and control over Native sovereignty. Although Native defiance was strong and sustained, enslavement was a key part of effectively tipping the balance of power. It stole away Indian men, women, sons, and daughters and demoralized entire communities. It disrupted leadership lines, tore apart family units, destroyed towns, destabilized crop production, and damaged trading networks.

Fear of enslavement drove Native Americans to either fight more—which led to even more losses—or pull up roots and move farther inland. This also slowly helped to clear the land, which is precisely what English colonists wanted. Enslaving the regions' Indigenous people was not simply a strategy of "replacement"—shipping away Natives to replace them with enslaved Africans.[3] It was its own process of generating income, land, and Indigenous slaves that bolstered American colonial settlement for decades to come.

WAMPANOAG SOLDIERS DESCENDED ON the southeastern Massachusetts town of Swansea on June 24, 1675. The warriors, who were loyal to Philip, or Pumetacom, the sachem of the Pokanoket (part of the larger Wampanoag nation), quickly moved through the small string of wooden clapboard buildings, burning houses, destroying property, and killing nine colonists who dared to show themselves. In their later published narratives of the conflict often referred to as King Philip's War, English colonists wrongly claimed that this attack and the ensuing war were unprovoked. If anything, narrators acknowledged that perhaps Pumetacom's men were upset that a Plymouth court had recently executed three Pokanokets who were found guilty of the murder of John Sassamon, a Christian Indian and former scribe for Pumetacom.[4]

Local Pokanoket and Narragansett leaders harbored a vastly deeper set of grievances, which are still felt generations later among regional Indigenous people today. As Narragansett educator Lorén Spears has noted, the Swansea attack was the first salvo in what we should call the War for New England, an attempt to retake what invading colonists had been stealing from Natives since their arrival.[5] When Pilgrims first arrived, the Great League of Peace with the Wampanoag in 1621 had staved off outright conflict during the lifetime of the great

King Philip, published by S. G. Drake, 1827. Pumetacom, or King Philip, was a Pokanoket sachem.

Wampanoag leader Ousamequin, or Massasoit. In the decades after the Pequot War in the 1630s, English colonists and regional Dawnland tribes had uneasily lived side by side. When Ousamequin passed away in 1661, his son Pumetacom (Metacom, or King Philip, a title given by colonists) came to power. He was less tolerant of English land grabbing and seemed determined to respond to challenges to Wampanoag power and sovereignty. Tensions grew in the 1660s and early 1670s, and English leaders increasingly heard rumors of war.[6]

A week before the Swansea attack, Rhode Island deputy governor John Easton met with Pumetacom and forty of his men to try to understand why the Pokanoket were threatening war. Pumetacom relayed to Easton the deeper history of colonial presence, reminding them that when the English first arrived, colonists were like children who had to be taught how to plant corn and to survive. The Wampanoag were the first to do right, Pumetacom stated, and the English were the first to do wrong, repaying kindness with continual attacks on Wampanoag sovereignty.[7]

Colonists, Pumetacom asserted, stole Native land, animals, and food supplies. They continually politically humiliated Native leaders by forcing them into unfair land deals and treaties. They also treated the Wampanoag unjustly in court and demanded they hand over their firearms without any rationalization, which robbed Native men of efficient means of hunting and self-protection. Pumetacom further resented the attempts to evangelize his people since, from his experience, once Christianized, Natives had split allegiances and could no longer be trusted. To top it off, English traders encouraged Native inebriation, thereby creating debt dependence as well as easier land sales. For fifty years, puritans had chipped away at Native lives with a thousand little cuts. And Pumetacom and his people could take no more.[8]

New England's Indigenous people had another reason to deeply resent the English, one that John Easton did not record: ongoing Native enslavement and coerced Indian servitude. This was, in the estimation

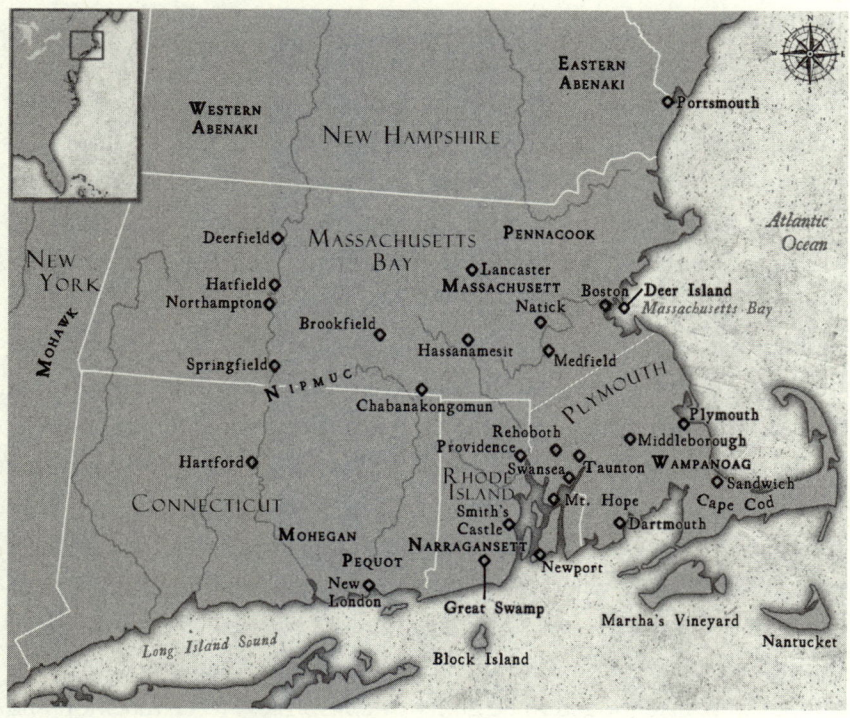

NEW ENGLAND IN 1675.

of Captain John Wyborne, "the chief if not the only cause of the Indians making war upon the English in New England." Coerced labor and enslavement were recurring aspects of wider Native American experiences in every New England colony. In the early 1670s, Massachusetts authorities punished public Indian drunkenness by shipping offenders to an island in Boston Harbor to serve for ten days doing hard labor, where they were sold more alcohol to keep them in debt and servitude. When Wyborne visited the island, he was shocked to see "hundreds" of Indians forced into hard labor in this way.[9]

IMMEDIATELY AFTER THE ATTACK ON SWANSEA, English magistrates turned the war into a slave-raiding and land-grabbing spectacle. Massachusetts, Connecticut, and Plymouth mustered their militias and took the war to every enemy Native town or encampment they could find. They convinced the Mohegan and Pequot to ally with the English, although these Native nations had their own reasons for doing so. Widespread dislike of Native Americans burst into outright anti-Indian fervor, with virtually all Natives viewed as legitimate targets of capture and enslavement. In the opening months of the conflict, colonists vastly preferred to ship Native captives out of the country rather than enslave them locally or pay to keep them in prisons or slave pens for months on end. A New England merchant named Captain Woly reported to a correspondent in England that colonists "do take and kill many of them" while others they send to "barbados & Neves & Jamecco & Spaine & sell them."[10]

The first large group of Wampanoags to be sold into slavery were not even combatants. Native forces attacked the towns of Dartmouth and Middleborough on July 8, 1675, burning approximately 51 houses. Shortly after the attack, 150 local Wampanoags who had not been involved in the raid turned themselves in to authorities, having been promised mercy. Instead, these surrendering Natives plus 10 more were taken to Plymouth, where all but 6 of them were promptly sold "out of the country" into slavery.[11] An additional 57 Natives who surrendered to authorities in Sandwich on Cape Cod in late August or early September were also judged to be guilty of conspiracy in the rebellion and were "condemned unto perpetuall servitude."[12] When Captain Spragg loaded up 178 Native captives on September 28, heading for Cádiz, Spain, at least 45 of them were surrenderers.[13]

Indigenous leaders were stunned. Enslaving combatants—horrible as it was—was one thing. Shipping off noncombatants, surrenderers, and women and children signified another level of unspeakable cruelty. Native individuals and leaders protested their mistreatment, and some colonists took up their cause in Boston. The Roxbury minister and missionary John Eliot recognized both the psychological terror of overseas enslavement—especially for those who surrendered—as well as the blowback from such policies. Early in the war, on August 13, 1675, Eliot warned Massachusetts governor John Leverett, "The terror of selling away such Indians unto lands for perpetual slaves, who shall yield up themselves to mercy, is like to be an effectual prolongation of the war."[14]

A rare voice of relative reason during wartime, Eliot argued that enslaving surrendering Indians violated the English colonists' Christian faith and, more pragmatically, was unwise.[15] But such sentiments were immensely unpopular. Both Eliot and his partner in evangelization, the judge Daniel Gookin, received death threats for defending Natives. Eliot also denounced the role land grabbing played in the conflict, suggesting "here is land enough for them and us too."[16]

To motivate enlistment, Plymouth and Massachusetts promised troops and military units that they would personally benefit from the plunder of Native property and the sale of Indigenous captives. Responders included several free-ranging militias known as the Jamaica privateers, who were authorized by the Massachusetts governor. One militiaman, Samuel Moseley, swaggered through Boston with the braggadocio of a hardened Atlantic privateer, having made his name by capturing several Dutch ships on the high seas of the Caribbean. Moseley and his henchmen quickly went to work. In July 1675 alone, they captured a total of one hundred Pocasset and Wampanoag Indians—most of whom were refugees, women and children trying to wait out the war.[17] As records and receipts show, Moseley and his accomplices—including a Dutch privateer named Cornelius—routinely received payment for Indians sold as slaves.[18]

Fear of enslavement and, more specifically, the fear of being sold as a slave out of the country, played a major role in the War for New England. In June 1676, the English captain Benjamin Church pressured Awashonks, the female sachem of the Sakonnet in Rhode Island, to join forces with him. When she demurred, he urged her to remember the Pequot—an ominous but unnecessary history lesson. Awashonks eventually agreed to have her men fight with the English on the condition that all of them, including the "Wives and Children," would not be killed and that "none of them transported out of the Country," echoing the plea of Wincumbone forty years earlier during the Pequot War.[19]

The fear of overseas enslavement was so palpable that it was used as a recruiting tactic by Pumetacom's warriors. The Massachusetts magistrate Daniel Gookin reported that Natives allied with Pumetacom sent "secret messages" to the Christian Indians warning "that the English designed, in the conclusion, to destroy them all, or send them out of the country for bond slaves."[20] And as Eliot had anticipated, the threat of foreign enslavement thus drove some Natives deeper into resistance against the English. When the Christianized Native James Quannapaquait, who was drafted into English service, suggested to some younger Indian warriors that they should stop fighting, they retorted, "Why shall wee have peace to bee made slaves, & either be kild or sent away to sea to Barbadoes."[21]

AT THE SAME TIME, colonists a thousand miles to the south in the growing patchwork of tobacco plantations carved out of Tsenacommacah's woods also provoked war with regional Native nations. A Virginia trader named Thomas Mathew failed to pay some of his Doeg Indian suppliers in the summer of 1675, and they retaliated by stealing his hogs. Mathew rallied his white neighbors and gave chase, hunting down the Doeg men and reclaiming his pigs. Frustrated by the persistent inequity of colonial justice, the Doeg struck back even harder, murdering the household of Mathew's herdsman, Thomas Hen.

That evening, Mathew assembled the Stafford County militia and marched through the night toward Doeg territory. In the morning, they attacked a Doeg settlement, killing close to a dozen Native inhabitants and taking captives, including the sachem's son. The militia unit moved on, assaulting the next Indian village and killing fourteen people. But they had inadvertently made a costly mistake. These Natives were not Doegs, but the newly arrived and powerful Susquehannock, who themselves were fleeing a losing war with the Haudenosaunee to the north.[22]

The Susquehannock, understandably incensed, furiously retaliated with counterraids, which turned local Virginians and Marylanders against them. In late September, one thousand militiamen laid siege to the Susquehannock fort on Piscataway Creek. When Susquehannock chiefs emerged to negotiate a peace treaty, colonists murdered all six of them in cold blood. After a six-week siege, the Susquehannock mostly vacated the region, traveling farther south to the Virginia border for the winter.[23]

In January 1676, the Doeg and Susquehannock regrouped, attacking a number of English plantations just south of James River Falls, kill-

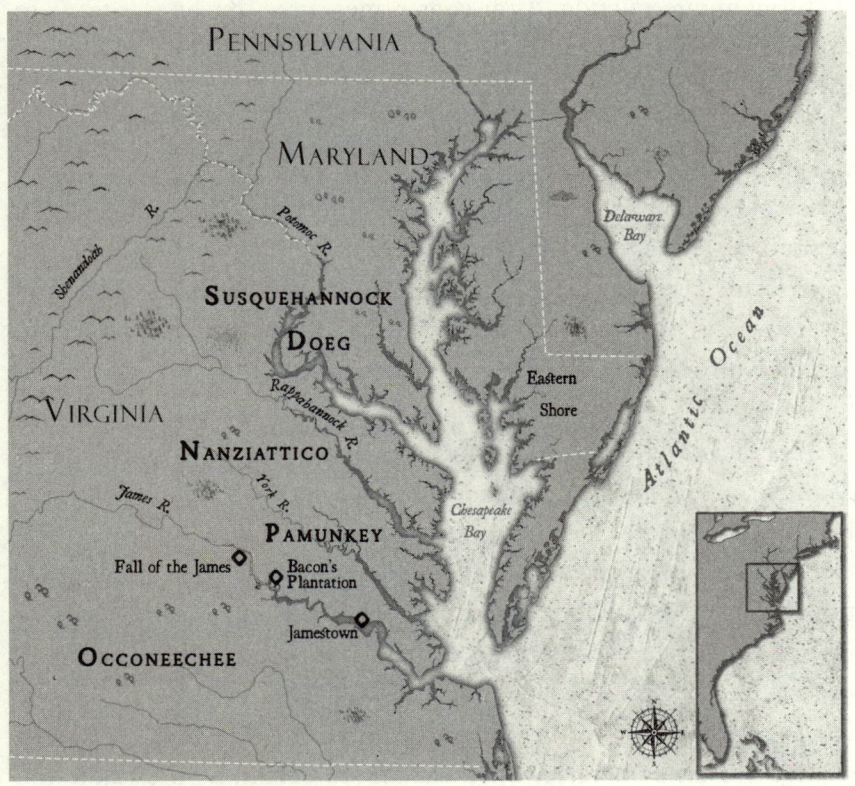

VIRGINIA IN 1675.

ing between thirty and sixty colonists. And on the way back to their encampment above the falls, they raided a few small plantations and Native trading outposts. One of them belonged to Nathaniel Bacon, a young, wealthy Virginia planter. Bacon, William Byrd, and a growing cluster of other colonists lived in what was then the backcountry of Virginia near present-day Richmond. Fifty miles west of Jamestown, they were pushing the line of settlement ever deeper into Indian territory. It was only a matter of time before these frequent small conflicts over boundaries detonated into a larger war.

Bacon and others were infuriated by this particular attack. Governor Berkeley declared war against all Natives who had committed "murthers, rapins and depradations" against the English, but he decided not to send a militia unit for counterattacks, much to the chagrin of Bacon and other aggrieved colonists.[24] Berkeley ordered a new string of forts built in the backcountry but kept tight control over frontier militias that sought direct action. As discontentment grew, Bacon was ready to unleash his full fury against local Natives, and he was backed by hundreds of backcountry planters.[25]

At a meeting on Bacon's plantation in March 1676, Bacon stirred the pot of anger until it boiled over. These anti-Native planters voted Bacon as their leader, and riding a wave of extreme anti-Indian fervor, he soon began leading vigilante raids against any and all nearby Native Americans. "Are not the Indians all of a Colour?" queried Bacon and his associates, drawing a distinctly racialized line between all whites and all Native Americans. "We will have warr with all Indians. . . . We will spare none."[26]

This racialized violence continued to spiral as two months later in May, Bacon and his men persuaded the Occaneechi to raid the Susquehannock. With the Susquehannock punished, Bacon turned on the Occaneechi, slaughtering over one hundred of them and taking captives.[27] One Occaneechi captive was the chief's daughter, who—as reports insinuated—soldiers raped after capturing, an all-too-common experience for Native women during war.[28] After taking captives, the troops marched on to the Virginia capital of Jamestown and confronted Governor Berkeley with clamorous demands to escalate the war against all Indians, a request that would soon be granted.

THE OUTBREAK OF INDIGENOUS WARS in New England and Virginia was not coordinated or directly connected so far as we know. Native nations in both places acted independently to address the pressures that colonization put on their communities. And yet colonists who knew that Native Americans were attacking English settlements in New England, Maryland, and Virginia believed Indians were all working together. Governor Berkeley certainly thought so, as did Nathaniel Bacon and even Barbados governor Jonathan Atkins, who heard reports of the "dayly devastations made by the Indians," which were "catching like a Contagion spreading it self over all the continent *from New England*."[29]

Fear of an East Coast pan-Indian conspiracy seemed even more worrisome as Pumetacom's successes in New England surged in late 1675. Between June and December, Pumetacom's troops torched villages in southern and central Massachusetts, including Rehoboth, Taunton, Dartmouth, Middleborough, Brookfield, Deerfield, Springfield, and Hatfield, sending colonists scurrying for protection in towns closer to Boston. Native bands targeted tangible signs of detested colonial intrusions by slaughtering and disemboweling pigs and cattle, mutilating English bodies, and ripping apart an Indigenous-language translation of the Bible page by page.[30]

By December 1675, the New England colonies were desperate for a change in strategy. Accusing the Narragansett nation of secretly aiding Pumetacom's men and withholding refugees, the United Colonies mustered a combined force of 1,000 soldiers from Connecticut, Massachusetts, and Plymouth, which included 150 Pequots and Mohegans. They marched through a snowstorm from Pettaquamscutt, Rhode Island, to the Narragansett fort in a large swamp on December 19, 1675, led by a Narragansett captive named Peter. After breaching the wall and burning everything inside, including 500 wetus, many of which contained women and children, the colonists captured 350 Natives and later sold them into slavery—some out of the region.[31] Between 500 and 1,000 Narragansetts and members of other regional nations died in the battle. The rest disappeared into the woods and found refuge with other Native communities.

The English had gravely miscalculated. This unprovoked attack,

WEEDEN FAMILY FLEEING NARRAGANSETT FORT, BY TALL
OAK WEEDEN, UNDATED.

which was rightfully called the Great Swamp Massacre, galvanized
rather than intimidated the Narragansett, driving them more firmly to
Pumetacom's cause.

Bolstered by Narragansett support, Pumetacom's troops began
attacking English towns with a new vigor. Lancaster, Massachusetts,
fell in February 1676, as did Northampton and Medfield, with English
captives taken by Natives. This included Mary Rowlandson, who
famously later wrote about her experiences traveling with Pumetacom's
troops.[32] Bostonians debated the possibility of erecting a wall around
their city to protect it. By the end of the month, Pumetacom's troops
were assaulting towns within ten miles of the city.[33] Rhode Island, too,
paid dearly for aiding the attack on the Narragansett stronghold. Narragansett and Pumetacom-allied Natives burned Providence to the
ground on March 29, 1676, and within a few months had torched every
English town on the west side of the Narragansett Bay.

Christianized Natives who affiliated with one of the fourteen "praying towns" in Massachusetts and northeastern Connecticut found
themselves caught in the middle.[34] Despite the creation of these English-
style mission villages in Connecticut and Massachusetts and a transla-

tion of the Christian Bible in the Massachusett-Wôpanâak language in 1663, English colonists and Pumetacom's men alike viewed "praying" Natives with suspicion.[35] The Massachusetts government began sending groups of Christianized Indians to Deer Island and Long Island, both in Boston Harbor. Authorities claimed it was for their own protection, but Natives feared this as a stopping point in a process that would lead to them being transported from the region as slaves.[36]

Christian Native men were recruited from their exile in Boston Harbor to serve as translators, guides, and soldiers—which only further confirmed to nonpraying Natives that these Christians had sold themselves out to the English. Those who remained in the temporary internment camp barely survived the cold winter of 1675–1676 on small, fairly barren islands with no real protection from the brutal winter wind and snow.

The War for New England began to turn in favor of the English when the powerful Mohawk in New York refused to join Pumetacom.[37] As military recruitment efforts flagged, Massachusetts officials continued to mobilize the general population against Natives in February 1676 by offering a reward of three pounds for any person who captured

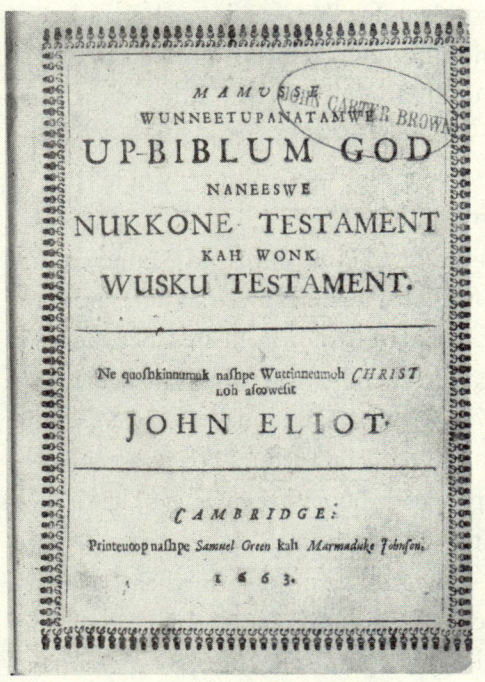

TITLE PAGE OF THE 1663 WÔPANÂAK-MASSACHUSETT TRANSLATION OF THE FIRST EDITION OF THE FIRST BIBLE PRINTED IN THE AMERICAS.

an Indian.[38] New Hampshire offered the same reward for any Native brought in, dead or alive.[39]

As had happened during the Pequot War, the United Colonies sent companies of English soldiers and allied Natives—Christian Indians, Mohegans, and Pequots—marching throughout Indian country in order to systematically root out Natives from swamps and forests. Major John Talcott took thirty-three captives at Chabanakongomun, just outside of what is now Webster, Massachusetts, and another twenty-nine near Lancaster. English forces raided Narragansett country in Rhode Island, killing thirty Indigenous men on the spot and taking forty-five women and children captive.[40]

Finally, on August 12, 1676, English troops caught up with the elusive Pumetacom, who had returned to his homelands at Mount Hope, in what is now Bristol, Rhode Island. He ended up surrounded by enemies in a swamp, where a Christian Wampanoag sharpshooter named John Alderman pulled the trigger that launched the fatal bullet. In fact, Pumetacom had already died a thousand deaths, watching his community and world dismantled around him. Benjamin Church commanded an Indian executioner to cut up Pumetacom's body for bragging rights and posted his head on a pike in Plymouth, where it stayed for decades.[41] Pumetacom's wife, Wootonekanuske, and their son languished in prison for months before officials decided to banish them into slavery, joining the hundreds of others who suffered the same fate. The records are not clear, but later historians and Native oral traditions suggest that they were likely sent to Bermuda, where, like so many others, they vanished without a trace.[42]

Fighting and sporadic raids in New Hampshire and Maine continued after Pumetacom's death in August 1676. A month later, under the pretense of a peace ceremony, Richard Waldron hosted between 350 and 400 regional Pennacooks and other Natives who had fled northward to find refuge from the War for New England at Cocheco, on the border of what is now Maine and New Hampshire. For two weeks, he wined and dined them on his property. Behind their backs, he orchestrated the arrival of part of the Massachusetts army, with perhaps as many as 200 soldiers, who surrounded and disarmed the approximately 250 women and children, 80 fighting men, and 20 or so older men. Waldron had 7 tried and hanged and sent the rest—perhaps as many as 200—to Boston as captives to be sold as slaves.[43] Such actions prolonged the war in New Hampshire and Maine.

English troops continued to round up refugees and bands of Indians. Known Indian enemy leaders were simply executed, often publicly, including approximately 50 Native men on the Boston Common.[44] Others were shipped overseas. In September 1676, Plymouth and Boston magistrates authorized Captain Thomas Smith to load 180 Natives onto his ship, the *Seaflower*. Two certificates made out to Smith confirmed these Indians had been condemned to "Perpetuall Servitude & slavery."[45] The Natives were transported out of Boston Harbor and disappeared into the wider world of Atlantic slavery.

The aftermath of the war quickly turned colonial towns into colossal Native slave-trading hubs. Massachusetts officials held several public auctions of enslaved Indians in Boston on August 24 and September 23, 1676, where they found ready buyers for nearly two hundred captives.[46] Leaders parceled out hundreds of Native Americans to soldiers who had been enticed into service with the promise of captives. Some soldiers and commanders conducted private sales of Natives they had in their possession.[47] In Providence, over thirty of the key men involved in the defense of Rhode Island during the war—including Roger Williams—were rewarded with a substantial share of the total proceeds of the sale of Indians.[48] Limited records of these sales indicate a wide range of acceptable payments and prices for Native captives, including specie (average of two pounds silver), sheep, cotton, twenty-two bushels of corn, and "three fat sheep."[49]

In a disgraceful betrayal, leaders in each colony consigned to limited-term slavery Natives who had responded to offers of leniency if they would surrender. Providence assigned between seven and twenty-five years of service for surrendering Natives based on their ages.[50] Newport magistrates preferred a simple, limited-term enslavement length of nine years.[51] Similarly, Connecticut parceled out noncombatant Indians into local English households to labor as servants for ten years, with an annual tribute of five shillings per male, as "an acknowledgment of their subjection to this gouernment of Connecticut."[52]

VIRGINIANS HOPED TO REPLICATE New England's victories. Determined to wield even greater power in his raids against Native communities, Bacon marched into Jamestown with four hundred men on June 23, 1676, and confronted Governor Berkeley and the members of the Virginia Assembly at gunpoint. Bacon demanded a commission as general and commander-in-chief with full power to raise forces for and to fight an "Indian warr."[53] The governor refused, but the assembly overruled him. Bacon received his commission.

Propelled by Bacon's anti-Indian fervor, the Virginia Assembly passed a series of laws—known as Bacon's Laws—in June that incentivized the taking of Indian captives and land. Soldiers could keep such captives and any other physical plunder, or they could sell them for personal profit. Either way, these captured Indians would be "accounted slaves dureing life"—that is, considered lifelong slaves.[54]

Newly empowered, from June 1676 onward, Bacon's men indiscriminately attacked Native communities, regardless of any previous alliance or tributary relationship with Virginia. They terrorized Indigenous towns on the frontier—burning villages, killing Natives, and taking captives. Desperate for additional manpower, Bacon and his men promised freedom for servants and slaves who joined them. They attacked the Virginia-allied Pamunkey in early September, destroying their villages, killing eight people, and taking forty-five captives. Along the way, soldiers also carted off loads of valuable assorted furs, skins, wampum, and cloth, all claimed as part of the promised spoils of war.[55] The Virginian army ranged the woods for a few weeks and eventually tracked down the Nanziattico, another Indian nation that was tributary to Virginia. They took a few more captives, plundered the village, killed a half dozen Natives, and moved on.[56]

The stately and sagacious Pamunkey leader Cockacoeske watched as Bacon's men marched into her territory with a genocidal fury in September 1676. She fled with as many of her people as were able, deep into the swamps of the Dragon Run watershed on the south bank of the Rappahannock River. Bacon and his men made repeated incursions into the densely wooded swamplands, but the Pamunkey and Rappahannock evaded detection by staying off the main trails and using a system of knocking on tree trunks and whistling to remain hidden.[57]

When the Virginia Assembly demanded that Cockacoeske appear before them, she complied, bravely choosing to stake her claim and protect her nation's future. She appeared before the assembly on her own terms, as the rightful ruler of her fiercely independent people. Dressed in a crown of shell beads and a long deerskin cloak, she commanded the room by insisting on speaking only in her own language with an interpreter. When she was given the floor, Cockacoeske spoke for a full fifteen minutes, denouncing the violence against her people and reminding the assembly of the Pamunkeys' loyalty to Virginia. It was a bold and effective move of self-preservation. After the war, she signed the Treaty of Middle Plantation that allowed the Pamunkey to continue as a Virginia tributary.[58]

Throughout the war, Native captives were sold locally or shipped out of Virginia for profit. In just one instance of many, forty-five captured Pamunkeys were paraded in front of a jeering crowd in Jamestown in September 1676 before being sold into slavery. Fragmented bits of information about individuals were sometimes noted in local records. One unnamed Native girl was captured by Bacon and his soldiers during a raid in 1676. Bacon sold her to a Mr. Ingram, who turned around and sold her to William Sloane. Wanting to make his purchase official, Sloane registered the deed of sale for an "Indian girle" with the Henrico County Court on January 22, 1677.[59] From there the paper trail disappears, but lifelong enslavement—perhaps with multiple sales

BRONZE STATUE OF COCKACOESKE, A PAMUNKEY LEADER, THAT IS PART OF *VOICES FROM THE GARDEN: THE VIRGINIA WOMEN'S MONUMENT*, IN RICHMOND, VIRGINIA.

and transfers—would have been the norm for most of the Susquehannock, Occaneechi, Pamunkey, and others taken during the war.

Bacon's actions provoked a strong backlash from regional Native
nations. Reprisals and raids at the hands of Natives on the border of
Virginia and Maryland led Maryland's English leadership to feel like
their colony too was under attack. Cecil Calvert, the second Lord Baltimore, raised some troops and marched on the Native bands they saw as
responsible. As in Virginia, these troops raided Indian towns and took
captives. But instead of allowing the soldiers to share in the plunder—
furs, skins, wampum, and Native captives—Baltimore instead sold the
captured Indians to Caribbean merchants, who took them to Barbados. Maryland residents were upset, not because Native Americans
had been enslaved but because they felt they had been cheated.[60]

Bacon's Indian War came to an abrupt halt in late October 1676
when Bacon, still out in the Virginia forests hunting down Natives, suddenly grew ill and passed away, most likely from typhus, an infectious
disease common during wars.[61] After his death, Governor Berkeley
attempted to regain control of Bacon's army and the colony. In dying,
Bacon escaped Berkeley's wrath and royal judgment, but his other
coconspirators were not so lucky. Dozens of English colonists who had
fought with Bacon were placed on trial and convicted—not of slave
raiding, but of sedition—including a few women, perhaps unusually,
whom Bacon had reportedly used to "preach Rebellion."[62] The English
Crown was appalled at Berkeley's inability to retain control, and the
arrival of royal troops from England in late January 1677 signaled the
end of his governorship.

Historians have called the events of 1676 in Virginia Bacon's Rebellion, which highlights the political contest between Bacon's men and
the royally appointed Governor Berkeley. But Bacon, his contemporaries, and even the Virginia legislature afterward called it the "Indian
warr," which seems more appropriate.[63] Bacon had led an all-out
assault on Natives, rarely caring if those he was murdering or enslaving
were the colony's allies or not. His war had widespread backing among
the populace and, to a limited extent, in the Virginia Assembly, and it
reflected a strong anti-Indian undercurrent that was quickly coming to
dominate the English colonies.

The Crown might have found it convenient to demonize Bacon,

but colony leaders and plantation owners alike recognized the value in enslaving Native Americans to provide financial benefit, land, and labor. In February 1677, the legislature allowed Bacon-allied soldiers—those supposedly treasonous traitors—to "keep all such Indians slaves, or other Indian goods" as an "encouragement" for their service, a measure it affirmed two years later. The legislature also desired the newly freed lands to be sold for public profit in order to pay for the war and tried to pass legislation to this effect.[64]

Bacon's own estate represented in microcosm the material and bodily benefits of his Indian war. The Virginia officials who inventoried his estate recorded three servants and seven Indigenous slaves between the ages of one year and forty years old. Most of Bacon's associates also personally benefited from enslaving and selling Native people. William Byrd, who became one of the principal enslavers in Virginia, led raids into Native territory and sold off Indigenous captives for profit. At least some of the enslaved Natives remained in the family, for his son, William Byrd II, counted Indigenous people among his enslaved population nearly twenty-five years later.[65]

WHAT WAS IT LIKE TO BE TRANSPORTED out of one's homelands as a slave? Such devastating shipments were a prominent feature of the wars in both Massachusetts and Virginia. In October 1675, Massachusetts troops under John Gorham and Matthew Fuller kidnapped thirteen noncombatant Indians from Chippaquasett (Prudence Island) in the Narragansett Bay. Some of them, including "Indian Jack" and his family, were serving as resident tenant laborers on the estate of William Paine. Gorham and Fuller swiftly shipped these Natives to Faial in the Azores before their owners could produce proper documentation.

Jack and his family must have been filled with dread as they were forced beneath the deck of a ship leaving the region. After weeks at sea, perhaps they could sense the ship approaching the westernmost of the nine primary islands of the Azores, Ilha das Flores and Corvo, before reaching the island of Faial. Within a few days of their arrival, these captive New England Natives were sold to planters and landowners on the islands and were added to the workforce of the ever-growing plantations that for more than two centuries had mercilessly used up one enslaved life after another.[66]

The Azores was only one destination for enslaved Natives. Virginians and New Englanders forcibly shipped Indigenous men, women, and children to Bermuda, Barbados, Jamaica, Antigua, Mexico (Yucatán Peninsula), Cádiz and Málaga (Spain), Calais (France), Tangier (North Africa), and possibly Madagascar.[67] In Tangier, some served as galley slaves in the Royal Navy, while others were forced to build the breakwater in the harbor. In 1683, John Eliot wrote to the president of the New England Company (a missionary society based in London), asking for help in returning some Natives from Tangier to New England, but we have no evidence that his request was fulfilled.[68] At least one shipload of New England Indians arrived in Cádiz and Málaga, where Squanto had been forcibly taken in 1614.[69] As many as three additional shipments of Natives arrived in Faial in the Azores, where New England Indians were sold as slaves.

The twenty "stout" New England Natives who were shipped as slaves to the Bay of Campeche on the Yucatán Peninsula joined a multiethnic labor force felling logwood trees, but they longed to return home. At the first opportunity, they murdered their overseer and attempted to make their way back to New England.[70] The archives are silent regarding the rest of their story, but it is tempting to imagine them finding a sympathetic ship captain to return them to the Dawnland.

In most cases, these North American Natives mostly vanished into a Caribbean slave market where tribal and geographical origins were not recorded. On certain English islands, however, they became a feared presence. Between August 1675 and December 1676, the largest English island colonies—Jamaica, Barbados, and Bermuda—passed laws prohibiting the importation of enslaved Indians. Jamaica and Barbados specifically restricted the arrival of New England Native captives.[71] This was no abolitionist campaign, nor was it a rejection of Indigenous slavery in general. Instead, these laws were passed out of fear, driven by the perception that all North American Indians had conspired to overthrow the English. Temporarily banning importation of these supposedly rebellious Native captives was a desperate attempt to stop any "revolts" from spreading to these colonies.[72]

EVEN FOR THOSE WHO were not shipped overseas, colonial policies regarding enslavement were traumatically disruptive to Native families and communities. Children of Indigenous captives and surrenderers were routinely separated from their parents.[73] Massachusetts parceled Indian children out to English families. Children of Natives accused of being in open rebellion were often enslaved for life. Even the children of Christianized Natives—including the children of Native men who had served the English in the war—were often removed from their parents and "ordered to be put forth to English service" as servants and slaves.[74]

Native families tried to reunite as much as possible, attempting to track down family members who had been enslaved. Usually this required vigilant letter-writing to magistrates, appearances in local courts, and even scrounging together money to buy back their wrongfully enslaved family members.[75] Peter Freeman, a Narragansett Indian who served as a guide for General Josiah Winslow during the War for New England, returned home from his service to the devastating news that his daughter had been taken by enterprising English soldiers and sold into slavery. He pleaded with the Massachusetts court to find his daughter, but in 1685—a full ten years later—all they could offer was the compensation of two coats, two pairs of stockings, and two pairs of shoes for him and his wife.[76] There was no further recourse for such an injustice.

It is challenging to reliably tabulate how many Indian captives were taken during Bacon's Indian War in Virginia. The number is likely in the hundreds, but it could easily be closer to a thousand. Many captives were shipped abroad, but others were retained locally. In the decades following the war, Indigenous slaves made up an astonishing 40 percent of the enslaved people in the towns along the James River.[77] The same was true in New England, where colonists slaughtered between three thousand and six thousand Natives and sold into slavery at least two thousand more, with half enslaved locally and the rest shipped overseas. Thousands more were chased from their lands and forbidden to return.[78]

Even in victory, English officials lamented that New Englanders had killed so many Indians instead of enslaving them. Edward Randolph, a royal investigator sent by the Crown to investigate the causes of the war, considered one of the greatest losses on the English side to be that of potential labor. Approximately three thousand Natives had been killed outright, Randolph estimated—all of whom were potential slaves that "if well managed would have been very serviceable to the English."[79]

As with earlier wars, these conflicts permitted an immediate expansion of English territory. Connecticut and Rhode Island both claimed vast tracts of former Narragansett lands in what is now central and northern Rhode Island and squabbled for decades over boundary lines. Connecticut and Massachusetts took former Nipmuc territory and gave huge tracts of land to English veterans of the war. Plymouth seized Pokanoket territory, including the ideally positioned peninsula of Mount Hope in the northeastern reaches of the Narragansett Bay. And Massachusetts sequestered even more land previously occupied by praying towns and tribes to the south and west of Boston.[80] In Virginia, the war further destabilized local tribes, allowed for regional expansion, and opened up the southern section of the colony to squatters and a more vigorous trade with large southern Indigenous confederacies.

This massive land grab was perhaps the point all along. In his written justification of the War for New England, Increase Mather, a puritan minister and future president of Harvard College, said in 1676 that "the Lord God of our Fathers" had given to the puritans Native American land "for a rightful Possession."[81] With this profound sense of divine entitlement that would continue to grow and flourish into Manifest Destiny by the 1840s, seemingly any enslavement or slaughter of Indigenous people and theft of lands could be justified as God's will.

DRIVING SOUTH ON ROUTE 2 in southern Rhode Island today takes one past the site of the Great Swamp Massacre. The entrance is completely unmarked, and the multiple warning signs against trespassing deter all but the most persistent visitors. A mile into the swampy woods stands a granite obelisk surrounded by four large boulders representing the four colonies that participated in the December 1675 attack: Massachusetts, Plymouth, Rhode Island, and Connecticut. Erected in 1906, it is the only public recognition of the massacre and dispossession imposed on the Narragansett by the War for New England. Absent from this memorial and most other markers of the war in the region is any indication of the massive slave raiding and shipment of Natives out of the area that resulted from this battle and the larger

GREAT SWAMP MASSACRE MONUMENT,
SOUTH KINGSTOWN, RHODE ISLAND.

"Indian Warr." Missing, too, are the stories and experiences of Native peoples—not just in the battle but in the centuries since.

The sacred lands of the Great Swamp were finally returned to the Narragansett Indian Nation in 2021 after being in the hands of colonizers for nearly 350 years. The Rhode Island Historical Society—which had been gifted the five acres from the slaveholding Hazard family in 1906—formally deeded the land back to the Narragansett during a discreet ceremony in October 2021. As a fire of remembrance burned in front of the gathered assembly, Narragansett medicine man John Brown reflected on the meaning of the transfer: "There has been a lot of sorrow surrounding those lands. . . . It was important to the generations before us, so it is important to us now."[82]

By 1680, the active, direct enslavement of Native Americans through warfare had tapered off considerably in New England and Virginia. But in the Carolinas, it was only getting started in ways that connected the wider English empire, from Massachusetts south to Barbados, through an even greater exportation of Native American slaves.

Six

RESISTANCE IN THE SOUTHEAST

THE CATACLYSMIC EVENTS THAT OCCURRED BETWEEN 1675 AND 1677 in New England and Virginia reverberated throughout the colonies, especially among Indigenous communities. But both of these were regional conflicts, one-off wars triggered by attempted settler expansion. After these conflicts were over, the large-scale enslavement and shipment of Natives largely subsided in these colonies.

Within a decade, however, an entirely different Indigenous slave trade in North America unfolded. It was an intentional, regularized traffick in Native captives spurred by Carolina merchants. For the first time in North America, English merchants and traders began arming Indigenous allies in large numbers for the primary purpose of slave raiding other Native nations for captives to be sold to the English. Carolina traders spun a web of conflict and slave trading that stretched in all directions. Francis Le Jau, an Anglican missionary serving the Goose Creek parish (located in present-day South Carolina), bluntly stated that the English encouraged Native men "to make War amongst themselves to get Slaves which they give for our European goods."[1] It was a distinct echo of the African slave trade, albeit conducted on American soil.

The results were catastrophic. Over the course of a half century, Carolina traders armed, traded with, and then turned on one Native nation after another. International conflict with the Spanish and the French created additional opportunities for the English to encourage devastating Native raids against Spanish Indigenous mission towns in Florida and French-allied Natives to the west. The impact on Native communities and families was profound, separating parents from children and damaging community cohesion. A Muklasa man reflected some of this trauma when he noted that, during the English-sponsored slave raids, "men take the women and children away and sell them to the English, each person being traded for a gun."[2] It was a devastatingly cruel and effective system that ensnared as many as fifty-one thousand captives, flooding Carolina plantations with so many enslaved Natives that colonial leaders began to export them to nearly every English colony and, temporarily, import fewer enslaved Africans.[3]

Indigenous nations were not merely pawns in these damaging processes. Although they might have been motivated by English trade goods and alliances, Native leaders used these events to accomplish their own goals within the complex web of regional Native alliances and networks that preexisted European invasions. And although the English did not recognize it at first, they were not actually in control. As Native nations realized the collective destruction wrought by decades of slave raiding, they banded together in resistance and nearly succeeded in destroying the Carolinas in the process.

IN THE DECADES AFTER BACON'S INDIAN WAR, Virginia expanded south and west into fertile Indigenous lands that colonists viewed as available for the taking. The colony saw the vast, coastal low country teeming with powerful Native nations to the south as under its purview and an important part of its trade. But colonial backers in London had other plans. In 1663, some proprietors in London received a patent from King Charles II for a large swath of land they called Carolina, which remained a single colony until 1712, when it was split into two. It was carved out of Native territory between southern Virginia and the upper reaches of what the Spanish claimed as part of *La Florida*. Like other colonial patents, and in line with John Smith's map of New England, it was a fictive imposition of English authority on the homelands of tens of thousands of Indigenous peoples. But such realities were of little concern to London officials.

Carolina grew quickly with the founding in 1670 of Charles Town, named after its royal patron. Located at the site of modern Charleston, South Carolina, this tiny outpost became a bustling port city and an important entrepôt in the English Atlantic trade. Perhaps even

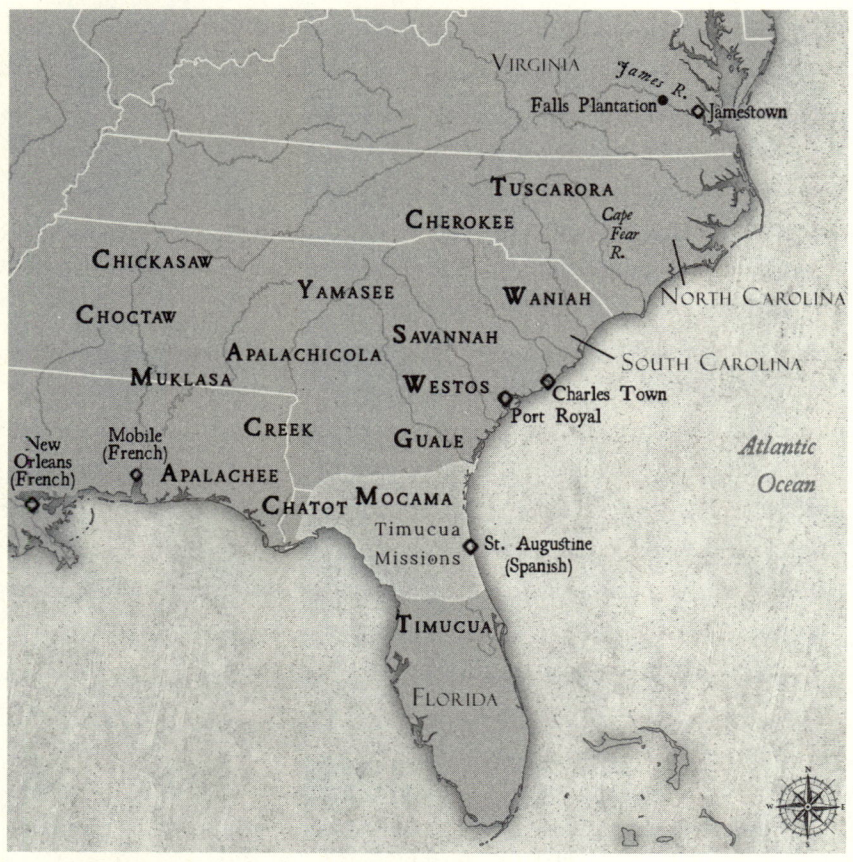

SOUTHEASTERN NATIONS AND COLONIES, CA. 1700.

more than any other North American English colony, Carolina had a direct tie to the Caribbean. Many of the founders and early colonists arrived from overcrowded Barbados, which made it, in the words of one scholar, a "colony of a colony."⁴ Planters and colonists poured into Carolina in its first decade, bringing enslaved men, women, and children with them. Many of these Barbadian immigrants were seasoned planters, and they knew that the core of a profitable plantation was enslaved labor. The transported enslaved population would have surely included Native Americans, even if their identities have been concealed or lost.

Large Indigenous polities of the Southeast initially tried to incorporate Virginia and Carolina traders into existing networks of trade and alliance. English merchants welcomed this regular and profitable trade with regional tribes. Native Americans desired cotton cloth and other material of vibrant colors, in addition to a wide array of manufactured goods, including mirrors, combs, ribbons, axes, and hoes. They especially prized guns, bullets, and gunpowder.[5] Native nations engaged in this trade tried to keep up with the heavy English demand for beaver pelts, deerskins, and other kinds of furs.

But many Natives soon learned that what English traders valued most highly were Indigenous captives. An adult could be sold for roughly the same price as two years' worth of deerskins, making it far more efficient for Indigenous traders to offer Native slaves rather than deerskins to the English. And pound for pound, even Indigenous youth were a much quicker path to trade goods: Native children were more valuable than their weight in skins.[6] With plenty of regional enemies to raid, Native warriors' capacity to conduct such a trade seemed to be a perfect match to dogged English pressure for Indigenous captives.

Carolina traders first relied on the Westo as their partners in the Indigenous slave trade starting in the 1670s. This large, powerful nation found in the English newcomers an important regional ally that gave them leverage against the Cherokee and the Savannah, two other sizable powers in the area. To provide Native captives to English traders, the Westo primarily slave-raided the Guale and Mocama Indians to the south, who were mostly allied with the Spanish.[7] Some of these hundreds of captives were sold as slaves to Carolina planters, but many more were sold to captains and merchants in Charles Town, who dispatched them to other English colonies or sold them on the wider Atlantic slave market.[8]

The Indigenous slave trade was not entirely invented by the English, but they expanded it in formidable ways and made it an integral part of English society in the region. Well before the arrival of English traders to Carolina, the Indigenous nations of the Southeast had engaged in cycles of raids and warfare that had their own cultural significance but at times were bewildering to outsiders. Native war parties took captives for revenge, to replace loved ones, and to bolster their own populations. Their reasons for slave raiding were distinctly different than those of the English, who sought captives for their monetary value, to clear the land, and to add to the colonial labor supply. But captive taking and captive giving were also rooted in Native practices of alliance building and the creation of kinship networks. Indigenous leaders attempted to incorporate English traders into their networks of trade and kinship as well, sometimes by offering them Native women or an Indian slave as a sign of alliance.[9]

As powerful, sovereign nations that had their own reasons for slave raiding, Indigenous nations like the Westo were not easily controlled by the English. Before long, Westo slave raids struck Native communities closer to Charles Town—including some who were allies of the colony.[10] To rein in the uncooperative Westo, colony magistrates and traders made a treaty with the powerful Savannah Indians, who agreed to raid the Westo into submission. As the Savannah attacked, the Westo fought back and fled, knowing full well what happened to captives taken by English allies. As Ariano, a Westo elder, told Carolina officials in April 1680, they were afraid they would be "sent in shipps beyond the seas and sold for slaves."[11]

Ariano was right. During and after what became called the Westo War (1680–1682), the Carolina colonists seemed determined to completely destroy this particular nation, as New Englanders had attempted to do with the Pequot decades earlier. English-allied slave raids ensnared approximately two thousand Westo captives, most of whom were sold to local traders who in turn either sold them into slavery locally or shipped them to the Caribbean. Hundreds of other Westos fled the region to escape the enslaving furor of the English. Many Westo men were killed in battle, executed in the field, or later condemned to death, as had been the practice during the previous Indian wars in Virginia and New England. Women and children were especially targeted for enslavement.[12] Within a few years, some traders reported only fifty Westos remained in the area. The rest had been slave-raided or had fled the region.

The dreadful war against the Westo set a pattern for the Southeast, in which English merchants turned Indigenous nations on each other. It was a tactic that the Spanish had used in their conquest of large Indigenous nations and was one that Virginia Colony secretary Edward Waterhouse had suggested in 1622 as a future model for the English.[13] In this fashion, between 1670 and 1715, the Carolina colony armed the Westo against the Guale and Mocama (1675–1679); the Savannah against the Westo and Waniah (1680); the Yamasee against the

Guale and Timucua (1680–1690); the Yamasee and Muscogee (Creek) against the Apalachee (1702–1704); the Muscogee against the Chatot (1706); the Yamasee, Chickasaw, and Muscogee against the Choctaw (1690–1710); and the Yamasee and Muscogee against the Tuscarora (1711–1712).[14]

Almost immediately, the Virginia legislature also embraced the Carolina Indian slave trade. In 1682, it ordered that all "Negroes, Moors, Mollattoes or Indians" who were brought into the colony and all Indians sold from neighboring Indian nations or any others, would be "taken to be slaves," presumably for life, something it reaffirmed in 1705.[15] Later in the eighteenth century, Virginia courts would interpret these provisions as functionally outlawing Indian slavery, but that was not the intention.[16]

BETWEEN 1685 AND 1700, English traders in Virginia and Carolina put pressure on their Native allies to keep up the trade in enslaved Indians, furs, and deerskins. The Savannah and Yamasee continued punishing raids into Spanish Florida, instilling terror in mission villages and threatening to upend the whole Catholic project.[17] In February 1685, some Scottish traders living at Port Royal (fifty miles south of present-day Charleston in South Carolina) paid the Yamasee to slave-raid the Catholic mission towns of the Timucua. During the raids, the Yamasee burned several towns, including the chapel and the house belonging to the resident Franciscan missionary. As promised, the Yamasee also brought back twenty-two Timucuan captives, whom they sold to the Scots as slaves. But they also stole another curious specimen that the Yamasee specifically mentioned more than three months later: a manuscript prayer book, written in Spanish and Latin, which was a small reminder of the collateral damage to Spanish Catholics resulting from the slave trade.[18]

The English-driven Indigenous slave trade also surged westward, deep into Chickasaw territory close to French settlements in Louisiana. As a powerful inland Native confederacy numbering close to seven thousand in 1685, the Chickasaw ranged widely across a huge swath of land between what is now Georgia and the Mississippi River.[19] Despite their reservations about the monetization of Native captive taking, the Chickasaw recognized in an English partnership the opportunity

TIMUCUA INDIAN VILLAGE IN FLORIDA SHOWING FOOD
TRANSPORTATION BY CANOE, BY THEODORE DE BRY,
ENGRAVING, CA. 1600.

to gain leverage over the Cherokee, Muscogee, and Choctaw.[20] English traders' efforts won out, and they retained a Chickasaw alliance primarily through continually supplying desired trade items. First, this meant guns—usually smoothbore muskets. But the Chickasaw also eagerly traded for metal tools like knives, needles, and hatchets—items that were more durable than their own bone or stone versions—in addition to cloth items like blankets and shirts.[21]

In return, English traders asked for two main things from the Chickasaw: animal skins and Indigenous slaves. The demand for leather in the colonies and in England created a booming market for deerskins in particular. Thousands of hides were hauled to Charles Town each year, brought by expert Native hunters. Because Indigenous women performed the time-consuming work of cleaning and drying the deerskins and other hides, they arrived at trading posts in ideal condition to be sold and used locally or shipped to England and other European markets. In the hands of English craftspeople, deerskins were transformed into a variety of leather products, including shoes, gloves, book covers, and military clothing and equipment.[22] But Indigenous captives were even more highly valued by the English, with one Indian slave worth as much as 160 deerskins. This incredible valuation ensured that Indigenous captives remained a vital part of the trade.[23]

The process of slave raiding Indian towns could be a complicated one, full of ritual, planning, and violence. An English trader and Indian agent (a colony-appointed official) named Thomas Nairne gave a surprisingly detailed account of a Chickasaw raiding party in 1708. An entourage of older warriors, younger men, and women marched overland or canoed down rivers to a rival's territory. More experienced warriors led the way, often with medicine bags full of roots, feathers, bones, and locks of hair from former victims—powerful tokens to ensure success. After stealthily approaching a targeted town, they spread out in a semicircle and attacked all at once, giving a "War Whoop" and creating a cacophony of noise to drive out victims from the village. As they encircled and closed in on victims, the fighting intensified. Chickasaw women sang songs and supported the warriors, urging them to victory. Enemy men were often killed outright. Women, children, and older boys were rounded up and bound together using special interconnected rope harnesses tied around their necks to keep them from escaping. Captives were then marched back to Chickasaw towns and later transported to more central locations to be sold to English traders.[24]

Using the Chickasaw as proxies, the English were able to slowly destabilize French alliances with large Native nations like the Choctaw located in what is now Mississippi. The human cost of the slave trade encompassed much more than the number of enslaved Natives alone. Indigenous people on both sides died during these raids: in extreme cases, as many as three Natives died for every Indigenous person who was enslaved, according to one observer.[25] As Chickasaw tribal member and scholar Chase Bryer notes, what English records omit is "the true horror and fear Chickasaws (my ancestors) felt by the oppressive and genocidal regime they were forced to reckon with. If they did not comply with colonial demands and interests, that meant cultural erasure and genocide of Chickasaws."[26]

THIS ENGLISH-DRIVEN INDIAN SLAVE TRADE dramatically escalated when war erupted between England and Spain in 1701. England joined with Austria against Spain in the contest over who would replace Spain's king Charles II, which is why it was called the War of Spanish

Succession. As with most wars in Europe, alliances and antagonisms quickly transferred to the Americas. In North America, the conflict was known as Queen Anne's War and pitted English colonies against Spanish and French ones. English colonies in the American Southeast suddenly had Crown approval to sack and raid Spanish Florida—and Spanish-allied Native nations, something that had been previously discouraged. Indigenous captivity and enslavement soon played a major role in how the English flexed their military power and increased their presence.

Carolina magistrates, now entirely unrestrained, immediately plotted slave raids to Florida. In January 1704, James Moore Jr., the son of the former governor of South Carolina, led fifty English soldiers and one thousand Yamasee, Apalachicola, and Muscogee soldiers into northern Florida on a massive slave-raiding expedition. They marched straight for Nuestra Señora de la Purísma Concepción de Ayubale, one of the largest mission towns in Apalachee territory, taking it after a bloody battle. Over several weeks, Moore's marauding force burned fourteen Spanish mission villages among the Apalachee, capturing and killing hundreds of Natives, while sending hundreds more fleeing for their lives into the Florida backcountry. Survivors reported that soldiers tortured mission Indians by forcing burning embers into open wounds, skinning individuals alive, and burning others at the stake.[27]

Moore bragged that he and his Native allies took 325 Apalachee men and 4,000 Apalachee women and children "as slaves," all with the loss of only four English and fifteen Native soldiers.[28] His report highlights yet again the targeting of women and children in these raids, which undercut surviving communities in tangible and long-term ways. The entourage marched the captives back to South Carolina, where they were sold into lifelong slavery, both locally and to Caribbean traders. Moore's exploits became an instant sensation, with newspapers as far away as Massachusetts hailing his successes.[29]

Over the next four years, English, Muscogee, and Yamasee forces continuously raided Spanish mission towns in Florida. By 1708, the Spanish governor of Florida, Francisco de Córcoles y Martínez, complained that an astonishing ten thousand to twelve thousand Florida Natives had been slave-raided by the Muscogee, Yamasee, and English.[30] Queen Anne's War was partially to blame, but the war simply intensified what had already been taking place. English magistrates relocated thirteen hundred surrendering Apalachees to Savannah Town, where the Westo had once lived. Four hundred or more Apalachee refugees fled to the French in Louisiana. The combination of war and slave raids demolished the expansive mission town system in Florida. Most remaining Spanish-allied Native groups moved to southern Florida, and some even tried fleeing to Cuba to escape the punishing raids.[31]

LICENSED BY QUEEN ANNE'S WAR, active Native enslavement briefly emerged again in New England. Since France was allied with Spain, New Englanders targeted French colonies to the north. Although the New England front of the war did not result in a large Indigenous slave trade like in Carolina, colonial governments offered Native captives as enlistment incentives as they had done during the War for New England. Officials also reintroduced the bounty system, with rewards for soldiers and civilians alike who captured or killed Natives.[32] This policy remained unchanged as one war transitioned into another into the eighteenth century, except that the bounty rates went up, and dramatically so.

With war on their doorstep, the Massachusetts Assembly quickly passed a law in 1703 incentivizing Indian killing and enslavement for private and public benefit. It first offered ten pounds per Indian scalp for enlisted soldiers and twenty pounds as a bounty for civilians. If taken alive, Native captives or the proceeds of their sale into slavery were to be divided among the company of volunteers. Even Indigenous children under the age of ten were authorized as targets for capture and sale into slavery, though they were to be sent "out of the country."[33] By 1707, as the war dragged on, the bounty was increased to one hundred pounds per captive, which was more than a year's income for most colonial Americans.[34]

New England magistrates tried to entice their Native allies into slave raiding for them but had far less success than in the Carolinas. Near the beginning of the war, Massachusetts officials recruited one hundred Mohegan, Pequot, and Niantic Indians to attack Abenaki forces in Maine. To sweeten the deal, the Mohegans were promised twenty pounds for every Native killed, or, if they could take captives, they would receive the money from the sale of those captives in addition to one shilling per day.[35] The surviving records do not permit an accurate count of Native captives taken, but the colonial impulse was the same in the Northeast and Southeast: arm Native allies against other Indigenous nations and incentivize slave raiding.

Queen Anne's War created an influx of Indigenous captives in New England, although the numbers were far smaller than in the American Southeast. English soldiers took hundreds of Wabanaki and their allies captive in the war and killed hundreds more. Some captives were kept by officials in Boston, under lock and key—usually to serve as bargaining chips for exchanges to get English captives back from the French and other Native nations.[36] In other cases, Indigenous captives were kept by soldiers or sold into slavery and transported to other colonies. In 1703, a number of "Eastern Indian" (which is how colonists referred to Native nations in what are now New Hampshire and Maine) captives were taken to Rhode Island as slaves. By January 1704, Rhode Island magistrates caught wind of such slave importation and tried to halt it.[37]

THE CAROLINA INDIGENOUS SLAVE TRADE created a veritable torrent of enslaved Natives through Charles Town. Some Native captives were purchased and enslaved by local planters and merchants, substantially adding to the colony's enslaved demographics. In 1708, South Carolina magistrates reported the total number of enslaved Natives in the colony to be 1,400: 500 men, 600 women, and 300 children. This was compared to 4,100 enslaved Africans, in addition to 3,960 white colonists and 120 white servants. It is not clear from the report if this includes the influx of 1,050 enslaved Indians, but it seems unlikely, given the availability and presence of Indian slaves in the colony before 1708.[38] This means that enslaved Native Americans accounted for between 25 percent and 34 percent of South Carolina's enslaved labor force in 1708.[39]

But Charles Town merchants soon drummed up a lucrative business trafficking Native captives elsewhere, too, as part of the wider English intercolonial trade. Ship captains placed enslaved Natives into their holds along with raw materials that were bound for virtually every port in the English Atlantic empire. Carolina magistrates informed the Board of Trade in 1708, "We have also Commerce with Boston,

TO be Sold at the Sign of the Blue Anchor in *Boston*, Four Carolina Indians, *viz.* A Lad, Two Men and a Woman.

"To Be Sold," *Boston News-Letter*, March 29, 1708.

Rhode Island, Pennsylvania, New York and Virgina, to which places We Export Indian Slaves, Light Dear skins drest, some Tanned leather, Pitch, Tar, and a small Quantity of Rice."[40] Enslaved Native Americans were also shipped to the wider Caribbean, including Bermuda, Barbados, Antigua, and Jamaica, and likely to Dutch, Spanish, and French colonies.[41]

Port cities along the eastern seaboard of North America received an influx of transported enslaved southeastern Indians. Boston's brand-new newspapers—the first durable ones in the North American colonies—soon began advertising Natives for sale. On March 29, 1708, the *Boston News-Letter* listed four Carolina Indians—a boy, two men, and a woman—to be sold next to the Blue Anchor Tavern in Boston.[42]

Some trafficked Natives from the Southeast promptly freed themselves by running away. A "Tall Lusty Carolina Indian Woman" named Sarah, approximately twenty-five or twenty-six years of age, ran away from her enslaver in the Boston area. Her legal owner placed an ad in the Boston newspaper, dated September 8, 1707, describing Sarah as having long, straight black hair tied up with a red "hairlace," with a red- and blue-striped homespun jacket, a black-and-white silk petticoat, a white shift (long undergarment), and a white apron.[43] Like many self-emancipated people, no records indicate if Sarah and others were successful in their escape or were found and forced to return to their owner.

THE CAROLINA INDIAN SLAVE TRADE created a highly volatile and unstable situation in the Southeast, mostly at the hands of profit-seeking English traders.[44] Members of the South Carolina Assembly worried that slave-raiding allied Indigenous nations were going to lead the colony "into one Indian warr," where all of the nations would rise up against the English.[45] By turning Native nations on each other and by making enemies of virtually all nations through slave raiding, English slave traders in Virginia, North Carolina, and South Carolina had created enough hatred and ill will that the entire Indigenous Southeast had become a powder keg.

The large and formidable Tuscarora nation (in present-day North Carolina) reached the same point of exasperation with colonists that Pumetacom in New England and Opechancanough in Virginia had reached decades before. Their presence and power long predated English arrival in Virginia, and for almost a half century, the Tuscarora had successfully limited colonial expansion in Virginia and North Carolina, keeping colonists mostly confined to the area near the Albemarle Sound. Although initially distrustful of Virginia and later Carolina colonists, the Tuscarora soon traded with and slave-raided other nations in order to get a share of the English trade.[46]

Almost immediately, tensions increased as a continuing influx of immigrants carved farms out of Tuscarora lands.[47] Once settled, colonists then prohibited the Tuscarora from hunting on their former lands and punished them when they shot and consumed English cattle that roamed freely through the countryside.[48] Equally vexing for the Tuscarora was the fact that some of their towns were also now targets for slave raids urged by English traders, placing their women and children in grave danger. It was an untenable situation.

Rather than fight, the Tuscarora first considered moving out of the area entirely. In June 1710, a delegation of chiefs traveled to Conestoga, Pennsylvania, to request permission to move to that colony to escape predatory Carolina colonists. The three main Tuscarora delegates— Iwaagenst, Terrutawanaren, and Teonnotein—presented Pennsylvania Colony leaders with eight wampum belts, each one symbolizing the various subgroups within the community who lived in fear of enslavement and death. The second wampum belt was especially poignant. It was given on behalf of Tuscarora children—those born and those yet to be conceived—that they might "sport & Play without danger of Slavery."[49]

When their pleas fell on deaf ears, the Tuscarora returned home and staged a violent revolt. On September 22, 1711, Tuscarora leaders brutally murdered the North Carolina land surveyor John Lawson in a symbolic act of defiance. Lawson was an important intermedi-

STRING AND BELT WAMPUM, CA. 1890.

ary between the colony and the Tuscarora, but as a surveyor, he represented the intertwined connections between the Indian slave trade and dispossession. The Tuscarora tied up Lawson and stuck him full of "small splinters of torchwood," then slowly lit them on fire, one by one, until he passed out from the pain and eventually died.[50]

News of this grisly murder spread quickly, perhaps serving as a signal for action, and Tuscarora bands began attacking nearby Carolina settlements, including those surrounding New Bern. On the same day as Lawson's murder, the Tuscarora and Coree struck towns between the Pamlico and Neuse Rivers, laying waste to dozens of houses and killing 130 colonists.

Perhaps most distressing to the colonists who returned to bury their dead was the careful mockery of English culture displayed through the positioning of the dead bodies. One woman was propped up on her knees against a chair, with her hands up as if in prayer. Her husband was stretched out on the floor nearby, with a clean pillow under his head, wearing his wife's bonnet, his stockings over his shoes, and neatly covered with new white linens. Other mutilations were less symbolic and—while disturbing—more common: pregnant women were slain, with their fetuses cut out of the womb and draped over tree branches. These tactics—used by English and Natives alike—were intended to mock and instill terror, which they did effectively.[51]

Stunned, the colonists wasted no time in mobilizing. As in most other colonies, this war was generically referred to as the "Indian warr," but it was an all-out assault against the Tuscarora and their allies.[52] Colonial militias used a string of garrisons as bases for raids against Tuscarora towns and immediately began taking Tuscaroras and other Natives captive and selling them as slaves.[53]

As the war stagnated, North Carolina desperately recruited help from South Carolina in the form of John Barnwell, a veteran of Indian slave raids against Spanish and Indian settlements in Florida during Queen Anne's War.[54] He and South Carolina Indian agents succeeded in turning a large number of regional Native nations against the Tuscarora with promises of profit from the sale of Tuscarora captives as slaves. At the start of his February 1712 expedition, Barnwell counted 528 soldiers, only 30 of whom were English. The remaining soldiers were drawn from approximately 19 different Native nations, including the Yamasee and Esaw (who provided 158 and 155 men, respectively) and the Apalachee and Catawba.[55] Barnwell knew the entire expedition depended on the skill and efficiency of Native soldiers, noting that the Indians "are more dextrous than us at taking slaves."[56]

With Barnwell's entry into the war, the Tuscarora fears of enslavement were fully realized. With a command from North Carolina officials to effect the "reduction or Extirpating [of] these Indians," Barnwell adopted a "total war" approach, indiscriminately killing and enslaving but also destroying villages, towns, and food supplies.[57] In addition to taking dozens of captives, Barnwell had two Natives "burned alive," as he proudly reported to his superiors. In early 1712, he and his men destroyed five Tuscarora towns. In each place, Barnwell first admired the landscape, orchards, houses, and food stores—including an impressive two thousand bushels of corn—before systematically setting fire to it all, sparing only the fruit trees.[58]

After months of vicious fighting and slave raids, the Tuscarora petitioned for peace.[59] But on the way back to South Carolina, Barnwell and his entourage attacked an unsuspecting group of Tuscarora who had been lured to a peaceful meeting, killing 40 to 50 men and taking

200 women and children to be sold into slavery.[60] The Tuscarora and their allies were rightly incensed at this breach of the peace agreement and renewed attacks on English towns. Finding themselves once more on the defensive, North Carolina magistrates in March 1713 again pleaded with South Carolina, promising that if the colony would send 1,000 men, they would have "the great advantage of slaves, there being many hundreds of (them) women & children may we believe 3 or 4 thousand."[61] South Carolina managed to cobble together yet another military unit of 113 English and 760 Native soldiers under Captain James Moore to hunt down the Tuscarora.

Moore went straight for the jugular, marching to the Tuscarora town of Nooherooka (near present-day Snow Hill, North Carolina) in mid-March 1713. Taking the massive fort at Nooherooka was infinitely harder than Moore anticipated. It was an engineering marvel. Tucked into one of the lazy bends of Contentnea Creek, the fort was surrounded by water on three sides and occupied a full acre and a half. A deep trench surrounded the edifice, with protected platforms and towers around the perimeter to give Tuscarora soldiers the maximum advantage for firing guns and shooting arrows. The main front wall angled outward to prevent easy scaling, and two large underground bunkers protected women, children, and the elderly.[62]

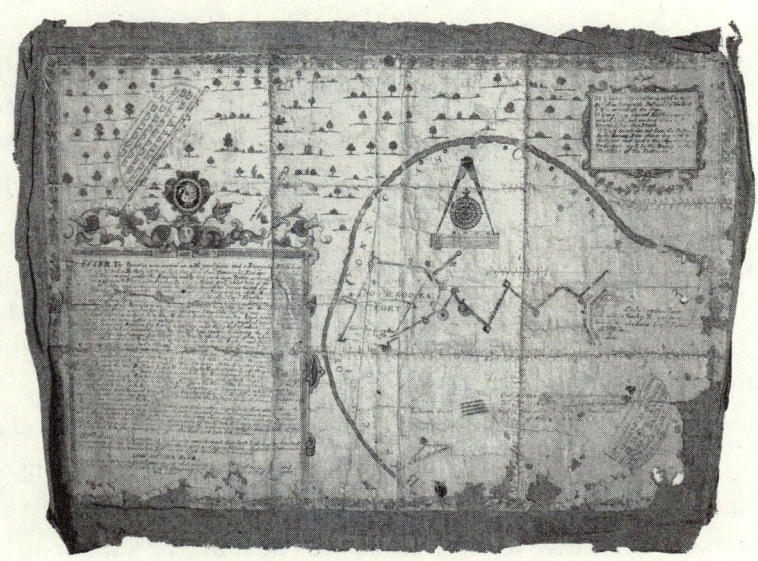

MAP OF NOOHEROOKA FORT, CA. 1713.

On March 20, after a failed attempt to breach the walls with a massive gunpowder bomb, Moore's army launched an all-out direct attack on the Tuscarora fort. On the third day, the fort finally fell, and Moore and his men destroyed the impressive edifice and ravaged the large town during three bloody days of fighting. They killed many Tuscarora men, took women and children as captives, and then torched the fort's bunkers, burning hundreds more alive. Moore estimated that over 550 Tuscaroras and their Indian allies were murdered, and another 398 were taken as captives, destined for sale into slavery.[63]

The war was a crushing blow to the Tuscarora.[64] In total, the English enslaved approximately seven hundred and killed almost as many more. Perhaps another five hundred to one thousand Tuscarora allies were enslaved by English Native allies, although those numbers are far more difficult to tabulate. For a nation of two thousand or so fighting men, the losses were devastating.[65] The war caused a massive dispersal, with hundreds of Tuscaroras and their allies fleeing to local Native nations, where they managed to piece together an ongoing tribal identity in the wake of a near-genocidal attempt to exterminate them. The fears they expressed in their plea to Pennsylvania officials had proven correct: the English were able to clear the land through a ruthless policy of warfare and enslavement and at a terrible cost to the Tuscarora.

THE EFFECTS OF THE TUSCARORA WAR reverberated throughout Indian country in the Southeast. English traders, emboldened by their victories, continued to press the Muscogee, Yamasee, Choctaw, and other regional nations for Native captives and terms of commerce that favored the traders. Leaders of the powerful Cherokee nation, perhaps seeing into the future more clearly than Carolina leaders, had long cautioned English officials that they should stop the "trade of Indians or slave making" and instead trade for "skins and furs."[66] Rather than relenting, English traders pushed harder.

Then suddenly, catastrophically, the decades-long system of slave trading imploded, nearly destroying the Carolinas. In the spring of 1715, a Coweta headman, or chief, called Brims sent several runners to the hundreds of Native towns that dotted the hills and valleys of the Southeast. At each town, they excitedly described an emerging plan to

avenge the misdeeds of the traders and the enslavement and murder of
their kinsmen. Would they join? Towns that agreed tied a knot in one
of three six-foot-long lengths of deer hide carried by the runners. By
the time the runners returned to Brims, there were a remarkable 161
knots representing the pledges of each of the towns willing to rise up
and send men into battle to punish the English.[67]

To discuss a plan of action, Brims convened regional leaders and
participants at the Yamasee town of Pocatalico in early April. Word
of the meeting, however, found its way back to Charles Town, and officials sent longtime South Carolina agent Thomas Nairne to Pocatalico together with a handful of other traders. On Good Friday, the
Yamasee struck. They killed some of the men and seized Nairne, tied
him to a post, stabbed him with dozens of burning wooden splinters,
and slowly burned him to death, thereby reprising earlier torture of
English traders.

Word of these murders spread like wildfire among the allied Native
nations of the Southeast. Other Indian towns understood this to be a
declaration of war against the English and followed suit. One by one,
Indigenous nations—the Upper Muscogee, Choctaw, Cherokee, and
Catawba—systematically executed dozens of English traders who lived
among them and were central to the trade that had so disrupted the
region's Native communities. Southern Indigenous nations formerly
allied with the English did the same: the Coweta, Tallapoosa, Abihka,
and Alabama slaughtered traders by clubbing them to death or sending
them fleeing for their lives into the woods.[68] Even the Chickasaw murdered fifteen English traders, though they mostly remained neutral in
order to maximize their position between the English and French.[69] It
was a stunning repudiation of the Indian slave trade and dispossession,
processes that the traders and surveyors represented.

In the Yamasee War, as the resulting conflict was later called, the
Yamasee, Muscogee, and their allies had a similar aim as Pumetacom had in 1675 in the Dawnland: expel the English from the region
entirely. When confronted by dumbfounded Carolina magistrates, the
allied anti-English Native nations relayed a lengthy list of resentments
and complaints. Continual encroachment on Native land was part of
the offense, but the vast majority of the complaints were related to
the expansive Indigenous slave trade.[70] The Yamasee and their allies

were also understandably incensed at the treatment of their children, who were sometimes sent to colonial homes for education or indentureship and then were sold out of the colony as slaves.[71] There would be no peace.

The war unfolded slowly at first, as the Yamasee and Muscogee spent several months strengthening a coalition that drew in most of the Native nations in the Southeast. Over time, the Yamasee, Upper Muscogee, Choctaw, some Cherokee, Catawba, Tallabosee, Abihka, Alabama, Euchee, Apalachee, Savannah, and even Seneca from farther north all turned against the English. Equally as important, the Muscogee and Yamasee sent envoys to Spanish leaders in St. Augustine and Pensacola, Florida, and to French officials in Mobile, on the Gulf coast of what is now Alabama, to secure alliances against the English. The Yamasee War had become a pan-Indigenous war of Native resistance to the Indian slave trade.

The Yamasee and their allies wreaked havoc on South Carolina, returning the devastation colonization had brought to Indian country. As had been the case during the War for New England, colonists fled from the interior settlements closest to Native towns toward the coast, looking for strength in numbers. By the end of 1715, colonial refugees streamed into Charles Town, and the area surrounding the city hosted most of the English settlers from the region.[72] As Native war bands raided English settlements, they took everything of value, including enslaved Africans. Some they likely kept, but Native soldiers sold hundreds to the French and the Spanish to strengthen alliances.[73]

Although the initial colonial response was weak, South Carolina eventually pulled together a ragtag army of volunteers from Virginia, North Carolina, and South Carolina, as well as—notably—some Cherokee warriors and even African soldiers. Militia units marched through the backcountry, engaging the Yamasee and their allies and taking captives to enslave wherever they could.

From the vantage points of Charles Town, New England, and even London, these developments terrifyingly threatened the entire English colonial enterprise. Newspapers reported that "all the Indians there are joined together."[74] The Carolina proprietors warned the English king George I in July 1715 that if the Spanish and French continued to side with the Yamasee and their allies, not just Carolina but "all the

British Settlements on the Continent of America" were in danger of being overrun.[75] Colonial reinforcements poured into South Carolina from Maryland, Virginia, and North Carolina in late summer of 1715, and by October, help was on the way from London in the form of two regiments of marines and a small squadron of ships.[76]

The war slowed to a halt in 1717 as the Carolinas regained their military strength and negotiated peace treaties with the majority of the Indian nations fighting with the Yamasee.[77] When the smoke slowly cleared over South Carolina, allied Native raids had exacted revenge by killing four hundred colonists, or roughly 7 percent of the colony's population. Remarkably, Natives systematically targeted English traders to Indigenous nations, murdering ninety of the one hundred who lived in Indian country. The lesson was clear. The uprising was unmistakably a war on English traders and the Indian slave trade.

IRONICALLY, THE WAR TO END the Indian slave trade initially greatly increased it. In every battle, English soldiers took as many captives as possible, with Indigenous women and children targeted for capture and sale into slavery.[78] While hundreds of captives were sold into local or regional slavery, many more were marched to Charles Town for sale or shipment out of the region. In the early summer of 1715, Colonel Alexander Mackay captured forty Native prisoners and sent them as "*slaves for Jamaica.*"[79] Another such shipment took place in early 1716, when Carolina magistrates reported to the Board of Trade that seventy-five Natives were shipped from South Carolina.[80] But most enslaved Natives were transported in smaller groups, chained and placed alongside everyday trade items destined for other English cities on the East Coast, the Caribbean, or any number of other international ports.[81] So vigorous was the Carolina Indigenous slave trade from the Yamasee War that, during its peak, merchants shipped more Indian slaves out of Charles Town than they imported enslaved Africans.[82]

English raids on the Yamasee and their allies produced yet another influx of enslaved Indians into colonial slave markets from Virginia to Massachusetts. However, northern English colonies soon became wary of imported enslaved Carolina Indians and those they called "Spanish" Indians, fearing they were "enemies," and passed laws prohibiting their importation. In Pennsylvania, the legislature created several laws to "prevent ye Importation of Indian Slaves," but eventually they gave up. In March 1715, they decided to tax the Indian slave trade, having been unable to prohibit it.[83]

New England colonies, too, attempted to regulate this Indigenous slave trade, mostly out of fear—not because they opposed Native enslavement. Between 1712 and 1715, Massachusetts, New Hampshire, Rhode Island, and Connecticut all passed laws against importing Carolina Natives that focused on their potential for leading a rebellion.[84] Even so, hundreds of enslaved Native Americans from the Carolina region were imported into New England before and after these laws took effect. One month after the passage of Rhode Island's law, local officials made an exception for one shipment and—tellingly—referred to the fifty-pound fee as a "duty," which implied that importation of Carolina Indians was a taxable activity, not an illegal one. This was at least the second time such an exception had been made.[85]

Carolina and Spanish Indians and their descendants in New England infused the region's labor force, as evidenced in wills, inventories, and newspaper advertisements. Three Carolina Indian slaves ran

Advertisements.

RAn away from their Masters in Boston, the 15th of this Instant September, at Night, Three Carolina Indians, viz. Two Men-Servants and One Woman, they speak but broken English, about 30 Years of Age or above ; one from Mr. *Samuel Adams* Malster, named *James*, well sett, he hath a Leather Jacket, black Stockings. Another of them Servant to Mr. *Nehemiah Yeals* Ship-Carpenter, named *Robin*, with double Breasted Jacket, Leather Breeches ; they both have other Cloaths with them. The Indian Woman Servant to Mr. *Thomas Salter* Cordwainer, named *Amareta*, pretty Lusty, she hath a strip'd home-spun Jacket, blue Petticoat. Whosoever shall take up the abovesaid Runaway Servants, and them or either of them Convey to their abovesaid Masters in Boston, shall have Forty Shillings Reward besides all necessary Charges paid.

THese are to give Notice, That the House in Winter Street, Boston, now in the Occupation of Mrs. *Willard*, Widow, is to be Sold on reasonable Terms, Inquire of Mr. *Richard Bill*, Merchant, and know further.

"RUNAWAY" ADVERTISEMENT, *BOSTON NEWS-LETTER*, SEPTEMBER 24, 1716, P. 3.

away together from their masters in Boston in 1716. James, Robin, and Amareta belonged to Samuel Adams, Nehemiah Yeals, and Thomas Salter, respectively, likely living in close urban proximity. But on September 15, 1716, they all ran away, taking only some garments. James had on a leather jacket and black stockings. Robin was wearing a double-breasted jacket and leather breeches.[86] They were among many who attempted to escape. In July 1717, William Bourden of Newport, Rhode Island, ran an advertisement in the *Boston News-Letter* for two "Carolina Indian Men-Servants" who had run away from his estate. Bourden noted that both of them were identifiable, in part, because he had his initials branded on their cheeks: one side was marked with a "W" and the other with a "B."[87]

THE END OF THE YAMASEE WAR of resistance signaled the slow demise of the regularized, fifty-year-long Indian slave trade in the southeastern region of North America. The war had shown English merchants and magistrates that continuous slave raiding destabilized the entire region and hurt them as well. As they rebuilt towns and expanded ever deeper into former Native territory, English planters focused more on importing enslaved Africans to replace the volume of the Indian slave trade.

Deerskins, not Native captives, soon become the most vital trade commodity in North and South Carolina—and Georgia, after its founding in 1732.[88] This shift in trading patterns in the 1720s did not mean that Carolina planters and colonists suddenly stopped using enslaved Native Americans.[89] Thousands of Indian slaves continued to labor on southern plantations, and when they had children, they too were claimed as slaves, as were their grandchildren.[90] And although Georgia initially was founded as a slave-free state, within a few decades it too embraced southern-style plantations, which also included enslaved Indigenous and African people.

Additionally, colonial records suggest that a more informal and ad-hoc trade in enslaved Natives continued at the local level. Captain John Hoyter—a Chowanoc Native—sold an Indigenous slave to James Sitterson after the war.[91] Surely hundreds of similar transactions occurred silently and without incident or record. Some English traders tried to revive the Indigenous slave trade in small-scale ways that would preserve both relationships with allies and the stability of the region. In October 1720, a group of sixteen traders made some concrete proposals to the South Carolina governor and council to permit the buying of nontributary and nonallied Native captives as slaves. Authorized deputies would sell and "transport them to the Islands"—instead of selling them within the colony, likely for safety reasons.[92]

More generally, Indigenous leaders and traders still knew the value of an enslaved Native even in a slave market increasingly dominated by African captives. As an Okfuskee chief noted to Tobias Fitch from South Carolina in 1726, "I have heard that the Choctaws makes as good slaves as Negroes."[93]

DEEP IN THE OPEN FIELDS of North Carolina's rural farmland stands a monument to Tuscaroran resistance to the Indigenous slave trade. A fifteen-foot-high metal arch rises sharply out of the surrounding acres of soybeans alongside the meandering two-lane Route 58 that cuts from the Atlantic Ocean northwest through the state. Even today, the monument feels remote, situated between small towns sixty miles southwest of Raleigh. The marker is simple: the narrow silver arch—meant to represent the entrance to a longhouse, a large Native gathering hall—stands in front of a small, landscaped circle filled with bricks and gravel. Subtle symbols mark the site, including bronze plaques depicting wampum, six tree logs representing the six nations of the Haudenosaunee Confederacy, and a stainless-steel rock pile behind a tall leafy tree in the center.[94] On the low, earth-colored walls in front of the arch are written two words in Tuscarora and English on either side of the opening:

Skaru:rę?   Neyuhorú:kę
Tuscarora   Nooherooka

The site feels sacred, although the serene surroundings mute both the colonial violence and the bravery of the Tuscarora.

The pan-Indian resistance to the Indigenous slave trade triggered by the Tuscarora ultimately proved effective. Still, the cost to every Native nation involved was immense. Tens of thousands had been stolen—

NOOHEROOKA MONUMENT, SNOW HILL, NORTH CAROLINA.

leaders, mothers, fathers, and children—with thousands more murdered. The Indian slave trade caused an existential fracturing of kinship
networks and clans. Native bands, families, and towns were displaced,
often hundreds of miles away, where they reconstituted communities
and sometimes formed new tribal identities. Most of the Tuscarora,
who narrowly escaped extermination at the hands of the English,
moved to New York in 1722 to become the sixth nation of the Haudenosaunee Confederacy.[95] The Yamasee War also created a rift between
the Muscogee and Cherokee that spun into several decades of wars and
reprisals between the two nations.[96]

The Indian slave trade imploded in the Carolinas, even as Indigenous slavery itself continued. But American merchants and traders
were inventive and persistent; before long they manufactured another
Native slave trade with a large, powerful Indigenous nation in the
Caribbean on the Central American coast that discreetly fed a stream
of Native captives to American colonies.

Seven

THE MISKITU TRADE

IN MOST HISTORIES OF NATIVE SLAVERY IN COLONIAL AMERICA, the story trails off rather quickly after the Yamasee War in the Southeast. Some Indigenous slaves remained, the narrative goes, but there were few importations of enslaved Natives into the American colonies.[1] And yet there is a mystery that demands resolution. Throughout most of the eighteenth century, "Spanish Indians" appear in colonial records, in newspapers as advertised for sale or having run away, or listed in wills and estate inventories of the deceased. Some of these enslaved Natives were recently trafficked, evidenced by their limited facility in the English language.[2]

A Mexican official named Don Francis Lopes stumbled upon a scandalous situation in 1733 that provides a clue. As the governor of the Tabasco region of the Yucatán in Mexico, Lopes had sailed to the British colonies of Virginia and Jamaica that year on a diplomatic trip. In each place, he was appalled to find enslaved Mayans and other Natives from Mexico and Central America. In the bustling port city of Hampton, Virginia, located on the southern tip of a long peninsula at the mouth of the Chesapeake Bay, Lopes spotted a few enslaved Mayans, who were readily recognizable among the enslaved Africans and North American Natives who were also in the city.[3]

From Virginia, Lopes then navigated to Jamaica and was further outraged to see at least fifteen Mayans and other Indigenous people he could not precisely identify enslaved on the streets of Kingston. Two younger Mayan girls said that they had been kidnapped six years earlier during a devastating raid on their town near Campeche on the Yucatán Peninsula in which "an entire Peoples" had been sold into slavery on the coast. These girls reported to Lopes that there was an "infinity of Indians" enslaved in Jamaica, victims of this same process. One enslaved Mayan woman told Lopes she was a Christian, having been catechized and baptized by Spanish missionaries. For Lopes, this only added to the injustice.[4]

These Mayans and other "Spanish Indians" had been caught up in an enormous and often overlooked Indigenous slave trade on the Central American coast. As in the Carolinas, it was largely driven by British merchants, who in this case were based in Jamaica and partnered with the Miskitu nation to conduct ongoing slave raids on Spanish-allied Indians and Spanish mission towns. This slave trade led to the capture of thousands of Indigenous people who were then shipped by English merchants throughout the wider Atlantic world, arriving in places like Barbados, Bermuda, Jamaica, and virtually every British North American colony. The Miskitu Indigenous slave trade took on international importance during times of warfare between England and Spain, straining diplomatic relations and prompting a strong rebuke from the Spanish ambassador to British officials in 1733. The Jamaican government halfheartedly tried to outlaw the trade in 1741 but to no avail.

These trafficked Central American Natives were usually called Spanish Indians in the records, and scholars have often assumed them to be from Spanish Florida, taken during the Carolina wars in the 1710s. But many of them were a result of the Mosquito Shore Indian slave trade,

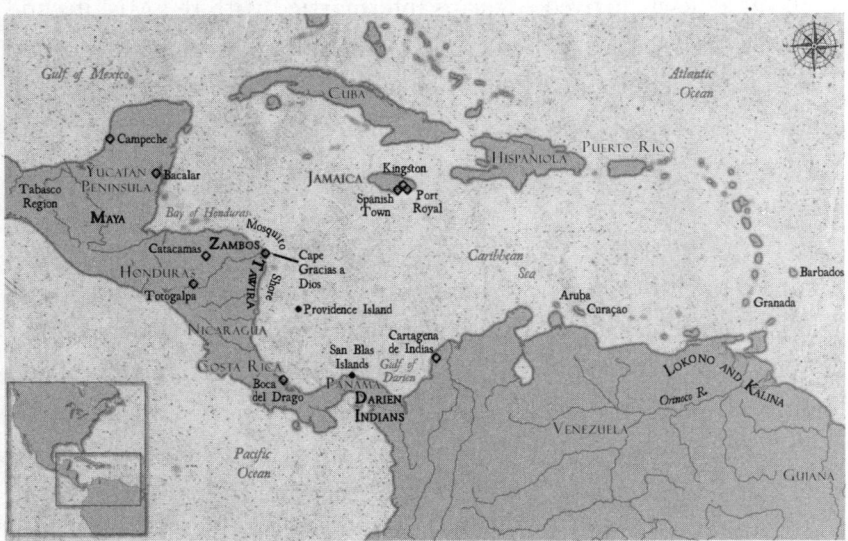

THE MOSQUITO SHORE AND SURROUNDING AREA, CA. 1700.

which came to dominate the British trade in Native American captives after 1720. This particular slave trade reveals the importance of understanding the British Empire in its hemispheric dimensions, beyond the thirteen colonies that later became the United States. Notably, the trafficking of thousands of Indigenous slaves from the Spanish Caribbean in this period meant that enslaved Natives were continually imported and present in the American colonies up through the 1770s and beyond in ways that we have not fully recognized.

ENGLISH MERCHANTS HAD BEEN DRAWN TO the five-hundred-mile stretch of white sand beaches on the western shores of the Caribbean Sea from the moment they laid eyes on the region. Situated in present-day Honduras and Nicaragua, the Mosquito Shore was home to the powerful Miskitu nation, with an estimated population of twenty thousand to thirty thousand at the time of English contact in the early seventeenth century.[5] By the eighteenth century, the Miskitu were made up of two related groups: the Tawira Miskitu and the Zambo Miskitu (often referred to collectively as the Miskitu). The Tawira Miskitu were the original inhabitants. The Zambo Miskitu were mixed-race African and Indigenous, the result of either a shipwreck or a mutiny of enslaved Africans in the 1630s, depending on who was telling the story.[6] Before long, these newly arrived Africans intermarried with the Miskitu and became a distinct but related group. Although English merchants and governors largely treated them as one polity, by the early eighteenth century, the Zambo Miskitu became more dominant and controlled the northern portion of the Mosquito Shore, while the Tawira Miskitu remained to the south.[7]

English governors of Jamaica found the numerous Tawira and Zambo Miskitu to be unconquerable as adversaries but willing allies against the Spanish. The Miskitu had experienced more than a century of Spanish merchants pillaging their shores and extracting natural and human resources from their homelands. Recognizing a strategic opportunity with English traders and merchants in the 1630s, the Miskitu chiefs, or headmen, soon came to favor the English over the Spanish. These alliances grew stronger over the years, and by 1687, Miskitu leaders traveled to Jamaica for every installation of a new English gov-

VIEW OF THE PORT OF BLACK RIVER IN THE TERRITORY OF POYAIS, BY WILLIAM HOME LIZARS, 1822, SHOWING A SCENE ALONG THE MOSQUITO SHORE.

ernor to receive official commissions for their leadership positions. The Jamaica governor received the Miskitu headmen as dignitaries, gifting them with fine clothing and presents, along with a reaffirmation of their titles, all as signs of the ongoing allegiance between the two nations.[8] By the 1750s, the Mosquito Shore was considered to be one of the "Dependencies" of Jamaica, although it never became an official colony. It became a haven for privateers, pirates, disaffected British settlers, and a wide range of people who preferred to live outside the scrutiny of the law.[9]

Central to British–Miskitu diplomatic relations was a vibrant trade that included Native captives. As in Carolina, English merchants traded guns, blankets, and shirts for specific items, in this case cacao, sarsaparilla, and turtle shells. But soon enough, the Miskitu Natives realized that Indigenous captives were prized above all. And the Miskitu were eager to provide captives as that activity dovetailed with their methods of maintaining power in the region. They positioned themselves as the coastal gatekeepers of dozens of interior Native nations, bands, and tribes that were a mixture of old enemies and tributaries. The Miskitu generally looked down on their numerous regional neighbors in the interior, calling them *Alboawinneys*, or "slave meat." Raiding for captives was a way for the Miskitu to maintain their population as well as keep tributaries in line and enemies at bay. These periodic raids against Spanish-allied Indians created a steady supply of enslaved Natives for British traders.[10]

A merchant on the Mosquito Shore observed firsthand the process of preparing for and executing slave raids. First, the Zambo and Tawira soldiers and headmen would meet together to plan individual or joint assaults. In a process steeped in ritual, they would often drink emetics or other traditional beverages, which they believed would give their shaman and leaders the ability to foretell the outcome of their plans. After being assured of success, they would then load into large canoes and paddle either inland up the rivers to Spanish mission towns or paddle or sail up and down the Central American coast and launch surprise nighttime attacks on Spanish-allied Native villages. While raiding food stores and cacao for trade, they often took captives to be sold to English traders.[11]

With constant British demand and an endless landscape of Spanish towns and traditional enemies to raid, the Mosquito Shore Indigenous slave trade grew steadily year by year. By the late seventeenth century, Miskitu raids ranged up and down the Central American coast from the Yucatán Peninsula to Costa Rica. Miskitu parties also intruded deeper into the central highlands of Honduras and Nicaragua, far from the coast, attacking Spanish mission towns and carrying off Indigenous captives to be sold into slavery.[12] Spanish officials angrily described how Miskitu raids destroyed Native mission towns, stole innocent (and Christianized) Indigenous women and children, and generally crippled Spanish missionary efforts.[13] British merchants were not solely responsible for these events, but they were mostly happy to harass the Spanish and gladly supported these actions by creating an active Indigenous trade and slave market for those captured by Tawira and Zambo warriors.

English merchants trafficked these Native captives to Jamaica and from there to farther destinations, such as Bermuda, Barbados, Virginia, and even New England.[14] These trafficking networks followed the usual trade routes between British colonies in North America and the Caribbean. A New England merchant named Thomas Steel purchased an enslaved Native man named Robin from an unrecorded tribe in Jamaica in 1698 or 1699. Steel took Robin to Virginia, where he sold him to a colonist named John Higgins. Once in Virginia, Robin disappears from the records, but it seems highly likely that Robin—so named by the British—had originally been caught up in the Miskitu Indian slave trade and taken to Jamaica, where Steel purchased him.[15]

MISKITU SLAVE RAIDING might have remained on the periphery had not periodic international wars between England and Spain thrust it into the spotlight. Between 1700 and 1760, recurring European wars licensed and gave great urgency to what was an otherwise shadowy trade. Driven by merchants and mostly licensed by the Crown, the Mosquito Shore Indigenous slave trade quickly rose in prominence to become the largest and longest-running Native slave trade in the eighteenth-century English Caribbean. British merchants and privateers quickly pounced on the War of the Spanish Succession (1701–1714) to officially encourage Miskitu slave raids on Spanish Indians in Honduras, Nicaragua, and Costa Rica.[16] Such raids resulted in hundreds, if not thousands, of Indian captives being taken throughout the war, most of whom ended up in various English colonies.

Desperate to counter these devastating raids, Spanish magistrates made a bold attempt to stop them. In 1709, a sizeable Spanish fleet brazenly invaded the Mosquito Shore. Leaving their large ships anchored in deeper waters, Spanish troops packed into smaller shallops and canoes to venture up the river toward Miskitu settlements. But the Miskitu were expert fighters on their own land. They set an ambush on the river, with hundreds hiding along the riverbanks. When the Spanish canoes passed, the Miskitu attacked, cutting them off and killing every Spanish soldier. The Miskitu warriors then sailed back down the river and launched a crippling attack on the poorly defended Spanish ships offshore. There they killed every sailor but one, sending him back with a warning not to invade their territory again.[17]

Even after hostilities between England and Spain subsided in 1714, the Miskitu kept raiding their traditional enemies, still motivated by the British alliance and demand for captives and trade goods.[18] Most of the targeted tribes remain unidentified, but occasionally specific communities were recorded. The Buccatora nation, for example, was among those hunted down by the Miskitu Indians and their English allies.

When the Buccatora fled their villages and hid out in local caves, the Miskitu built fires in the entrances, filling the caves with thick plumes of toxic smoke. Those who refused to surrender died from asphyxiation. The ones who emerged, coughing, stumbling, eyes burning from the fumes, were taken captive by the Miskitu, transported to the coast, and sold to the British.[19]

Between 1710 and 1721 alone, the Miskitu took more than two thousand Native captives in their raids against Spanish towns, as reported by regional Spanish officials. These, too, silently entered the British colonial labor supply through Jamaica traders.[20] Some were retained by captains and merchants to serve on tall-masted vessels that circled the globe. One "Miskito" man who was claimed by Captain John Watling disappeared while hunting in the woods of the Juan Fernandez Islands off the coast of Chile. Watling left him behind.[21]

THE MOSQUITO SHORE Indigenous slave trade remained continuous even during times of peace, in part because it was paired with a vibrant trade in turtle shells. In Carolina, English traders wanted deerskins and Indigenous captives; on the Mosquito Shore, they demanded turtle shells along with Indian slaves.

Turtle fishing had a long history among the Indigenous peoples of the Caribbean. Europeans quickly learned from Native Americans the nutritional value and delicious taste of turtle meat. Turtles also soon became an essential caloric support in European waterborne colonial activity. Green turtles weighing between two hundred and five hundred pounds could be caught and kept alive on long voyages and eventually slaughtered and cooked to supplement other onboard—and often less tasty—provisions, like the flavorless, brittle flour-and-water crackers known as hardtack.[22] Daniel Defoe's main character in *Robinson Crusoe* (1719) narrated the salvation of finding turtles on the Atlantic island where he was stranded, describing turtle meat as "the most savoury and pleasant that ever I tasted in my life."[23] Turtle dishes dotted the menus of London restaurants and became desired culinary additions in places like Philadelphia and Kingston, Jamaica. Merchants also found a valuable and marketable commodity in the huge turtle shells, which could be manufactured into beautiful, decorative handles for combs and brushes to be sold in Europe.[24]

TURTLE FISHING IN
THE CARIBBEAN,
SHOWN IN *PESCHE
DES TORTUES*, BY
LAURENT, 1764;
THE BOTTOM PANEL
DEPICTS A MAN
TURNING OVER A
TURTLE.

This robust turtle trade went hand in hand with the Indigenous slave trade. Each season, two hundred or more Miskitus (often Zambos) would depart in a flotilla of twenty piraguas, or large canoes, containing ten to fifteen men each. The Miskitus were trailed by several merchant ships, and the sailors aboard quickly purchased the live turtles and processed the shells on the spot before sailing the fourteen days back to Jamaica. British officials noted the incredible fishing range of the Miskitus, from the northern tip of the Yucatán Peninsula in Mexico a thousand miles south to the islands off the coast of Panama.[25]

Notably, the geographies of Miskitu coastal slave raiding and turtle hunting were exactly the same. In many instances, the trips to turtle-nesting destinations also involved taking Indigenous captives. In approximately 1727, the Miskitu sailed north and west to the Yucatán on one of their many turtling and slaving expeditions. On the trip, they sacked the Bacalar region (likely Chetumal or Asención Bay, Mexico) and took a staggering nine hundred Natives as captives. Unbeknownst to the Miskitu or British merchants, the Bacalar prisoners were carrying smallpox, likely from the Spanish. The results were devastating: one

by one, Miskitus began to contract the deadly disease through exposure to their Native captives, whether on the voyage back or through
daily contact with captives incorporated into households. Within a few
years, perhaps as many as half of the Miskitu contracted the dreaded
disease and perished.[26]

After the Bacalar disaster, the Tawira and Zambo preferred to hunt
for turtles and to slave-raid down the coast to the south instead of to
the north. In the 1730s and 1740s, the two Miskitu nations embarked on
turtling and raiding expeditions south at least as far as Boca del Drago
Bay and the Gulf of Darién, on the northern shore of Panama. Most of
the captives were sold to English merchants, but some of the Miskitu
leaders retained a few slaves for their personal use. This was in keeping
with much older Native practices of captive taking, enslavement, and
adoption that predated the coming of Europeans. The Zambo Miskitu
headman claimed several enslaved Natives in 1757, as noted by the British superintendent of the Mosquito Shore, Robert Hodgson.[27]

It is almost impossible to know how many raids on Spanish Indians
went unrecorded or how many enslaved Natives changed hands along
the lengthy coast of Central America. Fragments and descriptions of
these transactions appear from time to time in the archives, as do complaints from the Spanish about this trade. But compared to the African slave trade (with which the Mosquito Shore Indian slave trade had
distinct resonances), or even the ways that Carolina officials candidly
discussed the Indian slave trade in their midst, this western Caribbean
shoreline was almost entirely unregulated, only loosely monitored by
European authorities, and poorly documented.

DON FRANCOIS LOPES'S DISCOVERY of Mayan slaves in Virginia
and Jamaica in 1733 provoked an international controversy that took
years to resolve. Lopes first appealed directly to officials in Jamaica
in 1734, demanding that local officials reclaim the enslaved Mayans
from their masters. British officials demurred since there was no law
against Indian slavery to justify such a repossession. English Jamaica
had served as a crossroad for the traffick in enslaved Native Americans for more than seventy years. The Mosquito Indigenous slave trade
provided a steady stream of human capital into Jamaica, supplement-
ing the largely enslaved African labor force and enabling diplomatic

relations with the powerful Miskitu Indians. Jamaican officials had no motivation to anger planters by taking away slaves that were, for British purposes, legally purchased.[28]

Jamaican officials wouldn't budge, but Lopes wasn't giving up. He next wrote to Spanish officials, lodging an official complaint at the royal court. The king of Spain was equally incensed and leaned on the Spanish ambassador to England, Conde de Montijo, to do something about it. The ambassador, in turn, wrote a stern letter protesting Indigenous slavery to Thomas Pelham-Holles, Duke of Newcastle, who was serving as the British secretary of state. Pelham-Holles had taken on oversight of the affairs of the colonies, which in the 1730s meant calming down an increasingly agitated Spain.[29]

The Spanish ambassador's damning letter outlined his perspective on the contours of the Mosquito Shore Indigenous slave trade. Everyone knew that profit-seeking British merchants were to blame for the Miskitu raids, as Spanish leaders had long suspected. English captains were often caught red-handed by Spanish privateers who found Native captives as part of the human and material cargo in the hold. Such was the case in the early 1730s when a Spanish merchant captured a British ship sailing from Campeche. In the ship's belly were six captive Natives from the Yucatán, but they could have just as easily come from Honduras, Nicaragua, or other parts of Mexico.[30]

Montijo's 1734 letter to Pellem-Holles demanded immediate action. He insisted that Jamaican officials pass a law prohibiting this ongoing Indian slave trade because it was draining Spanish mission towns of their converts and allies. He also required Jamaican officials to track down enslaved Natives from Spanish territories who resided in Jamaica, Virginia, and other English colonies and return them to their rightful homes on the Spanish mainland (Central America). To refuse to do so, Montijo stated, would be a breach of the "reciprocal friendship and good correspondence" between Spain and England.[31]

Although this was perhaps a slightly idealized description of the relationship between the two countries, the Spanish ambassador clearly understood the political nature of the Indian slave trade, as well as the injustice of Indigenous slavery itself. But he also underestimated the extent to which "Spanish Indians" had been shipped throughout the British Empire and how impossible it would be to return them.

Upon receiving Montijo's letter, in 1735, Pelham-Holles wrote to Lieutenant Governor William Gooch of Virginia about the enslaved Mayans in that colony. Gooch, in his reply, dismissed charges of the intentional enslavement of Spanish Christianized Indians, although he acknowledged that the enslavement of free people from any Christian country was against the law. But Gooch defended the particular mechanisms of the Mosquito Shore Indigenous slave trade. Purchasing captives that were taken in what he saw as legitimate wars between rival Native nations was entirely defensible according to the "law of nature and of nations." In that case, the "right of the conqueror is freely transferr'd by the purchase."[32]

Gooch's invocation of the law of nations echoed debates regarding Native slavery by Juan Ginés de Sepúlveda and other Spanish jurists in the 1540s. Ironically, this English magistrate was now turning the Spanish jurists' proslavery arguments back on the Spanish, two hundred years later. And like the Spanish jurists who defended Indian slavery in the 1540s, Gooch had plenty of reasons to preserve an Indigenous slave trade based on the purchase of captives. After all, this was exactly the system that undergirded the British-sponsored Indigenous slave trade out of the Carolinas and Virginia between 1670 and 1720, the Guiana coast prior to that, and now the Mosquito Shore and the Bay of Mexico.

Even more important, this logic of the transfer of the right of the captor was the backbone of the transatlantic African slave trade. The entire plantation system of enslaved labor was dependent on upholding a slave trade—whether Indigenous or African—that permitted the legal sale of already-captured people to Europeans and then the resale of those slaves to others. Gooch admitted that sometimes Africans who, by this definition, should not have been enslaved were caught up in the system.[33] But as a whole, Gooch believed this structure could not be challenged. The entire Atlantic colonial plantation complex—and the accompanying revenue streams from the British colonies—depended on it. As Charles Hayes noted in 1744, "Will not every British Planter in America, and every West-India Merchant in England grant, that the Negroe Trade on the Coast of Africa is the chief and fundamental Support of the British Colonies and Plantations in America?"[34]

Gooch was unmoved by Indigenous slave trading in Virginia. The same was true for British officials in Jamaica who paid no attention to the sharp rebuke from Montijo. In any case, nothing of substance was done about it immediately. Throughout the 1730s, Tawira and Zambo Miskitu continually raided Spanish-allied Indian nations and towns throughout most of Central America.[35] In May 1738, Miskitu forces sacked the Spanish town of Catacamas, deep in the interior of present-day Honduras. After plundering the town, including the chapel, the Miskitu carried off fifty-nine captives, whom they presumably marched back to the Mosquito Shore and sold as slaves.[36] For the moment, at least, this slave trade seemed unchallenged.

BRITAIN SHRUGGED OFF the Mosquito Shore Indigenous slave trade until it threatened their own interests only a few years later. Tensions between England and Spain grew stronger in the late 1730s until finally England declared war on Spain in October 1739. Spain reciprocated a month later, initiating the War of Jenkin's Ear (1739–1748), as it was later called due to the severing of Captain Robert Jenkin's ear by a Spanish soldier.

Wartime privateering instantly expanded, drawing in merchants from as far away as New England to sack Spanish ships and towns in the Caribbean. Captain Joseph Powers from Newport, Rhode Island, raided some Spanish towns on the Orinoco River in Venezuela in the fall of 1740, along with a pair of Dutch ships. In addition to their lucrative haul of gold and silver coins and plates, they also captured sixty enslaved Indigenous and African people and likely sold them when they arrived in Jamaica a few weeks later.[37] Four years later, the *Prince Charles of Larraine* out of Rhode Island attacked a Jesuit mission town on the Oyapock River in French Guiana. After taking five Lokono captives, the privateers scoured the coastlines and rivers looking for additional towns to sack before heading to Barbados to sell Indigenous and African captives into slavery. Such exploits were celebrated in North America, where the *Pennsylvania Gazette* heralded their taking of "9 Indians, 2 Negroes, [and] a Mulatto Wench" during the raid against the French.[38]

The war expanded slave-raiding operations on the Mosquito Shore as well. Jamaica governor Edward Trelawney sent Robert Hodgson to the Miskitu to reaffirm their alliance with the British in this new war.

Hodgson arrived on the Mosquito Shore in 1740 and met with some Miskitu chiefs, including King Edward, south of Gracias a Dios. They held an elaborate ceremony that renewed Miskitu allegiance, provided additional commissions for Miskitu headmen, and issued a broad (and long-sought) conveyance of the Mosquito Shore to the British.[39] That year, English officials encouraged at least three different Miskitu raids on Spanish towns west of Miskitu territory, each raiding party heading inland to Spanish territory via one of three rivers.[40]

As war with Spain dragged on, British officials fixed their eyes on an even bigger prize: Cartagena de Indias. Situated on the Caribbean coast of Colombia, Cartagena was a flourishing crown jewel of the Spanish Empire. It was the one location that, if taken, could permanently cripple the Spanish in the Americas. In order to conquer it, the English would need the help of Native allies in the Bay of Darién and Panama region. But as British officials soon found out, the Bay of Darién was one of the slave-raiding destinations for the Miskitu and their English merchant allies, which had created strong anti-British sentiment in the region.[41]

Suddenly, the Mosquito Shore Indigenous slave trade became a problem for British magistrates since, in the midst of a war with Spain, they desperately needed additional Native allies in Central America. In early 1741, the Jamaica Governor's Council formed a committee to investigate accusations of aggressive Indigenous slave raiding in that region. The issue was not the Miskitu per se, but rather English traders and buccaneers from Jamaica who incentivized Miskitu raids all the way down to the Bay of Darién. This created opposition from Native nations in the region to permanent British settlement and alliance in the war against Spain.[42] If an alliance with Indians in the Bay of Darién could be cultivated, Cartagena would fall to the British in no time.[43]

Accordingly, a bill to remedy this specific wartime diplomatic crisis was drafted in the Jamaica Assembly and revised three times before being passed on May 7, 1741, as "An Act for Recovering and Extending the Trade with the Indian Settlements in America, and preventing for the future Some Evil Practices formerly Committed in that Trade."[44] It was a curious piece of legislation, marked more by wartime interests than humanitarian concern. Its scope was narrowly focused on a politically disruptive Indigenous slave *trade*; Indigenous *slavery* was left untouched.[45] To disincentivize the Mosquito Shore slave trade, the act declared that after June 1 all Indigenous people who were transported to Jamaica as slaves would be free. At the same time, it explicitly protected colonists who already owned enslaved Natives, allowing them to retain or trade them.[46]

The law also required an Indian slave registry in Jamaica, with the names and sexes of all such slaves to be submitted to the clerk of each parish vestry by December 28, 1741. Unfortunately, no records of such a slave registry survive. More than likely, owners and masters refused or simply reclassified Indian slaves as Black or mulatto in order to get around the reporting requirement.

Though Jamaica officials might have persuaded the Miskitu to stop slave raiding so far south, they continued to slave-raid other regions with or without the permission of the assembly.[47] Instead of scaling back the Indigenous slave trade, the Miskitu escalated it. One of their favorite targets for more than a half century had been Totogalpa, a small region in present-day northern Nicaragua. Franciscans had attempted a mission in the region in 1696 but had withdrawn after funding shortages and the murder of a missionary. In 1744, they were back again and succeeded in setting up an Indian mission town at Xicaques. But the Zambo repeatedly harassed them during periodic raids, making life difficult and instilling terror. In 1749, the Zambo Miskitu raided one of the new mission towns, killing the Spanish missionary and thirteen Indians and carrying off seventy more as slaves. Six years later, after additional raids, the Franciscans gave up and vacated the area, convinced that only a military escort would make the region safe for missionary work.[48]

Spanish officials noted with alarm the increased slave-raiding activity in the late 1740s and early 1750s. In October 1753, the Miskitu Indians attacked a Spanish settlement called Carpenter's River, ransacking it and taking with them various recorded items of plunder. Within a few years, the volume of Indigenous captives raided from Spanish territories was so immense that officials compared it to the African slave trade, noting that British traders were buying and selling Indians "as if they were Negros."[49]

But Spanish officials turned a blind eye to the ways that enslaved Natives saturated the labor market, even in territories under their own jurisdiction. One promoter of the region of Caledonia in Panama wrote to an official at Hispaniola in the 1750s that the land was so "extreamly fruitfull" that "a man may have an Estate without Negroes by means of the natives who will work and aughment your plantation, & their Labour will cost you only a few Cloths for them."[50] The need for enslaved labor on plantations was a given, with the availability of enslaved Natives equally so.

THE MOSQUITO SHORE Indigenous slave trade continued well after the 1741 law. In rare instances, communities subjected to Miskitu raids complained to British authorities. In 1762, fifty-three Woolva women and children were chased down, tied up, and forced to march the one hundred miles to the Caribbean coast. An English merchant named Abraham Trenawston was behind the raid, having hired two Miskitu captains named Tilas and Dick Allen.[51] The Woolva nation was large and powerful—second only to the Miskitu on the Mosquito Shore, according to British authorities in the area. English merchants and the Miskitu had overstepped.[52]

Outraged, a Woolva chief named Garrison complained to British officials at Bluefields, a coastal settlement at the southern end of the Mosquito Shore. Finding no sympathy from pro-Indigenous slave-trading officials there, he secured a ride on a Jamaican merchant ship and arrived in Kingston. There Garrison met with a colonist and occasional Mosquito Shore resident named Richard Jones and relayed the desperate situation to him. Jones heard his complaint, promised to act, and offered to take him to Spanish Town to meet the governor of Jamaica. After repeated delays in actually seeing the governor, Garrison abandoned his mission and slipped away, hopping on a ship named *Betsey*, presumably to return home.[53]

Garrison's complaints in 1762 garnered eventual attention. His accusation against English merchants slave-raiding allied tribes coincided with rumors that these traders routinely flaunted the 1741 act by trafficking Native captives into Jamaica. The assembly formed an investigative committee, which gathered witnesses and produced a report in a few months. What they found was an underground market for enslaved Natives in which sales were conducted through word of mouth.

This secrecy contrasted sharply with the widely publicized sales of African captives. When a ship full of enslaved Africans sailed into Bridgetown (Barbados) or Kingston (Jamaica), the subsequent public sale of its human cargo was usually advertised in local newspapers several days in advance, thereby giving the captains time to go through quarantine if necessary, complete the required paperwork, and prepare the captive Africans for sale. Slave factors (local agents) Jones and Moe in Bridgetown, for example, advertised the sale of a "Cargo of the best SLAVES from the Gold-Coast" on September 25, 1770.[54] But there are few, if any, such shipments of Indigenous captives advertised, partially because the Indian slave trade into Jamaica was technically illegal after 1741 and operated in smaller quantities. Knowledge was passed through local networks and traders known to be willing to trade in Indigenous slaves.

An underground slave-trading network is how Edward Glasse was offered an enslaved Native for purchase. Glasse, a resident of Port Royal, was approached by James Lawrie, a trader with connections to the Mosquito Shore. Lawrie informed Glasse of the availability of Native slaves for sale. Glasse in turn told Richard Jones—perhaps to ingratiate a friend with some insider news. Jones took a look but declined to buy any of the Natives and told Glasse to do the same. Instead, the enslaved Indians were sold to another planter named Jasper Hall.[55] Thus, as individuals or smaller groups, enslaved Indians continually entered into the larger enslaved labor force of Jamaica and the wider Caribbean, often off the books, through personal connections, and almost entirely unregulated.

Under scrutiny, Jamaican captains and merchants also learned to be savvy about offloading their human cargo. In places where selling Indian slaves was either illegal or frowned upon, English merchants called Indian slaves "servants." In Jamaica, although some Natives were still sold as slaves, many were sold as indentured servants or apprentices for a specific number of years. "By that clandestine method," Superintendent Lawrie reported, "they are kept in Slavery in Jamaica or wherever they are carried to."[56]

On hearing all of this testimony, the Jamaica Assembly assigned another committee to find out exactly how many enslaved Natives had been sold on the island. The committee was also charged with returning any Natives who had been recently purchased and prosecuting both the sellers and buyers of enslaved Indians.[57] There is no evidence that this was done, however, nor is it clear that it was even possible. Through racial shifting and documentary genocide, enslaved Indians disappeared into the larger mass of enslaved Africans in the decentralized plantation system of Jamaica.

THIS CENTRAL AMERICAN INDIGENOUS slave trade remained an incredibly important, even if largely invisible, source of enslaved Natives in the American colonies. When English merchants purchased or directly raided enslaved Natives from Central America, they packed them alongside other trade items and sold them in other British colonies on their regular trade routes, whether Jamaica, Barbados, Virginia, or Massachusetts. Privateers did the same. In 1719, an English privateer out of Jamaica captured a Spanish ship and sailed it to Virginia, where the captain sold some enslaved Spanish Indians and Africans before heading to New York to offload the rest.[58]

Although Natives raided from the Central American coasts were often stripped of their tribal identities and were labeled simply "Spanish Indian," in some cases they were identified as having come from the Mosquito Shore. Such was the case with an enslaved Indian named Jack, who ran away from his master Robert Field in Burlington County, New Jersey, in 1767. Jack was described as a "Musqueto Shore Indian Slave," approximately five feet, six inches tall, twenty-one years old, with black long hair that he usually wore tied in a ponytail. He could play the fiddle, and when he left, he was wearing a "lightish coloured Stuff Coat, a blue Broadcloth Waistcoat, Ozenbrigs Shirt and Trowsers, a Pair of old Shoes, with Brass Buckles."[59] Although no details are given as to when he had arrived in New Jersey, it is surely the case that he was just one of thousands of enslaved Indians from Central America who were slave-raided by the Miskitu and taken to English colonies in the Caribbean and North America during this hundred-year-long slave trade.

Others in North American colonies were occasionally noted as having arrived from Jamaica. In approximately 1747, an enslaved Native woman named Paupouse was taken from Jamaica to Virginia by her legal owner. The records are silent about how she ended up in Jamaica

> ## TEN POUNDS Reward.
>
> RUN-away from the SUBSCRIBER, the 13th of *June last*, a Negro Man, named, RICHARD or DICK, aged about 25 Years, about 5 Feet 9 Inches high, of a yellowish Complexion, and grave Countenance, very stout and well set, walks a little stooping, is a good Farmer :——Had on, when he went away, a good dark-coloured Nap Coat, with Mohair Buttons, Oznabrigs Shirt and Trowsers, a Pair of new Shoes, and a good Felt Hat.
>
> AND, on the 24th Day of July, a Musqueto-shore Indian, named JACK, about 21 Years of Age, 5 Feet 6 or 7 Inches high, thick set, with long black Hair, which he generally wears tied behind. He is a Farmer, and had on a good Felt Hat, a short yellowish-coloured Homespun Coat, a blue Broadcloth Waistcoat, without Sleeves, Oznabrigs Shirt and Trowsers, a Pair of good Shoes, with Steel Buckles. He stole, and took with him, a good Beaver Hat, a new fine Shirt, and a buff-coloured Cloth Waistcoat, with Lapells, and yellow Buttons.
>
> Whoever takes up said Slaves, and secures them in any Goal, so that they may be had again, or brings them to the Subscriber, at Whitehall, Burlington County, West Jersey, shall have the above Reward, or FIVE POUNDS for either of them, and reasonable Charges paid by
>
> ROBERT FIELD.
> N. B. All Persons are forwarned harbouring or employing them, and all Masters of Vessels taking them off, at their Peril.

"RUNAWAY" AD FOR JACK, FROM THE MOSQUITO SHORE, IN *PENNSYLVANIA CHRONICLE, AND UNIVERSAL ADVERTISER,* AUGUST 24, 1767.

as a slave in the first place. Her name—*papoose* meant "child" in some Native languages and was used widely by colonists—suggests that perhaps she had been enslaved as a young girl, likely from Central America. But eventually Paupouse ended up in Virginia, where her enslavement continued with no apparent controversy in the 1740s.[60]

More generally, dozens of "Spanish Indians" are listed in self-emancipated and for-sale advertisements in North American British colonies throughout the eighteenth century. This was especially true after 1720, when the Carolina Indian slave trade had largely ended. In Boston alone, 54 percent of the newspaper ads for Indigenous people (both for sale and runaways) between 1704 and 1770 were related to either Carolina or Spanish Indians.[61] A "Young Spanish Indian Woman," for example, was advertised for sale in March 1732 by Captain Thomas James on Second Street in Philadelphia. Although few details are given about the twenty-year-old girl, she was defined by her gendered labor capacity, advertised as being "very fit" for various types of household work.[62] Another Spanish Indian slave named James Don-bar emancipated himself by running away in March 1764 near Great Egg Harbor in southern New Jersey (sixty miles southeast of Philadelphia). He was on the shorter side—five feet, three inches tall—with his long straight hair tied back and likely carrying an Indian blanket and a large blue overcoat.[63]

Other enslaved Natives from the Caribbean were forced to serve on ships, disappearing into the increasingly multiethnic world of sailors in the Atlantic. Such was apparently the case with an unnamed "Spanish Indian man," who slipped away into the streets of Philadelphia in June 1741. He had arrived on a small merchant vessel named *Lancashire Witch*, presumably as a bound member of the crew. While at port, he ran away and likely found refuge among the city's laboring class of free and enslaved people of color. Notably, this enslaved Native man only spoke a few words of English. His legal masters offered twenty shillings for his return.[64]

Enslaved Natives from Spanish territories were also taken by their owners to England, where they mostly labored in households. Some such Natives even retained Spanish names, giving evidence of their being trafficked. Francis de Silvo ran away from his enslaver, Christopher Gibson, in London on March 13, 1732. The twenty-one-year-old Francis had long black hair and was dressed exceptionally well, wearing a light-colored, blue-trimmed frock and a nice hat with gold lace. He took with him a livery suit—the clothing of slaves and servants who accompanied coaches.[65]

DUE TO THE QUASI-LEGAL NATURE of this activity, it is impossible to know exactly how many Natives were trafficked from the Central American coast during this time. But the volume was substantial, far larger than we have realized. A modest estimate is that the Mosquito Shore Indigenous slave trade placed as many as twenty thousand Native captives in the hands of English traders during its one-hundred-year duration. It flourished during the cyclical wars between England and Spain from 1700 to the 1750s, when such slave-raiding activity increased.[66]

More broadly, this incredible flow of human bodies at the peak of these larger English slave trades were not only tied to English traders' demands for trade goods. The Yamasee, Westo, Miskitu, and other nations had their own reasons for slave raiding and refused to be controlled by the whims of British officials. These various Indigenous slave trades ensured that enslaved Natives remained a vital part of the labor landscape in all English colonies up through the American Revolution and beyond.

Part Three

TRANSITIONS

1750–1820

THE PERIOD BETWEEN 1750 AND 1820 WAS ONE OF THE most formative eras in American history. The colonies threw off the political subjugation of the British Crown and aggressively pushed westward into Indigenous land, even as southern states steadily grew and expanded slavery's reach. At the same time, the transatlantic African slave trade grew phenomenally for a period, powered by the ascendancy of British and American merchants who temporarily eclipsed the earlier trading powerhouses of the Portuguese and the Dutch.[1] But the era of the legalized Atlantic slave trade came to a sudden halt in 1808 in both the United States and Britain.

The meteoric rise and ensuing fall of the African slave trade often overshadows the steady presence of Indigenous slavery in the American colonies and early United States. The peak years of English Native slave trading between the 1630s and 1760 had placed tens of thousands of enslaved Native Americans into homes and plantations in every English colony from New York to Jamaica. From the mid-eighteenth to the early nineteenth century, Indigenous enslavement featured prominently in American life but often in rather everyday kinds of ways. The exception was during times of war, including in the era of the American Revolution, when more aggressive captive taking and land grabbing resurfaced. Native Americans trapped in servitude of various forms were kept there by custom, racism, and the law.

Rather than enslaved African labor edging out Native slavery in this period, the records suggest that Indigenous and African slavery existed side by side in overlapping ways for the entire colonial period and well into the early American republic, along with other forms of servile labor, such as white indentured servitude. Even where African slavery had grown rapidly, as in Virginia, enslaved Natives were still enslaved and sometimes imported throughout the eighteenth century and into the early nineteenth century.

The American colonies, and later the United States, continued to grow and flourish at the expense of Native nations, all while imposing enslavement and servitude on Indigenous peoples in less visible but equally insidious ways. But something else was growing as well—even though it took a long time to really take root: the idea that Indigenous people were naturally free. This did not mean that Americans viewed Native nations as equal in any sense of the term, but it did create additional legal space for Indigenous people to pursue their freedom in courts.

Eight

EVERYDAY OPPORTUNISM

NOT ALL NATIVE SLAVERY INVOLVED LARGE-SCALE SLAVE TRADING or genocidal wars. If we could enter the houses, plantation slave quarters, and courts in eighteenth-century Connecticut, Pennsylvania, or Georgia, we would see the ways that Americans continuously kept some Natives enslaved through less visibly violent means of everyday life.

On June 20, 1746, for example, justices of the peace in Amelia County, Virginia, ordered that four Native American children—Charles, Jemmy, Bobb, and Isaac—be taken away from their mother, Deborah, and bound out to local white planters.[1] Deborah was listed as "belonging to" Samuel Jordan, who was the owner of a 1,360-acre plantation along the south bank of the Nottoway River, fifty miles south of Richmond; so it is likely that Deborah was part of the estate's enslaved population. There is no indication of how Deborah was enslaved in the first place. Notably, the court-ordered separation and binding out of her four children gave no contract or length of time for service. It seems to have been the case that on rural Virginia plantations, Indigenous children like these were often enslaved for life.

The stealing of Deborah's children reveals what I am calling the "everyday opportunism" of Indigenous enslavement and servitude in the American colonies. Everyday opportunism refers to the myriad ways that Indigenous people almost invisibly and continuously were forced into servitude and enslavement in the eighteenth century through legal and extralegal processes. This opportunism came in different forms. It could involve enslavement for falling into debt or being poor or for being accused of a crime. Native parents were also pressured—sometimes even required—to place their children into white homes through indenture, which catastrophically shattered families. With each generation, it became more difficult to break out of family enslavement, especially when Natives were racially recategorized as "mulatto" or "Black."

This opportunistic impulse to steal and coerce Natives was on full display during imperial warfare through the bounty system, when the public was financially incentivized to capture or murder Natives. Newspapers, too, played an insidious role when they published Indian runaway slave advertisements, listed Natives for sale, published notices of bounties on Indigenous bodies and scalps, and otherwise normalized the Natives as enemies and appropriate targets of enslavement.

All of these factors created immense challenges to Native sovereignty and concern for everyday living—fear of arbitrary enslavement for debt and minor infractions, of having one's children stolen, of being hunted down by colonists during war, of white people constantly questioning one's freedom, and of being denied one's Native identity and community.

Despite the repeated protests and occasional violent resistance of enslaved Indigenous people, Native enslavement and servitude did not wane in the eighteenth century. There was no difference between northern and southern colonies on the issue of slavery; that distinction would only become meaningful in the decades following the American Revolution. Instead, there was a steadily increasing view of Natives as enslavable, bolstered by the power of the law and popular perception. Native enslavement continued unabated, not even edged out by the substantial growth in the transatlantic African slave trade.

INDIGENOUS CHILDREN like those stolen from Deborah continued to be the most vulnerable group throughout the British colonies.[2] They served, invisibly, in surprising numbers in every colony and in some cases in the homes of colonial leaders. Pennsylvania governor William Markham, a Quaker and cousin of the colony's founder, William Penn, kept an enslaved Native boy in his household, who he freed in his will when he died in 1704.[3] By the eighteenth century, one primary legal tactic targeting children was indenture, or being bound out to a (usually) white legal master for a trade. Sometimes this was voluntary, but in many cases it was imposed on families.

Indentures, even when centered on a specific trade, separated children from parents, where legal masters tried to force them to be less Indian and more English in terms of language, dress, and habits of the mind. And by dissociating Indian children from tribal lands, within a generation colonists hoped to free up territory for colonial expansion while slowly eroding Native populations on the borders of British settlements. In Massachusetts, missionary Gideon Hawley reported that "there is scarcely an Indian boy among us not indetted to an English Master."[4] The same was true farther south, where indentured Natives commonly served in colonial households in the Chesapeake region.[5]

Indentures were slippery business, as Indian parents quickly found out. There was the real danger of being treated like a chattel slave—whipped, beaten, or raped. Even worse, after a while an indentured Indigenous person might find it difficult to extract themselves or their children from cycles of indentured servitude and coerced labor. A Native boy named James was lured into contract servitude as a young man by the offer of five pounds (cash), a horse bridle, a saddle, and two suits

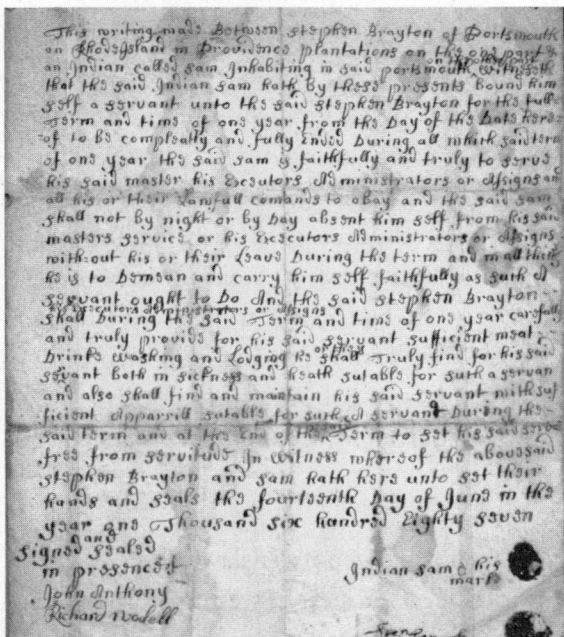

INDENTURE FOR
SAM, PORTSMOUTH,
RHODE ISLAND,
1687.

of clothing. The terms of service set by his master, Marcus Andrews, in Maryland, were long—thirty years—although such arrangements were somewhat common in the region. But Andrews turned around and trafficked James across colony lines to a Mr. Nicholas of Philadelphia for fifteen pounds (presumably as a slave). In this case, Andrews was caught and fined because James belonged to an unnamed "Friend" Native nation, but the record is silent on the status of James himself and whether or not he found his freedom.[6] Many other such examples exist in the archives.[7] One can imagine the scores of verbal transactions, sales, and agreements that were never recorded or were improperly filed with local authorities.

Sometimes Native parents chose to indenture their children after being driven into poverty and desperation by colonialism. In February 1729, a Pequot woman named Abigale indentured her seven-year-old daughter, Sarah, to William Morgan of Groton until she reached the age of eighteen. In cases of official indenture (as with this one), there were specific reciprocal obligations that, in theory, could be enforced by law. Sarah agreed to generally obey and not run away; Morgan agreed to provide Sarah with food, clothes, and English-language instruction and to not abandon her if she should get sick. Most importantly, Morgan promised at the end of the term "to give his said apprentice her freedom."[8] As with most such indentures, there are no records indicating whether this actually happened.

In many cases, repeated patterns of stealing children in this manner prompted protests, especially when governments put pressure on families to indenture their children. Indigenous families in New York complained that binding out their children to British legal masters meant losing them forever. When Native parents went to redeem their children again, they found that they had been "transferred to other plantations and sold for slaves." Indigenous parents filed their objections with local officials, and soon word got back to the British secretary of state for the Northern Department, Charles Townshend, who attempted to prevent the practice.[9]

THE EVERYDAY OPPORTUNISM of Indigenous enslavement also came in the form of punishments for alleged crimes. In western cultures, the law is imagined to be a neutral arbiter of justice, but that is rarely how colonized peoples experienced it. Colonial laws upheld and supported racialized slavery, created inequities, and kept non-whites and lower classes in the societal "stations" deemed appropriate by white men in power. Indigenous nations who found themselves shoehorned into American colonies and legal systems quickly learned this valuable lesson and tried to shape it and use laws to their benefit.

In the eighteenth century, laws permitting slavery as a punishment for various crimes became even more important as a means for controlling Indigenous people and enslaving them. The court records of almost every British colony are strewn with cases in which Natives were sold as slaves or shipped out of the country for relatively minor infractions. For example, in 1725, an enslaved Indigenous man named Dick in the home of Peleg Smith of Newport, Rhode Island, was accused of assaulting a colonist. The court decreed that Dick should be sold out of the colony "never to return again," with the proceeds of his sale to be given to his accuser.[10]

Natives who were otherwise free could be taken before a local court, accused of owing a debt or stealing something from a white colonist, and be sentenced by a local magistrate for a limited time of servitude. In 1724, an Indigenous man named Charles was accused of owing money to Samuel Edgecomb of New London and Charles Arcott of Saybrook, both in Connecticut. When Charles could not pay back the debts immediately, the New London County Court ordered him to pay off his debts through servitude to both men, one at a time: Edgecomb for six months and twelve days, and Arcott for two years, three months, and twenty-five days.[11]

But once enslaved—even for a specified time—Native Americans and people of color could have their service extended, either officially or unofficially. Punishable infractions included running away, getting pregnant (or getting someone else pregnant) out of wedlock, and theft, among other things.[12] Arbitrarily extending time of service or enslavement was also a common strategy used by enslavers after wars, when colonial governments sold Natives—surrenderers and combatants—as "servants" for a specified period of service. But because these limited-term enslavement arrangements did not always come with as clear a paper trail as did voluntary indentures, it became difficult to prove one's freedom, especially after a decade or two.

This question repeatedly surfaced in New England in the decades following the War for New England. In May 1721—a full forty-five years after the end of that war—Connecticut attorney Peter Pratt petitioned the Connecticut General Assembly with a dilemma. The children who had been put into English houses as limited-term slaves and servants had over time grown into adults and had children of their own. Pratt's questions were straightforward: Should the children of enslaved Native women from King Philip's War also be "deemed Slaves as ye Negroes"? Or should these children instead be "deemed free at ye age of thirty years or Some other certain age"? Pratt strongly urged the latter—that the "said Children ought to not be Slaves at their masters pleasure." Nonetheless, Pratt did not think it wise to just set them free immediately. Pratt's proposed compromise—limited-term enslavement of no more than thirty years—simply repeated the enslavement practices after King Philip's War in the next generation of Indian children, thereby continuously separating Native children from reservations, families, and kin.[13]

DEBT WAS A FREQUENT MECHANISM for initiating and perpetuating the enslavement of Indigenous people.[14] In New England, such tactics became so onerous that in 1700 a group of Wampanoags on Cape Cod petitioned the Massachusetts Bay Colony officials, asking for help. These Natives outlined plainly how this informal system of debt servitude worked. English merchants would allow Indians to buy items on credit—too much credit. When Indigenous people ran up debts and could not repay them, merchants would take the debtor before a colonial official and have the Indian—or his child—assigned to colonists to pay off the debt. The labor terms demanded by the white creditors were oppressive, the Indians complained—not at all consistent with the small debts that were owed. These Natives petitioned colonial authorities to pass a law stating that no Indigenous person be allowed to be "taken as a Servant" unless examined and permitted by two justices of the peace.[15]

The debt-to-enslavement pipeline became so well used that Massachusetts had to repeatedly pass laws against it well into the eighteenth century, even as late as 1758.[16] Rhode Island too recognized the "greedy and covetous Design" of white residents who overextended credit to

Native peoples in order "get the said *Indians* to be bound to them for longer Time than is just and reasonable."[17] The Rhode Island Assembly passed a law in 1730 requiring the consent of at least two justices of the peace or wardens in order to bind out a Native person.

The problem of debt servitude or debt peonage was widespread across the British colonies and lasted well into the nineteenth century in various forms. In some regions, merchants were especially brash. English traders in New York began demanding Native children as human collateral for trade goods. An Indigenous person might desire a certain quantity of clothing or guns and—lacking any suitable item to barter—the trader would demand one of their children as a guarantee. In theory, when the debt was paid off, either by the labor of the Indian child or by an outright payment or another exchange, the parents could redeem the child. In reality, Native parents often found their children had instead been sold into slavery. The problem became so great that in 1750, New York governor George Clinton ordered that all Indian children held as pledges be returned to their families.[18] As usual, it is unclear how thoroughly this order was enforced.

AMERICANS ALSO RELIED ON the legal fabrication of *partus sequitur ventrem* to keep Indigenous and African people in multigenerational slavery. This mechanism allowed enslavers to claim as property the offspring of enslaved women, whether Indigenous or African. It remained in effect throughout the entire course of American slavery. In January 1709, a case came before the Anne Arundel County Court in Maryland that demonstrated the ongoing power of *partus* to keep Natives enslaved. An Indigenous woman had been captured and enslaved thirty-four years earlier, as a result of the English raid on the Susquehannock Fort in 1675 during Bacon's Indian War. During her enslavement, she gave birth at least once, to a boy who was claimed by Captain William Harbert as a slave. This Indian woman died, likely in the early 1700s. Harbert went to the county court with an important question: should the boy be considered a lifelong slave as his mother had been? The court's answer was a resounding affirmation: like his mother, he should be a "slave During life."[19]

Maryland was not alone. Like Virginia had done in 1662, Georgia ensconced this principle in law a century later, stating that "all negroes, Indians . . . mulattoes, or mestizoes" and "all their issue and offspring . . . are hereby declared to be and remain forever hereafter absolute slaves, and shall follow the condition of the mother."[20]

The imposition of *partus* can be seen in wills and probate records, where the children of Indigenous enslaved women were also presumed to be slaves. When James Parrish of Brunswick County, Virginia, wrote his will in 1753, he left three enslaved girls—Cheny, Phillis, and Farthing—to his daughter Mary. Cheny and Phillis were Africans, while Farthing was Indigenous. But Parrish's will clearly stated that his daughter would have the benefit of any future children they might bear as well.[21] *Partus* was also applied to Natives who were serving in term-limited enslavement (for a set number of years). A May 1723 Virginia law stated that children born to any "female mullatto, or indian" with a fixed term of service would also be forced to serve until they, too, reached the age of thirty.[22]

And yet enslaved people did not simply accept laws and practices they saw as fraudulent. An Indigenous man named Will complained in April 1724 to the Henrico County Court in Virginia that his mother was supposed to have been enslaved for thirty years and then freed. And Will, when he was born, had also been claimed as a slave. But now, at the age of twenty-three, he believed that he should be freed. The court disagreed, decreeing that he continue to serve his legal master, William Rowlett, until the age of thirty, just like his mother.[23] To settle further disputes, Virginia later tied a child's required time of service to the length of servitude of the mother. If the mother had to serve thirty-one years, the child would have to serve that length as well.[24]

There was no formal law in New England that enacted *partus sequitur ventrem*. But it was so deeply embedded into wider English and Atlantic enslavement practices that it required no official legalization. It was simply assumed. On May 12, 1733, a man named John Kent passed away in Suffolk County, Massachusetts. Listed among his estate belongings were "1 Indian girl & child," valued at eighty pounds. The brevity of this record raises many questions, few of which can be answered. The relatively high monetary value assigned as well as the records listing them on the same line seems to indicate that this enslaved Indigenous girl had already given birth and her child had also been claimed as a slave. Tellingly, the probate records did not challenge this claim in the least.[25]

YET ANOTHER OPPORTUNISTIC STRATEGY for keeping Natives enslaved was to question their Indianness through changing racial terminology. This approach, too, had a deeper colonial history that became more common in the eighteenth century. Charles McLamore experienced it firsthand. McLamore was a Cherokee man with some African ancestry who served as a packhorseman during a period of warfare between the Cherokee and Carolina colonists in 1760. Like many mixed-race individuals, he found colonists constantly changed his racial classification based on their imprecise perceptions. In the records, he is variously described as a "mulatto" and "half-breed" and occasionally an "Indian." One witty commentator even suggested, playing with his last name, that he should be called "Mac la-Moor," emphasizing his African ancestry ("moor" had long been used as shorthand for North Africans).[26]

This documentary genocide and clerical race-shifting consistently happened in every colony and sometimes had dire consequences for Native people. Enslavers often minimized Native ancestry—usually of mixed-race individuals—and instead emphasized African "blood" to increase enslavability.[27] An enslaved man named Will self-emancipated from his enslaver, Dr. Graeme, just outside of Philadelphia in mid-January 1749. Graeme described him as a "Molattoe man" in the runaway ad he placed in the *Pennsylvania Gazette*. But in the same ad, Graeme noted that Will had "a Negroe father, and an Indian mother."[28] Will was equally as Indigenous as Black, but by branding him a "Molattoe man," Graeme ensured Will's enslavability.

Presumed owners had other ways of questioning racial authenticity, noting that their runaway slaves were of the "Indian breed" or that they claimed to be of an "Indian extraction" or were half Indian or were "mulatto" with long, straight black hair or looked like an Indian—all of which cast doubt on authentic Indigenous identities.[29] As had been happening for more than a century, presumed owners often identified Natives with a Black slave population, thereby erasing their kinship connections and tribal origins from the records. But Indigenous people knew. They asserted their identity in court cases, fled from enslavers to nearby Indigenous communities, and passed along stories about their Native American ancestors to their children.

In some cases, colonial officials explicitly imposed this racial collapsing and erasure. In 1705, the Virginia legislature moved to eliminate Native identities in mixed-race individuals by stipulating that the child of an Indian and an African or the child, grandchild, or great-grandchild of an African would be "taken to be a mulatto."[30] Similarly, North Carolina magistrates and merchants enacted laws to control who counted as an Indian. In 1715, the Carolina House of Commons proposed legislation that functionally eliminated the category of "mustee"—a term often used for an individual of Native American and African descent. Instead of preserving this mixed racial reality, the proposed act erased Indigenous identity that they deemed to be not "pure," ordering that "all and every such slave who is not entirely Indian, shall be accounted and deemed as negro."[31]

These acts and actions had far-ranging legal implications that solely benefited planters and enslavers. Africans and African-descended peoples—including "mulattos"—were generally presumed to be more legally enslavable than were Native Americans. In later years, the general assumption of some slave colonies was that "negros" and "mulattos" were enslaved unless they could specifically prove their freedom. By erasing Indian parentage, colonists could ensure the absolute enslavability of Indigenous people caught in bondage and protect against any uncertainties regarding their status.[32] But this racial erasure had significant and long-term effects on Indigenous people: by undercutting Native claims to Indigenous identity, colonial authorities also undermined Native claims to land.

Colonists who shifted the race of enslaved people were also motivated by financial considerations. In most colonies, enslaved Africans and their descendants were valued more highly than enslaved Native Americans, in part because Africans were seen as hardier, more disease averse, and stronger workers. Even at the peak of the Indian slave trade in the Carolinas, for example, enslaved Africans generally sold for more than twice the price of an enslaved Native, whether man or woman.[33] Indigenous people were valued for other reasons and more highly in certain contexts, but probate records and deeds of sale consistently demonstrate higher valuation for "negroes" and "mulattos." Therefore, by erasing or minimizing Indigenous lineage, enslavers could increase their total net worth and command more on the market for the sale of enslaved men and women.[34]

TIMES OF WARFARE AFFORDED AN even more public and forthright opportunism for Indigenous enslavement and slave raiding. Between 1720 and 1765, the American colonies participated in a series of imperial wars involving Britain, Spain, and France. English colonies in North America once again incentivized enlistment for white Americans by promising financial rewards, or bounties, for capturing Native Americans or killing and scalping them. Notably, these bounties were an explicit attempt to get private citizens—not just soldiers—to grab a gun, take to the woods, and hunt down an Indian, whether to kill and scalp or to take to Boston or Richmond or Philadelphia as a captive destined for sale into slavery. Offering large bounties for Indigenous captives and scalps became so commonplace that Edward Cornwallis, the governor and commander in chief of Acadia in Canada, called it the "custom of America" in 1750.[35]

During Dummer's War (1722–1725), named after the Massachusetts governor William Dummer, the Massachusetts and New Hampshire legislatures passed laws that promised a large sum of money for capturing or killing an "enemy" Indian. New Hampshire offered one hundred pounds—a stunning two year's wages for a decently paid worker—for an Indian prisoner or an Indian scalp taken during the war. Massachusetts offered one hundred pounds per scalp and fifty pounds per captive. In both colonies, the law allowed those who captured Native Americans to have the added benefit of the use of the captives or the profit from their sale in addition to the reward money.[36]

With such an enticing bounty at stake, an enterprising New Hampshire resident Captain John Lovewell sprang into action. He organized a company of dozens of volunteers (up to eighty at one point) to range the woods in search of Native Americans. On three separate occasions between late 1724 and March 1725, they marched north into Abenaki territory in New Hampshire and Maine and tracked down Natives to capture and kill. Boston newspapers approvingly reported their exploits in detail.[37] Their first raid into Abenaki territory was lethally successful. On January 5, 1725, Lovewell and his men paraded into Boston with one scalp and a fifteen-year-old captive Native boy, taken approximately forty-four miles north of Lake Winnipesaukee in New Hampshire. For their efforts, the General Assembly granted them the advertised £150 to be split among the group.[38]

This cash windfall immediately inspired other citizens–turned–Indian hunters to roam the woods of New Hampshire, similarly looking for Abenakis. Lovewell rounded up more recruits and on their third expedition killed some Natives—perhaps "enemies," perhaps not. They also stole ten guns, twenty sets of snowshoes, and a pile of beaver pelts, all of which was theirs to keep and split.[39] Lovewell, ever the performer, returned to Boston in March 1725 and again sauntered through the streets with ten Indian scalps worth £1,000 in bounty money on full triumphant display. Lovewell himself wore a grotesque wig fashioned from the scalps of Abenakis he had murdered.[40] His violence and greed were eventually answered by Chief Paugus and the Pequawket band of Abenaki in Maine, who raided regional British settlements in response to the attacks. Lovewell and eleven other English soldiers were killed just outside of what is now Fryeburg, Maine, in a battle with the Pequawket.

In his death, Lovewell was memorialized in American literature by the likes of Nathaniel Hawthorne, Henry Wadsworth Longfellow, and Henry David Thoreau as a forerunner of nineteenth-century frontiersmen to be admired. Today in Fryeberg, Maine, a simple wooden fence encloses a small space at the edge of a pond renamed after Lovewell. A large metal marker crafted in 1904 and attached to a boulder commemorates Lovewell and his soldiers. There is no mention of his Indian slave raiding or lucrative scalp taking. Instead, Lovewell is portrayed as a fallen hero: "The Indians were repulsed and their chief killed." Recent residents of Fryeburg have considered how to interpret the space that might include an "Indigenous people's perspective."[41] Not surprisingly, there is no marker or memorial for Chief Paugus.

It is perhaps unexpected, however, that bounties for Native captives and scalps remained an enduring part of American colonial warfare, becoming ever more profitable. During King George's War (part of the War of the Austrian Succession) in New England in the 1740s, Massachusetts magistrates offered an astonishing £250 in 1747 for Indian

LOVEWELL'S MONUMENT,
FRYEBURG, MAINE, 2022.

captives, with the money to be divided between the various members of the company or scouting party.[42] The same was true during the French and Indian War (1754–1760), which was part of the global Seven Years' War fought from 1756 to 1763. Virtually every colony offered bounties for Indian scalps and slaves during that war, with incredible sums of up to £320 per Indian captive offered by Massachusetts in 1756.[43]

Such fantastically rewarding bounties emboldened colonists to plumb new depths in their mistreatment of Native people. Samuel Taylor and Ebenezer Crawfoot dug up a previously interred Indian corpse near Stockbridge, Massachusetts, cut off the head, and brought it to local authorities in 1754, hoping to cash in on the bounty. Disinterring the corpse was madness enough. The two men then had to rinse and scrub the severed head to make it presentable to local authorities. The freshly cleaned Native head didn't pass muster, however, and instead of a reward, Taylor and Crawfoot were fined and sentenced to a humiliating public whipping: thirty lashes for Taylor and twenty for Crawfoot.[44]

The bounties for scalps and captives were especially motivating during wars that targeted Native American nations. During the Anglo-Cherokee War of 1759, fought on the western borders of Virginia and the Carolinas, North Carolina governor Arthur Dobbs suggested to South Carolina governor William Lyttelton that soldiers should abduct

"BY HIS HONOUR
SPENCER PHIPS,
ESQ; LIEUTENANT-
GOVERNOUR AND
COMMANDER IN
CHIEF, IN AND OVER
HIS MAJESTY'S
PROVINCE OF THE
MASSACHUSETTS BAY
IN NEW-ENGLAND:
A PROCLAMATION,"
1755.

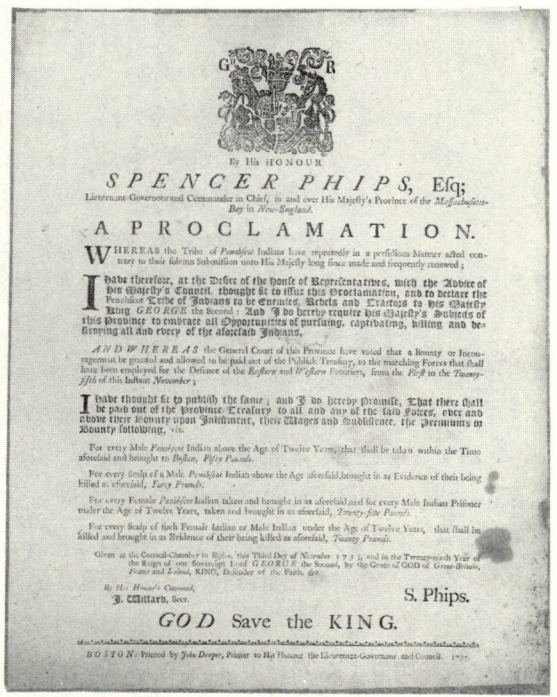

Cherokee "Wives & Children and sell them in the Islands for Slaves."[45] Both governors promptly offered the taking of Cherokee slaves as an incentive for colonial participation in the war. The Assembly of North Carolina passed a law in 1760 allowing soldiers who captured enemy Cherokees and other Natives to keep them as slaves. The language was strong: "That each of the said Indians who shall be taken a Captive . . . is hereby declared to be a Slave, and the Absolute Right and Property of who shall be the Captor of such Indian."[46] South Carolina followed suit.[47]

The same was true during an Indigenous war of resistance that broke out on the western frontier of colonial settlement in 1763. With the removal of the French after the end of the Seven Years' War that same year, Indigenous nations along the Ohio River Valley chafed at their interactions with British commanders who were less adept at diplomacy than the French had been. An Odawa warrior named Pontiac organized a massive Indian resistance to colonization, based on visions and instructions from a deity called the Master of Life. American colonists watched with horror as Pontiac and his men took fort after fort in what is now Ohio.[48]

To help regain control of the region, some colonies offered large sums of money for everyday men and women to take up arms against Indigenous people who were thought to be connected to the uprising. In 1764, Pennsylvania offered 150 Spanish dollars for prisoners or the scalps of adult Native men and lesser amounts for children and women. The purpose of the bounty, as the Pennsylvania Council minutes noted, was to "prosecute the Indian War with more vigour, and to spirit up the People to pursue and harrass the Savages in their own Country."[49] By turning everyday Americans against Pontiac and the Shawnee, colonial militias and the British army violently squelched his war of resistance within a year. Contemporaries and later historians called it Pontiac's Rebellion, but Native peoples on the edge of colonial settlement saw it differently. Indians were fighting to protect themselves, their communities, and their territories against slave-raiding colonists.[50]

These bounty proclamations—printed in newspapers across the colonies—were incredibly damaging for Native nations and individuals. They were official, governmental statements that shaped the public discourse and action regarding Indigenous peoples. They both reaffirmed and added to a widespread hatred of Indians that spiked in the 1750s and 1760s in North American English colonies. These pronouncements were reinforced by newspaper cartoons, stories of Indian attacks, narratives of enslavement at the hands of Natives, and generally degrading language about Indians (what one scholar has called an "anti-Indian sublime").[51] Taken as a whole, these various bounty policies across colonies were invitations to exterminate particular Indian populations through enslavement and murder, which, as always, had a direct negative impact on tribes' abilities to sustain their communities and retain their land base.

THE RISE OF COLONIAL NEWSPAPERS played a surprisingly pernicious but overlooked role in perpetuating Indigenous slavery throughout the eighteenth century. Although often assumed to be relatively benign, the newspaper industry actively demonized Indigenous people and normalized their existence as targets of raid, capture, and enslavement. This was true even during times of peace. From the moment of their publication in the early eighteenth century, American colonial newspapers contained advertisements that offered a monetary reward—not entirely unlike a bounty—for the return of an escaped enslaved person to their owner.[52]

The first long-lasting newspaper appeared in Boston on April 24, 1704, with the printing of the *Boston News-Letter*. The advertisement of enslaved Native people immediately followed. Captain John Aldin posted the first advertisement for an Indigenous person in the June 19, 1704, edition of the paper. An "Indian Man" named Harry had escaped from Aldin's Boston household. Harry was, according to Aldin, nineteen years old and was wearing a black hat, brown pants, and a jacket when he left.[53]

These newspaper advertisements—with hundreds of copies distributed in major cities up and down the East Coast—leveraged the power of ordinary citizens against these self-emancipated individuals. Self-emancipating was brave, but the advent of newspapers made it exponentially more dangerous and opened newly free Indigenous men, women, and children to capture, reenslavement, and punishment. As part of an emerging surveillance regime, most "runaway" slave advertisements called for readers—ordinary men and women—to "take up and secure" self-emancipated Black or Indigenous people. In this way, newspapers deputized their readers to vigilantly police the mobility of people of color in the course of everyday life. Newspaper advertisements warned that self-emancipated people might "pretend to be free"—thereby licensing white people everywhere to question the legitimacy of Indigenous and Black claims to freedom.[54]

Furthermore, the advertisements encouraged citizens to act directly, to detain suspected runaways and return them to the owner (or their agent) to receive the promised reward. No constables, no sheriffs—just white citizens acting on their own.[55] For Native Americans (and other people of color), this created an early and constant state of fear, even for free Natives operating in white society, who could be accused of being runaways, apprehended, and forced into (or back into) slavery.

These newspaper advertisements also confirmed that colonists continued to hold Native Americans as slaves and servants in surprisingly large numbers across the British colonies throughout the eighteenth

RUN away from Caleb Ferris, of East-Chester, in the Province of New-York, some Time before last Christmas; a lusty likely Man Slave, named Joe, aged about 25 Years: He is of a yellow Complexion, being mixed Indian and Negroe, much of an Indian Countenance, speaks altogether English, he is well set every Way, about five Feet ten Inches high, understands all Sorts of Plantation-Work, and is an excellent Hand to make Stone-Wall; he was born of a Slave, and brought up by Martha Clark, of W. Chester, and since her Death he is often running about, he sometimes pretends to be free, and it is supposed that a vile Fellow has given him a Pass; He is a great Fidler, and when he went away he took his Fiddle and a Bundle of Cloaths. Whoever will take up said Servant and secure him, so that his Master may get him again, shall have THREE POUNDS Reward, and all reasonable Charges paid by me,
 Jan. 24   CALEB FERRIS.
 All Persons are hereby forewarned from harbouring or carrying off said Servant.

"Runaway" ad for Joe, who "pretends to be free,"
New-York Gazette, January 24, 1757.

century. A close investigation of newspaper advertisements contained in just one database (America's Historical Newspapers) reveals 1,066 newspaper advertisements between 1704 and 1804 for Indigenous people, whether advertised for sale or as having run away. After accounting for repeated advertisements for the same people, 416 unique Native individuals appear in these records. This is only a sample of the total runaway slave ads as it is far from a tabulation of all newspapers in this period. And these individuals represent only a small percentage of the actual number of enslaved Indigenous people in the American colonies since these ads only mention those who ran away or were for sale.

In this sample, it is possible to identify clear trends. Notably, the number of self-emancipated Indigenous people listed as runaways is steady year by year, without a large drop-off at any point in the eighteenth century. Equally important, the average ages of people advertised trend *downward* over the years, which suggests that the Indigenous enslaved and unfree population was not simply static and aging. Rather, it was being constantly replenished through the ongoing importation of enslaved Natives from the Caribbean, the capture and enslavement of Natives in times of war (encouraged by bounties), and the enslavement of new generations (through *partus*); legal mechanisms like debt and punishment; and other random instances of kidnapping and capture.[56]

With every enslaved Indigenous person who was advertised for sale or as having run away, the legality and everydayness of the enslavement of Native Americans was more firmly planted in the psyche of colonial Americans. With newspaper proclamations offering extraordinary sums of money for their capture or scalps, these publications subtly vilified all Native people and turned the public against them in ways that cemented negative views of Natives and created lasting harm.

THESE FORMS OF EVERYDAY OPPORTUNISM meant that American colonists continued to view Natives as potential servants and slaves, with or without legal approval. Native individuals found themselves abducted and trafficked across colony lines and sold away from their communities. Such was the case with an Indian woman named Phebe and her child. In 1765, Phebe was taken on board the ship of Captain William Woolcut of New Haven, Connecticut; shipped to South River, South Carolina; and sold as a slave to Edmund Whithall for £100. In time, Phebe complained to Craven County officials and claimed that she had been born free. Phebe and her child were placed in the care of John Howard and John Tomlinson, who posted a £500 bond that Phebe and her child would "not be sold nor shipt out of the country till such time as the matter be determined" by the magistrates.[57]

For Natives living in or near English colonies, the threat of enslavement formed an ever-present fear of simply existing on their own land. In 1722, tributary Indians in Virginia were prohibited from traveling outside a specific region bounded by the Potomac River to the north and the Blue Ridge Mountains to the west. The penalty was dire: "death, or be transported to the West-Indies, there to be sold as slaves."[58] Throughout Indian country, the message was the same. In the 1730s, Mohican and River Indians of western Massachusetts told the British missionaries that "[the English] Religion is not a good one, and that [the English] design only to make Slaves of them."[59] In 1749, the Nanticoke asked the Haudenosaunee to help them move from Maryland to Pennsylvania because, in Maryland, colonists "make slaves of them and sell their Children for Money."[60]

NO MATTER WHERE THEY CAME FROM or how they were enslaved, Natives were largely subjected to the same kinds of dislocation and violence that characterized African slavery in British colonies. They were legally considered to be property and movables, on par with donkeys, pigs, steers, and horses—living things necessary for plantation work.[61] The quotidian humiliation and relentless violence often went unrecorded, save some rare glimpses from surviving documents. Such was the case with a twenty-three-year-old "Spanish Indian" named Caesar enslaved in Rehoboth, Massachusetts. He self-emancipated in August 1730 still wearing an iron collar made of pothooks that had been attached by his enslaver.[62] Cruel devices like this were common, even if only rarely noted.

As always, enslaved Natives endured the same punishments inflicted on the wider Black enslaved population. In September 1753, an "Indian slave" named Sam was accused of breaking into the house of William Fraser of Chesterfield County, Virginia. The county court ordered him to stand at the pillory for one hour with both ears nailed to the wood. Afterward, one ear was to be cut loose, and then he was still assigned to receive the dreaded and painful thirty-nine lashes—seemingly with the other ear still nailed to the wood.[63]

Exasperated with the brutality of their owners and the injustice of bondage, enslaved Natives and Africans found ways to resist, sometimes violently. Even as colonists enslaved Indigenous people, some were nervous about having them in their households, perhaps because they could more easily seek revenge or even murder their enslavers and return to their communities.[64] An enslaved Native woman in the house of New England minister Peter Thacher dropped his infant on the floor—perhaps an intentional carelessness meant as retaliation to the Thacher household. In response, Thacher was merciless, beating her "severely."[65] In 1711, an enslaved Native woman named Maria seemingly murdered her own young child by "letting it fall" into the outhouse. While hard to fully comprehend from our modern perspective, Maria's actions not only robbed her enslaver, William Hutchinson, of the child's future labor but also spared the child from a lifetime of enslavement.[66]

Farther south, during a cold winter night in January 1708, an enslaved Indian named Sam and an enslaved African woman snuck from bedroom to bedroom in their enslaver's house in Newton, Long Island, systematically killing William Hallett Jr., his pregnant wife, and their five children. The murders sent shockwaves through the region.[67] New York authorities were determined to make an example of the two avengers. After hastily assembling a special commission and holding a trial, they burned the enslaved African woman alive at the stake—a horrific and inhumane spectacle. "Indian Sam" was placed in a gibbet, or an elevated metal cage, and forced to painfully straddle a sharpened metal beam. Deprived of food and water, Sam slowly went insane as he starved and bled to death.[68] So deeply did the murders spook colonial officials that they passed a law in October of the same year titled "An Act for preventing the Conspiracy of Slaves," which specifically mentioned the murders of the Hallett family.[69] Such acts of dire retribution were rare, but they reflect deep grievances felt by enslaved people.

Enslaved Indigenous people were also part of the first "successful" enslaved uprising in the mainland American colonies. At midnight on April 6, 1712, approximately thirty enslaved men—including at least two "Spanish Indian" slaves named Husea and John—met in the back alleys of New York City and systematically turned on their enslavers. Within a few short minutes, nine New Yorkers lay dead, with another five or six bleeding and wounded. Shaken to the core, residents quickly rounded up suspected culprits. Twenty-seven were found guilty. Authorities executed twenty-one of them, either by public burning, hanging (including from chains in the town), or being tortured to death—in this case, broken on the wheel, a medieval torture that slowly pulled apart the victim.[70] Husea and John were reprieved by the governor.[71]

More common was the fate of an enslaved Native named Salvadore, who was accused of organizing an uprising in James City, Virginia, in 1710. He and a coconspirator named Scipio were condemned to be executed and beheaded and to have their corpses cut into pieces and placed on display to discourage other enslaved people from doing the same.[72]

IN 1764, the lieutenant governor of Massachusetts, Thomas Hutchinson, published the first volume of his monumental history of the Massachusetts Bay Colony. A royally appointed magistrate, Hutchinson had family lines that traced back to the first generation of puritan invaders of the Dawnland. Written as an attempt at serious and objective history, Hutchinson was unflinching when it came to treatment of

Native Americans.[73] "We," he stated, inserting himself and his family in this indictment, "are too apt to consider the Indians as a race of beings by nature inferior to us, and born to servitude."[74]

The long history of colonialism had proven Hutchinson correct. Most Americans viewed Indigenous people as inferiors—worthy to be servants and slaves and unworthy to be on their lands. In the half century prior to the American Revolution, this was manifested in the everyday opportunism of colonists, who enslaved and commandeered the labor of Indigenous people. It was then intensified through print media in ways that normalized and rapidly multiplied this racialized thinking.

Even as enslavement and servitude continued, something profound started to shift, at least in the realm of the law, making freedom appear a bit more attainable for enslaved Native American men and women in the British Empire.

Nine

A KING'S PROCLAMATION

RATHER UNEXPECTEDLY, JUST AS SLAVERY WAS REACHING ITS apex in the British Empire, a chorus of voices erupted to challenge its morality. Although there were a few high-profile court cases in England and the American colonies regarding African and Indigenous people, most of the antislavery activism called attention to the horrors of the transatlantic slave trade—which had always been notoriously inhumane. The increasingly overburdened ships driven by profit-seeking merchants were so full of noxious odors and diseases that thirteen out of every one hundred African captives died en route to the Americas.[1] In some instances, the mortality rate was closer to 50 percent. Over the course of the eighteenth century, that trade would bring nearly 2 million enslaved people to the British Caribbean, with approximately 350,000 of them shipped to North America.[2] Antislavery activists believed that although abolition was perhaps too radical, if they could at least regulate or, better yet, shut down the transatlantic slave trade, millions of African lives could be spared from slavery or premature death.

Consequently, when an Indigenous delegation arrived in London in 1775 describing a Native American slave trade that was "similar to that of negroes from the Coast of Africa," Crown officials were understandably flummoxed.[3] The delegation that had made the arduous five-thousand-mile journey from the Mosquito Shore consisted of three Miskitu leaders—Prince George, Richard, and John—along with an English merchant named Jeremiah Terry. The delegation minced no words, accusing British traders of going rogue in their slave raiding, targeting the Miskitu themselves and other Native allies. To prove their point, Terry, a longtime resident of the Mosquito Shore, produced two Indigenous captives he had recently purchased. Their message was simple: the Indigenous slave trade in the British Caribbean should be abolished.

The news came as an affront to most London officials and members of Parliament, who likely assumed that the Mosquito Shore Indigenous slave trade had ended and who were only vaguely aware of ongoing Indigenous slavery in their colonies. The delegation's descriptions of an African-like Indigenous slave trade eventually reached Lord Dartmouth and individuals in the administration of King George III. Against all odds, the Miskitu delegation eventually got what it came for: a royal proclamation that, for the first time in the history of the English empire, expressly forbade the active enslavement of Native Americans.

The king's proclamation seemed bold, at least on the surface. It stated that the Indigenous slave trade from the Mosquito Shore was "in violation of the Common Feelings and Rights of Humanity, and also of the obvious Principles of Sound Policy," in addition to violating the "Personal Rights of the Said Native Indians."[4] But it only focused on the Indigenous slave trade and not Native enslavement itself. Still, it was a major victory for the Miskitu headmen, and its language mirrored wider anti–slave trade rhetoric in the 1770s.

The usual story of the early British and American antislavery movement is that it emerged in the 1770s among religious protesters in the centers of power in England and in particular American colonies and that it focused exclusively on Black slavery and the African slave trade. But Native slavery was part of this debate and was vocalized by a wider array of people who also recognized this practice as part of the problem. Famous abolitionists in London like Granville Sharp wrote about African *and* Indian slavery together; the first person that the earliest antislavery society in the American colonies, the Pennsylvania Abolition Society, worked to free was Indigenous; and in 1775, the king of England released a proclamation against the Indigenous slave trade in the Caribbean. In the instance of the Miskitu headmen, the protests came from Indigenous people themselves on the farthest fringes of the British Atlantic Empire.

Of course, to have Miskitu headmen complain about the slave trade was ironic, given their nation's own participation in the nearly 150-year-long Native slave trade conducted out of their lands. But when it was their own people who were enslaved—and by the English no less—the Miskitu chiefs had to do something. Prince George and his fellow leaders laid most of the blame on John Hodgson, the corrupt and self-serving superintendent of the Mosquito Shore, whom George called "the foremost trafficker of Indian slaves."[5]

Miskitu complicity in the trade also gestures toward the wider moral complexity of these early British and American antislavery movements—more of a series of stutter steps in the direction of antislavery rather than outright abolition. Despite wide and conflicting views and motivations, the seeds of doubt regarding slavery would later grow to become a flourishing movement of abolitionism in ways that once again highlighted Native American slavery. For the moment, the king had only theoretically outlawed the Indigenous *slave trade*. Indigenous *slavery* itself proved much harder to curb, in part because it was so deeply enmeshed in the very fabric of American and British Caribbean society.

THE NEW ANTISLAVERY MOVEMENT built on a long legacy of continuous, even if at times marginal, protests against slavery. Enslaved people themselves often led the objections, whether through petitions and direct actions (like running away, waging war, or murdering their enslavers) or joining with some Anglo-Europeans who also questioned slavery and the slave trade.

One of the earliest organizational stances against slavery in colonial America came from the Society of Friends, or Quakers, an English religious movement founded in the 1640s. As early as 1688, Quakers in Germantown, Pennsylvania, questioned the buying and selling of other humans based on the Golden Rule (from the New Testament). Although no formal action was taken, the annual meeting of the same group in 1696 recommended to its members "not to encourage the bringing in of any more negroes." This suggestion was repeated periodically by Quaker Meetings throughout the eighteenth century, even as some members continued their slaveholding.[6] In 1721, Quaker leaders specifically instructed members to "not buy or sell Indian slaves."[7] The Boston judge Samuel Sewall's famous critique of slavery in 1701, *The Selling of Joseph*, although focused more on African slavery, caused transitory ripples throughout the English slaveholding world. As he noted years later in his diary, his concern was for both Indian and African enslavement.[8]

Indigenous enslavement often raised more questions about its legality and morality, perhaps because it revealed the hypocrisy of European Christian aspirations for Christianizing Natives versus their violent actions. Early voices like the Spanish reformer Las Casas had left an important imprint on Indigenous slavery's regulation, an outcome shaped by Native protests. Throughout much of the English colonial period, however, when officials expressed reservations regarding Indigenous slavery, these concerns were often less about the immorality of slavery per se than about public safety, or the disruption of wider diplomatic relations with Natives, or individual monetary gains. In 1713, for example, the Board of Trade and Plantations wrote to the governor and deputies of Carolina complaining that the Indian slave trade was only padding the pockets of individuals and was not benefiting the empire as a whole.[9]

Over the course of the eighteenth century, there were signs that judges and juries, especially in the Northeast, were increasingly willing to consider the testimony of Indigenous people who claimed to be wrongfully enslaved. On the night of October 3, 1743, an enslaved Indigenous woman named Ann emancipated herself by running away from Stephen Gardner's household in Norwich, Connecticut, along with three of her children. Ann had been trafficked to Newport, Rhode Island, in 1714 or 1715, likely as part of the trade of Native captives out of the Carolinas. After their escape, Ann and her three children were soon tracked down and taken to court, where the judge gave Ann the floor to explain herself. After calling witnesses, in December 1743 the court determined she was a free-born Mohawk as she claimed and that she and her children had been wrongfully enslaved.[10]

Native American manumissions (official releases from slavery) such as Ann's were not necessarily a sign of antislavery, but their increasing frequency throughout the eighteenth century hints at a slowly shifting legal landscape. In Virginia, one attorney estimated that "hundreds of the descendants of Indians" had received their freedom by 1770.[11] This was also true in the Caribbean colonies. An elderly Indigenous woman named Elizabeth Johns was set free in Kingston, Jamaica, on July 6,

1761. Her four mixed-race children—Catherine Johns, Jane Todd, Thomas Vere, and John Vere—were set free at the same time.[12] Jamaican officials, seeing so many Africans, "mulattoes," and Natives receiving their freedom, began to require parishes (towns) to set up registries of free persons to record who was being emancipated.

Indigenous people also shifted their tactics for greater effectiveness. Although for well over a century Native Americans could secure their freedom by proving that they or their ancestor had been wrongfully enslaved, by the 1770s, a few Natives petitioned for their freedom based on the simple fact that they were Indians and therefore should never have been enslaved. Surprisingly, American courts were sometimes open to this line of reasoning. Still, no colony issued a general proclamation of Indian emancipation.

PROTESTS AGAINST SLAVERY—and especially the inhumanity of the African slave trade—became stronger in the 1770s. Influential antislavery books and pamphlets by Quaker Anthony Benezet in Philadelphia in 1772 and the minister John Wesley in 1774 revealed the unjust origins of African captivity and the horrors of the slave trade.[13] Later tactics included appalling images of enslaved Africans jammed together side by side on multiple levels in the putrid bellies of slave ships. Stories of enslaved people rotting in their own excrement, or being too malnourished to stand, or giving birth while in chains swayed a wider British public who had little direct experience with slavery.[14]

And yet concern for Indigenous slavery was present in these debates, too. In 1769, the antislavery activist Granville Sharp published *A Representation of the Injustice and Dangerous Tendency of Tolerating Slavery* in London.[15] Sharp was a self-made scholar who began his career as an antislavery advocate by taking up the case of an enslaved man named Jonathan Strong who had been trafficked to London and badly beaten by his master.[16] In his stridently antislavery tract, Sharp repeatedly mentioned both Africans and Native Americans when discussing antislavery justice and the reach of the law. In particular, he cited and argued against colonial laws that stated no "Negro, Mulatto or Indian slaves" could be set free except under certain strict conditions. Additionally, Sharp argued that "a Negro or Indian Slave" who was born outside of the United Kingdom and arrived in England would

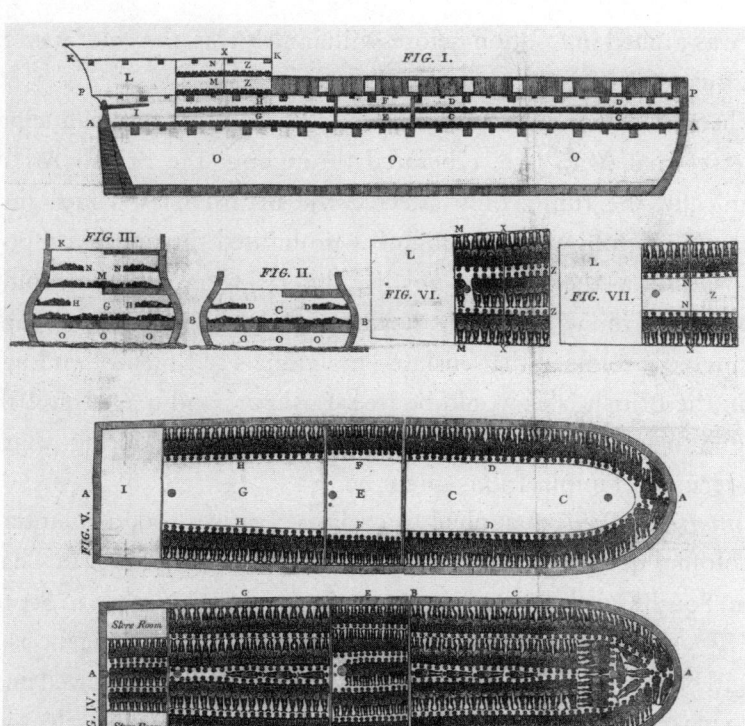

DIAGRAM OF A SLAVE SHIP, 1821.

be considered a subject and therefore protected by the Habeas Corpus Act of 1679, which required English courts to prevent unlawful imprisonment.[17]

In 1772, Sharp got the chance to turn his pamphlet into precedent when he helped prosecute the case *Somerset v. Stewart*. The controversy had started when an enslaved Black man named James Somerset had been taken by his legal master, Charles Stewart, from Virginia to London in 1768. Although there is no record of Somerset's reaction to London, one thing he surely noticed was the lack of an oppressive slavery regime like the one he had experienced in Virginia. London contained twenty thousand Black people in various forms of servitude and freedom, according to contemporary estimates, but nothing Somerset saw compared to the horrors of plantation slavery. In 1771, he ran away, refusing to serve as Stewart's slave. Stewart had him tracked down, arrested, and thrown in prison. Sharp was involved with the case as it was argued in London before William Murray, the chief justice of the Court of King's Bench in the spring of 1772.[18]

When the ruling was handed down in favor of the self-emancipated Somerset that May, it reverberated throughout the British Atlantic. Technically, the ruling only affected the British Isles. Chief Justice Murray's carefully worded judgment prohibited the forcible deportation of slaves as there was no positive slavery law in England. Colonial enslavers and the wider public, however, along with some newspapers, interpreted it to mean that enslaved individuals setting foot on English soil in the British Isles would be free. Enslavers and magistrates from Virginia to Jamaica must have reacted anxiously, wondering what the long-term legal implications might be.[19]

Somerset v. Stewart applied to enslaved Natives too, as planters in the colonies quickly comprehended. One unnamed enslaver in Charles Town, South Carolina, tried to sell his two enslaved Natives in September 1773, shortly after the *Somerset* case. The enslaved Indigenous boy and girl both spoke English well and, even at a young age, showed potential to make able house servants. "The only Reason" for the sale, the ad read, was "because there are no *Slaves* allowed by LAW in *England*."[20] If this owner took his enslaved Native Americans to England, he risked losing them, so he sold them in South Carolina instead.

For some antislavery activists like Sharp, the question of African slavery was inseparable from Indigenous slavery. Even as *Somerset v. Stewart* was gaining national and international attention, Sharp wrote to Frederick North, the Second Earl of Guilford, again affirming the linked issues of Indigenous and African slavery, noting that "there is no instance whatever which requires more *immediate redress* than the present miserable and *deplorable slavery of* Negroes and Indians, as well as white English servants, in our colonies."[21]

Sharp's interest was especially piqued by the aggressive manner in which British colonists in St. Vincent in the Caribbean's Lesser Antilles had invaded the lands of the so-called Black Caribs, who were a numerous mixed-race tribe that had withstood several centuries of colonization. By the 1770s, colonists had the effrontery to petition the British government to forcibly remove this large Indigenous community from the island entirely (which did in fact happen in the 1790s). Sharp blamed the violent standoff on the longtime English practice of enslaving Natives in the Caribbean basin, "a practice which has rendered the Caribbee Indians irreconcileable to us ever since."[22]

In the years following the *Somerset* decision, true to his name, Sharp became known as an incisive legal defender of enslaved Indian and African men and women. He sheltered and took on the cases of multiple enslaved individuals, including at least one unnamed Native American in England.[23]

THE QUESTION OF INDIGENOUS SLAVERY was an increasingly pressing issue in the American colonies as well. American enslavers closely guarded their rights to enslave and saw potential Crown impositions on slaveholding as just one of many increasing grievances during the early 1770s.

In 1772—the same year Somerset received his freedom in London— controversy over Indigenous slavery erupted in the Virginia court system. That year, twelve Native Americans filed a complaint against a Virginia planter named John Hardaway for "trespass, assault, and battery." At the heart of the case was an assertion of freedom based on Indigenous lineage. Robin, Hannah, Daniel, Cuffie, Isham, Moses, Peter, Judy, Autry, Silvia, Davy, and Ned all claimed to be descended from a Native woman named Judith Coleman (also called Judy or Indian Judith in the records). As heard by the court, their story had started more than a half century earlier.[24]

Sometime between 1708 and 1715, a Virginian planter named Coleman from Dinwiddie County had traveled to South Carolina to purchase slaves for his planned move to a bigger estate. Among the enslaved individuals purchased was Judith, a young Native woman who was one of the tens of thousands of Natives enslaved in the Southeast between 1680 and 1720. Colonists who knew Judith understood her mother to be Apalachee, from Spanish Florida, likely one of the thousands of Apalachees taken prisoner and enslaved by English soldiers and their Native allies during raids on Spanish mission towns. Coleman purchased Judith, who was approximately thirteen or fourteen years old at the time, for twenty-five pounds and returned home to Virginia.[25]

Over the years, as happened so frequently for other enslaved Indians and Africans, Judith bore children who were also enslaved, as were the children of their children. The twelve Native Americans named in the resulting court case, *Robin v. Hardaway*, were descended from Judith, spanning two generations.[26] At least two of them were her daughters.

The case immediately became a lightning rod, drawing regional, colonywide, and international attention. Robin and the rest of the plaintiffs were represented by Thomson Mason, the younger brother of the famous Virginia statesman George Mason. The young Virginia luminary Thomas Jefferson sat in on the case as well and provided legal input.[27] In prosecuting the case, Mason waded deep into the realm of international law as well as the history of Virginia Indian slavery laws.

In particular, Mason ventured a distinctive interpretation of important Virginia laws that dealt with Native Americans in 1691 and 1705. In his view, the 1691 law legalized free trade with Natives, which Mason interpreted as implying that Natives should be free, not enslaved (only free nations could be in a free-trade arrangement with the English). The 1705 law prohibited Indian slavery, according to Mason, with the major exception of those who had been brought by sea. Mason mistakenly reasoned that since only Africans arrived by boat, the act was intended to end all future incidences of Indigenous slavery.[28]

Mason's interpretations of these laws contradicted the original intent of the Virginia legislature and the ways that colonists at that time interpreted them. He also was ignoring—or was not even aware of—the history of Indigenous trafficking from the Caribbean, as well as the decades of ongoing post-1705 enslavement of Native Americans in Virginia. His legal opinions were shaped by the nascent antislavery—including Indigenous antislavery—sentiment, but his reinterpretation of the past surely would have shocked Virginia planters who had held Indigenous slaves throughout the colony from 1705 to the 1770s and beyond, with full support of the law.[29]

But Mason went a step further. He argued that Native Americans, as historically free political entities in the Americas, were naturally free and could not be enslaved without positive slave law. In this way, he powerfully invoked the natural-rights language that the American revolutionaries would employ just a few years later when writing the Declaration of Independence. Conversely, and without any evidence or logic, Mason argued that the natural condition for Africans was enslavement, so no positive slave law was needed for them. Such a seemingly arbitrary distinction was influential and held weight in the 1770s, marking a growing and important distinction between African and Indigenous enslavability in the colonies. In the end, the court awarded freedom to the twelve Indigenous plaintiffs and compensated them a measly one shilling each for their troubles, plus their court costs.[30]

The rationales given in 1772 *Robin v. Hardaway* revealed the changing attitudes toward Natives over the course of the eighteenth century. Every European power had always viewed Native Americans as justifiable objects of enslavement under certain conditions, even though in each empire and colonial context and in almost every generation officials had to revisit questions regarding the legitimacy of such enslavement. But this 1772 court case suggested there was no situation in which Native enslavement was defensible. Like *Somerset v. Stewart* earlier that year, *Robin v. Hardaway* signaled a new, more positive legal era for enslaved Indian men and women, though it boded poorly for African claims to freedom. Even if it did not lead to a general abolition of Native slavery, the case set a precedent that reverberated in the courts for decades to come.

News about the *Robin v. Hardaway* ruling likely spread quickly among the networks of enslaved Native men and women in the region. Almost immediately, additional enslaved Natives demanded that they too should be freed. Jim, for one, jumped at the opportunity. He was enslaved on the plantation of Paul Michaux in Cumberland, Virginia, due west of Richmond, was twenty-seven years old, and was short and stocky. Jim had unmistakably long black hair, likely reflecting his Native heritage since his father, Cheshire, was Indigenous and seemingly free, while his mother was probably African. His owner had designated him a "Mulatto," placing him in a category of firmer legal enslavement while also increasing his value. Jim knew his Native parentage, however, and on hearing about the *Robin v. Hardaway* outcome, decided to make his case directly to the courts. On October 10, 1772, he slipped off into the Virginia backcountry and traveled the one hundred miles to Williamsburg, then the capital of the colony. Jim's aspirations were no secret. Michaux strongly suspected he was "gone to the General Court [to] seek for his Freedom," as was reportedly confirmed by others who saw him en route.[31]

David, too, was similarly stirred by the *Robin v. Hardaway* decision. He was enslaved on the plantation of William Cuszens in Dinwiddie,

Virginia, south of Richmond. As with Jim, the twenty-two-year-old
David was described as a "mulatto" but claimed Indian parentage. On
April 1, 1773, David took off for Williamsburg to sue for his freedom at
the General Court. Three months later, Cuszens had heard of no outcome and took out three separate newspaper advertisements in July to
track down David.[32] Other enslaved Indians must have also sought their
freedom in this way, as suggested by the increase in runaway Native
slave ads and freedom suits in Virginia following 1772.[33]

ANTISLAVERY SENTIMENTS WERE harder to fully translate into
immediate changes on the Mosquito Shore. The Miskitu chiefs with
Indigenous slaves in tow had dramatically escalated the concern in
London in 1775 regarding Indian slavery just as Granville Sharp and
other antislavery activists were doing the same. The king had taken
action, forcing the resignation of the Mosquito Shore superintendent
Hodgson and issuing a 1775 royal proclamation prohibiting Native
slave trading.

It fell to a magistrate named James Lawrie to transform the king's
prohibitions into policy. When Lawrie took over as the British superintendent of the Mosquito Shore in 1776, he found a territory that
appeared virtually lawless. The basic structures of empire and
colonization—governmental agents, legal organization, courts, officials to record wills—were all absent, due in part to the intense isolation of English settlements up and down the five hundred miles of
coastline.[34]

Like his predecessors, Lawrie found an active, ongoing Indigenous
slave trade still firmly in place, even after the king's proclamation. It
was still largely conducted by the Miskitu against their own longtime
enemies as well as Spanish-allied Natives in the interior. In a complaint
to Jamaica governor Basil Keith, Lawrie described a process that had
been in place for more than a hundred years: English merchants regularly arrived on the Mosquito Shore, eagerly expecting to purchase
Indian slaves along with other raw trade goods, and the Miskitu Indians were content to comply. They constantly raided for Indigenous
captives in the interior—both for their own purposes and to meet the
demands of British traders.[35]

Under pressure from Keith, and perhaps motivated by his own

reasons to impose greater control, Lawrie drafted and then pushed through the Mosquito Shore Council an act forbidding the ongoing Indian slave trade in the region. The August 22, 1776, Mosquito Shore act used nearly the exact wording of the 1741 Jamaica act and was similarly framed in terms of protecting the larger "British Interest" in the region.[36] The law declared any enslaved Natives who were bought or sold after October 22, 1776, would be deemed free. But like its 1741 predecessor, the act was not intended to change the position of Indians already enslaved nor did it address the question of the status of children born to enslaved Natives.[37]

As part of his attempts to regulate Native enslavement, Lawrie also tabulated a registry of Indigenous slaves on the Mosquito Shore. It is an exquisite and rare piece of documentation of Native American slaveholding within British colonies. With careful penmanship on lined paper, the registry meticulously lists the name, age, sex, and owners of 256 enslaved Natives, with a few comments regarding places of origin.[38] But these were only the enslaved Indigenous people that planters felt obligated to reveal. Many dozens of colonists and merchants up and down the five hundred miles of the Mosquito Shore and dozens more logwood cutters in the interior likely felt no compulsion to report their enslaved Natives.

Despite being only a partial record, this registry provides unusually

"RETURN OF INDIANS REGISTERED ON THE
RECORDS OF THE MOSQUITO SHORE," 1777.

rich insight into the social mechanisms of Indigenous slavery as well as its geographical spread. Colonists held enslaved Natives from at least ten different regional Native nations in Central America, largely from the interior of the vast area that now covers Mexico to Panama. Only a small percentage of the Natives listed have tribal identifications recorded, which means that the actual tribal and geographical spread was likely even greater. Notably absent from the registry are Miskitus, although complaints from Native leaders suggests that colonists occasionally held them as slaves as well.[39]

Additionally, the registry reveals that some families labored together under enslavement. In most cases, Indigenous children born into slavery were claimed by their legal owners, as was often the case with African slavery in keeping with *partus sequitur ventrem*. Lorena, Lucinda, Phillis, and Dorinda, four of the twenty-three Indigenous people claimed by William Anderson, are noted in the registry as "Children born in the family" and retained as slaves.[40] The parents' information is not provided. The passive, anonymizing word "born" leaves open the possibility of repeated rape by Anderson of his enslaved Indigenous women that resulted in offspring. It is also possible that the children were born within a Native or Native-African relationship on his plantation.

Other family units are clearly indicated—sometimes, it would seem, due to a more careful owner who made sure such relationships were entered into the records. Nine different families of enslaved Natives labored on the estate of Joseph Wood—a full thirty-six of his thirty-eight Indigenous slaves belonged to such family units. Seven of the families consisted only of a mother and her children; two had both the father and mother listed.[41] The registry also reveals that women and girls outnumbered men and boys by a ratio of two to one (87 males, or 33.2 percent, and 175 females, or 68.8 percent), and almost all of the younger enslaved Natives were women, likely desired for their childbearing capacity. Two-Spirit (Indigenous nonbinary) individuals, if they were present, were not recognized as such.

The presence of this 1777 Mosquito Shore registry in all of its detail is a glaring reminder of the absence of other accounts recording the long-term Indian slave trade out of the region over the previous one hundred years. This same dearth of recordkeeping regarding Native slavery can be found in almost every English colony, making a true accounting of the scale of Indigenous enslavement especially challenging to reconstruct.

As LAWRIE WAS TABULATING family enslavement on the Mosquito Shore, an enslaved Indigenous family in Pennsylvania caught the attention of antislavery activists in Philadelphia. In April 1775, a group of Philadelphia Quakers and antislavery sympathizers learned about the experiences of a mixed-race Native woman named Dinah Nevil and her children, who claimed to be wrongfully enslaved. Nevil and her four children had been serving in the household of a wealthy, well-connected family in Flemington, New Jersey. In the winter months of 1772–1773, Nevil and her children were sold by Nathaniel Lowry of New Jersey to a Virginia merchant named Benjamin Bannerman. When Bannerman's ship arrived in Philadelphia, Nevil used that opportunity to protest that she and her children—Bontury, Jane, and two others whose names were not recorded—had been wrongfully enslaved and should be free.[42]

Her powerful complaints attracted immediate attention. The mayor of the city took Nevil and her children into custody and sent them to Philadelphia's workhouse, where enslaved people who did not have obvious owners were often placed. Some Philadelphia Quakers learned about Nevil's situation and tried to secure her freedom in court. In early 1775, however, a Pennsylvania jury ruled that Nevil and her children should remain enslaved. This ruling was in line with the long practice of Native enslavement in the colony, but it went against a small but growing sentiment of antislavery in Philadelphia.[43]

In response to the denial of freedom for Nevil and her children, in 1775, these Philadelphia Quakers formed the Society for the Relief of Free Negroes Unlawfully Held in Bondage (later called the Pennsylvania Abolition Society). The society's name reveals the ways in which people of color were collapsed into the category of "negro"—a point especially demonstrated by the fact that in organizing around the aid for Nevil, they recognized that they were helping an Indigenous person.[44] The society filed a complaint with the Grand Jury that Nevil's enslavement had been a violation of the 1725 Pennsylvania law prohibiting the enslavement of Native Americans.

Members of the new society also visited Nevil and found her and her children in abysmal circumstances. Two of Nevil's children had died in the workhouse, and she and her remaining children were emaciated from malnutrition. Society members arranged to have them released into the custody of Thomas Harmon, who cared for Nevil and her eight-year-old daughter and ten-year-old son and incorporated them into his family. Their case lingered on, and Harmon eventually bought Nevil's and her family's freedom from Bannerman, though in 1786 he requested reimbursement from the society for his care of Nevil and her children.[45]

The attempt to free Nevil through the courts illustrated the antislavery impulse of Philadelphia Quakers, but the court's unwillingness to free the family showed the limits of such activism. It was a sharp contrast with the conclusions of the Virginia courts in the *Robin* case only a few years earlier.

So important was Dinah Nevil's case that the talented American painter Jeremiah Paul committed it to canvas in 1795. In his rendering, Nevil kneels on the floor before her Quaker sponsors. Her visage is portrayed in a way that forefronts her Indigeneity. Her light skin is contrasted with the darker skin of two Africans in the immediate

MANUMISSION OF DINAH NEVILL, BY JEREMIAH PAUL, 1795.

AM *I NOT A MAN AND A BROTHER?* ANTISLAVERY SEAL, WOODCUT ON WOVE PAPER, 1837.

background, who are also slightly exoticized as possible North African Muslims.[46] Notably, Paul depicts her as kneeling in the same posture as a kneeling African man in the seal used by the Committee for the Abolition of the Slave Trade, founded in 1787 by Quakers in Philadelphia. In this seal, which was famously used and widely circulated by abolitionists in the nineteenth century, the enslaved African man, chained hands held out, asks, "Am I not a man and a brother?"[47] Nevil is the exact parallel and opposite to this famous image: Indigenous, a woman, and forgotten.

Even if slightly romanticized in its tone, Paul saw clearly the importance of this moment: an enslaved Indigenous woman was the focus of the very first antislavery society in America. But Nevil was freed because antislavery activists purchased her freedom, not because Pennsylvania courts believed it was wrong to enslave Native Americans. The pockets of the new abolition society were not deep enough to purchase the freedom of the many thousands who remained enslaved.

IF PHILADELPHIA COURTS WERE unmoved by Indigenous slavery, so too were most residents on the Mosquito Shore. British officials in Jamaica, perhaps under more pressure after the king's proclamation, viewed the September 1776 Mosquito Shore Indigenous slave trade law as too timid. The Jamaica Assembly passed its own vastly more aggressive law against the Indian slave trade on December 22, 1776, which also revised the original 1741 Jamaica law. This amended law, unlike the 1776 Mosquito Shore version, declared that any Native Americans who had been shipped to Jamaica after December 28, 1741, should be considered free people, along with their descendants. It levied a hefty penalty of £500 for buying and selling Indian slaves in Jamaica. Stunningly, the penalty the law imposed for trafficking Indigenous slaves in and out of Jamaica was death.[48]

The incredible stridency of this 1776 law is a testament to the antislavery sentiment circulating in English colonies from London to Boston, from Philadelphia to the Mosquito Shore. Yet this 1776 Jamaican act seems to have been largely ignored. Although the law opened up a window for legal action for Natives, there was no mechanism for actual emancipation: no census, no investigation into numbers and ownership, no plans to reimburse owners of Indians who had to set them free. There is neither evidence of a generalized Indian slave emancipation nor of anyone being convicted and executed for Indian slave trading.

Perplexingly, the Miskitu were equally to blame for the perpetuation of Indigenous slavery and the slave trade. British officials could pass laws, but on the periphery of empire, large Indigenous nations like the Miskitu were still in charge. As Superintendent James Lawrie admitted to Governor Basil Keith in January 1777, "It is impossible for me totally to prevent the Mosquito Indians from invading and making Slaves of sundry Neighbouring Tribes of Indians."[49] Although there is not much commentary from Miskitu leaders on the 1776 anti–Indian slavery law, one of them told Lawrie directly that he reserved for himself the right to continue to exact "Justice" on the Spanish and their Indian allies by raiding them as necessary, which almost always involved taking captives.[50]

The Miskitu felt that British laws targeted the Indigenous slave trade without addressing aspects that affected them. They were most concerned by the nefarious and unequal trading practices by English merchants who lured Miskitus into functional slavery through overextension of credit. This had been, in essence, the thrust of the Miskitu chiefs' complaints in London in 1775. British colonies and merchants extended generous amounts of credit to Miskitus, but when they could not repay their debts, demanded that either the debtor or one of their children or a regional proxy (a captured Native from another tribe) be given over as a servant or slave for compensation. Superintendent Lawrie's solution focused only on Miskitu debtors instead of English merchants. In November 1776, he ordered that the Miskitu chief Colvil Briton convince his people to no longer accept the offers of British credit.[51]

The request surely put Briton in a bind, as his rather tortured yet dutiful proclamation in late 1776 suggests. On the one hand, he wanted to protect his people from additional enslavement, and running up debts with English merchants was a quick path to servitude. But Briton also must have known that to cut off credit was essentially to isolate the Miskitu from the trade goods on which they had come to rely. It might also undermine trade relations. So Briton instead reframed the problem around his own interpretation and protected his community. In his statement, he prohibited British colonists from extending credit to the Miskitu, set out terms to protect his men who were serving on British vessels, and asserted control of the turtle-shell trade.

While Briton tried to prohibit the debt slavery of his own people, he still embraced Native slavery in general. His proclamation ended with an offer of a "Young able Indian Slave" as a reward to "any White Man" for catching Indians selling valuable turtle shells to English merchants.[52] Indian slave raiding and trading was so integral to the Mosquito Shore that the Miskitu chiefs had a hard time envisioning a society completely free from it.

These Miskitu headmen were excellent diplomats, however, just like the Haudenosaunee in New York, the Powhatan in Virginia, and the Narragansett in Rhode Island. At the same time they were maintaining good relationships with the British in 1777, they were also negotiating with the Spanish, who proposed a treaty that would halt Miskitu raiding on Spanish towns and Spanish-allied Indians. The Miskitu refused most of the terms and suggested new ones, asserting the primacy of their allegiance with the British. With their own amendments in place, the Miskitu also insisted on exchanging "Canes"—perhaps sugar-cane stalks or carved treaty sticks—as a way of ratifying the agreement with the Spanish instead of signing the written document.[53] The Miskitu chiefs had no intention of complying with either Spanish or British dictates that went against their own interests.

What British colonial officials failed to see—or chose to ignore—is that by retaining the Miskitu as allies, they were enabling ongoing slave raiding and captive taking. The Miskitu chiefs were consistently transparent about this. In a large meeting between Lawrie, other British officials, and two of the main Miskitu chiefs in 1780, they affirmed their loyalty to the English but preserved their right to conduct traditional methods of warfare: "distress[ing]" their enemies, burning their towns, and carrying off their slaves and cattle. Their whole motivation was "hopes of Plunder."[54] Essentially, this was what the Miskitu had been doing throughout the interior since before the arrival of Europeans, something the 150 years of English alliance and trade partnership helped enable. Ending Native slave trading sounded clear-cut and ethical in London, Boston, and even Kingston perhaps, but it was virtually impossible to enforce on the edges of empire.

THE STRUGGLE OVER THE EXISTENCE of Native slavery and the Indigenous slave trade in England, the American colonies, and the British Caribbean was an essential part of broader antislavery activism. In the 1770s, British officials seemed determined to end the British Indian slave trade in the Caribbean, and other antislavery activists hoped to end the slave trade, both Native and African, everywhere. And yet slavery was so deeply entrenched that antislavery remained a radical position, with most northern colonies still upholding the basic legality of keeping Native Americans and Africans in bondage.

The Miskitu were not alone in their vacillating views and actions surrounding slavery and the slave trade. Others too had complicated associations. On the way home from London in 1775, on a trade ship called the *Morning Star* bound first for Jamaica, the Miskitu leaders met another such conflicted soul named Olaudah Equiano. A recently freed African man, Equiano would later become one of the most famous critics of slavery, publishing a riveting and influential narrative of his life in 1798 that would catapult him to international fame and galvanize the antislavery movement. But in 1775, he was just trying to improve his condition as a free Black man, even if that meant joining in a plantation venture on the Mosquito Shore with enslaved men and women to work it.

Equiano, as a devout Christian convert, made the Miskitu chiefs his evangelistic project during the voyage, paying special attention to Prince George. One wonders if they talked about slavery, whether about Miskitu enslaving practices or Equiano's experiences while enslaved or his planned slave-based plantation. In Jamaica, Equiano assisted in the purchasing of a group of enslaved Africans before continuing on to the Mosquito Shore—still in the company of George and the Miskitu headmen. The Miskitus disembarked at Dupeupy on February 18. Equiano continued with his plantation project at Cape Gracias a Dios on the Mosquito Shore but never again saw the Miskitu headmen who were similarly against and for slavery, depending on the situation.[55]

Even American colonies were not unified on these questions surrounding slavery, and they were not necessarily in lockstep with antislavery activists in England or in Philadelphia. As King George III's American colonies turned from rascally to rebellious, these differences and tensions intensified in ways that both harmed and benefited Indigenous people.

Ten

REVOLUTIONARY
RAGE CONTRE-INDIENNE

WHATEVER GAINS WERE MADE REGARDING ANTISLAVERY IN THE
early 1770s, the period of the Revolutionary War created additional
hardships and opportunities for many Native nations. The long buildup
of tensions over taxes and imperial imposition between the belliger-
ent American colonies and the British Crown boiled over into outright
military conflict starting in 1775. But these events and the subsequent
war that resulted in a successful American bid for independence over-
shadow equally important developments to the interior.

If we shift our gaze from soggy crates of tea in Boston Harbor to
the verdant hills of Cherokee homelands, we can see that the American
Revolution was actually two wars in one. The first one—more familiar
to most—was the war of American independence against the British
between 1776 and 1783. The second was a prolonged conflict between
Native nations and Americans on the periphery of western settlement.
Waged from Georgia to New York, this war started earlier and lasted
longer. Eager for land and furious that many Indigenous nations sided
with the British, Americans attacked the Cherokee, Shawnee, Delaware, and other nations with a disturbing ferocity, putting Indigenous
people on the defensive to protect their lands. From Native perspectives, the American Revolution was merely part of what we might call
the longer War of Indigenous Sovereignty, one phase in a series of wars
to defend their homelands between 1763 and 1795.

Throughout this period, anti-Indian sentiment was palpable all
along the western frontier of American settlement. Twenty days after
the signing of the Declaration of Independence in July 1776, William
Henry Drayton, a leading South Carolina royalist-turned-patriot, hast-

ily scrawled a letter to Francis Salvador, who was in the backcountry leading a company of 1,151 American militia volunteers against the Cherokee Nation. Salvador was a prominent Jewish member of the provincial congress who was later called the southern Paul Revere for riding through the expansive low-country piedmont on horseback, alerting Americans of the arrival of the British fleet in Charles Town harbor in late June 1776.[1] In response to Cherokee counterraids on new American settlements at Wachovia, Watauga, and Holston (in present-day North Carolina and Tennessee) in May, June, and July, Drayton urged action.

In his July 24, 1776, letter to Salvador, Drayton called for slave raiding and a devastating war of total destruction against the Cherokee: to "cut up every Indian corn-field, and burn every Indian town." Notably, he directed "that every Indian taken shall be the slave and property of the taker; that the nation be extirpated, and the lands become the property of the public."[2] Salvador died a week later while carrying out Drayton's commands, but not before viciously cutting a swath of destruction through Cherokee territory, destroying every village in his path, burning corn and other food supplies, and taking captives.[3]

Salvador and his troops were only one of scores of American militias who invaded Cherokee, Shawnee, and Delaware lands during the era of the American Revolution, leaving a similar path of devastation and severed family connections in their wake. Scholars of the American Revolution have noted the Americans' *rage militaire*, a French phrase meaning "passion for arms." It refers to the groundswell of enthusiasm for war with Britain in the early years of the war.[4] But Americans also exhibited what I am calling a *rage contre-indienne*, or a "passion against Indians." Nearly all of the Indigenous nations on the western edge of colonial settlement sided with the British Crown, which they viewed as more likely to restrain the American colonists' encroachment on Native lands.

Americans, in turn, demonized Natives, seeing them as an impediment to claiming desirable lands. Most American leaders hoped that the terrorizing, murdering, and enslaving of Native nations would push British-allied Indigenous people westward, whether "beyond the mountains," as Drayton wished, or "beyond the Mississippi," as Thomas Jefferson dreamed. Such sentiments were widespread: the American

general Charles Lee, for his part, planned to "crush" Indigenous people, while the North Carolina delegates to the Continental Congress
believed the United States should "extinguish the very race of them."[5]

These genocidal attitudes partially explain why Indigenous slavery
and servitude continued as a constant reality during the longer revolutionary era and its immediate aftermath, even if it goes against the conventional view of the revolution as a political contest in which Native
peoples played a minor part.

After the American Revolution, the United States debated the role
slavery should play in the new nation. Americans later rewrote the history of the era to focus solely on the conflict with the British. The *rage
contre-indienne* and the war against Native nations was an inconve-
nient aspect of the period that later Americans found less celebratory
and so conveniently left out of the telling of this history.

THE SHARPSHOOTING DANIEL BOONE—often idealized as a self-
made frontiersman—started his career in 1769 by illegally leading a
party of settlers onto Native lands in what later became Kentucky.[6] At
the end of the Seven Years' War against the French and their Native
allies in 1763, the British Crown had drawn an imaginary serpentine
boundary called the Proclamation Line of 1763 that ran north to south
from Canada to Georgia, officially prohibiting colonists from buying
and selling land or settling to the west of this border. Americans were
furious about royal limitations on westward development, and this
indignation became a major cause of the American Revolution, even
if taxation without representation continues to get more attention and
to be taught in most history texts. Revolutionary leaders no less than
George Washington were heavily invested in western land speculation
and personally motivated to be free from British rule to pursue their
own land-based financial interests.[7]

Blatantly defying the British Crown, frontiersmen like Boone, hailing from Virginia, Pennsylvania, Georgia, and the Carolinas, crossed
over the Proclamation Line and into Indian Territory to terrorize
Native towns and leaders into either moving or ceding land. Colonists
petitioned the Virginia Assembly from 1769 onward in an attempt to

THE UNITED STATES, 1776.

lay claim to Native lands.[8] Cherokee, Delaware, and Shawnee leaders at first responded to these invasions with diplomatic solutions, but by late 1773, when Boone led yet another party of would-be settlers into Kentucky, a collection of Natives from the three nations attacked Boone's group and killed six of them, including his son. American colonists sprang into action, attacking a half dozen Native settlements up and down the Ohio River Valley in early 1774.[9] The eventual mythology of

Daniel Boone as an iconic American smoothed the rough edges of the ubiquitous land grabbing and captive taking that was central to American expansion.

These backcountry skirmishes and raids over land and settler encroachment escalated in the summer of 1774 when Virginia's royal governor, John Murray (Lord Dunmore), ordered the Virginia militia to march on Shawnee towns along the Scioto River in what is now Ohio. Dunmore's instructions were clear: to "make as many Prisoners as they can of Women and Children" and to "reduce the Savages to sue for Peace."[10] Two Virginia regiments totaling 2,500 militiamen invaded Native territory, including one regiment Dunmore led himself. After several bloody showdowns on the Ohio River, the troops forced the Shawnee leader Cornstalk to relinquish any claim to the Shawnees' sizable traditional hunting grounds in Kentucky and return all white captives. Before leaving the area, Dunmore's army attacked a nearby Seneca town and took more Native prisoners.[11]

Boone and others continued to fixate on taking Native lands. In March 1775, he negotiated the purchase of a huge tract of land in what is now Kentucky and northern Tennessee. The acquisition was secured from the Cherokee on behalf of the Transylvania Company at the Treaty of Sycamore Shoals. This transaction further divided the Cherokee, however. At the treaty proceedings, among the speeches and giving of £2,000 worth of trade goods, the Cherokee chief Tsiyu Gansini, or Dragging Canoe, openly opposed the land sale. In a passionate speech, he accurately prophesied that Americans would steal and barter for Cherokee land until, left with no hunting land, the Cherokee would be forced to "seek a retreat in some far distant wilderness."[12] When Boone and others proceeded to take possession of the fertile Kentucky plains, a band of Cherokees attacked, defending their lands. Incensed, colonial militias in turn targeted any and all nearby Native settlements, spiraling the region into violence.

ALTHOUGH BRITISH ROYAL GOVERNORS and American colonists had united against Native raids in 1774, a growing divide between Britons and Americans during the first half of 1775 quickly reshaped allegiances. On April 19, American militiamen from the Massachusetts countryside mobilized against advancing British Regulars to protect the ammunition stockpiles held at Lexington and Concord—warned a few hours in advance by Paul Revere and others who rode to "spread the alarm / Through every Middlesex village and farm," as Henry Wadsworth Longfellow would famously depict eighty-five years later.[13] Two months after Revere's ride, on June 17, 1775, American colonists again clashed with the British army occupying Boston at the Battle of Bunker Hill, just north of the city in what is now Charlestown. With the thirteen colonies again convening in Philadelphia for the Second Continental Congress and the American Continental Army commissioned with the young Virginia general George Washington at its head, royal governors and Loyalists began to see all Patriot colonists as traitors and rebels.

Virginia's royal governor, Lord Dunmore, who had previously led American colonial troops against the Cherokee in 1774, had been chased out of Williamsburg by the fall of 1775 with the threat of a Patriot militia invasion. American colonists, not the Cherokee, were now his biggest problem, and he intended to unleash their own enslaved population on them. From the safety of his anchored vessel in Norfolk Harbor, Dunmore issued a proclamation on November 7, 1775, that all "*indented servants*, *Negroes*, or others" held by American Patriots were free so long as they would fight with the British against the Americans.[14] As many as twenty thousand enslaved people responded to royal offers of freedom by the war's end, fleeing from their owners by land and by sea to British ships, forts, and encampments, likely ecstatic at the prospect of freedom and the chance to punish their former enslavers.[15]

No doubt the news of Dunmore's proclamation circulated orally through networks of trade and kinship and spread quickly among the enslaved and laboring classes of the American colonies. Likely there were hundreds of Native people who similarly fled, given the large number of enslaved and indentured Indigenous and mixed-race Indigenous people in colonies. Harry, a thirty-year-old mixed-race Native man, was one of them. He was noted as a sharp dresser with a blue greatcoat and with skills as a carpenter, wheelwright (making and repairing wooden wheels), potter, and painter. Less than three weeks after Dunmore's offer of freedom, Harry ran away with three enslaved Blacks on

"LORD DUNMORE'S
PROCLAMATION," 1775.

By His Excellency the Right Honorabe JOHN Earl of DUNMORE, His
Majesty's Lieutenant and Governor General of the Colony and Dominion of
Virginia, and Vice Admiral of the same.

A PROCLAMATION.

AS I have ever entertained Hopes that an Accommodation might have
taken Place between GREAT-BRITAIN and this Colony, without being
compelled by my Duty to this most disagreeable but now absolutely necessary
Step, rendered so by a Body of armed Men unlawfully assembled, firing on His
Majesty's Tenders, and the formation of an Army, and that Army now on
their March to attack His Majesty's Troops and destroy the well disposed Subjects of this Colony. To defeat such treasonable Purposes, and that all such
Traitors, and their Abettors, may be brought to Justice, and that the Peace, and
good Order of this Colony may be again restored, which the ordinary Course
of the Civil Law is unable to effect; I have thought fit to issue this my Proclamation, hereby declaring, that until the aforesaid good Purposes can be obtained, I do in Virtue of the Power and Authority to ME given, by His Majesty, determine to execute Martial Law, and cause the same to be executed
throughout this Colony: and to the end that Peace and good Order may the
sooner be restored, I do require every Person capable of bearing Arms, to resort
to His Majesty's STANDARD, or be looked upon as Traitors to His
Majesty's Crown and Government, and thereby become liable to the Penalty
the Law inflicts upon such Offences; such as forfeiture of Life, confiscation of
Lands, &c. &c. And I do hereby further declare all indented Servants, Negroes,
or others, (appertaining to Rebels,) free that are able and willing to bear Arms,
they joining His Majesty's Troops as soon as may be, for the more speedily
reducing this Colony to a proper Sense of their Duty, to His Majesty's
Crown and Dignity. I do further order, and require, all His Majesty's Leige
Subjects, to retain their Quitrents, or any other Taxes due or that may become
due, in their own Custody, till such Time as Peace may be again restored to this
at present most unhappy Country, or demanded of them for their former salu-
tary Purposes, by Officers properly authorised to receive the same.

GIVEN under my Hand on board the Ship WILLIAM, off Norfolk,
the 7th Day of November, in the sixteenth Year of His Majesty's Reign.

DUNMORE.

(GOD save the KING.)

November 26, 1775. His owner was certain they had all run off to join "Lord Dunmore."[16] American colonists were so angered by Dunmore's actions that they mentioned these "domestic insurrections" in the long list of resentments against King George III as part of the Declaration of Independence half a year later.

Meanwhile, the cycles of frontier raiding and counterraids between the Cherokee and state militias and renegade settlers continued unabated into early 1776, with Native captives continually being taken. The General Council of Virginia ordered on June 26, 1776, that four-teen pounds and eleven shillings should be set aside for clothing to be given to Indigenous captives in Frederick County.[17] Americans in Charles Town, South Carolina, believed the Cherokee coordinated their frontier attacks with the arrival of the British navy in their city on June 28, 1776.[18] The British navy was rebuffed, and one American field commander wrote to his superiors that he hoped to likewise defeat the Indian attacks on the frontiers.[19]

ON JULY 4, 1776, American separation from Britain became official when an assortment of fifty-six wealthy, white plantation owners and merchants representing the thirteen colonies assembled in Philadelphia and signed the Declaration of Independence. Drafted by Thomas Jefferson, it famously proclaimed that "all men are created equal, that they are endowed by their Creator with certain unalienable Rights, that among these are Life, Liberty and the pursuit of Happiness."[20]

Enslaved people and free Native nations on the American frontier must have scoffed at such hypocritical platitudes when they caught wind of them, but the creation of the United States was an arresting development. From the perspective of large Native nations on the violent edge of American colonial settlement, it only intensified the stakes of a war they had already been waging for several years. Both Britons and Americans vied for the allegiance of Native nations, but Indigenous people filtered the conflict through the lens of their own communities' concerns. The British Crown seemed like a better bet than land-hungry, enslaving American colonists. As the Cherokee leader Dragging Canoe told British agent Henry Stuart in March 1776, the Cherokee "had but a small spot of ground left . . . to stand upon," and he feared that the Americans intended "to destroy [the Cherokee] from being a people."[21]

The American Revolution provided potential leverage against the Americans for the Shawnee, Delaware, Cherokee, and other Native nations along the Proclamation Line. A younger faction of the Cherokee hoped that they could reject the American settlers who continually invaded their lands and help to shape the outcome of the conflict. In July 1776, the Cherokee mounted a three-pronged attack on American settlements on and surrounding Cherokee lands, targeting encroaching towns and villages on the frontier of Virginia, North Carolina, and South Carolina in what colonists perceived to be a coordinated assault.[22]

Reports from new settlements and territories described the effectiveness of these Cherokee raids. The minister James Creswell, writing from the North Carolina outpost named Ninety-Six (which still exists today as a town), reported to William H. Drayton in South Carolina that American "plantations lie desolate, and hopeful crops are going to ruin. . . . Fences are thrown down, and many have already suf-

MILITARY COMMISSION
GRANTED TO CHIEF
OKANA-STOTÉ OF
THE CHEROKEE BY
GOVERNOR LOUIS
BILLOUART, CHEVALIER
DE KERLÉREC,
FEBRUARY 27, 1761.

fered great loss."[23] In August 1776, the same month that the US Continental Army fought British regulars on Long Island and in New York City, Dragging Canoe led a war party of six hundred men to attack outlying American settlements between Georgia and Virginia.[24] This ensured that a second major front of the Revolutionary War remained active for the Americans, in Indian country, one that would continue throughout the duration of the war.

This fresh eruption of violence poured gasoline on the fire of *rage contre-Indienne*. Americans in the South used the Native raids as a justification to pursue an all-out war against the Cherokee and other regional tribes. With the Continental Army's battles against the British taking place in the northern states, southern state militias eagerly looked westward to Indian country. Within weeks, North Carolina, South Carolina, and Virginia raised a massive army of five thousand men that roved across Cherokee country that August, burning villages, towns, and fields overflowing with vegetables and fruit waiting for harvest.[25] American militias chased Cherokees from their homes and villages, killed those they could, and took women and children as captives. Virginia's General Council was ecstatic about the success of its "Indian expedition" and spent months reimbursing merchants and traders for the costs of the war as well as the transportation of Native captives they took along the way.[26]

Americans were not just satisfied with Native land; they burned with wartime fervor for scalps and captive bounties in order to purge Natives from the region. In what had become standard wartime procedure, state leaders again incentivized military participation and rogue violence with the prospects of capturing or killing Natives for personal gain. In early November 1776, the North Carolina General Assembly offered "considerable rewards" for the scalps of Indians and allowed Native children under a certain age to be taken prisoner as slaves.[27] By 1780, Pennsylvania officials offered the incredible sum of $3,000 for the capture of each Indian prisoner or Loyalist soldier fighting with them or $2,500 for every Indian scalp.[28] These astonishing rates—many times the annual wages for average individuals—illustrate the governmental willingness to enact Charles Lee's vision of complete annihilation.[29]

Soldiers who enlisted took these incentives seriously, as American military commanders soon discovered. During one expedition in 1776, Captain William Moore was sent by General Griffith Rutherford to burn the towns of the Chickamauga, or Lower Cherokee. Moore arrived at the town of Too Cowee in western North Carolina with ninety-seven men after an all-night march, found the town mostly empty, and proceeded to burn the twenty-five houses and food stores. His troops killed and scalped several Cherokees and eventually succeeded in capturing three alive.[30]

At the first opportunity, Moore's men expected to cash in on their bounties. The scalps were the easiest to redeem, along with other items of plunder they sold. But when Moore demurred regarding the sale of Cherokee captives, his men threatened a revolt. Most of the men told Moore that if he would not allow the Cherokees to be sold as slaves "upon the spot," they would kill and scalp the Indians and claim the scalp bounty instead. Moore was forced to relent, and three Cherokees were sold for £242. All told, Moore's men walked away with more than £1,100, or nearly $3,000 at the time, to be split among them—direct profit from enslaving and killing Indians.[31]

Other military units also took captives in Cherokee country. Colonel William Christian's troops raided and looted Cherokee supplies and trade items, including cattle, horses, and "other Rich plunder." According to William Dells, a soldier on the expedition, they also took more than fifty captives—mostly Cherokees but also a few whites and Blacks (likely enslaved) who lived with the Indians.[32] Brigadier General Andrew Williamson's men took several Natives captive during an expedition in 1776, and as late as 1786 still held two Cherokee children in slavery after the war, according to Cherokee reports.[33] After a raid in 1778, the Cherokee bitterly complained that American soldiers had taken several of their relatives and sold them as slaves.[34]

Captives taken during raids were sometimes sold in Virginia and other colonies at slave markets. During the 1776 raids against the Cherokee, American soldiers captured a Cherokee woman and her daughter. They killed the mother, named Olufletoy, but took the young girl and possibly other captives with them and sold her into slavery in Virginia, where she showed up in the records as "Nancy." Subsequent bills of sale for Nancy reveal how colonists justified the holding, selling, and purchasing of enslaved Natives in places like Virginia, where courts increasingly saw Natives as free. One bill of sale called Nancy a "Negro Girl, mixture of the Indian Breed"; another claims she was brought from the East Indies—thereby morphing her Cherokee identity into an Asian one. Nancy was sold again thirty years after her initial sale into slavery. She was moved around and had children and grandchildren— all of whom were claimed as slaves by southern planters in Tennessee and other places. There is no indication she ever received her freedom, unless she lived long enough to be freed by the Civil War.[35]

Innumerable individuals scooped up Native children and refugees as servants and slaves. A colonist named James Miller of North Carolina claimed a Cherokee boy.[36] Other Americans used the chaos of war as a cover for brazen stealing of Natives. In December 1782, John Garland busted through the front door of James Manley, a free Native man who lived near New Bern, North Carolina. Garland tied up Manley and sold him as a slave to Colonel Levi Dawson for one hundred pounds. Outraged, Manley petitioned for his freedom, but the outcome is unclear.[37] Family members sometimes tried to track down enslaved loved ones, but often in vain. One Native man successfully sleuthed out the location of his sister who had been enslaved by

General Griffith Rutherford, but when he arrived, he learned she had recently died.[38]

As Americans felt the war slipping away, they turned their full fury on Native nations in Pennsylvania and New York, determined to punish them for loyalty to Britain. When the congressional commissioners traveled to Fort Pitt (now Pittsburgh) in 1778 to attempt a treaty with the Delaware, the chiefs and headmen complained that "it is the design of the [United] States . . . to extirpate the Indians and take possession of the country."[39]

None other than General George Washington confirmed Americans' intentions to extirpate and possess. The brash young Virginian had weathered the starving winter in Valley Forge, Pennsylvania, in 1777–1778, only to face a losing war on the northern frontier to British-allied Native nations. In response to several raids on American towns in 1778 in northern Pennsylvania and southern New York, Washington ordered a scorched-earth campaign against the Haudenosaunee in New York as punishment for aiding the British. In his written orders to General John Sullivan on May 31, 1779, Washington exuded desperate fury, ordering "the total destruction and devastation of their settlements, and the capture of as many prisoners of every age and sex as possible." He explained further that "it will be essential to ruin their crops now in the ground and prevent their planting more."[40]

In what was later called the Sullivan-Clinton campaign after the two generals who led the two main prongs of the attack, 4,300 Continental Army soldiers converged on the vast stretches of Haudenosaunee territory in 1779 and proceeded to burn crops and houses and destroy food supplies. Soldiers took 33 Onondaga men prisoner in the first of 16 or so violent assaults on Haudenosaunee towns in eastern and central New York between April 21 and October 6, 1779. Word spread quickly, and Haudenosaunee families fled the region. American soldiers shifted to outright extermination, as troops simply murdered the approximately 500 remaining Natives who had not escaped.[41]

Most Americans have forgotten Washington's betrayal of Indian country, but Indigenous people have not. To this day, his nickname among the Haudenosaunee is "Town Destroyer."[42]

Colonists perpetrated countless other acts of frontier violence. In

March 1782, Pennsylvania militias ranged across the Ohio River Valley, seeking to punish Indigenous people they blamed for ongoing raids on American settlements. Coming up empty, some soldiers under the command of Lieutenant Colonel David Williamson instead turned their fury on a pacifist Moravian mission village at Gnadenhutten, ninety miles west of Pittsburgh. Despite finding no evidence of Moravian participation in raids, the bloodthirsty soldiers lined up the Natives and took turns systematically murdering them, one by one.[43]

By the time the slaughter stopped, ninety Natives—twenty-nine men, twenty-seven women, and thirty-four children—lay dead, their bodies mutilated.[44] Outraged Wyandotte, Shawnee, and Delaware men avenged the murder of their kin by attacking local American towns. They also sought militiamen, whom they captured and burned at the stake as punishment. The pain and betrayal lingered for years, mentioned frequently by Native leaders in later treaty negotiations.[45]

THE BRITISH, TOO, SOMETIMES ENSLAVED Native Americans during the war, as Oliver Fry Sr. and Oliver Fry Jr. experienced. Early in the conflict, this Indigenous father and son joined the many American privateers who were tasked with harassing British shipping lines. In the late 1770s, the two men were serving on the *Saratoga* out of New London, Connecticut, when it was captured by a British ship.[46] As was often the case, the people of color on the ship were claimed as slaves as part of the privateering bounty, and the Frys were taken to Jamaica and sold.[47] In Jamaica, the father was purchased by one plantation owner, while Oliver Fry Jr. was obtained by another planter named Walter Ogilby, who added him to his large, enslaved labor force.

The Frys, however, knew their enslavement was wrong. Oliver Fry Sr. resisted by self-emancipating, disappearing into the silence of history. Perhaps he found a home in the mountains among the maroon communities or made his way out of Jamaica and even back to New England. Oliver Fry Jr., however, remained unsuccessful in his attempts to secure his freedom. Finally, in 1792, long after the war's conclusion, he was able to get the attention of some sympathetic Jamaican colonists. After hearing his story, they agreed to write to the Pennsylvania Abolition Society in Philadelphia to solicit help.[48] The Abolition Society, in turn, wrote to the Providence Society for Promoting the Abolition of Slavery (in Rhode

Island) in January 1793 for aid.[49] There, Moses Brown, a Quaker convert and former partner of the slave-trading Brown family, was able to confirm Fry Jr.'s story and found that his mother, Mary Fry, was a free Native living in Providence.[50]

Brown assembled the necessary legal depositions and documents to prove Fry Jr.'s freedom. A series of missteps left him stuck in Jamaica, for reports in May 1796 confirmed that he was still laboring as a slave in that colony.[51] Unfortunately, we don't know how Fry Jr.'s saga ended. Nevertheless, his case suggests another way that the American Revolution imposed enslavement on Native Americans, even those who weren't fighting Americans on the frontier. Enslaved Indians could still be trafficked across international borders, as they had been since 1492. The difference was that by the 1790s, the combination of legal precedents and abolition groups ensured enslaved Native Americans more legal support in their attempts to secure their freedom.

AMERICAN POLICIES TOWARD Indigenous peoples during the Revolutionary era were deeply contradictory. Americans attacked and took captive individuals from Native nations on the westward edge of American settlement. But they sometimes offered freedom in exchange for military service to enslaved Native individuals in areas already occupied by the United States. One of the most prominent examples of this was the 1st Rhode Island Regiment. The Rhode Island Assembly in 1778 offered freedom for every "able-bodied negro, mulatto, or Indian man slave" who would fight the British, with financial compensation of up to £120 for their owners—a Rhode Island version of Dunmore's proclamation. A total of 225 enslaved men enlisted as a result, 85 of whom were clearly identified as Native American.[52] Even more of these volunteers were likely mixed-race Native men listed by Rhode Island officials as "mulatto." They served in high-profile skirmishes, as well as the Battle of Yorktown in 1781.[53]

After the war, most of the Natives who had served in the 1st Rhode Island Regiment received their freedom papers and tried to integrate into whatever community of color they could find. In some cases, this meant the Narragansett reservation in Charlestown, Rhode Island. Others, like Daniel Perry, started new lives. After his discharge from the regiment on December 25, 1783, with his freedom secured through military service, Perry married a free Black woman named Ruth and settled in South Kingstown, Rhode Island.[54]

Some Natives self-emancipated from their enslavers during the war and enlisted in local militias as newly free persons. This was the case for a mixed-raced Indigenous man named Sam, who was enslaved by William Davenport of West Point, New York, fifty miles north of New York City on the Hudson River. Sam was an active twenty-eight-year-old who was known to be smart and articulate as well as highly social and notably good at singing and dancing. His figure and visage were distinctive; he stood six feet tall, had a small scar on the side of his nose, another larger one on his stomach, and a pinhead-sized black speck on the white of one eye. In 1780, during the war, Sam vanished overnight and turned up in Danbury, Connecticut, with a new name—Job—and a new assignment in the regiment of Colonel Samuel Canfield. After the war, Davenport advertised—likely in vain—for Sam's return.[55] Dozens of similar advertisements for self-emancipated Native Americans dot the newspapers during and after the American Revolution.

"ORIGINAL WATERCOLOR OF AFRICAN-AMERICAN SOLDIER OF THE RHODE ISLAND REGIMENT, AND THREE OTHER SOLDIERS IN AMERICAN UNIFORMS; MOUNTED IN MANUSCRIPT DIARY," BY JEAN BAPTISTE ANTONINE DE VERGER, 1778, IN *JOURNAL DES FAITS LES PLUS IMPORTANTS, ARRIVÉS AUX TROUPES FRANÇAISES AUX ORDRES DE* MR. LE COMTE DE ROCHAMBEAU, CA. 1781–(1784).

FOR SOME ENSLAVED NATIVES, the Revolutionary War meant unwanted relocation out of the country. Just one example of this was the forced peregrinations of Hector—also called James Wright—who was an enslaved Indigenous man approximately four years old at the start of the American Revolution. Hector was a fourth-generation enslaved Native; his great-grandmother, Diana, belonged to an unknown Native nation in the American Southeast. Diana had been purchased as a young girl by a white colonist named Jonathan Fitz, who had integrated Diana into his household as a slave, where she served as a seamstress in Charles Town, South Carolina. When she grew up, Diana had a daughter with an African man. She named her Mary, and eventually Mary reached adulthood and had a daughter named Phillis, who later bore Hector—all of whom were also claimed as slaves.

During the American Revolution, Phillis and Hector's enslaver, James D. Yarborough, moved from Charles Town to Jamaica and later to the Mosquito Shore. Yarborough's decision to flee the United States was an option that thousands of Loyalists chose during and after the war, uprooting their households and moving to other parts of the British Empire. Collectively, these loyalists also took a total of 15,000 enslaved Africans and Indians with them.[56] Many went to Canada, but most slaveholding Loyalists scattered throughout the British Caribbean, including the Bahamas, Jamaica, British Honduras (now Belize), and the Mosquito Shore. When Yarborough left the United States, he joined 3,000 white Loyalists who went to Jamaica, along with 1,359 enslaved people they forced to accompany them. Yarborough followed 66 Loyalists who continued on to the Mosquito Shore with 143 enslaved people in tow.[57]

Yarborough surely thought he had escaped the nightmare of the American Revolution by moving to one of the most remote outposts of the British Empire, but the reverberations of the conflict rippled out globally. In the Treaty of Versailles (1783), Spain—which had sided with the United States—and Great Britain agreed that British logwood cutters in Spanish Central America should all relocate to a swatch of land between the Belize and Hondo Rivers, roughly where British Honduras was already established.[58]

American Loyalists who had just arrived on the Mosquito Shore, like

Yarborough and his household, which included Hector, were incensed to learn that they had to move yet again. Nonetheless, in 1787, Yarborough and 537 Mosquito Shore residents packed up their 1,667 Native and African slaves and livestock and set sail along the Caribbean coast of Central America to British Honduras.[59] In this way, the Indigenous slavery so prevalent on the Mosquito Shore followed the colonists to British Honduras, where it would create legal ripples and spur freedom suits in the decades to come. In 1822, Hector joined a much larger group of enslaved Indigenous people who sued for their freedom. Hector did so based on the unjust enslavement of his great-grandmother, Diana Fitz.[60]

THE AMERICAN REVOLUTION EXPOSED the massive contradiction between the lofty rhetoric of freedom and the reality of slavery, including for Indigenous people. State after state followed the Declaration of Independence in its pretensions of equality. "All men are by nature equally free and independent," thundered the Virginia Declaration of Rights in 1776, even as its residents held almost half a million Africans and Natives in slavery. Massachusetts, Pennsylvania, and every other state proclaimed the same while also keeping thousands of people enslaved.[61]

The reality was that were no free states in 1776, or even 1783, at the war's conclusion. Every state in the newly formed country retained enslaved Natives and Africans, and not a single state freed all enslaved people in the era of the Revolution. Most white American statesmen reconciled such contradictions by applying these ideals to members of the body politic—to citizens. This essentially meant only white men who owned land, which of course had previously been Native land. Consequently, the question of slavery was left unresolved at the national level. The Articles of Confederation of 1777, which functioned as the United States' first constitution, said nothing about slavery, deferring to individual states on this and many other matters.[62]

Although every state permitted slavery, a slow differentiation emerged between northern and southern ones by the 1780s. Many northern American states were already taking steps to end the slave trade and even slavery itself, including Indigenous slavery, often in response to petitions by enslaved people.[63] New Englanders were in a bind, however, since few white Americans wanted an immediate general emancipation, nor could most white Northerners imagine a society where people of color were equals.

Instead, they concocted a compromise solution. One by one, most northern states passed laws between 1780 and 1804 called "gradual emancipation" acts that prevented the enslavement of any child born after a particular date (the exact date varied by state). Over time, slavery would end by attrition as enslaved people died off, ran away, or were freed by their enslavers because no additional Natives or Africans could legally be enslaved, although Black and Native children could be indentured or forced to labor until adulthood.[64]

Most of the gradual emancipation acts were worded broadly enough to include the children of Native, Black, and mixed-race enslaved people. Pennsylvania's Act for the Gradual Emancipation of Slavery (1780), the first of such acts, covered "all persons, as well Negroes and Mulattoes as others."[65] Other states eventually followed suit: Rhode Island in 1784, Connecticut in 1784, New York in 1799, and New Jersey in 1804.[66] Vermont's republic constitution (1777; admitted as a state in 1791) prohibited slavery for those over the age of twenty-one for men and eighteen for women, although the state's slave population was not large in the 1770s. New Hampshire's Bill of Rights was silent regarding slavery, while Massachusetts interpreted the 1780 state constitution as not allowing slavery in the first place, forcing enslaved people to prosecute their owners for wrongfully enslaving them.[67]

Americans in New England and other northern states later convinced themselves in retroactive instances of self-righteousness that they had taken radical steps immediately following the American Revolution to eradicate slavery and that slavery had never been an important part of their histories.[68] But these gradual emancipation acts neither freed existing slaves nor offered them any promise of future freedom. Only the future *children* of enslaved women would be free, although even they would be forced to labor as indentured servants for a set number of years.[69] Abolitionists and cartoonists ridiculed the conservative notion of gradual emancipation and its British corollary of the "gradual abolition" of the slave trade.[70]

In response to gradual emancipation laws, some legal owners relabeled enslaved people (and their children) as indentured servants or

THE GRADUAL ABOLITION *off the Slave Trade or leaving of Sugar by Degrees.*

THE GRADUAL ABOLITION OFF THE SLAVE TRADE OR LEAVING OF SUGAR BY DEGREES, BY ISAAC CRUIKSHANK, PUBLISHED BY S. W. FORES, APRIL 15, 1792.

term-limited slaves to keep them under their control, though they continued working in functional slavery. In Pennsylvania, this conversion from lifelong slavery to term slavery was made explicit, since the 1780 gradual emancipation act required all owners to register their enslaved people and permitted designating them as slaves for life or term slaves until the age of thirty-one years old. Pennsylvanians registered 6,312 enslaved Black and Native people in response to this act, thereby making official their ongoing enslavement.[71] Abel Hodson, for example, of East Nottingham, registered two Native Americans: Jam, twenty-eight years old, who would remain a servant until the age of thirty-one (the maximum age allowed by the law), and Sarah, twenty-four years old, who was registered as a slave for life.[72] In 1788, presumably in response to demands from enslavers, the state legislature permitted owners to also claim the children of either lifelong or term slaves as slaves for up to twenty-eight years, thereby extending slavery in Pennsylvania well into the nineteenth century.[73]

And yet, even as they phased out slavery, northern states invested more heavily in the growing behemoth of slavery in southern states. Northern companies produced millions of dollars' worth of farming tools that were sent to be used on southern plantations. New England's textile mills soon used cotton from the South to make clothing for enslaved people ranging from Virginia to Louisiana. Northern states' indirect involvement in the business of slavery continued right up to the Civil War.[74]

INDIGENOUS NATIONS WEST OF official US settlement often fared the worst after the Revolution. With the British relegated to Canada, Indian nations were forced to accept one-sided and unfair treaties imposed by the US Congress. Native nations were continually subjected to encroachment and raids by state militias. Indigenous families requested the return of family members who had been stolen away by militias and soldiers, but these petitions were rarely responded to or even possible to carry out.

This desire to have loved ones returned was made more explicit in a 1785 treaty between the Cherokee and the United States, which stipulated that all captives on both sides taken during the Revolutionary War must be returned.[75] But enforcement on the American side was difficult as many Native captives had already been sold out of the region into slavery. Federal officials spent months and years trying to track down individual Indians who had been enslaved by Americans. R. Caswell wrote to North Carolina officials in December 1786 looking for a particular Cherokee Indian boy who had been captured and enslaved and then vanished. Most such requests languished, unanswerable.[76]

Indian country on the western edge of American settlement smoldered with resentment in the years following the Revolution. As Americans poured into Indian Territory, sporadic raids and conflicts soon erupted into what scholars call the Northwest Indian War (1785–1795). Most of the regional Indian nations along the Ohio River were drawn into its vortex, especially the Delaware, Shawnee, and Miami. The War of Indigenous Sovereignty continued.

Captive taking and enslavement, too, accompanied these ongoing conflicts. In early 1789, a seemingly self-appointed militia from the Washington District of western North Carolina marched into Cherokee territory and carried off "a considerable number of prisoners." The expedition was driven by captive taking since no Natives were killed and little other damage was done. The federal commissioners noted with disapproval that such activities would make it very hard to effect a permanent peace.[77]

Similar expeditions occurred, many of which went unreported. Four years later, Colonel George Doherty led 180 volunteers on horses into Cherokee territory, murdered 12 Cherokees, and took 16 women as prisoners. This specific mission to capture only Cherokee women suggests purposes both sexual and domestic. Unusually, no children were reported to have been captured.[78]

Confederated Native nations won a major victory in November 1791, with the stunning defeat of American major general Arthur St. Clair in the Battle of the Wabash, later known as St. Clair's Defeat. Despite this and other Indigenous successes, Americans finally gained the upper hand in the Battle of Fallen Timbers in 1794 and negotiated the Treaty of Greenville in 1795, which declared peace and a truce while requiring captives taken by both sides to be returned.[79] This temporarily concluded a thirty-year war waged by Native nations on the edges of European settlement—first against the British and then the Americans. The Revolutionary War had been just one phase in that larger war of Indian resistance.

Officially, at least, the United States neither permitted nor outlawed Indigenous slavery. But officials understood Indigenous slave raiding created resentment with Native nations. This is partially why, when the federal government began eyeing the enormous tract of Native land south of the Great Lakes (termed the Northwest Territory), it carefully theorized the need for good relations with Natives, including outlawing slavery and involuntary servitude. The Northwest Ordinance of 1787 laid out in fourteen sections and six articles the general principles behind this massive extension into Indian lands. It promised that the "property, rights, and liberty" of Natives would never be "invaded or disturbed."[80]

This optimism was colossally farcical. According to Article 3 of the Northwest Ordinance, official wars against Natives nullified all of these idealistic guidelines. Notably, Article 6 contained wording that would later be borrowed for several western state constitutions and the

Thirteenth Amendment in 1865: there should be "neither slavery nor involuntary servitude in the said territory, otherwise than in the punishment of crimes whereof the party shall have been duly convicted." The second part of Article 6 functioned as an early fugitive slave act, allowing owners to follow and reenslave any claimed enslaved people who escaped into the territory.[81]

The massive loopholes and exceptions for slavery in the 1787 ordinance allowed Americans who moved into the region to perpetuate both Indian and African slavery under different names, such as long-term indentures, rental contracts, and "servitude."[82] This was on full display in Detroit—the largest and most important outpost in the Northwest Territory—which remained a growing center of Native American slavery. By 1800, there were between three hundred and six hundred enslaved people in Detroit, the majority of whom were Indigenous. Even by a conservative estimate, the enslaved population in Detroit was roughly two-thirds Native and one-third African. A surprising number of these enslaved individuals were recorded in the registry of Saint Anne's Church, which in the 1790s alone showed a total of ninety-four slaves: sixty-eight Indians and twenty-six Blacks.[83] Indian and African slavery continued unabated in the Northwest Territory, and it would continue for decades.

THE AMERICAN REVOLUTION HAD SET the United States and Great Britain on two different tracks regarding slavery. In England, antislavery activists amassed heartwrenching testimony of the horrors of the Middle Passage from Africa to the Americas as part of the so-called Triangle Trade. Outright emancipation was immensely unpopular because it was the most radical position among a wide variety of options proposed by antislavery activists. Abolitionists instead poured their energies into legislation that would end the transatlantic African slave trade, with stiff opposition from companies who directly benefited from that trade.[84] Americans were divided over this same question. Northern states like Rhode Island, while slowly emancipating Natives and Africans, embraced the profits of its privateering middlemen who carted human cargo from Africa to the American South and the British Caribbean. In response to growing antislavery protests, both countries agreed on one thing: the transatlantic slave trade needed to end at some future date.

Eventually, both the United States and Great Britain did terminate the legal transatlantic slave trade, which also had implications for the long history of Indigenous slave trading. In Britain, the 1807 Act for the Abolition of the Slave Trade intended to halt the flow of human bodies out of Africa and into British colonies. But this act gestured toward Native slavery as well. The law explicitly prohibited the sale and movement of peoples "from any Island, Country, Territory, or Place whatever, in the West Indies," which potentially affected long-standing Native slave trades in the region.[85] For the moment, the transfer of African and Indian slaves *between* British colonies was still legal, although the Slave Trade Act of 1824 eventually curbed this practice too.

The United States followed suit, approving its own law intended to end the transatlantic slave trade. Passed in March 1807 as the Act Prohibiting Importation of Slaves, it went into effect on January 1, 1808. As part of a series of compromises in 1789 and as a concession to southern enslavers, this was the earliest allowable date for such a ban according to the US Constitution. Although an illegal slave trade rose as a partial replacement, this law ended the legal African slave trade into the United States.

The language of this American act was broadly inclusive, prohibiting the importation of persons "from any foreign kingdom, place, or country, any negro, mulatto, or person of color," with the intent to sell or force them into labor.[86] This capacious wording meant that Indigenous people too were no longer allowed to be trafficked from the Caribbean into the United States. The prohibition against different kinds of servitude, not just slavery, undercut the devious practices previously used to enslave Native Americans (and some Africans), particularly in the North following the gradual emancipation acts.[87]

These British and American acts might have outlawed the *slave trade*, but they did not prohibit ongoing *enslavement* of both Native Americans and Africans. Although British and American officials made no note of it, separating the slave trade from slavery itself was deeply rooted in a longer history of Native American enslavement. For one hundred years, between 1675 and 1775, English officials in various colonies had occasionally attempted to halt the various Indigenous slave trades for political reasons without intending to end Indigenous slavery. So when the American and British governments outlawed the slave trade in 1807 and 1808 while continuing to legalize slavery itself, they drew—unconsciously or not—on longer precedents rooted in Indigenous enslavement regulation in the Americas.[88]

But is it possible that ending the legal African slave trade actually increased the Caribbean Indian slave trade within British colonies and the United States? The ink was barely dry on the 1807 act when at least some merchants and magistrates in the British Caribbean considered the "Traffic in Indian Slaves" as a "substitute for the abolished African Slave trade."[89] Some—perhaps many—enterprising merchants and slave traders began eyeing the large and numerous Native nations within British colonial boundaries as possible sources for ongoing enslavement and revenue.

The same was true for Americans. Deprived of the legal Native slave trade from the Caribbean, proslavery Americans exploited potential Indigenous labor from within the bounds of the North American continent. In this way, the ending of the African slave trade very likely *increased* incidences of Native slavery in both the British Caribbean and the United States.

Added to this was an ongoing illegal slave trade that likely included Indigenous captives. Americans continued to illegally import enslaved Africans after 1808. It seems certain that the Caribbean Indigenous slave trade to North America also continued in some form, and perhaps even more so, since Native enslavement and trade was a form of slavery that had almost always operated on the legal fringes of colonial society.[90]

THE INTENSITY OF THE *rage contre-indienne* during the American Revolution set a precedent for the new United States, one that would continue as Americans steadily colonized westward for the next century. The War of Indigenous Sovereignty reverberated throughout Indian country and was far from settled with the firm strokes of the pen by distant white leaders in the Treaty of Paris and the Treaty of Versailles in 1783 or even the Treaty of Greenville in 1795.

Indigenous slavery was not outlawed in either the United States or in the extensive network of colonies still attached to the British Crown. In the decades following 1808, enslaved Indigenous people and Africans would have to continue the fight for their freedom in courtrooms. Increasingly, the courts in most states were again becoming receptive to the argument that Native Americans and their descendants should not be enslaved.

Eleven

A SURGE OF FREEDOM

IN THE DECADES FOLLOWING THE AMERICAN REVOLUTION, ENSLAVED men and women enacted their own emancipatory revolution in the courts. Scholarship has described such activity among enslaved Black populations in the first half of the nineteenth century, which led to substantial free Black communities in the American South.[1] But it has been slow to fully acknowledge that during the fifty years after the American Revolution, Native American legal protests of their enslavement grew to a crescendo in the United States and parts of the British Caribbean.[2]

Enslaved Native Americans directly advocated for their own freedom through what we might term "Indigenous legal activism."[3] Using personal and word-of-mouth networks of kinship and patronage that stretched across state lines, Indigenous people found attorneys, ministers, and philanthropists willing to navigate the law in an attempt to secure their freedom. These legal protests led to the emancipation of thousands of Indigenous people, often in larger family units—multiple generations of Indians who claimed their freedom based on having descended from a free Native maternal ancestor.

Southern enslavers despised these court cases for freedom—freedom suits, as they are often called—and were especially worried that successful Indigenous claims to liberty would weaken the rationale for all slaveholding. Proslavery lawyers articulated this forthrightly during courtroom arguments, as in the fascinating case of *Butt v. Rachel and Others* in 1813–1814. In this freedom suit, an Indigenous woman named Rachel and some of her relatives sued their enslaver, Mr. Butt of Virginia, for wrongful enslavement. They were descended from a Native woman who had been trafficked to Jamaica and then to Virginia in 1747, where all of her children and grandchildren had also been claimed as slaves. The case landed in the Virginia Supreme Court in 1813, where in the Richmond courthouse Rachel's attorney, Mr. Wirt, argued—perhaps with *Robin v. Hardaway* and other cases in mind— that "Indians are naturally entitled to freedom." In a stunning admission, the proslavery prosecutor, Mr. Wickham, agreed but then retorted, "So are negroes; but this does not prevent their being slaves." To free enslaved people whose enslavement had been recognized by laws and customs for decades was "dangerous," Wickham believed, because "it leads to the emancipation of all slaves concerning whom there is no special act of assembly."[4]

After hearing both sides, the Virginia Supreme Court ruled in favor of Rachel and her relatives in March 1814. But Wirt and Wickham both verbalized a powerful idea, one that would grow, blossom, flourish, and eventually edge out legal slavery in all corners of the western hemisphere: *Native Americans and Africans are naturally entitled to their freedom.*

This admission proved to be a potent seed of hope sown by the injustice felt among enslaved Indigenous and Black people everywhere. But

RICHMOND, *FROM THE HILL ABOVE THE WATERWORKS*, ENGRAVED BY W. J. BENNETT AFTER A PAINTING BY G. COOKE, CA. 1834.

freedom would not grow equally well in the soils of the United States and the British Caribbean. In the British Empire, antislavery activism first prompted attempts to improve the conditions and treatment of slaves, a movement generally referred to as Amelioration, before finally leading to full emancipation in 1834 (with a four-year indentureship period until 1838 in most colonies). In the United States, the spread and growth of slavery in the American South would only be halted through a vicious civil war nearly thirty years later. Freedom would come in both places but through vastly different processes.

For the moment, Indigenous claimants faced an uphill battle. In both the United States and the British Caribbean, the torrent of Native freedom suits in the late eighteenth and early nineteenth centuries prompted enslavers to increasingly emphasize the Black ancestry of multiracial Natives and downplay or ignore their Indigeneity. But Native people pushed back, strongly asserting their connections to their communities and to the lands from which they had been stolen. And courts grudgingly conceded, at least in many cases.[5] These Native freedom suits and accompanying Indigenous emancipation spurred debates about slavery and freedom for all enslaved people.

IT TOOK NERVES OF STEEL to protest one's enslavement. Indigenous plaintiffs faced the rage of their enslavers during and—for unsuccessful cases—after court cases. When an enslaved Indigenous man named Abner sued for his freedom in Virginia in the 1810s, his legal owner, Thomas Hardeway, simply murdered him.[6]

Successful freedom suits required tapping into a network of sympathetic white Americans and knowledgeable enslaved and free people of color to navigate a system that was firmly tilted in favor of enslavers. Enslaved Natives and others in bondage learned how to build such networks and glean information, keeping tabs on the changing legal contexts of their particular states and communities.

Enslaved Native Americans likely learned about local and national laws and court cases from people in the households where they lived and served, as did an enslaved African woman named Bett in Massachusetts. Bett served in the house of a judge named John Ashley in 1781 and learned through overheard conversations that the Massachusetts legislature had functionally rendered slavery illegal. She sought out Theodore Sedgwick, a young local attorney who was fortunately sympathetic. Instead of reporting her to Judge Ashley, Sedgwick took up her case and won.[7] Still, it was a tiring and humiliating process that required finding legal experts who were willing to help navigate a complex court system and line up the necessary witnesses, evidence, and depositions.[8] And after all that, some unfortunate claimants still lost their cases, although the law seemed to be increasingly on their side.

Native American freedom suits were complex, usually requiring written proof and oral testimony that traced back several generations. It almost always took at least one enslaved Native to get things started. In the case of Rhoda's family, that person was her son Hampton.[9] At first, the case may have seemed simple. In the late 1780s, Hampton sued Jonathan Hall Jr., a Connecticut resident, for selling him as a slave to Robert Martin, even though his grandmother was a free-born "Spanish Squaw" (*squaw* was a common term for an Indigenous woman). This first case was heard by a jury in the Connecticut Superior Court, which ruled in favor of Hall.

Hampton remained enslaved, but he did not give up. He next filed a suit of assault against Samuel Clark and John Martin, who as the executors of the estate of Robert Martin had also held him as a slave. This time the jury ruled in favor of Hampton, which triggered additional lawsuits by other enslaved people who were also descended from Rhoda. Some white enslavers were unconvinced about Rhoda's identity (was she really Indigenous?) and original status (was she free or enslaved?), which was the legal crux of the issue. If Rhoda was determined to be free, her descendants would be granted their freedom. But if she had been legally enslaved, her descendants would remain in slavery. These white enslavers petitioned the Connecticut General Assembly for help, and the assembly formed a committee on December 29, 1790, to investigate the matter.

A year and a half later, the committee had the full story. The family saga had started with an unnamed Indigenous woman who had either been trafficked from the Caribbean or the Carolinas into Virginia, likely in the 1710s when the Carolina and Mosquito Shore slave trades were in full swing. Somehow, she found her freedom and gave birth to a multiracial daughter named Rhoda, who was also free. At a young age,

Rhoda had been bound out as a servant to a man named Adam Hurd in 1741. Hurd, in turn, proved himself the nightmare incarnate of every Native parent when he sold the adolescent Rhoda as a slave to Mary Wheeler in 1747. Wheeler subsequently married Stephen Judd and on April 6, 1751, sold Rhoda to Joseph Hall. Rhoda remained enslaved in the household of Hall for almost thirty years, bearing four children named Lilly, Hampton, George, and Peter.

Beginning in 1779, Rhoda's family was torn apart through a series of sales, perhaps prompted by the stresses of the American Revolution. Rhoda was sold twice in quick succession before being purchased on April 5, 1784, by her husband, a free Black man named Dick Bristol. Her four children—Lilly, Hampton, George, and Peter—who were no longer under her care, were likewise repeatedly sold and resold. Lilly was sold to John Lewiss in 1779, who then sold her to John Robins Jr. in 1786; George was sold four times before also being purchased by John Robins Jr. in 1785; Peter was sold three times and landed in the household of Samuel Bellamy in 1780. And Hampton—the Indigenous man who prompted the series of court cases—remained in the household of Joseph Hall until Hall's death in early 1786. At that time, Jonathan Hall Jr., as his father's executor, sold Hampton to an attorney named Simeon Bristol. But within a month, in February 1786, Bristol sold Hampton to Robert Martin. When Martin passed away, Hampton was held by the executors of Martin's estate, which is when Hampton sued for his freedom.

The Connecticut committee had sorted through the reams of testimony and paper trails when it convened in 1792. They determined that Rhoda was indeed "born free," which meant her children—including Hampton—were free. This determination also invalidated all of the many sales and transactions involving her children between 1751 and the 1780s. The committee told each purchaser to chase down the owed money from the previous purchaser, thereby daisy-chaining the responsibility to the enslavers back to the source. In cases where a seller had since died, the committee mandated that the estate should pay. Having stipulated who owed whom and how much, the committee declared that the case be "forever quieted."

This bewildering case with its intricate family details and long listing of sales was common for such freedom suits. These realities are a window into the enormous disruption, dislocation, and humiliation that enslaved Indigenous people endured over the course of their life-times and into successive generations.

INDIGENOUS LEGAL ACTIVISM posed a threat to the legal foun-dations of Black slavery, as enslavers and judges understood. Not all courts were sympathetic to claims of freedom. In the 1790s, prosecu-tors for the state of New Jersey brought a habeas corpus case against a member of the Van Waggoner family before the state's lower courts.[10] Although the records do not say, the enslaver might have been John Van Waggoner from Patterson Township in New Jersey, since four years later he advertised for an enslaved man named Ben who had self-emancipated.[11] The state's prosecutors argued in court that Van Wag-goner's enslavement of an Indigenous woman named Rose was not legal under New Jersey laws. Rose's mother was known to be a "North Carolina squaw" and had been purchased by a colonist named Vang-eson, likely in the 1720s or 1730s. When Rose was born in the 1740s, Vangeson also claimed her as a slave, and later Rose was purchased by the Van Waggoner family.

The case made it to the New Jersey Supreme Court in April 1797 as *State v. Van Waggoner*, where the state's prosecuting attorney, Eli-sha Boudinot, argued that there were no positive slave laws in New Jersey to affirm Indian slavery. Reiterating the rhetoric of *Jenkins v. Tom* (1792), which asserted the essential freedom of Native peoples, Boudinot repeated what was becoming a strong anti-Black orthodoxy: Blacks were presumed to be enslaved unless they could prove other-wise; Indigenous people "must always be presumed free." The defense attorneys for the enslaving Van Waggoner family were more honest historians, however, and in their rebuttal, they laid out before the court multiple examples from 1713 to 1769 of slavery-related laws in New Jersey that included Native Americans in the common triad of "negro, Indian, or mulatto slave." With this litany of historical documents, the defense attorneys asserted, "The slavery of Indians, therefore, by our laws, stands precisely upon the same footing, and is to be governed by the same rules as that of Africans."[12]

With the fate of African and Indigenous slavery as a whole seem-ingly at stake, the New Jersey Supreme Court justices deliberated care-fully. C. J. Kinsey, in delivering the opinion of the court against Rose, warned that abruptly undoing previous state laws regarding slavery would dangerously destabilize the entire institution of slavery. It would be a blatant "violation of the rights of property," he reasoned, "to establish a contrary doctrine at the present day, as it would in the case of Africans." Given the past laws in New Jersey, as well as the alarming precedent Indian freedom could set for enslaved Africans, the Supreme Court justices denied the state's demand that Rose be set free.[13]

Part of the challenge in many of these cases was that the litigants were multiracial. Most Indigenous freedom seekers claimed and proved their Indigenous ancestry, but that lineage was constantly called into question by enslavers and defense attorneys. This was consistent with the emerging racialized language of the nineteenth century, when there was a slow shift toward using "coloured" to describe almost any non-white person. Coupled with "mulatto," these terms continued the previous English colonial practice of obscuring and blurring racial identities, particularly Native American ones. Virginia made this official in 1792 by affirming an earlier colonial law stipulating that any individual (including an Indian) who had even just one "negro" grandparent should be "deemed a mulatto."[14]

Faced with mixed-race claimants, the courts increasingly affirmed slavery as based on visible racial identification. This unfairly privileged very light-skinned people, who were categorized as "white" and therefore presumed to be illegally enslaved. When an enslaved Native woman named Jackey Wright contested the right of Holden Hudgins to enslave her and her children, the case made it all the way to the Virginia Supreme Court. In 1806, the court found the Wrights to be free and affirmed a legal precedent that had surfaced elsewhere: slaves who looked white should be considered naturally free. The inverse was also true: slaves who looked darker or Black should be considered slaves unless they could prove otherwise. This created a legal environment in which the claims to freedom of lighter-skinned Natives and their descendants were taken seriously, while the claims of mixed-race Indigenous and Black people were usually disbelieved or contested.[15]

Indigenous litigants also pressed courts to acknowledge their claims of Native heritage by accepting the oral testimony of relatives and others who knew the family. This insistence pushed the courts to create new legal precedents, such as the admissibility of hearsay evidence when it came to determining racial lineage. Enslavers tried to keep mixed-race Indigenous people in bondage by claiming that their ancestors were Black and therefore had been legally enslaved. This happened on the Eastern Shore of Maryland to an Indian man named Walkup, who sued his enslaver, Henry Pratt Jr., for his freedom in 1818.[16] Like so many other freedom suits during the previous century, Walkup's case rested on his claim that his grandmother Violet was a free Indian woman. As the court learned, Violet had been enslaved as a child in the 1730s by Philip Feddeman. Walkup produced witnesses that testified that some of Violet's owners knew she was supposed to be free and that her children were free. In fact, one owner declined to beat Violet for misdeeds as she would have done to enslaved Blacks because she knew Violet and her children were free.

When Walkup's case first came before the Maryland court, the jury decided against him, deeming his grandmother and mother to be Black, not Indigenous. But Walkup appealed, and in 1820, the Maryland Appeals Court heard his case. After sorting through the evidence, it overturned the county court decision, calling Violet a "free Indian woman." Walkup, the appeals court ruled, should be free. Walkup's case was important, in part because it set a legal precedent for the admissibility of the hearsay evidence of race and family lineage in cases of pedigree.[17] It resonated throughout the courtrooms of the day and was recorded as notable in legal journals and summaries of precedents. While perhaps benefiting Walkup, hearsay evidence could easily work against Indigenous people. For this reason, owners were deeply invested in discrediting evidence of Native ancestry and lining up witnesses who would testify that Natives were "negro" and therefore enslavable.

As INDIGENOUS PEOPLE WERE finding success in their freedom suits on the East Coast, the United States suddenly became the inheritor and the perpetuator of thousands of additional enslaved Indigenous men, women, and children in the center of the continent. The preposterous "purchase" of the 530 million acres of Indigenous land in the Louisiana Territory in 1803 nearly doubled the domain claimed by the United States. These newly claimed lands encompassed some of the most fertile acreage on the entire continent, from the bayous of present-day Louisiana to the rugged mountains of Montana in the north, with the muddy, serpentine Mississippi River and the towering Rockies providing the eastern and western boundaries. So vast was this territory that it encompassed part or all of seventeen American states later carved out of the diverse terrain.

But above all, this was the homeland of approximately one million Native Americans, including the Sioux, Cheyenne, Kiowa, Osage, and other nations who had for millennia cultivated the landscape and traded from the Great Lakes to the west coast—long before the influx of European invaders, traders, and enslavers.[18] By the early nineteenth century, French and Spanish traders had spent more than two centuries journeying up and down the many riverways, trading for Native captives and sometimes slave-raiding Indigenous nations directly. These Indigenous communities had as a result suffered the loss of thousands of captured kin along the Missouri, Arkansas, and Mississippi Rivers.[19]

The United States was the third foreign empire in quick succession to claim the Louisiana Territory, which led to a complicated legal

NORTH AMERICA, BY R. WILKINSON, 1804, A MAP
HIGHLIGHTING THE LOUISIANA TERRITORY.

morass for enslaved people seeking their freedom. French traders had established a permanent presence in Louisiana as early as 1682. New Orleans, founded in 1718, quickly became an international port and entrepôt of commerce, shipping, and slavery. From the beginning, Indigenous slavery formed an important core of the region's economy. The French benefited from a Native slave trade from the interior, just like the English had in the Carolinas between 1670 and 1720.

When the Spanish took over the territory in 1768 as part of the negotiations after the Seven Years' War, Spanish officials at first tried to prohibit Indigenous slavery in keeping with Spanish policies elsewhere in the Americas. This led to a number of Native freedom suits in Louisiana in the 1790s, but planter pushback prompted the Spanish governor to halt the court cases, functionally leaving Indigenous enslavement intact.[20] After Louisiana was transferred to the United States in 1803, it did not take long before the question of the legality of Indigenous slavery again emerged in the courts. And the particular history of Louisiana's European transfers—French to Spanish to American—made it all the more confusing.[21]

Indigenous legal activism—and the closely related question of African slavery—was catapulted into national prominence in Louisiana as well, but with layers of international complexity. When the Louisiana Supreme Court heard the suit brought by an enslaved Native American named Seville in 1817, it was at the very end of a twenty-five-year-long fight for justice.[22] His family saga started in 1765, when a French trader named Duchene had taken an enslaved Indian woman to Opelousas, a town half an hour west of what is now Baton Rouge. Duchene sold the unnamed Indian woman to Chretien Sr., the father of the man who claimed Seville in 1817. This enslaved Indian woman died before long, but first gave birth to a daughter, Agnes, who Chretien also kept as his slave.

As Agnes grew, she lived through the Spanish takeover and perhaps even observed that officials declined to free enslaved Indians in the colony, despite Native slavery's illegality in Spanish territories more generally. In the early 1790s, she took advantage of a trip with her enslaver to New Orleans and sued for her freedom with the Spanish government, then led by Baron Francisco Luis Héctor de Carondelet. Her freedom suit disappeared into the labyrinth of the Spanish bureaucracy. Dejected, she returned to Opelousas with Chretien Sr. Later, Agnes birthed several children, including Seville, who were all claimed by Chretien as slaves.

In 1803, Agnes watched as yet another imperial power took over Louisiana. This time it was the United States, which had no federal guidelines concerning the enslavement of Natives. Shortly after 1803, Chretien Sr. died, and Agnes and her children—including Seville—once again sued for their freedom, this time under the laws of the United States and the territorial government in Louisiana. The initial case was decided against Agnes, but she appealed to the Superior Court of the Territory of Louisiana, where she was given a jury trial. The jury ruled in her favor, but the judge set the case aside due to some unnamed misconduct and ordered a new trial. The case languished until Louisiana received statehood in 1812, but then it was again temporarily set aside by the judge.

When Seville's freedom suit finally made its way to the Louisiana Supreme Court as *Seville v. Chretien* in 1817, it was at least the third time under two national governments that he or his family members had pressed for their freedom. The most urgent question was the hardest: under whose laws should Seville's case be considered? Seville's grandmother had been enslaved by the French in the eighteenth century, which the court acknowledged was legal. Seville's attorney proposed that the case should be tried under Spanish laws, which seemed like a solid strategy since Spain deemed Indian slavery illegal. But rather perplexingly, the Spanish governor Baron de Carondelet had specifically returned some Indigenous slaves to their claimed owners in 1794, which the court considered to be evidence of his approval of Native enslavement.[23]

The Louisiana Supreme Court also considered the laws of the United States and those of the British colonies prior to 1776. It found that Indigenous enslavement was accepted and practiced in all of the colonies, including ones in the Caribbean, even without an official legal, empirewide mandate. This implicitly carried over to the United States, the court reasoned, where Native people were enslaved by custom, even in the absence of specific laws authorizing Indigenous slavery.

After this remarkable tour of earlier legal precedent that covered four different national contexts (British, French, Spanish, and American), the Louisiana Supreme Court ruled against Seville, denying him his freedom. The principle was clear: a change in governance between international powers should not alter the condition of enslaved peoples. But a wider concern lurked in the background. One could almost hear the justices wondering, *If we free Seville, are enslaved Africans next?*[24]

INDIGENOUS LEGAL ACTIVISM SOON ERUPTED in the British Caribbean. In the early 1820s, a case of scandalous mistreatment of an enslaved Indigenous woman in British Honduras (modern Belize) grew into a mass protest against Indian slavery. These cases eventually gripped the imaginations of legal experts and the wider public from London to Jamaica and shaped conversations about the nature of all slavery, hastening its demise.

This process started when an enslaver in British Honduras named Duncannette Campbell viciously flogged Kitty, an enslaved Indigenous woman, with a cowskin for allegedly "behaving with the greatest insubordination." Cowskin whips were as dreadful as they

BRITISH HONDURAS AND THE MOSQUITO SHORE, 1820.

sound: long sections of the thick skin of a cow that had been dried into leather and then softened with oil just enough to be flexible. Soft human flesh was no match for the thickness of the leather and coarseness and hardness of the tips; even one or two lashings drew blood. The repeated whippings Kitty endured left deep gashes on her upper body. Other parts of her body, too, suffered from the blows. One ear had been sliced in half by the hardened leather whip, and one of the lashes had found its way around Kitty's arms that were protecting her face and dug into her eye, which soon became swollen and infected. In between floggings, Campbell chained Kitty in the loft of her house, with the chains wrapped so tightly around her legs she couldn't move or stand up.[25]

British Honduras had long been on the periphery of the British Empire, and enslavers like Campbell likely believed they were insulated from imperial laws. The settlement had become more populated after 1716, when British logwood cutters were pushed out of the Laguna de Términos on the Yucatán Peninsula. Belize City, the capital, was situated on the eastern edge of the colony at the mouth of the Belize River, facing the Caribbean. It was protected by a series of hidden and dangerous shoals, sandbars, and small islands that required local knowledge to navigate.[26] The colony received an unexpected boost in 1787, when 537 British colonists and their 1,677 enslaved Native Americans and Africans evacuated the Mosquito Shore as part of the post–Revolutionary War settlement between Britain and Spain.[27] British Honduras grew steadily after 1811, when a colony census tabulated an estimated 200 whites; 500 free Blacks, Native Americans, and people of color; and approximately 3,000 enslaved Africans and Indigenous people.[28]

Reports of Kitty's hellish treatment in 1820 soon made their way to Superintendent George Arthur and prompted an investigation and jury trial. When brought to court, Campbell argued that, as Kitty was her property, she was allowed to punish her for disobedience as she saw fit. The jury agreed. In fact, the entire case hung not on the gory details— which were revealed by witnesses on the stand—but on whether it was probable that Campbell whipped Kitty more than thirty-nine times, which since Roman times was seen as the maximum number of lashings the human body could withstand and still survive. This standard

A View in Belize, 1829.

was ensconced in the Jamaica Consolidated Slave Law of 1788, which extended to British Honduras. These laws were largely seen as a product of the Amelioration movement that intended to protect enslaved people from cruel owners.[29] But they failed Kitty, and miserably. The jury debated a mere ten minutes before deciding that Campbell had done nothing wrong.[30]

Within a year, in the sweltering late summer months of 1821, a second high-profile case attracted Superintendent Arthur's attention. This involved the appalling mistreatment of Peggy, another enslaved Indigenous woman. Her enslaver, a colony magistrate named Manfield William Bowen, severely flogged and then handcuffed her in the basement of a store he owned. The space was so infested with rodents, mosquitos, and biting insects that it was not fit for human habitation. But when the jury met in September 1821, they could not cite a single law that Bowen had broken.[31]

Bowen's exoneration was infuriating, and Kitty's and Peggy's return to slavery was devastating. From enslaved people's perspectives, the courts were failing to protect them. Enslaved Natives decided to use a different tactic: challenging their enslavement, not just mistreatment, based on being descended from a free maternal Native ancestor. Perhaps predictably, enslavers in British Honduras dismissed these claims of freedom and Indigeneity, calling them "negros" in the court records.[32]

Fortunately, these enslaved Natives found a particularly sympathetic ally in the person of Superintendent Arthur, who wrote to the attorney general of Jamaica, William Burge, in November 1821, asking him to provide legal counsel regarding slaves in British Honduras who had Indigenous parentage. Arthur's questions were direct: Can Native Americans be held as slaves? What about Indigenous people who were transferred to British Honduras from the Mosquito Shore in 1786? Can British citizens be compelled to give up enslaved Natives? Finally, should freed Native slaves be given any compensation for being wrongfully enslaved?[33]

Arthur's letter was timely, since it arrived on the desk of the learned and slaveholding attorney general Burge just as he was considering a spate of Native freedom suits in Jamaica. In St. James Parish, on the northwestern coast of the island, eight enslaved individuals had been granted their freedom in July 1821 by a court that determined they were "descendants of Indians."[34] In another case a little to the south, in the parish of St. Elizabeth, four enslaved Natives disappeared from their enslaver's plantation that same year. When they were finally caught and questioned, John Turner, William Clark, Harry Royal, and Burnet Green all said that they were descended from an Indian woman and therefore had been wrongfully enslaved.[35] Unfortunately, no resolution is recorded. It is likely that they received their freedom since Burge firmly believed that no colonists could or should legally hold enslaved Natives or their descendants.

Burge's terse response to Arthur was decisive. With a few strokes of his pen, this royal attorney completely vindicated the claims of enslaved Natives in British Honduras with four main points. The most important one was the first, which stated, "British Subjects cannot, under any circumstances, hold in Slavery the Native Indians of the Continent of America, or their Descendants." Burge's subsequent points declared the transfer of Indigenous slaves from the Mosquito Shore in 1787 to have also been illegal. Any colonist who persisted in holding any Natives in slavery would be subject to "criminal Prosecution." Furthermore, illegally held slaves would be eligible for compensation from their former enslavers—"Damages," as the attorney general's letter stated it. To bolster his view, Burge referred to original documents held in the archives in Jamaica, including the 1776 anti–Indian slavery proclamation made by Sir Basil Keith, then governor of Jamaica, which had made trafficking Indigenous slaves a capital offense.[36]

Empowered by such a clear directive, Arthur met several times with British planters, who initially seemed willing to work with him to secure the freedom of their enslaved Natives. But as some of the owners and planters began examining the past laws and proclamations, including the 1741 Jamaican act and the 1776 act of the Mosquito Shore Council, many of them began to resist, querying the basis of the Jamaican attorney general's sweeping denunciations. At a meeting on December 31, 1821, the planters produced copies of several historical documents, including the 1777 Registry of Slaves on the Mosquito Shore—a tally of enslaved Indians that was taken *after* the 1776 law and even after King George III's 1775 prohibition of the slave trade. Surely if the Mosquito Shore Council registered and did not free these enslaved Natives, they and their descendants currently held in British Honduras should not be freed.[37]

Arthur moved swiftly—too quickly, the planters complained. With Belize City on edge and the city's slaveholders nervously watching, Arthur set up a Board of Commissioners on January 5, 1822, which he appointed to investigate the claims of Indians and their descendants (often referred to as the Board of Indian Claims).[38] When this body first convened four days later, it decreed that the burden of proof for legal enslavement would fall to the owner and that, if freed, formerly enslaved people and not their former owners would be compensated.

The presumption that Native people were free unless proven otherwise was in stark contrast with the assumption in other British colonies that Black people should normally be considered slaves. Officials in most colonies confirmed that "the colour of the Negro is a presumption of slavery" unless it was proven otherwise (by a manumission letter, badge, seal, or other tangible legal means).[39] But in this new legal environment in British Honduras, the opposite was true for Indigenous people. Enslaved Indians were presumed to be wrongfully enslaved if they claimed their freedom, and it was up to the enslavers to produce evidence of their legal enslavement.

With the British Honduras Board of Indian Claims in place, enslaved Indigenous people began petitioning for their freedom by the dozens, giving astonishingly detailed narrations of family histories. Most of the families traced their ancestors to the Mosquito Shore, often stretching back fifty years or more.[40] Samuel Potts was born into slavery in approximately 1776 on the Corn Islands, fifty miles or so off the Mosquito Shore. He was the son of a Native woman enslaved by Mr. Potts.[41]

Another petitioner, Peggy—now just over forty years old—and her brother George were the children of Betty, a Native woman enslaved by Major Campbell on the Mosquito Shore. Peggy was also petitioning for the freedom of her seven children—Charles, Billy, Violet, Betty, Darby, Eleanor, and Rose. Similarly, Fidelia Lawrie brought a petition for herself and her two children, Smart and Phoebe. Fidelia was the daughter of an enslaved Native on the Mosquito Shore named Rose. Notably, her enslaver was none other than James Lawrie, at that time the superintendent of the Mosquito Shore territory.[42]

On and on the petitions continued. Within a month, more than one hundred enslaved Indigenous people had submitted evidence for their wrongful enslavement, with dozens of additional family members listed as well.[43] And each story was a variation on the same theme. Cumberland Winter filed a petition for an additional twenty-two enslaved Indians who traced their family line to Isabella, an enslaved Indian whose claimed owner was Stephen Winter on the Mosquito Shore. Cumberland's family was so extensive and complicated that he submitted a genealogical table with his petition, as did others.[44]

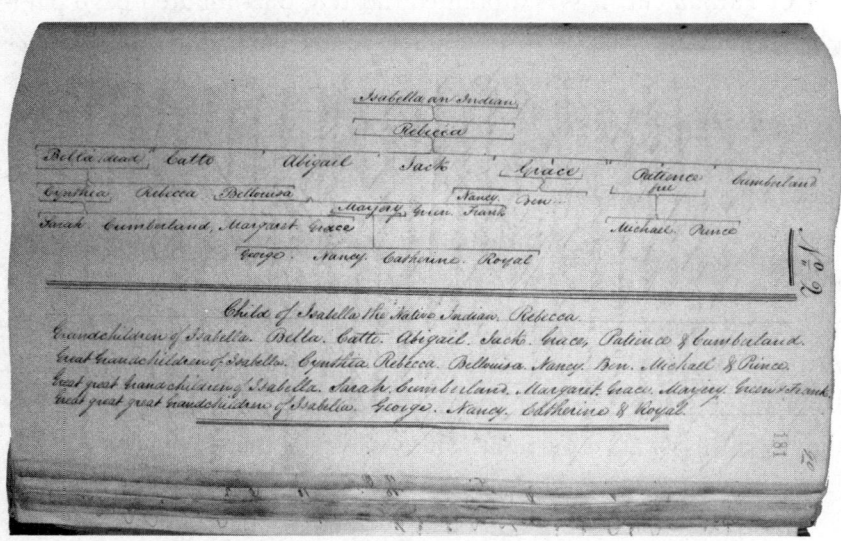

ISABELLA'S FAMILY CHART, 1821.

Despite the mountains of testimony, Arthur quickly lost control of the situation. To expedite the process, he issued a proclamation in early 1822 declaring all Indigenous slavery to be illegal in British Honduras and guaranteeing due process for Indians claiming freedom.[45] The planters erupted with anger, driving Arthur into hiding. As a final salvo in this fight for emancipation, Arthur sent his version of the proceedings to administrators in England, which caused an immediate uproar. London newspapers reported a summary of the proceedings in which they characterized British Honduras enslavers as determined to hold onto their "Indian slaves except taken by force."[46]

Spurned by their enslavers, the claims of these enslaved Natives gripped the national attention in England. Even the aged William Wilberforce, who as a member of Parliament had led the campaign to end the African slave trade in the 1780s and 1790s, joined the fray, giving a rousing speech in Parliament on July 11, 1823, demanding their freedom. The "Indians at Honduras," Wilberforce argued, "were free by birth, and nothing could legally deprive them of this freedom." He urged Parliament to appoint a committee to look into the matter, which it did.[47]

Undeterred, the claimed owners of enslaved Indigenous people in British Honduras retaliated. In 1824, they published a scathing critique of Arthur's handling of the Native slavery situation. To ensure wide distribution, they had it printed in Jamaica and sent to every member of Parliament. It was a pointed, heated, one-hundred-page pamphlet that took Arthur to task, as the title indicated: *The Defence of the Settlers of Honduras against the Unjust and Unfounded Representations of Colonel George Arthur*.[48] The book was mostly propaganda made official-looking with elaborate documentation, but it demanded a rebuttal.

John A. Armstrong, a settlement chaplain in British Honduras, published a thorough refutation of the settlers' complaint in 1824, titled *A Candid Examination of "The Defence of the Settlers of Honduras."*[49] Armstrong's main point was that the intent of the 1741 and 1776 laws was to strike down all Native slavery, even if the letter of the law did not always state it outright. The enslavers followed the letter of the law; Arthur understood its spirit.

The overly defensive planters were right in one regard: there was really no logical defense of a slave system that liberated people of one race and kept another in bondage, which had been the crux of the controversy in the United States. That illogic had always been there, of course, but the Native freedom suits inescapably brought this to the fore. Freeing Indigenous slaves solved one problem, but it immediately created others. Enslaved Blacks who could not trace Indigenous lineage began looking around and wondering why they too could not be freed. It was the precise scenario enslavers had been trying to avoid.

These public debates soon attracted the attention of the eminent Commissioners of Legal Inquiry, who in 1826 were swiftly redirected from Bermuda to British Honduras to resolve this dilemma.[50] After reviewing all of the available evidence, the commissioners made the rather progressive recommendation that all Native peoples who had petitioned for their freedom should, in fact, be set free and the planters be compensated for their losses.[51] Planters dragged their feet, and it wasn't until April 1830 that the Board of Treasury in London declared that the British Honduras Natives formerly held in bondage "must now be considered as lawfully and unconditionally free."[52]

At long last, the saga of these Indigenous people in British Honduras was over. But in the end, the enslavers in the colony also won a victory of sorts. They had protested the financial loss of these Indigenous people loudly enough that the Department of Treasury in London agreed to pay them for the forfeiture of the people they had claimed as slaves.[53]

This process of compensating enslavers for the emancipation of their Native slaves set an important precedent for a far larger mass emancipation that was beginning to loom over the British colonies in the late 1820s and early 1830s. In the past, some former enslavers of emancipated African slaves had received compensation from the royal Treasury. But Indigenous emancipation and owner compensation in British Honduras was on a larger scale and precisely at a time when magistrates and colonists were beginning to wonder what a larger, universal manumission process might look like.

OTHER ENSLAVED PEOPLE in the British Caribbean did not have to wait long to receive their freedom. Movements and protests by enslaved people throughout British colonies along with other political and economic currents persuaded British Parliament to end slavery. This included the Christmas Rebellion in Jamaica in 1831, in which thousands of enslaved people pressed for their freedom and wages for their labors.[54]

On August 1, 1834, the 750,000 enslaved men, women, and children in the British Empire were declared free, as mandated by the 1833 Act for the Abolition of Slavery throughout the British colonies. The fifty-year-long debate about slavery in the British colonies was finally resolved, and soon Caribbean planters would turn to indentured servants from the subcontinent of India to fill their labor demands (who the records also referred to as Indians). But slavery did not end immediately, at least not in most places. Emancipation imposed the detested burden of six years of indenture for all former slaves—which was soon reduced to four years.[55] Only a few colonies, including Bermuda, chose immediate emancipation.[56]

Importantly, as had been done for Indigenous owners in British Honduras, the British Abolition Act made provisions for the compensation of enslavers, requiring British citizens to report the number of slaves in their households and on their plantations. Planters in approximately twenty colonies in the Caribbean and every other British slaveholding colony in South and Central America, South Africa, and the Indian Ocean meticulously recorded the names, ages, employment skills, and total number of their enslaved men, women, and children. These precise population tallies were then assigned per-person values to calculate the total amount to be reimbursed by the British Treasury to each former enslaver.[57]

Notably, thousands of Indigenous and mixed-race Indigenous people were freed through British emancipation, although the clerical erasure of Native Americans in the records prevents us from ever fully knowing exactly how many. As part of the slave registries for compensation, enslavers recorded the perceived racial identification, or "color," of each enslaved person. Most individuals were noted as "black," but other racial designations abounded, including "sambo," "mulatto," "quadroon," and "mustee." Any one of these racial designations could refer to mixed-race people of Indigenous or African descent. Even so, Indigenous people dot the compensation claims, even if their official racial designation is erased. One sixteen-year-old enslaved youth in Barbados was listed with "Indian" for his name and "Black" for his color. The same was true for a thirty-one-year-old enslaved man listed as "Tom Indian," who was similarly listed as "Black."[58]

Bermuda's 1834 slave registry is a good example of this clerical erasure. Despite its history of receiving Indian captives and slaves from North America and the Caribbean, there are no "Indians" listed in 1834 (or for many previous years).[59] But it seems impossible that enslaved Indigenous people were not present, given that in Bermuda today there is an entire community on St. David's Island whose lineage traces back to North American Native nations and whose oral histories describe post-emancipation life. Even the archives gesture toward this reality. As late as 1829, an enslaved Indigenous man from North America was married to a free woman in Bermuda.[60] One presumes that this Native man, along with many others, received his freedom in 1834 when Bermuda voted to embrace Parliament's Emancipation Act.

ENSLAVERS AND PROSLAVERY OFFICIALS in the United States followed these and other previous developments with great trepidation. The successful overthrow of French rule by enslaved people in Saint-Domingue (Haiti) in the 1790s led to the creation of the first independent former slave colony in the western world, putting American enslavers on high alert for any liberatory activity. And as British Parliament debated a general emancipation act in early 1833, American newspapers bristled with reports of similarly aimed machinations in the United States. The *Newbern Sentinel* in North Carolina and the *Richmond Telegraph* in Virginia ran articles with the headline "ALARMING CONSPIRACY!!" that alleged the formation of a countrywide society whose *"main object seems to be to procure a general emancipation of slaves through out the United States."*[61] Defiant American enslavers in southern states doubled down, becoming increasingly determined to forever protect the system of slavery that they called their "peculiar institution."[62]

The ongoing success of enslaved Natives demanding freedom through American courts only added to the alarm of southern enslavers. Indigenous emancipation erupted in the national consciousness in October 1834—just two months after British emancipation—when an enslaved Native woman named Marguerite sued for her and her familv's freedom in the Missouri Supreme Court. Rather unusually, this case eventually made its way to the US Supreme Court. Her family's saga began in 1731 when a Natchez woman named Marie Scipion was taken to Fort Chartres (just south of St. Louis) and sold as a slave to a French family and then handed down to the family of Joseph Tayon. Marie Scipion passed away in 1802, in the household of Madame Chauvin, who was Tayon's daughter. When Scipion's children and grandchildren began exerting increasing independence, Tayon sued them in 1806 in order to confirm his legal ownership of them.[63]

Even so, Marie Scipion's children and grandchildren held on to the hope of justice. In May 1826, two of Scipion's descendants, Catiche and Sophia, received their freedom in a ruling from the Missouri Supreme Court.[64] Two years later, in 1828, Scipion's granddaughter Marguerite also sued for her freedom from her enslaver, Pierre Choteau. After several rounds of suits at the state level, the Missouri Supreme Court in 1834 overturned lower-court rulings in favor of Marguerite. A desperate Choteau appealed to the US Supreme Court, which heard the case in January 1838 as *Pierre Choteau, senior v. Marguerite, a woman of colour*. After hearing all the evidence, the court determined that Tayon had essentially given up his right to Scipion and her descendants back at Fort Chartres in the 1760s, when he had apparently declined to register Scipion as his slave. The US Supreme Court deemed Marguerite to be free on March 6 and sent the case back to the Missouri Circuit Court to follow their instructions.[65]

Marguerite's case was part of one of the longest-lasting series of Indigenous freedom suits in the history of the United States and, before that, the English colonies. Like most freedom suits, its long and meandering pathway through the judicial system demonstrated the incredible resolve of some enslaved Indigenous families to secure their freedom. It was a stunning victory and added to the growing conviction that, with patience, slavery could be overturned.

Not all Indigenous people who sued for their freedom were successful. American courts seemed fixated on whether or not enslaved people *looked* Black and were therefore doomed to enslavement instead of freedom. In 1827, the Virginia Supreme Court denied the freedom suit of an enslaved man of Indian ancestry named James Baugh based on the freedom of his grandmother, Indian Sibyl. The justices ruled that some witnesses testified that Sibyl looked Black and, based on her reportedly dark skin, was presumably enslaved, thereby justifying Baugh's enslavement.[66]

THE INTENSITY OF Indigenous legal activism revealed the incredibly high stakes for enslaved people everywhere. One astute American judge in the 1827 *Vaughan v. Phebe* Indigenous court case noted, "Freedom in this country is not a mere name. . . . It is something substantial. It embraces within its comprehensive grasp, all the useful rights of man."[67] Enslavers and enslaved alike could see plainly that freedom was highly prized, something to pursue at all costs.

In the British Empire, this demand for freedom brought an end to slavery in 1834. Enslaved Indigenous people had played important roles in these immense changes, taking their mistreatment and wrongful enslavement to the courts in places like Jamaica and British Honduras. The situation was different in the United States. Although hundreds of Native Americans from Connecticut to Virginia and elsewhere had found freedom, southern states clamped down on enslaved people in response to freedom suits and British emancipation. Indigenous legal activism was a powerful movement, but in the United States, Indigenous and African enslavement would continue to dramatically expand in numbers and geographical scope before it could be rooted out.

Part Four

RESURGENCE

1820–1880

THE SURGE OF NATIVE FREEDOM SUITS WAS POWERFUL, BUT it did not end Indian slavery in the United States. Instead, a completely unexpected new round of assaults against Native nations erupted in the United States from the 1830s through the 1870s. As Americans colonized southward and westward, they began enslaving Indigenous people in even greater numbers as they stole increasingly large quantities of territory. The United States had been founded on the aggressive desires of Americans for Native land, as seen in the flaunting of the Proclamation Line of 1763 and the wars against the Cherokee, Shawnee, and Delaware between the 1760s and the 1790s. Though the term *Manifest Destiny* was not coined until 1845, from the beginning, Americans remained continually convinced that they were divinely entitled to Native lands.

There were important precedents that encouraged Americans to think and act in this way. Leaders in all three branches of the federal government, for example, often supported such views. One powerful Supreme Court case in 1823, *Johnson v. M'Intosh*, ludicrously claimed that Native Americans had only ever been "occupants" of North American soil, not rightful owners of it. Europeans, including the English and Americans, Chief Justice John Marshall reasoned, had rights to the land by virtue of discovery and conquest. This Doctrine of Discovery became an insidious rationale that threaded its way into court cases even into the twenty-first century.[1] Marshall also later referred to Native tribes as "domestic dependent nations," a dismissive designation that cast aside Native sovereignty and self-determination.[2] And when the law sometimes tried to set limits on colonial expansion, presidents like Andrew Jackson ignored restrictions placed on him by the Supreme Court and simply went rogue, enacting the mass removal of Indigenous populations. Throughout, Congress generally affirmed one-sided treaties and imposed legislation, including the Indian Removal Act of 1830.

Stealing land continually went hand in hand with stealing people. Starting in the antebellum South, potentially hundreds of thousands of Indigenous people were captured during removals, were abducted as part of the internal slave trade, or remained enslaved on plantations. And after the Mexican–American War, which lasted from 1846 to 1848, delivered vast regions of the West to the United States, Americans who surged westward discovered and expanded systems of slavery, peonage, and bondage of Native people, even in supposedly free territories and states like New Mexico and California.

So entrenched were these systems of Indigenous enslavement and servile labor that Americans in these regions convinced themselves that this servitude was categorically different from Black southern slavery. Consequently, they ignored the Thirteenth Amendment at the close of the Civil War, forcing Congress to pass an act in 1867 to specifically deal with the ongoing enslavement and peonage of Indigenous people in the West.

Twelve

REMOVALS AND PLANTATIONS

THE CUSTOMARY STORY OF AMERICAN SLAVERY IN THE FIRST HALF
of the nineteenth century is the rapid expansion of *Black* slavery in
the South. After the Revolutionary War, Americans quickly claimed
land and created new states, starting with Kentucky in 1792 and Tennessee in 1796. As Americans streamed to the deeper South, they
expanded slavery's geographical reach as well as the number of people enslaved. The enslaved population mushroomed from 1.1 million
in 1810 to nearly 4 million by 1860—and that was without the supply
of the legal transatlantic slave trade from Africa or the Caribbean.[1]
As scholars have shown, slavery's expansion was central to American
capitalism, with both northern and southern states benefiting equally
from its growth through slave-produced cotton for textile production
and financial markets backed by enslaved collateral.[2]

All of this is true, but the stealing of Indigenous land and labor was
central to this history in two specific ways that are often overlooked.
First, all of the newly claimed territory was originally Indigenous land.
It did not just casually fall into the hands of Americans. Instead, it
was coercively and violently taken from large Native nations in the
American South and Midwest through a series of removals and expulsions during the first half of the nineteenth century. Although removal
affected dozens of Native nations from Florida to the Great Lakes, the
largest and most notable expulsions cleared millions of acres of land in
the South that were in climates highly desirable for the rapidly expanding and lucrative cotton industry. These lands allowed the United States
to create the plantation powerhouses of Alabama, Mississippi, Arkansas, Louisiana, and Texas—places that by 1860 produced two billion

pounds of cotton per year and shipped it to destinations throughout the Americas and Europe.[3]

Second, and less well known, is the fact that Americans actively enslaved Native Americans and mixed-race Indigenous people in these slaveholding states. Their enslavement directly contributed numerically to the meteoric growth of southern slavery. In some cases, this simply meant continuing to enslave generation after generation of Native American and mixed-race Indigenous people in households and on plantations. But Americans also stole Native peoples from their lands and trafficked them southward to be sold at slave auctions in Mississippi and Louisiana as part of the domestic slave trade. Indian removal too led to new enslavement as Indigenous people were kidnapped and claimed as slaves during the wars that preceded removal, during removal itself, and even on their new lands after being expelled from the United States. Enslaved Indigenous people were part of every aspect of antebellum slavery.

Mostly, though, Americans have overlooked this reality because they have equated antebellum southern slavery with Black slavery, which is what the official records usually indicate. The 1860 federal census states, for example, that there were 3,953,760 enslaved people in the South, all of whom were simply listed as "slaves" or at times "blacks" and "mullatoes."[4] But we know from other sources that a multitude of Native Americans and mixed-race Indigenous people also labored on plantations, even if they were not noted as such. Although exact tabulation is impossible, I estimate that between 2 percent and 5 percent of the enslaved population was mixed-race Indigenous or had direct Native American parentage. This means that as many as 80,000 to 200,000 of the nearly 4 million enslaved people in the South on the eve of the Civil War were Native Americans or Native-descended people.[5]

While this number may seem unexpectedly high, it is likely a rather conservative estimate. In the 1920s, Melville Herskovits, an anthropologist at Northwestern University, reported in one study that more than 27 percent of Black Americans reported having Native American ancestors. If Herskovits is right, enslaved Indigenous people in the American South might have numbered more than a million.[6]

Riviana Boynton was just one example of a Native person enslaved on a southern plantation. She was born into slavery in approximately 1847 on the property of John and Mollie Hoover just outside of the sleepy town of Ulmer in south-central South Carolina. Riviana's father and mother were both enslaved by the Hoovers; her father was Native American, but her mother was sold away when Riviana was very young—too young to have any recollection of her or her ancestry. As a young child, Riviana had to thin cotton blossoms in the expansive fields and keep flies off the food in the house, which she did with big leafy branches taken from a tree. Her aunt and uncle—both also Native— were enslaved on the same property, and in the evenings, she slept in a rough shed that her uncle had built. The shack was sparsely furnished; long bunk beds lined one wall, with only coarse burlap sacks nailed down to cushion the uneven wooden boards. For warmth on cool evenings, Riviana and her family members used thick rugs that she had woven with the scraps left over from the looms on the property.[7]

Most histories of southern antebellum slavery in the United States do not include Indigenous people like Boynton. This is partially because records reflect the "one drop" racial ideology, which viewed mixed-race Indigenous people as Black and not Indigenous. But scholars have also contributed to the invisibility of enslaved Natives in the antebellum South by following the erasures of Native presence and identities in the archives and in the present day.[8] Enslaved Natives and mixed-race Indigenous men and women cleared fields, brought in harvests, were brutally whipped, and sometimes chose to self-emancipate, chancing the rough terrain, trained dogs, and slave catchers who awaited them along the route to freedom.

We need a more racially nuanced and expanded history of slavery in the American South in the nineteenth century, one that recognizes Indigenous presence. Mixed-raced people—then and now—can have multiple and overlapping identifications and affinities, as both scholars and people of mixed ancestry have argued.[9] Mixed-race Indigenous people in this period retained the dual sense of their identities.[10] A mixed-race Indigenous person with a Choctaw mother and a Black father is no less Indigenous than Black, even if their enslavers and some records have told us otherwise.[11]

BEFORE THE SOUTH BECAME the center of American slavery, it was home to hundreds of thousands of Native Americans who had withstood three centuries of French, Spanish, and English colonization. Some of these peoples formed large nations and confederacies, like the powerful Choctaw, Cherokee, and Muscogee, whose total population neared fifty thousand by the early nineteenth century.[12] Immediately following the American Revolution, presidents like George Washington and Thomas Jefferson believed that Native Americans had far more land than they needed, and if properly "civilized," they might be persuaded to give up most of it for American expansion.

The new United States government and state officials placed intense pressure on Native nations to relinquish their land and follow white American gender and cultural norms (which included farming for the men and domestic duties for women). The focus was increasingly on five large Indigenous nations—Cherokee, Choctaw, Chickasaw, Muscogee, and Seminole—whose ancestral homelands were precisely where Americans saw the most agricultural promise for new cotton planta-

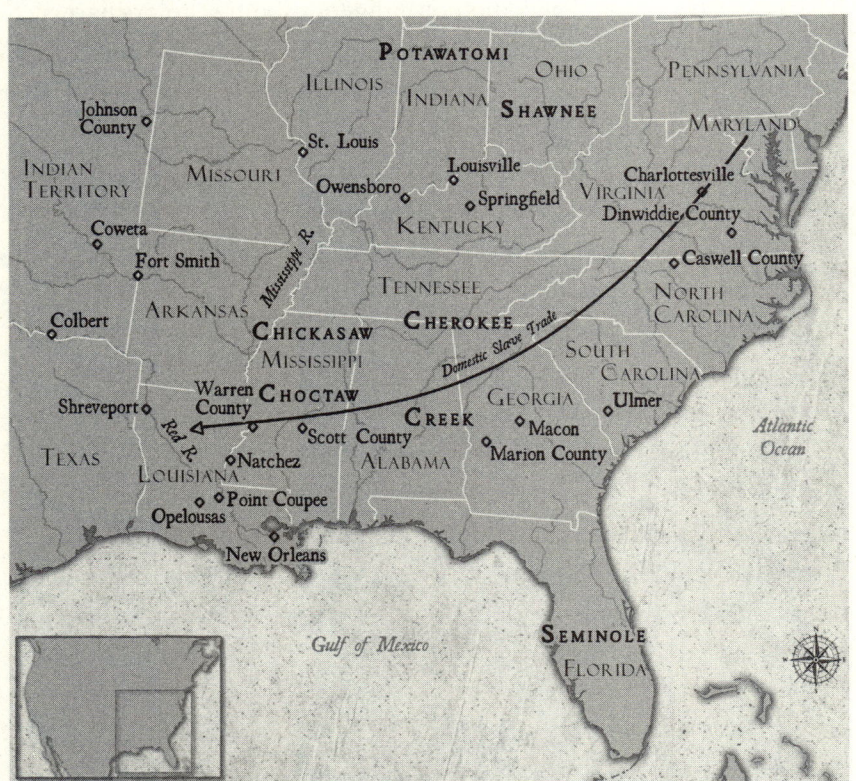

THE ANTEBELLUM SOUTH, 1830.

tions. As a strategy of survival and self-determination, these Indian nations adopted visible signs of "civilization" as defined by whites and became more Americanized. This included reorganizing tribal governance and adopting a constitution modeled after the US Constitution, as well as accepting American Christian missionaries who opened schools and churches on Native lands. The Cherokee soon developed their own system of writing, published their own bilingual newspaper called the *Cherokee Phoenix*, and translated parts of the Bible into Cherokee. All of these efforts led outsiders to refer to these five nations as the Civilized Tribes.[13]

Yet it was not enough to prove them "worthy" inhabitants of their lands. The US government coerced more than a dozen treaties with these Indigenous nations between 1814 and 1835 that ceded millions of acres of land in what is now Alabama, Georgia, Florida, Mississippi, and Tennessee.[14] One of the earliest and most significant of these treaties was the Treaty of Fort Jackson in 1814 between the Muscogee nation and the United States, formally ending the Red Stick War, which

Cherokee Phoenix,
New Echota, Georgia,
April 10, 1828.

was a subset of the War of 1812. This settlement ceded to the United States a staggering twenty-three million acres of land spanning parts of Alabama and Georgia.[15] Impatient white Americans who desired to take even more land immediately threatened violence and even enslavement. Andrew Jackson—who was then a decorated military general—assured a group of Choctaw headmen at a treaty conference that president James Madison would protect them from the "threats of white men" who wanted to make them "slaves."[16]

Despite these land cessions, Americans would not be satisfied until Natives were entirely cleared from the region. The Indian Removal Act of 1830 under President Andrew Jackson was designed to do just that and came with the full weight of the federal government behind it. When the US Supreme Court ruled in *Worcester v. Georgia* in 1832 that Georgia's laws regarding the removal of the Cherokee were unconstitutional, Jackson colluded with state officials and proceeded to expel Native peoples anyway, hiring private contractors and mobilizing the US Army and state militias. The process divided Native nations, with pro- and antiremoval factions in almost every community.[17]

To force Native nations into accepting removal, state militias sometimes waged war on them, which involved instances of slave raiding and captive taking. During the prolonged conflict with the Muscogee prior to removal, including in the Second Creek War (1836–1837), Native parents desperately tried to keep their infants and young children out of the hands of soldiers who wished to claim them. When infants' cries threatened to reveal their families' hiding places, frantic Muscogee parents reportedly suffocated them by stuffing their noses and mouths with dry grasses and moss, leaving their bodies to be discovered by pursuing soldiers. One party of fleeing Muscogee reportedly poisoned their children during the night, likely believing death was better than a lifetime of slavery at the hands of whites. Their fears were well founded; soldiers who captured Muscogee infants and children kept them as slaves.[18]

In the Battle of Pea River (1837), Alabama troops fought an all-out war that mirrored the Pequot War's Mystic Massacre exactly two hundred years earlier. Soldiers cornered a band of Muscogees in a fetid swamp and indiscriminately murdered everyone they could lay hands on—men, women, and children. In the end, all the Indian men were executed, and the surviving women and children were enslaved, often claimed by soldiers as a reward for military service. Perhaps especially prized were the two children of the Muscogee leader Cheske Micco.[19]

All of this understandably led to Natives associating removal with fear of enslavement at the hands of southern whites. In 1835, as the forcible removal of the Muscogee loomed, the federal government contracted with a removal company founded by the ardent anti-Indian US representative from Georgia, John W. A. Sanford. Rumors swirled that the Muscogee would be led farther west, enslaved, and forced to work on cotton plantations.[20] When the removal contractor Moses K. Wheat rounded up some Muscogee in Coosa and Tallapoosa Counties and tried to march them to a temporary holding site, many of the Natives violently resisted and disappeared, fearing they were "going to be chained and sold as slaves."[21]

An unknowable number of Native survivors of military campaigns against southern Indigenous tribes during removal were stolen and sold into slavery. In the 1830s, when the US military was forcibly removing the Choctaw from their homelands in Mississippi, one particular skirmish left a small band devastated. A small Choctaw girl, the daughter of a chief named Red Bird, was the sole survivor. The soldiers took her with them and sold her to a Dr. Jernigan, who raised her on his plantation along with the rest of his slaves. She married an enslaved man who had been illegally trafficked directly from Africa, and their children too were claimed as slaves on the Jernigan plantation. She and her children did not receive their freedom until Union soldiers liberated the entire plantation near the end of the Civil War.[22]

The enslavement of hundreds of other Native Americans during removal was rarely documented by militias and governments, but families and kin were painfully aware of their absence. Muscogee leaders reported to American officials that children from their nation had been stolen and enslaved during the chaos of removal. This was confirmed in January 1846, when some government contractors hired to remove any remaining Muscogees from Alabama reported a significant but unknown number of Native children kept by white planters "who hold them for the benefit of their present and future services."[23] A scout named Luther Blake toured former Muscogee territory in Alabama in 1846 and found Natives, many of whom were "orphans," held as slaves in Barbour, Henry, Dale, Covington, and Pike Counties.[24]

As late as 1848, after being forcibly expelled to Oklahoma, the Muscogee chief named Cochemy traveled back to his former home-land in Georgia and Alabama to round up an additional sixty-five peo-ple, including some of his own relatives, who had not yet moved west. Cochemy was unable, however, to free a number of enslaved Mus-cogees scattered across central Alabama plantations since the threats from their enslavers caused him to give up temporarily. The enslaved included an unknown number of Muscogees held by a minister named William Hays in Autauga County.[25] A few Muscogee captives taken during the Second Creek War in the 1830s lived as slaves and servants among white families even up through 1870, well past the Civil War.[26]

Additionally, the wars of removal created an influx of an untold number of Native Americans into military prisons and forts across the American South. The status and fate of these thousands of cap-tives are not entirely clear. After the Creek Wars, military command-ers and officers at various forts were instructed to submit listings of "Indians, Indian Negros, and slaves" who had been taken captive.[27] In the chaos of wartime and its aftermath, who was to ensure that for-merly free Native people were not claimed by soldiers or locals or sold into slavery? Mixed-race Indigenous people were especially vulnera-ble to slavery.

Similarly, after the series of wars waged against the Seminole Indi-ans in Florida in 1838, hundreds of Seminoles, Black Seminoles, and Blacks languished in prison at Fort Marion in St. Augustine. Nineteen died, perhaps from wounds or unsanitary conditions. At least sixteen escaped the fort, perhaps (as others would later do) by scraping out the mortar in between the coquina (shell) blocks to create enough of a toehold to scale the walls and find escape routes. Hundreds were relo-cated, shipped by boat to Louisiana and then marched north to prison reservations in Indian Territory. Rather suspiciously, however, more than two hundred men, women, and children were taken to Charles-ton, presumably for sale into slavery. More than likely these included mixed-race Indigenous captives who the military presumed could be sold off without notice.[28]

Legal protests, treaties, campaigns by missionaries, and wars of resistance ultimately proved ineffective. To enforce the Removal Act, the US military marched in and violently moved Native communities en masse, often at gunpoint, forcing them to walk for months until they reached their federally appointed destinations. The Cherokee Trail of Tears in 1838–1839 is the most famous and heartbreaking of these military-escorted removals from their homelands to Oklahoma,

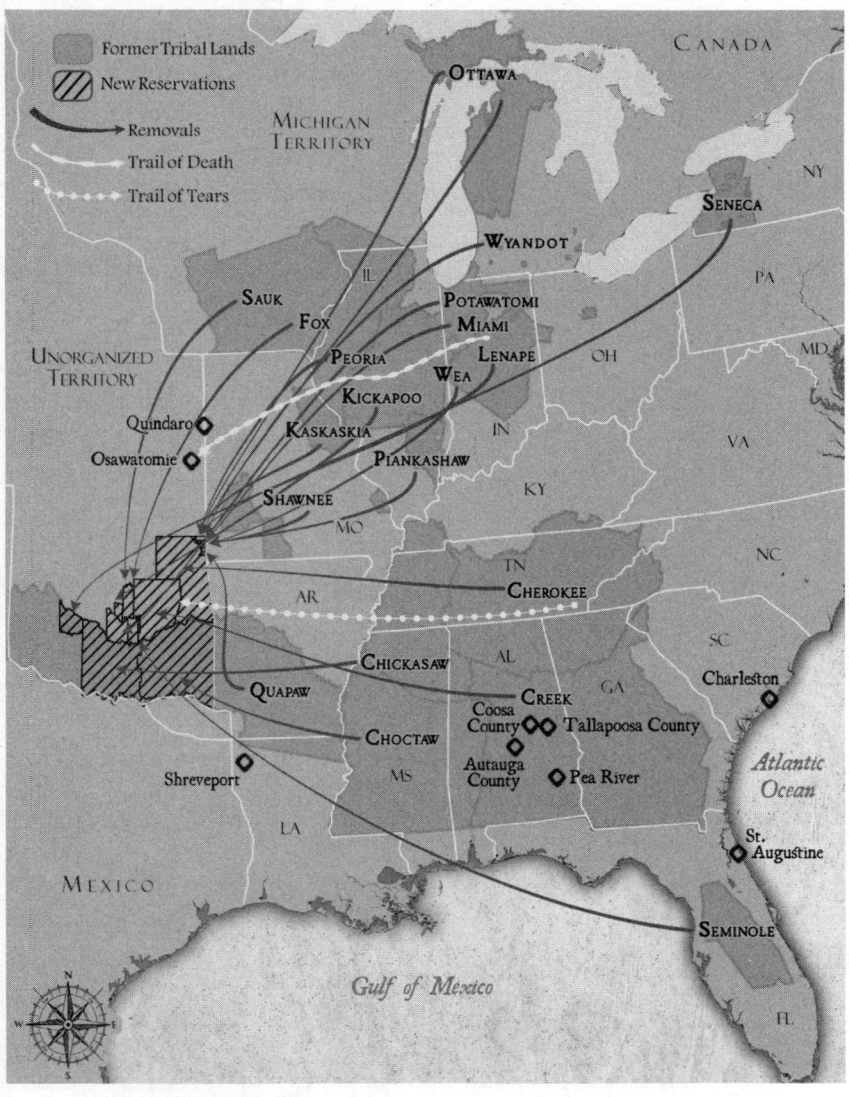

FORCED REMOVALS OF INDIGENOUS NATIONS, CA. 1830.

and perhaps the most deadly, with as many as four thousand to six thousand fatalities along the way.[29]

These southern removals were only one part of dozens of such forced routes westward. Between the 1810s and the 1840s, the US federal government colluded with states, courts, and local officials to force the expulsion of several dozen Native nations westward, ranging from the Quapaw in Arkansas to the Potawatomi in Michigan and Indiana. By the late 1840s, the United States had moved 130,000 Native Americans from their homelands in eastern parts of the United States to new reservations west of the Mississippi.[30] It was a stunning, unprecedented mass expulsion that served as a dangerous example for global genocidal regimes for the next one hundred years.[31] American colonists swooped into these newly vacant lands, sometimes even sleeping in beds that were still warm from recently removed Native bodies.[32]

INNUMERABLE INDIVIDUAL STORIES of family trauma and enslavement emerged from this devastating upheaval, many of which were only preserved in family oral histories. In the 1830s, John Hawk, who was Sauk, and his wife, Rachel, who was Choctaw, lived with their three daughters among the towering elm, sycamore, and maple trees in the fertile Wabash River Valley.[33] For millennia, this five-hundred-mile waterway, stretching from western Ohio through Indiana and along the Illinois border to the Ohio River, had provided ample planting and hunting grounds for numerous Indigenous nations. By the 1810s, Indiana officials began systematically purchasing and claiming land out from under the Miami, Potawatomi, Lenape, Kickapoo, and Wea. Even before the 1830 Indian Removal Act, the federal and state governments removed individual clans and communities of Indigenous nations from Indiana, including most of the Potawatomi, Miami, and Shawnee, with new lands assigned to them in western territories.

These sporadic expulsions continued for decades, and John and Rachel were caught up in a violent and deadly removal in 1838, when the federal government forced the remaining enclave of approximately eight hundred resisting Potawatomis from their homelands. The US military marched them along a 660-mile pathway through western Indiana, Illinois, and Missouri into new reserved lands in Kansas.

Later called the Trail of Death, more than forty children and elderly members died en route.

Somehow, John and Rachel escaped. Instead of being marched to Kansas, they and their three children, Courtney, Lucy, and Rachel, joined a much smaller contingent of Natives who fled nearly three hundred miles southeast to Alabama. When they arrived, they were taken in by some enslaved Blacks working in the sugarcane fields on the plantation of Patent George. This act of hospitality led to the Indigenous family being claimed as slaves by George. John arrived in poor health and soon died. Rapes soon followed as the George men preyed on the newly enslaved and vulnerable Native American women. Patent George's son, Ford, raped Courtney, who eventually gave birth to a daughter named Eliza. Patent George raped John's widow, Rachel, who gave birth to a son named Patent George Jr. These children were added to the count of enslaved Natives held by the George family.

In approximately 1850, the George family moved their entire plantation to Kentucky, where Ford George raped his enslaved daughter, Eliza. When she found out she was pregnant by her own father, Eliza plotted her revenge. A few days later, Ford George was found dead, with a sharp stick or knife shoved through his heart, and Eliza had disappeared. By the time they tracked her down in Alabama, she had already delivered her baby. When Eliza was forced back to the George plantation, Ford's widow named Eliza's baby Ford George after her murdered husband and the baby's incestuous father. Within a few years, with both George men now in the grave, the matriarch of the family freed all her slaves sometime around 1856.

As FEDERAL TROOPS AND MILITIAS forced out Native nations, white Americans claiming these stolen lands quickly chopped down trees to create enormous plantations based on slave labor. These new plantations soon had a labor crisis. The problem was that American enslavers could no longer simply purchase more enslaved men, women, and children from the transatlantic African slave trade or the Caribbean Indigenous slave trade since both had been banned in 1808. Instead, they had to improvise to expand slavery, using four specific means: "negro stealing," the domestic slave trade, "slave breeding," and raiding Native homelands and reservations. Each one involved Indigenous people, marking their hidden presence in the central aspects of antebellum slavery.

"Negro stealing" and the domestic slave trade went hand in hand. Both were notoriously brutal. Slave traders scoured the upper South for enslaved people offered for sale, as well as free or enslaved Indigenous, African, and mixed-race people they could abduct and sell across state lines for profit. When slave traders collected enough captives to sell, they marched entire gangs of men, women, and children mile after endless mile along dusty or muddy roads from Maryland, Virginia, and Georgia to Alabama, Mississippi, and Louisiana. Groups of ten and twenty captives, called coffles, chained together at the necks, hands, and feet, were forced to march with minimal caloric intake. Muscles cramped; iron shackles chafed and rubbed to the bone; people fainted from exhaustion and the heat. At each stop, potential buyers would prod bodies, pry open mouths and legs to inspect teeth and genitalia, and forcibly inspect people as they would domesticated beasts of burden.[34]

The final destination was often a slave auction in the deep southern slave states, though white drivers of slave coffles sold enslaved people at various points along the way to the highest bidder. An astonishing one million enslaved men, women, and children were trafficked across state lines to the newly claimed lands of the deep South in this way between 1800 and 1865.[35]

A man named Pink was one of thousands of Native Americans subjected to the indignity of the domestic slave trade. Pink was born free on Indian lands in Mississippi and was a "full-blooded" Native American, perhaps Choctaw or Chickasaw, although the exact tribe is not recorded. One day a band of white "negro stealers" raided his community, chased Pink down in the woods, and added him and other captured Natives to the coffle of captives who had been stolen from elsewhere. The man in charge of the slave raiding was Joseph Crews, a notorious trader from South Carolina who made his living kidnapping and trafficking people of color across the American South in the 1840s and 1850s. With Pink in tow, Crews marched his gang of stolen captives around the southern states, driving them like cattle and stopping at plantations along the way to find prospective buyers. Pink was

SLAVE TRADER, SOLD TO TENNESSEE
DEPICTS A SLAVE COFFLE, CA. 1853.

eventually purchased by Joe Patterson, a plantation owner in western South Carolina along the Enoree River. Pink later married a white Irish servant on the plantation. When the couple had children, they too were claimed as slaves.[36]

Entire families were sometimes stolen all together. In 1828, a Muscogee woman named Elizabeth Mordecai and her family were engaged in everyday activities in Muscogee Nation territory when a group of armed white men ambushed them and "chained them with irons." These men marched them from "their native forests and dear relations," as she later recounted, south into Louisiana, where they were sold to a plantation owner named John Baird of Pointe Coupee Parish. Once in Louisiana, the Mordecai family petitioned the local courts, explaining the circumstances of their unjust enslavement. Additionally, they demanded the remarkable sum of $10,000 in compensation for their humiliation and enslavement. The judge believed this Indigenous family, for he freed them without a trial, although he denied their requests for compensation.[37] They were fortunate in their success considering that kidnapped and stolen individuals often struggled in vain to secure their freedom.

Stolen and enslaved Natives were also sold at auctions—"on the block," as it was called—in southern cities like Shreveport and New Orleans. The auction block represented both formal and informal locations for slave auctions, where enslaved people were forced to mount a platform before a raucous audience of prospective buyers to be sold by an auctioneer to the highest bidder. The auction block exemplified sites of immense dehumanization, as enslaved people were often forced to strip naked for inspection. Auctioneers often split up families, focusing on whatever sales strategy would bring the highest price. John Rudd, a mixed-race Indigenous man, later reflected on the terror and sadness of being sold: "If'n you wants to know what unhappiness means," Rudd mused, "stand on the Slave Block and hear the Auctioneer's voice selling you away from the folks you love."[38]

Family separations were common. When a Native man named John W. H. Barnett was a child, his entire family—mother, father, and ten

SALE OF ESTATES, PICTURES AND SLAVES IN THE ROTUNDA, NEW ORLEANS, BY WILLIAM HENRY BROOKE, PRINTED BY J. M. STARLING, 1842, DEPICTS A SLAVE AUCTION.

children total—was sold on the block in New Orleans. One enslaver purchased the parents and the four oldest children; the youngest six were parceled off to different buyers. Barnett had Native ancestry on both sides; his father was a mixed-race Native man from the Eastern Shore of Maryland, and his maternal grandmother was an Indian woman.[39] The sale of an entire Native family into slavery was seemingly entirely routine.

In many instances, abductions and trafficking of Indigenous children and adults went unrecorded at the time and were only sometimes revealed in later oral histories or court records. In December 1845, an Indigenous woman named Peggy Perryman was visiting friends in Arkansas when she was violently assaulted, gagged, and kidnapped by people she did not know. She was trafficked farther west to Missouri, where she was sold as a slave to Joseph Philibert of St. Louis. She was held as a slave until 1848, when she was able to lodge her complaint in the St. Louis Circuit Court.[40] A Choctaw girl named Sallie was sold at auction in Mississippi when she was twelve years old. It is unclear how she had been stolen and separated from her family. She was purchased by a Mr. Martin and taken to Helena, Arkansas, where she eventually married an enslaved Muscogee man named Bob. Together, Bob and Sallie had seven children, all of whom were Indigenous and who remained enslaved on the Martin plantation until the end of the Civil War in 1865.[41]

Like many enslaved Blacks in the antebellum South, Native Americans also experienced rape and forced-breeding practices by enslavers who sought to expand slavery. Wylie Nealy, a Choctaw-Cherokee-Black man born into slavery on a South Carolina plantation in 1853, stated it bluntly: "The master mated the colored people."[42]

Chloe Ann experienced this as a mixed-race Indigenous woman enslaved on the plantation of Wash Hodges. She and an unnamed Muscogee man who was free but seemingly laboring on the Hodges plantation were partners or perhaps even married by custom or common law. Before long, they had a child they named Lulu; Hodges immediately claimed her as a slave as well. When Chloe Ann—who was far younger than her Muscogee husband—did not quickly bear additional children, Hodges blamed her husband's age and turned a pack of dogs on him to run him off the plantation. In his place, Hodges forced a younger enslaved man to regularly rape Chloe Ann over the next few decades. A distraught Chloe Ann gave birth to not just one child but *nineteen* mixed-race Indigenous children, all of whom were added to Hodges's slave roster. Adding to the pain and trauma, Hodges financialized Chloe Ann's offspring. When she was out in the field working, he would quietly sell off a child or two and pocket the money, to Chloe Ann's unspeakable anguish.[43] Other enslaved Indigenous people reported similar occurrences.

In addition to forced breeding, southern plantation owners sometimes found other opportunities to silently incorporate free Native Americans into their enslaved population. Virginia Newman was one of many free Natives who was drawn into plantation life and enslaved. Newman's maternal grandmother was a "pure bred Indian woman" named Sarah Turner. Newman was raised in her grandmother's old log cabin out in the endless bayous of southern Louisiana. Newman grew up learning to climb trees and hunt, kill, and cook everything that moved, including rattlesnakes, which she learned to skin, dice, stew, and serve with copious amounts of brown gravy.[44]

Newman's family was free, but she did not remain so for long. When Newman was old enough, her mother, Eli Chivers, and her grandmother suggested she indenture herself on the nearby Foster plantation in Franklin—an avenue for learning a marketable skill but one that came with risks. The plantation was an escape from the solitary bayou for the young Newman, and she was quickly incorporated into plantation life, which included singing, dancing, and cultural immersion alongside the harsh whipping of enslaved workers. Newman likely did not realize it, but her claim to liberty was slipping away a bit more each year she remained on the plantation. This freedom evaporated entirely when she married an enslaved man from the nearby Lewis plantation in Opelousas—an arrangement often granted to meet the demands of enslaved people. The three children she bore were evidently claimed as slaves on the Foster plantation. The transition from free Indigenous woman to multigenerational enslavement was silent and complete. Newman and her children would only be freed at the end of the Civil War.[45]

Other Indigenous families also stumbled into de facto enslavement on white southern plantations, often driven by poverty. Jerry Sims was born in Natchez, Mississippi, in 1859, into a functionally enslaved

Indigenous family. Sims's paternal grandfather had been a "full blod" Indian chief, and his mother was Choctaw. Sims's parents labored on two different plantations in Mississippi: his mother worked on the Quill and Sely Whitaker property, and his father worked "like a slave" for a white man named John Rob. According to Sims, his parents were poor and were incorporated into plantation life as slaves, perhaps because they had no other means of supporting themselves.[46]

Some enslaved Indigenous people resisted by running away, risking recapture and the intense anger of their enslaver and possible torture or death. In the decades before 1865, enslaved Natives appeared in dozens of runaway slave ads in the Mid-Atlantic and southern states from Maryland to Louisiana.[47] Tom Indian, as he called himself, ran away multiple times from various claimed owners in Caswell County, North Carolina, who advertised for his return in regional newspapers. Similarly, an enslaved Indigenous man named Abraham Camp self-emancipated in September 1835. His claimed owner, Joseph Waggoner, in Davidson County, North Carolina, ran an ad in the *Raleigh Register* that offered one hundred dollars for Abraham's return if he was alive. If Camp resisted, Waggoner instructed people to simply murder him, for which Waggoner would pay ten dollars.[48]

INDIGENOUS PEOPLE WERE NOT ONLY enslaved by whites. In some cases, they were enslaved by Native American and mixed-race Indigenous planters belonging to the so-called Five Civilized Tribes who owned large plantations driven by enslaved labor.[49] These startling developments had their roots in the early eighteenth century, when enslaved Africans frequently ran away to the large Native nations of the Southeast. Sometimes they found refuge, but in other instances they were either handed over to white authorities or retained as servants, slaves, and adopted family members by these Indian nations.[50]

By the late eighteenth century, some elite members of the Five Civilized Tribes increasingly embraced slaveholding. Perhaps this was partly an attempt to perform "civilization" within the context of southern culture, but it also showed the dynamism of Native nations that adapted to a continually changing colonial context. Enslaving Africans allowed some Native individuals to compete economically with plantation owners around them. Within a few decades, dozens of wealthy individuals from these tribes had large plantations with thousands of enslaved Africans and mixed-race Indigenous people laboring on them.[51]

During removal, Native farmers—some of whom were wealthy plantation owners and enslavers—took their slaves with them and immediately set up estates based on coerced labor in their new homes in what soon became Oklahoma. These enslaved populations continued to grow and included mixed-race Indigenous people. In the 1860 census, the Choctaw, Cherokee, Muscogee, and Chickasaw numbered approximately 59,000, and collectively they held a total of 7,369 people in slavery. The average Native enslaver held approximately 6 slaves, with some Native plantation owners holding as many as 227 enslaved people.[52]

Benjamin Franklin "Frank" Colbert, for example, was a Chickasaw man who had been forcibly removed from Mississippi to Oklahoma with the rest of his nation in the 1830s. His expansive plantation was near what is today Colbert, Oklahoma, within the modern-day boundaries of the Chickasaw reservation. Colbert was a savvy investor and operated a ferry across the Red River and a stagecoach stand in addition to extensive property worked by enslaved people. At the center of his plantation sat an imposing log mansion, with six rooms connected in the middle by a large open hall. The rear of the building held a large kitchen and a smokehouse stocked full of various meats and lard. Colbert kept at least twenty-five enslaved people, who lived in log cabins on his property behind the house.[53]

An unknown percentage of slaves held by Native enslavers like Colbert were Indigenous. A Chickasaw woman named Temene (or Tamena) was enslaved as part of the Logan plantation in the 1840s on Chickasaw lands in Oklahoma. She eventually had several children, including Aleck Brown and Sebbie Johnson, born from at least two different men who were also enslaved. Logan passed away during the Civil War, leaving the status of the enslaved population in limbo. Temene took her children to Kansas to wait out the war. She returned to Oklahoma in 1866, where Aleck and Sebbie eventually petitioned to join the Chickasaw Nation as both blood citizens and freedmen (a term applied to formerly enslaved people held by the Five Civilized Tribes).[54]

Similarly, Sarah Wilson was born in 1850 and raised on a plantation in Cherokee territory in Oklahoma. Sarah's grandmother and her mother, Adeline, were both owned by the same person, Ben Johnson, who was married to a Cherokee woman and was part of the Cherokee nation. Well before Sarah was born, they had likely followed the tribe as they were forcibly removed in the 1830s to Oklahoma Territory, where Johnson and his Cherokee wife set up their plantation just west of present-day Fort Smith on the Oklahoma-Arkansas border. At some point, one of Johnson's sons began raping Adeline, which is how Sarah was conceived. Throughout her life, Sarah maintained that she was one-quarter Cherokee. After the war, she and her mother returned to Cherokee territory (from Texas, where they had been relocated by Johnson as he fled the Union Army) and took their place on Cherokee land as blood citizens and freedmen.[55]

Indigenous slaveholding entwined family-slavery relationships in ways that outsiders found confusing. A mixed-race Muscogee-Black woman named Polly from Coweta, Oklahoma, was married to a Black man named John. Even though they were married, Polly was his legal owner. In another situation, when the parents of two young Muscogee children died, they became the young owners of an enslaved Black woman who was also their primary caretaker.[56] American officials often didn't fully understand these networks of kinship and slavery, and family members had to negotiate their position in these tribes, especially after the Civil War.[57]

THE TERROR OF ENSLAVEMENT FOLLOWED Indigenous nations even after expulsion from their lands. Instead of a safe haven, Indian reservations in Oklahoma became a hunting ground for slave traders who entered tribal lands, abducted children and other vulnerable Native Americans, and trafficked them into slavery.[58] James Boyd was born in an "Indian hut" in Oklahoma Territory, likely in the late 1850s. Even though Native people had been forced onto large reservations, white settlers still invaded Indigenous land and provoked fights and skirmishes. Boyd lived with his Indian father, Blue Bull Bird, who had been raised in Oklahoma, and his mother, Nancy Will, who was Indigenous Mexican and had come north with Mexican president Antonio López de Santa Anna during a battle and somehow found her way into Oklahoma.

One day the young Boyd (when he was a "real li'l feller," as he later recalled) was fishing on the Cherokee River in southern Oklahoma just north of the Texas line when a band of white men moved through, yelling and shooting, perhaps intending to terrorize and intimidate the tribe. Boyd took his fishing rod and hid in the bushes along the side of the river, hoping to avoid detection. He was spotted by a white man named Sanford Wooldridge, who stole (under the guise of protection) and enslaved him on his large 1,600-acre plantation in Texas.[59]

Spence Johnson was also captured on his own homelands and years later vividly recalled the details of his kidnapping from the Choctaw Nation at the age of three. Johnson was born and raised free on reserved Choctaw lands in Oklahoma Territory. On a hot summer day in 1859, Spence's mother took her five younger children to the river near a town named Boggy Depot to wash clothing. As Spence and his siblings played nearby, a large carriage stopped along the side of the road. The Choctaw mother was too preoccupied with the laundry to notice the men inside offering the irresistible gift of candy to the young children. After the first child received candy harmlessly, the other four flocked to the carriage for some, too. Two other men slipped out from the carriage and snuck up on the mother.

In a flash, the trap was sprung. The men near the carriage grabbed the children and locked them inside while the other assailants wrestled the mother to the ground. The mother fought back, screaming, biting, and flailing, until one of the men clubbed her over the head. They lugged her unconscious body into the carriage and drove south out of Oklahoma, from Boggy Depot across the Red River into Texas and eventually into Louisiana to Shreveport, a major center of the southern slave trade. There, Spence, his mother, and two of his siblings were placed on the auction block and sold to the highest bidder, Riley Suratt, who paid $3,000 for all four of them. The other two children were sold to a different owner. No one seemed to care that a visibly Native American family was sold at the auction block in the late 1850s. There is no record of protest, no objection, and no effort at concealment, despite the supposed illegality of Native enslavement in Louisiana.[60]

This slave raiding of Native reservations became so frequent that the US representative from Arkansas, Alfred B. Greenwood, proposed

Spence Johnson, Age over 87, ca. 1936–1938.

in 1860 that Congress take action by "providing by law for the indictment and punishment of persons for the stealing of slaves in the Indian country." At first, US representative John Sherman from Ohio objected because he thought that the resolution was intended to prevent "abolition negro thieves" from stealing enslaved Blacks held by Indian slaveholders (like the Cherokee and Choctaw, for example). And Sherman, as a northern antislavery Republican, seemingly approved of such radical abolitionist actions. The ensuing discussion revealed that the resolution was intended to protect free Native Americans who were being kidnapped and trafficked from reservations and sold into slavery. When Sherman realized the purpose was to punish "pro-slavery negro thieves" and protect Native nations from slave raiding, he gave his full support.[61]

UP THROUGH THE END OF the Civil War, Indigenous people—especially mixed-race individuals, who were seen as Black—were enslavable in southern slave states. In 1858, an unnamed Muscogee man ran a popular ox yoke manufacturing shop in Quindaro in the free state of Kansas. Quindaro was located just west of what is now Kansas City, Missouri, and was on a major westward trail leading to California, Oregon, and Utah. In late August 1858, this Muscogee artisan was helping a family move from Johnson County, Kansas, approximately ten miles from the Missouri state line, when a group of armed men from Missouri, a slave state, surrounded his wagon and claimed that he was a fugitive slave from Missouri. He was apprehended by these vigilante whites and jailed in Missouri, where local whites attested that he had been "running at large" without an owner. A Kansas attorney named John W. Wright tried to secure his freedom, but the outcome of the case is inconclusive.[62]

Occasionally, kidnappers were brought to justice. In June 1859, a wiry man named Abel R. Burks hoped to make a quick profit by kidnapping Indians and selling them as slaves. Burks was born in Georgia and practiced law in Mississippi. Standing nearly six feet tall, with black eyes and even blacker hair, the fast-talking, twenty-eighty-year-old Burks likely made quite an impression in courthouses. On June 15, 1859, Burks ambushed and kidnapped two free Native Americans named Sally and Terrell Cash in Scott County, Mississippi, and carried them one hundred miles west to Warren County on the banks of the Mississippi River, where he sold them into slavery.

But somehow the word got out, and a warrant was issued for Burks's arrest on January 2, 1861. He was eventually caught, placed on trial, and sent to the state prison, much to the horror of his wife, children, and family friends. The enslaver had become the enslaved, sentenced to hard labor at the Mississippi Penitentiary. Outraged, he and his friends immediately began petitioning for his release as if there was nothing wrong with kidnapping free Native Americans with the intent to sell them as slaves. In an angry, pitiful letter sent from prison on May 7, 1762, Burks described his situation, which closely mirrored the condition he had imposed on Sally and Terrell Cash: "I am now powerless, completely in the hands of others, deprived of liberty, character, home, wife & children."[63]

WALKING THE STREETS OF the French Quarter in New Orleans today with its ornate buildings and distinctly French creole cuisine and culture, it is hard to imagine its former life as a bustling southern center of the domestic slave trade. At approximately fifty-two sites across the city, tens of thousands of enslaved men and women were placed on an auction block and sold to the highest bidder. How many Native Americans and mixed-race Indigenous people passed through the hands of auctioneers between 1811 and 1862? We may never know, in part because they were not usually noted as Native.

Such erasures continue today. A recently installed historical marker acknowledging the domestic slave trade and New Orleans' auction sites, posted at the corner of Esplanade Avenue and Chartres Street, is silent regarding the Indigenous people trafficked and sold in the city's markets and dispersed into the wider regional countryside.[64]

Through various means, the stealing and enslavement of Native Americans and mixed-race Indigenous people continued in the years before the Civil War, even if scholars have not usually included this reality in most histories of the period. Indigenous people in the South were assailed on all sides: they were kidnapped and enslaved, had their homelands stolen, and were physically removed to a new, unwanted land. And in these new, unchosen homes in exile, white Americans continued to slave-raid and kidnap them and their children.

A surprising new drama was just starting to unfold as Americans continued to colonize westward past the Mississippi. American settlers carried their anti-Indian biases with them, spreading older forms of chattel slavery and embracing newer versions of servitude that mirrored southern slavery. A massive expansion of Native American slavery in the United States was still on the horizon.

Thirteen

A NEW AMERICAN SLAVERY

AS AMERICANS WERE EXPANDING SLAVERY'S SOUTHERN REACH ON Native lands, an equally monumental process was unfolding in the West. Determined to claim the remainder of the western regions, Americans seized land from Mexico in a short, decisive war between 1846 and 1848. Afterward, American colonialism went into hyperdrive.

What is often called westward expansion was basically a repeat of English and American colonization compressed into just a few short decades, with devastating results. Between 1840 and 1870, invading Americans stole, enslaved, removed, or murdered tens of thousands of Indigenous people in New Mexico, Arizona, Utah, Colorado, and California, and forcibly sequestered tens of thousands more onto reservations in the Upper Midwest and the Pacific Northwest. In many cases, this was done by the state and federal authorities in addition to the actions of private citizens. The atrocities were so systematic, so intentional, that one scholar has rightfully referred to the treatment of California's Indians as an American genocide.[1]

John Sutter, often hailed as the founder of American California, embodied this colonial violence. Sutter was a Swiss American entrepreneur who had arrived in New York City in 1834 before moving west, staying for a period in the slave state of Missouri, where he saw firsthand that the wealthiest citizens were slaveholders and fur traders. Taking advantage of Mexico's openness to foreign settlement, he followed trade lines through Native territory to the city of Santa Fe. From there, he traveled northwest to the Mexican province of Alta California (a large area that covered what is now California, Nevada, and Utah) in 1839, where he received an enormous governmental grant of nearly fifty thousand acres that he called New Helvetia.

Commandeering the labor of local Nisenan and Miwok Natives, he built an adobe compound he named Sutter's Fort, which later grew into the city of Sacramento and later still, the state capital. He continued to expand his influence by purchasing a huge estate named Fort Ross from a Russian company in 1841, which nearly quadrupled his landholdings. Like other such purchases, these territories were the traditional home-lands of thousands of Native Americans. The lands were unceded, and Nisenan, Miwok, and other Indigenous peoples still lived on them.[2]

Sutter quickly turned his estate into a southern-style plantation using the coerced labor of hundreds of Indigenous people. Overseers stood by with whips as Nisenans and Miwoks planted and harvested vast acres of grain, wove blankets, trapped for furs, and hunted and fished to provide food for the compound.[3] Mealtimes were a feeding frenzy that Sutter designed to make Indigenous people feel like ani-mals. Visitors reported seeing wooden troughs three to four feet in length that were placed on the ground and filled with the leftovers from the estate: slaughterhouse entrails, morsels, and grain rejects. Indige-nous laborers were forced to squat on the ground around the troughs and eat with their hands.[4] One visitor in July 1845 reported that Sutter "keeps 600 or 800 Indians in a complete state of Slavery."[5]

Sutter's Fort also became a major center of a regional Indigenous

SUTTER'S FORT, SACRAMENTO, CAL. 1847, CA. 1866.

slave trade. Sutter routinely abducted Natives and sold them as slaves to ranchers in the wider region. He later reminisced that it was "common in those days to seize Indian women and children and sell them." They were even used as currency: in 1845, Sutter sent thirty-one emaciated enslaved Natives to his creditor Antonio Suñol as payment for a debt. Dozens more were sent to family and friends.[6]

Sutter's slavery-based estate in California was only one of hundreds of such plantations founded by Americans in the Southwest and West between 1840 and the 1880s. Sutter and others like him should cause us to question why we have drawn a firm distinction between the slaveholding American South and the West in the antebellum period, since in both regions slavery-based labor regimes were common. The primary difference was that Sutter and other western enslavers used Natives almost exclusively, even in territories and states that had outlawed slavery.

Americans at the time—and later historians—liked to blame the Spanish, Mexicans, and larger Indian nations for a system of Native peonage and slavery that Americans inherited after 1848 when it took these lands from Mexico.[7] But the truth is that the new colonizers quickly Americanized and expanded these regimes of Indigenous labor. Americans were so willing to capitalize on such enslavement, in part, because they had been enslaving and dispossessing Indigenous people across the continent since the first arrival of the English. Instead of shutting down these practices, they firmly embraced and expanded them, applying previous methods of enslavement to a new context.

To justify their actions, Americans convinced themselves and officials in Washington that these forms of Indigenous servitude and slavery were categorically different from southern slavery. This helps explain why California was admitted as a free state in 1850 despite rampant Indigenous enslavement and peonage. It also sheds light on why New Mexico could pass a short-lived slave code in 1859 that applied only to African-descended enslaved individuals despite the presence of thousands of enslaved Native Americans in the territory and why Mormons in Utah were able to justify their large-scale and intentional purchase of Native children and impose indentures.

By defining slavery and servitude narrowly in terms of Black chattel slavery, these newly arrived American colonists created a powerful, self-serving distinction that allowed Indigenous enslavement to thrive in western territories and states for decades. This fiction, along with nationalistic mythologies about rugged, self-made American settlers, has hidden the central role of Native American slavery and servitude in westward colonization.

SUTTER HAD SUCCESSFULLY FULFILLED the expansionist fantasy held by thousands of Americans in the 1830s and early 1840s. Americans increasingly believed it was ordained by God that they should eventually control most of the North American continent, from the Atlantic to the Pacific. The journalist John O'Sullivan called this growing sentiment the "manifest destiny" of the United States in 1845, and the phrase stuck.[8] This powerful idea gave religious and cultural jus-

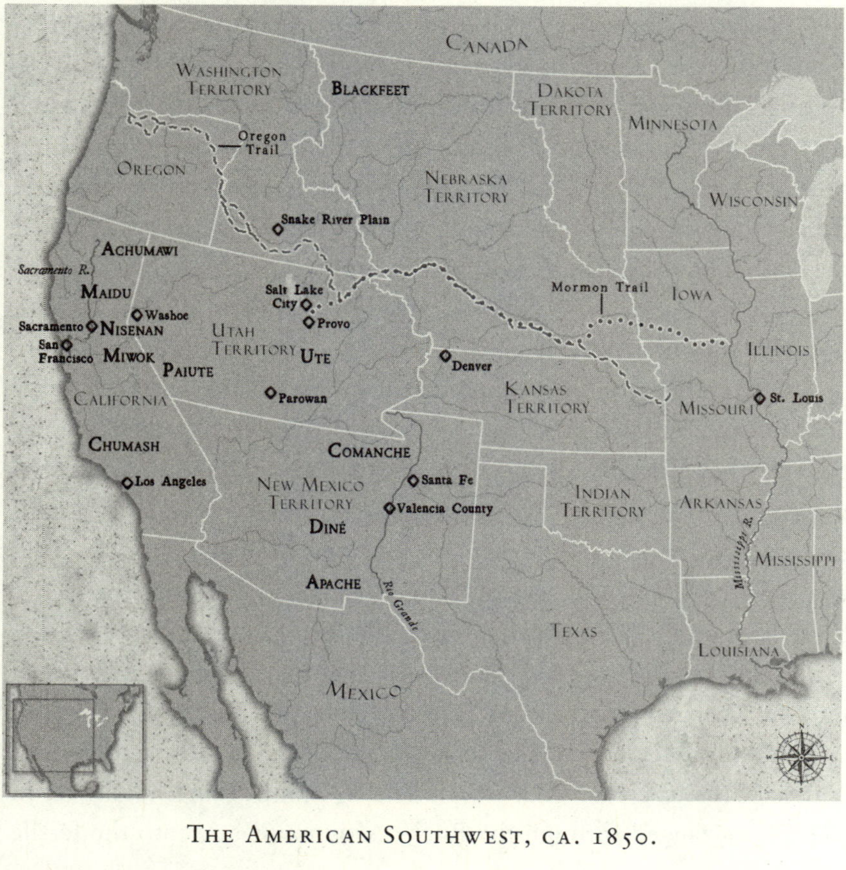

THE AMERICAN SOUTHWEST, CA. 1850.

tification to the tens of thousands of Americans who coveted the vast western third of the continent.

As Americans soon realized, the regions from the Great Plains westward contained a stunning array of topographies, as well as large and powerful Native nations that ranged and traded over hundreds of miles. From the soaring ranges of the Rockies and Sierra Nevada to the vast deserts and canyons of the Southwest, to the fertile central valley of California and the extensive coastal maritime culture where the continent meets the Pacific Ocean, the West was a world unto its own. Large nations like the Arapaho, Kiowa, Cheyenne, Sioux, and Comanche commanded the regional trade on horseback from Texas to the Dakotas, while Mandan and Hidatsa farmed along the upper Missouri River. The Diné (Navajo), Apache, and Ute controlled much of the Southwest, from New Mexico to California's Sierra Nevada range, with at least fifty thousand Native Americans living in what later became the New Mexico Territory.

California's expansive terrain was home to as many as one hundred thousand Native Americans, including large tribes such as the Miwok, Nisenan, Konkow, Yokut, and others who had successfully navigated centuries of Spanish and Mexican imperialism.[9] North of California, the Nez Perce, Walla Walla, Yakima, and Chinook nations hunted and fished along the coastal inlets and the Snake River. The western half of the continent was teeming with Native presence.

These were not empty lands, as white Americans liked to believe, nor were they unprofitably used.[10]

Americans were initially somewhat restrained by the invisible treaty lines of the Louisiana Purchase that formed an international boundary between the United States and Mexico. Starting in the 1830s, Americans moved into Texas, which became a growing outpost of American traders, ranchers, and would-be plantation owners hoping to extend southern slave economies westward. After Texas seized its independence from Mexico in 1836 (despite Americans being routed at the Alamo earlier that year), even more traders and squatters ventured farther west into the Mexican territories of Nuevo Mexico and Alta California.[11]

Farther north, in Independence, Missouri, Americans took over Native paths to create their own overland trail heading northwest in 1840. It zigzagged through the Rocky Mountains and into the fertile valley of the Snake River plain in southern Idaho before curving gently northwest into the Oregon Territory. Plodding caravans of American colonists invaded Native lands, setting up towns and trading posts all along the Oregon Trail.

As Americans traveled more frequently to Nuevo Mexico and Alta California in the early 1840s, they sent back reports and even published guides to the region. These early descriptions confirmed that, although slavery was technically illegal in the country of Mexico, a robust and widespread system of cheap, slavelike labor formed the backbone of the workforce in the area. Often called peons, Natives (and sometimes poor Mexicans and mixed-race individuals) were hired to work in exchange for basic clothing and some food. This system of peonage was predicated on racking up debts that the laborer could never fully pay, thereby justifying ongoing servitude, which was often enforceable not only by coercion but also by the law. These Natives were in "absolute vassalage," a proslavery and future Confederate soldier named Lansford Warren Hastings wrote in an 1845 guidebook to Oregon and California, and in conditions "even more degrading, and more oppressive than that of our slaves in the south."[12]

THE WAR WITH MEXICO starting in 1846 marked the beginning of the American military conquest of the West, and with it came a sharp spike in Native American enslavement and land theft that continued for decades. With their usual braggadocio, the American army marched into regions dominated by powerful sovereign Native nations and tried to intimidate them into submission. The seasoned military general Stephen W. Kearny was tasked with invading Mexican territory. He captured Santa Fe in August 1846 and established a territorial government for the United States. Viewing the large, regional Indigenous nations as a menace, Kearny freely licensed American and Mexican residents to wage war against the Diné (called Navajo by the Spanish). He also encouraged attacks on other tribes as retribution for raids against ranches and towns. As in previous American wars, this almost always involved taking Diné and other Natives captive, forcing them into servitude.[13]

Kearny's troops soon made their way to California in July 1846, determined to extend their land claims to the Pacific Coast. With a stern visage and imposing commander's uniform, Kearny was installed as the military governor of the newly claimed territory of California on March 1, 1847. Americans and military units who streamed in after him saw local Native populations as subservient peoples on whom to prey for labor and land. In early 1847, a group of Californians rode into a local Native town in Sonora, east of San Francisco, at the foot-hills of the Sierra Nevada, and tried to kidnap all the Indian children and women they could find. These Natives fought back, killing one of the slave traders and forcing the rest to make a hasty retreat.[14]

The end of the Mexican–American War brought massive changes for Natives and Mexicans living in the New Mexico and California ter-ritories. The Treaty of Guadalupe Hidalgo in 1848 transferred a colos-sal amount of land from Mexico to the United States—portions of the present-day states of New Mexico, Arizona, California, Nevada, Utah, and Wyoming. The jagged imaginary line that defined the new US–Mexico border sawed in half a larger region that had been relatively unified by culture and language. Thousands of Mexicans and Indige-nous peoples suddenly found themselves in the United States, with the option to migrate south to Mexico or, for Mexicans, to become citi-zens of the United States, an option not offered to Native Americans. These Mexican and Indigenous populations did not cross the border into the United States; instead, in the words of Choctaw and Cherokee scholar Eileen Luna-Firebaugh, "The border crossed us."[15]

With Mexico defeated, Americans moved into the vast, unceded lands of the Diné, Ute, and Nisenan and quickly Americanized a centuries-old system of raiding, captive taking, and enslavement. For genera-tions, large Native nations in the Southwest had raided their Indian enemies and had taken captives, mostly rooted in kinship and adop-tion practices and rituals, as well as amid contests for regional power. Americans jumped at these opportunities by claiming land, intermar-rying with wealthy Mexican ranching families, and trying to replicate structures of mastery and vassalage over the Indigenous population. Newly arrived Americans also purchased Indigenous and Mexican cap-tives, participated in slave raids, and experienced the power and stealth of Indian retaliatory attacks on their farms and towns. Notably, how-ever, Americans purchased Native captives and worked them in ways that closely resembled southern Black chattel slavery.[16]

The US military was an integral force in this embrace and expansion

of Indigenous slavery. Repeating well-rehearsed tactics of outright conquest and subjugation, the United States waged war against the powerful Diné nation that occupied large sections of New Mexico Territory
(which included present-day Arizona). In August 1849, the new American governor and military head of New Mexico, Colonel John M.
Washington, led a series of expeditions against the Diné. A Virginian
by birth and distant cousin of George Washington, he was a veteran of
the wars of removal against the Seminole and Muscogee. Unsurprisingly, his explicit purpose was to subjugate the Diné and force them
to agree to a subservient treaty like the ones the United States had
imposed on the Muscogee, Choctaw, Seminole, and other larger Native
nations in the Southeast.[17] Under his watchful eye, militias and settlers
unleashed rounds of slave raiding and captive taking.

This policy of military submission was pursued by subsequent
American governors, including James Calhoun, who assumed the New
Mexico Territory governorship in January 1851. A round-faced, sullen-
looking man, Calhoun was born in Georgia during Indian removal and
slavery's expansion. He was elected as a Georgia state representative
in 1830, and he took his seat that November as the legislature systematically deprived Muscogee and Cherokee communities of their lands
through unfair treaties and military force. He served as a lieutenant colonel during the war with Mexico and stepped into the governorship of
the New Mexico Territory determined to badger the Diné and Apache
into submission.[18] Calhoun immediately handed out licenses to individuals and militias to raid and plunder, which Mexican and American
traders interpreted as a license to slave-raid as well.[19] Abolitionist journalists on the East Coast were outraged when they heard about Calhoun's actions. "Scoundrelism in Our Territories: Kidnapping under a
Governor's License" blasted the National Era headline in Washington,
DC, in 1851, describing how licenses were used to "purchase Indian
children as slaves, for the benefit of persons in New Mexico."[20]

These government-licensed traders and raiders brought in hundreds
of Diné men, women, and children. Captives who were sold as slaves
and peons were valued based on "age, sex, beauty, and usefulness,"
according to Calhoun. Younger girls and women were valued the most
highly, at perhaps $100 to $150 each, because of their potential for agricultural, domestic, and reproductive work. Male captives were only

worth half as much, even if they had useful or marketable skills.[21] By January 1852, Diné headmen told American federal agents in Santa Fe that more than two hundred Diné children had been carried off. "My people are yet crying for the children they have lost," one leader named Armijo stated. "Is it American justice that we must give up everything and receive nothing?"[22] Apparently, the answer was yes.

Somehow, inexplicably, this veritable eruption of conquest and enslavement barely registered back East, where antislavery debates were reaching a crescendo. Local newspapers like the *Santa Fe Weekly Gazette* taunted northern abolitionists for focusing so exclusively on African slavery in the South. The situation in New Mexico was "much more worthy of the efforts" of abolitionists, asserted an editorial on July 20, 1852. "Thousands" of Indigenous women and children had been "stolen from their families and sold into slavery, worse than *Southern Slavery*."[23] Local officials occasionally prosecuted seemingly random cases, as with the enslavement of an unnamed twelve-year-old Diné girl held by a wealthy woman residing in Valencia County, New Mexico, who was set free by a local judge after seven years of slavery.[24] But most of the enslaved Natives remained untouched.

In CALIFORNIA, Americans eagerly coopted a decades-old *rancheria* system that dominated the landscape, powered primarily by Indian labor. This network of large-scale plantation-like farms emerged after the secularization of the Spanish mission system in 1834. Spanish missionaries had arrived in the 1770s, starting with the Franciscan Junípero Serra, and eventually set up a string of a dozen mission towns that used a combination of punishments and rewards to coerce the labor and allegiance of Native communities.[25]

When the missions closed sixty years later, resident Natives were evicted—a betrayal that lingered for decades and left somewhat adrift the thousands of Natives who had become dependent on the system. Mission lands were converted to rancherías, with former mission Natives used as laborers in varying degrees of servitude and enslavement. Rancho Petaluma was one such example. It lay north of San Francisco, spreading over 104 square miles, and used a sizable Native workforce to grow produce, raise livestock, and manufacture products. Francisca Benicia Carrillo de Vallejo built a veritable empire at Rancho

Petaluma from 1834 until 1857, directly on the backs of Indigenous slaves and servants.[26]

Rancho Petaluma may have been one of the largest, but many other such rancherías built on Indigenous labor extended across the California landscape as Americans moved into the region. Wage labor was expensive in the 1840s and 1850s, with talented mechanics demanding between two and five dollars per day. Even unskilled white laborers usually commanded a slightly lower rate of one to three dollars daily. White Americans quickly learned that they could rather easily force Indigenous people into lopsided, coercive labor contracts for pen-

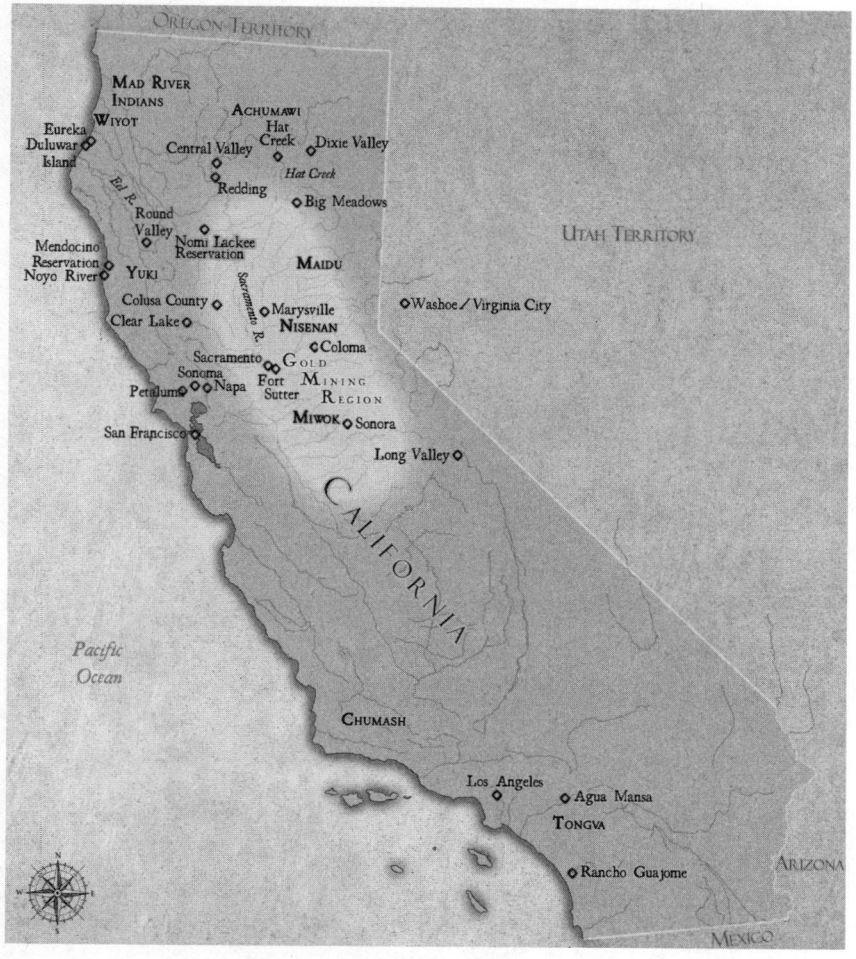

CALIFORNIA, 1850.

nies. In particular, rancheros found they could impose a barter system rather than pay cash wages, requiring full-time labor for mere trifles: a shirt or trousers or perhaps some meat or a little bit of food. But each "purchase" in this system added more owed labor, and the markup of items kept Natives perpetually indebted. Some ranchers had up to four hundred Natives "employed" in this fashion.[27]

As during other eras of American history, debt peonage and other forms of coerced labor were scarcely or not at all better than outright enslavement. James Calhoun, at the time the federal Indian agent in New Mexico, stated plainly in 1850, "*Peons*, you are aware, is but another name for *slaves* as that term is understood in our Southern States." Native peons could be bought, sold, and inherited and could only be redeemed by buying out their monetary value, just like enslaved Black and Indigenous people in the American South. And as in slave states, New Mexico residents felt an absolute right to buy and sell peons, and "no human power can disturb that right."[28]

Indigenous people resisted these new impositions in numerous ways, sometimes violently. In 1847, two Americans named Andrew Kelsey and Charles Stone bought a ranching operation on Clear Lake, fifty miles northwest of Sacramento. They inherited and added to a sizable labor force of several hundred Natives whom they treated like slaves. Visitors noted their ruthlessness in whipping Indigenous people, shooting at them for sport, and punishing them by hanging them by their thumbs for days on end.[29] Kelsey and Stone terrorized local Native communities by conducting a small-scale Indian slave trade out of the region. In 1848, they raided local Indian towns and sold 172 Natives southward to ranches in Napa and Sonoma.

Resentment soon reached a boiling point. In 1849, Kelsey and Stone hatched a plan to round up all local Natives for usable workers, sell some, and forcibly remove the rest eastward to the Sacramento River. The two Americans compelled their Indigenous captives to craft ropes to be used to tie groups of enslaved Natives together to ensure safe transport. While they were making the ropes, the captives must have been devising plans as well. While Kelsey and Stone were out working one day, the Native women they kept as sex slaves and household domestics filled the men's guns with water, making it almost impossible to quickly load and fire. The next morning, in December 1849, a group of Natives raided the adobe house of their despised enslavers and slaughtered them with arrows and stones.[30]

THE DISCOVERY OF GOLD in central California soon turned a westward trickle of American colonists into a torrent of often greedy, violent treasure seekers. On January 24, 1848, a man named James Marshall discovered gold near Coloma, on land claimed by John Sutter. Marshall, like so many other Californians, turned to Indigenous laborers from the Nisenan nation to help mine the gold. Although it would take almost a year for it to be verified, Marshall had unknowingly stumbled upon an enormous vein of gold (called a mother lode) 120 miles long and a few miles wide. When suddenly rich Californians began sauntering through American cities slinging around bags of gold dust, the imagination of the entire world was aroused. The discovery was confirmed by President James Polk, who in late 1848 declared it to be a bona fide mother lode, inaugurating an official gold rush.[31]

Within a year, the non-Indigenous population of California skyrocketed from ten or twelve thousand to ninety-four thousand. Would-be prospectors poured in from Oregon, as well as from the South and Southwest, all heading to central California to pry and sift a metallic fortune from the earth. Americans and others hoping for a shortcut to prosperity came by land and sea. Indigenous people and locals watched as more than six hundred ships sailed into the San Francisco Bay from all over the world. Photographs from 1849 depict a crowded and chaotic harbor with masts stretching in every direction but not a person in sight. Crazed by gold, sailors completely abandoned their ships, leaving them bobbing lifelessly in the harbor.[32]

These invasive "Forty-Niners" created a devastating shockwave for California's numerous Indigenous peoples, something that is often forgotten in the lore of this most famous of gold rushes. Gold-frenzied Americans came primed for violence against Natives, even coercing them into slavery. Overland travelers who had nervously cradled their rifles on the trails to Oregon or Salt Lake City imported their fears and Indian hatred to California. As they rode toward gold-rich Coloma, these Americans presumed every Indian to be an enemy, shooting them on sight or, at other times, indiscriminately raiding and enslaving as they went.

Shew Daguerreotype Panorama,
by William Shew, ca. 1852,
shows abandoned ships in the San Francisco Bay.

Conflicts escalated, and soon white immigrants to the region sought to exterminate the local Nisenan Indians—on whose homelands gold had first been discovered. In late February 1849, a roving band of sixty gold seekers from Oregon hunted down and took as prisoners two hundred to three hundred Nisenan tribal members, whom they blamed for the death of approximately thirty settlers. An ad-hoc trial was set up at Sutter's Mill, and thirty Nisenans were executed.[33]

Indigenous laborers were at the center of the quickly escalating gold rush. Some seemingly worked willingly in the early months, seizing the chance to share in the wealth of a metal so valued by the invaders. Two prospectors named Charles M. Weber and William Daylor relied on the labor of a thousand Natives near Coloma in the first few months, most of whom were Nisenan. Others were forced into servitude and slavelike conditions, performing the heavy manual labor of carrying, building, and dredging that could lead to the discovery of gold.

When the worker supply dwindled, some white prospectors simply marched into local Nisenan towns and forced men and boys to labor in the mines. In 1848, three white men brought thirty or forty Indians to Coloma to dig for gold, with daily quotas set and a vicious whipping awaiting those who could not find enough gold. Those who ran away were hunted down and brought back and treated, in the eyes of one observer, "like slaves."[34]

By the end of 1849, perhaps as many as four thousand California Natives labored in the mining industry, most of them in various states of servitude and slavery. Thousands more were pulled into coercive labor situations across the state to replace the innumerable free farmhands and artisans who had decamped to central California to prospect for gold.[35] Four hundred years after the Spanish had enslaved Natives and forced them to work in gold mines, Americans were doing the same, with equally devastating effects.

The gold rush profoundly altered the landscape and ecology for the Native communities in the region. The large Indian nations of the Central Valley, including the Nisenan and Miwok, foraged for wild onions, sweet potatoes, and acorns. They fished clams and mussels from estuaries and salmon from the rivers, and hunted bear, deer, and small animals.[36] White Americans roamed over the landscape, devouring everything in sight. Additionally, the never-ending process of digging, sifting, and diverting waterways for gold-mining operations clogged rivers with silt and killed off local fish populations. Farms and ranches soon began spreading across the countryside, and "No Tres-

CALIFORNIA INDIGENOUS
GOLD MINERS, CA. 1850.

passing" signs turned familiar territory into forbidden landscapes.[37] When Natives responded to this invasive colonial presence by purloining cattle, towns and counties formed militias to raid Indian villages, setting off a deadly cycle of counterattacks that usually favored the white invaders.

THIS SLAVERY-POWERED GOLD RUSH paradoxically propelled California into statehood—and into being deemed a free state at that. While Native peoples worked in slavelike conditions in the gold mines, California took center stage in a national debate about the spread of slavery into new states. But when legislators in Washington, DC, discussed slavery, they meant southern Black slavery. The coerced labor, enslavement, slave raids, and peonage of Native peoples was so hidden it did not factor into the heated deliberations. In 1849, California petitioned to enter the Union as a free state—fast-tracked, in part, because of its newly important role as the guardian of the most important gold supply in North American history.

Southerners vehemently objected to the admission of California as a free state, fearing an imbalance of free and slave state representation in Congress. Northerners, for their part, would not tolerate the extension of slavery into a region they (mistakenly) saw as free from slavery and so championed California's proposed free status. Orin Fowler, a US representative from Massachusetts, during a speech in Washington, DC, on March 11, 1850, unknowingly and without irony thundered, "To extend slavery—American slavery—(the worst kind of slavery that ever existed on the face of the globe, since Adam fell)—into territory now free, is a wrong done to humanity—to the rights of humanity, to the friends of humanity."[38]

The result was what politicians called the Compromise of 1850. In exchange for admitting California as a free state, Southerners secured a draconian Fugitive Slave Act, which gave them the power to pursue runaway slaves across state lines into free states, even in the North, and into western territories. Antislavery activists made other gains like abolishing the internal slave trade in Washington, DC.

This national politicking reshaped the geography of the American West. In addition to California being admitted as a free state, two rugged desert and mountainous territories were also created: Utah and New Mexico, both of which would briefly legalize slavery. The New Mexico Territory stretched from the Texas border to California, including what is now New Mexico and Arizona. The Utah Territory included what is now Utah, Nevada, eastern Colorado, and a small portion of Wyoming.

In all the national debates over keeping slavery out of California, legislators conveniently ignored the open secret of ongoing Indigenous enslavement taking place there. California's constitution, written in 1849, made a mockery of the lived reality of thousands of Native Americans. Ratified on November 13, 1849, Section 18 of Article 1 of the California Constitution declared, "Neither slavery, nor involuntary servitude, unless for the punishment of crimes, shall ever be tolerated in this State."[39] These words were borrowed from the Northwest Ordinance of 1787, which was the first experimental "free" territory carved out of Native land after the American Revolution.[40] As had been true in the Northwest Territory, the statute gave a perception of antislavery while creating enormous loopholes that American colonists repeatedly maximized.[41]

California state legislators were well aware of coerced Indigenous labor in their state. Instead of eliminating it, they decided to regulate it. The new California legislature passed—with relatively little debate— "An Act for the Government and Protection of Indians" on April 22, 1850, a full five months before California officially became the thirty-first state. The title was a farce; instead of providing protection, its statutes reeked of an American-style colonialism designed to subjugate the Native populations by imposing white law.

In theory, according to the 1850 act, Natives were supposed to be "unmolested in the pursuit of their usual avocations for the maintenance of themselves and families." But the law allowed white Americans to buy and sell Indian lands and impose American "justice" in Native communities, including public whipping for stealing cattle.[42] Notably, this law gave local justices of the peace enormous power to assign Native individuals to residents who paid the bond of any Native convicted of a crime (also called convict leasing).[43] Additionally, Indigenous people who were perceived to be either loitering in public places or vagrants could also be rounded up and—in the short span of twenty-four hours—sold to the highest bidder for the term of four months.[44]

Even more notable, any person could bring an Indian minor before a justice of the peace and, with the "permission" of the child's parents or friends, have that child formally assigned to them as a servant or slave until adulthood. Such enslavers were legally required to provide basic food and clothing to their Indian servants and not "inhumanly treat" them. The law stipulated that such guardianships or indentures would end at the age of fifteen for girls and eighteen for boys. As elsewhere, terms of service were ignored, and abuse was common.

This 1850 law accelerated an already vibrant traffick in Native servants, slaves, and peons. Merchants in the northern regions of the state—as far north as the coastal mining town of Eureka—kidnapped, abducted, and in other ways obtained Indigenous children from local tribes and sent them south, where they were sold as functional slaves. A Sacramento Valley rancher named John Bidwell reported that Indians were "all *among* us, *around* us, *with* us—hardly a farm house—a kitchen without them."[45] Thomas Henley, the California superintendent of Indian Affairs, reported in April 1856 that "Hundreds of Indians" had been brazenly kidnapped from Native lands, taken to American towns, and sold as slaves. Henley knew of instances where entire Indian villages and tribes were rounded up and sold into slavery.[46] This happened so frequently that the *Daily Alta California* in 1854 noted, "This practice has become quite common."[47] Notably, the short article did not call for regulation or an end to it. It simply stated it as fact.

By some estimates, as many as ten thousand to twenty thousand Indigenous people were indentured, sold, or functionally enslaved in the "free" state of California between 1850 and 1865.[48] Native slaves and servants formed the core of a broader labor market that increasingly included Chinese laborers, poor Mexican Americans, and even a surprising number of enslaved Blacks who had been smuggled into the state.[49]

SEVEN HUNDRED MILES EAST of California, a different group of white American settlers also began trading in Native captives. On a hot day in July 1847, the first Mormon scouts—called the Mormon Vanguard Company—traversed the Rocky Mountain range and arrived in the hauntingly beautiful and rugged lands of the Ute nation. Within a few months, they began to attract attention from local Utes who wanted to trade. In the fall of 1847, some Utes led by a thin leader named Batiste rode up to the Mormon camp on horses, bringing with them two Pi band Indigenous children—an emaciated young woman named Pidash and an unnamed boy. Despite communication challenges, it was obvious what the Utes wanted: trade items for the captives. When these early Mormon settlers demurred, the Utes spurred on the negotiations by killing the captive boy. To spare Pidash, a Mormon scout named Charles Decker traded her for a gun.

Decker turned over this newly purchased Native captive to his sister, Clara, and her husband, Brigham Young, the leader of the Mormon Church. The Youngs renamed her Sally and kept her as a long-term servant or slave.[50] Despite the pretense of family adoption heralded by the Mormons in such situations, Sally labored for three decades as a functional slave in the Young household, cooking, cleaning, and caring for children in Salt Lake City's Temple Square. Tellingly, she was listed as "Sally, Indian" and a "servant" in Brigham Young's household in the 1860 federal census, without even the dignity of the Young family name.[51]

These Mormons were part of a new religious group that had been formed in upstate New York in the 1820s and 1830s. Its founder, Joseph Smith, reported he had received access to gold plates inscribed with a holy language that required special lenses to interpret.[52] The resulting translation was an entirely new religious text, the Book of Mormon, which Smith published in 1830. That same year, Smith organized his new church (officially the Church of Jesus Christ of Latter-day Saints), which American Christians saw as illegitimate due to its claims to direct revelation from God and its practice of polygamy. This triggered a multidecade saga of religious pressure and persecution that drove Smith and his followers ever farther west, from New York to Ohio, Missouri, and eventually Illinois.

By the mid-1840s, they had moved beyond the formal boundaries of the United States and entered the Great Salt Lake Basin, in what would later be called Utah. Native Americans played a central role in Mormon theology because in the Book of Mormon they were portrayed as the descendants of the Lamanites, a fallen tribe of Israel. Perhaps conveniently for Mormons arriving in Native lands, the church believed that Natives could be redeemed through church followers settling on their lands and teaching them their "true" history as described in the Book of Mormon.[53]

When Mormons first arrived in Utah in July 1847 during the Mexican–American War, they had wandered into a massive Indigenous territory with a deep and complex history that they did not control or understand.[54] The Mormons, then led by Young, sparred with local Utes and other Native bands but quickly tried to position themselves as trading partners in an effort to preserve their nascent settlement and accomplish one of their missions—the conversion of regional Native nations. Attempts to secure Native allegiance included securing food and provisions for Wakara, the prominent leader of the Western Ute, as well as tending to sick Natives who had contracted measles from other colonists heading west.[55]

Early on, the Mormons discovered and then adapted to a preexisting vibrant Indigenous slave trade, just as white Americans streaming into New Mexico and California had done. Over the course of several years, Brigham Young and his followers tried to turn away the Mexican American slave traders who had been entering the region and purchasing captives from the Ute. This included confronting a well-known Mexican slave trader, Don Pedro Léon Luján, a contest that escalated into the federal court case *United States v. Pedro León et al.* (1851–1852).[56] Young preferred that the Mormons rather than Mexican Americans control and benefit from the regional trade in Native children and women.

By the early 1850s, Young seemed to have allied with the Ute raider Wakara, even providing him with a church-sponsored "permission" pass to "trade horses, Buckskins, and Piede [Paiute] children."[57] Young encouraged Mormons to "buy up the Lamanite children as fast as they could and educate them and teach them the gospel."[58] Mormons responded and quickly became major purchasers of Native captives from the Ute and Mexican traders. This practice made a mockery of their earlier prosecution of the Mexican trader León Luján for slave trading. Mormon individuals eagerly handed over guns, livestock, blankets, and saddles for Native children slave-raided by the Ute and other nations, who soon learned the incredible value of a captive Native child. A Utah resident named Jacob Hamblin bought a six-year-old

Native boy for a gun and some ammunition while John D. Lee traded a horse for a young eight-year-old Native girl. Purchased Native captives were bought and sold between colonists, traded among friends, and given as gifts.[59]

But Mormons also directly waged war on Ute and other Indigenous bands, taking captives and servants who then served as functional slaves. When Utes and Paiutes stole cattle for food, Mormons retaliated by trying to track down the perpetrators and, failing that, entering local villages and taking captives. During the especially harsh winter of 1849–1850, some Timpanogos stole cattle from the settlement at Parowan, in southern Utah. The Mormons cobbled together one hundred men and chased down the suspected Natives, killing approximately thirty men and taking the women and children captive.[60] Young wrote to Lieutenant General Daniel Wells of the Utah militia, asking him to bring the "little Indian children" and "peaceful women and children" to Salt Lake City.[61] Ongoing skirmishes with the Ute in 1852 similarly resulted in additional Indian captives being parceled out to Mormon households.[62]

In a January 1852 speech before the Utah House of Representatives in Salt Lake City, Young tried to legitimize Mormon purchases of Native captives while distancing that practice from both southern plantation slavery and the Native slave trade in New Mexico and Cal-

STREET IN GREAT SALT LAKE CITY, LOOKING EAST,
BY JAMES ACKERMAN AND HOWARD STANSBURY, 1851.

ifornia. Young believed slavery to be a divine institution—pointing
to the Old Testament as a rationale—and soon convinced officials
to make Utah a slaveholding territory.[63] Additionally, prompted
by Young's speech, the Utah legislature quickly passed "An Act for
the Relief of Indian Slaves and Prisoners" on January 31, 1852. But
instead of outlawing Indian slavery and servitude, it created an official
apparatus for twenty-year Native indentures, couched in the language
of Mormon paternalism.[64]

As they took Indigenous captives into their families as servants and
slaves and then educated and Christianized them, Mormons convinced
themselves that their mission was not primarily about labor or ideol-
ogies of colonization but was obedience to the religiously mandated
improvement of an entire race.[65] The motivations, no matter how
divinely inspired, were insidiously harmful to Native nations. As Elder
E. T. Benson noted in July 1855, the hope was cultural erasure. Discussing his own purchased "little Indian boy and girl," Benson stated of the
boy, "True, he yet has some of his Indian traits, and I presume it will be
some time before they are all erased from his memory."[66]

Between 1847 and 1900, Mormons officially recorded the purchase or
capture of at least four hundred Paiute, Gosiute, Shoshone, Diné, and
Ute Natives by the Mormon faithful, who incorporated them as servants in their families.[67] The numbers were likely far higher since such
transactions were not always recorded and some children died before
their purchases were documented.[68] Moreover, non-Mormons in Utah
and the surrounding area bought and sold Indian captives, too, which
the church did not tabulate. Newspapers reported that in January 1858
some Nebraska residents had traveled to Utah, purchased Indian captives from Mormon residents, and then returned to Nebraska, where
they held their Indians in "slavery."[69]

THE CORE ISSUE IN MOST OF THESE regions was that white Americans in California, Utah, and New Mexico, as elsewhere, simply could
not envision a society with Native Americans as equals. Many preferred to have no Natives at all. In 1848, the *Californian* newspaper
stated outright that many residents "desire only a white population
in California." The column went on to explain that "Indians are more
of a nuisance than a benefit to the country; we would like to get rid

of them."[70] Members of California's diverse non-white populations, including Chinese, Blacks, Mexicans, and workers from Central and South America, all experienced varying degrees of racism, but Californians for the moment seemed fixated on eradicating Native Americans from their midst.[71]

While they were clearing the land by stealing and enslaving Native Americans, some California legislators reprised earlier American strategies of forcibly moving entire bands and communities to small, confined reservations. Pressuring Indian communities to sign removal treaties, federal agents told Native tribes in the 1850s that it was impossible for them to remain on their current lands as they were considered to be "a barrier to the rapid settlement of the State." Federal agents promised Indians protected lands with government support for farming and subsistence. Quixotically, the US government imagined segregated enclaves of Indians that would become entirely self-sufficient through their own labor.[72]

Native oral histories recall how whole towns were "herded like cattle" onto the reserved lands in a Californian version of the Cherokee Trail of Tears, with elderly and younger children dying along the way.[73] Only a small percentage of Native communities agreed to their removal, however. By 1856, the commissioner of Indian Affairs in California reported that ten thousand Indigenous people had been taken to seven reservations. Another estimated sixty-four thousand remained on their lands and at large in the vast state, leaving officials to ponder their options.[74]

Ironically, the specter of removal alarmed California residents who relied on ongoing Indian slave raiding and servitude for labor. One Mexican American rancher named Fernando Féliz near Petaluma recognized this quandary in 1851. He was poor and elderly but had a "horde of Indians" associated with his property who were visibly underdressed and underfed but made his farming possible. When he learned of the plan to forcibly move the Indians to reservations, he noted that he "should be utterly ruined were the Indians to be removed" since comparably inexpensive labor was impossible to find. Yet according to others, he treated his Indigenous workforce like thieves "who had killed his cattle and eaten his crop."[75]

For the moment, instead of a widespread military campaign to effect removal, California eliminated any remaining restrictions on white residents to enslave Natives. In 1860, the state radically amended the "Act for the Government and Protection of Indians" of 1850, gutting it of any feigned accountability to tribes. Permission or consent for Indigenous guardianship was no longer required, allowing almost any California resident to have any Native indentured with virtually no questions asked. This included Indian minors as well as adults who might be deemed vagrants, prisoners of war, or otherwise nonproductive members of society (as defined by whites), all without any consent from Native family or friends. The length of indenture was extended as well, for up to thirty years old (or for ten years for those already older than thirty). And now legal masters were given complete control over all aspects of the "indenture," including any possible earnings.[76]

The result was catastrophic, as local newspapers had predicted.[77] Enterprising white Californians kidnapped Indian children in the early 1860s by the hundreds and took them before local judges in Los Angeles, Sacramento, and San Francisco, where the judges would then assign the whites as "guardians" until adulthood and beyond. Vigilante slave-raiding organizations formed, each with its own president, secretary, and treasurer, to more efficiently systematize slave raids. Some slave raiders rode the coattails of official California militias and US Army troops—swooping in after a battle and seizing Indian children to sell in the Indian slave trade.[78] Once secured, enslaved Natives could be trafficked across state lines. A former US Indian agent named Vincent E. Geiger convinced the court to sign over eighty Native Americans to him as "apprentices" in early 1861 based on the new law. Geiger planned to take his newly acquired labor force eastward into what is now Nevada and to set up shop in the lucrative mining district of Washoe, or Virginia City, where his captives were surely treated as slaves.[79]

Observers who saw the various coercive Indian labor systems in place—peonage, apprenticeship, servitude, and outright enslavement—almost always compared them to southern slavery. Edward A. Stevenson, an agent for Indians in California, reported the widespread use of peons on ranches and farms surrounding the Nome Lackee Reservation a hundred miles north of Sacramento. When conditions got too harsh, Indigenous people often fled from their ranchero enslavers and sought shelter on the reservations. Their enslavers almost always

LITHOGRAPH DEPICTING DOWNEY BLOCK ON THE CORNER OF
SPRING STREET AND TEMPLE STREET, LOS ANGELES, 1875–
1885. LOS ANGELES INDIGENOUS MARKET BUILDING.

hunted them down, demanding absolute rights over them and their
labor, just as southern enslavers had over enslaved Black and Indigenous laborers. Like so many others who observed western Indigenous
enslavement, Stevenson believed this kind of Native slavery was even
worse than southern Black enslavement as the "Indians claim to be the
rightful owners of the soil."[80]

Indigenous people being enslaved on their own lands had long been
a core feature of American colonialism, but it was especially reprehen-
sible when it happened in a free state that was founded to offset the
growth of southern slavery.

IN DOWNTOWN LOS ANGELES TODAY, a gleaming white, seventeen-
story building with imposing vertical lines completely mutes the importance of the site to California's Indigenous slavery history. Built in the
1930s as the largest federal building in the West, the US Courthouse
at 312 North Spring Street stands today where California's longest-
running Indigenous slave market operated from 1850 to 1870.[81] For

two full decades, California residents streamed to this spot to purchase Indigenous children who were stolen by residents or orphaned by raids and massacres at the hands of whites. No memorial marks this American slave market; no stories of Native children are recounted at the site.

Still, California has officially recognized parts of this ignoble history. In 2019, state leaders finally apologized for the "violence, mistreatment and neglect inflicted upon California Native Americans throughout the state's history."[82] Some California residents took direct action a year later, forcing the removal of the statue of one of the earliest American colonists, John Sutter, from the Midtown neighborhood of the state's capital, Sacramento, the former site of Sutter's Fort. They also toppled the statue of Father Junípero Serra. To replace the Serra statue, Sacramento installed in 2023 a bronze sculpture of twentieth-century Miwok elder William "Bill" Franklin, as a monument to California's 338 Native American tribes who survived centuries of Spanish, Mexican, and American colonization.

By 1860, the American Southwest and West had become sites of new American barbarism and colonialism, which included the widespread enslavement and forced servitude of Indigenous peoples. As the nation descended into a disturbing and divisive war to end slavery, western Americans seized the opportunity to expand their stealing of Native land and labor.

Fourteen

PARADOXICAL CIVIL WARS

THE ERUPTION OF NATIVE ENSLAVEMENT DURING THE AMERICAN invasion of western Native lands soon received an unexpected boost from a dreadful war that tore the nation in two. On December 20, 1860, South Carolina became the first state to officially secede from the Union in response to the election of Abraham Lincoln as president. On that same day, California senator Milton Latham proposed a bill in Congress to aid militias in California that were fighting and enslaving Native Americans.[1] The results of both events led to a paradoxical Civil War that ravaged and dramatically reshaped the nation in four short years.

The petition for funding from Senator Latham did not include many details about California's wars, perhaps because they were too grisly. In one of the most egregious raids, a white militia had viciously attacked several hundred Wiyot, Eel, and Mad River Indians on Duluwat Island in the Humboldt Bay, near Eureka. Under the cover of early morning darkness, on February 29, 1860, the militiamen stabbed wildly at bodies, wielded axes with skull-crushing might, and sank hatchets into anything that moved. The rising sun presented a grim tableau: "The wounded, dead and dying were found all around, and in every lodge the skulls and frames of women and children cleft with axes and hatchets, and stabbed with knives, and the brains of an infant oozing from its broken head to the ground."[2] Local newspapers counted fifteen separate murder-massacres that killed at least four hundred Natives and led to the capture of an additional six hundred more who were presumably destined for slavery.[3]

Senator Latham successfully convinced Congress to fund this slave-raiding Indian war in California. By March 1861, when his $400,000 was finally approved, six additional southern states had already joined South Carolina in seceding from the Union and had formed the Confederate States of America. Less than a month later, on April 12, the newly formed Confederate Army fired on the Union-held Fort Sumter in South Carolina, officially marking the start of military engagements in the American Civil War. Simultaneously, three thousand miles away, Captain Charles S. Lovell of the US Army, flush with congressional funds, led a multipronged expedition into northern California that routed out "enemy" and friendly Indians alike. Within a few months, more than two hundred Indigenous people had been massacred and many more children seized by the US soldiers to be sold into functional slavery.[4]

Bizarrely, the Union Army was now fighting two wars: one in the South to end slavery and one in the West that perpetuated slavery.

The American Civil War was one of the most defining events in American history, but it is often narrowly understood as a battle between the North and South regarding Black slavery.[5] Just as the American Revolution was simultaneously a war against the British and a war against Indigenous people on the frontier of settlement, so too the Civil War was really two wars in one. The first was the familiar war of the Union Army against the seceded proslavery Confederate States of America, leading to the emancipation of nearly four million enslaved people. The second and much less familiar one was a war of enslavement and removal against Native American nations in the West, funded and propelled by the same Union Army. This western crusade against Native nations put the army in the position of both liberator and enslaver.[6]

The continent's Indigenous people experienced the Civil War in vastly different ways. Some of the slaveholding tribes in Oklahoma joined with the Confederacy and were punished after the war as "conquered peoples."[7] For the hundreds of thousands of Native Americans who were enslaved on southern plantations, the war led to their liberation. But for Native American nations in the large territories and states of the American West, the Civil War era unleashed on them an enslaving and genocidal fervor. This activity was in sharp contradistinction to President Abraham Lincoln's rhetoric regarding the dignity and freedom of individuals, as well as the eventual Emancipation Proclamation and the Thirteenth Amendment, which proclaimed liberty. If we understand the Civil War only as a North–South battle to free African-descended people, we miss a surprising and relentlessly devastating story of enslavement and attempted extermination of Native Americans in the West that was occurring at the same time.

THE ONGOING VIOLENCE IN the American West described by Senator Latham was largely overshadowed by the crisis of secession. Despite the federal government's careful negotiation of growing separation between those who supported slavery and those who wished to halt its spread or—even more radically—end it completely, the country lurched toward a grim sectional divide that seemed irreconcilable. The economies of the North and the South were intertwined, and despite posturing by Northerners, racism was a cancer that had become a national disease.

But antislavery and radical abolitionism increasingly combined with a "free soil, free labor" ideology that made the stringent defense of slavery in the South feel increasingly morally unacceptable and economically retrograde.[8] A series of events convinced antislavery Americans that Southerners were aggressively spreading slavery and infringing on

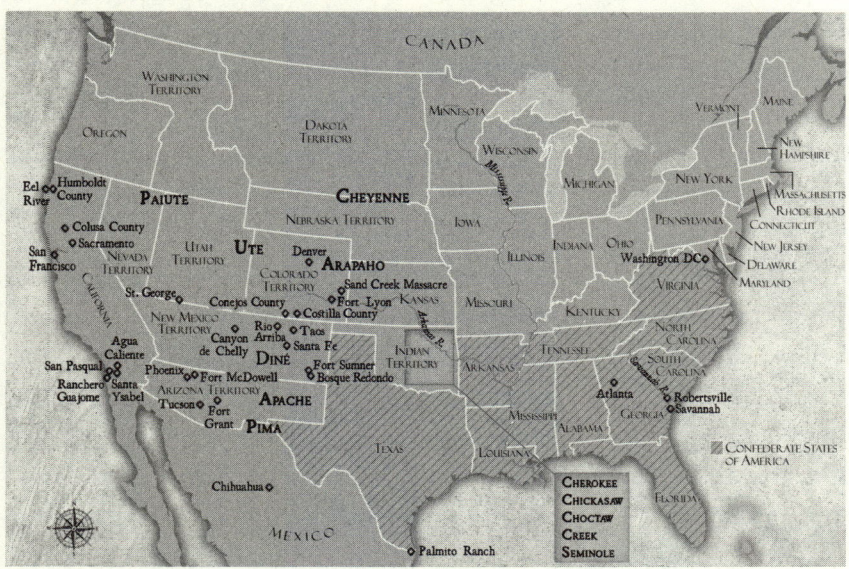

WESTERN THEATER OF THE CIVIL WAR.

free states' rights. This included the forceful southern prosecution of the 1850 Fugitive Slave Act, which permitted enslavers to chase down freedom seekers who had taken refuge in free states and territories. Additionally, the passage of the Kansas-Nebraska Act in 1854 represented the potential expansion of slavery into western territories that antislavery legislatures felt had previously been prohibited.

Popular backlash in the North led to the founding of the Republican Party in 1854, which brought together a wide coalition of smaller factions through a strongly antislavery agenda. Additionally, the US Supreme Court's ruling in 1857 that an enslaved man named Dred Scott could be deprived of citizenship and protection of the law, despite having lived in a free territory, angered abolitionists and antislavery advocates who saw it as another sign of proslavery overreach.

But Southerners had long believed their rights as slaveholders were under attack. The final straw was the 1860 election of Abraham Lincoln, who ran on a Republican ticket that was firmly antislavery. Despite Lincoln's assurances that he was only interested in halting the spread of slavery, not outlawing it entirely, southern states seceded one at a time. By February 8, 1861, the seceding states declared themselves independent, as the Confederate States of America.

When Confederate troops attacked Fort Sumter, it represented the eruption of tensions and disagreements that had been building for well over half a century. The resulting Civil War was destructive for the landscape and the people of the South. Cities burned and young men died by the hundreds of thousands all across southern states as the Confederacy defended to the death their right to keep men and women of color in a state of slavery.[9]

AMONG THE UNTOLD STORIES OF the Civil War are the experiences of tens of thousands of enslaved Native Americans on southern plantations who lived through the full range of hardship and liberation the war brought. For some of them, as with enslaved Blacks, the Civil War created an escape hatch. Some enslaved Indigenous people simply disappeared from plantations and headed north to join the Union Army. Among them was John Anderson, who had been born into slavery on a Cherokee plantation in Oklahoma in approximately 1832. His father was Cherokee, his mother was Black, and he spent almost thirty years of his life enslaved. That changed suddenly in late 1861, when Anderson, inspired by the start of the war, self-emancipated and enlisted in the Union Army.[10]

Some enslaved Indigenous men in the South were forced to fight for the Confederacy. Occasionally, they fought beside their enslavers. James Boyd, who had been trafficked from Indian Territory in Oklahoma to Texas as a young boy, was required to serve in the Confederate Army alongside his legal master, Sanford Wooldridge. Boyd's first battle was in Halifax, North Carolina, and he traveled with the troops all the way to the Battle of Vicksburg, Mississippi, in 1863. Boyd was shot in the chest and took six months to recover. He was still in Vicksburg three years later when news arrived that the North had won.[11]

As Union soldiers marched through the American South, they actively recruited enslaved Indigenous and Black boys and men. Wylie Nealy, an enslaved, mixed-race Cherokee-Choctaw-Black youth, was only twelve years old when a regiment of the US Army swept through Gordon County, South Carolina, in 1864. Nealy was walking along the road when some Union soldiers took him to their camp near Calhoun, South Carolina. Young as he was, he served for nine months in a "colored" regiment and traveled for a short while with the well-known army of Union general William Sherman on its take-no-prisoners "march to the sea" from Atlanta to Savannah. Nealy served until August 1865, surviving on army rations until he moved to a farm owned by a former Union officer in Arkansas, where he worked as an underpaid wage laborer.[12]

Union soldiers aggressively destroyed southern property and devoured the food and resources on these plantations. Mollie Moss, a Cherokee mixed-race girl who was enslaved on the Billy Cain plantation in Campbell County, Tennessee, was forced to crawl underneath the house to retrieve the chickens after soldiers shot them.[13] Wylie Nealy recalled the plantation and countryside stripped of all edible farm animals: not a chicken, hog, or cow could be found for miles.[14] Plantation owners frantically hid or buried their valuables and money in advance of the arrival of the northern army. Some of them burned piles of their harvested cotton to rob Union troops of any possible profits.[15] An enslaved mixed-race Native girl named Riviana Boynton remembered that her legal owner, John Hoover, asked his slaves to help dig holes in the ground to hide the potatoes and then cover the ground with cotton seed.[16]

As the war began to turn in favor of the North, Congress grew bolder. It passed a series of proclamations and laws aimed at freeing enslaved men and women that also applied to enslaved Indigenous people on plantations throughout the South. In April 1862, Congress freed enslaved people in Washington, DC. In June 1862, Congress outlawed slavery in all western US territories, and on January 1, 1863, President Abraham Lincoln famously issued the Emancipation Proclamation, which declared "all persons held as slaves" in Confederate states to be "forever free."[17] With the stroke of a pen, Lincoln legally freed more than 3.5 million people held in bondage.

Enslaved Native Americans and their children serving on plantations understood that they were included in these measures. Celia Henderson, an Indigenous-Black woman laboring on a plantation in Mississippi, recalled that when the Emancipation Proclamation was read out to the slaves, they celebrated by dancing around and yelling.[18] Others were freed outright by plantation owners, who perhaps found themselves on the geographical and ideological margins of the Confederacy. A mixed-race Sauk man named Joe Higgerson was born into slavery in 1845 on a plantation in central Missouri. A few months after the Emancipation Proclamation on January 1, 1863, the plantation owner gathered the men and women he had enslaved and read the news that they were free. Higgerson traveled north to Boonville, Missouri, and decided to join the Union Army. He did so on November 23, 1863, as part of the mostly "colored" 25th Corps, 2nd Division, under Major General Godfrey Weitzel. Higgerson served through the remainder of the war, even fighting in the Battle of Palmito Ranch in Texas on May 12–13, 1865, which was considered to be one of the final battles of the Civil War.[19]

Other enslaved men and women took direct action to free themselves, perhaps inspired by the Emancipation Proclamation. On February 25, 1864, seven enslaved people ran away from the plantation of David D. Allen of Black Rock, North Carolina. The group included an enslaved Indigenous man named London, who was listed as twenty-six years old, the "color of an Indian," with straight hair. Allen believed the escapees were all trying to join the Union Army and offered a $200 reward per person for their return.[20] Tens of thousands of enslaved men, women, and children—which would have included Indigenous and mixed-race Indigenous people—self-emancipated during the war.[21]

SUCH EMANCIPATIONS CONTRASTED sharply with the experiences of Indigenous people in the West who were at the same time being enslaved by the congressionally funded Union Army. The US Army had long been the primary arm for the American colonization of Native lands in the Louisiana Territory. It was actively involved in forcing Plains nations into treaties throughout the first half of the nineteenth century. After the war with Mexico ended in 1848, the army turned its attention to coercing treaties with Indigenous nations in newly annexed lands and, when strongarm diplomacy failed, militarily forced them to submit to reservations and reduced land. The start of the Civil War meant an increase in funding and an expanded mission of keeping the Confederate States of America from controlling additional territory in New Mexico, California, and Oregon. The army's actions during the Civil War were consistent with previous US policies regarding Native nations that were anti-Indian at their core.

With the US military as a model and federal funding liberally flowing, Californians felt fully empowered to prosecute their war against Natives in the state. In May 1861, several self-organized raiding parties of whites—"citizens," as they were reported—rode through Long Valley and brazenly stole forty to fifty Indian children from their parents. When confronted, the raiders scoffed that "the law cannot reach [us]" and sold the Indian children to rancheros in and out of the county.[22]

In October 1861, three enslavers were caught near Marysville (north of Sacramento) with nine Native children between the ages of three and ten. They later explained to the court that they planned to indenture the children to white families as an act of charity since their parents were dead. When the court inquired what happened to the parents, one slaver admitted that he had killed them.[23] The *Boston Evening Transcript* accurately reported that California Indians were "being hunted *for their children*. . . . The settlers make war for the young ones, so as to take them and sell them."[24]

The superintendent of Indian Affairs for the northern California district, George Hanson, lamented in 1861 that the kidnapping of Indians had become "quite a business of profit." But it was more than that. Slave raiding massively destabilized the region and made it easier to take Native land. Indigenous nations often retaliated, leading to perpetual cycles of warfare as Indian communities fought back. Hanson believed Indigenous slavery was behind the Native wars that California and the federal government spent so much money trying to prosecute. To help resolve these resentments, Hanson proposed repealing the 1850 law (and the 1860 amendment) that had vastly increased the stealing and enslaving of Native Americans, especially children.[25]

The Civil War also soon bolstered the US Army's wars against the Diné in New Mexico. Two decades of an intrusive white American colonial presence had created a cycle of Diné and Apache raids on American and Mexican American homes and towns that spurred counterraids, captive taking, and enslavement of Natives by American and territorial militias. The American military began roving under Colonel Edward Canby, organizing expeditions, hunting down Diné bands, raiding villages, and taking livestock and captives.[26] Desperate to gain the upper hand and with fresh mandates from Washington, DC, Brigadier General James H. Carleton and Lieutenant Colonel Kit Carson gathered a one-thousand-strong New Mexico regiment to wage a total war against the Diné in 1863–1864.

American troops and Native allies started with raids on numerous bands of both Ndé (Mescalero Apache) and Diné throughout the first half of 1863. Carson, who was the primary commander on the ground, attempted every possible way to force the Diné into submission. As in so many earlier wars fought against Natives in North America, Carson's men burned villages, crops, and food supplies, attempting to render the Natives' homelands uninhabitable. He invited Ute warriors to serve as guides and raiders of Diné towns, with the incentive that they could keep Diné captives taken during the raids to be sold or traded into slavery for profit.[27]

Starting in August 1863, General Carleton wrote letter after letter to military commanders in the region, instructing them to slaughter all Diné and Apache men (including boys old enough to bear arms) and to take women and children captive.[28] By the end of the year, the US military reported murdering more than three hundred Diné and taking captive seven hundred women and children.[29] An unknown number of these captives, particularly those taken by American-allied Ute raiders, were subsequently sold into slavery and eagerly purchased by residents of New Mexico. The result was an enormous surge of Indian enslavement at the hands of the same Union Army that was supposed to be fighting slavery. Michael Steck, superintendent for Indian Affairs in New Mexico, reported in January 1864 that Diné children were being "stolen, bought, and sold by our people."[30]

In the face of this expansive campaign against them, the Diné retreated to the spiritual center of their lands: Tséyí, or Canyon de Chelly, a stunning eighty-three-thousand-acre labyrinth of thousand-foot-high, red-walled canyons etched into the mile-high desert highlands of northeastern Arizona. With a seasonally fertile and spacious canyon floor, Canyon de Chelly had nurtured Indigenous peoples for nearly five thousand years. Even today, visitors to the canyon can view the remnant structures of houses on the ledges of the canyon walls that were built by ancestral Puebloan people a thousand years ago. Petro-

FORTRESS ROCK, CANYON DE CHELLY, ARIZONA, DINÉ RESERVATION, 2023.

glyphs and rock paintings from Anasazi, Hopi, and Diné artists remain throughout the winding canyon walls. For hundreds of years, the Diné had lived and worked the land in the canyon, harvesting crops and grazing cattle on the canyon floor.

Although the newly invading Americans found the imposing cliffs and maze of slot canyons and side fissures utterly confusing, Carson and US military commander Albert H. Pfeiffer conducted a two-pronged invasion of Canyon de Chelly in the fall and early winter of 1863 in an attempt to force the Diné into submission. Diné families were on their own turf and temporarily had the advantage. Retreating one hundred to two hundred feet up the canyon walls into houses and dwellings built in cracks and on outcroppings, they fired through portals and rained down rocks and boulders on the American soldiers hunting them.[31] One group of two hundred Diné banded together atop a large rock outcropping they called Tsélaa in the northern arm of the canyon—a formation today called Fortress Rock. Using long ponderosa pine tree trunks and footholds carved into the canyon walls, they strapped babies and food supplies to their backs and scaled the sheer cliff face, where they camped out for weeks eating dried fruit and meat.[32]

Carson, Pfeiffer, and their men, frustrated with their inability to reach the Diné, staged a lethal siege from below, destroying crops, killing or stealing livestock, and taking captive any stray Diné they could find. Carson and three hundred Union soldiers found a large field of unharvested corn on the canyon floor and spent an entire day destroying it. His troops also demolished a large orchard with three thousand peach trees cultivated by the Diné. The military stripped the canyon floor bare of any living thing that could give sustenance to the Diné, including thousands of sheep and goats.[33]

By the time the first snows fell on January 6, 1864, Diné bands and clans faced starvation and certain death in the freezing highlands. They emerged from the canyon walls and began surrendering at Fort Defiance, just southeast of Canyon de Chelly. Five thousand emaciated Diné arrived between January and March 1864, completely overwhelming the resources of the US military stationed there. The goal had always been removal, to forcibly relocate the Diné to Bosque Redondo near Fort Sumner, or Hwéeldi, a military outpost four hundred miles southeast of the Diné homelands. Accordingly, in the late winter, spring, and summer of 1864, as the US military continued to hunt down Diné and Ndé bands, thousands of Diné were forced to take what they later preserved in their oral histories as the "Long Walk." It was the western equivalent of the Cherokee Trail of Tears or the Potawatomi Trail of Death in the 1830s.[34]

On March 4, 1864, one group of 2,138 Diné headed for their new prison reservation with 473 horses and 3,000 sheep; other such bands soon followed.[35] As they set out at gunpoint across the rugged desert landscape on foot, with thousands of head of sheep and cattle in tow, only the elderly and young children were permitted to ride in wagons.[36] As additional groups followed, temperate spring turned to stultifying summer, provisions were in short supply, feet blistered, wagons broke, and supervising military officers grew impatient.

Some Diné silently escaped en route, hoping for freedom but preferring death or capture by Utes or local residents to American captivity. Marauding bands of Mexicans, whites, and other Native nations, including the Ute, preyed on sporadic and poorly guarded trains of prisoners, stealing stragglers as slaves. By the middle of 1864, 8,477 Diné—including more than 3,000 children—along with nearly 500 Mescalero and Gila Apaches had been forcibly relocated to Bosque

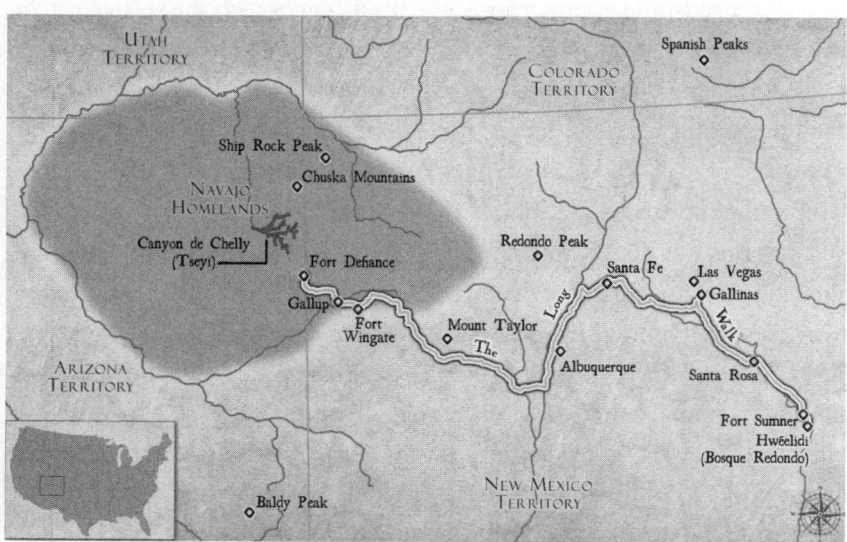

THE DINÉ LONG WALK TO BOSQUE REDONDO, NEW MEXICO, IN 1864.

Redondo, where the federal government held them as prisoners on a new military-run reservation.[37]

Rumors circulated, as later reported by regional newspapers like the *Santa Fe Gazette*, that the purpose of the Diné roundup and forced removal was to sell them into slavery.[38] And, indeed, the plan was to keep them in quasi-plantation slavery: the government hoped to turn Bosque Redondo into a model self-sustaining reservation built on the agricultural labor of the Diné captives.[39] Survivors of their captivity at Hwéeldi recalled their time as akin to slavery. Everybody was forced to work in one capacity or another under close watch by soldiers.[40] Diné women were required to serve in food preparation and cooking, while men, women, and children all were tasked with growing wheat, oats, corn, beans, pumpkins, sorghum, and watermelons in both private and collective gardens to aid in the enormous task of feeding the nine thousand prisoners.[41]

Anna Haney, from the Bit'ahnii clan (Under His Cover People), grew up hearing stories of her great-grandmother, who was captured by the army and taken to Hwéeldi as a slave, where she was kept, barefoot, cooking for the soldiers every day. She eventually grew weary of her forced servitude and ran away to her homelands at Ch'óshgai, or the Chuska Mountains, on the border of present-day Arizona and New Mexico, just east of Canyon de Chelly. When her feet blistered on the three-hundred-mile escape route, she used *tsin bi jeeh*, or spruce pitch, on her sores and kept placing one foot in front of the other until she arrived home.[42] The traumatic story of her enslavement and escape was just one of many passed down through generations.

Thousands of Diné and Apache were silently carried off in these raids and removals. In December 1864, with nearly 9,000 Natives in captivity at Bosque Redondo, an additional 3,000 to 4,000 Diné remained unaccounted for. Stories circulated of some Diné captives being taken away as slaves by unnamed parties. Superintendent Steck estimated—likely conservatively—that at least 2,000 of them were serving as slaves in New Mexican homes and on ranches. Baptismal records from New Mexico in the 1860s record approximately 2,500 Native servants and slaves baptized in Catholic churches alone—most of them newly introduced to the area through an Indigenous slave trade. On February 20, 1864, as just one example of thousands, Antonio Vaca and Simona

NATIVE AMERICANS AT FORT SUMNER, NEW MEXICO, 1863,
SHOWS BOTH DINÉ AND NDÉ AT THE FORT.

Valdez brought a seven-year-old Diné child renamed J. Maria Baca, to their local parish church for baptism.[43] Some of those baptized were young and had been enslaved only a short time. Others were elderly, having "served from childhood to old age." Perhaps as many as 1,000 captive Diné do not appear in these church records, likely serving in non-Catholic households.[44]

The source of Diné enslavement wasn't only rogue Mexican American militias and raiding parties. A wide array of public officials and federal agents in local, territorial, and state offices also claimed Native people as servants and slaves.[45] Kit Carson held two Diné in his household in December 1860.[46] Two years later, Albert Pfeiffer, by then an American agent to the Ute at Abiquiu, New Mexico, "adopted" a five-year-old Indian girl and a seven-year-old Indian boy who had almost certainly been slave-raided by the Ute and given or sold to Pfeiffer.[47] In 1864, Colorado newspapers reported an Indian slave trade in Diné out of New Mexico into southern Colorado, with a white "Indian agent" at the center of the buying and selling of Natives.[48]

Thus the Union Army, its officers, and federal agents led the way in sustaining ongoing Native enslavement in the Southwest during the Civil War even as the same government and military fought to eradicate chattel slavery in the South.

THE AMERICAN CIVIL WAR UNLEASHED anti-Indian fury in other American territories as well. In the summer of 1862, tribal members from the Dakota nation in the upper Midwest lashed out at local American settlers. The causes were complex, but the biggest complaint was frustration with the US government not providing promised rations and support in return for land cessions. In response to Dakota raids, the Union Army and local militias hunted down and rounded up two thousand Dakota men, women, and children and marched them to Fort Snelling (in present-day Minnesota). As they marched through each frontier town, Americans cursed, attacked, kidnapped, and murdered the Dakotas who were supposed to be under the protection of the US military.

At Fort Snelling, hundreds of Dakota men were put on trial and condemned to die. In December 1862, just weeks before the Emancipation Proclamation, Lincoln personally read the trial transcripts and commuted the sentence of all but thirty-eight Dakota men. The remaining prisoners were hanged on December 26, 1863, in what was—and still is—the largest mass execution in American history.[49]

In Colorado, territorial governor John Evans turned American residents against the Indigenous people around them. Responding to raids by Diné, Ute, and Apache bands, on July 26, 1864, Evans declared that "all citizens of Colorado," either individually or in organized war parties, were authorized to hunt down all "hostile Indians" on the plains. As in virtually all earlier colonial wars (English and American), soldiers were incentivized by a bounty system that rewarded raiding and ransacking the persons and possessions of Native Americans. Evans instructed Colorado residents to "kill and destroy" and "to take captive, and hold to their own private use and benefit" Natives and their property, taken as a "reward" for their service.[50]

Governor Evans's licensing of slave-raiding Natives in July 1864 was Colorado's version of the war against the Diné to the south. And in terms of enslaving Natives, Colorado residents were way ahead of him, thanks to an Indigenous slave trade out of the New Mexico Territory. The *Daily Commonwealth* in Colorado had reported in May 1864 that Diné captives were "held as slaves, and are bought and sold as chattels."[51] In the two southernmost Colorado counties, Costilla and Conejos, residents had purchased or directly captured one hundred Diné, Utes, and Apaches. In 1864, perhaps partially in response to Governor Evans's order, they purchased or captured an additional fifty-three, and another six in 1865.[52] Only these two tabulations survive, but likely hundreds more Natives were enslaved throughout the rest of Colorado.

Today, one of the most important military sites in early Colorado colonial history has been memorialized as the Fort Garland Museum and Cultural Center. Nestled into the San Luis Valley of the lower Rocky Mountains three dozen miles north of the New Mexico border, the town of Fort Garland is little more than a small grid of houses containing five hundred or so people. During the Civil War, it was a primary recruiting station for Union Army soldiers heading south and east to fight the Confederate Army. It also played a major role in supplying troops for the 1862 Battle of Glorieta Pass in New Mexico, often called the Battle of Gettysburg of the West due to its importance as a victory that secured New Mexico for the Union.

But Fort Garland also has a history intertwined with Indigenous enslavement, a legacy that their 2021 museum exhibition revealed. None other than the infamous Native fighter and slave raider Kit Carson commanded the fort for a brief period after the war, and until recently, the fort used Carson's bravado to elevate its own importance. But instead of perpetuating the Carson myths, this modern exhibit turned its gaze to the enslaved Native peoples in the region, including Carson's own captive Diné boy, Juan Carson.[53] The lists of enslaved Natives from Costilla and Conejos Counties feature prominently around the site, a sobering reminder to visitors of the long legacies of trauma caused by American invasions, warfare, and enslavement.

While residents in Colorado and New Mexico were taking Native captives and adopting Indigenous children, California legislators in April 1863 finally repealed the thirteen-year-old law permitting Indian peonage and functional slavery. But this 1863 act only prohibited future indentures and enslavement; those who were already caught up in the system were left untouched. In this way, it was more like the 1741 Jamaica Indian slave trade law or the gradual emancipation acts in New England states in the 1780s. It merely meant to prevent future enslavement, not to grant freedom to those already enslaved or indentured.[54]

As California was taking small steps to limit Indian slavery and

JUAN CARSON, CA. 1870.

indenture, the newly formed (and Union-controlled) Arizona Territory was embracing it, which was yet another sign of how Americans in the Southwest successfully differentiated Native servitude from Black slavery and created mechanisms for it to thrive. In November 1864, the Arizona territorial legislature passed an act titled "Of the Support of Poor Persons, and Orphan Children of Indians."[55] The contrast between the treatment of white and Native children was stark. Poor white children were to be placed with relatives and, if necessary, supported by public funds. Indian children, however, could be bound out "to service" to whites until the age of eighteen for girls and twenty-one for boys. This included any "captive Indian child of a hostile tribe" as well "any minor Indian child" of any tribe at all. The individual who had such a Native child only had to come before a probate judge or justice of the peace and have the child signed over to them.[56]

This measure placed Arizona's treatment of Indigenous children firmly in line with laws and practices in California, New Mexico, and Utah. As in these other states and territories, indenturing of Native children could be easily exploited and turned into functional enslavement, even though Arizona was supposed to be a free territory. Surreptitiously coercing Native labor was a practice with a long history that would continue into the twentieth century.

AFTER FOUR SOUL-WRENCHING YEARS, fighting on the southern front of the Civil War slowly ground to a halt in the spring and summer of 1865. The South was utterly depleted, its railroads and infrastructure in ruins, plantations stripped of valuables, and the wealth formerly bound up in enslaved humans gone. The surrender of General Robert E. Lee and the Confederate Army of Northern Virginia to General Ulysses S. Grant of the Union Army at the courthouse in Appomattox, Virginia, on April 9, 1865, signaled the beginning of the end of the Confederacy, even as holdouts in the deep South initially refused to accept the surrender, making the actual end of the war far murkier.[57]

Plantation by plantation and town by town, news of the defeat of the Confederacy created a groundswell of relief among enslaved populations that swept through the South. The news was greeted with celebrations by freed Black and Indigenous men, women, and children. People left the fields, poured into the streets, "crying, praying, singing, shouting, yelling," destroying property and shooting off guns, as a formerly enslaved mixed-race Native woman later recalled.[58] Others were afraid to celebrate too noisily lest they draw the anger of their former enslavers.[59] After years of enslavement, newly freed people traded stories that exposed enslavers and the Confederacy, perhaps trying to make sense of their experiences. The mixed-race Cherokee and Chehaw William Sherman later relished the rumor that former Confederacy president Jefferson Davis had been captured sneaking around in his wife's dress and bonnet to avoid detection.[60]

Enslaved Indigenous people experienced the end of slavery in different ways. For some, the Union victory meant immediate freedom. Cato Carter, a mixed-race Indigenous man, recalled the day his legal owner, Oll Carter, returned to his Alabama plantation from fighting with the Confederate Army. The war had taken a toll; Oll Carter's clothing was in tatters, and he was visibly gaunt. He called the enslaved workers into the yard in front of his plantation house and announced, "Mens and womens, you are today as free as I am. You are free to do as you like, 'cause the damned Yankees done 'creed you are."[61]

Some enslavers brazenly hid the outcome of the Civil War from their enslaved people or refused to grant them freedom. Indigenous and Black men and women reported being held in bondage up to four years after the passage of the Thirteenth Amendment.[62] A mixed-race Indigenous girl named Lulu Wilson, who was enslaved by Wash Hodges on a plantation in Texas, testified that Hodges returned home after his tour of duty and lied to his family and those he had enslaved. He asserted that the Confederate troops had "done whop the hell out them blue bellies"—referring to the dark navy Union uniforms. Eventually, Union soldiers began prowling the region, and one enslaved man confronted Hodges, who changed his story, saying that adult slaves were free but children had to serve until some unspecified age of adulthood—an additional lie that was likely impossible to maintain for very long.[63]

Other plantation owners moved farther into territories and areas that were less regulated. Cato Carter reported enslavers and entire plantations moving south to Texas or to western territories with their enslaved populations in tow, out of the reach of the "Fed'rals."[64] Similarly, Virginia Newman was an enslaved Indigenous woman on the Foster plantation in Franklin, Louisiana, deep in the Louisiana bayou between Lafayette and New Orleans. In the early 1860s, fear of the arrival of the Union Army prompted Foster into action. He packed up his entire plantation on carts hauled by oxen and marched everything and everyone 435 miles to Brazos County, Texas—the eventual home of Texas A&M University.

The trip took an entire miserable year. All the enslaved people had to walk, barefoot, over terrain so tough their feet blistered, causing open sores that festered for months. There were no tents or protections from the elements; enslaved people slept out in the open air, exposed to the heat and cold, soaking rain, and bugs, snakes, and vermin. The mud got so deep it stopped the oxen and carts in their tracks. Newman recalled having to carry her two sons, Jonah and Simon, the entire time since they were still infants and could not walk on their own. Even such a dramatic move could not forever stave off the results of a Union victory in 1865.[65]

California was an especially effective hideaway for southern plantation owners who found the remote hinterlands of the huge state entirely unregulated. They hauled their enslaved Blacks and Native Americans over the rugged Great Basin and set up plantations and ranches that exactly mirrored the ones they had had in Mississippi, Arkansas, and Louisiana. So many white, southern, slaveholding Democrats arrived in Colusa County that this north-central area became known as California's "banner Democratic county" in the 1850s and the "South Carolina of California" during the Civil War.[66]

California had been a supposedly free state since 1850, so the end of the war there was far less dramatic than in the South. No Union troops liberated plantations because the army did not consider the rancherías and farms with Indigenous servants and slaves as sites of relevant slavery. In this environment, southern plantation owners who were lying low in the state managed to keep their enslaved populations under their control for an additional five to six years without interference. One planter had a small plantation in Agua Mansa, in San Bernardino County, where in the late 1860s he still had five or six enslaved laborers to work a rudimentary sugar mill like those in Louisiana and Arkansas. Eventually, enslaved populations like his sued for their freedom and were finally released. The planters then turned to coerced Indian labor, but over time those Natives also secured their freedom.[67]

In more extreme cases, enslavers murdered the people they held in slavery rather than grant them their freedom. Lucy Thomas, who was enslaved on William Baldwin's Texas plantation, was fourteen years old when the war ended. Years later, she recalled with vivid detail how the mistress of a neighboring plantation, an Indigenous widow named Mrs. Haggerty, started poisoning the three hundred enslaved people on her plantation, one by one. At night, Thomas could hear the wails and mournful cries of the living grieving the dead.[68] Some former owners too met sudden deaths after the end of the war, perhaps through acts of retribution from formerly enslaved people. Ben Johnson, a white enslaver married to a Cherokee woman on Cherokee lands, died shortly after freeing his slaves, and rumors swirled that he was poisoned by the people he had kept in bondage.[69]

Such an abrupt release to freedom was often jarring and economically unviable after decades of enslavement since most newly freed people had nothing to their name. Most of them owned no tools or land, had received minimal literacy instruction, and possessed only the frailest of legal standing. White southern owners, who had invested most of

LUCY THOMAS,
AGE 86, CA. 1936.

their wealth in the ownership of other human beings and who looked poverty in the eye after the war, tried to scare newly freed men and women into staying and working for them. One newly poor plantation owner named Sanford Wooldridge taunted his former slaves when they threw their hats in the air to celebrate their freedom by sneering, "How you gwine eat and git clothes and sech?"[70]

Some newly freed men and women looked at the economic chaos and charred remains of plantations and towns across the South and decided to keep working for their former owners until things stabilized. Joseph Samuel Badgett, an Indigenous mixed-race man who was a year old when the South was liberated, recalled that his mother was unusually fortunate because her former owner, John Badgett, gave her forty acres of his Dallas County, Arkansas, plantation, along with a mule.[71]

After the war, formerly enslaved people looked in vain for some compensation for their years of enslavement. Rumors spread that plantations would be divided up among the newly freed people, or that the government would give them mules and they wouldn't have to work, or even that Queen Victoria in England was going to send barrels full of money, but all of this proved to be a chimera.[72] Most newly freed people received nothing. In the words of Cora Gillam, a mixed-race Cherokee woman, after the war, former slaves "didn't have nothing but their two hands to start out with." Some people worked as sharecroppers—by which they were supposed to be given a reasonable portion of the profit from the plantation—only to be told that their labor merely balanced the debt they owed the plantation owner for the seed, food, housing, and costs of running the plantation. "Why didn't you work harder?" white plantation owners asked. For Gillam and many others, share-cropping was merely a new kind of slavery: "We was just about where we was in slave days."[73]

Some newly freed Natives took more direct action to lay claim to the wealth accumulated by their previous enslavers. A mixed-race Indigenous man named Hall had been enslaved on the plantation of the fabulously wealthy Benjamin Roach Jr. of Mississippi. Hall was still enslaved when Lieutenant Francis Barlow's military unit rode through the state in April 1863, liberating slaves and claiming stacks upon stacks of cotton bales for the North. Hall immediately saw an opening and tried to take it. Now freed, he followed the federal officers who had loaded up the bales of cotton onto wagons and transported them to the river. At the water's edge, Hall made an audacious claim: some of the cotton belonged to him, since he was Roach's business partner and had not been enslaved. Challenged by his former overseer, Hall backed down in the moment but later sued in court, where the case languished until 1875 when it was finally dismissed.[74]

The former slaveholding Native nations—Muscogee, Cherokee, Choctaw, Chickasaw, and Seminole—who had signed treaties with the Confederacy and fought against the Union Army were treated like conquered people. The federal government required them to accept the thousands of their formerly enslaved people into their tribes as citizens, called "freedmen"—a convenient solution for the United States since it offloaded support of such people to tribes. But it was also a practical mandate since many freedmen were connected to those tribes through kinship. Generations of freedmen since that time have had to navigate their status and position in communities, and up until the present in some cases.[75]

For Native Americans and Indigenous-Blacks who had been enslaved and then set free during the Civil War, freedom was life changing, even as daily existence remained hard and racism ubiquitous. Decades later, formerly enslaved Indigenous men and women reflected on the meaning of their freedom. Moses Mitchell noted, "Here's the idea, freedom is worth it all."[76] And Mattie Logan, commenting on her life postslavery, reported, "I'm my own boss, get up when I want, go to bed the same way. Nobody to say this or that about what I do. Yes, I'm glad to be free!"[77]

WITH THE END OF THE CIVIL WAR, a distinct phase of Black and Indigenous enslavement in the South was officially over. But the same war threw the lives of tens of thousands of Native Americans in the Southwest and West into turmoil through outright warfare, captive taking, enslaving, and forced removals to reservation prisons. Native Americans were still viewed by US officials as an immense threat, especially west of the Mississippi.

James Harlan, the secretary of the Department of the Interior, reflected this persistent racism when he sat down in October 1865 to write a lengthy annual report regarding the state of Indian affairs in the United States. Virtually every tribe west of the Mississippi had sided with the Confederacy in the war, Harlan claimed with disgust—although this was not quite true. Harlan, ignoring the fact that the United States was the primary aggressor in the West, asserted that Native American involvement prolonged the war and considerably increased expenses for the United States. What should be done?[78]

One proposal made by "gentlemen of high position" was a war of extermination against the 350,000 Native Americans within the borders of the United States. Harlan spent three whole paragraphs weighing the pros and cons of such a murderous policy. On the one hand, he reasoned, Native nations deserved such destruction, for not only fighting against the Union in the Civil War but also refusing to be shuttled onto reservations, resistance that resulted in the loss of property in the West for caravans of American colonists, supply lines, settlements, and even the new railroads that cut through Indian country. On the other hand, the "total destruction of the Indians" would be too costly, leading Harlan to dismiss the "inauguration of such a policy." Harlan also acknowledged the unconscionable loss of life of 350,000 Indians and how indefensible such mass murders might be to the outside world. It would also be, as he acknowledged, a violation of "Christian duty."[79]

Still, it was telling that the possible genocide of the entire Native population in the United States was worth even a moment's consideration by the head of the federal agency whose job it was to oversee Indigenous nations. This persistent anti-Indian mentality, even at the highest levels of the federal government, helps explain why American callousness toward ongoing Native enslavement, peonage, and servitude persisted well after the Civil War and soon required yet another federal intervention.[80]

Fifteen

ABOLISHING PEONAGE

IN AMERICAN NATIONAL MEMORY, THE CIVIL WAR BROUGHT A DECI-
sive end to all slavery everywhere in the country.[1] While this was
legally—even if incompletely—true for southern slavery, Indigenous
slavery and servitude in the American West were essentially untouched.
From New Mexico to California, residents interpreted the Thirteenth
Amendment in 1865 as not applying to the slavery and servitude of
Native Americans. Quite the opposite, in fact, since Indigenous people
in these areas had experienced an *expansion* of enslavement during the
war, and it continued unabated afterward.

In these regions, the buying and selling of Native captives continued as usual. Two months after Lee surrendered to Grant on April 9,
1865, the brother of a high-ranking government official in Bernalillo,
New Mexico, purchased an enslaved Native woman for the price of
a cow and ten goats. She was far from alone, according to the Catholic bishop of New Mexico, Juan Baptiste Laney, who reported that
thousands of Diné captives were kept as servants and slaves by New
Mexican families. The same was true for thousands more Indigenous
people in the other expansive and unregulated regions of the Southwest and West.[2]

It was not supposed to be that way. In the waning months of the
war, with a Union victory all but certain, Congress had passed the
Thirteenth Amendment on January 31, 1865. It declared, echoing
the language of the Northwest Ordinance of 1787, "Neither slavery nor involuntary servitude, except as a punishment for crime
whereof the party shall have been duly convicted, shall exist within
the United States, or any place subject to their jurisdiction."[3] But

the Thirteenth Amendment contained a major omission: it did not specifically mention Native Americans.

In the months and years following the Confederacy's demise, officials in Washington slowly realized the full extent of ongoing Native enslavement and servitude in the Southwest and West. Three related events forced the nation to finally address these issues. First, as direct testimony and reports circulated regarding rampant Native enslavement, Americans in the western region of the country could no longer argue for a unique and privileged status of Indian slavery and peonage after the Civil War. Second, the postwar federal zeal for eradicating all forms of servitude, called Reconstruction (1865–1877), widened to include Indigenous enslavement, which put pressure on western slaveholders to comply.

Third, and perhaps most important, ongoing Indian slavery and servitude were seen by federal administrators as an obstacle to an orderly conquest of western regions by the federal government. The repeated cycles of captive taking, purchasing, and enslaving threatened the systematic "settlement" of New Mexico, Arizona, and California desired by federal government and state and territorial leaders. As New Mexico's Indian Affairs superintendent Michael Steck noted in 1868, in regard to the ongoing Native slave and captive trade, "No permanent peace could be had with [the Indians] as long as this evil is permitted."[4]

Especially influential was a five-hundred-page report published by a special congressional subcommittee in early 1867 on the treatment of Native tribes in the United States. It contained reams of testimony regarding Indigenous slavery and peonage, which meant that US legislators could no longer ignore the issue. Although Congress eventually passed an act targeting the practice in March 1867, American enslavers in the Southwest and West dug in their heels, and the federal government, half a continent away, mostly gave up. This failure of enforcement combined with deep-seated anti-Indian racism allowed Native slavery to persist long after the American Civil War, leaving Native families vainly searching to reconnect with stolen relatives well into the 1880s and beyond.

IT TOOK A VICIOUS MASSACRE TO jolt Congress into exhibiting concern for western Native nations. In the early morning chill of

November 29, 1864—just five days after the nation observed the second annual Thanksgiving celebration led by President Lincoln—nearly one thousand soldiers from the US Army departed from Denver at the base of the towering Rocky Mountains. Stealthily, this formidable entourage marched nearly two hundred miles southeast to the small military outpost of Fort Lyon. Passing this Union stronghold, they finally approached their destination: an encampment of five hundred or more peaceable Cheyenne and Arapaho families who had sought refuge at the fort.

Seeing the imposing column of mounted soldiers approaching Sand Creek in the early dawn hours, a Cheyenne leader named Black Kettle quickly hoisted a US flag as well as a white flag, universally known to signal surrender. The American troops ignored these gestures. They continued their march toward the camp, even firing on a federal Indian agent named John S. Smith who ran out to intercede.[5] For six hours, the US soldiers systematically slaughtered every Indigenous person in sight. When a group of one hundred Cheyenne and Arapaho people—

DEPICTION OF THE SAND CREEK MASSACRE, BY EUGENE RIDGELY SR. (EAGLE ROBE), ELK HIDE ARTWORK, 1994.

mostly women and children—took refuge under a wide earthen over-
hang along the river, the soldiers cut off all escape routes and fired until
more than seventy of them had been murdered.

When the rifles and howitzers finally ceased blazing, the mutilated
bodies of more than a hundred Cheyenne and Arapaho men, women,
and children lay lifeless on the shores and in the shallow waters of Sand
Creek. Their corpses bore testimony to intense hatred and violence.
These peaceable Natives weren't just killed; their bodies had been cut to
pieces, stabbed, scalped, and bludgeoned beyond recognition by axes,
hatchets, swords, and the blunt end of guns and pistols. Infants, young
children, women, the elderly, men—all were indiscriminately hacked to
death. Federal Agent Smith was summoned to see if he could identify
the corpses of any known Native leaders, but he could only recognize a
few of the disfigured faces. So deep was their animosity toward Natives
that when US soldiers then found out Smith had a mixed-race Indian
son named Jack in his living quarters, they burst in and killed the boy
in cold blood.[6]

Local newspapers praised the slaughter of the Cheyenne and Arapaho as one of the most "brilliant feats of arms."[7] Washington officials,
however, were alarmed and took decisive action. Governor Evans was
eventually forced out of office, and a commission was established to
learn the whole truth, ultimately calling it what it was: a massacre.

The final report on the Sand Creek murders, titled "Massacre of

DETAIL FROM EUGENE RIDGELY SR.'S DEPICTION
OF THE SAND CREEK MASSACRE, 1994.

the Cheyenne Indians," was sent to Congress on January 10, 1865, in the waning months of the Civil War. Its depositions and details were so horrific and the massacre so outrageous that President Lincoln and Congress felt compelled to discover what really was happening to Indigenous nations in the West.

To find out, on March 3, 1865, a joint committee composed of members from both houses of Congress was appointed to consider the condition of Indian tribes west of the Mississippi.[8] Headed by Wisconsin Republican senator James R. Doolittle, the committee's seven members divided up the various western states and territories for investigation. They relied on a combination of in-person visits and interviews, reports, and letters sent in from various locales, as well as depositions taken in Washington from officials summoned from territories like Colorado and New Mexico. The reports they heard only reinforced the dual realities of the ongoing outrages against Indigenous nations and the immense colonizing work that still remained if the United States wished to fully control western territories.

The Doolittle Committee, as it was called, was not specifically tasked with inquiring about Indigenous slavery and bondage, but it was barraged with evidence of these practices taking place everywhere, especially in regions in and surrounding New Mexico. It is impossible to know how Lincoln would have responded to the reports of ongoing Indian slavery as he was assassinated on April 15, 1865, before the committee's investigation was complete.

His vice president, the southern Democrat Andrew Johnson, entered office committed to speeding up Lincoln's plan of cautiously reintegrating southern states. While President Johnson was at times ambivalent about the treatment of Indigenous nations, he appointed a Republican and close friend of Lincoln, James Harlan, as the secretary of the Department of the Interior. With both the report of the Sand Creek Massacre and stories of Indigenous slavery arriving on his desk, Harlan decided the Department of the Interior needed an overhaul. He immediately began firing corrupt federal Indian agents and making replacement appointments.[9]

Harlan also gave President Johnson the early reports and correspondence of the committee showing that Indigenous slavery was rampant in New Mexico. As Harlan later noted, forcing Indians to labor was a violation of their personal liberty and "should not be tolerated in a country professing to be free."[10] On June 9, 1865, Johnson issued an executive order targeting these practices, noting "Indians in New Mexico have been seized and reduced into slavery." Importantly, President Johnson's order recognized the role of American federal agents and military officers in the ongoing enslavement and servitude of Native Americans. He commanded that all governmental "subordinates, agents, and employés" in the New Mexico Territory "discountenance the practice aforesaid" and called on those same people "to take all lawful means to suppress the same."[11]

Harlan had no idea what an uphill battle he faced. Ranchers in New Mexico, Utah, and California had long defended Indian peonage, servitude, and enslavement as different from southern plantation slavery. When questioned, Felipe Delagado, the superintendent of Indian Affairs in New Mexico, who held at least six Native Americans as slaves and servants, admitted to his superiors in Washington, DC, that there was "a large number of Indian captives" still held—in July 1865—by the residents of New Mexico, most of whom had been purchased from the Ute, Diné, and other regional Native nations. The point was not to enslave them, Delagado argued rather pathetically, but to provide what he defined as humanitarian uplift. Like so many others, Delagado pointed toward a 150-year-old practice of captivity and servitude in the region, which he defined as different from outright slavery. Delagado's defense was flimsy at best, as even he surely must have known, since he also reported that he instructed his Indian Affairs agents not to permit any further purchases of Native captives.[12]

Harlan soon discovered that Colorado was another hot spot of ongoing Native slavery and captivity. When Lafayette Head, a federal Indian agent, and E. R. Harris, a US deputy marshal, toured Colorado, they found 149 captured or purchased Native servants and slaves (plus an additional 9 children tabulated separately) in Costilla and Conejos Counties alone, acquired between 1831 and 1865. Most of these enslaved Natives were listed as Diné, along with Ute, Paiute, Apache, and even one "California" Indian who had been purchased in 1831. Women and girls were disproportionately represented, at 62 percent and 69 percent of the captives in Costilla and Conejos Counties, respectively. Most of the Natives in these counties were under the age of twenty; the youngest in Costilla County was a four-year-old Diné boy named Juan who had been purchased from Mexican traders as an infant in 1862. Most of the Natives—109 in all—had been captured and sold into slavery during the Civil War, and they were still enslaved even after the war had ended.[13]

Officials agreed these enslaved Natives should be emancipated. The challenge was what to do with them. They were casualties of an entrenched American colonial system, severed from families, and potentially with no homes to return to. A few older enslaved Diné had memories of their former lives and were eager to return home. Younger children purloined as infants were unable to give specifics about their family's names or tribal origins, leaving them in relational limbo.[14]

Meanwhile, the Doolittle Committee continued to make progress in revealing the full scope of Native slavery and servitude. Committee members took dozens of depositions from high-ranking territorial offi-

"LIST OF INDIAN CAPTIVES ACQUIRED BY PURCHASE,
AND NOW IN THE SERVICE OF THE CITIZENS
OF CONEJOS COUNTY," JULY 1865.

cials and federal agents in New Mexico and the surrounding area. The chief justice of New Mexico, Kirby Benedict, testified on July 4, 1865, that at least two thousand to three thousand Native Americans were still claimed by Americans in New Mexico. Other residents believed the number to be much higher. A physician named Louis Kennon gave sworn testimony on July 4, 1865, that he estimated the actual number of Diné Indians held in slavery and servitude to be between five thousand and six thousand—double what territory officials reported.[15]

By this time, Harlan's investigators realized they were dealing with a system of lifelong, heritable slavery that had escaped the notice of the nation during the Civil War. Local officials testified that Natives had been bought and sold by residents "as their servants and slaves," held as "fixed domestic servants without their being the recipients of wages."[16] General Carleton, in a separate statement, believed that three-quarters of Natives held in bondage in New Mexico were Diné. Such bondage was multigenerational, with the children of peons—whether perpetrated through rape or other means—also retained as peons.[17] This slavery, Kennon averred, was worse than southern slavery that he had seen in Georgia before the Civil War because it was entirely unregulated and owners felt no compulsion to properly provide for their enslaved Natives or care for them after they could no longer work.[18]

INDIGENOUS PEONAGE AND SLAVERY were rampant in California, too. Officials there acknowledged in 1864 and 1865 that as many as six thousand Native girls and boys under the age of seventeen lived in non-Native households—with most held as servants, peons, or slaves.[19]

Individual rancheros and farmers saw themselves well within their rights, even in a state that billed itself as free, and treated Natives in myriad inhumane ways. In early August 1865, a rancher named Robert Hildreth chased down one of his Native servants who had hired himself out to another rancher to pick barley. Enraged, Hildreth bound the boy's hands behind his back, tied a short rope from the boy's hands to his saddle, jumped on the horse and dug his spurs deep into the horse's sides. Spooked, the horse took off, bucking off Hildreth and dragging the Indian youth across the road and over two ditches before stopping. The youth, described by local newspapers as "terribly mangled," did not survive. Hildreth was arraigned, but locals doubted he would be convicted.[20] In a separate incident that same summer, a white farmer that local papers called "an Indian slaveholder" shot and maimed an enslaved Native man for resisting a whipping.[21]

One California rancher who embodied the American perpetuation of Indian peonage and functional enslavement in the 1860s was Cave Johnson Couts. He had arrived in California as part of the US military occupation of California in the late 1840s. Couts's marriage to Ysidora Bandini also put him in charge of a 2,219-acre estate called Rancho Guajome (named after the Luiseño word *wakhavumi*, meaning "place of the frogs"). It lay forty miles north of San Diego and was the site of the abandoned Mission San Luis Rey. Originally an enslaver from Tennessee, Couts quickly used the 1850 indenture laws in California to exploit the labor of dozens of Native Americans, placing himself at the center of the Indian indenture trade, even serving as the local justice of the peace in charge of assigning Native children to himself and others.[22]

Couts was an inveterate recordkeeper. His account books tracked his cattle, horses, and sheep each year, noting when he started sheep shearing along with who exactly trimmed them. In letter books and diaries, he recorded observations and tracked the activities of his property. He meticulously tracked his finances, both personal and business, as well as the number of days he spent on Indian affairs.[23]

But most of all, Couts kept razor-sharp accounts of his laborers. Each year, Couts listed who worked for him, how much he paid them, how much they owed him, and what their total indebtedness was. His servant account books, as he called them, are models of debt peonage in action. Cucensia, for example, was listed in 1853 as "an Indian" and was paid fifteen dollars per month, or roughly thirty-one cents per day. But, as with his other indebted servants, Couts added to her account an inflated cost for every item he provided for her. He charged her one dollar for a bottle and four dollars for a blanket, and when she got sick, he added two dollars for medicine. Month by month, Cucensia's debt accrued, with no hope of her ever paying it off. When she ran away on December 20, 1853, Cucensia was in debt to Couts for fifty-seven dollars and fifty cents.[24]

Couts flouted the law repeatedly. In 1865, he had more than a dozen Native and Black "servants" working at Guajome. These servants—

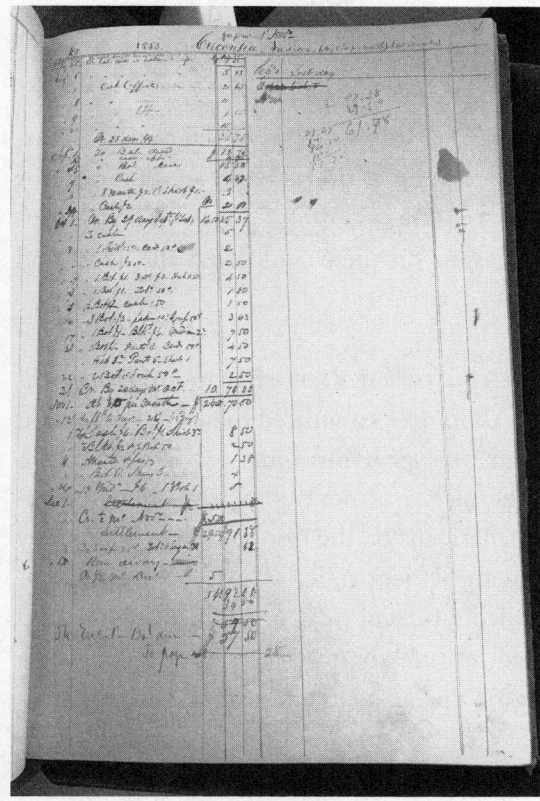

CUCENSIA
ACCOUNT,
CAVE JOHNSON
COUTS PAPERS.

most of whom were likely legally bound to him—complained of mistreatment. One Indian boy in particular, named Reyes, was being held long past his appointed time of service. Like other Natives caught in peonage, Reyes was getting paid twenty-seven cents per day, but Couts continually charged small items to Reyes's account. His parents complained to the justice of the peace, who declined to act, concluding that Reyes was reasonably well cared for.[25]

Fortunately for the parents, an Indian agent named John Quincy Adams Stanley searched the justice of the peace's record books and found out that Reyes had only been "sentenced to serve" Couts for one year. Stanley wrote to Couts in December 1865, demanding that he "at once liberate the boy" and return Reyes to his father.[26] Instead, Couts flew into a rage, brazenly asserting virtually unlimited rights as legal master: "No servant of mine can be taken from me on the ord of any 'Especial Indian Agent.' "[27] Stanley appealed up the chain of command

and got an order from the justice of the peace and the Indian superintendent. There is no direct evidence that Couts complied, but Reyes
was not listed among Couts's forty-five "servants" in 1867.[28]

Couts may have been especially stubborn in so flagrantly violating the law, but he was not alone in his actions. Many more rancheros
silently extended the time of service required of Natives on their properties, imposing functional slavery on them and using the 1850 and
1860 laws for justification.

ON THE OTHER SIDE OF THE CONTINENT, after months of gathering evidence the Doolittle Committee submitted their final report on
January 26, 1867. It contained a ten-page introduction by Doolittle in
which he candidly blamed the dire treatment of Natives on the continuing aggression of white Americans on the frontier, often abetted by
governmental agents and structural ineptitude.[29]

As proof, Doolittle appended a torrent of depositions, reports, and
correspondence that cascaded relentlessly onto the 532 pages that followed. The direct testimony of dozens of territorial and federal officials, New Mexican residents, three Diné, and one Apache (all four
Natives were prisoners at Bosque Redondo) that revealed, among other
things, a deeply entrenched Indian slavery and peonage system perpetuated by whites, Mexicans, and Natives alike. Multiple sources suggested there were as many as six thousand Diné alone held as slaves
in New Mexico and the surrounding area.[30] These enslaved Natives
were central to the labor economy of the region. New Mexico residents were staunchly opposed to the proposed reservation for the Diné
especially because "there will be no more tribes from which they can
capture servants."[31]

Doolittle was candid, but his exposé of the mistreatment of Natives
and their ongoing enslavement angered those who were implicated.
Members of Congress, individuals in the US Army and the Department of War, and former employees of the Department of the Interior
claimed the report slandered them.[32] This explains, in part, why Doolittle sat on the report for a year before finalizing it. But amid the controversy, one thing was clear: the situation in the American West was
starkly at odds with the aggressive attempts to eradicate all vestiges of
slavery in the American South.

By 1867, the Republican-controlled Congress increasingly bypassed the southern-sympathizing President Johnson to enact a stronger set of requirements in the former Confederate states, known as Radical Reconstruction. The aggressive antislavery Republicans who pushed for the military occupation of noncompliant southern states leveraged the findings of the Doolittle Committee and other reports to bring the issue before Congress. Massachusetts senator Charles Sumner—who famously had been beaten with a cane on the floor of Congress by a southern senator in the fractious time leading up to the Civil War— and Senator Henry Wilson, also from Massachusetts, led the charge. They demanded that Congress, in Wilson's words, pass a bill that would "abolish and forever prohibit the system of peonage."[33]

Within two months, they succeeded. On March 2, 1867, President Johnson signed into law "An Act to abolish and forever prohibit the System of Peonage in the Territory of New Mexico and other Parts of the United States." It outlawed "the voluntary or involuntary service or labor of any persons as peons, in liquidation of any debt or obliga- tion." A hefty $5,000 fine would be levied against anyone participating or aiding in the ongoing coercion of Indians in this way. Military and civil servants who continued in the trade and use of peons would be court-martialed and dishonorably dismissed.[34]

As with most laws passed in Washington, the news of what was termed the Peonage Abolition Act was transmitted from east to west in waves, carried by telegraph lines, trains, and express mail carriers. Newspapers reprinted extracts of the act, noting that Congress had abolished the system of "Peonage," which was "a mild name for a very bad system of slavery."[35] Federal authorities sent strongly worded letters to governors and agents in the rugged, barely controlled New Mexico Territory and the surrounding territories and states.

Governors gestured toward compliance with the new prohibition. New Mexico governor Robert B. Mitchell issued a proclamation that in theory set free all peons and those "held to service or labor by any stat- ute or custom heretofore in force."[36] Most legal masters, however, were unmoved considering they had long convinced themselves that the Civil War and its prohibitions regarding slavery referred to *Black* slavery, not Indigenous slavery and servitude. Mitchell left office, and a year later, on June 10, 1868, the new governor, Herman M. Heath, issued another

NEWSPAPER REPORT
OF THE PEONAGE
ABOLITION ACT,
IN "PEONAGE
ABOLISHED,"
FREEDOM'S CHAMPION
(ATCHINSON, KS),
MAY 16, 1867.

> ## "Peonage" Abolished.
>
> On the 2d of March last the President approved an act of Congress abolishing the system of "Peonage," (a mild name for a very bad system of slavery,) in the Territory of New Mexico, and prohibiting it throughout the United States. The law makes it the duty of all civil and military officers of the Government to see that its provisions are duly and strictly enforced. In accordance therewith, Gov. ROBERT B. MITCHELL, of the Territory of New Mexico, has promptly issued a Proclamation declaring all persons held to service or labor by any statute or custom of that Territory, (except on conviction for crime,) free, and stating that any one found guilty of violating the law of Congress, will be severely dealt with.

proclamation that condemned slavery "in every name and form," along with "peonage and every other class of involuntary servitude."[37] And still New Mexico residents remained largely unswayed.

In other places, too, Indigenous captives continued to be bought, sold, and seen as a means of barter and exchange in the local economy. At Fort McDowell, a few miles northeast of Phoenix, US soldiers continued a steady trade in Native captives and slaves as late as 1867. Reports reached Washington that Indigenous captives brought by Pima and Marian Pac Indians to Fort McDowell were used as functional currency to barter, trade, and exchange for goods. Government officials ordered an investigation.[38]

Faced with such brazen disregard for federal policy, American officials attempted to dismantle Indigenous slavery and peonage one case at a time. William W. Griffin, a special commissioner for Indian Affairs and a radical antislavery Republican; New Mexico US attorney Stephen B. Elkins; and US marshal John Pratt seemed especially determined to stamp out Indigenous servitude in all of its various forms. Griffin had lived in New Mexico for almost a decade and knew the networks and key families there. He and Pratt immediately tracked down enslavers.[39]

Between March and November 1868, Griffin brought 363 cases against 224 households of residents in Taos, Santa Fe, and Rio Arriba Counties in north-central New Mexico. It was one of the most astonishing mass legal prosecutions of Native slavery and servitude in American history, and it took place after the passage of both the Thirteenth Amendment (1865) and the Peonage Abolition Act (1867). Fully 81 percent of the people listed in bondage, or 292 Natives, were deemed to be enslaved, while 19 percent, or 70, of the cases dealt with debt peonage or other kinds of perpetual, long-term labor arrangements. More than half of the households prosecuted had only one Native American, but some households had between 2 and 4, with several having between 8 and 10.[40]

The accused slaveholders were a cross section of New Mexico society, including territorial assembly members, farmers, and merchants. Juan Trujillo was found to have two Diné women named Rosa and Maria in his possession, one of whom had young children who were also claimed as servants and slaves. Trujillo had purchased these Diné women eight years earlier, and they labored without pay for maintaining the house. Juan Santistevan held an Indigenous girl named Dolores as well as two additional Native slaves, and Santistevan's mother, Rosalia Medina, also held at least two Indigenous slaves, a Native woman and her four-year-old child.[41] José Benito Martinez, who had served in the New Mexico Assembly, was charged with holding six enslaved Natives.

Griffin claimed to have set free these Native Americans, but local juries refused to convict enslavers or punish them.[42] The wide availability of Native captives and servants meant that some residents simply acquired others as replacements. This was especially true for wealthier inhabitants, including those who were well connected and enmeshed in territorial leadership. Juan Benito Valdez was serving in the upper house of the New Mexico Assembly in 1868 when Griffin took him to court for holding ten "Indian slaves." Local newspapers reported that Griffin "liberated the slaves" and held Valdez on bail.[43] Valdez was swiftly acquitted, however, and two years later, in the 1870 census, he listed two Native domestics in his house: Maria Refugio and Soledad, ages thirty and thirty-one.[44]

High-ranking socialites, some of whom came from deeply entrenched Mexican American families, seemed especially immune to

Griffin's emancipatory attempts. Martinez was accused by Griffin of slaveholding and two years later was still listed in the 1870 New Mexico census as having eight Indigenous people in his household, some of whom were specifically called "Domestics." His real estate was valued at $1,750, but his personal estate was worth $4,175, some of which presumably was due to these Native servants and slaves.[45] Local Catholic priests were also accused by Griffin, including Father Mariano Lucero, who had four enslaved Natives in 1868. Although he was apparently excommunicated by 1870, Lucero is listed in the census with a staggering $15,000 of personal property and four Indian domestics: Manuela Martínez, Juan Antonio, Andres, and Luisa, ranging from six to fifty-five years old.[46]

In almost every region, Americans defiantly continued to enslave and coerce Natives. Scandalously, parish and census records show a steady *increase* in Indigenous slaves and servants in New Mexico households during and after these federal investigations.[47] Griffin and Elkins claimed to have won the battle, but New Mexico residents won the war.

Mormons, too, believed themselves to be exempt from federal regulations. This was partly because they lived in a parallel society where polygamy and other specific Mormon religious and cultural norms reigned supreme. Believing they were fulfilling religious mandates, they convinced themselves that their system of adopting and indenturing Indian children was not slavery or peonage.

Federal officials thought otherwise. Hundreds of Native Americans lived in Mormon households across Utah, some of them teenagers who had been purchased and "adopted" in the 1850s. Wilford Woodruff, a Mormon apostle and future head of the Mormon Church, had purchased a six-year-old Paiute captive named Saroquetes in 1857. As he grew into young adulthood and perhaps more fully comprehended his situation, Saroquetes (or Sarakeets) grew more resistant to his Mormon claimed masters and family. He stole items from the Woodruffs, disappeared for days, and in 1868 left the household completely.[48]

The trade in Indigenous captives slowed significantly by the late 1860s, although some Mormons around St. George in southern Utah continued to trade sporadically with Natives for captives into the 1890s, with adoptions persisting into the twentieth century.[49]

Federal zeal for eradicating all forms of slavery extended to Native nations that still held enslaved individuals from other tribes. Tribes in the Oregon Territory of the Pacific Northwest were well known for slave raiding each other and keeping captives, which was reported by American residents in the region as resembling chattel slavery.[50] At a council held at the Warm Spring Reservation on the Columbia River, south of The Dalles, Oregon, in July 1871, the Native chiefs and headmen from the Wascoe, Tenino, and Warm Springs (Upper Deschutes band) nations met with an Indian agent named Captain John Smith. One by one, the Native chiefs reflected on proposed impositions from the US government. In particular, agents targeted the long-standing practice of slave raiding and captive taking among Natives in the Northwest. The "white men had a great war," Felix R. Brunot explained. "Many people were killed, but now we all have the same laws. . . . If there are any slaves among these Indians the President wants them sent back to their friends."[51]

Federal agents and missionaries who visited tribes in Oregon and Washington reported mixed success. In some instances, Native enslavement of other tribes seemingly had ended; in other cases, agents reported that "a mild form of slavery" still existed among the Makah Natives in Washington, with Natives from other tribes "held as slaves." As a sign of the very different sort of slavery in Indian country, however, the federal Indian agent at the Neah Bay station, E. M. Gibson, noted that the enslaved Natives fare "as well as their masters, and will not leave them."[52]

FEW PEOPLE FELT the collective suffering of captivity more acutely than the imprisoned Diné. The forced prolonged captivity of nearly nine thousand Diné and Ndé by the US military at Hwéeldi was a humanitarian disaster of heartbreaking and historical dimensions. Oral histories of Diné survivors record inhumane conditions, raids by Apache and New Mexico residents, diseases that ravaged the community, and extremely limited portions of flour, meat, beans, and other rations provided by the federal government.[53] General James Carleton wrote to his superiors in Washington, describing the destitute circumstances of the Diné he had rounded up, asking especially for clothing for the women and children to survive the winter months.[54]

For a nation that expertly raised cattle and sheep and annually coaxed corn, fruit, and other crops from the desert, the transition to a largely flour-based diet was deleterious. When the flour rations first arrived, famished Diné ate it raw, sometimes mixed with water, and got sick.[55] As Mayla Benally, a Diné woman from the Tsénahabilnii clan stated succinctly, "The Navajos suffered at Hwéeldi."[56]

Although the federal government hoped that Diné captivity at Bosque Redondo would result in a permanent reservation away from Diné lands, by 1868 the tide of public opinion had turned against the prison camp. Local newspapers reported with outrage the staggering cost of $750,000 per year for keeping the Diné and Ndé in captivity, with no benefit of captives for white households or livestock for New Mexico residents.[57] Diné leaders were relieved and reported it to be the "unanimous wish of all the chiefs to go back to their old country."[58]

In June 1868, the United States signed a treaty with Diné headmen that legally disenfranchised them from vast acres of their homelands but allowed them to leave the detested and deadly Hwéeldi. At the treaty table, surrounded by federal agents, the Diné spokesperson Barboncito refused to simply sign over the land. Instead, he demanded an answer for the thousands of "Navajo children held as prisoners" in the households of New Mexico residents. When asked how many Diné were held as slaves, Barboncito informed them, "Over half the tribe."[59] Barboncito's estimate was easily possible. Only three years earlier, federal reports surmised six thousand Diné had been taken as captives and slaves, and the actual number could have been much higher.

Barboncito received no satisfactory response from federal officials regarding the return of his stolen kin, however. The final treaty he and others were compelled to sign contained no stipulations about the return of enslaved Diné children and other captives. Instead, Americans continued to turn a blind eye to the effects of American colonization and blamed Diné leaders, forcing them to agree that they would never again raid Americans and Mexican Americans.[60]

One by one, bands of emaciated Diné vacated their prison of four years and retraced the path of the Long Walk, back across the rugged New Mexico terrain to Fort Defiance on the edge of their government-mandated reservation, and from there to their homelands, now surrounded by Arizona. The Diné nation's territory was reduced to a reservation that was only a portion of their former lands, although it did include their treasured, red-walled spiritual fortress of Canyon de Chelly. The land the United States had stolen from them was a fertile, mineral-laden territory of inestimable value, as reported by military leaders and federal agents.[61]

Diné complaints about their stolen relations and lands attracted the attention of the Freedmen's Bureau, a federal agency created by President Lincoln in March 1865 to provide relief and support to formerly enslaved people. That the bureau's head, General Oliver Otis Howard, concerned himself with Indigenous enslavement in the Southwest was yet another sign that officials in Washington had finally acknowledged the similarities between western and southern slaveries.

In 1872, Howard traveled to Arizona to meet with Diné headmen, where he was told by Hasting Ch'il Haajini, also called Manuelito, that many Diné children were still kept by Mexicans and Americans. Diné saw firsthand their children in households in New Mexico as they traveled around and visited white ranches and towns. Worse still, American enslavers psychologically terrorized the children, telling them that their real parents would only kill them if they escaped to Diné territory.

HASTING CH'IL
HAAJINI, OR
MANUELITO, DINÉ, BY
E. A. BURBANK.

Native children likely didn't believe this lie, for many desperately still wanted to return home.[62]

When Howard asked how it was that Diné children were in American households, Manuelito rebuked him: "You know very well how they come to be there. . . . When all the Nations came against us, then we lost our children (eight years ago)."[63] The devastating total war against the Diné at the hands of the US military in 1863–1864 was largely to blame and remained fresh in their minds.

BY THE 1870S, IT WAS CLEAR that Americans in the West had mostly defended their right to keep Native Americans in slavery and servitude. Thousands of Indigenous people served in New Mexican households, even in the homes of prominent state and federal officials. The extended family of José Francisco Chávez, the New Mexico delegate to the US Congress, remained one of the largest holders of Indigenous slaves, peons, and captives into the 1870s.[64] Territorial newspapers pilloried Chávez and other Republicans in 1869 for betraying their party's antislavery stance by having "peons and Indian slaves . . . about their houses, in their fields, with the herds and with their trains, in the same condition of subjection and servility that they had them before the passage of the laws abolishing the institutions."[65] The 1870 census of New Mexico meticulously tabulated the ongoing presence of hundreds of Native "domestics" in households, with likely hundreds more unreported.[66]

Part of the problem was that the US military was still fighting wars against Native nations, which occasionally led to captive taking and enslavement. In Arizona, an American-led and Papago-aided expedition of 142 men from Tucson marched across the desert at night and attacked a sleeping Apache camp at sunrise on April 28, 1871. The bloodthirsty crew tore through the sleeping tents, clubbing bodies indiscriminately in the early dawn light, hacking some to pieces and smashing heads over rocks. Those who tried to escape were shot or hunted down and beaten to death. Approximately 144 Apaches were killed, mostly women and children. The raiders took 29 Apache children captive and marched them back to Tucson, where they were sold into slavery. The Apache survivors suspected as much and pleaded with American leaders: "Get them back for us. Our little boys will grow up slaves, and our girls, as soon as they are large enough, will be diseased prostitutes, to get money for whoever owns them."[67]

The Camp Grant Massacre, as it was rightfully called, was met with national outrage and denunciation from federal officials. President Ulysses Grant called the attack "purely murder" and threatened to place the entire territory under martial law. A five-day federal trial ensued, but the local Arizona jury declined to find anyone guilty.[68]

Abandoned by the federal government, Indigenous people in New Mexico continued to labor as servants and functional slaves up through the 1880s and perhaps even into the twentieth century. In 1877, a federal agent named Alexander G. Irvine reported that Diné—and especially women—were "held as servants" in New Mexico and Colorado with nothing more than food and clothing in return.[69] Census records in Colorado, Arizona, and Utah continued to show the presence of Indian women and children in American households throughout the following decades.[70] In one case, three individuals charged by Griffin in 1868 for holding Indigenous slaves were by 1880 all living together and listed five domestic servants ages fourteen to thirty, three of whom were noted as "Indian."[71]

The same was true in California. Even after the 1863 repeal of these laws, and despite the 1867 Peonage Abolition Act, rancheros and legal masters across California continued these forms of Indian servitude for decades. In his annual report to the secretary of the interior, the Board of Indian Commissioners secretary Vincent Coyler reported in 1871 that the Natives of southern California, having been stripped of their lands by white Americans, largely labored on ranches in relatively unacceptable conditions. "To the rich rancheros," he reported, "they are slaves in all but the name."[72]

BY 1877, THE PROJECT OF Reconstruction had largely failed nationally, not just in the West. There were some distinct gains, most notably in the successful passing of two additional constitutional amendments that cemented the rights and freedoms of formerly enslaved people. The Fourteenth Amendment (1868) granted citizenship to Black Americans and guaranteed their equal protection, even while notably excluding "Indians not taxed," meaning on reservations. The Fifteenth

Amendment (1869) in theory guaranteed the right of all male citizens (even formerly enslaved ones) to vote. Members of Native nations were excluded from citizenship and were denied voting rights.

But the withdrawal of federal troops from the South in 1877 unleashed a wide-ranging series of restrictions on the mobility and political involvement of Black and mixed-race individuals all over the American South. These are usually called Jim Crow laws, named after a caricatured minstrel character. Southern whites and local governments increasingly capitalized on loopholes in the Thirteenth Amendment and the sale of incarcerated labor to essentially introduce, as one scholar has termed it, "slavery by another name."[73] The repurposing of some plantations to prisons, where hundreds of Black and mixed-race Indigenous prisoners worked in fields in which they had toiled as enslaved people only a decade earlier, was proof enough for many that Southerners were not yet ready to fully give up slavery. The end of slavery was not so immediate and complete in either the South or the West.

The several decades of vicious colonization and slave raiding in the West resulted in a colossal loss of lands and life. California's Indigenous population plummeted from 150,000 in 1845 to between 16,000 and 20,000 by the time of the 1880 census.[74] California had become the nation in a microcosm, with these processes taking place in a compressed time frame. The genocide, removal, and enslavement of Native Americans took centuries in other parts of the country; Californians managed it at a dizzying speed, in a mere quarter of a century.

No wonder some California Natives longed for a "future Spirit land where deer and fish abound." Americans had stolen their children, murdered their relatives, driven them off their lands, and forced them onto reservations that were more "a hell than a home." The future Spirit land they dreamed of was a special place free of all these injustices, and one where "the white man can never get there."[75]

Part Five

TRANSFORMATIONS

1880–1978

I N THE YEARS AFTER THE AMERICAN CIVIL WAR AND THE 1867 Peonage Abolition Act, taking Native captives through warfare slowly declined. This was especially true after what is often called the "last" western Indian war in 1890, the Battle of Wounded Knee, in which the US Army slaughtered three hundred Lakotas. Sporadic, smaller armed conflicts persisted through the 1920s, including continual harassment of the Apache by the US military that mostly subsided after 1924. Soldiers took captives at times, but the era of outright slave raiding was largely over.

Instead, new forms of stealing Native Americans and their land gradually rose to prominence. Federal and state governments focused more intently on forced assimilation through two long-lasting programs. The first was an expansive federally sponsored boarding school system that enrolled tens of thousands of Native children throughout its 180-year history. It had at its core the exploitative labor of Indigenous youth. The second was a series of adoption programs in the twentieth century that systematically placed tens of thousands of Native children in white homes, often against the wishes of parents and tribal leadership. Together, these programs stole hundreds of thousands of Indigenous children from families and reservations between 1800 and 1980, forcing them into white homes and institutions. The purpose was no secret: Americans aimed to fully and completely assimilate Indigenous people into American society, eradicating their cultures and presence in the process.

The effect of these policies was the slow removal of children from Native communities across the nation that intertwined with land grabbing. Children had often been targeted for stealing and enslavement in American history, but this nationally concerted effort was the broadest ranging in its attempt to completely assimilate Natives and seize their land. It robbed families of their children, deprived communities of their future leaders, and sent generations of Native youth into a cultural tailspin that left them drifting between two worlds.

Despite the incredible damage caused by these programs, white Americans did not succeed, at least not completely. Thousands of Native children survived; grew into well-educated, savvy adults; and returned to tribal lands to fight for sovereignty and the future. Building on long traditions of resistance, Native American communities fought back—this time not through raids and war but by using the tools of the oppressors, including petitions and lawsuits, in addition to channeling public pressure and staging nonviolent protests. The result was an astonishing set of victories that, while not complete, ushered in an important era of self-determination that halted the draining of children from reservations and restored sovereignty and some territory to tribes.

Sixteen

THE PRIMER
AND THE HOE

THE COLOSSAL TAKEOVER OF INDIGENOUS LAND THROUGH ENSLAVE-
ment and removal throughout the country left deeply etched scars in
Native communities from the Wampanoag to the Nisenan. But alongside military campaigns against Native Americans, another form
of imposed servitude and dispossession had been quietly growing
throughout the nineteenth century. The means to accomplish this—
schools and education—were benign on the surface, but in the hands
of religious leaders and the federal government became insidious tools
for compulsory labor, cultural eradication, and land loss.

A five-year-old Hopi youth was just one of tens of thousands of
Native children forced to attend American boarding schools. In 1901,
armed police arrived at his house in Oraibi, Arizona, and loaded him
into a wagon with seven other Hopi children. They traveled thirty
miles southeast in a horse-drawn wagon on a long, dusty road to a
foreboding complex of three-story brick buildings. The next day, white
officials snatched away his only possession, a striped blanket from his
grandfather; cut his untouched, youthful, long black hair; and forced
him to put on an uncomfortable blue shirt, mustard-colored pants, and
heavy, stiff shoes.[1] To complete the transformation, he and other gathered children were given new names. The one assigned to the stolen
child from Oraibi who had lost his colorful blanket was Emory.

Emory's new home was Keams Canyon Boarding School, funded
by the US government on the Hopi reservation in Arizona. It was
founded in 1887 at the site of an old trading post as part of a national
effort by the federal government to funnel Native American youth into

THE *MOQUI INDIAN SCHOOL, KEAMS CANON*
[I.E. *CANYON], ARIZONA, 1905.*

government-funded boarding schools. Forced labor was central to this education, which federal agents in 1818 had characterized as a combination of the "primer and the hoe."[2] Students usually studied remedial English, math, and literature for half of the day; the rest of the hours were spent laboring on unfamiliar, gender-specific chores. Native girls sewed, scrubbed floors, cleaned windows, and cooked, while boys learned American-style agriculture (which was not the traditional role of Native men), grew crops to supply the school, and dabbled in other "industrial arts." Emory spent the next thirteen years in the federal boarding school system, which included stints at the Sherman Institute in California and the Phoenix Indian School in Arizona.

Emory was part of a much larger scheme that has been rendered invisible in much of American memory. Between 1801 and 1980, an astonishing 523 Indigenous boarding schools across the country focused on the elimination of Indigenous cultures through so-called education. "Kill the Indian, save the man" was the rallying cry coined in 1878 by Colonel Richard Henry Pratt, one of the pioneers of the off-reservation boarding schools.[3] At least 408 of those schools were financially supported or directly operated by the federal government. They were located in 37 states or territories and included 21 schools in Alaska and 7 in Hawai'i.[4]

The Canadian government pursued parallel policies, with approximately 139 governmentally sponsored Indigenous boarding schools established by religious and nonreligious organizations between the 1880s and the late twentieth century (with earlier religious schools starting in 1831).[5] In both countries, sexual exploitation was rampant, with molestation, rape, and other forms of sexual assault perpetrated by school officials, leaders, priests, and nuns.[6]

Indigenous boarding schools in the United States were not all the same. They were an assortment of institutions that ranged widely in terms of proximity to reservations, funding streams, and religious affiliation. But the nearly universal aspects of all boarding schools in this 180-year period were fourfold: to strip Native children of their language and culture by separating them from their parents and communities; to exploit manual labor as a core component of that reeducation; to work in lockstep with the federal government, which funded many of the schools and was highly motivated to dissolve tribes and incorporate Natives into white society; and, ultimately, to break the spirit of Native communities by stealing the next generation of leaders so that they, too, would accept the imposed program of assimilation.[7]

As fewer Natives remained on reservations, the government put more pressure on tribes to give up additional land. The result was a dual theft of Native children and Native lands through labor-focused "education," with the hope of eradicating Native Americans as a distinct people. It's no wonder that Ojibwe scholar Brenda Child has suggested that "the boarding school as an institution is symbolic of American colonialism at its most genocidal."[8]

It is hard to fully comprehend how immensely difficult and traumatic these experiences were for Native children and families. For many Indigenous people today, the labor focus of the boarding schools, including the outing system, represents yet another chapter in the hidden history of Indigenous slavery. As one tribal member commented in 2019, it seemed that "Native boys and girls were being

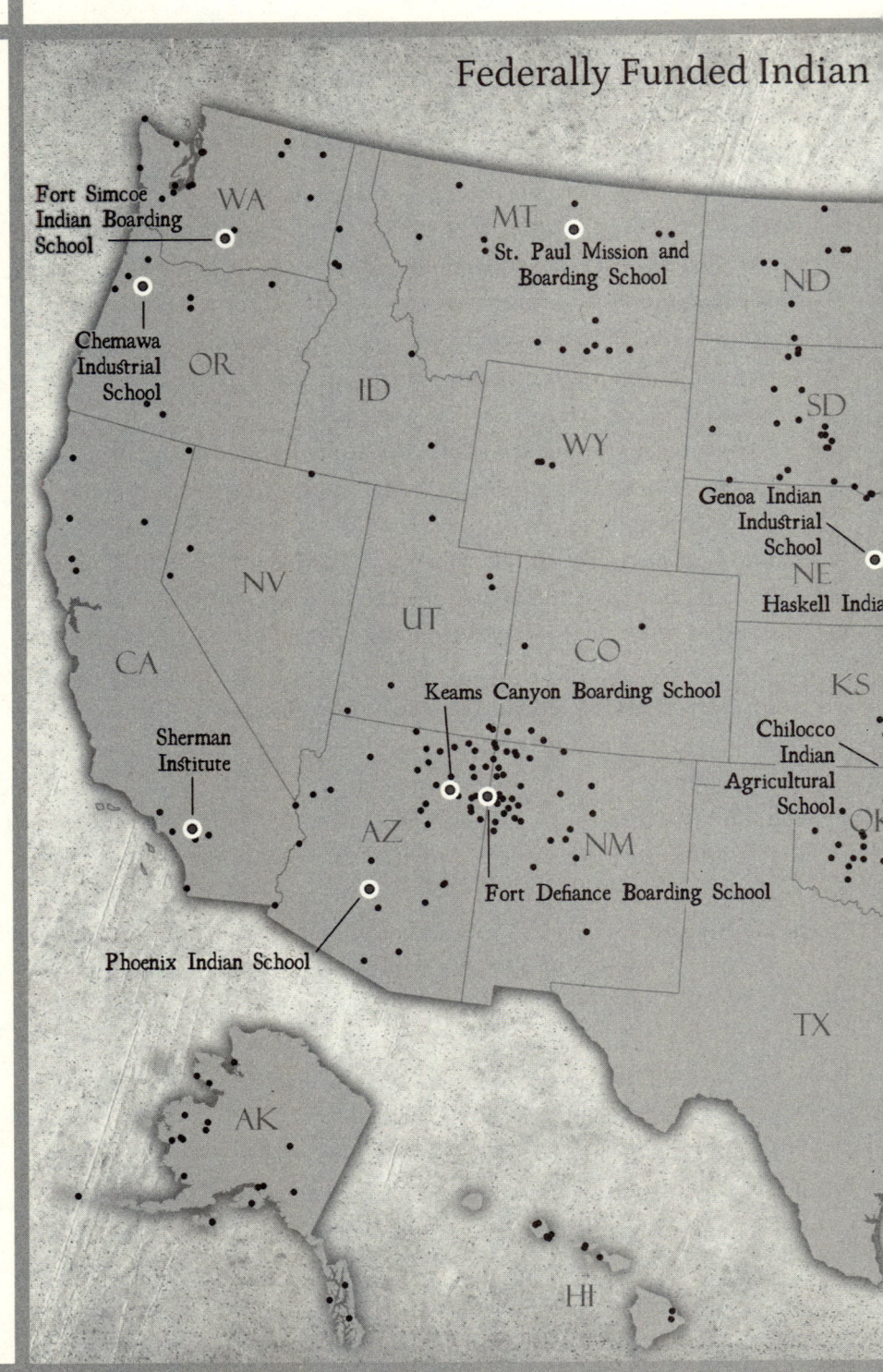

Fort Simcoe
Indian Boarding
School

Chemawa
Industrial
School

St. Paul Mission and
Boarding School

Genoa Indian
Industrial
School

Haskell India

Keams Canyon Boarding School

Chilocco
Indian
Agricultural
School

Sherman
Institute

Fort Defiance Boarding School

Phoenix Indian School

WA

OR

ID

MT

WY

ND

SD

NE

NV

UT

CO

KS

CA

AZ

NM

OK

TX

AK

HI

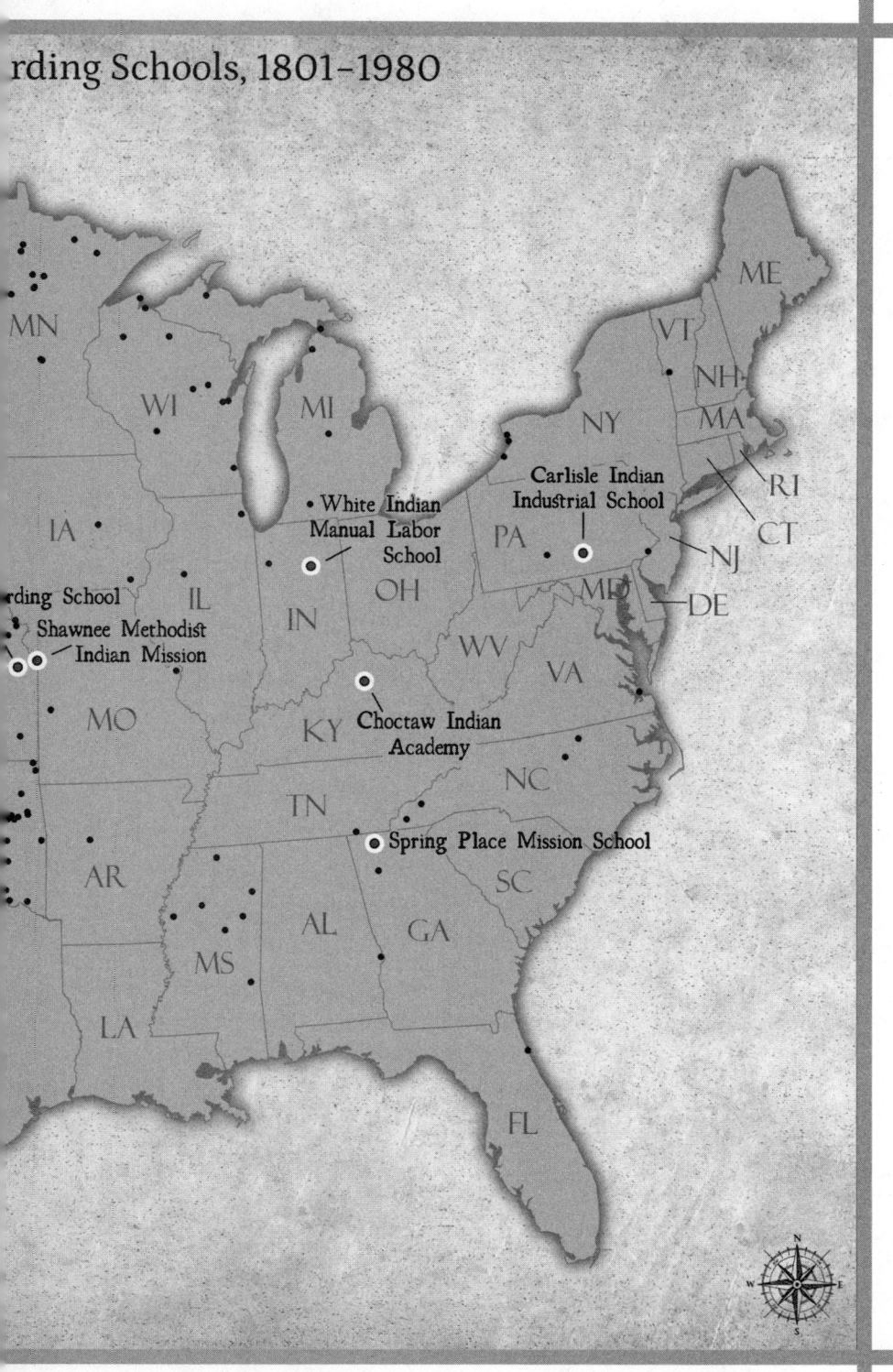

rding Schools, 1801–1980

trained to be slaves."[9] Eventually, the protests of parents and communities led to attempts at reforms in the 1930s and, finally, the agonizingly slow dissolution of the federal boarding school system over the next half century.

THE USE OF EDUCATION AND LABOR to reshape Native cultures was as old as colonization itself. Harvard Indian College in Massachusetts, founded in 1655, was one of the most prominent early institutional attempts, although it did not last long. Native students there, too, were put to work, staffing the printing press at Harvard College.[10] Virginia soon followed suit by founding the Brafferton Indian School, which was associated with the College of William and Mary (founded in 1698), but Indigenous parents were afraid to send their children there lest they be "transported (as they say) to other Countrys and sold as Slaves."[11]

In the 1740s and 1750s, two schools opened in New England that envisioned a combination of "Learning & hard Labour" for Native children. The founders of the Stockbridge Indian School (1748) and Moor's Indian Charity School (1754) hoped Native students could be sent as missionaries to their home communities and other Native nations. Some students revolted when they were subjected to a strict, jarring regime of religious services, classical education, and manual labor.[12] One Lenape youth named Hezekiah Calvin at Moor's Indian Charity School accused its founder, Eleazar Wheelock, of financial mismanagement and keeping students—even Native girls—"close to work, as if they were your slaves."[13]

In the decades following the American Revolution, education that targeted Indigenous people for the purposes of assimilation quickly gained popularity.[14] This involved persuading Native American nations to adopt American markers of civilization—education, labor, gender norms, and religion—and give up their own. Religious organizations proved to be effective conduits of American assimilation. And after the successful multidecade tenure of the Moravian Springplace Mission and school among the Cherokee starting in 1801, the US government turned to churches and missionary societies to enact its "civilization" mission of dispossession.[15]

This partnership between American churches and the government was made explicit with the passage of the Indian Civilization Fund Act of March 3, 1819, which allocated $10,000 annually to encourage Natives Americans to adopt "habits and arts of civilization" by employing "capable persons, of good moral character, to instruct them."[16] The Office of Indian Affairs (later the Bureau of Indian Affairs) was created in 1824, as part of the Department of War, with a primary task of distributing the Indian Civilization Fund, which mostly went to churches and religious bodies. By 1824, these federal funds supported 32 schools and more than 900 Native children. Six years later, that number had risen to 52 schools and 1,512 students.[17] Encouraged by governmental support, the number of religious day and boarding schools grew steadily over the next century.[18]

DURING THE PEAK OF NATIVE EXPULSIONS and removals between 1810 and 1840, the federal government founded Indigenous boarding schools among Native American nations that had been forced to move westward. These schools, often imposed by treaties, were blatantly exploitative, using the labor of Native children to create profits for superintendents and other officials. The Shawnee Methodist Mission and Indian Manual Labor School in Fairway, Kansas, was founded in 1839 among expelled tribes as part of an agreement between the Office of Indian Affairs and the Methodist Episcopal Church. It opened on October 29, and by March 1840, the school's director, Thomas Johnson, reported sixty-seven Indian children enrolled—thirty-five boys and thirty-two girls—from nine different tribes: the Shawnee, Delaware, Potawatomi, Peoria, Kickapoo, Kansas, Gros Ventre, Piankashaw, and Munsee.[19]

Students at the school were occupied for twelve hours per day: six hours dedicated to classroom learning and six hours to manual labor. The thirty or so Native girls cooked for the entire boarding school compound, including the seventy students in attendance by the fall of 1840, plus a staff of twenty people. They also washed the dishes, cleaned the buildings, and made clothing for all students. Native boys were forced to learn rudimentary mechanical skills but mostly toiled in the vast acreage of the school's farmland, planting, tending, and harvesting wheat, corn, oats, and potatoes, plus taking care of hundreds of head of livestock.[20] This agricultural focus was reflected in the expenditures of the school in the first year, with a full $2,200 spent on "livestock, wagons and farming utensils" and no money spent on books or other traditional classroom materials.[21]

It was a veritable southern-style plantation in the free state of Kansas, exploiting the labor of Native American boys and girls. Within a few short years, the Shawnee Manual Labor School began to turn a sizable profit. Situated along the Santa Fe and Oregon Trails, the school was well positioned to access a large market for the wagon parts, lumber, clothes, and food supplies the Native students produced. The sawmill and gristmill made close to $6,000 in 1847, with the farm store, wagon, blacksmith, and shoe shops turning out an additional $1,600 in revenue. Johnson also took in white students who were the children of Indian agents and Methodist leaders in the region and collected substantial rent and tuition in return.[22]

Shawnee and Delaware parents and leaders grew increasingly disgusted with the school. In 1850, three Shawnee leaders named James Captain, Charles Fish, and John Fish sent a lengthy complaint to Orlando Brown, the US commissioner of Indian Affairs. "From a small beginning," these tribal leaders noted, the school "has become an immense money making concern. Its managers have become rich and powerful." These Shawnee leaders especially noted the outrage over two Native students falling ill and passing away. They had been quietly buried, and their parents were not informed. A few months passed, and the parents came looking for their children only to learn the truth.[23] The silent burial of Native children in unmarked graves at boarding schools would become all too commonplace in the movement as it expanded, rendering eternal the children's separation from kin.

IN THE YEARS AFTER THE CIVIL WAR, the United States became more mercenary in its attempts to force Native Americans to abandon their language, culture, and land. Off-reservation federal boarding schools featured prominently in these efforts. Dakota Territory governor Newton Edmunds articulated a growing sentiment among American officials and white missionaries when he suggested in 1866 that "a plan that will separate pupil from parent I believe the one most likely to be attended with satisfactory results."[24]

The ideal of the off-reservation boarding school dovetailed with several other federal initiatives that shared parallel goals of assimilation and taking Native land. One of them was the deceptively titled "Indian Peace Policy" announced by President Ulysses Grant in 1868. Grant claimed the right of the US government to commandeer tribal lands and move the numerous and large Native nations from all across the Great Plains, Southwest, and West onto reservations, where they would be provided for, educated, and "civilized" by churches and denominations.[25] As before, this "peaceable" option was backed with the uncompromising power of the US military, which continued to wage wars against Native nations who refused to leave their homelands. Three years later, in 1871, the US government decreed it would no longer enter into treaties with Indigenous nations, which reversed nearly 250 years of precedent dating back to the English colonial period. Although dictated terms and brute military force became the norm, Native leaders still negotiated what they held to be enforceable treaties with the federal government.[26]

Off-reservation boarding schools soon emerged as an essential component of these processes of coerced assimilation. They became a national sensation in 1879, when Richard Henry Pratt founded the Carlisle Indian Industrial School. Rather tellingly, its immediate inspiration was a military prison for Native Americans in Florida. After the Red River War of 1874, the US government sent seventy Kiowa, Cheyenne, Arapaho, Comanche, and Caddo prisoners to Fort Marion in St. Augustine. Pratt, a veteran of both the Civil War and the ongoing western Indian wars, was placed in charge of them. As was common in most other Indigenous boarding schools (and prisons), Pratt cut the incarcerated men's hair, made them wear military uniforms, and ran the prison like a military camp with a strictly regimented schedule.[27]

Pratt intertwined forced manual labor with education. He taught the men English, invited ministers to teach the basics of Christianity, and arranged for the prisoners to spend most of their time laboring: polishing beans; making canes, bows, and arrows for sale to the local public;

cr being hired out as agricultural laborers, railway workers, or farm-hands.[28] Refusing to be completely reeducated, these prisoner-students also turned their energies in artistic directions, producing vivid and riveting drawings and paintings of their communities' ceremonies, wars, and their families in leftover financial ledger books. These ledger drawings were purchased by visitors at the time and are now part of archives and private collections around the country.[29]

Even though Pratt was a latecomer to Indigenous boarding school education, he was a masterful self-promoter. He heralded the Native prisoners at Fort Marion as a model for what "uplifting the Indians" might look like, and they became a spectacle for visitors far and wide.[30] After Fort Marion was deemed no longer necessary in 1878, Pratt continued his experiment by transferring some of his prisoner-students to the Hampton Institute in Virginia, which provided similarly assimilative education for formerly enslaved African Americans. He soon petitioned the Bureau of Indian Affairs and Washington superiors to fund his own school for Native American children. They granted him an unused military barracks in Carlisle, Pennsylvania, with the funding and authorization to start with 125 students.

Central to Pratt's vision was the removal of Native children from their communities. When the Carlisle Indian Industrial School opened

OMAHA DANCE AT ST. AUGUSTINE,
BY ETAHDLEUH DOANMOE, CA. 1870S.

its doors on November 1, 1879, most of the students were drawn from the Sioux reservations at Pine Ridge and Rosebud in the Dakotas, joined by eleven of his original student-prisoners from Fort Marion. It was not easy to convince Sioux and other tribal leaders and parents to send their children 1,500 miles away to be "educated" by whites. In subsequent years, Pratt also recruited from East Coast nations, including the Mashpee Wampanoag, Narragansett, and Eastern Band of Cherokee.[31]

Similar to other schools, Native children at Carlisle were forced to have their hair cut and to trade in their comfortable leather and cloth traditional clothing for wool military uniforms. Some students resisted, as they had at other schools. The Lakota writer Zitkála-Šá (also known as Gertrude Simmons Bonnin) recalled that when she was first at the White's Indian Manual Labor Institute in Wabash, Indiana, she hid under her bed and had to be dragged out and pinned down while her braids were hacked off, since in Lakota culture only cowards and captured Indian enemies had their hair cut.[32] Students at Carlisle were prohibited from speaking their Native languages and instead were given lessons in English. Pratt carefully documented the transformation of

STUDENT BODY ON THE PARADE GROUND AT THE CARLISLE INDIAN SCHOOL WITH BUILDINGS IN THE BACKGROUND, TAKEN IN MARCH 1892, ATTRIBUTED TO JOHN N. CHOATE.

CHIRICAHUA APACHES ARRIVING AT THE CARLISLE
INDIAN SCHOOL, 1886.

Native students through photos taken on arrival at Carlisle and a few months into their enrollment, mostly for fundraising.

Pratt's most brazen innovation was what he called the outing system. This program placed older Native boys and girls in the homes and on farms of white Americans for the summer months or the entire year, where they labored either in exchange for their room and board or sometimes for low wages.[33] After a trial run during the first few summers, and despite complaints of students that they felt lonely and isolated, by 1885, Pratt had placed 250 Native American children in non-Indigenous homes during the summer, with 100 of them kept there year round.[34]

Skeptical white families warmed to the idea, and soon the demand for Native children swelled. This was especially true for religious families, like the Quakers, who felt they were doing tangible good to "help" Natives. Farmers and other white Americans enthusiastically relished the supply of cheap labor. By 1903, Carlisle had placed an astonishing 948 Native children in white homes, on farms, and even in factories.[35] In 1909, Mrs. Joseph V. Peck, of Tullytown, Pennsylvania, 138

*CHIRICAHUA APACHES FOUR MONTHS AFTER
ARRIVING AT CARLISLE, 1886.*

miles east of Carlisle, noted that her farm had been cultivated almost
exclusively by 45 "Indian boys" over 17 years, all from Carlisle's outing system.[36]

Carlisle's off-reservation placement and outing system inspired
Congress and the Bureau of Indian Affairs to set aside funds specifically for the outing program in 1882. Two years later, they contributed
more funds to help with transportation costs to get students to and
from their labor assignments.[37]

The government-funded outing system rose to national prominence in lockstep with a different but related policy known as allotment. Both the "great educational program for the Indians" and
"breaking up of tribal lands into allotments" worked to effect the
"abolition of the old tribal relations and the treatment of every
Indian as an individual," federal agents later asserted.[38] This detrib-
alizing policy was made official at the national level with the General Allotment Act of 1887, often called the Dawes Act after its
sponsor, Henry Dawes, a US senator from Massachusetts. It was

part of a wider push to assimilate Native Americans by fracturing reserved lands—which had been promised to them through treaties—by assigning one tract per Native family and selling the rest to non-Indigenous Americans. As Native leaders rightly predicted, the effects were devastating. Ninety million acres of land—nearly two-thirds of Native reservations—were funneled into the hands of Americans, both the federal government and private citizens.[39] As the next generation of Native children was assimilated through the boarding schools, federal leaders reasoned, they would have no future need for reservations.

WITHIN A FEW YEARS, opportunistic Americans founded additional schools based on the outing system. Local white populations readily embraced this model too. When Bureau of Indian Affairs commissioner Thomas Morgan visited the greater Phoenix area in October 1890 looking for a new federal boarding school site, he found local demand for cheap Native labor from eager Arizona residents. Owners of large orchard companies informed Morgan of the plentiful labor opportunities on their farms, while Phoenix housewives imagined Indigenous girls in their households to take care of menial chores. Local newspapers exulted: "The establishment of this school will furnish cheap and efficient labor in quantity to warrant the growing and manufacture of cotton here in the valley."[40]

At the opening of the Phoenix Indian School in September 1891, Morgan celebrated the school's mission by stating publicly what had by then become an American truism: "It's cheaper to educate Indians than to kill them."[41] Within two years, the school began to place its first Native children into the local workforce. With much less oversight and accountability than Pratt instituted at Carlisle, Hall placed Native children in Phoenix family homes to labor five to six days per week, returning to the school on Saturday only to head back into the workplace on Monday morning. Indigenous children in the outing system were underpaid, earning only eight dollars per month on average, at a time when the usual monthly pay for domestic labor was between 30 percent and 300 percent higher than that.[42] By 1900, the school placed approximately two hundred Native students each year into the wider Phoenix region as low-wage household servants, agricultural laborers, and construction workers.[43]

Other schools followed suit. The Perris Indian School was founded in 1891, seventy miles east of Los Angeles, as the first off-reservation boarding school in California. It was soon renamed the Sherman Institute after California congressman James S. Sherman and was moved twenty miles north to Riverside, California, which was a bustling center of agriculture and industry. The relocation was in part to be closer to an urban center that offered a wider array of outing opportunities for Native students.[44]

Immediately, the Sherman Institute's outing program grew into an on-demand servant mill for regional businesses and households. The school privileged the desires of these customers and employers far more than the welfare of its own students. Native girls made up the vast majority of students in the outing system, and all of them had their room and board deducted from whatever small amount of money they earned.

The Sherman Institute director, Harwood Hall, formerly at the Phoenix Indian School, functioned as a regional broker in this Indigenous servant trade, offering returns and trade-ins to the overseers of Native students who underperformed and promising that they were "accustomed to taking orders, and will come to you with that understanding—not only in work, but in general conduct as well." He also "lent" Native students as laborers to family members and friends and allowed "employers" to pass students around as needed. Riverside residents were overwhelmingly enthusiastic about the school, especially since they could secure Native girls between the age of ten and thirteen for a mere one dollar per month, from which was also deducted room and board.[45]

The Sherman Institute was perhaps the most egregious offender in California, but it was only one of a dozen Indian boarding schools in the state supported by the federal government, in addition to other schools targeting Native children. By the 1890s, a full half of the Indigenous children in California—more than twelve thousand—attended day and boarding schools, both off and on reservations.[46]

SHERMAN INSTITUTE INDIGENOUS
ORANGE-PACKING WORKERS, 1909.

As "EDUCATION" DEVOLVED INTO drudge labor, Native students grew impatient, as did their parents. Indigenous tribal leaders and parents saw plainly the government's scheme to empty the reservations by stealing their children and using their labor for profit. And indeed, the output of some schools on the backs of Native children was staggering. Carlisle reported that in 1881 alone its students produced "8,929 tin products, such as cups, coffee broilers, pans, pails, and funnels" in addition to a host of other marketable items, including nine spring wagons and two horse carriages that were valued at $6,333.46 when sold to the public.

Sewing departments powered by Native girls produced mounds of clothing and household goods for in-house use and to be sold. At the Albuquerque Indian School in New Mexico, sixteen Native girls produced in 1890 alone "170 dresses, 93 chemises, 107 hickory shirts, 67 boys' waists, 261 pairs of drawers, 194 pillowcases, 224 sheets, 238 aprons, 33 bedspreads, and 83 towels." Boarding school residents also tilled, planted, and harvested crops from thousands of acres of farmland each year, well in excess of what the students and staff needed for themselves. In just one year, Native students at the Genoa Indian Industrial School in Nebraska planted 300 acres of corn, oats, wheat, potatoes, and sorghum, much of which was presumably sold for profit.[47]

For many students, the physical demands of the long days of laboring edged out meaningful classroom learning. Henry Roe Cloud, a Ho-Chunk youth who was required to manually crank a washing machine for two years, recalled detesting labor without compensation. "Such work is not educative," he later wrote. "It begets a hatred for work, especially where there is no pay."[48]

For students in the year-round outing system, classroom education evaporated completely. An Eastern Band of Cherokee youth named Simon Johnson arrived at Carlisle from Cherokee, North Carolina, in September 1899 at the age of fifteen. He spent two five-year terms at Carlisle, but during the second term, his classroom education stagnated since he was out working year-round. School administrators recorded his educational level at the fifth grade in 1904 at the start of his second term, and still only at the fifth-grade level when he aged out in 1909. He died two years later of illness in Trenton, New Jersey.[49]

When possible, Indigenous children were their own advocates. Schoolteachers didn't anticipate that with literacy came the ability to write home and expose the school's mistreatment.[50] Loneliness and exploitation plagued students in the homes of white Americans, and students were candid about this to their families and to school supervisors. One Native student placed into a white household wrote to Pratt: "I have never been so lonesome in all my life and I hope I never will again." Other students reported lower-than-expected wages, hard labor, and racism. "She always calls us Dunce, careless, lazy, ugly, crooked, and have no senses," another student complained to Pratt.[51] Others wrote directly to the Indian Affairs Office. Charles Peters, a Mashpee Wampanoag youth from Massachusetts, requested dismissal from Carlisle on December 1, 1913, for family reasons, but also because he felt that he could no longer "waste my time like this" working out in the country only in exchange for a place to live.[52]

The ultimate expression of self-determination was to run away, which Native children frequently did. This powerful protest had been used by Indigenous people who had been stolen or coerced by Europeans for centuries. At Carlisle alone, between 1883 and 1918, approximately 1,842 Native children self-emancipated—which represented nearly 20 percent of the total students who attended.[53] And that was just at one school. These numbers were multiplied by the thousands of children in the hundreds of federal boarding schools throughout the United States.

But self-emancipation came with potential consequences. At Fort Defiance Boarding School in Arizona, children who were captured while running away were spanked, whipped, locked up in a room in quasi-solitary confinement, or forced to perform public acts of shame.[54] The Haskell Indian Industrial Training School in Lawrence, Kansas, had a basement dungeon for recaptured runaway Native girls, with one covered window, a single mattress, and a bucket for a toilet, where they were forced to stay for a month or more at a time.[55]

Abuse in all forms was a recurring experience in these boarding schools. Sexual assault was especially difficult for younger students to resist or report. Jay, a member of the Assiniboine and Gros Ventre tribes, attended the St. Paul's Mission and Boarding School in Hays, Montana. He was raped at the age of eleven by a Jesuit father in a shack out in the woods and was told he would "go to hell" if he ever told anyone. Geraldine Charbonneau Dubourt was repeatedly raped and eventually impregnated at the age of sixteen by a Catholic priest at the Marty Mission School in Marty, South Dakota. When her pregnancy became known, Catholic nuns associated with the school arranged for a doctor to perform an abortion.[56] Thousands of other incidents of rape and assault prior to the mid-twentieth century went unreported or were suppressed.

Later investigations have revealed the immensity of this horrific problem. A 2024 initial survey of the eighty Catholic-run boarding schools found more than a thousand children had been sexually assaulted, most of them in the 1950s and 1960s.[57]

The sustained assault against Native children in these schools—physically, sexually, and culturally—resulted in severe psychological trauma and devastation for survivors. Irene Stewart, a Diné attendee, remembers a childhood of "inferiority and insecurity," marked by irrational fears of darkness, people, and lightning; unexplained illnesses that lasted for months at a time; and hallucinations.[58] Being stolen or removed to boarding schools often meant missing out on important community rites of passage that normally punctuated Indigenous childhood and transition to adulthood. Stewart later noted with regret that her attempts to maintain continuity with "the traditional Navajo way of life was chopped up with school life." She never got to participate in the four-day "customary puberty ceremony" because she was away at school.[59]

Indeed, from the government's perspective, that was part of the point: missing out on such rites of passage disrupted the sense of community, membership, and belonging. The hope was that Native children who felt adrift would gravitate toward white society and turn their back on all things Indigenous. And some did. But far more carried that loss with them for the rest of their lives, struggling to feel fully at home either on the reservation or in wider white society.

And an unknown number never had the chance to return home. At Carlisle alone, five hundred Native children—5 percent of those who enrolled—died from disease, malnutrition, loneliness, or abuse, separated from their families and loved ones.[60] Hundreds more perished in other schools around the country.

NATIVE PARENTS AND TRIBAL LEADERS often protested and sometimes withdrew their children from schools. But they were also trapped by treaties that Native leaders had been forced to sign requiring them to accept missionaries and schools on or close to their reservation, with mandated attendance. This started early in the nineteenth century and continued through the end of the treaty era in the 1870s. One of many examples of this was the Yakama, who live in what is now south-central Washington state. In 1855, the Yakama were made to sign a treaty consigning them to a reservation. It also mandated their children's attendance at an Indian boarding school at Fort Simcoe.[61] Noncompliance led to withheld rations and annuity payments, so they assented.

Indigenous leaders tried initially to embrace what they must have seen as the only path forward. The Diné headman Manuelito, who in the 1860s and 1870s had repeatedly told the federal government that Diné children were still enslaved in American homes, also told his people by 1880, "My grandchild, education is the ladder. Tell our people to take it."[62] Like so many others in previous centuries, many Native parents initially believed that the boarding school system might provide some practical help in dire times, such as housing, food, clothing, and rudimentary job training. So determined were parents to have their children gain an advantage in life that many encouraged them to learn a trade, even supporting the outing system, at least initially.[63]

To ensure universal compliance, in 1891, a federal law required all Native American children between the ages of seven and eighteen to attend school at least nine months out of the year.[64] Families that refused to comply faced starvation since federal agents were authorized to withhold food rations and annuity payments (both of which the government was bound to provide by treaty stipulations).[65] Notably, compulsory education for non-Indigenous children was determined by states, not the federal government. Education for whites also did not include a mandated half day of labor. Instead of spending money to build quality public schools nearby or on reservations, the government poured millions of dollars into the Indian boarding school system, believing it accomplished the desired goals of assimilation. In 1877, the federal budget for the Indian schools was $20,000, but by 1900, it had dramatically increased to almost $3 million.

Tribal leaders and parents tried to shape these unprincipled institutions into something serviceable for their own communities. Rather unusually, at the Santee Normal Training School, founded in 1870 in Nebraska, Santee Sioux students were permitted to speak, read, and write in their own language. The Santee Sioux (Dakota) had been forcibly relocated to this Nebraska reservation after the Dakota War in 1862 and the hanging of thirty-eight Dakota men as additional punishment for their "revolt." As one option for the school's half-day labor requirement, Native boys could work on the printing press, which churned out two newsletters, one in English, called the *Word Carrier*, and one in Dakota, called *Iapi Oaye*. Both had wide distribution and ran for nearly seventy years.[66] Indigenous students also provided the labor to produce a wide array of "Christian literature" for distribution to regional tribes. The Congregationalist administrators boasted to their sponsors in 1873 that the press produced more than 1.1 million pages that year.[67]

Santee was not typical and was often targeted by white officials who believed sustaining Native languages undercut assimilation. Bureau of

Indian Affairs commissioner John D. C. Atkins, a Tennessee resident and former enslaver, increasingly pressured Santee and other schools to uniformly prohibit the use of Native languages and especially not to teach Native youth in their own language. But Santee parents and students somehow evaded this order.[68] The ability to retain languages throughout the boarding school era was a rare and transformative experience for Native children and their families.

Other small windows of opportunity afforded cultural continuities. In 1906, the federal government blamed a Hopi chief named Tawaquaptewa for causing a division in his community at Oraibi, Arizona. As punishment, they required him to either attend the Phoenix Indian Boarding School or the Sherman Institute or be sent to prison. Despite the humiliation of being sent to a boarding school as a prominent community leader, he chose the Sherman Institute. The presence of Tawaquaptewa was greatly encouraging for the Hopi students in attendance there. He—although a student himself—met with the younger Hopi pupils and tried to help them retain cultural traditions and memory, including music and dances. As part of a public performance of the eagle dance at the school, Tawaquaptewa ordered a large number of important regalia and traditional items from Oraibi, including Hopi skins, skirts, beads, feathers, rattles, and belts.[69] But most students did not have a Tawaquaptewa to mentor and sustain them at their boarding schools.

BY THE TURN OF THE TWENTIETH CENTURY, churches and governments heralded the boarding schools and the outing system as an unmitigated success. At the center of this triumph was the creation of a class of low-wage Indigenous servants for the wider population. As Estelle Reel, the federally appointed head of the government-sponsored boarding schools, told the *New York Mail* in 1889, "The demand for these Indian servants is very great in southern California and Arizona, and indeed the supply is not equal to the demand."[70]

Major newspapers reported with approval the influx of Native American laborers into white households. This was especially true when it came to Native American girls who were house servants. The *New York Times* in 1905 reported the waves of "graduates" from governmental boarding schools who had been trained in "domestic science" and were helping to solve the "servant girl problem" in Wisconsin. Noting just a few of the feeders for the program, the report promised a soon-to-be-ready batch of "thirty to forty" more Native girls from the Oneida reservation.[71]

Throughout the first quarter of the twentieth century, the federal boarding school system continued to grow. Carlisle recruited nearly 10,000 Native students during its forty years of operation. The Chemawa Indian Training School (founded in 1880) in Salem, Oregon, enrolled 1,000 students in 1926 from at least 12 nations; the Genoa Indian Industrial School (1884) in Nebraska enrolled 500 students per year; the Phoenix Indian School (1891) had 1,000 students by 1900; by the 1920s, the Chilocco Indian Agricultural School (1884) in Newkirk, Oklahoma, had nearly 900 students from 40 nations.[72] The outing system remained strong as well. In 1924, the Sherman Institute sent 272 Native boys and 264 girls out into the region as a cheap labor force.[73]

Americans also hoped to export their "civilization" schemes internationally to new sites of American colonialism. Reel wrote a three-hundred-page manual titled *Course of Study for the Indian Schools of the United States* to standardize the schools' curriculum.[74] Three thousand copies were printed for the North American Native boarding schools, and another six thousand were sent to the United States' expanding overseas empire, particularly the Philippines, Hawai'i, and Puerto Rico—demonstrating the essential continuity between "Americanizing" Indigenous populations at home and globally. The curriculum was "intensely practical," Reel explained, with an emphasis on "manual labor, agriculture, trades, and 'civilized,' but not too fancy, domestic life."[75]

WITHIN A FEW DECADES, HOWEVER, the federal government could no longer turn a blind eye to the tidal wave of critiques regarding the boarding school system. A growing mountain of multigenerational evidence revealed US federal policies to be massively destructive, with the boarding schools at the center of the problem. As part of wider Progressive Era reforms, Native American activists finally began to make headway. This included winning the right to citizenship for all Native peoples in 1924. Among other efforts to focus more on Native concerns, and in response to widespread complaints, leaders of the Bureau of Indian Affairs began advocating a return to reservation day schools instead of boarding schools and ensuring greater Native inclusion in regular public schools.[76]

Two years later, the government hired the Brookings Institution to study "the economic and social conditions of American Indians." The lengthy final report, published in 1928 and titled *The Problem of Indian Administration* (usually referred to as the Meriam Report after its principal author, Lewis Meriam), described throughout the more than 850 pages all of the ways that government policies generally "operated against the development of wholesome [Indian] family life." In particular, the report blamed the hundreds of government-funded boarding schools that "involved the permanent breaking of family ties." Students lived in squalid dormitory conditions, struggled with chronic illnesses, and were malnourished. Notably, the report criticized the ongoing requirement of substantial labor of Native children that by the 1920s likely violated child labor laws. The work demanded of children was self-serving and not useful to Native children: "Very little of the work provided in Indian boarding schools is directly vocational," the report admitted.[77]

The Meriam Report was damning and hard to ignore. Reformers within the Department of the Interior and the Bureau of Indian Affairs used it as a platform to make important national changes, even as the country suffered during the Great Depression and into the era of the New Deal in the 1930s. One of the most important governmental figures who responded to the concerns of Native nations and the Meriam Report was John Collier, who was appointed as the new commissioner of Indian Affairs in 1933 by President Franklin D. Roosevelt. Collier had extensive experience in Indian country and had long been a vocal critic of US Indian policy. One of his first acts was to undertake a nationwide listening tour of Native nations in the form of a series of "congresses." Although Native leaders were not unified on every issue, the core message he heard throughout Indian country was twofold: they desired a return to greater sovereignty over their own tribal affairs, and they wanted the United States to abide by former treaties, which had largely been disregarded.

The resulting Indian Reorganization Act of 1934 as part of the "Indian New Deal" was a direct response to both the Meriam Report and the complaints voiced by Native leaders to Collier.[78] The four sections of the act symbolized the primary areas of grievance and injury from the previous centuries: Indian Self-Government, Special Education for Indians, Indian Lands, and the Court of Indian Offenses.[79] Its passage led to the transfer of control over some schools to Native leaders and a slow reduction in the number of off-reservation boarding schools. Additionally, the Johnson-O'Malley Act passed that same year created greater opportunities for Native American students to attend public schools. The persistent issues were not all resolved and the harms were not undone, but it was a start.

It took years to dismantle such a well-funded and misguided system. The Seneca Boarding School in Wyandotte, Oklahoma, was one of the last federal schools to close, in 1980, after 108 years of operation.

NATIONAL AMERINDIAN CONFERENCE IN THE USA IN 1934 SHOWS JOHN COLLIER WITH NATIVE LEADERS, JUNE 3, 1934.

The school's buildings and 189 acres were given back to the Wyandotte nation, with whom they should have remained all along.[80]

THE SUN WAS STILL RISING over the hills of South Dakota on July 16, 2021, when a somber delegation crossed the Missouri River from Nebraska en route to Yankton Sioux tribal lands. The caravan was on the final leg of a long overdue trip home for the remains of nine Lakota children who had died at the Carlisle Indian Industrial School 140 years earlier. Lucy Takes the Trail, Rose Long Face, Ernest Knocks Off, Dennis Strikes First, Maud Little Girl, Friend Hollow Horn Bear, Warren Painter, and Alvan and Dora Her Pipe were all commemorated and their remains interred with proper funerary rituals on the homelands they had been separated from for so many years. "These spirits will be able to join up with their families and won't have that lost-soul feeling, like there's a disconnect," enrolled Rosebud Sioux and South Dakota state representative Shawn Bordeaux stated. "Now, there's a re-connect."[81]

The federal boarding schools are not merely history for many Native Americans today. There are an unknown number of survivors with stories of multigenerational forced attendance, alienation from communities, and loss of language and culture. In the absence of a federal process of information gathering and healing, survivors have created associations and online forums for sharing stories and reconnecting.[82]

Some survivors today focus more on what they were able to take away from the experience, not what was taken away from them in the process. In the midst of the family separations and forced labor, Native American students often created meaning for themselves where none might otherwise be found. They connected meaningfully across tribes, learned about each other's traditions, and used the tools meant for their cultural destruction to forge new identities, connections, communities, and careers.[83]

The reparative work is still ongoing. As Laura Tohe, a Diné survivor of the boarding school system, noted in her memoir, "In the end there are no winners; there are only the victims and the survivors of an inhumane system, whether they are the colonizer or the decolonized."[84]

Seventeen

LOST SPARROWS AND SELF-DETERMINATION

WHITE AMERICANS COMPLETELY UNDERESTIMATED THE STRENGTH and vitality of Indigenous nations. The inability of the government to fully assimilate or exterminate them was commonly called the "Indian problem." Rather typical of the time was a headline from the *Santa Fe New Mexican* in 1924: "The Indian Problem Is Turning Uncle Sam's Head Gray." And what exactly was the problem? Indigenous people themselves, according to federal officials, in all of their vast diversity and numbers—then estimated to be 340,000 people spread across 193 tribes who spoke 53 languages. "Every Indian tribe is a problem and every Indian in the tribe is also a problem," proclaimed the secretary of the Department of the Interior, Hubert Work.[1] This sentiment had emerged in the nineteenth century but grew to a crescendo after World War II as the federal government desperately tried to deal with incredible Indigenous resilience and the failure of its own policies.

As boarding schools declined, Americans turned to the large-scale fostering and adoption of Indigenous children. These were part of yet another round of mid-twentieth-century policies and practices devised to forcibly assimilate tribes. In some instances, methods were stunningly aggressive. A Dakota Sioux mother experienced this firsthand in 1946, when two men burst into her house in South Dakota, stole her infant from the babysitter, and placed him in the "papoose house" of the Tekakwitha Indian Mission in Sisseton. When the mother demanded the return of her son, the nuns in charge of the orphanage had the mother and babysitter arrested.[2]

For five years, this Dakota Sioux child was kept by his captors at the mission, where he was renamed Dennis, fed, clothed, and instructed to be a good American Catholic. At the tender age of five, Dennis was essentially sold for ten dollars by the mission's supervising priest, Father John Pohlen, to a white couple in Wheaton, Illinois, named Malcolm and Suzanne Seely. Dennis was treated as a household servant upon his arrival. He swept and mopped the floor among other tasks, all in exchange for his room and board. "I was cheap Indian labor," Dennis later reflected. The Seelys falsified his birth certificate to claim him as their own, thereby erasing any Dakota Sioux connection. "It took my identity," Dennis later lamented. "I had lost everything."[3]

Dennis was just one of a number of Native children stolen and trafficked through the Tekakwitha Indian Mission, and one of tens of thousands nationally caught up in adoption, fostering, and placement programs targeting Indigenous children in the mid-twentieth century. These programs arose as part of a wider emphasis on transracial adoptions at the national level, which included programs like Operation Brown Baby and others that focused on adopting Korean War orphans.[4] But the particular emphasis on Indigenous adoptions and placement was massively out of proportion to other racial adoption programs. Conveniently, targeting Native children contributed to the slow emptying of tribal lands.

The numbers are staggering. In 1968, the Association on American Indian Affairs meticulously surveyed Native communities nationally. They found that 25 percent to 35 percent of all Native American children in the United States had been forcibly removed from their homes due to fostering, placement, adoption, or boarding schools. In the case of fostering and adoption, this was usually because federal and state social workers had erroneously deemed the child's home life inadequate.[5] Most commonly, the children were placed in non-Indigenous families or other white institutions. These misguided processes were conducted by a whole range of federal, state, and religious organizations, with devastating results.

This was yet another manifestation of a longer, targeted stealing of Native American children, whether through captivity and enslavement in the Powhatan Wars in Virginia from the 1620s to the 1640s, or the Pequot War in 1636–1637, or the sale of California Native American children into functional slavery in the 1850s, or the forced attendance at boarding schools in the nineteenth and twentieth centuries.

This twentieth-century push to assimilate Indigenous children through adoption had global manifestations, with similar active programs in Canada, New Zealand, and Australia.[6] Contemporary survivor networks and published testimonies are worldwide in their reach.

Native communities, parents, and children again mobilized for action. But this time was different. The outrage at the stealing of their children coincided with a massive, unstoppable movement nationally to once and for all return sovereignty and self-determination to Indigenous nations. Indigenous parents used the courts when they could to get back their children—who were often called "lost birds" or "lost sparrows."[7] Native leaders increasingly insisted on the right to determine whether their children should be removed from their homes in the first place and where they should be placed if they could not remain with their parents or families.

This fundamental Indigenous revolution for self-determination reshaped all of Native American life, including the eventual passage of the Indian Child Welfare Act in 1978, which returned the rightful authority regarding Native children to tribal leadership and parents, even if it could not undo the decades of harm and trauma caused by previous adoptions and placements.

IN THE YEARS FOLLOWING WORLD WAR II, American state and federal legislators more aggressively tried to assimilate Native Americans into wider white society. Most often, this involved reversing initiatives from the 1930s Indian New Deal era that had intended to increase Native American self-determination.[8] At the same time, the federal government decided it no longer wanted to be financially responsible for the well-being of Native American nations, despite clear treaty obligations. Since its founding, the American government had promised large annuity payments as compensation for stolen land and forced relocations. But by the early twentieth century, the annualized costs to the US government were ballooning, and by the 1950s, it wanted to remove itself from fiduciary responsibility. Instead of creating more opportunities for Native nations to strengthen tribal leadership and cultural systems, the American government wanted them dismantled entirely or turned over to the states, without any federal liability for their oversight.

The most egregious of these policies involved the termination of Native American tribes. Starting in 1953, the US Congress officially dissolved approximately one hundred smaller tribes, affecting thirteen thousand Native Americans, declaring the government to be free of financial responsibility for them. Some smaller nations had been pushing for a severing of this relationship as a way to escape government restrictions on land use. But the results generally were not favorable for Native peoples. Public Law 280 offloaded to individual states the costs and responsibility of dealing with tribes, thereby removing constitutionally mandated federal protections. Termination of Native nations led to the stealing of enormous amounts of communally held tribal property, approximately 1,365,801 acres, or 3 percent, of valuable Native land.

Additional programs of government-sponsored relocations incentivized Native people to move off reservations to more industrialized and urban areas.[9] To coordinate the massive federal relocation effort, the government turned to Dillon Myer, the leader of the Wartime Relocation Authority during World War II, which had directed the relocation and internment of approximately 120,000 Japanese Americans. During his brief tenure as the commissioner of Indian Affairs, Myer fixated on cutting off federal funding for reservations, moving thousands of Natives to American cities, and funneling Native lands into federal and private hands.[10]

At this precise moment, a host of federal, state, and religious agencies turned to the large-scale fostering and adoption of Native American children. This new emphasis was consistent with termination policies, and agents saw this as a more effective and financially viable method of assimilation than boarding schools.[11]

The adoption of Native children had a deeper history in North America, but never before had it been so systematically pursued by governments and religious bodies. Starting in the early seventeenth century, colonists in both Virginia and Massachusetts—urged by colonial governments—had sought out Native children to take into their households, usually with intermingling motives of Christianizing them and benefiting from their practical household help. This adoption impulse intensified in the nineteenth century, when white Americans frequently adopted Indigenous children orphaned by the wars of removal and conquest waged against Native nations by the US government.[12]

During the boarding school era, the outing system that sent students to white homes served as a form of short-term adoption. This common aim was noted by Superintendent of Indian Schools Estelle Reel in 1901: "As an Indian child adopted at an early age into a good white family will grow up as much civilized as any of his white playmates, so a lengthy outing has to a degree a similar effect, for the principle is the same."[13] Having Indigenous children "adopted" in the labor-focused outing program set a troubling work expectation for all future adoptees, even those outside of boarding schools.

It is little wonder that Americans turned to adoption of Native American children at the same time boarding schools were falling out of favor. Americans might have convinced themselves that their motives were charitable, but the goals were largely unchanged: to solve the "Indian problem" by assimilating them, one child at a time. Very few white families encouraged Native adoptees to maintain their linguistic and cultural connections with their tribal communities. As Mary Francis Isaac, the president of the Central Maine Indian Association, astutely noted, placing a Native child in a white home was "almost equal to the termination of Indian-ness."[14] Adoption was simply a new form of an older agenda of attempting to eradicate Native cultures through long-term stints of living and working in white American families.

American federal and religious leaders justified this new adoption program by pointing to the supposedly impoverished and broken-home lives on reservations. And in truth, reservation life could be challenging. But the federal government—not Native nations—was to blame. Federal policies had crippled Native nations by forcing them onto reservations, stealing land and the next generation. By tearing apart family units, they restricted traditional lifestyles and gender roles and created constant barriers to sovereignty and self-determination. The resulting trauma led to increased rates of depression, substance abuse, and suicide. Despite these challenges, most Native families and communities persisted in finding ways to care for children and community members, even if that care was deemed inadequate by biased social workers.

IN 1947, A DINÉ TEENAGER named Helen John became the test case for an aggressive and expansive Mormon program of Native child fostering and adoption.[15] Helen grew up just outside of Phoenix, as the third of thirteen children born to Rose Toucha and Willie John. Her family had deep roots in the region that included painful experiences with American colonialism. Helen's great-grandfather had found refuge with his family in the towering red walls of Canyon de Chelly as an eight-year-old when Kit Carson and the US Army hunted down the Diné in the winter of 1863–1864; he eventually made the Long Walk to Bosque Redondo in 1864 with thousands of other Native prisoners. While imprisoned at Bosque Redondo, Helen's great-grandmother, who had also been forced to go there, soon refused to remain a captive. She escaped and was later reunited with her family after the military allowed the Diné to return home in 1868.

Helen's mother was born during the off-reservation boarding school era and, when she had her own children, experienced the trauma of raising children with the constant fear that they would be taken away. In the 1930s, when US officials were still entering reservations and carting off Native children to boarding schools, Helen hid with her sister when agents came too close to their house. She escaped capture, but her uncle Clarence was abducted and taken to the Phoenix Indian School without his parents' permission. The family found themselves sinking into poverty—in part due to federal policies such as reducing the number of sheep allowed on Diné lands. Helen's parents eventually sent her to the Tuba City Boarding School in northern Arizona, where she remained on and off for five years.

When Helen returned home as a teenager, her desire for education as a way out of field labor for whites led her to connect with a local Mormon family near Glendale who introduced her to other Mormon families and leaders. A Mormon elder named Spencer Kimball who had been newly appointed to the General Lamanite Committee (tasked with outreach to Native Americans) convinced Golden and Thelma Buchannan in Richfield, Arizona, to take in the seventeen-year-old

Helen. Although Helen was free to come and go and was enrolled in a local school for a time, she was immediately trained in housework and eventually did most of the household labor for the Buchannans.[16]

This "successful" placement of Helen inspired in Kimball and other Mormon leaders a vision of hundreds of additional supposedly destitute Native children being placed or adopted into Mormon families. The resulting Indian Student Placement Program became an official Mormon church program in 1954, and it soon expanded rapidly, with an estimated forty thousand to seventy thousand Native children placed with white families between 1947 and 1996.[17] Even *Time* magazine covered the program on September 7, 1959, and suggested that the placement of Diné, Zuñi, Hopi, Apache, and Hualapai children in Mormon homes was a "signally successful experiment," at least through the lens of middle-class white Americans.[18] Church of the Latter-day Saints maps from the 1970s show with bold arrows the steady stream of children from their home communities into neighboring states.[19]

In theory, Mormon families were supposed to take in voluntarily offered Indigenous children and treat them like family. But the system was rife with abuse. It soon came to more closely resemble the exploitative outing program at boarding schools. Such placements also were a distinct echo of the Mormon Indigenous captive trade during the second half of the nineteenth century, in which Mormon families purchased Native captives from Ute traders and retained them as household adoptees, servants, and slaves. In both instances, Native children were completely separated from their families and kept in Mormon households, where they were evangelized, educated, and taught to work in ways that reflected the values and methods of white Americans.

Such an incredible traffick in the placement of Native children could not go unnoticed. Accused by the Indian tribes like the Diné as well as the Bureau of Indian Affairs of "stealing" Native children from reservations and putting them in unlicensed foster and adoptive homes, the Mormon Indian Student Placement Program was brought under the direction of the Mormon Relief Society, which was already licensed to handle white Mormon adoptions. Nevertheless, Mormon adoptions of Native children continued.[20]

PARTIALLY INSPIRED BY THE Mormon program, in the 1950s the federal government began encouraging direct and permanent adoption of Native children, not just placement and fostering. This included support from the Bureau of Indian Affairs, which had a powerful voice in legitimizing such activities at the national level. Religious organizations, state adoption societies, and local institutions soon joined in, creating a massive, chaotic national effort to funnel Native American children off reservations and into white American homes. These efforts were stunningly effective and devastatingly harmful.

In 1958, the Bureau of Indian Affairs and the Child Welfare League of America initiated the federally sponsored Indian Adoption Project. Their aim was to find white families, mostly on the East Coast, to offer permanent homes for Native American children whose parental situations were deemed inadequate. Originally designed as a three-year "experiment," the Indian Adoption Project started by finding fifty Native children who were at least one-quarter Indian, since they were deemed to be ideal candidates for removal and permanent adoption into a "non-Indian adoptive home."[21]

The process was plagued with profound issues from the start. "Welfare workers" were the main on-the-ground decision makers, and they were often untrained. Even worse, they almost always carried with them unhealthy doses of prejudice regarding Native families and culture. Biased against Native reservations, these social workers, as later government reports admitted, had virtually no understanding of Indigenous cultures and were miserably equipped to make life-altering decisions about the adequacy of individual parents' child-rearing capacities.[22]

Traveling deep into reservations and visiting families individually, these social workers claimed the final authority to determine the inadequacy of a Native family's home environment. Parental abuse or neglect was almost never cited. Instead, workers claimed Native parents were too poor or otherwise unable to raise families according to white, middle-class American standards. Especially vulnerable were families with only one parent in the household, teenage parents, general impoverishment, or children in the care of extended family networks, including aunts, uncles, and grandparents.[23]

If a household was deemed inadequate, social workers were supposed to convince Native parents or relatives to sign paperwork, often in English and with confusing language, that effectively terminated all parental rights. This distressing determination would then be confirmed through local courts. In countless cases, social workers forcibly took Native children with no signed paperwork or notification of relatives. In North Dakota, a social worker found some Sioux children home alone at their grandparents' house and simply seized custody of them, carting them off without informing the grandparents or tribal leadership.[24] Tribal leaders and parents understandably grew deeply suspicious of "well-meaning" whites, telling their children to run away at the very sight of any white person on the reservation to avoid abduction.[25]

Once a Native child was in custody, these same courts—relying on inadequately trained social workers—decided on the placement of the child, whether through fostering or, more commonly, outright adoption. In instances of secret abduction, when relatives demanded information, federal authorities told them adoption information was confidential. The process effectively permanently cut Native parents out of their children's lives and slowly stripped Native children of the opportunity to continue their community's cultures and customs. Social workers and courts greatly preferred to place Native children into white American homes, which they did with incredible success.[26]

Wounded Cougar (Karen Ann) Jefferson, a Choctaw tribal member, experienced this harmful practice in the early years of the adoption craze. She was born to her seventeen-year-old mother, Charlotte Louise Jefferson, in 1950. Charlotte's family had recently been relocated by the federal government from Oklahoma to Sacramento, and when she became pregnant, the federal social worker swooped in and quickly pressured her to give up her child for adoption, which she did. Karen Ann, as the baby was renamed, was adopted by a young Air Force major and his wife, Donn and Evelyne. Under their care, Karen Ann grew up experiencing intense emotional and sexual abuse and was often called "wild" and "a savage." After high school, she found an escape in the navy but was discharged for pregnancy. She was horrified when, in the disorienting moments after giving birth to her son, Jonathan, the hospital shoved adoption papers in her face leading to a separation she could not undo. "I have been robbed of my life by the United States Government, Department of Welfare Services," she later lamented.[27]

Adopting or fostering Native American children soon became a national obsession, just as having Native American girls as housemaids through boarding school outing programs had been a half century earlier. Newspapers and wire service stories heralded Native American adoption as attractive and successful, causing a rush of thousands of families to line up for such adoptions.[28] Articles crafted idealized stories of the purportedly successful adoptions of infants and toddlers who were happy and experienced no prejudice in their new, mostly white adoptive communities.[29]

Adopting a Native infant or child became fashionable among East Coast whites: "Adoption of Indian Children 'In Thing' among Well-to-Do," stated a headline on July 11, 1968.[30] As just one example among many, a widow in Connecticut adopted a young Native brother and sister to fill her empty nest after her four biological sons had all left for college.[31] Still, there were strong hints of resistance and doubt regarding these adoption programs, which some newspaper reports admitted. "Not all tribes in the nation accept the adoption of Indian children by white families," an otherwise cheery article on the Indian Adoption Project noted in 1962.[32]

As young adoptees grew older, they began to better understand the ways that adoptions were an inhumane solution to a situation created by a century or more of federal policies. Anecia Tretikoff was born in a Seattle hospital in 1961 to a single Alutiiq Sugpiaq mother who had been sent one thousand miles from her Alaskan community to attend a boarding school in Oregon. Pregnant, young, and cut off from her family network, she was pressured to put up her daughter for adoption—but did so sobbing while signing the papers. Tretikoff was adopted by a strict Christian family in Olympia, Washington, who told her she was a "damned sinner damned to hell." She felt out of place and never totally accepted by her family or their community. It was only in college when she met another Native student that she began to more fully understand her past and was able to reconnect with her Alaska Native family, including her mother. For Tretikoff, the overt positivity of the national media that fueled adoptions in the 1960s and 1970s glossed over the

NEWSPAPER
ARTICLE ON
ADOPTIONS,
POPLAR STANDARD,
AUGUST 3, 1962.

Interest Said Growing in Adopting Indian Children

The following story, written by Jack Zygmond of Associated Press, may be of interest to this area. During the past decade there have been many programs to promote the adoption of children—the handicapped child, the child in the older age group; even children of racial groups both within the United States and from foreign lands.

All but the Indian child. For the most part, he has been left "forgotten," left unloved and uncared for on the reservation without a home or parents he can call his own.

Now there is change — increasing interest on the part of the American public in the adoption of Indian childen. To facilitate that interest the Montana Public Welfare Department has jo.ned the Child Welfare League of America, Inc., in a prjoect to broaden adoptive resources for Indian children in need of homes and parents.

It is not that adoption of Indian children by non-Indian families is a new phenomenon. Public and private agencies, where there are Indian populations, have planned for Indian children in adoption.

Also, non-Indian families have gone to reservations for the purpose of finding Indian children to adopt on an independent basis. But this has been limited.

Arnold Lyslo, director of the Indian adoption project for the Child Welfare League, estimates there are hundreds of Indian children legally free for adoption today who are living in all types of substitute care, because adoptive families have not been found for them.

Last year in Montana, the Welfare placed 150 youngsters up for adoption — 50 of them being Indian. The board presently has about 300 children in foster homes. Many of these are Indian. Only about half may be able to go back to their own homes — if the conditions that warranted their removal are changedf or the better.

Through the Indian adoption project, the Welfare department and the League hope to select for purposes of adoption from 50 to 100 or more homeless Indian children from all parts of the country. To implement that program, Lyslo was in Helena this week to discuss movement of Indian children

isolation and trauma experienced by many, if not most, adopted Native children. Reports also ignored state and federal policies that separated her mother from her home community in the first place.[33]

In addition to official programs, an untold number of stealings and forced adoptions were undertaken by white Americans on their own. Charlene Summers, a mother on the Standing Rock Sioux Nation reservation in North Dakota experienced the audacity of these rogue adoption agents. Summers had given birth to Marcia Marie Summers on Christmas Day in 1975. When Marcia was only a few months old, a white couple from Indiana offered to provide childcare services for Summers while she attended school. Summers agreed and was persuaded to sign a document that, likely unbeknownst to her, transferred power of attorney to the Indiana couple. Within a few days, the couple disappeared, taking the infant Marcia with them. The Standing Rock Tribal Court intervened and ordered the return of the child, but when that was ignored, they filed a writ of habeas corpus to have the child returned. In this case, the actions of the tribal court proved success-ful.[34] So many others were not.

SLOWLY, NATIVE PARENTS and tribal leaders mounted a powerful resistance. Indigenous leaders knew they and their children were being unfairly targeted. In state after state, the adoption and fostering rate of Native children was astronomically higher than that of non-Native children. In Michigan, Indigenous children were 370 percent more likely to be forced into adoption than non-Native children, and the fos-tering rate was 710 percent greater than among their non-Native peers. In Minnesota, the adoption rate of Native kids was 390 percent higher and the fostering rate 1,650 percent more than among the non-Native population.[35]

The Navajo Tribal Council established a Tribal Welfare Commit-tee that asserted a "Tribal Policy on Adoption of Navajo Orphans or Neglected and Abandoned Children" in 1960. The policy demanded explicit approval from the tribal council for any Diné child to be removed from the reservation, with the only exception being for pro-grams by the Bureau of Indian Affairs. But Mormon and other adop-tion agents could be conniving, sometimes convincing Diné parents to sign papers that they could not fully read or comprehend.[36]

The groundswell of Native resistance to adoptions and placements also coincided with national protests of federal policies by Indigenous people who demanded the right of self-determination. With protests and movements regarding the Vietnam War and civil rights erupting around the country in the 1960s and early 1970s, Native activists and leaders founded the American Indian Movement (AIM) in 1968 as part of the Red Power Movement. These organizations brought national vis-ibility to Indigenous issues through direct protest and action, including the occupation and military standoff with state and federal agencies at places like Alcatraz in San Francisco Harbor (November 1969 to June 1971) and Wounded Knee in South Dakota (February to May 1973).[37]

Many of these activists were survivors of boarding schools and adoption programs or had relatives who were survivors. Dennis Banks, an Ojibwe tribal member and the cofounder of the American Indian Movement, had been taken from his parents in the 1940s when he was only four years old and sent to the Pipestone Indian School in south-western Minnesota, more than three hundred miles away from his home on the Leech Lake Indian Reservation in northern Minnesota. For six years, Banks was cut off from all communication with his family and punished harshly when he repeatedly ran away.[38] Banks survived the boarding school experience and emerged as a vocal critic of federal policies, including boarding schools and adoption programs. He helped lead a movement that powerfully centered Native concerns and sovereignty.

Indigenous activists successfully enlisted the support of President Richard Nixon, who came into office in 1969 just as Red Power was increasing in visibility and activism. Nixon appointed Mohawk tribal member Louis Bruce as the head of the Bureau of Indian Affairs, met with AIM activists, and in a 1970 speech to Congress outlined the end of federal termination policies and a new era of Native American self-determination.[39]

TIPI WITH SIGN
"AMERICAN INDIAN
MOVEMENT" ON
THE GROUNDS OF
THE WASHINGTON
MONUMENT DURING
THE "LONGEST
WALK," JULY 11,
1978.

Tribal empowerment, parental protests, and the Red Power Movement soon brought greater awareness to the national crisis of the stealing of Native American children from reservations and families. Outraged Native parents and tribal leaders increasingly pressured the federal government for action in response to the ongoing placement and adoption of children. They also solicited the help of advocates, social workers, and psychologists who warned against the trauma and social dislocation of placement programs, which at times included the outright kidnapping of children.[40]

Adding to the crisis of Indigenous adoption and placement, the boarding schools continued to target Native children in ways that demanded attention. Four decades after the Meriam Report, the Senate Committee on Labor and Public Welfare published an important update in 1969.[41] Known as the Kennedy Report, named for its first chairman, Robert F. Kennedy, the 200-page document counted a bewildering 35,309 Native American children still enrolled in federal boarding schools operated by the Bureau of Indian Affairs, with another 16,139 in day schools on reservations.[42]

The criticisms of the adoption and placement programs, largely generated by Indigenous tribal leaders and parents, led to direct intervention by the US Congress in the 1970s. Congress set up a series of hearings along with federally funded studies that had Native American representation. A nine-year-old Native child from Fallon, Nevada, tearfully testified before a Senate subcommittee in 1974 that her brother was abused in their foster home—the traumatic reality for an estimated 75 percent of all Native adoptees.[43]

At another set of hearings in 1977, tribal leaders lined up to communicate the damaging effect of intrusive Indian adoption programs on Native tribes and families nationwide. Calvin Isaac, the tribal chief of the Mississippi Band of Choctaw Indians, speaking also in his capacity as a member of the National Tribal Chairmen's Association, stated it plainly: "If Indian communities continue to lose their children to the general society for adoptive and foster care placement at the alarming rates of the recent past, if Indian families continue to be disrespected and their parental capacities challenged by non-Indian social agencies as vigorously as they have in the past, then education, the tribe, Indian culture have little meaning or value for the future."[44]

Similarly, a 1976 report of the Association on American Indian Affairs, reflecting the experiences and complaints of tribal leaders and Native parents, recounted some astounding numbers to the US Senate. In the 13 states they surveyed, 11,157 Native American children had been adopted between 1964 and 1976, with another 6,700 in foster care.[45] Added to that were the 29,000 Native children in boarding schools run by the Bureau of Indian Affairs and the 40,000 to 70,000 Indigenous children removed through the Mormon Indian Placement program. All told, Native parents and leaders were looking at between 87,000 and 117,000 Native children removed from their families and homes (out of an estimated 333,650 Native children under the age of 21 in the United States).

As the Association on American Indian Affairs report noted, these numbers did not include informal placements of Native children, private boarding school programs (which involved thousands of western Native children), Native placement programs, and the unknown thou-

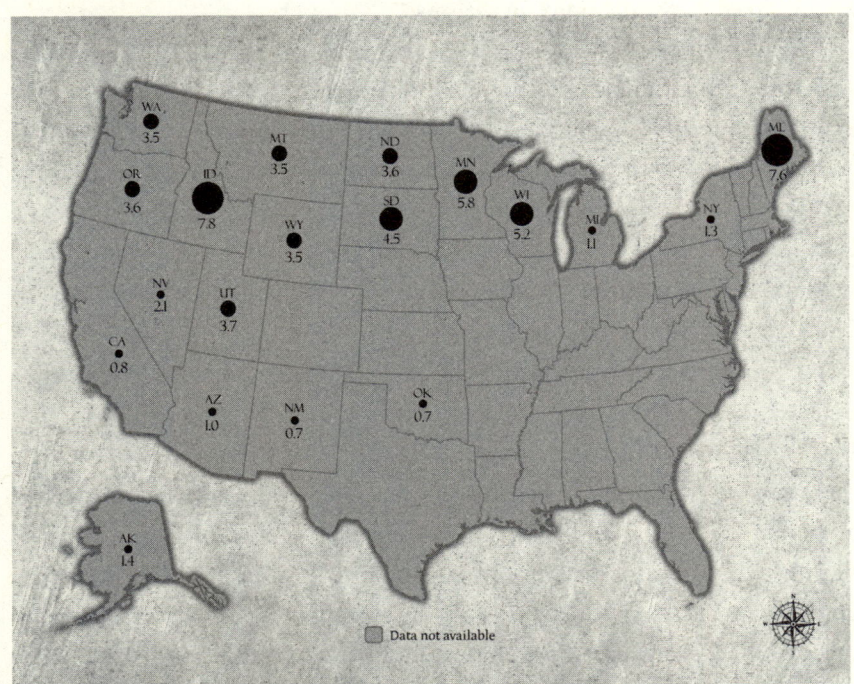

FOSTER RATE OF NATIVE CHILDREN UNDER 21 IN 1976 RELATIVE TO NON-NATIVE POPULATIONS. Drawn from data given in *Report on Federal, State, and Tribal Jurisdiction: Task Force Four* (1976).

sands of Native youth in "correctional institutions."[46] Almost completely omitted from these various reports were the experiences of non–federally recognized tribes and non-reservation Indigenous people, who numbered in the tens of thousands. The situation was even more dire than these reports suggested.

In seeking recommendations, Congress looked to Task Force Four, a subcommittee of the American Indian Policy Review Commission, which had intentional Indigenous representation. Its final report in 1976 was uncompromising: "The issue of the custody of an Indian child," the commission decreed, should be under the "exclusive jurisdiction of the tribal court."[47] After dozens of reports and hearings, the Senate Committee on Indian Affairs drafted a bill called the Indian Child Welfare Act of 1977. It listed a damning summary of findings, which contained an admission of everything that Native parents and leaders had protested.[48] Importantly, it blamed the federal government, which "has chosen to allow these agencies to strike at the heart of

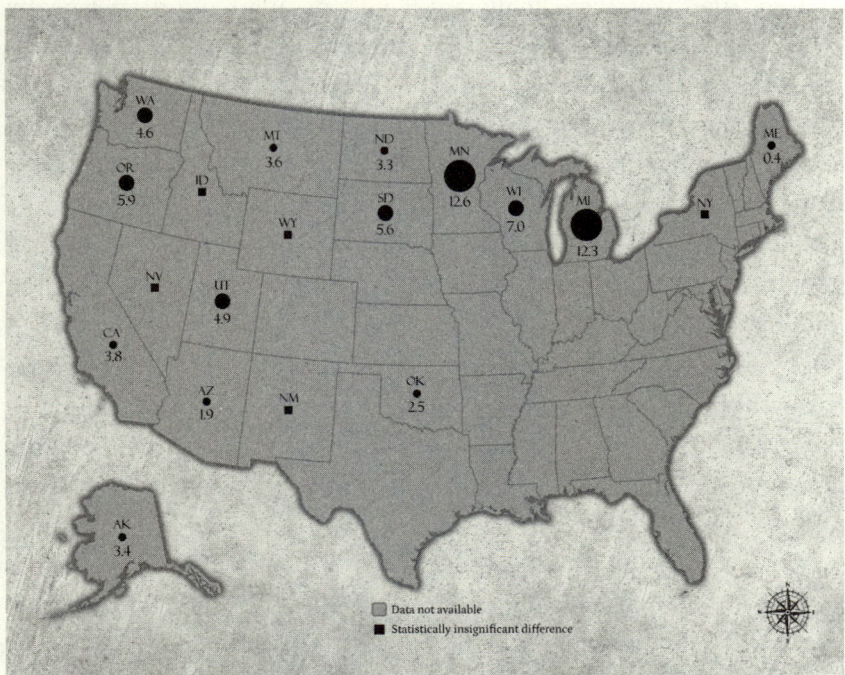

ADOPTION RATE OF NATIVE CHILDREN UNDER 21 IN 1976
RELATIVE TO NON-NATIVE POPULATIONS. Drawn from data given in *Report on Federal, State, and Tribal Jurisdiction: Task Force Four* (1976).

Indian communities by literally stealing Indian children." The report continued, soberly, "It has been called a cultural genocide."[49]

This coordinated remonstrance against stealing through adoption, fostering, and boarding schools led to the passage of legislation the following year. Called the Indian Child Welfare Act of 1978, it echoed the concerns of tribal leaders by emphasizing that Native children were "vital to the continued existence and integrity of Indian tribes." It gave Native nations "exclusive jurisdiction" in matters of custody for Native children, which was what tribal leaders demanded, but this applied only to children "domiciled" on reservations—an unfortunate clause that would lead to later lawsuits and clarifications regarding Native children living off of reservations. But even for off-reservation Native children, state courts were supposed to defer to tribal courts. And in all cases, Native custodians—not just parents—and tribal leadership were given the right "to intervene at any point in the proceeding."[50]

It was a resounding victory for Native nations, communities, parents, and sovereignty that has had real effects nationally. This included eastern tribes who were finally receiving federal attention after nearly two centuries of outright neglect, since they were generally seen as being "successfully" assimilated.

But it came forty years too late for tens of thousands of children and should never have been necessary in the first place. The same year President Jimmy Carter signed the bill into law, two adopted Native Crow brothers died on railroad tracks in New York. Bobby, who was thirteen years old, and Tyler, who was eleven, were two of five Native children adopted by the wealthy and already large Billing family in 1971. When Bobby and Tyler's younger sister, Lana, told them that their adoptive father was sexually molesting her, the boys ran away in June to their homelands in Montana to seek help. Authorities speculated they arrived at the train tracks in hopes of traveling westward but instead were run over and killed.

Wracked with guilt and anguish, Lana ran away as well, eventually making it to North Carolina, where, although still haunted by trauma, she slowly built a new life. The Billings' biological son, Chris, who was sixteen at the time of the boys' deaths, later became a journalist and filmmaker and directed an investigation into the incident, titled *Lost Sparrow* (2010), so named for the Crow term to describe Indigenous children stolen from the reservation. Chris also arranged to have the remains of Bobby and Tyler taken home to the Crow reservation and interred with dignity and ceremony.[51]

Despite the importance of the Indian Child Welfare Act, it did little to protect federally unrecognized Native nations, communities, and non-reservation peoples. Additionally, some adoption agencies and individuals found ways to subvert the tribal sovereignty the law intended to protect. Six years after the passage of this important legislation, agencies estimated that 80 percent of Native placements in white homes were still done without informing tribal leadership or the secretary of the interior. The Mormon Indian Student Placement program officially continued until 1992, with the last student phasing out in 2000.[52] Even with increased compliance over time, newspapers reported in 1996 ongoing workarounds to the law, including agencies simply not telling adoptive parents that the infants or young children were Indigenous.[53] As recently as 2023, white parents attempting to adopt a Diné child took their case to the US Supreme Court, which ruled in support of the Indian Child Welfare Act.[54]

THE EFFECTS OF THESE family separations followed Native children for decades. Many survivors are still living today and have formed support groups to try to recover what they feel are the "stolen generations."[55]

Justice has ultimately proved elusive in many cases. In 2010, survivors of the Tekakwitha Indian Mission banded together to sue the Catholic Diocese of Sioux Falls in a class-action lawsuit, but the South Dakota Supreme Court dismissed the case a year later. A different lawsuit brought by survivors of the St. Paul's Indian Mission on the Yankton Sioux Reservation was also dismissed by the South Dakota Supreme Court in 2012, based in part on a 2010 law meant to impose a statute of limitations on such claims.[56]

Despite the limitations of the Indian Child Welfare Act, it has been transformative for many communities. Paula Peters, a Mashpee Wampanoag tribal member, described how she was able to adopt young Mashpee Wampanoag twins who were born to parents unable to care for them. In previous generations, these infants might have been commandeered by state or religious adoption agencies and placed in non-Indigenous homes, perhaps even separated from each other. Working through the Indian Child Welfare Act, officers at the tribal and state levels allowed the twins to find a loving and specifically Wampanoag home. "They are very proud Wampanoag children," Peters told me in 2024, and are "glad to have been placed in their community."[57]

Epilogue
FORGETTING AND REMEMBERING

> "It is in remembering that our power lies, and our future comes. This is the Indian way."

> —Anna Lee Walters
> (from "Come, My Sons")[1]

ONE OF THE PUZZLES REGARDING THE STEALING OF AMERICA—BOTH the people and the land—has been its virtual invisibility in narratives of United States history. How did the long saga of Indigenous enslavement and its role in American colonialism become so forgotten and remain so hidden?

One insight into this mystery comes from comparing the reception of two books published in the 1880s by the poet and writer Helen Hunt Jackson. As a well-traveled New Englander, Jackson was jolted into action in 1879 when she heard Ponca chief Standing Bear describe to a Boston audience his nation's forcible removal at the hands of the US military. Perplexed, she dove into the archives and in 1881 published *A Century of Dishonor*, a scathing critique of United States policy regarding Native Americans. Despite Jackson sending a copy to every member of Congress, the book was largely ignored.

Determined to try again, Jackson published *Ramona* three years later. It was an earnest novel about a multiracial Indigenous-white girl in a Mexican family who navigated servitude and loss during the American invasion of California. The book was an instant success. The *North American Review* called it "the best novel yet produced by an American woman" and praised its "clearness of conception, purity of tone." Jackson passed away that same year, but she would have been utterly flummoxed to learn that the book had sold more than six hundred thousand copies by the mid-twentieth century and remains in print.[2]

What accounts for the vastly contrasting reception of Jackson's two books? Fiction usually sells better, of course, but the reasons were more nuanced. *A Century of Dishonor* directly indicted the United States, describing in unflinching detail failed policies that included wars against Natives and forced removal to reservations. It was a harsh assessment that demanded action. *Ramona*, on the other hand, was set during and after the Mexican–American War. It has Spanish-named characters, making it seem like Mexican, not American, history. The servitude and hardship Ramona faces feel endemic to Indigenous life and not the fault at all of the white Americans who swarmed California.

Jackson hoped *Ramona* would awaken a reading public to the horror of Native slavery much like *Uncle Tom's Cabin*, published in 1852, had provoked outrage about Black slavery. But there was no national surge toward Native justice after *Ramona*. Americans read it, but they saw the events as purely fictional.

Jackson's two books and their varying receptions suggest a larger reality: Americans have an enduring attraction to Native American history and culture, but they have completely disassociated themselves from their destructive roles in that history. Americans have long cast Native American experiences as a national tragedy that is no one's fault. Native land loss and "disappearance" are often naturalized instead of being understood as the direct consequence of an unrelenting assault on Native presence and culture for more than five hundred years at the hands of European and American citizens, soldiers, legislators, ministers, and educators. There is simply no room in this rewritten history—nor appetite from the American public—for a serious reckoning of the persistent and cyclical enslavement of Indigenous peoples and the theft of their lands.

Generations of Americans have repeatedly suppressed this history, refusing to include it in the narrative of the United States and its development. In a way, after spending centuries stealing America, these new Americans also stole the truth.

———

AMERICANS HAVE ALWAYS TRIED to make their stealing and mis-treatment of Native Americans and their land part of a distant past. This revisionism started in the era of the American Revolution, when in 1772 Virginia courts falsely asserted that Native slavery had been outlawed in that colony after 1705.[3] It continued when the future third American president, Thomas Jefferson, wrote in *Notes on the State of Virginia* (1785), "An inhuman practice once prevailed in this country, of making slaves of the Indians." Jefferson conveniently relegated Indigenous slavery to a European colonial past when in reality it was still part of his American present.[4] This denial contin-ued during and after the Civil War, when American leaders framed the Thirteenth Amendment to apply only to enslaved Black people, thereby necessitating the passage of the Peonage Abolition Act two years later in 1867.

This disregard for Indigenous slavery in American history burst to the forefront during the quadricentennial commemoration of Colum-bus's invasion. As newspapers considered the meaning of 1492, they briefly mentioned a long-ago period of Indigenous enslavement con-ducted by the Spanish in the Caribbean and by the French along the Mississippi River. In both cases, according to the journalists, Native slavery faded quickly and was replaced by the African slave trade.[5]

Rather surprisingly during this period of denialism, there was one scholar who saw more clearly. In 1913, a Columbia University PhD recip-ient named Almon Lauber published his dissertation: *Indian Slavery in Colonial Times within the Present Limits of the United States.*[6] It was a tour-de-force survey of archival and printed material in three differ-ent languages that cataloged the myriad ways early American colonists enslaved Natives up through the American Revolution. But this prescient volume was too far ahead of its time to be accepted. Its presence only registered briefly in newspapers and academic journals and was mostly dismissed. A review of Lauber's book in the *Mississippi Valley Histor-ical Review* in 1914 condescendingly noted that the subject of Native American enslavement "is rather narrow and not of high importance."[7] Historians mostly dropped the topic for nearly a century.[8]

In contrast, Americans were perfectly comfortable acknowledging Indigenous slavery when Native people were the enslavers and whites were the liberators. During the fifty-year commemoration of the start of the Civil War, newspapers in 1911 recounted the history of "Indian slavery," by which they meant the slaveholding of the Cherokee and other tribes in Oklahoma. This practice, writers noted, was terminated by victory of the Union Army at the end of the Civil War.[9]

The same focus on Native people as enslavers was present in early 1916, when dozens of newspapers from New York to Alaska proclaimed the passing of the "Last Indian Slave" in the United States.[10] Articles recounted with great flourish the experiences of Schickulash (Humptulips) Pete, who had been enslaved in the early nineteenth century by an Indigenous tribe near Grays Harbor in what is now the state of Washington. Pete remained enslaved until the United States persuaded Native nations in the Pacific Northwest to release their Indigenous servants or slaves. This aged man was nearly 110 years old when he passed away in his home in Hoquiam, Washington, on January 9, 1916.[11]

This and other "last of" instances of Indian enslavement touted in the newspapers made Native nations, not Americans, the perpetrators of Indigenous enslavement.[12] It also reinforced the idea that Natives themselves were dying off and slowly fading away. This language of "the last of," as White Earth Band of Ojibwe scholar Jean O'Brien has

AN EXCERPT FROM THE *MONMOUTH INQUIRER*, FEBRUARY 1916, ENTITLED "LAST INDIAN SLAVE, 110 YEARS OLD, DIES."

LAST INDIAN SLAVE, 110 YEARS OLD, DIES

HOQUIAM, Wash. — Schnickulash Pete, reputed to be 110 years old and the last of the Gray's Harbor Indian slaves, is dead. The aged Indian came here in 1840 with a war party from the Columbia river to attack the Gray's Harbor Indians.

The Harbor Indians attacked the invading party and the last big Indian battle in this vicinity was fought. Most of the invaders were killed or captured.

The captives were held as slaves, but were freed several years later under a treaty made with the Indians by Governor Stevens.

noted, has long been used as a powerful tool of erasure by white Americans in the reinscribing of a white-centric history.[13] James Fenimore Cooper's best-selling *The Last of the Mohicans* in 1826 was both representative of this genre and its popularizer.

TO REPLACE THIS hidden and suppressed history of stealing, popular culture fed a potent narrative that valorized Americans and demonized Indigenous people. For generations, Americans grew up with plays, novels, radio segments, silent films, and finally, full-color movies and television shows that romanticized brave Americans on the "frontier." These same media depicted Indigenous nations as poverty-stricken terrorizers rather than powerful, sovereign nations militarily displaced by the US government. Such portrayals obscured the role of aggressive American colonialism in the enslavement of Natives and the theft of their lands, while also naturalizing and justifying a clean and rational westward march of "civilization."

One early version of this was Buffalo Bill's Wild West, a fabulously popular stage show that started in 1883 and toured the country for thirty years. It was the brainchild of William Cody, alias Buffalo Bill, who was a complex individual with years of colonizing experience in the American West as a soldier and buffalo hunter. The show tapped into and popularized a romanticized version of western territories with the supposedly heroic, Indian-fighting cowboy at its center. Central to the show's attraction was an entourage of Indigenous people Cody paid to reenact typical showdowns, like an attack on a westward-bound stagecoach full of white Americans. Cody used his many contacts with Native Americans to get them to feature in his show, even hiring the Hunkpapa Lakota chief Sitting Bull for a short time before he was executed by the US military in 1890.[14]

This pop culture fixation on Native Americans as terrorists and villains who attacked caravans and trains heading westward quickly became the standard way everyday American men and women viewed Indigenous people. These themes were on full display in children's literature too, like the *Little House on the Prairie* series, which was published between 1932 and 1943. In Laura Ingalls Wilder's hands, Native Americans appear at times as wild, brutish, and barely human, with dark glittering "snake's eyes." But the main protagonist, young Laura,

SITTING BULL AND BUFFALO BILL, BY D. F. BARRY, 1885.

reflected a powerful sentiment: a deep, inexplicable urge to "have" a Native baby or two. When a line of innumerable Osage men, women, and children on horseback file by their home, Laura notes the beauty of one Osage infant's eyes and immediately blurts out, "Pa, get me that little Indian baby! . . . Oh, I want it! I want it!" Although Pa gently reminds Laura that "the Indian woman wants to keep her baby," it is an incredibly telling moment.[15] This longing to "have" an exoticized Native child was powerfully planted in the minds of millions of readers for the next half century as the nation embraced Native adoptions.

Movies quickly became an even more powerful medium. Few films more effectively cemented the narrative of rogue Native villains than *Stagecoach* in 1939. In this full-length, black-and-white movie about a group of Americans journeying across the Southwest, the climax shows a prolonged attack on a single stagecoach by a band of Apache on horseback. The Apache attackers are generally nameless, faceless entities—a generalized, fiendish specter. Such portrayals reinforced the belief that Natives were not sovereign nations and rightful possessors of their lands but irrationally savage peoples who needed to be tamed, suppressed, and "civilized." A new genre of western films soon took over the televisions and movie theaters, continually and fictitiously repeating these truisms that both strengthened American justification for the country it had become and buried its own violence even deeper.

NATIVE AMERICANS, HOWEVER, have not forgotten this long history of injustices nor their role in shaping this continent's history. For centuries they have served as the collective memory keepers of their own communities as well as for the nation, refusing to allow these histories to be completely buried. At innumerable points during repeated attempts to steal America, Indigenous leaders have reminded the English and Americans of the wrongs they have perpetrated. This included Pumetacom, who recounted to puritans a long list of English aggressions against the Wampanoag in the weeks before the War for New England began in 1675. Manuelito too stood in this truth-telling and memory-keeping tradition when he reminded federal negotiators that Americans had stolen Diné children during the American Civil War. The Ponca chief Standing Bear did the same when he bravely traveled East in 1879 to describe the US military's mistreatment of his people.

Dozens of Native parents and leaders who met with John Collier in the early 1930s also described the long history of unjust US poli-

STILL HERE, BY GAIA, 2018, DOWNTOWN PROVIDENCE,
RHODE ISLAND, 2018.

cies and the stealing of their children and land. And Indigenous members of the American Indian Policy Review Commission in the 1970s took down testimony from Native Americans throughout the country regarding their mistreatment. Native leaders have continually forced non-Indigenous Americans to confront historical and present-day injustices they would rather forget.

This deep and powerful work of remembering has been at the center of a groundswell of Indigenous cultural revitalization movements over the past century. The effort toward renewal and recovery was always present in previous eras, but the distinct legal and federal gains from the early twentieth century onward have been significant and lasting, despite cyclical policy setbacks. The protests, the petitions, the court cases, the sit-ins, and the ongoing efforts locally and nationally to preserve Native American sovereignty have been continuous means of reminding non-Indigenous Americans: *We are still here. These are our people. This is our land. We remember.*[16]

This important work of memory keeping continues on full display during tribal petitions for federal recognition. Since the official rollout of this process in the late 1970s, 574 Native American nations have successfully proved their longevity, history, and sovereignty. But the imposed standards of recognition are not possible for all Native communities to meet, especially those who have been most affected by waves of European and American colonization for the past five hundred years.[17] And yet they too continue to tell their stories and hold the United States accountable for this history of stealing and dispossession.

Native nations repeatedly remind non-Indigenous Americans about this history of land loss when they insist that the United States honor treaty obligations, as seen in the modern surge of land reclamation projects, including the Land Back movement. The federal government, forced to acknowledge land ownership preserved in nineteenth-century treaties, has relinquished symbolic acreage in past decades. More recently, the Land Buy-Back Program for Tribal Nations that ran from 2012 to 2022 returned nearly three million acres in fifteen states to tribal ownership.[18] Many more millions of acres have been recovered through court cases and legal processes. And at the state and local levels, tribes continue to successfully buy land in an attempt to restore their land base.

This work of remembering and memory keeping is tenderly continued in the Missing and Murdered Indigenous Women movement. Through personal storytelling, collection of information, and legal action, this effort seeks to highlight the four thousand to six thousand Indigenous women who have been stolen from their home communities in recent years. Indigenous women and children have always been the most vulnerable in the centuries-long history of American colonialism, and this program connects that deeper history to the present. Their families still await justice from the federal government since direct prosecutions by tribes are usually not permitted.[19]

Indigenous reformers for carceral justice continue to point out that Native Americans are still stolen by judicial processes, too. The incarceration rate per capita for Indigenous people in state and federal prisons is twice as high as the national rate and four times higher than for white Americans.[20] As scholars and activists have noted, prisons are hidden sites of ongoing legal slavery and involuntary servitude, as permitted by the Thirteenth Amendment and by approximately twenty state constitutions, which still allow slavery and involuntary servitude as punishment for a "duly" convicted crime. High Indigenous incarceration rates are a product of the long and traumatic histories of

MURDERED
AND MISSING
INDIGENOUS WOMEN
SIGN.

stealing, displacement, and racism. Native nations all across the country continue to advocate for judicial sovereignty in prosecuting crimes committed by outsiders on reservations as well as promoting reservation methods of justice that promote healing and reintegration.[21]

Perhaps most powerful in this work of remembering is the reshaping of storytelling and scholarship in the realm of education. A new generation of Native American scholars and educators continues to speak the truth about the past and inspire future generations toward reclamation, healing, and hope. They are supported by professional societies like the Native American and Indigenous Studies Association, founded in 2009 to ensure a space for specifically Native-centric scholarship.[22] Native American professionals graduate from the nation's top schools and are present in every sector of society, including law, medicine, and academia.

At the local level, many Indigenous communities have regained control of their own education through tribal high schools and colleges. In Albuquerque, the Native American Community Academy has taken over the buildings of the old Albuquerque Indian School, which for decades served as a federal boarding school. Founded in 2006, this Indigenous-run primary and secondary charter school offers curricula that "affirm and draw from each student's traditional culture and language."[23] Students tend a greenhouse with tribally relevant herbs and vegetables and run medicinal experiments; in literature classes, they discuss racism with a Native American instructor, and middle-schoolers write Native-themed rock songs.

The school's high graduation rates and the academic success of its students have allowed it to grow into a collective of thirteen campuses in five states. "In 150 years, we've moved from a foreign, abusive, violent structure to now, where our communities have something to say about where education is going," notes former executive director Anpao Duta Flying Earth. "We're leading these schools. We're in the classrooms. It's not just maintaining status quo. It's how we're pushing the edge of what's possible."[24]

THE UNITED STATES HAS YET TO fully acknowledge the extent of the harm and trauma caused by the interrelated histories of enslavement, stealing, and dispossession. The appointment of Deb Haaland (Pueblo of Laguna) as the first Native American secretary of the Department of the Interior in 2021 was an important step forward in recovering these hidden histories. Under her leadership, the federal government conducted a self-study of Indigenous boarding schools and initiated a "Road to Healing" listening tour. To at least be aware of these histories, to tell these difficult truths, and to fully acknowledge Native American presence, rights, and cultural vitality in the present can only be the first step, not the last.

These histories and ongoing realities continue to weigh on Native American communities today as they wrestle with historical trauma, deal with the ongoing need to prove and legitimize their Indigeneity, and struggle against erasures. But the source of these troubles is crystal clear to Native peoples. As Narragansett elder Dawn Dove notes, "We did not inflict this upon ourselves; this is the direct result of the theft of our land, the enslavement and indenture of my people by the colonizers. . . . This pain, these scars, these wounds are so deep that they have yet to be healed."[25]

The story of Native peoples' history, current existence, and future flourishing are chapters of a millennia-long existence that will continue to be written by these communities. Native nations continue to persist, survive, and thrive, asserting their sovereignty and rights in local and federal courts, recovering languages and rituals that were banned and outlawed, continuing weaving and other art forms that run generations deep, and nurturing community traditions that have sustained their tribes and nations since before Columbus first stepped foot on Guanahani in 1492. Native peoples have not vanished, nor have they been defeated, as symbolized through annual powwows, like the reconnection powwow in Bermuda in 2018; through sovereignly governed lands; and through presence in US Congress, state legislatures, and every professional arena.

The Chickasaw nation's motto sums it up well: "Unconquered and Unconquerable."[26]

AUTHOR'S NOTE
What Now?

IN THE SPRING OF 2024, A GROUP OF MY IMMEDIATE NEIGHbors, who had read a draft of this book, gathered around my dining room table for a meal and a discussion. Among the many understandable comments—it is too long and about unfamiliar people and places—was an earnest query: what do you want people to do after reading this?

It's a fair question. I wrote this book to illuminate the repeated patterns of settler colonialism in American history, largely centered on the enslavement and coercion of Indigenous people. The central but overlooked role of Native slavery contributed in concrete ways to the loss of Native lands, thus allowing for the growth of the United States. So my main purpose was just to tell a more honest version of these histories and to remind non-Native readers that Indigenous people have survived, are still here, and are still owed justice.

Throughout, I wanted readers to be informed about how many Indigenous people have experienced the nonstop colonialism and stealing we call "American history." Most Native Americans today experience the United States as a settler colonial state with policies that continue to disadvantage and divide Native communities. Most non-Indigenous Americans do not realize the countless ways that the American federal and state governments *actively* restrain and oppress Native American nations and communities. This happens when governments stifle exertion of sovereignty by restricting fishing rights, land purchases, or casino construction, or constrain access to health care, funding, or education. This is not the past for these communities; it is their present, and ours too, if we are willing to see it.

Most non-Indigenous Americans do not really know the incredible array of histories of Native peoples or their perspectives on the past, or understand the innumerable ways that Native peoples have been vitally active in US history, constantly present and shaping the outcomes of events. Even when one is fully informed, it is hard to know what to do. Calls for decolonization and land acknowledgments feel hollow without real restitution and change.

What I propose is that, as a simple starting point, every non-Indigenous reader could commit to three concrete actions: self-educate, listen, and advocate.

Self-educate. Native Americans today should not have to bear the weight of educating non-Native people about the history of settler colonialism. It is up to people living in actively colonized spaces to first educate themselves, whether by reading the documents of the past (treaties, newspaper articles, books) or by reading the works of scholars who have tried to write more honest histories of these events and processes.

Indigenous-centered surveys of Native American history are good starting places, including Kathleen DuVal, *Native Nations: A Millennium in North America* (2024); Pekka Hämäläinen, *Indigenous Continent: The Epic Contest for North America* (2023); Ned Blackhawk, *The Rediscovery of America: Native Peoples and the Unmaking of US History* (2023); David Treuer, *The Heartbeat of Wounded Knee: Native America from 1890 to the Present* (2019); and Roxanne Dunbar-Ortiz, *An Indigenous Peoples' History of the United States* (2015).[1]

In terms of original sources, the Library of Congress and the National Archives have reams of materials on the United States' role in this history. Digital projects like Stolen Relations (stolenrelations.org) make primary sources and individual stories related to Native enslavement available to the public.

Self-educating will likely mean revising preconceived notions of Native peoples today. They are not indigent, reservation-bound populations but sovereign nations and entities within the United States, with nation-to-nation diplomacy, treaty obligations owed to them, and land rights. Thousands of Native Americans live outside of reservations but maintain strong ties to family and homelands. Non-Native people can research which Native nations and communities are in their area, learn whose land they are on, and read tribal websites thoroughly to understand their long history and presence. For educators (and the wider public), a terrific starting place for a Native-centric framework of American history is *Why You Can't Teach United States History without American Indians* (2015), an edited collection of topical essays.[2]

Listen. For too long, colonizers have told Indigenous people what they need, or who they should be, or what they should (or should not) do. One basic thing each non-Native reader of this book can do is listen to Indigenous voices in order to understand. Read the literature, art, poetry, autobiographies, and nonfiction writing of Native artists and scholars (the Dawnland Voices project—which exists as a book and an online anthology—is a great example); attend powwows and respectfully engage artisans, attendees, and performers; watch Native-directed shows and movies; find, visit, and support local and regional museums run by tribes and Indigenous people (including the National Museum of the American Indian in Washington, DC).

Readers who want to dig even deeper can learn about the history of federal Indian law through the writings of Maggie Blackhawk (Fond du Lac Band of Lake Superior Ojibwe) and Steve Newcomb (Shawnee-Lenape) or of decolonization through the Māori (New Zealand) scholar Linda Tuhiwai Smith's *Decolonizing Methodologies*. Reading Indigenous news outlets (such as Indian Country Today and Native News Online) is a helpful way to get a sense of the current events that are important to Native nations.[3]

Advocate. Although Federal Indian Law and legal processes feel beyond the influence of most people, there are ways that each person can serve as an ally at the local level. Each of us can support local and state ballot initiatives that concern Native rights and land, including state recognition; support tribes' efforts to build casinos (which can help bring financial independence) and have land returned to them; ask local leaders running for office what their views are on current issues facing Native communities today; hold state and local leaders accountable for treaty rights and other provisions promised Native nations and communities; and financially contribute to local Indigenous museums and advocacy groups. At the national level, readers can research how each candidate for president or Congress views and relates to Indigenous nations and incorporate that information into their voting deliberations.

Doing these things will not change the past, but they can help us be more honest about the harms that have been done and provide space for more restorative conversations and better policies to take root.

APPENDIX
Timeline

25,000 BCE–1492	Pre-contact period in which Indigenous people made these vast continents their homes.
1492	Columbus lands on Guanahani; initiates widespread enslavement of Native Americans.
1500–1501	Portuguese explorer Gaspar Corte-Real enslaves Abenakis from Maine.
1539–1541	Hernando de Soto invades the Southeast.
1542	Spain passes the New Laws, which target the mistreatment of Natives.
1552	Bartolomé de Las Casas publishes *A Brief Account of the Destruction of the Indies.*
1576–1578	Martin Frobisher steals at least four Inuits from Baffin Island (Canada).
1580	Beginnings of English, French, and Dutch colonization, which includes captive taking.
1585–1587	The English attempt to colonize Roanoke (North Carolina).
1607	The English found Jamestown, Virginia.
1609	Bermuda shipwreck.
1610–11	First Powhatan War (Virginia).
1612	Epenow and others are captured on Cape Cod.
1614	Squanto and twenty-three other Wampanoags are captured on Cape Cod.
1619	First importation of enslaved Africans to Virginia.

1620	"Pilgrims" found Plymouth Colony.
1622	Second Powhatan War (Virginia), with active enslavement of Native peoples.
1626	English colonists murder and enslave Kalinagos on St. Kitts.
1627	Kalinago captives are brought to Virginia.
1630	Massachusetts Bay Colony is founded by nonseparating puritans.
1630	Providence Island Colony is founded (Caribbean).
1636	Barbados and St. Kitts institute race-based slavery.
1636–1637	Pequot War (Connecticut).
1641	Body of Liberties (Massachusetts).
1643	Governor Kieft's War in New Netherlands (New York).
1644	Third Powhatan War (Virginia).
1662	Virginia codifies multigenerational slavery.
1675–1677	King Philip's War (War for New England).
1675–1676	Bacon's Indian War in Virginia.
1680	Pueblo Revolt (New Mexico).
1680–1620	Southeast Indigenous slave trade.
1680–1780	Mosquito Shore Indigenous slave trade (Central America).
1702–1713	Queen Anne's War.
1704	English slave raids on Apalachee mission towns in Florida.
1711–1715	Tuscarora War (North Carolina).
1715–1717	Yamasee War (Carolinas).
1729	Natchez revolt (Louisiana).
1741	Jamaica Indigenous slave trade law.
1754–1761	Seven Years' War.
1763	Odawa chief Pontiac's War (Ohio).
1763–1795	War of Indigenous Sovereignty.

1772	*Robin v. Hardaway* court case (Virginia).
1774–1776	Cherokee frontier wars.
1776–1783	American Revolution.
1780–1830	Peak of Indigenous freedom suits.
1801–1980	Federally funded boarding schools in the United States.
1803	Louisiana Purchase.
1807/1808	Ending of the transatlantic African slave trade.
1830	Indian Removal Act.
1834	British Emancipation.
1838	*Pierre Choteau, senior v. Marguerite, a woman of colour* court case (US Supreme Court).
1838–1839	Cherokee Trail of Tears and Potawatomi Trail of Death.
1846–1848	Mexican–American War.
1849	California gold rush.
1850	California licenses the mass indenture of Native children.
1861–1865	Civil Wars (South and West).
1863–1864	Diné Long Walk (New Mexico).
1865	Thirteenth Amendment officially ends slavery in the South.
1866	Freedmen are required to be given tribal citizenship (Treaty of 1866).
1867	*Condition of the Indian Tribes* is released.
1867	Peonage Abolition Act.
1879	Carlisle Indian Industrial School is founded.
1887	Dawes Act (allotment).
1924	Indian Citizenship Act.
1928	*The Problem of Indian Administration* (Meriam Report).
1930	Senate committee report on boarding schools.
1934	Indian Reorganization Act.

1947	Mormon adoption program starts.
1958–1967	Indian Adoption Project.
1968	American Indian Movement (AIM) is founded in Minneapolis.
1970s	Congressional hearings on adoptions and boarding schools.
1978	Indian Child Welfare Act.
2007	United Nations Declaration on the Rights of Indigenous Peoples.
2016	Murdered and Missing Indigenous Women movement.

ILLUSTRATION AND MAP CREDITS

IMAGES

Frontispiece and part opener illustrations by Silvermoon LaRose.

99   Courtesy of the John Carter Brown Library, Providence, RI.

105   From Book of Wills, vol 3., pt. 2, 178–180. Courtesy of the Bermuda Archives.

109   Photo by Linford D. Fisher.

112   Courtesy of the John Carter Brown Library, Providence, RI.

114   From Benjamin Church, *The History of Philip's War, Commonly Called the Great Indian War, of 1675 and 1676* . . . (Thomas B. Wait, 1827). Courtesy of the John Carter Brown Library, Providence, RI.

122   Courtesy of the Weeden family and the John Hay Library, Brown University, Providence, RI.

123   From John Eliot, *Mamusse Wunneetupanatamwe Up-Biblum God* (Cambridge, MA: Samuel Green, 1663). Courtesy of the John Carter Brown Library, Providence, RI.

127   Photo by Randy Duchaine/Alamy Stock Photo.

133   Photo by Linford D. Fisher.

140   Prisma Archivo/Alamy Stock Photo.

145   Courtesy of the American Antiquarian Society, Worcester, MA.

147   Native American Photographs at Select List No.16, National Archives at College Park, MD.

149   From the Maps/Plats Collections (32-05-09), South Carolina Historical Society, Charleston.

154   Collection of the Massachusetts Historical Society, Boston.

157   Photo by Linford D. Fisher.

161   Courtesy of the John Carter Brown Library, Providence, RI.

165   Courtesy of the John Carter Brown Library, Providence, RI.

171   Courtesy of the American Antiquarian Society, Worcester, MA.

183   Collection of the Newport Historical Society, FIC.2020.132, Newport, RI.

193   Photo by Daymond Steer, *Conway Daily Sun*. Used with permission.

194   Collection of the Massachusetts Historical Society, Boston.

197   Accessed through Readex/Newsbank.

207   From Thomas Clarkson, *Le cri des Africains contre les Européens, leurs oppresseurs, ou, Coup d'oeil sur le commerce homicide appelé traite des noirs Londres* (G. Schulze, 1821). Courtesy of the John Carter Brown Library, Providence, RI.

213   Courtesy of the National Archives (UK), CO 123/31/130b.

216   Private collection, photo by Gavin Ashworth. Used by permission.

217   From John Greenleaf Whittier, "Our Countrymen in Chains," broadside, 1837. Library of Congress, Prints and Photographs Division, LC-USZC4-5321.

228   Courtesy of the Library of Virginia.

230   From the *Bureau of Rolls and Library, Miscellaneous Manuscripts, ca. 1756–*

378   Richard Henry Pratt Papers, Yale Collection of Western Americana, Beinecke Rare Book and Manuscript Library, New Haven, CT.

379   Cumberland County Historical Society, PA-CH2-41, Carlisle, PA.

380   National Archives (US) (593347).

381   National Archives (US) (593352).

384   Image 40 of [Sherman Institute; US Indian School, Riverside, Calif.], Library of Congress.

392   Keystone-France, Getty Images.

404   Montana Historical Society Library and Archives, Helena, MT.

406   Photo by Warren K. Leffler. Library of Congress, Prints and Photographs Division, 2011646498.

416   Public domain.

418   Library of Congress.

419   Courtesy of the Tomaquag Museum.

421   Nadeera photos, Shutterstock.

MAPS

All maps created by Lynn Carlson, Compass Cartographic, 2026.

ACKNOWLEDGMENTS

THE FAMED HUNKPAPA LAKOTA HOLY MAN SITTING BULL once remarked, "It does not take many words to tell the truth." In this, I have failed. But if this book contains truth in its too many words, it is only because of the indispensable input of tribal members, knowledge keepers, students, friends, colleagues, and collaborators over the past fifteen years.

First and foremost, this includes the tribal representatives for *Stolen Relations: Recovering Stories of Indigenous Enslavement in the Americas* (stolenrelations.org). I have had the privilege of serving as the principal investigator since its founding in 2015 and, beginning in 2019, collaborating with tribally appointed representatives from more than a dozen regional nations and communities. Although its home is the Center for Digital Scholarship at Brown University, Stolen Relations is a project that belongs to Native nations and communities whose history and ancestors it attempts to recover. Special thanks to those who have served as tribal representatives for Stolen Relations over the years and who have shaped my thinking on this history. My thanks to Ashley Champagne and the Center for Digital Scholarship and Brown Library staff for their support and input as well.

One of the distinct rewards of a protracted book project is the number of people one meets and learns from. With apologies to those I have inadvertently omitted, this book has benefited from numerous colleagues who lent their insights and expertise, including Carolyn Arena, the late Trevor Bernard, Arne Bialuschewski, Ronnie Chameau (Bermuda Native), Anjali DasSarma, Nives Filice (Bermuda Native), Alan Gallay, Daniel Genkins, Becky Goetz, Rae Gould (Hassanamisco Nipmuc), Jerome Handler, Scott Heerman, Karla Ingram (Bermuda Native), Katrina Jagodinsky, Heather Kopelson, Jason Mancini, Margaret Newell, Marjory O'Toole, Carla Pestana, Paula Peters (Mashpee Wampanoag), Daniel Richter, James Robertson, Brett Rushforth, Mack Scott (Narragansett), Lorén Spears (Narragansett), Patricia Stafford, Kimberly Toney (Hassanamisco Nipmuc), Brinky Tucker (Bermuda Native), Nancy van Deusen, the late Tall Oak Weeden (Pequot and Wampanoag), Sophie White, and Cory Young.

I am especially grateful to people who graciously gave of their time to read chapters or drafts of the book in two different phases. Those who read portions or all of the first draft in 2018–2019 include participants in the departmentally sponsored book manuscript workshop in January 2019: Philip Deloria (Standing Rock Sioux), Susan Ferber, Karen Kupperman, Emily Owens, Robert Preucel, Andrés Reséndez, and Seth Rockman. Other first-draft readers included my faithful and treasured Providence Early America Group (PEAG): Edward Andrews, Charlotte Carrington-Farmer, Owen Stanwood, and Adrian Weimer. Still others who read some or all of this early version include Randy M. Browne, Alejandra Dubcovsky, Jo Fisher, Tim Lehnert, Chad Martin, Raymond Memery, Max Mueller, Marjory O'Toole, David Silverman, and Keith Woodman.

In 2024–2025, additional friends and colleagues provided helpful feedback after reading parts or all of a second draft, including Reni Bartl, Chase Bryer (Chickasaw), Kimonee Burke (Narragansett), Steven Byler, Charlotte Crozier, Ann Daly, Geoff Decker, T. J. DeMarco, Eden Fisher, Jo Fisher, Rebecca Friedman, Jeff Hirsch, Hal Horvat, Joanne Jahnke-Wegner, Drew Jepson, Richard McGee, Joanne Melish, Brian Murphy, Paula Peters (Mashpee Wampanoag), Ed Rafferty, Tarika Sankar, Mack Scott (Narragansett), Vikram Tamboli, and Khanh Vo.

Over the past decade and a half, I have had the privilege of working with nearly two dozen high school, undergraduate, and graduate research assistants on this book, including Sam Boss, Benjamin Buka, Erin Calfee, Claire Fishman, Eric Gottlieb, Brooke Grasberger, Henk Isom, Rose Lang-Maso, Jane Lichacz, Marley-Vincent Lindsay, Kailash Muthukumar, Tamsin Rankine-Fourdraine, Heather Sanford, Lindsay Schakenbach Regele, Evan Sherman, Michael Simpson, Samuel Skinner, Daniel Tatar, Theodore Vial, Daniel Wayland, and Gwenyth Winship.

I have presented portions of this work at more venues than I can fully recall, and questions from engaged audiences at every location have made this project stronger. I have also leaned on the help and work of excellent archivists at more than two dozen repositories, including the American Antiquarian Society, Bahamas Department of Archives, Barbados Department of Archives, Barbados National Library, Bermuda Department of Archives, Bermuda National Library, British Library, Connecticut Historical Society, Connecticut State Library, Huntington Library, Jamaica Archives, Jamaica National Library, John Carter Brown Library, Library of Congress, Massachusetts Archives, Massachusetts Historical Society, National Archives (UK), National Archives and Records Administration (US), Newberry Library, Newport Historical Society, Providence City Archives, Rhode Island Historical Society, Rhode Island State Archives, and the South Carolina Historical Society.

This project benefited from the robust financial support of key institutions. First and foremost, this funding has been local to Brown: the Department of History, John Carter Brown Library, Native American and Indigenous Studies Initiative, Office of the Vice President for Research, Population Studies and Training Center, Ruth J. Simmons Center for the Study of Slavery and Justice, and Social Sciences Research Institute. Fellowships and awards from external institutions have allowed sustained research time since 2011: American Antiquarian Society, American Council of Learned Societies, Massachusetts Historical Society, National Endowment for the Humanities, and Newberry Library.

Brown University has been a warm community of scholars and friends who have nurtured and supported this book at every stage. My colleagues in the Department of History in particular deserve special mention, for modeling teaching, scholarship, service, and activism in admirable and inspiring ways. Colleagues and fellows at the John Carter Brown Library, the Simmons Center, the Center for Digital Scholarship, the Brown Library, and the Native American and Indigenous Studies Initiative have all played key roles.

The images in this book help to better tell the story, and I'm indebted to all of the institutions and individuals that granted permission for their use. I'm especially grateful to Cassie Staudinger (Hassanamisco Nipmuc) for alerting me to the Nipmuc basket designs used as text dividers in each chapter, and with thanks to Sonksq Cheryll Toney

Holley for permission to use them. The talented Silvermoon LaRose (Narragansett) agreed to create a poignant piece of art that adorns the cover and some interior pages. Her interpretation of this complex history means a great deal to me, and I hope the image moves readers of this book as well.

As this project inched toward completion, several people provided critical assistance. Pamela Haag performed heroic and much-needed work in two phases of developmental editing. Charlotte Crozier, a wonderful Brown University undergraduate, was an incredibly helpful and dedicated conversation partner regarding maps, images, permissions, copyright, and fact checking. Her involvement and steady presence brought order to a process that can be quite chaotic. Two other Brown undergrads, Derek Block and Emma Weech, also provided careful fact-checking assistance. My wonderful mapmaker, Lynn Carlson of Compass Cartographic, patiently produced draft upon draft of the nearly twenty maps in this book, making the various geographies I discuss much clearer, I hope, to readers.

I am especially grateful to my editor, Bob Weil, for believing in this project from the moment we first chatted. His rather extraordinary and thorough editing of the first draft in the summer of 2024, along with subsequent conversations and comments, have been a critical part of making this book all that it can be. Working with the Norton team has been a pleasure, with special thanks to Luke Swann in particular, whose responsiveness and care ensured a thorough and smooth production process. My literary agent, Lauren Sharpe from Aevitas Creative Management, has been a steady guide through this process, for which I am immensely thankful.

To my amazing siblings—Ray, Ann, Martha, Wilma, Marlene, Twila, Lisa, and Tiffany—and my parents, Daniel and Priscilla, I owe a lifetime of love and thanks. I miss the incisive feedback that my brother Ray would surely have given had he not passed away in an accident in December 2020.

Most of all, my deepest gratitude goes to my wife, Jo, who has patiently endured nearly fifteen years of periodic absences due to research trips and presentations during some key parenting years. She has also uprooted to places like Chicago and London so that I could take fellowships and be near archives, turning these months into memorable family adventures for our kids. Her constant support has come in many forms, including countless conversations about all aspects of this history and the book itself in addition to patiently editing this manuscript at various points along the way. She and our four incredible and inspiring children—Eden, Elliot, Kieran, and Harrison—make this world an infinitely better place.

NOTES

ABBREVIATIONS USED IN NOTES

AAJ   *Acts of Assembly, Passed in the Island of Jamaica* (London: John Baskett, 1738)

AAS   American Antiquarian Society (Worcester, MA)

ADM   Admiralty, and Ministry of Defence, Navy Department (designation of records in the National Archives, UK)

AHN   America's Historical Newspapers and Periodicals, readex.com

ARCIA   *Annual Report of the Commissioner of Indian Affairs* (Washington, DC: Office of Indian Affairs)

ARMB   *The Acts and Resolves, Public and Private, of the Province of the Massachusetts Bay* (Boston: Secretary of the Commonwealth)

ARMU   *Acts, Resolutions, and Memorials Passed by the First Annual, and Special Sessions, of the Legislative Assembly, of the Territory of Utah* (Salt Lake City: Brigham H. Young)

BARD   Barbados Archives Recopied Deeds (St. James, Barbados)

BDA   Barbados Department of Archives (St. James, Barbados)

BL   British Library (London)

BMDA   Bermuda Department of Archives (Hamilton, Bermuda)

BSIC   Archibald Cameron Hollis Hallett, *Bermuda under the Sommer Islands Company* (Juniperhill Press, 2005)

CCHS   *Collections of the Connecticut Historical Society* (Hartford, CT)

CO   Colonial Office (designation of records in the National Archives, UK)

CRIHS   *Collections of the Rhode Island Historical Society* (Providence, RI)

CRNC   *Colonial Records of North Carolina* (Raleigh, NC)

CSA   Connecticut State Archives (Hartford, CT)

CSP   *Calendar of State Papers, Colonial Series* (London: H. M. Stationery Office)

CSPO   Colonial State Papers Online (Farmington Hills, MI: Gale)

DRCNY   *Documents Relative to the Colonial History of the State of New York* (Albany: Weed, Parsons, Printers, 1853–1887)

FAAC   "List of Indian Slaves, Free Indians, and African Americans," Free African Americans in Colonial Virginia, North Carolina, South Carolina, Maryland, and Delaware, freeafricanamericans.com

FWP   *Federal Writers' Project: Slave Narrative Project* (Works Progress Administration, Born in Slavery Collection, Library of Congress)

Hening   William Hening, *The Statutes at Large* (New York: R. & W. & G. Bartow)

HSP   Historical Society of Pennsylvania (Philadelphia)

JA	Jamaica Archives (Spanish Town, Jamaica)
JCCAS	Helen Tunnicliff Catterall and James J. Hayden, eds., *Judicial Cases Concerning American Slavery and the Negro* (Negro University Press, 1968)
JCSV	*Journals of the Council of the State of Virginia* (Richmond: Division of Purchase and Printing, 1931–1952)
JGCSC	*Journal of the Grand Council of South Carolina, August 25, 1671–June 24, 1680* (Columbia: Historical Commission of South Carolina, 1907)
LOC	Library of Congress (Washington, DC)
MBCR	*Records of the Governor and Company of the Massachusetts Bay in New England* (Boston: W. White, 1853–1854)
MHS	Massachusetts Historical Society (Boston, MA)
MPCP	*Minutes of the Provincial Council of Pennsylvania* (Philadelphia: J. Severn, 1851–1852)
MSAC	Massachusetts State Archives Collection (Boston, MA)
NARA	National Archives and Records Administration (Washington, DC)
NHPL	*Laws of New Hampshire: Province Period, 1702–1745* (Concord, NH: Rumford Printing, 1913)
NLJ	National Library of Jamaica (Kingston, Jamaica)
PAAS	*Proceedings of the American Antiquarian Society* (Worcester, MA)
PASP	Pennsylvania Abolition Society Papers (Historical Society of Pennsylvania, Philadelphia)
PCSM	*Publications of the Colonial Society of Massachusetts* (Boston, MA)
PRCC	*Public Records of the Colony of Connecticut* (Hartford: Brown & Parsons, 1850–1890)
PRSC	*Public Records of the State of Connecticut* (Hartford: Connecticut State Library)
RB	Record Book (in the Barbados Department of Archives)
RCNP	*Records of the Colony of New Plymouth* (Boston: W. White)
RCRI	*Records of the Colony of Rhode Island and Providence Plantations* (Providence: A. C. Greene)
RIHS	Rhode Island Historical Society (Providence, RI)
SCHS	South Carolina Historical Society (Charleston, SC)
SOC	*Statutes of California, Passed at the First Session of the Legislature* (San Jose, CA: J. Winchester)
SP	Records of the State Paper Office (designation of records in the National Archives, UK)
SRNC	*State Records of North Carolina* (Raleigh: P. M. Hale)
T	Treasury (designation of records in the National Archives, UK)
THL	The Huntington Library (San Marino, CA)
TNA	The National Archives (Kew, London, UK)
TPUS	*Territorial Papers of the United States* (Washington, DC: US Government Printing Office

PREFACE

1. Alan Gallay, *The Indian Slave Trade: The Rise of the English Empire in the American South, 1670–1717* (Yale University Press, 2002).
2. Linford D. Fisher, *The Indian Great Awakening: Religion and the Shaping of Indian Cultures in Early America* (Oxford University Press, 2012).
3. Tall Oak Weeden, personal conversation, November 13, 2020.

A NOTE REGARDING TERMINOLOGY

1. For a discussion of these various terms, see Brooke Bauer and Elizabeth Ellis, "Indigenous, Native American, or American Indian? The Limitations of Broad Terms," *Journal of the Early Republic* 43, no. 1 (2023): 61–74.
2. Kathleen DuVal, *Native Nations: A Millennium in North America* (Random House, 2024).
3. David Lewis, "Defining Slavery in Global Perspective," in *Writing the History of Slavery*, ed. David Stefan Doddington and Enrico Dal Lago (Bloomsbury, 2022), 20.
4. Christina Snyder, "Indian Slavery," *Oxford Research Encyclopedia of American History*, December 2, 2014, oxfordre.com.
5. "Proceedings at a General Congress held at Tebuppy," October 1, 1780, TNA CO 137/79/165.
6. See, for example, Casey Schmitt, *The Predatory Sea: Human Trafficking, Colonization, and Trade in the Greater Caribbean, 1570–1670* (University of Pennsylvania Press, 2025).
7. Sue-Ellen Jacobs, Wesley Thomas, and Sabine Lang, eds., *Two-Spirit People: Native American Gender Identity, Sexuality, and Spirituality* (University of Illinois Press, 1997); Gregory D. Smithers, *Reclaiming Two-Spirits: Sexuality, Spiritual Renewal and Sovereignty in Native America* (Beacon Press, 2022).
8. Chase Bryer, personal communication, April 15, 2024.

PROLOGUE

1. The descriptions of these events are drawn from my attendance at a powwow in Bermuda on June 9, 2018.
2. See Chapters 2 and 5 of this book for more details.
3. For the authoritative Bermuda Native narration of this history, see St. Clair "Brinky" Tucker, *St. David's Island, Bermuda: Its People, History and Culture* (St. Clair Tucker, 2009).
4. Nives Filice, personal interview, March 28, 2017, Hamilton, Bermuda.
5. A special thanks to the tribal collaborators for the Stolen Relations project, and especially to Lorén Spears, for this point.
6. Sven Beckert, *Empire of Cotton: A Global History*, repr. ed. (Vintage, 2015); Sven Beckert and Seth Rockman, eds., *Slavery's Capitalism: A New History of American Economic Development* (University of Pennsylvania Press, 2016);

Edward E. Baptist, *The Half Has Never Been Told: Slavery and the Making of American Capitalism*, 1st ed. (Basic Books, 2014).

7. Andrés Reséndez estimates there were 2.5 million to 5 million enslaved Indigenous people in the Americas (North, South, and Central America, and the Caribbean). Given the frequent procreation (which included a range of consensual and nonconsensual forms) between Africans and Natives (and sometimes Europeans) and later, their descendants, and given that multiracial Indigenous people are not usually counted in tabulations of Native slavery, I am proposing a new estimation of 3 to 6 million to account for these people, who were also Indigenous as much as they were Black or white. Reséndez, *The Other Slavery: The Uncovered Story of Indian Enslavement in America* (Houghton Mifflin Harcourt, 2016), 5.

8. Reséndez estimates that between 147,000 and 340,000 Native Americans were enslaved in North America, excluding Mexico. Reséndez, *Other Slavery*, 324. I have increased these estimates to 600,000 to account for enslaved, mixed-race Indigenous people. In the antebellum South alone, for example, I estimate that we have overlooked the presence of between 80,000 and 200,000 enslaved Native and mixed-race Indigenous people. These 600,000 individuals are part of the estimated 3 to 6 million enslaved Natives in the Americas as a whole.

9. Most of the 12.5 million enslaved Africans trafficked to the Americas were sent to the Caribbean and South America. According to the Slave Voyages website, the combined total of Africans trafficked to North America directly from Africa and indirectly through secondary voyages was 535,204 (tally as of January 2025). "Trans-Atlantic Slave Trade—Estimates," slavevoyages.org. For analyses of the Spanish and Portuguese trade, see Alex Borucki, David Eltis, and David Wheat, "Atlantic History and the Slave Trade to Spanish America," *American Historical Review* 120, no. 2 (April 1, 2015): 433–461; Ana Lucia Araujo, *Humans in Shackles: An Atlantic History of Slavery* (University of Chicago Press, 2024).

10. This framing can be found in virtually all of the scholarship on Black slavery. The otherwise excellent 1619 Project largely excludes Native American enslavement. "The 1619 Project," *New York Times*, August 14, 2019.

11. The few (and much older) books that tried to tell a wider story almost universally concluded with discussion of the eighteenth century. See, for example, Almon Wheeler Lauber, *Indian Slavery in Colonial Times within the Present Limits of the United States*, repr. ed. (Columbia University Press, 1913).

12. Alexis Moreis, presentation at the Stolen Relations Launch Symposium, Brown University, May 10, 2025.

13. For a sampling of the recent literature of Native enslavement in the regions that later became the United States, see Gallay, *Indian Slave Trade*; Margaret Ellen Newell, *Brethren by Nature: New England Indians, Colonists, and the Origins of American Slavery* (Cornell University Press, 2015); Kristalyn Shefveland, *Anglo-Native Virginia: Trade, Conversion, and Indian Slavery in the Old Dominion, 1646–1722* (University of Georgia Press, 2016); Benjamin Madley, *An American Genocide: The United States and the California Indian Catastrophe, 1846–1873*, repr. ed. (Yale University Press, 2017); James Brooks, *Captives and Cousins: Slavery, Kinship, and Community in the Southwest Borderlands* (University of North Carolina Press, 2002).

14. Mack Scott, personal correspondence, March 11, 2024.

15. Michael Rothberg, *Multidirectional Memory: Remembering the Holocaust in the Age of Decolonization* (Stanford University Press, 2009). I am grateful to Ed Rafferty for pointing me in this direction.

16. Susan Sleeper-Smith et al., eds., *Why You Can't Teach United States History without American Indians* (University of North Carolina Press, 2015).

17. Reséndez, *Other Slavery*. Reséndez's book has been vitally important in shaping the field.

18. Susanah Shaw Romney, " 'With & alongside His Housewife': Claiming Ground in New Netherland and the Early Modern Dutch Empire," *William and Mary Quarterly* 73, no. 2 (2016): 187–224; Lisa Brooks, *Our Beloved Kin: A New History of King Philip's War* (Yale University Press, 2018), 43.

19. Jennifer Morgan introduced this double labor concept for enslaved Black women. Morgan, *Laboring Women: Reproduction and Gender in New World Slavery* (University of Pennsylvania Press, 2004), 36.

20. Jean Baptiste Vourguignon D'Anville, *Amérique septentrionale* (Paris, 1763). John Carter Brown Library, Providence, Rhode Island.

21. Ruth Wallis Herndon and Ella Wilcox Sekatau, "The Right to a Name: The Narragansett People and Rhode Island Officials in the Revolutionary Era," *Ethnohistory* 44, no. 3 (1997): 437. See also Nancy E. van Deusen, "In the Tethered Shadow: Native American Slavery, African Slavery, and the Disappearance of the Past," *William and Mary Quarterly* 80, no. 2 (2023): 355–388.

22. Bermuda 1698 census, CO 37/2, 194. See also Virginia Bernhard, *Slaves and Slaveholders in Bermuda, 1616–1782* (University of Missouri, 1999), 98; Michael J. Jarvis, *In the Eye of All Trade: Bermuda, Bermudians, and the Maritime Atlantic World, 1680–1783* (University of North Carolina Press, 2012), 102.

23. Gloria McCahon Whiting, "Race, Slavery, and the Problem of Numbers in Early New England: A View from Probate Court," *William and Mary Quarterly* 77, no. 3 (2020): 405–440.

24. Jack D. Forbes, *Africans and Native Americans: The Language of Race and the Evolution of Red-Black Peoples* (University of Illinois Press, 1993).

25. Hening, 3:252; William L. Ramsey, *The Yamasee War: A Study of Culture, Economy, and Conflict in the Colonial South* (University of Nebraska Press, 2008), 166.

26. See Chapter 12 in this book for additional analysis. For the enslaved population in 1860, see Joseph C. G. Kennedy, ed., *Population of the United States in 1860* (Washington, DC: Government Printing Office, 1864), xii.

27. Frederic Denison, *Westerly (Rhode Island) and Its Witnesses: For Two Hundred and Fifty Years* (Providence: J. A. & R. A. Reid, 1878), 84.

28. "Federally Recognized American Indian Tribes and Alaska Native Entities," USA.gov, last updated September 24, 2024.

29. Nikki Khanna, " 'If You're Half Black, You're Just Black': Reflected Appraisals and the Persistence of the One-Drop Rule," *Sociological Quarterly* 51, no. 1 (2010): 100.

30. William Loren Katz, *Black Indians: A Hidden Heritage* (Alladin Paperbacks, 1997).

31. Patrick Wolfe, "Land, Labor, and Difference: Elementary Structures of Race," *American Historical Review* 106, no. 3 (2001): 866–905.

32. Deborah Bird Rose, *Hidden Histories: Black Stories from Victoria River Downs, Humbert River, and Wave Hill Stations* (Aboriginal Studies Press, 1991), 46.

33. Marcelo Dascal, "Colonizing and Decolonizing Minds," in *Papers of the World Philosophy Day*, ed. I. Kuçuradi (Philosophical Society of Turkey, 2009); Linda Tuhiwai Smith, *Decolonizing Methodologies: Research and Indigenous Peoples*, 5th ed. (Zed Books, 2002).

34. Waziyatawin and Michael Yellow Bird, "Introduction: Decolonizing Our Minds and Actions," in *For Indigenous Minds Only: A Decolonization Handbook* (SAR Press, 2012), 1–3.

35. Joseph P. Gone, "Reconsidering American Indian Historical Trauma: Lessons from an Early Gros Ventre War Narrative," *Transcultural Psychiatry* 51, no. 3 (June 1, 2014): 387.

36. Lorén Spears, personal communication, December 12, 2019.

Chapter 1. Colonial Templates

1. Christopher Columbus, *The Journal of Christopher Columbus*, ed. Clements R. Markham (London: Hakluyt Society, 1893), 39.

2. Elizabeth Horodowich and Alexander Nagel, *Amerasia* (Zone Books, 2023), 30–31.

3. William M. Denevan, ed., *The Native Population of the Americas in 1492*, 2nd ed. (University of Wisconsin Press, 1992), xxvii.

4. Columbus, *Journal of Christopher Columbus*, 38, 41.

5. Columbus, *Journal of Christopher Columbus*, 41.

6. Reséndez, *Other Slavery*, 22.

7. Reséndez, *Other Slavery*, 22–23; Lawrence A. Clayton and David M. Lantigua, *Bartolome de las Casas and the Defense of Amerindian Rights: A Brief History with Documents* (University of Alabama Press, 2020), 5–6.

8. Christopher Columbus et al., *Select Letters of Christopher Columbus* (London: Hakluyt Society, 1870), 15.

9. Alden T. Vaughan, *Transatlantic Encounters: American Indians in Britain, 1500–1776* (Cambridge University Press, 2006), 11.

10. Michael Guasco, *Slaves and Englishmen: Human Bondage in the Early Modern Atlantic World* (University of Pennsylvania Press, 2014), 14–18.

11. Simon P. Newman, *A New World of Labor: The Development of Plantation Slavery in the British Atlantic* (University of Pennsylvania Press, 2013), 17–18.

12. Christina Snyder, *Slavery in Indian Country: The Changing Face of Captivity in Early America* (Harvard University Press, 2012), 30; Neil L. Whitehead, "Indigenous Slavery in South America, 1492–1820," in *The Cambridge World History of Slavery: Volume 3—AD 1420–AD 1804*, ed. David Eltis and Stanley L. Engerman (Cambridge University Press, 2011), 248–272; James D. Rice, "War and Politics: Powhatan Expansionism and the Problem of Native American Warfare," *William and Mary Quarterly* 77, no. 1 (2020): 3–32.

13. Fernando Santos-Granero, *Vital Enemies: Slavery, Predation, and the Amerindian Political Economy of Life* (University of Texas Press, 2009); Denise I. Bossy, "Indian Slavery in Southeastern Indian and British Societies, 1670–

1730," in *Indian Slavery in Colonial America*, ed. Alan Gallay (University of Nebraska Press, 2009), 208–209.

14. See, for example, Brooks, *Captives and Cousins*.

15. J. Alexander, "Islam, Archaeology and Slavery in Africa," *World Archaeology* 33, no. 1 (2001): 45–46; Herman L. Bennett, *African Kings and Black Slaves: Sovereignty and Dispossession in the Early Modern Atlantic* (University of Pennsylvania Press, 2018).

16. Newman, *New World of Labor*, 37–38.

17. Paul Lovejoy, "Pawnship and Seizure for Debt in the Process of Enslavement in West Africa," in *Debt and Slavery in the Mediterranean and Atlantic Worlds*, ed. Gwyn Campbell, 1st ed. (Routledge, 2016), 63. For a fuller discussion of African practices, see Guasco, *Slaves and Englishmen*, 66. For northern Africa, see Chouki El Hamel, *Black Morocco: A History of Slavery, Race, and Islam* (Cambridge University Press, 2012).

18. Rebecca Anne Goetz, *The Baptism of Early Virginia: How Christianity Created Race* (Johns Hopkins University Press, 2012); Joyce E. Chaplin, *Subject Matter: Technology, the Body, and Science on the Anglo-American Frontier, 1500–1676* (Harvard University Press, 2001).

19. David Eltis, *The Rise of African Slavery in the Americas* (Cambridge University Press, 1999).

20. Columbus et al., *Select Letters*, 88.

21. Reséndez, *Other Slavery*, 23.

22. Columbus et al., *Select Letters*, 88.

23. Columbus et al., *Select Letters*, 88–89.

24. Reséndez, *Other Slavery*, 24–25.

25. Carol Delaney, *Columbus and the Quest for Jerusalem* (Simon and Schuster, 2011), 181.

26. Nancy E. van Deusen, *Global Indios: The Indigenous Struggle for Justice in Sixteenth-Century Spain* (Duke University Press, 2015), 2–3. On "cannibalism," see Rachel B. Herrmann, ed., *To Feast on Us as Their Prey: Cannibalism and the Early Modern Atlantic*, 1st ed. (University of Arkansas Press, 2019).

27. Erin Woodruff Stone, *Captives of Conquest: Slavery in the Early Modern Spanish Caribbean* (University of Pennsylvania Press, 2021), introduction.

28. Van Deusen, *Global Indios*, 5; Erin Stone, "War and Rescate: The Sixteenth-Century Circum-Caribbean Indigenous Slave Trade," in *The Spanish Caribbean and the Atlantic World in the Long Sixteenth Century*, ed. Ida Altman and David Wheat (University of Nebraska Press, 2019), 47–68.

29. Reséndez, *Other Slavery*, 44.

30. Van Deusen, *Global Indios*, 14–15.

31. As quoted in Hugh Thomas, *Rivers of Gold: The Rise of the Spanish Empire, from Columbus to Magellan* (Random House, 2013), 294. See also Lewis Hanke, *All Mankind Is One: A Study of the Disputation between Bartolomé de Las Casas and Juan Ginés de Sepúlveda* (Northern Illinois University Press, 1974), 4.

32. William L. Sherman, *Forced Native Labor in Sixteenth-Century Central America* (University of Nebraska Press, 1979), 85–87.

33. Hanke, *All Mankind Is One*, 6–7.

34. Bartolomé de las Casas, *The Spanish Colonie, or Briefe Chronicle of the Acts and Gestes of the Spaniardes in the West Indies*, Early English Books, 1475–1640/878:09 (London: Thomas Dawson for William Brome, 1583), A3, verso.

35. Bartolomé de las Casas, *Brevíssima relación de la destrucción de las Indias* (Sevilla: En casa de Sebastian Trugillo impressor de libros, 1552).

36. Reséndez, *Other Slavery*, 47.

37. Personal tour by author and promotional literature, November 2017.

38. Kendall W. Brown, *A History of Mining in Latin America: From the Colonial Era to the Present* (University of New Mexico Press, 2012), 62; Jeremy T. Hua et al., "Racial Differences in Respiratory Impairment, Pneumoconiosis, and Federal Compensation for Western U.S. Indigenous Coal Miners," *Annals of the American Thoracic Society* 21, no. 4 (April 2024): 551–558.

39. Araujo, *Humans in Shackles*, chap. 7.

40. John Stevens Cabot Abbott, *The History of Maine* (Augusta, ME: Brown Thurston, 1892), 24. See also Annette Kolodny, " 'This Long Looked for Event': Retrieving Early Contact History from Penobscot Oral Traditions," *Native American and Indigenous Studies* 2, no. 1 (2015): 94.

41. John de Verrazzano, "Verrazzano's Voyage," in *Collections of the New-York Historical Society: Second Series*, vol. 1 (New York: New York Historical Society, 1841), 44.

42. Guasco, *Slaves and Englishmen*, 174; Lauber, *Indian Slavery in Colonial Times*, 155.

43. Vaughan, *Transatlantic Encounters*, 2, 6–8.

44. Sir Walter Raleigh, *The Discovery of the Large, Rich, and Beautiful Empire of Guiana*, ed. Schomburgk (London: Hakluyt Society, 1848), 144–145.

45. E. G. R. Taylor, *The Original Writings and Correspondence of the Two Richard Hakluyts* (Printed for the Hakluyt Society, 1935), 2:332.

46. David Beers Quinn, *Set Fair for Roanoke: Voyages and Colonies, 1584–1606* (University of North Carolina Press, 2017), chap. 5; Malinda Maynor Lowery, *The Lumbee Indians: An American Struggle* (University of North Carolina Press, 2018), 24.

47. Michael Leroy Oberg, *The Head in Edward Nugent's Hand: Roanoke's Forgotten Indians* (University of Pennsylvania Press, 2010), chap. 1.

48. David Beers Quinn, *The Roanoke Voyages, 1584–1590*, vol. 1 (Hakluyt Society, 2010), 138.

49. Edmund S. Morgan, "The Labor Problem at Jamestown, 1607–18," *American Historical Review* 76, no. 3 (1971): 595–611.

50. Kim Sloan, *A New World: England's First View of America* (University of North Carolina Press, 2007).

51. Don Pedro Vique y Manrique to the [Spanish] Crown, Cartagena, April 5, 1586, in Irene A. Wright, *Further English Voyages to Spanish America, 1583–1594* (Taylor and Francis, 2011), 62. There are varying accounts as to how many ships Drake had with him. See also p. 227.

52. Pedro, Indian, précis of his deposition, Cartagena, February 16, 1587, in Wright, *Further English Voyages*, 226.

53. Walter Bigges, Lieutenant Croftes, and Nicholas Bourne, *A Summarie and True Discourse of Sir Francis Drakes West-Indian Voyage* (London: Nicholas Bourne, 1652), 30–31.

54. Wright, *Further English Voyages*, 173.

55. Juan de Posada to the Crown, San Agustin, September 2, 1586, in Wright, *Further English Voyages*, 206.

56. Kathleen Donegan, *Seasons of Misery: Catastrophe and Colonial Settlement in Early America* (University of Pennsylvania Press, 2013), 56; Oberg, *Head in Edward Nugent's Hand*, xiii–xiv.

57. Donegan, *Seasons of Misery*, 57–58; Oberg, *Head in Edward Nugent's Hand*, 106.

58. John Knox Laughton, *State Papers Relating to the Defeat of the Spanish Armada, Anno 1588* ([London]: Navy Records Society, 1895), 226–227. See also Garrett Mattingly, *The Defeat of the Spanish Armada* (Pimlico, 2000). For the stranding of the Roanoke colonists, see Donegan, *Seasons of Misery*, 60–61.

59. Andrew Lawler, *The Secret Token: Myth, Obsession, and the Search for the Lost Colony of Roanoke*, 1st ed. (Doubleday, 2018).

60. Sarah Cascone, "Archaeologists May Have Finally Solved the Mystery of the Disappearance of Roanoke's Lost Colony," *Artnet News*, November 6, 2020.

61. "New Discovery by Croatoan Archaeological Society Helps to Further Dispel the Myth of the Lost Colonists," *Island Free Press*, May 5, 2022.

62. Jonathan D. Hill and Neil L. Whitehead, eds., "Ethnogenesis and Ethnocide in the European Occupation of Native Surinam, 1499–1681," in *History, Power, and Identity: Ethnogenesis in the Americas, 1492–1992* (University of Iowa Press, 1996), 22.

63. See Nicholas Sanson, "Guiana and Caribana," ca. 1650, LOC. See also Carolyn Arena, "Indian Slaves from Caribana: Trade and Labor in the Seventeenth-Century Caribbean" (PhD diss., Columbia University, 2017).

64. Raleigh, *Discovery*, 39, 153, 179. I am grateful to Carolyn Arena for this reference. See also Whitehead, "Indigenous Slavery in South America," 256.

65. Raleigh, *Discovery*, 39–40.

66. Vincent Todd Harlow, *Colonising Expeditions to the West Indies and Guiana, 1623–1667* (Hakluyt Society, 1925).

67. Richard Hakluyt, *The Principal Navigations, Voyages, Traffiques and Discoveries of the English Nation* (J. MacLehose and Sons, 1906), 317; Robert Harcourt, *A Relation of a Voyage to Guiana* (John Beale, for W. Welby, 1613), 9–10; Alexander Brown, *The Genesis of the United States* (Boston: Houghton Mifflin, 1897), 27.

68. Hakluyt, *Principal Navigations*, 310.

69. Sir Everard Ferdinand Im Thurn and James Rodway, "The First English Colony in Guiana," in *Timehri: The Journal of the Royal Agricultural and Commercial Society of British Guiana* (J. Thomson, 1895), 22–23; Vaughan, *Transatlantic Encounters*, 35.

70. Colin G. Calloway, *Dawnland Encounters: Indians and Europeans in Northern New England* (University Press of New England, 1991), 32.

71. Henry S. Burrage, *The Beginnings of Colonial Maine, 1602–1658* (Marks Printing House, 1914), 43.

72. James Rosier and Henry S. Burrage, *Rosier's Relation of Waymouth's Voyage to the Coast of Maine, 1605* (Portland, ME: Gorges Society, 1887), 130–131.

73. Rosier and Burrage, *Rosier's Relation of Waymouth's Voyage*, 131, 161.

74. Rosier and Burrage, *Rosier's Relation of Waymouth's Voyage*, 131, 161.

75. William Shakespeare, *The Tempest, or, The Enchanted Island a Comedy, as It Is Now Acted at His Highness the Duke of York's Theatre.*, ed. William

D'Avenant, Early English Books, 1641–1700/877:25 (London: J. Macock, for Henry Herringman, 1676), 19. See also Alden T. Vaughan, "Shakespeare's Indian: The Americanization of Caliban," *Shakespeare Quarterly* 39, no. 2 (1988): 137–153.

76. Alfred W. Crosby, "Virgin Soil Epidemics as a Factor in the Aboriginal Depopulation in America," *William and Mary Quarterly* 33 (April 1976): 289–299.

77. David S. Jones, "Epidemics in Indian Country," in *Oxford Research Encyclopedia of American History* (Oxford University Press, 2014).

78. Van Deusen, *Global Indios*, 2; Reséndez, *Other Slavery*, 5.

CHAPTER 2. AMERICAN SLAVERY

1. Audra Simpson, *Mohawk Interruptus: Political Life across the Borders of Settler States* (Duke University Press, 2014), 11.

2. Engel Sluiter, "New Light on the '20. and Odd Negroes' Arriving in Virginia, August 1619," *William and Mary Quarterly* 54, no. 2 (1997): 395. For a broader perspective, see Paul J. Polgar, Marc H. Lerner, and Jesse Cromwell, eds., *Beyond 1619: The Atlantic Origins of American Slavery* (University of Pennsylvania Press, 2023).

3. John Smith, *The Generall Historie of Virginia, New England and the Summer Isles, the Travels of Captaine John Smith*, 2 vols. (J. MacLehose, 1907), 1:87.

4. Frank Marotti, "Juan Baptista de Segura and the Failure of the Florida Jesuit Mission, 1566–1572," *Florida Historical Quarterly* 63, no. 3 (1985): 276–278. See also Karenne Wood, "Paquiquineo, 1570," *South Atlantic Review* 77, no. 1/2 (2012): 177.

5. John Smith and Charles Deane, *A True Relation of Virginia* (Boston: Wiggin and Lunt, 1866), 31.

6. Thomas Dale to Salisbury, August 17, 1611, in Brown, *Genesis of the United States*, 1:503; Camilla Townsend, *Pocahontas and the Powhatan Dilemma* (Hill and Wang, 2004), 12.

7. George Percy, "Observations," in *Captain John Smith: Writings with Other Narratives of Roanoke, Jamestown, and the First English Settlement of America*, ed. James Horn (Library of America, 2007), 930.

8. H. R. McIlwaine, ed., *Journals of the House of Burgesses of Virginia, 1619–1658/59* (Colonial Press, E. Waddey Co., 1915), 29. For the deaths in August, see Percy, "Observations," 932–933.

9. John Smith, *New England's Trials*, 2nd ed. (1622), in *Capt. John Smith, Works, 1608–1631*, vol. 1, ed. Edward Arber (Birmingham: English Scholar's Library, 1884), 263.

10. Shefveland, *Anglo-Native Virginia*, 13.

11. Percy, "A Trewe Relacyon," in Horn, ed., *Captain John Smith: Writings*, 1103–1104.

12. Percy, "Trewe Relacyon," 1104–1105. For more on this raid, see Pekka Hämäläinen, *Indigenous Continent: The Epic Contest for North America* (Liveright, 2023), 64; Shefveland, *Anglo-Native Virginia*, 13.

13. William Strachey, "The Historie of Travell into Virginia Britania," in Horn, ed., *Captain John Smith: Writings*, 1046.

14. Thomas Dale to Salisbury, August 17, 1611, in Brown, *Genesis of the United States*, 1:505.

15. Townsend, *Pocahontas and the Powhatan Dilemma*; David J. Silverman, *This Land Is Their Land: The Wampanoag Indians, Plymouth Colony, and the Troubled History of Thanksgiving* (Bloomsbury, 2019), 65.

16. Silvester Jourdain, *A Plaine Description of the Barmudas, Now Called Sommer Ilands* (London: W. Stansby for W. Welby, 1613), 10–11.

17. Rowena Ryan, "Bermuda, the Shipwreck Capital of the World," news.com.au, September 30, 2014.

18. Jourdain, *Plaine Description of the Barmudas*, Early English Books Online, unpaginated.

19. Harcourt, *Relation of a Voyage to Guiana*, 38.

20. Heather Miyano Kopelson, " 'One Indian and a Negroe, the First Thes Ilands Ever Had': Imagining the Archive in Early Bermuda," *Early American Studies: An Interdisciplinary Journal* 11, no. 2 (2013): 272–313. For a wider history of Spanish oyster fishing, see Molly A. Warsh, *American Baroque: Pearls and the Nature of Empire, 1492–1700* (Omohundro Institute and University of North Carolina Press, 2018).

21. Robert Rich to Nathaniel Rich, May 25 (19?), 1617, in Vernon A. Ives, ed., *The Rich Papers: Letters from Bermuda 1615–1646* (University of Toronto Press, 1984), 17, 25.

22. Miles Kendall to Nathaniel Rich, January 17, 1619/20, in Ives, ed., *Rich Papers*, 122.

23. Robert Rich to Nathaniel Rich, May 25 (19?), 1617, in Ives, ed., *Rich Papers*, 17.

24. Trevor John Whitaker, "The Economic and Military Impact of Privateers and Pirates on Britain's Rise as a World Power" (MA thesis, Arizona State University, 2020), 35.

25. Bernhard, *Slaves and Slaveholders in Bermuda*, 19–20.

26. Nathaniel Butler to Nathaniel Rich, January 12, 1620/1, in Ives, ed., *Rich Papers*, 229.

27. Sluiter, "New Light on the '20. and Odd Negroes,' " 397–398.

28. John Thornton, "The African Experience of the '20. and Odd Negroes' Arriving in Virginia in 1619," *William and Mary Quarterly* 55, no. 3 (1998): 421; Sluiter, "New Light on the '20. and Odd Negroes,' " 395–396; *JCCAS*, 1:55–156.

29. Cassandra Newby-Alexander, "The Arrival of the First Africans to English North America," *Virginia Magazine of History and Biography* 127, no. 3 (2019): 190.

30. Sluiter, "New Light on the '20. and Odd Negroes,' " 395–396.

31. William Thorndale, "The Virginia Census of 1619," *Magazine of Virginia Genealogy* 33 (1995): 155–170. See also discussions in John C. Coombs, "The Phases of Conversion: A New Chronology for the Rise of Slavery in Early Virginia," *William and Mary Quarterly* 68, no. 3 (2011): 338; Goetz, *Baptism of Early Virginia*, 57; Guasco, *Slaves and Englishmen*, 202.

32. Peter Wilson Coldham, *English Adventurers and Emigrants, 1609–1660: Abstracts of Examinations in the High Court of Admiralty with Reference to Colonial America* (Genealogical Publishing, 1984), 181.

33. Linda M. Heywood and John K. Thornton, *Central Africans, Atlantic Creoles, and the Foundation of the Americas, 1585–1660* (Cambridge University Press, 2007), 28–32.

34. Kevin Bertelsen, "Indian Slavery in Colonial Virginia and South Carolina" (MA thesis, College of William and Mary, 1984), 11.

35. McIlwaine, *Journals of the House of Burgesses of Virginia, 1619–1658/59*, 10.

36. William Cronon, *Changes in the Land: Indians, Colonists, and the Ecology of New England* (Hill and Wang, 1983).

37. Smith, *Generall Historie of Virginia*, 2:2–3.

38. Smith, *Generall Historie of Virginia*, 2:4. See also Drew Lipman, *Squanto: A Native Odyssey* (Yale University Press, 2024), 91–93.

39. *Mourt's Relation or journal of the plantation at Plymouth* (Boston: J. K. Wiggin, 1865), 114.

40. Lipman, *Squanto*, 76.

41. David J. Silverman, *Faith and Boundaries: Colonists, Christianity, and Community among the Wampanoag Indians of Martha's Vineyard, 1600–1871* (Cambridge University Press, 2005), 1–3.

42. Smith, *Generall Historie of Virginia*, 2:5–6. See also William P. Cumming, "The Colonial Charting of the Massachusetts Coast," in *Seafaring in Colonial Massachusetts*, vol. 52 (Colonial Society of Massachusetts, 1980), 79–80.

43. See, for example, *The Pilgrim Fathers* (Portland, ME: Shirley, Hyde, 1830).

44. William Bradford, *Of Plimouth Plantation* (Boston: Wright and Potter, 1898).

45. Bradford, *Of Plimouth Plantation*, 99–103.

46. Bradford, *Of Plimouth Plantation*, 111.

47. Silverman, *This Land Is Their Land*.

48. Hämäläinen, *Indigenous Continent*, 65.

49. Hämäläinen, *Indigenous Continent*, 66.

50. Edward Waterhouse, "A Declaration of the State of the Colonie and Affaires in Virginia," in *The Records of the Virginia Company of London*, vol. 3 (Government Printing Office, 1906), 551. See also Smith, *Generall Historie of Virginia*, 1:279–281.

51. Alden T. Vaughan, " 'Expulsion of the Salvages': English Policy and the Virginia Massacre of 1622," *William and Mary Quarterly* 35, no. 1 (January 1978): 76.

52. "The First Africans in Virginia Landed in 1619: It Was a Turning Point for Slavery in American History—but Not the Beginning," *Time*, August 20, 2019.

53. As quoted in Guasco, *Slaves and Englishmen*, 183.

54. Waterhouse, "Declaration," 558–559.

55. John Martin, "The Manner Howe to Bring the Indians into Subjection," December 15, 1622, BL, Add. Ms. 12496, ff. 459–460.

56. Waterhouse, "Declaration," 558–559. See also Guasco, *Slaves and Englishmen*, 183.

57. Francis Wyatt, "Letter of Sir Francis Wyatt, Governor of Virginia, 1621–1626," *William and Mary Quarterly* 6, no. 2 (1926): 118.

58. Tessa Murphy, *The Creole Archipelago: Race and Borders in the Colonial Caribbean* (University of Pennsylvania Press, 2021).

59. James Alexander Williamson, *The Caribbee Islands under the Proprietary Patents* (Oxford University Press, 1926), 23; Vincent K. Hubbard, *A History of St. Kitts: The Sweet Trade* (Macmillan, 2002), 16–18.

60. Deposition of Lieut. Robert Choppin, December 18, 1675, TNA, CO 1/35/63ii. See also Vere Langford Oliver, *The History of the Island of Antigua* (London: Mitchell and Hughes, 1894), 1:xviii, lii.

61. Oliver, *History of the Island of Antigua*, 1:xviii.

62. Testimony of Nicholas Broune, N. Darnell Davis, ed., "Papers Relating to the Early History of Barbados," *Timehri* VI (New Series) (1892): 330. See also Jerome S. Handler, "The Amerindian Slave Population of Barbados in the Seventeenth and Early Eighteenth Centuries," *Caribbean Studies* 8, no. 4 (1969): 39–40.

63. Richard Ligon, *A True and Exact History of the Island of Barbados* (London: Humphrey Moseley, 1657), 23.

64. John Poyer, *The History of Barbados* (J. Mawman, 1808), 10.

65. Major John Scott and P. F. Campbell, "The Description of Barbados," in *Some Early Barbadian History* (Caribbean Graphics & Letchworth Ltd., 1993), 247; Davis, ed., "Papers Relating to the Early History of Barbados," (1892), 328, note, and 54; Handler, "Amerindian Slave Population of Barbados," 38–39.

66. Scott and Campbell, "Description of Barbados." John Scott's description of Barbados is undated, but the editor places it around the year 1677.

67. See Henry Powell's petition in Davis, "Papers Relating to the Early History of Barbados," 1891, 54–55. See also Richard S. Dunn, *Sugar and Slaves: The Rise of the Planter Class in the English West Indies, 1624–1713* (University of North Carolina Press, 2000), 71, 227; Handler, "Amerindian Slave Population of Barbados," 40–47.

68. Henry Winthrop to Emmanuel Downing, August 22, 1627, in *WP*, 5:357. See also Dunn, *Sugar and Slaves*, 227.

69. William Arnold, *Memoirs of the First Settlement of the Island of Barbados* (London: E. Owen, near Chancery-Lane, Holborn, 1743), 20. See also Jerome S. Handler, "Custom and Law: The Status of Enslaved Africans in Seventeenth-Century Barbados," *Slavery and Abolition* 37, no. 2 (April 2, 2016): 326.

70. Mark Peterson, *The City-State of Boston: The Rise and Fall of an Atlantic Power, 1630–1865* (Princeton University Press, 2019); Karen Ordahl Kupperman, *Providence Island, 1630–1641: The Other Puritan Colony* (Cambridge University Press, 1993).

71. Kupperman, *Providence Island*, 25, 28.

72. For Winthrop's famous sermon, see Daniel T. Rodgers, *As a City on a Hill: The Story of America's Most Famous Lay Sermon* (Princeton University Press, 2020).

73. *MBCR*, 1:83.

74. Justin Winsor and Clarence. F. Jewett, *The Memorial History of Boston: Including Suffolk County, Massachusetts, 1630–1880*, vol. 2 (Boston: Osgood, 1881), 123, 489.

75. William Hubbard, *A Narrative of the Indian Wars in New England* (Worcester, MA: Daniel Greenleaf for Joseph Wilder, 1801), 19–22.

76. Alfred A. Cave, *The Pequot War* (University of Massachusetts Press, 1996), 109; Philip Vincent [P. Vincentius], *A True Relation of the Late Battell Fought in New England (1637)*, ed. Paul Royster, Electronic Texts in American Studies (London: M. P. for Nathanael Butter and John Bellamie, 1637), 8–9.

77. Cave, *Pequot War*, 110–113, 115–118.

78. Cave, *Pequot War*, 150–151.

79. As quoted in Cave, *Pequot War*, 152.

80. John Mason, *A Brief History of the Pequot War* (Boston: S. Kneeland & T. Green, 1736), 84.

81. Newell, *Brethren by Nature*, 18.

82. Vincent [P. Vincentius], *True Relation of the Late Battell*, 12–13; Newell, *Brethren by Nature*, 33.

83. Israel Stoughton to John Winthrop, June 28, 1637, in *WP*, 3:435–436.

84. Hubbard, *Narrative of the Indian Wars*, 45–48; Cave, *Pequot War*, 158–159.

85. Cave, *Pequot War*, 160–161.

86. *WP*, 3:456–458. See also Newell, *Brethren by Nature*, 40–41.

87. *WP*, 3:450.

88. *WP*, 5:436–437.

89. Linford D. Fisher, Sheila McIntyre, and Julie A. Fisher, *Reading Roger Williams: Rogue Puritans, Indigenous Nations, and the Founding of America—A Documentary History* (Pickwick Publications, 2024), 96–97.

90. John Winthrop, *Winthrop's Journal "History of New England" 1630–1649*, ed. James Kendall Hosmer (Charles Scribner's Sons, 1908), 1:227–228.

91. "Book of Entries of ye Governor and Company of Adventurers for ye Plantation of the Island of Providence," TNA CO 124/1/123b. For the debate about their identity, see Linda M. Heywood and John K. Thornton, " 'Canniball Negroes,' Atlantic Creoles, and the Identity of New England's Charter Generation," *African Diaspora* 4 (2011): 76–94.

92. Winthrop, *Winthrop's Journal*, 1:260.

93. Roger Williams and Glenn W. LaFantasie, *The Correspondence of Roger Williams* (University Press of New England, 1988), 1:132–133.

94. For an authoritative version of the treaty, see Daragh Grant, "The Treaty of Hartford (1638): Reconsidering Jurisdiction in Southern New England," *William and Mary Quarterly*, 72, no. 3 (2015): 495–498.

95. Cave, *Pequot War*, 162–163.

96. Richard A. Radune, *Pequot Plantation: The Story of an Early Colonial Settlement* (Research in Time Publications, 2005), 48–49.

97. *PRCC*, 1:186.

98. Rice, "War and Politics."

99. Shefveland, *Anglo-Native Virginia*, 14–15; William L. Shea, "Virginia at War, 1644–1646," *Military Affairs* 41, no. 3 (1977): 142–143.

100. Shea, "Virginia at War," 142.

101. Clifford Lewis, "Some Recently Discovered Extracts from the List Minutes of the Virginia Council and General Court, 1642–1645," *William and Mary Quarterly* 20, no. 1 (1940): 69.

102. Lauber, *Indian Slavery in Colonial Times*, 301; C. S. Everett, " 'They Shalbe Slaves for Their Lives': Indian Slavery in Colonial Virginia," in *Indian Slavery in Colonial America*, ed. Alan Gallay (University of Nebraska Press, 2009), 71.

103. Hening, 1:324–326.

104. As quoted in Everett, " 'They Shalbe Slaves,' " 76.

105. Everett, " 'They Shalbe Slaves,' " 70.

106. Emmanuel Downing to John Winthrop, ca. August 1645, in *Collections of the Massachusetts Historical Society* (Boston, 1863), ser. 4, 6:65.

107. Everett, " 'They Shalbe Slaves,' " 71.

108. William Berkeley to Robert Smith, ca. 1668, in "Indian Slaves," *William and Mary College Quarterly Historical Magazine* 8, no. 3 (January 1900): 165.

109. Morgan, *Laboring Women*, 36; Romney, " 'With & alongside His Housewife.' "

Chapter 3. Thin Justifications

1. Joseph T. Murphy, "The British Example: West Indian Emancipation, the Freedom Principle, and the Rise of Antislavery Politics in the United States, 1833–1843," *Journal of the Civil War Era*, 8, no. 4 (December 2018): 621.

2. Holly Brewer, "Slavery, Sovereignty, and 'Inheritable Blood': Reconsidering John Locke and the Origins of American Slavery," *American Historical Review* 122, no. 4 (October 1, 2017): 1038–1078; Seymour Drescher, *Abolition: A History of Slavery and Antislavery*, 1st ed. (Cambridge University Press, 2009), 77–78.

3. "An agreement and contract," August 2, 1654, BMDA, Colony Records (manuscript), 2:98B; *BSIC*, 3:237.

4. *BSIC*, 3:192, 281.

5. Holly Brewer, "Creating a Common Law of Slavery for England and Its New World Empire," *Law and History Review* 39, no. 4 (November 2021): 765–834.

6. John Cotton, *An Abstract or the Lawes of New England* (London, 1641), 15; Worthington Chauncey Ford, *John Cotton's Moses His Judicialls and Abstract of the Laws of New England* (J. Wilson and Son, 1902), 10.

7. John Mark Mattox, *St. Augustine and the Theory of Just War* (Continuum, 2006).

8. "The Body of Liberties of 1641," in William Henry Witmore, ed., *The Colonial Laws of Massachusetts* (Boston: Rockwell and Churchill, 1889), 32–61. For the role that Cotton's laws played in the Body of Liberties, see Whitmore, *Colonial Laws of Massachusetts*, 5–9; Daniel R. Coquillette, "Radical Lawmakers in Colonial Massachusetts: The 'Countenance of Authoritie' and the Lawes and Libertyes," *New England Quarterly* 67, no. 2 (June 1994): 179.

9. Roger Williams to John Winthrop, June 21, 1637, in Williams and LaFantasie, *Correspondence of Roger Williams*, 1:86.

10. Newell, *Brethren by Nature*, 103.

11. T. H. Breen and Stephen Innes, " 'Myne Owne Ground': Race and Freedom on Virginia's Eastern Shore, 1640–1676* (Oxford University Press, 2005).

12. Newman, *New World of Labor*.

13. May 19, 1643 (entered Nov. 10, 1643), BDA, BARD RB 3/1, 68–70.

14. William Hillyard and George Standfast, March 20, 1653, BDA, BARD RB 3/5, 120–122.

15. Arnold, *Memoirs of the First Settlement*, 20. See also Handler, "Custom and Law," 243.

16. Kupperman, *Providence Island*, 172.

17. See, for example, Thomas Burton, *Diary of Thomas Burton* (London: H. Colburn, 1828), 255–257, 301.

18. Ligon, *True and Exact History*, 54–55. See also Frances Seymour Somerset, *The Story of Inkle and Yarrico: A Most Moving Tale from the Spectator* (London: J. Cooper, 1738).

19. David Brion Davis, *The Problem of Slavery in Western Culture*, repr. ed. (Oxford University Press, 1988), 12. Regarding Yarico's ethnic identification, see Roxann Wheeler, "Colonial Exchanges: Visualizing Racial Ideology and Labour in Britain and the West Indies," in *An Economy of Colour: Visual Culture and the North Atlantic World, 1660–1830*, ed. Geoff Quilley and Kay Dian Kriz (Manchester University Press, 2003), 37–39.

20. Hening, 2:280–281.

21. Joseph Merrill, *History of Amesbury* (Haverhill, MA: F. P. Stiles, 1880), 41.

22. "Deed transferred from William Baldwin Senior to William Baldwin Junior son of Thomas Baldwin," May 20, 1654 (entered June 9, 1654), BDA, BARD RB 3/2, 708–711.

23. See, for example, William Hilliard to George Standfast, March 20, 1653, and William Hilliard to F. Georges, August 12, 1645, BDA, BARD RB 3/5, 120–125.

24. Deed of Marmaduke and Robert Bulricke and Edward Leake, St. Michaels, Barbados, May 19, 1643, BDA, BARD RB 3/1, 68–70.

25. Royal proclamation regarding the Royal African Company with signatures, December 2, 1674, Saltonstall Family Papers, MHS. Similar examples dot the Barbados deed books in the 1640s.

26. *BSIC*, 3:265; Bernhard, *Slaves and Slaveholders in Bermuda*, 52.

27. *BSIC*, 3:267.

28. Hening, 2:299.

29. Jennifer L. Morgan, "*Partus Sequitur Ventrem*: Law, Race, and Reproduction in Colonial Slavery," *Small Axe* 22, no. 1 (April 3, 2018): 1–17. Morgan's discussion is exclusively regarding enslaved Africans.

30. Julia E. Mercer, *Bermuda Settlers of the 17th Century: Genealogical Notes from Bermuda* (Genealogical Publishing, 1942), 85.

31. Morgan, *Laboring Women*, 36.

32. Handler, "Amerindian Slave Population of Barbados," 53–54.

33. Hening, 2:170. For the wider context of this act, see Jennifer L. Morgan, *Reckoning with Slavery: Gender, Kinship, and Capitalism in the Early Black Atlantic* (Duke University Press, 2021), 1–4.

34. David Buisseret, *Jamaica in 1687: The Taylor Manuscript at the National Library of Jamaica* (University of the West Indies Press, 2008), 287.

35. Linford Fisher, "A 'Spanish Indian Squaw' in New England: Indian Ann's Journey from Slavery to Freedom," in *Hearing Enslaved Voices: African and Indian Slave Testimony in British and French America, 1700–1848*, ed. Sophie White and Trevor Bernard (Routledge, 2020).

36. Kristalyn Marie Shefveland, "The Many Faces of Native Bonded Labor in Colonial Virginia," *Native South* 7, no. 1 (2014): 71–74.

37. Hening, 1:396, 410, 455–456; Everett, " 'They Shalbe Slaves,' " 101n20.

38. Shefveland, "Many Faces," 74.

39. Shefveland, "Many Faces," 75.

40. *RCRI*, 1:243.

41. *RCNP*, 3:74.

42. Hening, 2:283.

43. Hayley Negrin, "Possessing Native Women and Children: Slavery, Gender and English Colonialism in the Early American South, 1670–1717" (PhD diss., New York University, 2018).

44. Hening, 2:155.

45. Hening, 2:260.

46. July 27, 1669, *RCRI*, 2:271–272.

47. Shefveland, "Many Faces," 82.

48. Shefveland, "Many Faces," 81.

49.   *Acts of the Commissioners of the United Colonies of New England*, July 15, 1646, in *RCNP*, 9:70–71.

50.   Lauber, *Indian Slavery in Colonial Times*, 205.

51.   Hening, 2:15–16; Everett, " 'They Shalbe Slaves,' " 76–77.

52.   Everett, " 'They Shalbe Slaves,' " 77.

53.   For the act concerning slaves, see TNA, CO 30/2/16–26. For the act concerning servants, see *Acts and Statutes of the Assembly, 1650–1682* (Transcript Acts), vol. 1, BDA, 258–270. See also Edward B. Rugemer, "The Development of Mastery and Race in the Comprehensive Slave Codes of the Greater Caribbean during the Seventeenth Century," *William and Mary Quarterly* 70, no. 3 (July 1, 2013): 438.

54.   Rugemer, "Development of Mastery and Race," 439.

55.   Rugemer, "Development of Mastery and Race," 430.

56.   *BSIC*, 1:471.

Chapter 4. The Erased Caribbean Trade

1.   Veta Smith Tucker, "Purloined Identity: The Racial Metamorphosis of Tituba of Salem Village," *Journal of Black Studies* 30, no. 4 (2000): 627; *ARMB*, 7:626–632.

2.   See "Trans-Atlantic Slave Trade—Estimates," slavevoyages.org.

3.   Tucker, "Purloined Identity," 630.

4.   Elaine G. Breslaw, *Tituba, Reluctant Witch of Salem: Devilish Indians and Puritan Fantasies* (New York University Press, 1997), 26; Elaine G. Breslaw, "Tituba's Confession: The Multicultural Dimensions of the 1692 Salem Witch-Hunt," *Ethnohistory* 44, no. 3 (July 1, 1997): 537.

5.   Jon Latimer, *Buccaneers of the Caribbean: How Piracy Forged an Empire* (Harvard University Press, 2009), 99; Kupperman, *Providence Island*, 278.

6.   William Jackson and Vincent T. Harlow, *The Voyages of Captain William Jackson (1642–1645)* (Royal Historical Society, 1923), 8–12, 28, 33. See also Bernhard, *Slaves and Slaveholders in Bermuda*, 55.

7.   William Jackson's journal shows that he was at "ye Musquitos" in 1643. Karl H. Offen, "The Sambo and Tawira Miskitu: The Colonial Origins and Geography of Intra-Miskitu Differentiation in Eastern Nicaragua and Honduras," *Ethnohistory* 49, no. 2 (May 1, 2002): 333; Stanley Pargellis and Ruth Lapham Butler, "Daniell Ellffryth's Guide to the Caribbean, 1631," *William and Mary Quarterly* 1, no. 3 (1944): 312–316.

8.   *BSIC*, 3:265.

9.   Carolyn Arena, "Indian Slaves from Guiana in Seventeenth-Century Barbados," *Ethnohistory* 64, no. 1 (January 1, 2017): 70–71.

10.   Arena, "Indian Slaves from Guiana," 70–71.

11.   Arne Bialuschewski, *Raiders and Natives: Cross-Cultural Relations in the Age of Buccaneers* (University of Georgia Press, 2022), 34.

12.   See, for example, Bill of Sale, Peter Handcock to John Hancock, May 30, 1654 (entered June 16, 1654), BDA, BARD RB 3/2, 717–718.

13.   Henry Whistler, "A Journal of a Voyage from Stokes Bay [1654]," in *Journal*

of the Institute of Jamaica, vol. 1 (Kingston: Institute of Jamaica, 1894), 291. See also "Appendix E: Extracts from Henry Whistler's Journal of the West India Expedition," in Robert Venables, *The Narrative of General Venables*, ed. Charles H. Firth (Longmans, Green, 1900).

14. Justin Roberts, "Surrendering Surinam: The Barbadian Diaspora and the Expansion of the English Sugar Frontier, 1650–75," *William and Mary Quarterly* 73, no. 2 (2016): 228–229, 233.

15. Hill and Whitehead, "Ethnogenesis and Ethnocide," 28; Arena, "Indian Slaves from Caribana," 5.

16. Roberts, "Surrendering Surinam," 237.

17. Ligon, *True and Exact History*, 22; Rugemer, "Development of Mastery and Race," 443.

18. Karl Henry Offen, "The Miskitu Kingdom: Landscape and the Emergence of a Miskitu Ethnic Identity, Northeastern Nicaragua and Honduras, 1600–1800" (PhD diss., University of Texas at Austin, 1999).

19. Ligon, *True and Exact History*, 54.

20. Jean-Baptiste Du Tertre, *Histoire generale des Antilles habitées par les François* (Paris: Chez Thomas Iolly, 1667), vol. 2, 484.

21. Oliver Cromwell to Major General Fortescue, November 1655, in Thomas Carlyle, *Oliver Cromwell's Letters and Speeches: With Elucidations* (New York: Charles Scribner's Sons, 1845), 3:237; Kupperman, *Providence Island*, 351.

22. Kupperman, *Providence Island*, 351.

23. "Appendix E: Extracts from Henry Whistler's Journal."

24. For a thorough account of the English takeover of Jamaica, see Carla Gardina Pestana, *The English Conquest of Jamaica: Oliver Cromwell's Bid for Empire* (Belknap Press, 2017).

25. Emmanuel Kofi Agorsah, *Maroon Heritage: Archaeological, Ethnographic, and Historical Perspectives* (Canoe Press, 1994); Mavis Christine Campbell, *The Maroons of Jamaica, 1655–1796: A History of Resistance, Collaboration and Betrayal* (Africa World Press, 1990).

26. Description of Jamaica by Governor Jacinto Sendeño Albornoz, in Francisco Morales Padrón, *Spanish Jamaica* (Ian Randle, 2003), 77.

27. Harcourt Fuller and Jada Benn Torres, "Investigating the 'Taíno' Ancestry of the Jamaican Maroons: A New Genetic (DNA), Historical and Multidisciplinary Analysis and Case Study of the Accompong Town Maroons," *Canadian Journal of Latin American and Caribbean Studies* 43, no. 1 (2018): 47–78. More precisely, the DNA testing indicated Native ancestry on the maternal side of the sample population tested in Accompong Town. Such tests cannot confirm or deny specifically Taíno ancestry, however. On the artifacts, see Agorsah, *Maroon Heritage*, 163–187.

28. Forbes, *Africans and Native Americans*, 231.

29. Journal of Edward D'Oyley, July 8, 1656, BL, Add. Ms. 12410, fol. 11.

30. Instructions to Edward D'Oyley, Governor of Jamaica, February 1665, TNA, CO 1/15, folio 11. See also MS. Rawl. A. 347, Bodleian Library, Oxford, folio 9.

31. *The Laws of Jamaica Passed by the Assembly and Confirmed by His Majesty in Council, April 17, 1684* (C. Harper, 1684), x. A narrated description of the seal can be found in TNA, CO 138/4, 220.

32. James Robertson, "Re-writing the English Conquest of Jamaica in the Late

Seventeenth Century," *English Historical Review* 117, no. 473 (September 1, 2002): 832; "Jamaica's National Symbols: Coat of Arms," Office of the Prime Minister (website), Jamaica.

33. "An Act for ye Punishing & ordering of Negro Slaves," undated, but likely early 1664, TNA, CO 139/1/53.

34. The 1660 company was rechartered in 1663 with a slightly different name: the Company of Royal Adventurers of England Trading into Africa. George Frederick Zook, *The Company of Royal Adventurers Trading into Africa* (Press of the New Era, 1919), 8, 13.

35. "An Act for the better ordering and governing of Negro Slaves," TNA, CO 139/1/66–69. See also Rugemer, "Development of Mastery and Race," 430.

36. George Warren, *An Impartial Description of Surinam upon the Continent of Guiana in America* (London: William Godbid, 1667), 26.

37. *BSIC*, 3:308–310.

38. Benjamin Worsley to the Duke of Buckingham? "Paper [no 9] on the importance of Jamaica and sugar, c. 1668," 244, Copy in "The 1661 Notebook of John Locke," entered under "Jamaica," 215–219, 232–252, Bodleian Library, MS Film 77. I am grateful to Caroline Arena for this reference. See also Thomas Leng, *Benjamin Worsley (1618–1677): Trade, Interest and the Spirit in Revolutionary England* (Boydell Press, 2008).

39. Arena, "Indian Slaves from Caribana," 211; Hill and Whitehead, "Ethnogenesis and Ethnocide," 30.

40. Captain Peter Wroth to Jonathan Kellicott, May 30, [1670], entered August 27, 1670, BDA, BARD, RB 3/8, 46–47.

41. Breslaw, *Tituba, Reluctant Witch of Salem*, 5.

42. Willoughby to Walker, February 2, 1668, TNA, CO 1/22/32; Willoughby to Arlington, July 29, 1668, TNA, CO 1/23/29. See also Handler, "Amerindian Slave Population of Barbados," 49–50.

43. Articles against James Davis, undated, TNA, CO 1/35/280.

44. Willoughby to Walker, February 2, 1668, TNA, CO 1/22/58.

45. Handler, "Amerindian Slave Population of Barbados," 50.

46. Thomas M. Truxes, *The Overseas Trade of British America: A Narrative History* (Yale University Press, 2021), 209.

47. *Merchants' Magazine and Commercial Review*, vol. 30 (New York, 1854), 560.

48. William Dampier, *Dampier's Voyages* (E. Grant Richards, 1906), 156. I am grateful to Arne Bialuschewski for this reference.

49. For details of this raid, see Arne Bialuschewski, "Slaves of the Buccaneers: Mayas in Captivity in the Second Half of the Seventeenth Century," *Ethnohistory* 64, no. 1 (January 1, 2017): 51.

50. Edwin G. Burrows and Mike Wallace, *Gotham: A History of New York City to 1898* (Oxford University Press, 1998), 88, 106, 126.

51. See, for example, Stuyvesant to the Vice-Director at Curaçao, July 5, 1660, DRCNY, 13:179.

52. Peter R. Christoph, Florence A. Christoph, and Charles T. Gehring, eds., *The Andros Papers, 1679–1680* (Syracuse University Press, 1991), 264–265. For a seeming draft of a similarly worded order in December 1679, see Christoph, Christoph, and Gehring, *Andros Papers*, 174–175. The draft from December 1674 originally had "Bay of Campechio and other forraigne parts," but "of

Campechio" was crossed out. The final version read "from the Bay and other forraigne parts," but the intended geographic referent was clear.

53. Molesworth to Blathwayt, August 8, 1687, TNA, CO 138/6/20-21.

54. List of Indian slaves imported and sold by James Barré, in Christoph, Christoph, and Gehring, *Andros Papers*, 3:173–174.

55. Lauber, *Indian Slavery in Colonial Times*, 317.

56. Sir Thomas Lynch to Lords of Trade and Plantations, September 29, 1682, TNA, CO 1/49/66i, 66ii.

57. Richard Coney to the Privy Council ("ye Committee"), January 3, 1685/6, TNA, CO 1/59/7; "Articles against Capt. Bartholomew Sharp," March 17, 1685/6, TNA, CO 1/59/165; Bermuda Governor and Council Minutes, January 4, 1687/8, *Bermuda Historical Quarterly* 2, no. 3 (1945): 118. See also Jarvis, *In the Eye of All Trade*, 102.

58. For some of the documents related to this case, see TNA, CO 1/59/7, 52, 54, 153.

59. Bermuda 1698 census, TNA, CO 37/2, 194. See also Bernhard, *Slaves and Slaveholders in Bermuda*, 98.

60. Jarvis, *In the Eye of All Trade*, 102.

61. Inventory of John Welsh Sr., BMDA, Book of Wills, vol. 2, pt. 2, 230.

62. Inventory of Boaz Sharpe, March 13, 1707, BMDA, Book of Wills, vol. 3, pt. 2, 178–180.

63. Meeting Minutes of the Board of Trade, August 10, 1698, TNA, 391/11/87b. See also Gallay, *Indian Slave Trade*, 300.

64. John Camden Hotten, *The Original Lists of Persons . . . Who Went from Great Britain to the American Plantations, 1600–1700* (London: Hotten, 1874), 438ff.

65. Oliver, *History of the Island of Antigua*, 1:137.

66. TNA, CO 318/2/81.

67. Dunn, *Sugar and Slaves*, 269–270.

68. "An Inventory of the Honble Major Genl James Banisters Negroes, Indians, Cattle Horses & Hogs at the Time of His Death," 1674, JA, Inventories, 1674–1675, 1B/11/3/1.

69. Inventory of Andrew Knight, JA, Inventories, 1677–1778, 1B/11/3/2. I am thankful to Trevor Bernard for this reference.

70. St. James Inventories, 1733, JA. I am grateful for Trevor Bernard for this lead.

71. John Taylor, "Multum in Parvo" (1683), NLJ, 2:538.

72. Carolyn Arena makes a good argument for this in Arena, "Indian Slaves from Caribana," 172–173.

73. John Taylor, "Multum in Parvo" (1683), NLJ, MS 105, vol. 2, 538; Ligon, *True and Exact History*, 54; Buisseret, *Jamaica in 1687*, 250.

74. Edward Long, *The History of Jamaica* (London: T. Lowndes, 1774), 2:240–242, 3:750, 757, 759.

75. Ligon, *True and Exact History*, 29–31.

76. Ligon, *True and Exact History*, 32.

77. Buisseret, *Jamaica in 1687*, 218; Hakluyt, *Principal Navigations*, 313–314.

78. "Concerning Hurricanes and their Prognosticks &c; observations of my own experience thereupon," no date, BL, Egerton Mss. 2395, f. 619–624. I am grateful to Evan Haefeli for alerting me to this source and providing a transcription.

79. Edward Long's many references to Native methods of doing various tasks even into the late eighteenth century demonstrates this. Long, *History of Jamaica*.

80.   Buisseret, *Jamaica in 1687*, 268.

81.   Paul H. Williams, "Jamaican Taino Chief Attends Third Annual Indigenous Peoples' Day Celebrations," *Gleaner*, October 31, 2023.

82.   Tucker, "Purloined Identity"; Henry Wadsworth Longfellow, *Giles Corey of the Salem Farms* (Houghton Mifflin, 1900), 11.

Chapter 5. Forced Diasporas

1.   The following account is drawn from a few letters, including TNA, ADM 3/276/50, ADM 106/311/161, 165, 167, and ADM 106/318/10–16.

2.   Captain Thomas Hamilton to the Admiralty, December 16, 1675, TNA, ADM 106/311, doc. 167.

3.   Wendy Warren, *New England Bound: Slavery and Colonization in Early America* (Liveright, 2016), 91.

4.   Silverman, *This Land Is Their Land*, 296–297.

5.   Lorén Spears, personal communication, August 20, 2023.

6.   Silverman, *This Land Is Their Land*, ch. 7.

7.   John Easton and Franklin Benjamin Hough, *A Narrative of the Causes Which Led to Philip's Indian War, of 1675 and 1676* (Albany: J. Munsell, 1858), 11–15.

8.   Easton and Hough, *Narrative of the Causes*, 11–15.

9.   "Minutes of the Committee for Trade and Plantations, December 1, 1675, TNA, CO 1/35/50.

10.   Morgan Lodge to Joseph Williamson, November 17, 1675, TNA, State Papers, Domestic, Charles II, 375, No. 34, Native Northeast Portal.

11.   Easton and Hough, *Narrative of the Causes*, 21, 21n2.

12.   *RCNP*, 5:173–174.

13.   Nathaniel Saltonstall, *The Present State of New-England with Respect to the Indian War* (London: D. Newman, J. Drake, 1675), 6.

14.   *RCNP*, 1:451–453. See also Joseph Barlow Felt, *The Ecclesiastical History of New England*, vol. 2 (Boston: Congregational Library Association, 1862), 569; MSAC, 30:173.

15.   See, for example, Depositions of Chachasijmes, Two Nipmuc Woman, and Keeweebhunt, June 1678 (1678.07.00.00), in Paul Grant-Costa and Tobias Glaza, eds., Native Northeast Portal.

16.   *RCNP*, 1:451–453. See also Felt, *Ecclesiastical History of New England*, 2:569; MSAC, 30:173.

17.   Newell, *Brethren by Nature*, 141–142.

18.   Mary White Rowlandson and Neal Salisbury, *The Sovereignty and Goodness of God* (Bedford Books, 1997), 146.

19.   Benjamin Church, Henry Martyn Dexter, and Thomas Church, *The History of King Philip's War* (Boston: J. K. Wiggin, 1865), 84; John Easton, "A Relation of the Indian War," in Easton and Hough, *Narrative of the Causes*, 20, note. See also William Hubbard, *The Present State of New-England: Being a Narrative of the Troubles with the Indians in New-England* (London: Tho. Parkhurst, 1677), 97.

20.   Daniel Gookin, "An Historical Account of the Doings and Sufferings of the Christian Indians in New England," in *Archaeologia Americana: Transactions*

and Collections of the American Antiquarian Society, vol. 2 (Cambridge, MA: Folsom, Wells, and Thurston, 1836), 462.

21. Linford Fisher, "'Why shall wee have peace to bee made slaves': Indian Surrenderers during and after King Philip's War," *Ethnohistory* 64, no. 1 (January 2017): 91.

22. James D. Rice, "Bacon's Rebellion in Indian Country," *Journal of American History* 101, no. 3 (2014): 733–734.

23. James D. Rice, *Tales from a Revolution: Bacon's Rebellion and the Transformation of Early America* (Oxford University Press, 2013), 4–7. See also Rice, "Bacon's Rebellion in Indian Country," 734–735; Hayley Negrin, "Cockacoeske's Rebellion: Nathaniel Bacon, Indigenous Slavery, and Sovereignty in Early Virginia," *William and Mary Quarterly* 80, no. 1 (2023): 68–69.

24. As quoted in Rice, *Tales from a Revolution*, 38.

25. Rice, *Tales from a Revolution*, 39–40.

26. As quoted in Rice, *Tales from a Revolution*, 44.

27. Rice, "Bacon's Rebellion in Indian Country," 740.

28. Negrin, "Cockacoeske's Rebellion," 70–71.

29. Governor Jonathan Atkins to Joseph Williamson, April 3, 1676, TNA, CO 1/36, doc. 70 (emphasis added). See also Rice, *Tales from a Revolution*, 36; Margaret Ellen Newell, "'The Rising of the Indians'; or, The Native American Revolution of (16)'76," *William and Mary Quarterly* 80, no. 2 (2023): 287–324; Maureen Meyers, "From Refugees to Slave Traders: The Transformation of the Westo Indians," in *Mapping the Mississippian Shatter Zone: The Colonial Indian Slave Trade and Regional Instability in the American South*, ed. Robbie Franklyn Ethridge and Sheri Marie Shuck-Hall (University of Nebraska Press, 2009), 98.

30. Jill Lepore, *The Name of War: King Philip's War and the Origins of American Identity* (Knopf, 1998), 105.

31. Reports varied regarding the number of Indians killed and taken captive in the raid against the Narragansett. Letter of Captain Oliver, January 26, 1676, in George M. Bodge, *Soldiers in King Philip's War* (Boston: Printed for the author, 1891), 126–127.

32. Mary White Rowlandson, *The Soveraignty and Goodness of God*, 2nd ed. (Cambridge, MA: Samuel Green, 1682).

33. Lepore, *Name of War*, xxvii.

34. Gookin, "Historical Account," 522.

35. Linford D. Fisher, "America's First Bible: Native Uses, Abuses, and Reuses of the Indian Bible of 1663," in *The Bible in American Life*, ed. Philip Goff, Arthur E. Farnsley II, and Peter Thuesen, 1st ed. (Oxford University Press, 2017), 44–45.

36. Gookin, "Historical Account," 476, 497–500.

37. George William Ellis and John Emery Morris, *King Philip's War: Based on the Archives and Records of Massachusetts, Plymouth, Rhode Island and Connecticut* (Grafton Press, 1906), 236–237.

38. MBCR, 5:72. For challenges in recruitment, see Jenny Hale Pulsipher, *Subjects unto the Same King: Indians, English, and the Contest for Authority in Colonial New England* (University of Pennsylvania Press, 2005), 163–165.

39. Nathaniel Bouton, ed., *Provincial Papers: Documents and Records Relating*

to the Province of New-Hampshire, from the Earliest Period of Its Settlement (Concord, NH: G E. Jenks, 1867), 1:318.

40. Ellis and Morris, *King Philip's War*, 241–42, 248.

41. Church, Dexter, and Church, *History of King Philip's War*, 150–153.

42. *The Correspondence of John Cotton Junior*, vol. 79, PCSM, 173, 175–76, 187–188. See also Christine M. DeLucia, *Memory Lands: King Philip's War and the Place of Violence in the Northeast*, 1st ed. (Yale University Press, 2018), 303; Ethel Boissevain, "Whatever Became of the New England Indians Shipped to Bermuda to Be Sold as Slaves?" *Man in the Northwest* 11 (Spring 1981): 103–114.

43. There are multiple conflicting accounts of these events. See, for example, "Articles of high misdemeanour exhibited against Richard Waldern, Richard Martyn, and John Gillman of New Hampshire," September 14, 1682, TNA, CO 1/49/203. The most thorough recent account is Brooks, *Our Beloved Kin*, 331–332. See also Christine DeLucia, "The Memory Frontier: Uncommon Pursuits of Past and Place in the Northeast after King Philip's War," *Journal of American History* 98, no. 4 (March 1, 2012): 988; J. Douglas Peters, " 'Removing the Heathen': Changing Motives for Indian Slavery in New Hampshire," *Historical New Hampshire* 58, no. 3 (2003): 72.

44. "Native American Executions on Boston Common," *Encyclopedia of Boston*, Boston Research Center, Northeastern University.

45. "To all People," September 12, 1676, Jamaica National Library, MS 1695. See also Lepore, *Name of War*, 150–151.

46. Entries of August 24 and September 23, 1676, John Hull Account Books, 2:390, 446. New England Historical and Genealogical Society, Boston, MA. I am grateful to Joanne Jahnke-Wegner for this reference.

47. Letter of Captain Oliver, January 26, 1676, in Bodge, *Soldiers in King Philip's War*, 126–127.

48. W. R. Staples, "Annals of the Town of Providence," *CRIHS* (Rhode Island Historical Society, 1843), 5:170.

49. Staples, "Annals," 5:170–171. Daniel R. Mandell, *King Philip's War: Colonial Expansion, Native Resistance, and the End of Indian Sovereignty*, 1st ed. (Johns Hopkins University Press, 2010), 113.

50. Staples, "Annals," 5:170.

51. *RCRI*, 2:549.

52. *PRCC*, 2:298, 482.

53. Hening, 2:349; Samuel Wiseman, *Samuel Wiseman's Book of Record: The Official Account of Bacon's Rebellion in Virginia, 1676–1677*, ed. Michael Leroy Oberg (Lexington Books, 2009), 32.

54. June 1676, in Hening, 2:346–347.

55. Rice, *Tales from a Revolution*, 45–46; Shefveland, *Anglo-Native Virginia*, 53.

56. Rebecca Anne Goetz, "The Nanziatticos and the Violence of the Archive: Land and Native Enslavement in Colonial Virginia," *Journal of Southern History* 85, no. 1 (February 2019): 33–60.

57. Gregory S. Schneider, "The Hidden Story of Native Tribes Who Outsmarted Bacon's Rebellion," *Washington Post*, September 20, 2024.

58. Negrin, "Cockacoeske's Rebellion," 73.

59. January 22, 1676/7, in FAAC, Henrico County Deeds, Wills, 1677–1692, 33.

60. Rice, *Tales from a Revolution*, 138.

61. Rice, *Tales from a Revolution*, 207.

62. Shefveland, *Anglo-Native Virginia*, 54–55.

63. Hening, 2:349, 373, 403; Everett, " 'They Shalbe Slaves,' " 88.

64. February 1677, April 1679, and June 1676, in Hening, 2:404, 440, 352.

65. Everett, " 'They Shalbe Slaves,' " 84, 80.

66. Deposition of James Sweet et al., October 8, 1675, MSAC, 30: 181. For a fuller account of this episode, see Newell, *Brethren by Nature*, 183–185.

67. See, for example, TNA, CO 1/18, no. 75, and CO 1/40, no. 80. See also SP 44/25, p. 3; TNA, CO 279/20, docs. 135, 136; Captain Thomas Hamilton to the Admiralty, December 16, 1675, TNA, ADM 106/311, doc. 167. See Samuel Drake's descriptions of these depositions, on p. 94 of vol. 2, in Hubbard, *Present State of New England*, 46; Hermann F. Clarke, "John Hull: Colonial Merchant, 1624–1683," *PAAS* 46 (1937): 214. See also Margaret Ellen Newell, "The Changing Nature of Slavery in New England, 1670–1720," in *Reinterpreting New England Indians and the Colonial Experience*, ed. Colin G. Calloway and Neal Salisbury (Colonial Society of Massachusetts, 2003).

68. John Eliot to Robert Boyle, 1683, *Collections of the Massachusetts Historical Society*, vol. 3, 1 (Boston: MHS, 1794), 183.

69. See, for example, TNA, CO 1/18, no. 75, and CO 1/40, no. 80. See also SP 44/25, p. 3.

70. Benerson Little, *The Buccaneer's Realm: Pirate Life on the Spanish Main, 1674–1688* (Potomac Books, 2007), 140.

71. For the Bermuda law, see "A law for making all Negroes, Indians, and Mulattos . . . " August 12, 1675, *BSIC*, 2:251–252. For Barbados, see Linford D. Fisher, " 'Dangerous Designes': The 1676 Barbados Act to Prohibit New England Indian Slave Importation," *William and Mary Quarterly*, 3rd ser., 71, no. 1 (January 2014): 99–124. For the Jamaica law, see Council at Port Royall, December 12, 1676, "Continuation of ye Council Book of Jamaica," TNA, CO 140/3, 535–536.

72. The Barbados June 1676 Act of Explanation is clear on this feared connection between New England Indians and African rebellions. "An Act of Explanation to the Act of Negroes, and to prohibite the bringing of Indians to this Island," *Acts and Statutes of the Assembly, 1650–1682 ("Transcript Acts")* (Barbados Department of Archives, n.d.), 421–423.

73. George Wyllys, *The Wyllys Papers*, CCHS, 21:257; PRCC, 2:482. See also Michael Leroy Oberg, *Uncas: First of the Mohegans* (Cornell University Press, 2003), 193.

74. Gookin, "Historical Account," 532; RCNP, 5:207, 223.

75. JCCAS, 1:474.

76. MBCR, 5:477.

77. Rice, "Bacon's Rebellion in Indian Country," 745. See also FAAC.

78. Thomas Hutchinson, *A Collection of Original Papers Relative to the History of the Colony of Massachusetts-Bay* (Boston: Thomas and John Fleet, 1769), 493.

79. Hutchinson, *Collection*, 493. See also Bouton, *Provincial Papers*, 1:342–345.

80. See, for example, Brooks, *Our Beloved Kin*, 321.

81. Increase Mather, *A Brief History of the Warr with the Indians in New-England* (Boston: John Foster, 1676), 9.

82. Katie Mulvaney, "Narragansett Indian Tribe Sees Return of Land Marking the Great Swamp Massacre," *Providence Journal*, October 27, 2021.

Chapter 6. Resistance in the Southeast

1. Francis Le Jau to the SPG Secretary, September 15, 1708, in Francis Le Jau, *The Carolina Chronicle of Dr. Francis Le Jau, 1706–1717* (University of California Press, 1956), 41.

2. Snyder, *Slavery in Indian Country*, 55.

3. Gallay, *Indian Slave Trade*, 299.

4. Peter H. Wood, *Black Majority: Negroes in Colonial South Carolina from 1670 through the Stono Rebellion*, reissue ed. (W. W. Norton, 1996), 14; William D. Hilton, *A Relation of a Discovery Lately Made on the Coast of Florida* (London: J. C. for Simon Miller, 1664).

5. Joel Martin, "Southeastern Indians and the English Trade in Skins and Slaves," in *The Forgotten Centuries: Indians and Europeans in the American South, 1521–1704*, ed. Carmen Tesser and Charles Hudson (University of Georgia Press, 1994), 312.

6. Martin, "Southeastern Indians," 308. See also Snyder, *Slavery in Indian Country*, 54.

7. Gallay, *Indian Slave Trade*, 56.

8. Snyder, *Slavery in Indian Country*, 48–49.

9. Denise Ileana Bossy, "The 'Noble Savage' in Chains: Indian Slavery in Colonial South Carolina, 1670–1735" (PhD diss., Yale University, 2007), 23.

10. *JCSV*, August 25, 1671–June 24, 1680, 84.

11. April 12, 1680, in A. S. Salley, *Journal of the Commons House of Assembly of South Carolina, November 20, 1706–February 8, 1706/7* (State Company, 1939), 83–84.

12. Snyder, *Slavery in Indian Country*, 49.

13. Waterhouse, "Declaration," 558.

14. Martin, "Southeastern Indians," 312.

15. Hening, 1:491–492; 3:447–448.

16. See Chapter 11 of this book for examples of Indigenous freedom suits.

17. John E. Worth, "Razing Florida: The Indian Slave Trade and the Devastation of Spanish Florida, 1659–1715," in *Mapping the Mississippian Shatter Zone: The Colonial Indian Slave Trade and Regional Instability in the American South*, ed. Robbie Franklyn Ethridge and Sheri Marie Shuck-Hall (University of Nebraska Press, 2009), 295.

18. "The declaration of severall Yamasee Indians," May 6, 1685, TNA, CO 5/287/70v. See also Emma Katherine Bilski, "Labor, Gender, and Violence at the Missions of Seventeenth-Century Florida" (PhD diss., Johns Hopkins University, 2023).

19. Snyder, *Slavery in Indian Country*, 65.

20. Snyder, *Slavery in Indian Country*, 51.

21. James Axtell, "Making Do: Trade in the Eighteenth-Century Southeast," in

Natives and Newcomers: The Cultural Origins of North America (Oxford University Press, 2000), 131–132; Jessica Yirush Stern, *The Lives in Objects: Native Americans, British Colonists, and Cultures of Labor and Exchange in the Southeast* (University of North Carolina Press, 2017); Snyder, *Slavery in Indian Country*, 52. See also Governor and Council to the Board of Trade, September 17, 1708, TNA, CO 5/1292/174.

22.   Wilma A. Dunaway, *The First American Frontier: Transition to Capitalism in Southern Appalachia, 1700–1860* (University of North Carolina Press, 1996), 33.

23.   Snyder, *Slavery in Indian Country*, 54.

24.   Thomas Nairne, *Nairne's Muskhogean Journals: The 1708 Expedition to the Mississippi River* (University Press of Mississippi, 1988), 42–43; Snyder, *Slavery in Indian Country*, 59.

25.   Snyder, *Slavery in Indian Country*, 61.

26.   Chase Bryer, personal correspondence, April 15, 2024.

27.   Robert Allen Matter, "Missions in the Defense of Spanish Florida, 1566–1710," *Florida Historical Quarterly* 54, no. 1 (1975): 33.

28.   Matter, "Missions in the Defense of Spanish Florida," 33.

29.   Martin, "Southeastern Indians," 312; Snyder, *Slavery in Indian Country*, 74. For an early newspaper account, see "South-Carolina Via New-York," *Boston News-Letter*, May 1, 1704, 2–3.

30.   Theodore W. Allen, *The Invention of the White Race* (Verso, 1994), 2:40.

31.   Snyder, *Slavery in Indian Country*, 50, 74.

32.   "For the Encouragemint of Lt. Elisha Andrews . . . ," November 6, 1690, MSAC, 36:218; "An Act for Encouragement of the Prosecution of the Indian Enemy and Rebels," October 18, 1697, MSAC, 30:435, 435a. See also *ARMB*, 1:292.

33.   "In the House of Representatives," November 25, 1703, MSAC, 70:664. See also *ARMB*, 1:530–531.

34.   *ARMB*, 1:600.

35.   Richard R. Johnson, "The Search for a Usable Indian: An Aspect of the Defense of Colonial New England," *Journal of American History* 64, no. 3 (1977): 630.

36.   *ARMB*, 8:614–615.

37.   *RCRI*, 3:482–483.

38.   Governor and Council to the Board of Trade, September 17, 1708, TNA, CO 5/1292/166.

39.   D. Andrew Johnson, *Enslaved Native Americans and the Making of Colonial South Carolina* (Johns Hopkins University Press, 2024), 93.

40.   Governor and Council to the Board of Trade, September 17, 1708, TNA, CO 5/1292/168–169.

41.   Gallay, *Indian Slave Trade*, 299–308; Everett, " 'They Shalbe Slaves,' " 92; Salley, *Journal of the Commons House of Assembly of South Carolina*, 33.

42.   *Boston News-Letter*, March 29–April 3, and April 12–19, 1708, Stolen Relations: Recovering Stories of Indigenous Enslavement in the Americas (website), Brown University.

43.   *Boston News-Letter*, September 8–15, 1707, Stolen Relations project.

44.   "T. Nairne to [? The Earl of Sunderland]," July 10, 1709, *CSP*, vol. 24.

45.   "T. Nairne to [? The Earl of Sunderland]," July 28, 1709 [? 1708?], *CSP*, vol. 24.

46. Bossy, "'Noble Savage' in Chains," 256.

47. Gallay, *Indian Slave Trade*, 262.

48. David La Vere, *The Tuscarora War: Indians, Settlers, and the Fight for the Carolina Colonies* (University of North Carolina Press, 2013), 50.

49. June 16, 1710, MPCP, 2:511–512. See also La Vere, *Tuscarora War*, 53–54.

50. Christopher Gale to South Carolina magistrates, November 2, 1711, SRNC, 1:826.

51. Christopher Gale to South Carolina magistrates, November 2, 1711, SRNC, 1:826–827.

52. SRNC, 2:113.

53. Christopher Gale to South Carolina magistrates, November 2, 1711, SRNC, 1:826.

54. Gallay, *Indian Slave Trade*, 261.

55. John Barnwell, "The Tuscarora Expedition: Letters of Colonel John Barnwell," *South Carolina Historical and Genealogical Magazine* 9, no. 1 (1908): 30–31. For a detailed analysis of the participating tribes listed by Barnwell, see Gallay, *Indian Slave Trade*, 267–268.

56. Barnwell, "Tuscarora Expedition," 41.

57. Barnwell, "Tuscarora Expedition," 34.

58. Barnwell, "Tuscarora Expedition," 34.

59. Baron Christoph von Graffenried and Julius Goebel, *Christoph von Graffenried's Account of the Founding of New Bern* (Edwards & Broughton, 1920), 244.

60. Sanford Winston, "Indian Slavery in the Carolina Region," *Journal of Negro History* 19, no. 4 (October 1, 1934): 432; Graffenried and Goebel, *Christoph von Graffenried's Account*, 245.

61. SRNC, 1:900.

62. La Vere, *Tuscarora War*, 165.

63. North Carolina governor Edward Hyde boasted that they had either "cut off" or taken captive between three hundred and four hundred Indians. Edward Hyde to Mr. Rainsford, May 30, 1712, SRNC, 1:850. See also La Vere, *Tuscarora War*, 169.

64. Graffenried and Goebel, *Christoph von Graffenried's Account*, 245. See also Winston, "Indian Slavery in the Carolina Region," 433; Graffenried and Goebel, *Christoph von Graffenried's Account*, 91.

65. Gallay, *Indian Slave Trade*, 298; Barnwell, "Tuscarora Expedition," 34.

66. Martin, "Southeastern Indians," 313.

67. Steven C. Hahn, *The Invention of the Creek Nation, 1670–1763* (University of Nebraska Press, 2004), 81; Alejandra Dubcovsky, "One Hundred Sixty-One Knots, Two Plates, and One Emperor: Creek Information Networks in the Era of the Yamasee War," *Ethnohistory* 59, no. 3 (July 1, 2012): 489–513.

68. Verner W. Crane, *The Southern Frontier, 1670–1732* (Duke University Press, 1928), 179, 181.

69. Snyder, *Slavery in Indian Country*, 77.

70. Crane, *Southern Frontier*, 165–166.

71. Caleb Heathcote to Lord Townsend, July 16, 1715, DRCNY, 5:432–433.

72. "Rhode-Island, June 10," *Boston News-Letter*, June 13, 1715: 2, AHN.

73. January 25, 1716/17, TNA, CO 5/1265/63.

74. "Rhode Island, September 2," *Boston News-Letter*, September 5, 1712: 2, AHN.

75. Petition from the Carolina Lords Proprietors, July 8, 1715, TNA, CO 5/1264/148.

76. See reports from September 5, September 26, and October 31, 1715, in *Boston News-Letter*, AHN.

77. Gallay, *Indian Slave Trade*, 338; Snyder, *Slavery in Indian Country*, 77.

78. "Rhode-Island, October 28," *Boston News-Letter*, October 31, 1715: 2.

79. "New York, July 11," *Boston News-Letter*, July 18, 1715: 2.

80. Chart of exports from South Carolina, undated, but likely early 1716. TNA, CO 5/1265/29(i).

81. Crane, *Southern Frontier*, 171.

82. Gallay, *Indian Slave Trade*, 7–8.

83. *MPCP*, 2:231, 583–584; "Slavery in Pennsylvania," *Middletown Transcript*, May 22, 1897, newspapers.com.

84. Winston, "Indian Slavery in the Carolina Region," October 1, 1934, 435; "An act prohibiting the importation or bringing into this province any Indian servant or slaves," passed May 15, 1714, *NHPL, 1702–1745*, 152–153. See, for example, *PRCC*, 5:516; *RCRI*, 4:193.

85. *RCRI*, 4:197–198, 185–186.

86. *Boston News-Letter*, September 17, 1716, Stolen Relations project.

87. *Boston News-Letter*, July 15–22, 1717, Stolen Relations project.

88. Martin, "Southeastern Indians," 313.

89. Snyder, *Slavery in Indian Country*, 78.

90. Johnson, *Enslaved Native Americans*, 116.

91. April 4, 1720, *SRNC*, 2:377–379.

92. Memorial from several merchants trading to Carolina, October 27, 1720, TNA, CO 5/358/50.

93. Alejandra Dubcovsky, *Informed Power: Communication in the Early American South* (Harvard University Press, 2016), 199.

94. These descriptions are based on an in-person visit by the author on August 5, 2018.

95. Stephen Feeley, " 'Before Long to Be Good Friends': Diplomatic Perspectives of the Tuscarora War," in *Creating and Contesting Carolina: Proprietary Era Histories*, ed. Michelle LeMaster and Bradford J. Wood (University of South Carolina Press, 2013), 140.

96. Bossy, " 'Noble Savage' in Chains," 325.

CHAPTER 7. THE MISKITU TRADE

1. See, for example, Newell, *Brethren by Nature*; Gallay, *Indian Slave Trade*; Johnson, *Enslaved Native Americans*, 117.

2. "Twenty Dollars Reward," *Boston-Gazette*, September 3, 1764; Stolen Relations project.

3. Memorial from the Conde de Montijo, 28 October/8 November 1734, TNA, CO 324/36/490–493. Translation assistance provided by Jo E. Fisher and Tamsin Rankine-Fourdraine.

4. Memorial from the Conde de Montijo.

5. Long, *History of Jamaica*, 1:314–316. On numbers, see Karl Offen, "Mapping Amerindian Captivity in Colonial Mosquitia," *Journal of Latin American Geography* 14, no. 3 (2015): 42.

6. Robert Hodgson to the Board of Trade, April 3, 1744, TNA, CO 323/11/67; John K. Thornton, "The Zambos and the Transformation of the Miskitu Kingdom, 1636–1740," *Hispanic American Historical Review* 97, no. 1 (February 1, 2017): 5–6.

7. Robert Hodgson to the Board of Trade; Thornton, "Zambos," 12–15.

8. The Duke of Albemarle to the Lords of Trade, February 11, 1687/8, TNA, CO 1/64/39, CO 138/6/42. See also Charles Leslie, *A New History of Jamaica* (London: J. Hodges, 1740), 276–277.

9. Governor Trelawney to the Board of Trade, July 17, 1751, TNA, CO 123/1/10v. See also Long, *History of Jamaica*, 1:314–316.

10. Kimberly Henke Breuer, "Colonies of Happenstance: The English Settlements in Central America, 1525–1787" (MA thesis, University of Texas at Arlington, 1993), 20–22.

11. M. W., "The Mosqueto Indian and His Golden River, Being a Familiar Description of the Mosqueto Kingdom in America [1699]," in *A Collection of Voyages and Travels*, eds. Awnsham Churchill, vol. 6 (London, 1732), 288. See also Daniel Richard Joseph Burnell, "The Betrayal of an Alliance: The Miskito and the British, 1687–1894" (MA thesis, University of Calgary, 1994), 43–44. See also Offen, "Sambo and Tawira Miskitu," 343–345.

12. Burnell, "Betrayal of an Alliance," 43–44.

13. Frank Griffith Dawson, "William Pitt's Settlement at Black River on the Mosquito Shore: A Challenge to Spain in Central America, 1732–87," *Hispanic American Historical Review* 63, no. 4 (1983): 679, 681–682.

14. Gallay, *Indian Slave Trade*, 300. January 30, 1710/11 and June 28, 1711, Jamaican shipping records, TNA, CO 142/14/28, 33. A total of nine Natives were transported on these two dates.

15. Westmoreland County (VA) Order Book, 1698–1705, 30a, FAAC.

16. Dawson, "William Pitt's Settlement at Black River," 681–682.

17. Robert Hodgson, "Description of the Mosquito Shore," ca. 1757, TNA, CO 123/14/24v.

18. Frank Wesley Pitman, "The Slaves," *Journal of Negro History* 11, no. 4 (October 1, 1926): 588–589.

19. *Slaves at Honduras: Correspondence Relative to the Condition and Treatment of Slaves at Honduras, 1820–1823*, House of Commons Parliamentary Papers 457 (London, 1823), 59.

20. Offen, "Miskitu Kingdom," 163n23; Forbes, *Africans and Native Americans*, 231.

21. "[Robinson Crusoe; Alexander Selkirk; Island of Juan Fernandes; Capt. Rogers; Duke and Dutchess]," *Northern Whig* (Hudson, NY) 11, no. 15 (April 6, 1819): [2]; AHN.

22. Sharika D. Crawford and Ana Isabel Márquez-Pérez, "A Contact Zone: The Turtle Commons of the Western Caribbean," *International Journal of Maritime History* 28, no. 1 (February 1, 2016): 68.

23. Daniel Defoe, *The Adventures of Robinson Crusoe* (London: S. O. Beeton, 1862), 76.

24. Crawford and Márquez-Pérez, "Contact Zone," 69.

25. Robert Hodgson to the Board of Trade.

26. Robert Hodgson to the Board of Trade; see also Offen, "Sambo and Tawira Miskitu," 335.

27. Hodgson, "Description of the Mosquito Shore."

28. Memorial from the Conde de Montijo, 28 October/8 November 1734, TNA, CO 324/36/490–493.

29. Memorial from the Conde de Montijo.

30. Memorial from the Conde de Montijo.

31. Memorial from the Conde de Montijo.

32. William Gooch to the Duke of Newcastle, May 26, 1735, TNA, CO 5/1337/175–176.

33. William Gooch to the Duke of Newcastle, May 26, 1735.

34. Charles Hayes, *The Importance of Effectually Supporting the Royal African Company of England Impartially Consider'd* (London, 1744), 3.

35. William Shuman Sorsby, "The British Superintendency of the Mosquito Coast, 1749–1787" (PhD diss., University of London, 1969), 11–12.

36. Sorsby, "British Superintendency," 11.

37. "Extract of a Letter from a Gentleman in Newport," *New-York Weekly Journal*, March 23, 1740, 1. See also Howard M. Chapin, *Rhode Island Privateers in King George's War, 1739–1748* (Providence, 1926), 83.

38. As quoted in Christopher J. Baldwin, *An Empire of Plunder: Conquest and Enslavement in the British Caribbean, 1700–1770* (University of Pennsylvania Press, forthcoming), 128–139.

39. Dawson, "William Pitt's Settlement at Black River," 684.

40. Offen, "Sambo and Tawira Miskitu," 343.

41. Regarding colonization attempts and Native relations at Darién, see Ignacio Gallup-Diaz, *The Door of the Seas and the Key to the Universe: Indian Politics and Imperial Rivalry in Darién, 1640–1750*, rev. ed. (Columbia University Press, 2005).

42. Francis Borland, *Memoirs of Darien* (Glasgow: Hugh Brown, 1715); Charles E. Nowell, "The Defense of Cartagena," *Hispanic American Historical Review* 42, no. 4 (November 1, 1962): 477–501.

43. Report of a committee, April 1741, TNA, CO 140/23/563.

44. TNA, CO 139/15/103; *AAJ* (Saint Jago de la Vega, Jamaica, 1769), 1:250–251. See also the brief commentary in Long, *History of Jamaica*, 2:344.

45. Regulating the "Indian trade" and keeping the peace for both practical and diplomatic reasons had been an ongoing concern for royal authorities for over a century. See "Col. Quary to the Council of Trade and Plantations, March 26, 1702," CO 323/3/120; CO 324/8/86–106 [March 26, 1702], CSPO.

46. *AAJ*, 2:193–194.

47. Robert Hodgson to the Board of Trade, April 3, 1744, TNA, CO 323/11/68.

48. Sorsby, "British Superintendency," 97–98.

49. TNA, CO 137/60/53; Sorsby, "British Superintendency," 93.

50. Dulac to the Count of Marillan ot Aquin, ca. 1755, TNA, CO 137/60/182v–183.

51. TNA, CO 140/40/379.

52. TNA, CO 137/72/94.

53. TNA, CO 140/40/378–379.

54. *Barbados Mercury*, no. 15, vol. 9, September 22, 1770, 2. Accessed at the AAS.

55. Testimony of Richard Jones to Jamaica Assembly, November 15, 1762, TNA, CO 140/40/378–379.

56. James Lawrie to Basil Keith, January 27, 1777, TNA, CO 137/72/97–98v.

57. Jamaica Assembly, November 17, 1762, TNA, CO 140/40/379.

58. William Gooch to the Duke of Newcastle, May 26, 1735.

59. "Run Away from the Subscriber," *Pennsylvania Gazette*, June 18, 1767. The same ad was run again on July 2, 1767, also in the *Pennsylvania Gazette*.

60. *Butt v. Rachel and Others*, March 5, 1814, 18 Va. 209; 1814 Va. LEXIS 26; 4 Munf. 209, all LexisNexis.

61. Peter Benes, " 'A [Useful] Spanish Indian Damsel': Native Caribbean Slavery in Boston before 1770," in *New England and the Caribbean*, Proceedings of the Dublin Seminar for New England Folklife Annual 2008 (Deerfield, MA: Dublin Seminar for New England Folklife, 2008), 82.

62. "A Young Spanish Indian Woman, to be Sold," *Pennsylvania Gazette*, March 23, 1732.

63. "Run Away, on the 26th of March last," *Pennsylvania Gazette*, April 12, 1764.

64. "Run away from the Snow Lancashire Witch," *Pennsylvania Gazette*, July 9, 1741.

65. "Run away from his Master," *Daily Journal* (England), March 14, 1732, Runaway Slaves in Britain database.

66. Estimates are my own, but for a recent discussion of numbers, see Daniel Mendiola, *The Mosquito Confederation: A Borderlands History of Colonial Central America* (University of Georgia Press, 2025), 28–29.

PART THREE: TRANSITIONS (1750–1820)

1. Stefan Goodwin, *Africa in Europe: Volume Two: Interdependencies, Relocations, and Globalization* (Lexington Books, 2009), 19–20.

CHAPTER 8. EVERYDAY OPPORTUNISM

1. "Indians to be Bound," June 20, 1746, Amelia County Virginia Order Book No. 2, 1746–1751, 9, FAAC.

2. David J. Silverman, "The Impact of Indentured Servitude on the Society and Culture of Southern New England Indians, 1680–1810," *New England Quarterly* 74, no. 4 (December 1, 2001): 622–666; Ruth Wallis Herndon and Ella Wilcox Sekatau, "Colonizing the Children: Indian Youngsters in Servitude in Early New England," in *Reinterpreting New England Indians and the Colonial Experience*, ed. Colin G. Calloway and Neal Salisbury (Colonial Society of Massachusetts, 2003); John Sainsbury, "Indian Labor in Early Rhode Island," *New England Quarterly* 48 (1975): 378–393.

3. "Slavery in Pennsylvania," *Middletown Transcript*, May 22, 1897, newspapers.com.

4. Silverman, "Impact of Indentured Servitude," 643.

5. William Hand Browne, ed., *Archives of Maryland, Vol. 25: Proceedings of the Provincial Court, 1698–1731* (Maryland Historical Society, 1905), 390–391.

6. Browne, ed., *Archives of Maryland, Vol. 25*, 390–391.

7. "Brought to the Work-House," *South Carolina Gazette*, April 21, 1767.

8. New London County Court Records, County Files, Native American, Box 1, Folder 29, CSA.

9. Lauber, *Indian Slavery in Colonial Times*, 200.

10. *RCRI*, 4:361.

11. Barbara W. Brown and James M. Rose, *Black Roots in Southeastern Connecticut, 1650–1900*, Gale Genealogy and Local History Series, vol. 8 (Gale Research, 1980), 479.

12. Accomack County (VA) Order Book, 1697–1703, 244, FAAC. See also Brown and Rose, *Black Roots*, 457; New London County Court Records, Native America, November 1689, CSA.

13. Memorial of Peter Pratt, May 1721, Native Northeast Portal.

14. Silverman, "Impact of Indentured Servitude"; Herndon and Sekatau, "Colonizing the Children."

15. June 18, 1700, Massachusetts Bay General Council Meeting Minutes, TNA, CO 5/787/367. See also Petition of May 24, 1700, MSAC, 33:108.

16. *ARMB*, 4:164.

17. June 1730, Rhode Island, in *Acts and Laws, of His Majesty's Colony of Rhode-Island* (Newport, RI: Widow Franklin, 1745), 153.

18. Lauber, *Indian Slavery in Colonial Times*, 200–201.

19. January 11, 1708/9, Anne Arundel County Court Proceedings, Maryland, as cited in Roberta Estes, "Indian Slaves in Maryland and Virginia," June 27, 2012, Native Heritage Project.

20. *Georgia Colonial Laws, 17th February 1755–10th May 1770: Savannah, James Johnston, 1763–1770* (Statute Law Book Company, 1932), 248–249.

21. Brunswick County, Virginia, Will Book No. 3, with Inventories and Accounts, 1751–1769, 135, familysearch.org.

22. Hening, 4:133.

23. Decision regarding Will, April 1724, Henrico County Court Minutes, 1719–1724, 333, FAAC.

24. Hening, 5:548.

25. Inventory of the Estate of Mr. John Kent, Deced May 12, 1733. Suffolk County (Massachusetts) probate records, vol. 31, 1732–1733, 1-548l [468]. Suffolk County Courthouse. My thanks to Jared Hardesty for this reference.

26. David Alexander Sicko, "'Runagadoes' and Beloved Men: Indian Traders in the American South, 1750–1800" (PhD diss., Florida State University, 1999), 153.

27. Herndon and Sekatau, "Right to a Name"; Daniel Mandell, "Shifting Boundaries of Race and Ethnicity: Indian-Black Intermarriage in Southern New England, 1760–1880," *Journal of American History* 85, no. 2 (September 1998): 466–501; Joanne Pope Melish, *Disowning Slavery: Gradual Emancipation and "Race" in New England, 1780–1860* (Cornell University Press, 1998).

28. "Run away, on the 16th instant," *Pennsylvania Gazette*, January 24, 1749, AHN.

29. See, for example, "Run away from the subscriber," *Virginia Gazette*, April 23, 1771, and June 20, 1773.

30. Hening, 3:252.

31. Ramsey, *Yamasee War*, 166.

32. For other examples concerning the illegality of Indian enslavement, see Felt, *Ecclesiastical History of New England*, 2:418; Col. Entry Bk., vol. 110, pp. 70–71, December 8, 1676, and Col. Papers, vol. 35, Nos. 56, 56i, CSPO; *BSIC*, 1:371.

33. Crane, *Southern Frontier*, 113.

34. I am grateful to Andrés Reséndez for pushing me on this point.

35. A. J. B. Johnston, *Endgame 1758: The Promise, the Glory, and the Despair of Louisbourg's Last Decade* (University of Nebraska Press, 2007), 40.

36. "An Act to Encourage the Prosecution of the Indian Enemy and Rebels, and to Repeal an Act of the Same Title Made and Past the First Day of September 1722," passed June 1, 1723, *NHPL*, 374; *ARMB*, 2:258.

37. Robert E. Cray, *Lovewell's Fight: War, Death, and Memory in Borderland New England* (University of Massachusetts Press, 2014), 12–14.

38. "On Tuesday Last," *New-England Courant*, January 11, 1725.

39. Cray, *Lovewell's Fight*, 17.

40. "On Tuesday Last," *New-England Courant*, January 11, 1725; "On Tuesday Last," *New-England Courant*, March 15, 1725; Calloway, *Dawnland Encounters*, 167.

41. Daymond Steer, "Lovewell Monument to Be Discussed Thursday," *Conway Daily Sun*, July 17, 2023.

42. Margaret Haig Roosevelt Sewall, "Grim Commerce: Scalps, Bounties, and the Transformation of Trophy-Taking in the Early American Northeast, 1450–1770," n.d., 251–252.

43. "In the House of Representatives, June 10, 1756," MSAC, 30:730. See also "New York, June 28," *Pennsylvania Gazette*, July 1, 1756.

44. December 1754, John Ballantine Diary [manuscript], 1737–1743, 1753–1774 (unpaginated), AAS, Mss. Octavo vols. B.

45. Kristofer Ray, "Constructing a Discourse of Indigenous Slavery, Freedom and Sovereignty in Anglo-Virginia, 1600–1750," *Native South* 10 (August 1, 2017): 29.

46. *SRNC*, 23:517.

47. *Newport Mercury*, March 25, 1760.

48. David Dixon, *Never Come to Peace Again: Pontiac's Uprising and the Fate of the British Empire in North America*, repr. ed. (University of Oklahoma Press, 2014), 136–137.

49. *MPCP*, 9:188–189.

50. Gregory Evans Dowd, *War under Heaven: Pontiac, the Indian Nations and the British Empire* (Johns Hopkins University Press, 2002), 78.

51. Peter R. Silver, *Our Savage Neighbors: How Indian War Transformed Early America* (W. W. Norton, 2008), 83.

52. I am grateful to Anjali DasSarma for her insights regarding the complicity of the newspaper industry.

53. "Ran away from Capt. John Aldin," *Boston News-Letter*, June 19, 1704, 2, AHN.

54. See, for example, "Run away from the Subscriber," *South-Carolina Gazette*, December 7, 1747; Stolen Relations project.

55. For a more in-depth analysis, see Anjali DasSarma and Linford D. Fisher, "The Persistence of Indigenous Unfreedom in Early American Newspaper Advertisements, 1704–1804," *Slavery & Abolition* 44, no. 2 (March 30, 2023): 267–291.

56. DasSarma and Fisher, "Persistence," 271.

57. Craven County, North Carolina, April 2, 1765, Book 2, 472, Digital Library on American Slavery, NC.CRA.2.472.1.

58. Hening, 4:104; *JCCAS*, 1:71.

59. Samuel Hopkins, *Historical Memoirs, Relating to the Housatunnuk Indians* (Boston: S. Kneeland, 1753), 19.

60. C. Hale Sipe, *The Indian Wars of Pennsylvania* (Telegraph Press, 1929), 136.

61. See, for example, John Stewart's deed to Hugh Agnew, August 2, 1701, RB 3/3, 196–199, BDA (see p. 199 for the inventory). The deed and inventory are largely repeated on pp. 202–204, with the same parallel method of recording names occurring on p. 204. (The name of Jack, the enslaved Indigenous person, is also repeated.)

62. *New England Weekly Journal*, August 30, 1731.

63. Chesterfield County Court Order Book, 1767–1771, 10, FAAC.

64. Louis Bond Mason, *The Life and Times of Major John Mason of Connecticut, 1600–1672* (Putnam, 1935), 145.

65. Malcolm Gaskill, *Between Two Worlds: How the English Became Americans* (Basic Books, 2014), 342.

66. Entry for May 4, 1711, in Samuel Sewall, *Diary of Samuel Sewall* (Massachusetts Historical Society, 1879), 2:308.

67. Lord Cornbury to the Board of Trade, February 10, 1707/8, DRCNY, 5:39; Junius P. Rodriguez, *Encyclopedia of Slave Resistance and Rebellion* (Greenwood, 2007), 1:352.

68. Edwin Hoey, "Terror in New York—1741," *American Heritage* 25, no. 4 (June 1974). See also Lord Cornbury to the Board of Trade, February 10, 1707/8, DRCNY, 5:39.

69. Andrea C. Mosterman, *Spaces of Enslavement: A History of Slavery and Resistance in Dutch New York*, New Netherland Institute Studies (Cornell University Press, 2021), 89.

70. Anne-Claire Faucquez, "'A Bloody Conspiracy': Race, Power and Religion in New York's 1712 Slave Insurrection," in *Fear and the Shaping of Early American Societies* (Brill, 2016), 204; DRCNY, 5:341–342.

71. Robert Hunter to the Board of Trade, June 23, 1712, DRCNY, 5:341–342.

72. Martha McCartney, *A Study of the Africans and African Americans on Jamestown Island and at Green Spring, 1619–1803* (Colonial Williamsburg Foundation and the National Parks Service, 2003), 114.

73. Lawrence Shaw Mayo, "Thomas Hutchinson and His 'History of Massachusetts-Bay,'" *PAAS*, October 1931, 331.

74. Thomas Hutchinson, *The History of the Colony of Massachusetts Bay*, 2nd ed. (London: M. Richardson, 1765), 1:283.

Chapter 9. A King's Proclamation

1. David Eltis, "A Brief Overview of the Trans-Atlantic Slave Trade: The Middle Passage," Slave Voyages website.

2. Estimates from the Slave Voyages website, slavevoyages.org. See also Trevor Burnard, "Plantation Slavery in the British Caribbean," in *The Palgrave Handbook of Global Slavery throughout History*, ed. Damian A. Pargas and Juliane Schiel (Springer International, 2023), 401; J. David Hacker, "From '20. and Odd' to 10 Million: The Growth of the Slave Population in the United States," *Slavery & Abolition* 41, no. 4 (October 1, 2020): 840–855.

3. TNA, T 1/527/148–149b. Alden Vaughan mentions this visit, but his sources omit the most important details. Vaughan, *Transatlantic Encounters*, 219–220.

4. "A Proclamation, By the King," November 29, 1775, TNA, CO 123/31/15.

5. George, Isaac, Richard, and John to Lord Dartmouth, November 10, 1775, *Calendar of Home Office Papers of the reign of George II: 1760–1775* (London: Longman & Co. and Tribner), 4:460.

6. Benton Sturges, "Dissensions in the American Churches over the Slavery Question; Especially as Illustrated in the Presbyterian and Methodist Episcopal Denominations," *Technology Quarterly* 4 (1891): 79.

7. "Slavery in Pennsylvania," *Middletown Transcript*, May 22, 1897, newspapers.com.

8. Samuel Sewall, *The Selling of Joseph*, Electronic Texts in American Studies, 26 (1700).

9. Board of Trade and Plantation to the Governor and Deputies of Carolina, September 30, 1713, TNA, CO 5/288/16.

10. Fisher, " 'Spanish Indian Squaw,' " 84.

11. *Robin v. Hardaway* (1772), in Thomas Jefferson, *Reports of Cases Determined in the General Court of Virginia* (Charlottesville: F. Carr, 1829), 116.

12. Kingston Registry of Free Persons, 1761–1795, JA, 2/6/277, 11.

13. John Wesley, *Thoughts upon Slavery* (London, 1774); Anthony Benezet and Capel Lofft, *Some Historical Account of Guinea* (London: J. Phillips, 1788).

14. Kevin Bales and Zoe Trodd, eds., *The Antislavery Usable Past* (Rights Lab, 2020), 123; Cheryl Finley, *Committed to Memory: The Art of the Slave Ship Icon* (Princeton University Press, 2018), 38.

15. Granville Sharp, *A Representation of the Injustice and Dangerous Tendency of Tolerating Slavery* (London: Benjamin White and Robert Horsfield, 1769).

16. Ruth Paley, "William Blackstone, Granville Sharp and the Case of Jonathan Strong," *Archives: The Journal of the British Records Association* 53, no. 137 (September 2018): 68–79.

17. Sharp, *Representation*, 46–57.

18. Gretchen Gerzina, *Black London: Life before Emancipation*, repr. ed. (Rutgers University Press, 1995), 33.

19. Steven M. Wise, *Though the Heavens May Fall: The Landmark Trial That Led to the End of Human Slavery* (Pimlico, 2006), 194–195.

20. "To be Sold, a very likely Indian Boy and Girl," *South Carolina Gazette*, September 6, 1773. The advertisement is repeated two additional times that same month.

21. Prince Hoare, ed., *Memoirs of Granville Sharp, Esq.* (London: Henry Colburn, 1820), 78–79.

22. Sharp, *Representation*, 146.

23. Hoare, *Memoirs of Granville Sharp*, 248.

24. *Robin v. Hardaway* (1772), in Jefferson, *Reports of Cases*, 109; Honor Sachs, "'Freedom by a Judgment': The Legal History of an Afro-Indian Family," *Law and History Review* 30, no. 1 (February 2012): 175.

25. Sachs, "'Freedom by a Judgment,'" 180.

26. Gregory Ablavsky, "Making Indians 'White': The Judicial Abolition of Native Slavery in Revolutionary Virginia and Its Racial Legacy," *University of Pennsylvania Law Review* 159, no. 5 (2011): 1457–1531; Kristofer Ray, "'The Indians of Every Denomination Were Free, and Independent of Us': Anglo-Virginian Explorations of Indigenous Slavery, Freedom, and Society, 1772–1830," *American Nineteenth Century History* 17, no. 2 (May 3, 2016): 139–159.

27. Sachs, "'Freedom by a Judgment,'" 183.

28. Ray, "Constructing a Discourse," 20.

29. Ray, "Constructing a Discourse," 20.

30. Sachs, "'Freedom by a Judgment,'" 188.

31. "Run away from the Subscriber, in Cumberland," *Virginia Gazette*, December 3, 1772.

32. "Run away from the Subscriber," *Virginia Gazette*, July 15, 1773.

33. Ablavsky, "Making Indians 'White.'"

34. James Lawrie to Basil Keith, January 28, 1777, TNA, CO 137/72/100.

35. James Lawrie to Basil Keith, January 28, 1777.

36. James Lawrie to Basil Keith, January 27, 1777, TNA, CO 137/72/98b. For Native slavery as an "inhuman trade," see James Lawrie to Lord Germain, May 28, 1777, TNA, CO 137/72/147.

37. For a copy of the 1776 law, see *The Defence of the Settlers of Honduras* (Jamaica: A. Aikman, Jun. 1824), 84–85.

38. "Return of the Registry of Indians on the Mosquito Shore in the year 1777," TNA, CO 123/31/123–132. See also *Slaves at Honduras*, 54–57.

39. TNA, T 1/527/148–149b.

40. "Return of the Registry of Indians on the Mosquito Shore in the year 1777," TNA, CO 123/31/124.

41. "Return of the Registry of Indians on the Mosquito Shore in the year 1777," TNA, CO 123/31/130.

42. Kirsten Sword, "Remembering Dinah Nevil: Strategic Deceptions in Eighteenth-Century Antislavery," *Journal of American History* 97, no. 2 (2010): 320–321.

43. Thomas Harmon, "To the Committee Appointed . . . ," no date (ca. 1780), PASP, 1748–1987, Collection 0490, Series II, Correspondence, Box 14, Folder 11.

44. Harmon, "To the Committee Appointed." Thanks to Scott Heerman for this document. See also Sword, "Remembering Dinah Nevil"; Dee E. Andrews, "Reconsidering the First Emancipation: Evidence from the Pennsylvania Abolition Society Correspondence, 1785–1810," *Pennsylvania History: A Journal of Mid-Atlantic Studies* 64 (1997): 230–249.

45. Harmon, "To the Committee Appointed."

46. Jeremiah Paul, *The Manumission of Dinah Nevill*, 1795, Milwaukee Art

Museum. My thanks to Kathleen Foster for alerting me to this painting's existence.

47. Virginia Raguin, "What the Statue of a Kneeling Enslaved Man in the Emancipation Memorial of 1876 Tells Us about Its History: An Art Historian Explains," *Conversation*, June 6, 2024.

48. "An act to explain and amend an act entitled, 'An act for recovering and extending the trade with the Indian settlements in America, and preventing for the future some evil practices formerly committed in that trade,'" TNA, CO 123/31/120–121. See also *The Laws of Jamaica: 1760–1792* (London: A. Aikman, 1802), 216–217.

49. James Lawrie to Basil Keith, January 27, 1777, TNA, CO 137/72/97–98; Lawrie to Lord George Germain, May 28, 1777, TNA, CO 137/72/148.

50. James Lawrie to Lord Germain, May 28, 1777.

51. Order of Colvil Briton, November 29, 1776, TNA, CO 123/31/17.

52. Order of Colvil Briton.

53. Letter from Colvill Cairns, April 3, 1777, TNA, CO 137/72/172.

54. General Congress with the Miskito Indians, October 1, 1780, TNA, CO 137/79/164b–165.

55. Olaudah Equiano, *The Interesting Narrative of the Life of Olaudah Equiano* (Norwich, 1794), 303–307, ProQuest.

Chapter 10. Revolutionary *Rage* Contre-Indienne

1. United States Congress, *Congressional Record: Proceedings and Debates of the 83rd Congress* (US Government Printing Office, 1953), A37. For the number of military volunteers, see Barnett Abraham Elzas, *The Jews of South Carolina: From the Earliest Times to the Present Day* (J. B. Lippincott, 1905), 75.

2. William H. Drayton to Francis Salvador, July 24, 1776, in Robert W. Gibbes, ed., *Documentary History of the American Revolution* (New York: D. Appleton, 1857), 29.

3. Elzas, *Jews of South Carolina*, 75.

4. Charles Royster, *A Revolutionary People at War: The Continental Army and American Character, 1775–1783* (University of North Carolina Press, 1979), 25; Robert G. Parkinson, *The Common Cause: Creating Race and Nation in the American Revolution*, 1st ed. (Omohundro Institute and University of North Carolina Press, 2016), 326.

5. Tom Hatley, *The Dividing Paths: Cherokees and South Carolinians through the Era of Revolution* (Oxford University Press, 1993), 193.

6. Jeffrey Ostler, *Surviving Genocide: Native Nations and the United States from the American Revolution to Bleeding Kansas* (Yale University Press, 2019), 49.

7. Ostler, *Surviving Genocide*, 53; Colin G. Calloway, *The Indian World of George Washington: The First President, the First Americans, and the Birth of the Nation*, illus. ed. (Oxford University Press, 2018), chap. 8.

8. "Petitions of the Early Inhabitants of Kentucky to the General Assembly of Virginia, 1769–1792," Cincinnati and Hamilton Public Library (online).

9. Ostler, *Surviving Genocide*, 50.

10. Lord Dunmore to John Conolly, June 20, 1774, in Peter Force, *American Archives: A Documentary History of the English Colonies in North America*, vol. 1, ser. 4 (Washington, DC: M. St. Clair Clarke and Peter Force, 1837), 473. See also Ostler, *Surviving Genocide*, 51.

11. Ostler, *Surviving Genocide*, 51–52.

12. Meredith Mason Brown, *Frontiersman: Daniel Boone and the Making of America* (Louisiana State University Press, 2008), 71.

13. Henry Wadsworth Longfellow, "Paul Revere's Ride," Paul Revere House.

14. "Lord Dunmore's Proclamation," 1775, Gilder Lehrman Institute of American History.

15. Maya Jasanoff, *Liberty's Exiles: American Loyalists in the Revolutionary World*, 1st ed. (Alfred A. Knopf, 2011), 8.

16. "Run away from the subscriber," *Virginia Gazette*, January 6, 1776.

17. *JCSV*, 1:47.

18. James Creswell to W. H. Drayton, July 27, 1776, in Gibbes, *Documentary History of the American Revolution*, 30.

19. A. Williamson to ?, July 22, 1776, in Gibbes, *Documentary History of the American Revolution*, 26.

20. "Declaration of Independence: A Transcription," NARA.

21. Ostler, *Surviving Genocide*, 55.

22. A. Williamson to ?, July 22, 1776, in Gibbes, *Documentary History of the American Revolution*, 27.

23. James Creswell to W. H. Drayton, July 27, 1776, in Gibbes, *Documentary History of the American Revolution*, 31.

24. Ostler, *Surviving Genocide*, 55.

25. See, for example, A. Williamson to William H. Drayton, August 22, 1776, in Gibbes, *Documentary History of the American Revolution*, 32.

26. *JCSV*, 1:82, 102, 133.

27. Lord George Germain to John Stuart, November 6, 1776, in William Laurence Saunders, ed., *CRNC* (Raleigh: P. M. Hale, 1886), 10:894.

28. Henry J. Young, "A Note on Scalp Bounties in Pennsylvania A," *Pennsylvania History: A Journal of Mid-Atlantic Studies* 24, no. 3 (1957): 214. This was in paper currency, which was valued lower compared to pounds sterling.

29. Hatley, *Dividing Paths*, 193.

30. Saunders, ed., *CRNC*, 10:896.

31. Saunders, ed., *CRNC*, 10:897.

32. Christina Snyder, "Andrew Jackson's Indian Son: Native Captives and American Empire," in *The Native South* (University of Nebraska Press, 2017), 86.

33. Snyder, "Andrew Jackson's Indian Son," 87.

34. Sanford Richard Winston, *Indian Slavery in the Carolina Region* (Association for the Study of Negro Life and History, 1934), 434.

35. Snyder, "Andrew Jackson's Indian Son," 86–87; Tiya Miles, "The Narrative of Nancy, a Cherokee Woman," *Frontiers: A Journal of Women Studies* 29, no. 2/3 (2008): 59–80.

36. Snyder, "Andrew Jackson's Indian Son," 87.

37. Wesley D. White Papers, Box 28/838, no. 18: Indian Slavery in North Carolina, 1690–1862, 29, SCHS.

38. Snyder, "Andrew Jackson's Indian Son," 87.

39. Ostler, *Surviving Genocide*, 61.

40. As quoted in Rhiannon Koehler, "Hostile Nations: Quantifying the Destruction of the Sullivan-Clinton Genocide of 1779," *American Indian Quarterly* 42, no. 4 (2018): 433.

41. For a detailed account of this campaign, see Max M. Mintz, *The Seeds of Empire: The American Revolutionary Conquest of the Iroquois* (New York University Press, 2001); Koehler, "Hostile Nations," 445.

42. Calloway, *Indian World of George Washington*, 256.

43. Earl P. Olmstead, *David Zeisberger: A Life among the Indians* (Kent State University Press, 1997), 334.

44. Olmstead, *David Zeisberger*, 334.

45. Olmstead, *David Zeisberger*, 335.

46. The details of this case come from "The Pennsylvania Abolition Society, Committee of Correspondence, Letter Book, 1794–1809," HSP. Thanks to Edward Andrews for this research tip and to Scott Heerman for copies of the documents.

47. William Weaver's testimony before the PAS, 1793, "The Pennsylvania Abolition Society, Acting Committee, Minutes, 1789–1797," 255, HSP. I am grateful to Scott Heerman for this and other Fry-related documents from the HSP.

48. Pennsylvania Abolition Society chairman James Pendleton noted in 1796 that he had first written to Rhode Island in 1793. The card catalog at the HSP indicates a letter on January 29, 1793, outlining the details of Fry's case. My thanks to Edward Andrews and Scott Heerman for their information and assistance.

49. James Pemberton to the Providence Society for Promoting the Abolition of Slavery, July 5, 1796, "The Pennsylvania Abolition Society, Committee of Correspondence, Letter Book, 1794–1809," HSP. The founding constitution of this society can be found in *Constitution of a Society for Abolishing the Slave-Trade* (Providence: John Carter, 1789).

50. Samuel Coates to William Weaver and Ebenezer Eddy, November 30, 1795, "The Pennsylvania Abolition Society, Committee of Correspondence, Letter Book, 1794–1809," HSP.

51. See a series of exchanges in "The Pennsylvania Abolition Society, Committee of Correspondence, Letter Book, 1794–1809," HSP.

52. Robert A. Geake and Lorén M Spears, *From Slaves to Soldiers: The 1st Rhode Island Regiment in the American Revolution* (Westholme, 2016), 39–40, 42.

53. Geake and Spears, *From Slaves to Soldiers*, 39–40, 42, 80–81.

54. Geake and Spears, *From Slaves to Soldiers*, 116.

55. "Five Pounds Reward," *New York Packet*, June 17, 1794, AHN.

56. Jasanoff, *Liberty's Exiles*, 9, 358.

57. "A Return of the American Loyalist & the number of Negro Slaves their Property now on the Mosquito Shore," TNA, CO 137/86/168.

58. Frank Griffith Dawson, "The Evacuation of the Mosquito Shore and the English Who Stayed Behind, 1786–1800," *The Americas* 55, no. 1 (1998): 66–68.

59. Dawson, "William Pitt's Settlement at Black River," 703.

60. *Slaves at Honduras*, 64.

61. "The Virginia Declaration of Rights," NARA.

62. "Articles of Confederation (1777)," NARA.

63. Christy Clark-Pujara, *Dark Work: The Business of Slavery in Rhode Island* (New York University Press, 2016), 61–62.

64. Melish, *Disowning Slavery*, chap. 3.

65. "Pennsylvania—An Act for the Gradual Abolition of Slavery, 1780," Avalon Project, Yale University.

66. Rhode Island, General Assembly, "Manumission Act, 1784," in Virtual Exhibits, Item #71, Rhode Island Virtual Archives.

67. Melish, *Disowning Slavery*; Francis Newton Thorpe, "Constitution of Vermont: July 8, 1777" (Government Printing Office, 1909; repr. December 18, 1998), 1777.

68. Margot Minardi, *Making Slavery History: Abolitionism and the Politics of Memory in Massachusetts* (Oxford University Press, 2010), 6–7; Melish, *Disowning Slavery*, xiii.

69. Melish, *Disowning Slavery*, 67.

70. Isaac Cruikshank, "The Gradual Abolition of the Slave Trade or Leaving of Sugar by Degrees," cartoon image, Prints and Photographs Division, LOC.

71. Cory Young, "A Just and True Return: Pennsylvania's Surviving County Slave Registries, 1780–1826," *Journal of Slavery and Data Preservation* 3, no. 1 (2022).

72. "Slavery in Pennsylvania," *Middletown Transcript*, May 22, 1897, newspapers.com.

73. Young, "A Just and True Return."

74. Seth Rockman, *Plantation Goods: A Material History of American Slavery* (University of Chicago Press, 2024); Clark-Pujara, *Dark Work*.

75. *SRNC*, 17:583.

76. *SRNC*, 18:796.

77. *SRNC*, 21:528.

78. *TPUS*, 4:305.

79. *Historical Collections: Collections and Researches of the Michigan Pioneer and Historical Society*, vol. 38 (State Printers, 1912), 142, 444; Melanie Fernandes, "'Under the Auspices of Peace': The Northwest Indian War and Its Impact on the Early American Republic," *Gettysburg Historical Journal* 15, no. 1 (2015), 175–176; Colin Calloway, *The Victory with No Name: The Native American Defeat of the First American Army* (Oxford University Press, 2014), 3.

80. Northwest Ordinance, July 13, 1787, Avalon Project, Yale University.

81. Northwest Ordinance, July 13, 1787.

82. Paul Finkelman, "Evading the Ordinance: The Persistence of Bondage in Indiana and Illinois," *Journal of the Early Republic* 9, no. 1 (1989): 22–23; Tiya Miles, *The Dawn of Detroit: A Chronicle of Slavery and Freedom in the City of the Straits* (New Press, 2017), 100; M. Scott Heerman, *The Alchemy of Slavery: Human Bondage and Emancipation in the Illinois Country, 1730–1865* (University of Pennsylvania Press, 2018), 3.

83. Miles, *Dawn of Detroit*, 120. For higher figures, see Marcel Trudel, *Canada's Forgotten Slaves: Two Hundred Years of Bondage*, trans. George Tombs, 1st ed. (Véhicule Press, 2013), 75, 83.

84. *Bermuda Gazette*, July 18, 1789 (also called *Royal Gazette*).

85. An Act for the Abolition of the Slave Trade, March 25, 1807, Public General Act, 47 George II session 1, c. 36, UK Parliamentary Archives.

86. "An Act to Prohibit the Importation of Slaves into Any Port or Place within the Jurisdiction of the United States, from and after the First Day of January, in the

Year of Our Lord, One Thousand Eight Hundred and Eight . . . March 2, 1810. Approved.," Rare Books and Special Collections Division, LOC.

87. *Constitution of a Society for Abolishing the Slave-Trade*, 12–19.

88. I'm grateful to Vikram Tamboli for pushing me on this point.

89. John Daly to [royal officials], February 20, 1811, TNA, CO 111/14/48.

90. David Head, "Slave Smuggling by Foreign Privateers: The Illegal Slave Trade and the Geopolitics of the Early Republic," *Journal of the Early Republic* 33, no. 3 (2013): 433–462; John Harris, *The Last Slave Ships: New York and the End of the Middle Passage* (Yale University Press, 2020).

CHAPTER 11. A SURGE OF FREEDOM

1. See, for example, Kimberly M. Welch, *Black Litigants in the Antebellum American South*, illus. ed. (University of North Carolina Press, 2018); Loren Schweninger, *Appealing for Liberty: Freedom Suits in the South* (Oxford University Press, 2018).

2. Some exceptions are Ablavsky, "Making Indians 'White'"; Sachs, "'Freedom by a Judgment.'"

3. Scholars have used this term more broadly. See, for example, Seán Patrick Eudaily, *The Present Politics of the Past: Indigenous Legal Activism and Resistance to (Neo)Liberal Governmentality*, 1st ed. (Routledge, 2004).

4. *Butt v. Rachel and Others*, Supreme Court of Virginia, March 15, 1814, 18 Va. 209 (Va. 1814), Nexis Uni.

5. Regarding the complexity of racial self-identification, see Martha Hodes, "The Mercurial Nature and Abiding Power of Race: A Transnational Family Story," *American Historical Review* 108, no. 1 (2003): 84–118.

6. *Abraham Vaughn v. Phebe*, January 1827, Supreme Court of Tennessee, Nashville, 8 Tenn. 5, Nexis Uni.

7. Jill Lepore, *These Truths: A History of the United States*, 1st ed. (W. W. Norton, 2018), 112.

8. Schweninger, *Appealing for Liberty*, 229–230.

9. The details of this case are drawn from *PRSC*, 7:225–227, 8:76–79.

10. Details of this case are drawn from *State v. Van Waggoner*, April 1797, New Jersey Supreme Court, 6 N.J.L. 374, Nexis Uni.

11. "20 Dollars Reward," *Centinel of Freedom* (Newark, NJ), September 1, 1801, New Jersey Slavery Records.

12. *State v. Van Waggoner*.

13. *State v. Van Waggoner*.

14. Thomas Jefferson to Francis C. Gray, March 4, 1815, in Thomas Jefferson, *The Papers of Thomas Jefferson, Retirement Series, Vol. 8: 1 October 1814 to 31 August 1815*, ed. J. Jefferson Looney (Princeton University Press, 2012), 310.

15. *Hudgins v. Wrights*, Supreme Court of Virginia, 11 Va. 134, 1806 Va. Lexis 58, 1 Hen. & M. 134, Lexis Nexis. See also "Supreme Court of Appeals: Hudgins *against* Wrights," *Virginia Argus* (Richmond), January 30, 1807, 4.

16. The details of this case are taken from *Walkup v. Pratt*, Court of Appeals of Maryland, Eastern Shore, 5H. & J. 51, 1820 Md. Lexis 7, June Term, 1820, Decided.

17. Samuel Want, J. Mercer Garnett Jr., and Daniel List Warner, *Maryland Digest Annotated* (M. Curlander, 1917), 5511.

18. American leaders—including Thomas Jefferson—notoriously misunderstood and underestimated the number of Native Americans in the region.

19. Kathleen DuVal, *The Native Ground: Indians and Colonists in the Heart of the Continent* (University of Pennsylvania Press, 2007); Daniel Usner, *Indians, Settlers, and Slaves in a Frontier Exchange Economy: The Lower Mississippi Valley before 1783* (University of North Carolina Press, 1992); Robert P. Wiegers, "A Proposal for Indian Slave Trading in the Mississippi Valley and Its Impact on the Osage," *Plains Anthropologist*, 33, no. 120 (1998).

20. Stephen Webre, "The Problem of Indian Slavery in Spanish Louisiana, 1769–1803," *Louisiana History: The Journal of the Louisiana Historical Association* 25, no. 2 (1984): 130–131.

21. Leila K. Blackbird, " 'It Has Always Been Customary to Make Slaves of Savages': The Problem of Indian Slavery in Spanish Louisiana Revisited, 1769–1803," *William and Mary Quarterly* 80, no. 3 (2023): 525–558.

22. The details in this case are drawn from *Seville v. Chretien*, Supreme Court of Louisiana, Western District, September 1817, 5 Mart. (o.s.) 275, 1817 LA Lexis 61; Wheeler, *Practical Treatise*, 12–17.

23. *Seville v. Chretien*; Wheeler, *Practical Treatise*, 17.

24. *Seville v. Chretien*; Wheeler, *Practical Treatise*, 16–17.

25. *Slaves at Honduras*, 4–5.

26. George Henderson, *An Account of the British Settlement of Honduras* (London: R. Baldwin, 1811), 15–20.

27. Dawson, "William Pitt's Settlement at Black River," 703.

28. B. W. Higman, *Slave Populations of the British Caribbean, 1807–1834* (University of the West Indies Press, 1995), 417. See also Henderson, *Account of the British Settlement of Honduras*, 85. (Henderson gives much lower estimates.)

29. *The New Act of Assembly of the Island of Jamaica* (London, 1789).

30. *Slaves at Honduras*, 4–5.

31. *Slaves at Honduras*, 12–18.

32. For two recent articles that also analyze these cases, see Nathaniel Millett, "Law, Lineage, Gender, and the Lives of Enslaved Indigenous People on the Edge of the Nineteenth-Century Caribbean," *William and Mary Quarterly* 78, no. 4 (October 2021): 687–720; Rajeshwari Dutt, "Emancipation and Imperialism in a Borderland: The Challenge to Settler Sovereignty over Slavery in Belize in the 1820s," *Americas* 80, no. 1 (January 2023): 1–31.

33. George Arthur to William Burge, November 26, 1821, in *Slaves at Honduras*, 20.

34. Return of Slaves, St. James Parish, 1824 1b/11/7/65/75 JA. I am grateful to Scott Heerman for providing a copy of this document.

35. *Slave Population, HCCP 347* (London: House of Commons, 1823), 133.

36. Letter from William Burge to George Arthur, TNA, CO 123/31/84–85.

37. Letter from George Arthur, February 28, 1822, TNA, CO 123/31/80.

38. Proclamation of George Arthur, January 10, 1822, in *Slaves at Honduras*, 24.

39. See, for example, the responses to the Commissioners of Legal Inquiry from St. Vincent and Dominica, 1826, TNA, CO 318/62 (unpaginated), as well as the responses from Demerara, Essequebo, and Berbice, 1828, TNA, CO 318/72/31–34.

40. Many of the petitions can be found at TNA, CO 123/31 (throughout). They have also mostly been reproduced in *Slaves at Honduras*.

41. *Slaves at Honduras*, 59.

42. *Slaves at Honduras*, 60.

43. TNA, CO 123/31/101v–106.

44. Isabella family genealogy, TNA, CO 123/31/181; *Slaves at Honduras*, 61–62.

45. Proclamation of George Arthur, January 10, 1821, in *Slaves at Honduras*, 24.

46. "Slavery: Condition and Treatment of Slaves at Honduras," *Times* (London), September 29, 1823, 3.

47. "Slaves at Honduras," *Aberdeen Journal*, July 23, 1823, 2.

48. *Defence of the Settlers of Honduras*. See also TNA, CO 123/35.

49. John Armstrong, *A Candid Examination of "The Defence of the Settlers of Honduras"* (London: J. Butterworth and Son and J. Hatchard and Son, 1824).

50. "Report of the Commissioners of Legal Inquiry on the Case of the Indians at Honduras," in *Papers Relating to the Slave Trade*, vol. 2 (1828), 3, House of Commons Papers, sess. 1828, vol. 26, paper 522. See also "Report of the Commissioners of Legal Inquiry on the Case of the Indians in Honduras," TNA, CO 318/67. I am thankful to Heather Sanford for these references.

51. "Report of the Commissioners of Legal Inquiry," 2:8.

52. *Returns Relating to Claims to Freedom by Descendants of Native Indians at Honduras*, vol. 21, House of Commons Parliamentary Papers 583 (London, 1830), 5.

53. *Returns Relating to Claims to Freedom*, 21:2–3.

54. Tom Zoellner, *Island on Fire: The Revolt That Ended Slavery in the British Empire* (Harvard University Press, 2020); David B. Davis, "James Cropper and the British Anti-Slavery Movement, 1823–1833," *Journal of Negro History* 46, no. 3 (July 1961): 154–173.

55. J. R. Ward, *British West Indian Slavery, 1750–1834: The Process of Amelioration* (Oxford: Clarendon, 1988), 233–235; Madhavi Kale, *Fragments of Empire: Capital, Slavery, and Indian Indentured Labor Migration in the British Caribbean* (University of Pennsylvania Press, 1998), 1, 7.

56. St. George's Parish Records, ANG/SG/PV-8/428, BMDA.

57. See, for example, the Barbados slave registry from 1834, TNA T 71/553/1.

58. Barbados slave registry, 1834, TNA T 71/556/25, 68.

59. Slave Registers, 1834, BMDA, RS/01/104.

60. Susette Harriet Lloyd, *Sketches of Bermuda* (London: James Cochrane, 1835), 98.

61. "Alarming Conspiracy!!" *Newbern Sentinel*, May 3, 1833, 1.

62. Kenneth Milton Stampp, *The Peculiar Institution: Slavery in the Ante-bellum South* (Vintage Books, 1656).

63. *Marguerite v. Chouteau*, in *Reports of Cases Argued and Determined in the Supreme Court of the State of Missouri* (E. W. Stephens, 1870), 3:286–303.

64. *Catiche and others v. The Circuit Court of St. Louis County*, 1828, in *Reports of Cases Argued and Determined*, 1:330–333. See also *Little v. Chauvin*, May 1828, JCCAS, 5:126–128.

65. *Marguerite v. Chouteau*, in *Reports of Cases*, 3:286–303; *Pierre Choteau, senior v. Marguerite, a woman of colour*, March 6, 1838, 37 U.S. 507, 9 L. Ed. 1174, 1838 U.S. LEXIS 368.

66. *Gregory v. Baugh*, February 14, 1827, Supreme Court of Virginia, 25 Va. 611, 1827 Va. LEXIS 4, 4 Rand. 611.

67. Wheeler, *Practical Treatise*, 400–401.

Part Four: Resurgence (1820–1880)

1. *Johnson v. M'Intosh*, US Supreme Court, 21 U.S. 543 (1823); Robert J. Miller et al., *Discovering Indigenous Lands: The Doctrine of Discovery in the English Colonies* (Oxford University Press, 2010), 3–4; 86–88.

2. Tim Alan Garrison, *The Legal Ideology of Removal: The Southern Judiciary and the Sovereignty of Native American Nations* (University of Georgia Press, 2009), 4, 268.

Chapter 12. Removals and Plantations

1. Kennedy, *Population of the United States in 1860*, ix.

2. Edward E. Baptist, *The Half Has Never Been Told: Slavery and the Making of American Capitalism*, 1st ed. (Basic Books, 2014); Rockman, *Plantation Goods*.

3. Baptist, *Half Has Never Been Told*, xxiii.

4. Joseph C. G. Kennedy, *Preliminary Report on the Eighth Census, 1860* (Washington, DC: Government Printing Office, 1862), 131.

5. This number is an estimate based on my reading of a wide array of sources in the period between 1750 and 1865, which give a deeper sense of patterns, intermarriage, and erasure. Court cases, newspaper advertisements, freedom suits, oral histories, family histories, and some later surveys all point toward a much larger Indigenous presence on plantations in the American South than most current histories account for.

6. Melville J. Herskovits, *The American Negro: A Study in Racial Crossing* (A. A. Knopf, 1928), 9. See also Tiya Miles, "Uncle Tom Was an Indian: Tracing the Red in Black Slavery," in *Confounding the Color Line: The Indian-Black Experience in North America*, ed. James Brookes (University of Nebraska Press, 2002), 145; Leonard Bloom, "Role of the Indian in the Race Relations Complex of the South," *Social Forces* 19, no. 2 (1940): 268–273.

7. Riviana Boynton interview, in *FWP*, Vol. 3: Florida (1936), 367.

8. For a thoughtful essay on these racially intertwined identities, see Robert Keith Collins, "How Africans Met Native Americans during Slavery," *Contexts* 19, no. 3 (August 1, 2020): 16–21.

9. Leila K. Blackbird, "Entwined Threads of Red and Black: The Hidden History of Indigenous Enslavement in Louisiana, 1699–1824" (MA thesis, University of New Orleans, 2018), 74–76.

10. Sophie Belle interview, *FWP*, Vol. 2: Arkansas, Part 1 (1936), 139.

11. For a discussion of the damage done by the racialization of Native Americans, see Kim TallBear, *Native American DNA: Tribal Belonging and the False Promise of Genetic Science* (University of Minnesota Press, 2013), 31–33.

12. Gary Clayton Anderson, "The Native Peoples of the American West: Genocide

or Ethnic Cleansing?" *Western Historical Quarterly* 47, no. 4 (November 1, 2016): 416.

13. Theda Perdue, *The Cherokees: Indians of North America*, heritage ed. (Chelsea House Publishers, 2005), 36–40.

14. Joshua D. Rothman, *The Ledger and the Chain: How Domestic Slave Traders Shaped America* (Basic Books, 2021), 104–105; Claudio Saunt, *Unworthy Republic: The Dispossession of Native Americans and the Road to Indian Territory*, repr. ed. (W. W. Norton, 2021), xv.

15. Baptist, *Half Has Never Been Told*, 68.

16. Robert Vincent Remini, *Andrew Jackson and His Indian Wars* (Viking, 2001), 196.

17. *Worcester v. Georgia*, US Supreme Court, 31 U.S. (6 Pet.) 515 (1832); Remini, *Andrew Jackson*, 255–258.

18. John T. Ellisor, *The Second Creek War: Interethnic Conflict and Collusion on a Collapsing Frontier* (University of Nebraska Press, 2010), 293–294.

19. Green Beauchamp, "Early Chronicles of Barbour County," *Alabama Historical Quarterly* 33, no. 1 (1971): 57–58; Ellisor, *Second Creek War*, 369–370, 423.

20. Ellisor, *Second Creek War*, 119.

21. Ellisor, *Second Creek War*, 427.

22. Chaney Mack interview, in Patrick Minges, *Black Indian Slave Narratives* (John F. Blair, 2013), 152.

23. Ellisor, *Second Creek War*, 427.

24. Ellisor, *Second Creek War*, 427.

25. Ellisor, *Second Creek War*, 428.

26. Beauchamp, "Early Chronicles of Barbour County," 58; Ellisor, *Second Creek War*, 425.

27. Letter of K. B. Gibbs, May 24, 1838, from St. Augustine, "Reports and Lists of Indians and Negroes" folder, Record Group 92: Records of the Quartermaster General, Brigadier General Thomas S. Jesup, NARA.

28. Letter of Thomas S. Jesup, May 8, 1838, from St. Augustine, Record Group 92: Records of the Quartermaster General, Brigadier General Thomas S. Jesup. Folder: 105377-013-0424, NARA.

29. William G. McLoughlin, *After the Trail of Tears: The Cherokees' Struggle for Sovereignty, 1839–1880* (University of North Carolina Press, 1993), 7. Anderson cites ten thousand for all removal fatalities, in "Native Peoples of the American West," 416.

30. Anderson, "Native Peoples of the American West," 416; Saunt, *Unworthy Republic*, xiii; John P. Bowes, *Land Too Good for Indians: Northern Indian Removal*, 1st ed. (University of Oklahoma Press, 2017).

31. Saunt, *Unworthy Republic*, xv–xvi.

32. Bowes, *Land Too Good for Indians*; Grant Foreman and Angie Debo, *Indian Removal: The Emigration of the Five Civilized Tribes of Indians*, 9th Bison Printing ed. (University of Oklahoma Press, 1974).

33. The following account is drawn from the George Fortman interview, *FWP*, Vol. 5: Indiana (1936), 84–95.

34. Baptist, *Half Has Never Been Told*, 22–23; Walter Johnson, *Soul by Soul: Life inside the Antebellum Slave Market*, 1st ed. (Harvard University Press, 1999), 54.

35. Rothman, *Ledger and the Chain*, 3.

36. George Patterson interview, *FWP*, Vol. 2: Arkansas, Part 5 (1936), 226.

37. Welch, *Black Litigants*, 182.

38. John Rudd interview, *FWP*, Vol. 5: Indiana (1936), 169–171. For a textured description of southern slave markets, see Johnson, *Soul by Soul*, chap. 2.

39. John W. H. Barnett interview, *FWP*, Vol. 2, Arkansas, Part 1 (1936), 107.

40. *Peggy Perryman, a woman of color v. Joseph Phillippi (Philibert)*, 1848, Washington University in St. Louis Library.

41. Josie Martin interview, *FWP*, Vol. 14: South Carolina, Part 3 (1936), 51–52.

42. Wylie Nealy interview, *FWP*, Vol. 2: Arkansas, Part 5 (1936), 192.

43. Lulu Wilson interview, *FWP*, Vol. 16: Texas, Part 4 (1936), 190–192.

44. Virginia Newman interview, *FWP*, Vol. 16: Texas, Part 3 (1936), 148–149.

45. Virginia Newman interview, *FWP*, Vol. 16: Texas, Part 3 (1936), 150.

46. Jerry Sims interview, *FWP*, Vol. 2: Arkansas, Part 6 (1936), 160.

47. As shown in the AHN database between 1804 and 1865. With thanks to Anjali DasSarma for sharing her research on this. See also the *Stolen Relations* project at Brown Univesity.

48. "$100 REWARD!!" *Raleigh Register and North Carolina Weekly Advertiser*, January 19, 1836.

49. For a succinct introduction, see Theda Perdue, *Slavery and the Evolution of Cherokee Society, 1540–1866* (University of Tennessee Press, 1979).

50. Barbara Krauthamer, *Black Slaves, Indian Masters: Slavery, Emancipation, and Citizenship in the Native American South* (University of North Carolina Press, 2013), 20–22.

51. Perdue, *Slavery and the Evolution of Cherokee Society*; Tiya Miles, *Ties That Bind: The Story of an Afro-Cherokee Family in Slavery and Freedom* (University of California Press, 2005).

52. Kennedy, "Introduction," in *Population of the United States in 1860*, xv. The Seminoles are specifically noted as holding no slaves, which contradicts other testimony.

53. Kiziah Love interview, *FWP*, Vol. 13: Oklahoma (1936), 192–199.

54. Aleck Brown et al., Chickasaws, Dawes Commission, no. 87, in "Five Civilized Tribes in Oklahoma: Reports of the Department of the Interior and Evidentiary Papers in Support of S. 7625, a Bill for the Relief of Certain Members of the Five Civilized Tribes in Oklahoma, Sixty-Second Congress, Third Session," January 1, 1909, 520–525.

55. Sarah Wilson interview, *FWP*, Vol. 13: Oklahoma (1936), 344–347.

56. Saunt, *Unworthy Republic*, 36.

57. Harmeet Kaur, "The Cherokee Nation Acknowledges That Descendants of People Once Enslaved by the Tribe Should Also Qualify as Cherokee," February 25, 2021, CNN.

58. Kiziah Love interview, *FWP*, Vol. 13: Oklahoma (1936), 198.

59. James Boyd interview, *FWP*, Vol. 16: Texas, Part 1 (1936), 117.

60. Spence Johnson interview, *FWP*, Vol. 16: Texas, Part 2 (1936), 228–229.

61. "Speech of Hon. T. C. Hindman, of Arkansas," *Memphis Daily Appeal*, February 16, 1860, 1.

62. "From Kansas, A Creek Indian Kidnapped and Enslaved," *Ohio State Journal* (Columbus), September 15, 1858, p. 4, AHN.

63. See the "Bill of Indictment," in *Burks v. Mississippi* (1860), Mississippi Department of Archives and History. I am grateful to staff there for sending scans of the documents. Sally and Terrell Cash were listed as Indians on the 1860 census of Scott County, MS.

64. "New Orleans, Slave Market of the South," Historic New Orleans Collection website; "New Orleans and the Domestic Slave Trade," Historical Marker Database website.

CHAPTER 13. A NEW AMERICAN SLAVERY

1. Madley, *American Genocide*.

2. Albert L. Hurtado, *John Sutter: A Life on the North American Frontier* (University of Oklahoma Press, 2006), 16–27, 67–68, 79–80.

3. Albert L. Hurtado, " 'Saved So Much as Possible for Labour': Indian Population and the New Helvetia Work Force," *American Indian Culture and Research Journal* 6, no. 4 (September 1, 1982): 64; Hurtado, *John Sutter*, 80.

4. Madley, *American Genocide*, 60.

5. James Clyman, *James Clyman, American Frontiersman, 1792–1881*, ed. Charles Lewis Camp (California Historical Society, 1928), 173.

6. Hurtado, " 'Saved So Much as Possible,' " 66–67; Clyman, *James Clyman*, 173.

7. See, for example, Brooks, *Captives and Cousins*; Reséndez, *Other Slavery*.

8. John O'Sullivan, "Annexation," *United States Magazine and Democratic Review* 17 (1845): 5–10.

9. E. F. Beale to Luke Lea, November 22, 1852, in Robert F. Heizer, ed., *Federal Concern about Conditions of California Indians, 1853 to 1913* (Ballena Press, 1979), 3.

10. Hurtado, *John Sutter*, 3–4.

11. Reséndez, *Other Slavery*, 258.

12. Lansford Warren Hastings, *The Emigrants' Guide to Oregon and California* (Cincinnati, OH: G. Conclin, 1845), 132. For Mexican slavery, see William S. Kiser, *Borderlands of Slavery: The Struggle over Captivity and Peonage in the American Southwest* (University of Pennsylvania Press, 2017), 44–45.

13. David M. Brugge, *Navajos in the Catholic Church Records of New Mexico, 1694–1875*, 3rd ed. (School for Advanced Research Press, 2010), 75.

14. George Harrison to Captain Dupont, March 17, 1847, in Robert F. Heizer, *The Destruction of California Indians* (University of Nebraska Press, 1993), 6.

15. Eileen M. Luna-Firebaugh, "The Border Crossed Us: Border Crossing Issues of the Indigenous Peoples of the Americas," in *Native American Voices*, ed. Susan Lobo, Steve Talbot, and Traci L. Morrison, 3rd ed. (Routledge, 2016), 128.

16. Ramón A. Gutiérrez, *When Jesus Came, the Corn Mothers Went Away: Marriage, Sexuality, and Power in New Mexico, 1500–1846* (Stanford University Press, 1991); Brooks, *Captives and Cousins*. See also Robert Francis Castro, "After the Slavers: Law, Liberation and Captive-Taking in the New Mexican Borderlands," *Slavery & Abolition* 28, no. 3 (December 2007): 369–386.

17. Brugge, *Navajos in the Catholic Church Records*, 77.

18. Sherry Robinson, *James Silas Calhoun: First Governor of New Mexico Territory and First Indian Agent* (University of New Mexico Press, 2021), 20–21.

19. Kiser, *Borderlands of Slavery*, 75–76.

20. Kiser, *Borderlands of Slavery*, 76.

21. James S. Calhoun, *The Official Correspondence of James S. Calhoun*, ed. Annie Heloise Abel (US Government Printing Office, 1915), 162.

22. Brugge, *Navajos in the Catholic Church Records*, 80–81.

23. "Message on Slavery," *Santa Fe Weekly Gazette*, July 20, 1852. As quoted in Kiser, *Borderlands of Slavery*, 42.

24. Lynn Robison Bailey, *Indian Slave Trade in the Southwest* (Tower Publications, 1966), 179.

25. Steven Hackel, *Children of Coyote, Missionaries of Saint Francis: Indian-Spanish Relations in Colonial California, 1769–1850* (University of North Carolina Press, 2005), 27–29.

26. Stephen W. Silliman, *Lost Laborers in Colonial California: Native Americans and the Archaeology of Rancho Petaluma* (University of Arizona Press, 2004), 12; Hackel, *Children of Coyote*.

27. Hastings, *Emigrants' Guide to Oregon and California*, 132.

28. James Calhoun to Orlando Brown, March 15, 1850, in Calhoun, *Official Correspondence*, 161–162.

29. Lyman L. Palmer, *History of Napa and Lake Counties, California* (San Francisco: Slocum, Bowen, 1881), 49–54; Reséndez, *Other Slavery*, 261; Max Radin and William Ralganal Benson, "The Stone and Kelsey 'Massacre' on the Shores of Clear Lake in 1849: The Indian Viewpoint," *California Historical Society Quarterly* 11, no. 3 (1932): 266–273.

30. Palmer, *History of Napa and Lake Counties*, 54–56. See also Reséndez, *Other Slavery*, 262.

31. Malcom J. Rohrbough, *Rush to Gold: The French and the California Gold Rush, 1848–1854* (Yale University Press, 2013), 17.

32. Madley, *American Genocide*, 76–78; Susan Sleeper-Smith, "Indians and the California Gold Rush," in Sleeper-Smith et al., eds., *Why You Can't Teach United States History*, 101–117.

33. Madley, *American Genocide*, 84.

34. Madley, *American Genocide*, 70.

35. Madley, *American Genocide*, 70–71.

36. Madley, *American Genocide*, 70–71.

37. American Friends Service Committee, ed., *Indians of California: Past and Present* (San Francisco: American Friends Service Committee, 1955), 5.

38. Orin Fowler, *Slavery in California and New Mexico* (Washington, DC: Buell & Blanchard, 1850), 2, THL.

39. Constitution of the State of California, 1849, *SOC, 1850*, 25.

40. Finkelman, "Evading the Ordinance."

41. Michael F. Magliari, "Free Soil, Unfree Labor: Cave Johnson Couts and the Binding of Indian Workers in California, 1850–1867," *Pacific Historical Review* 73, no. 3 (2004): 351.

42. "An Act for the Government and Protection of Indians," April 22, 1850, *SOC, 1850*, 408–410.

43. Reséndez, *Other Slavery*, 265.

44. "An Act for the Government and Protection of Indians," April 22, 1850, *SOC, 1850*, 408, 410.

45. Magliari, "Free Soil, Unfree Labor," 349–350, 358.

46. Madley, *American Genocide*, 162.

47. "Abducting Indian Children," *Daily Alta California*, no. 273, October 2, 1854, California Digital Newspaper Collection.

48. Heizer, *Destruction of California Indians*, 219. For the twenty thousand number, see Magliari, "Free Soil, Unfree Labor," 353.

49. Stacey L. Smith, *Freedom's Frontier: California and the Struggle over Unfree Labor, Emancipation, and Reconstruction*, repr. ed. (University of North Carolina Press, 2015).

50. Michael K. Bennion, "Captivity, Adoption, Marriage, and Identity: Native American Children in Mormon Homes, 1847–1900" (MA thesis, University of Nevada, Las Vegas, 2012), 65–66; Max Perry Mueller, *Wakara's America: The Life and Legacy of a Native Founder of the American West* (Basic Books, 2025). See also Sondra Jones, *The Trial of Don Pedro León Luján: The Attack against Indian Slavery and the Mexican Traders in Utah* (University of Utah Press, 2000), 124–125.

51. Mueller, *Wakara's America*.

52. For Smith and early Mormonism, see Richard Lyman Bushman, *Joseph Smith: Rough Stone Rolling* (Random House, 2007).

53. Stephen P. Van Hoak, "'And Who Shall Have the Children?' The Indian Slave Trade in the Southern Great Basin, 1800–1865," *Nevada Historical Society Quarterly* (Spring 1998): 12.

54. Jones, *Trial of Don Pedro León Luján*, 2.

55. Mueller, *Wakara's America*.

56. Sondra Jones, "'Redeeming' the Indian: The Enslavement of Indian Children in New Mexico and Utah," *Utah Historical Quarterly* 67, no. 3 (1999): 220–241; Kiser, *Borderlands of Slavery*, 77–78, 85. See also Jones, *Trial of Don Pedro León Luján*.

57. Van Hoak, "'And Who Shall Have the Children?'" 14; Bennion, "Captivity, Adoption, Marriage, and Identity," 92–93.

58. Brian Q. Cannon, "'To Buy Up the Lamanite Children as Fast as They Could': Indentured Servitude and Its Legacy in Mormon Society," *Journal of Mormon History* 44, no. 2 (2018): 5.

59. Cannon, "'To Buy Up the Lamanite Children,'" 7.

60. Reséndez, *Other Slavery*, 274.

61. Mueller, *Wakara's America*.

62. Bennion, "Captivity, Adoption, Marriage, and Identity," 90.

63. "Governor's Message," *Deseret News*, January 10, 1852; W. Paul Reeve, *Religion of a Different Color: Race and the Mormon Struggle for Whiteness* (Oxford University Press, 2015), 152.

64. *ARMU*, 91–94. For the labor component, see Elder E. T. Benson's comments on July 13, 1855, in Robert M. Muhlestein, "Utah Indians and the Indian Slave Trade: The Mormon Adoption Program and Its Effect on the Indian Slaves" (MA thesis, Brigham Young University, 1991), 50.

65. Bennion, "Captivity, Adoption, Marriage, and Identity," 92–93.

66. Muhlestein, "Utah Indians and the Indian Slave Trade," 50.

67. Bennion, "Captivity, Adoption, Marriage, and Identity," 3; Cannon, "'To Buy Up the Lamanite Children,'" 6.

68. Bennion, "Captivity, Adoption, Marriage, and Identity," 83–85.

69. "Indian Slavery in Utah," *Sacramento Daily Union*, vol. 14, no. 2134, January 28, 1858. See also "Indian Slaves," *Athens Post*, December 25, 1857, Chronicling America, LOC.

70. "Slavery in California," *Californian*, vol. 2, no. 44, March 15, 1848, 2, California Digital Newspaper Collection.

71. Smith, *Freedom's Frontier*.

72. E. F. Beale to George W. Manypenny, September 30, 1853, in Heizer, *Federal Concern about Conditions of California Indians*, 13.

73. American Friends Service Committee, *Indians of California*, 8.

74. Thomas J. Henley to George W. Manypenny, September 4, 1856, in *ARCIA, 1856* (Washington, DC: Government Printing Office, 1856), 796–797.

75. Henry Rowe Schoolcraft, "Journal of the Expedition of Colonel Redick M'Kee, United States Indian Agent, through North-Western California: Performed in the Summer and Fall of 1851," in *Information Respecting the History, Condition and Prospects of the Indian Tribes of the United States [Microform]*, vol. 3 (Philadelphia: Lippincott, Grambo, 1853), 105.

76. "An Act Amendatory of an Act entitled 'An Act for the Government and Protection of Indians,' passed April twenty-second, one thousand eight hundred and fifty," approved April 18, 1860, in *SOC, 1860*, 196.

77. See, for example, the extended analysis of the 1860 amendments published in the *Sacramento Union* in July 1860. "Apprenticing Indians," *Sacramento Daily Union*, vol. 19, no. 2915, July 31, 1860, California Digital Newspaper Collection.

78. George Hanson to Chas. E. Mix, July 23, 1861, in Heizer, *Destruction of California Indians*, 230–232.

79. Robert F. Heizer and Alan F. Almquist, *The Other Californians: Prejudice and Discrimination under Spain, Mexico, and the United States to 1920* (University of California Press, 1971), 40.

80. Edward A. Stevenson to H. Thomas J. Henley, July 31, 1856, in *ARCIA, 1856*, 802–803.

81. "Los Angeles' 1850s Slave Market Is Now the Site of a Federal Courthouse," PBS SoCal, September 2, 2016. For wider background on the Los Angeles region, see Kelly Lytle Hernández, *City of Inmates: Conquest, Rebellion, and the Rise of Human Caging in Los Angeles, 1771–1965* (University of North Carolina Press, 2017), chap. 1.

82. State of California, "Governor Newsom Issues Apology to Native Americans for State's Historical Wrongdoings, Establishes Truth and Healing Council," California Governor, June 18, 2019.

CHAPTER 14. PARADOXICAL CIVIL WARS

1. Madley, *American Genocide*, 289.

2. As quoted in Madley, *American Genocide*, 283. See also Michael F. Magliari, "Masters, Apprentices, and Kidnappers: Indian Servitude and Slave Trafficking in Humboldt County, California, 1860–1863," *California History* 97, no. 2 (May 1, 2020): 2–26.

3. Madley, *American Genocide*, 280.

4. Madley, *American Genocide*, 290–293.

5. For the most recent treatment of the Civil War as a continental affair, see Alan Taylor, *American Civil Wars: A Continental History, 1850–1873* (W. W. Norton, 2024).

6. Scott Manning Stevens, "American Indians and the Civil War," in Sleeper-Smith et al., eds., *Why You Can't Teach United States History*, 134–149.

7. Alaina E. Roberts, *I've Been Here All the While: Black Freedom on Native Land* (University of Pennsylvania Press, 2021), 37.

8. Eric Foner, *Free Soil, Free Labor, Free Men: The Ideology of the Republican Party before the Civil War* (Oxford University Press, 1995).

9. Taylor, *American Civil Wars*, chaps. 3–5.

10. "Was Indian Slave," *Tomahawk*, November 7, 1918, Chronicling America, LOC.

11. James Boyd interview, *FWP*, Vol. 16: Texas, Part 1 (1936), 118–119.

12. Wylie Nealy interview, *FWP*, Vol. 2: Arkansas, Part 5 (1936), 189–190.

13. Mollie Moss interview, *FWP*, Vol. 15: Tennessee (1936), 57.

14. Wylie Nealy interview, 188, 193.

15. Charlie Davenport interview, *FWP*, Vol. 9: Mississippi (1936), 39.

16. Riviana Boynton interview, *FWP*, Vol. 3: Florida (1936), 368.

17. "Transcript of the Emancipation Proclamation," NARA.

18. Celia Henderson interview, *FWP*, Vol. 12: Ohio (1936), 42–43.

19. Joe Higgerson interview, *FWP*, Vol. 10: Missouri (1936), 178. On the ending of the Civil War, see Michael Vorenberg, *Lincoln's Peace: The Struggle to End the American Civil War* (Knopf, 2025).

20. *Wilmington Journal* (North Carolina), March 10, 1864, University of North Carolina, Greensboro, University Library.

21. National Museum of African American History and Culture, "Part 4, Chapter 3: A Divided Nation Fights for Freedom," in *Slavery & Freedom, 1400–1877* (online exhibition).

22. Edward Dillon to Captain C. S. Lovell, May 31, 1861, in Heizer, *Destruction of California Indians*, 229.

23. George Hanson to William Dole, December 31, 1861, in *Report of the Commissioner of Indian Affairs for the Year 1862* (Washington, DC: Government Printing Office, 1863), 315. See also Madley, *American Genocide*, 295.

24. Jean Pfaelzer, *California, a Slave State* (Yale University Press, 2023), 186.

25. George Hanson to William Dole, December 31, 1861.

26. Brugge, *Navajos in the Catholic Church Records*, 88–89.

27. "Condition of the Indian Tribes: Report of the Joint Special Committee, Appointed under Joint Resolution of March 3, 1865: With an Appendix," 39th Cong., 2d Sess., Senate, no. 156 (Washington, DC: Government Printing Office, 1867), 345–348.

28. "Condition of the Indian Tribes," 129, 148.

29. "Abstract of the number of captive Indians and of produce raised on Apache and Navajo farms at Fort Sumner, New Mexico in the year 1865," Fort Sumner—Bosque Redondo Digital Collections, drawn from NARA, Record Group 94: Records of the Adjutant General's Office, 1762–1984, M619 Letters Received by the Office of the Adjutant General (Main Series), 1861–1870, Roll 561, Files 109-295 M.

30. Michael Steck to William P. Dole, January 13, 1864, in Brugge, *Navajos in the Catholic Church Records*, 96–97.

31. "Condition of the Indian Tribes," 97.

32. Cindy Yurth, "Proud Moment in Sad Legacy: Fortress Rock," *Navajo Times*, June 4, 2009.

33. Patty Chee et al., *Oral History Stories of the Long Walk = Hwéeldi Baa Hane* (Lake Valley Navajo School, 1990), 8; Lynn Robison Bailey, *The Long Walk: A History of the Navajo Wars, 1846–68*, 1st ed. (Westernlore Press, 1964), 166–167; Testimony of Kit Carson, "Condition of the Indian Tribes," 97.

34. Reséndez, *Other Slavery*, 290.

35. "Condition of the Indian Tribes," 260.

36. Chee et al., *Oral History Stories of the Long Walk*, 13, 35.

37. "Condition of the Indian Tribes," 316. For the number of children, see James H. Carleton letter, April 24, 1865, in "Condition of the Indian Tribes," 224–225.

38. "Captive Indians in New Mexico," *Santa Fe Weekly Gazette*, April 18, 1868, Chronicling America, LOC.

39. James H. Carleton letter, April 24, 1865, in "Condition of the Indian Tribes," 224–225.

40. "Condition of the Indian Tribes," 355.

41. "Abstract of the number of captive Indians," M619 Letters Received by the Office of the Adjutant General.

42. Chee et al., *Oral History Stories of the Long Walk*, 69.

43. Estévan Rael-Gálvez, "Identifying Captivity and Capturing Identity: Narratives of American Indian Slavery in Colorado and New Mexico, 1776–1934" (PhD diss., University of Michigan, Ann Arbor, 2002), 216.

44. Brugge, *Navajos in the Catholic Church Records*, 96–97. For the 2,500 and 1,000 figures, see pp. 105–106.

45. Reséndez, *Other Slavery*, 293–294.

46. Brugge, *Navajos in the Catholic Church Records*, 96.

47. Brugge, *Navajos in the Catholic Church Records*, 94; Kiser, *Borderlands of Slavery*, 65.

48. *Daily Commonwealth*, March 30, 1864.

49. Blackhawk, *The Rediscovery of America*, 293–294.

50. *ARCIA, 1863/1864* (Washington, DC: Government Printing Office, 1865), 230–231.

51. "A New Phase in the Navajo War," *Daily Commonwealth*, May 18, 1864.

52. "A List of Indian Captives acquired by purchase and now in the service of the citizens of Costilla County," July 1865, Letters Received by the Office of Indian Affairs, 1824–1881, NARA, M234, RG 75, Roll 197, frames 88–91, and Roll 198, frames 271–274.

53. Patricia Leigh Brown, "A Grim, Long-Hidden Truth Emerges in Art: Native American Enslavement," *New York Times*, December 17, 2021.

54. Heizer, *Destruction of California Indians*, 219.

55. The date of the act can be found in Arizona Legislative Assembly, Journals of the . . . Legislative Assembly of the Territory of Arizona, 1865, 246–247. For the full text of the act, see *Compiled Laws of the Territory of Arizona, Including the Howell Code and the Session Laws from 1864 to 1871* (Albany, NY, 1871), 505–507.

56. *Compiled Laws of the Territory of Arizona*, 505–507.

57. Vorenberg, *Lincoln's Peace*.

58. Patsy Moore interview, *FWP*, Vol. 2: Arkansas, Part 5 (1936), 124.

59. James Boyd interview, 118–119.

60. William Sherman interview, *FWP*, Vol. 3: Florida (1936), 297.

61. Cato Carter interview, *FWP*, Vol. 16: Texas, Part 1 (1936), 208.

62. See, for example, Zek Brown interview, *FWP*, Vol. 16: Texas, Part 1 (1936), 168.

63. Lulu Wilson interview, *FWP*, Vol. 16: Texas, Part 4 (1936), 194.

64. Cato Carter interview, 209.

65. Virginia Newman interview, *FWP*, Vol. 16: Texas, Part 3 (1936), 150.

66. Michael F. Magliari, "Free State Slavery: Bound Indian Labor and Slave Trafficking in California's Sacramento Valley, 1850–1864," *Pacific Historical Review* 81, no. 2 (2012): 162.

67. "The Sugar Industry," *Advocate* (Topeka, KS), January 31, 1894, 14.

68. Lucy Thomas interview, *FWP*, Vol. 16: Texas, Part 4 (1936), 90.

69. Sarah Wilson interview, *FWP*, Vol. 13: Oklahoma (1936), 352.

70. James Boyd interview, 117–118.

71. Joseph Samuel Badgett interview, *FWP*, Vol. 2: Arkansas, Part 1 (1936), 78–80.

72. James Boyd interview, 119–120. See also Hannah Travis interview, *FWP*, Vol. 2: Arkansas, Part 6 (1936), 351.

73. Cora Gillam interview, *FWP*, Vol. 2: Arkansas, Part 3 (1936), 27–33.

74. *Hall v. United States v. Roach*, 92 U.S. 27, October 1875.

75. Angela Y. Walton-Raji, *Oklahoma Freedmen of the Five Tribes* (History Press, 2023), 13–14.

76. Moses Mitchell interview, *FWP*, Vol. 2: Arkansas, Part 5 (1936), 116.

77. Mattie Logan interview, *FWP*, Vol. 13: Oklahoma (1936), 191,

78. *ARCIA*, 1864/1865, iii–iv.

79. *ARCIA*, 1864/1865, iii–iv.

80. *ARCIA*, 1864/1865, iii–iv.

Chapter 15. Abolishing Peonage

1. For the continuance of Black servitude in other forms, see Mary Frances Berry, *Slavery after Slavery: Revealing the Legacy of Forced Child Apprenticeships on Black Families, from Emancipation to the Present* (Beacon Press, 2024); Douglas A. Blackmon, *Slavery by Another Name: The Re-enslavement of Black Americans from the Civil War to World War Two* (Icon Books, 2012).

2. Robert Francis Castro, "Liberty like Thunder: Law, History, and the Emancipatory Politics of Reconstruction America" (PhD diss., University of Michigan, 2003), 64–66.

3. "13th Amendment to the U.S. Constitution: Abolition of Slavery (1865)," NARA.

4. Jones, *Trial of Don Pedro León Luján*, 32.

5. "Massacre of the Cheyenne Indians," in *Report of the Joint Committee on the Conduct of the War, 38th Cong., 2nd Sess.* (Washington, DC: Government Printing Office, 1865), iii.

6. "Testimony of Mr. John S. Smith, March 14, 1865," in "Massacre of the Cheyenne Indians," 4–12.

7.   Hugh J. Reilly, *The Frontier Newspapers and the Coverage of the Plains Indian Wars* (Bloomsbury, 2010), 23.

8.   "Condition of the Indian Tribes." A more comprehensive account of the committee's activities can be found in Harry Kelsey, "The Doolittle Report of 1867: Its Preparation and Shortcomings," *Arizona and the West* 17, no. 2 (1975): 107–120.

9.   Kelsey, "Doolittle Report of 1867," 108. See also Theodore Aubrey Walsh Vial, "Defining Freedom: New Mexican Debt Peonage and the Struggle to Define and Restrict Unfree Labor in the Post-Civil War Period" (Senior thesis, Brown University, 2020).

10. James Harlan to William P. Dole, June 12, 1865, in *ARCIA, 1865* (Washington, DC: Government Printing Office, 1865), 164.

11. "Order of the President of the United States," June 9, 1865, in *ARCIA, 1865*, 165; Bailey, *Indian Slave Trade in the Southwest*, 175–176.

12. Felipe Delagado to W. P. Dole, July 16, 1865, in *ARCIA, 1856*, 165–166.

13. "A List of Indian Captives acquired by purchase," Roll 198, frames 88–91, and Roll 198, frames 271–274.

14. Lafayette Head to John Evans, July 17, 1865, *ARCIA, 1865*, 180.

15. Deposition of Chief Justice Kirby Benedict, July 4, 1865; Deposition of Louis Kennon, undated, ca. July 1865, in "Condition of the Indian Tribes," 326, 334.

16. Deposition of Chief Justice Kirby Benedict, 326.

17. Deposition of Brigadier General James H. Carleton, July 3, 1865, in "Condition of the Indian Tribes," 325.

18. Deposition of Louis Kennon, July 4, 1864, in "Condition of the Indian Tribes," 334.

19. Smith, *Freedom's Frontier*, 190.

20. Robert F. Heizer and Alan F. Almquist, *The Other Californians: Prejudice and Discrimination under Spain, Mexico, and the United States to 1920* (University of California Press, 1971), 57–58.

21. Heizer and Almquist, *Other Californians*, 58.

22. Magliari, "Free Soil, Unfree Labor," 350–351; Lynne Newell Christenson and Ellen L. Sweet, *Ranchos of San Diego County* (Arcadia Publishing, 2008), 24; Smith, *Freedom's Frontier*, 121.

23. See the various account books of the Cave Johnson Couts Papers in THL.

24. Cave Johnson Couts, Cattle and Servants Account Book (1854–1857), Cave Johnson Couts Papers, CT 2543 (19), THL.

25. Cave Johnson Couts, Day Book (1865–1867), Cave Johnson Couts Papers, CT 2454 (6), THL. See also Magliari, "Free Soil, Unfree Labor," 384.

26. John Quincy Adams Stanley to Cave Johnson Couts, December 22, 1865, Cave Johnson Couts Papers, CT 2118, THL.

27. Cave Johnson Couts to John Quincy Adams, December 26, 1865, Cave Johnson Couts Papers, CT 2118, THL.

28. Cave Johnson Couts, Day Book (1865–1867), 151–152, Cave Johnson Couts Papers, CT 2454 (6), THL.

29. "Condition of the Indian Tribes," 5.

30. See, for example, Deposition of Chief Justice Kirby Benedict, July 4, 1865; Deposition of Louis Kennon, undated, ca. July 1865, in "Condition of the Indian Tribes," 326, 334.

31.   James H. Carleton to the Doolittle Committee, July 3, 1865, "Condition of the Indian Tribes," 324.

32.   Kelsey, "Doolittle Report of 1867," 117–119.

33.   As quoted in Kiser, *Borderlands of Slavery*, 162.

34.   *The Statutes at Large, Treaties, and Proclamations of the United States of America, from December, 1865, to March, 1867*, vol. 14 (Boston: Little, Brown, 1868), 546.

35.   *Freedom's Champion* (Atchison, KS), May 16, 1867, 2, Kansas Historical Society.

36.   William Kiser, "Alternative Slaveries and American Democracy Debt Bondage and Indian Captivity in the Civil War Era Southwest" (PhD diss., Arizona State University, 2016), 394.

37.   Kiser, *Borderlands of Slavery*, 165.

38.   "Noon Dispatches," *Memphis Daily Appeal*, July 16, 1867, 1.

39.   Larry D. Ball, *The United States Marshals of New Mexico and Arizona Territories, 1846–1912* (University of New Mexico Press, 1982), 51.

40.   W. W. Griffin, "Summary of Actions regarding Peons and Indian Slaves Held in Taos, Santa Fe, and Río Arriba Counties, New Mexico Territory, March 16 to November 28, 1868," in Papers Relating to the Cases of W. W. Griffin, Indian Commissioner of Territory of New Mexico, Indian Peonage, United States Senate Territorial Documents, New Mexico, record group 46, NARA. As cited in Brooks, *Captives and Cousins*, appendix C.

41.   Rael-Gálvez, "Identifying Captivity," 293–294, 310.

42.   Jerry D. Thompson, *A Civil War History of the New Mexico Volunteers and Militia* (University of New Mexico Press, 2015), 410.

43.   "John T. Russell, Editor and Proprietor: Peonage and Indian Slavery," *Santa Fe Weekly Gazette*, May 23, 1868, Chronicling America, LOC.

44.   1870 Census, Rio Colorado, Taos County, New Mexico, pp. 11–12, Familysearch .org. See also Rael-Gálvez, "Identifying Captivity," 313.

45.   Rael-Gálvez, "Identifying Captivity," 310, n591.

46.   Rael-Gálvez, "Identifying Captivity," 316–317.

47.   Robert F. Castro, "Plying the Liberty Trade: Law, Empire-Building, and the Enforcement of Antislavery Scriptures in the Reconstruction of New Mexico," *Political and Legal Anthropology Review* 30, no. 1 (2007): 122.

48.   Bennion, "Captivity, Adoption, Marriage, and Identity," 129–132.

49.   Bennion, "Captivity, Adoption, Marriage, and Identity," 149. See also Thomas C. W. Sale, to Honorable O. H. Irish, *ARCIA, 1864/1865*, 155.

50.   Leland Donald, *Aboriginal Slavery on the Northwest Coast of North America*, 1st ed. (University of California Press, 1997).

51.   Minutes of a Council Held at Warm Springs Reservation, Oregon Territory, *ARCIA, 1870* (Washington, DC: Government Printing Office, 1871), 130.

52.   E. M. Gibson to T. J. McKenny, September 1, 1871, *ARCIA, 1870*, 279.

53.   Chee et al., *Oral History Stories of the Long Walk*, 87.

54.   "Condition of the Indian Tribes," 157.

55.   Chee et al., *Oral History Stories of the Long Walk*, 29.

56.   Chee et al., *Oral History Stories of the Long Walk*, 35.

57.   "Captive Indians in New Mexico," *Santa Fe Weekly Gazette*, April 18, 1868, Chronicling America, LOC.

58.   "Condition of the Indian Tribes," 354.

59.   Brugge, *Navajos in the Catholic Church Records*, 92.

60.   Kiser, *Borderlands of Slavery*, 84.

61.   Testimony of Lieutenant Colonel Edward B. Willis, in "Condition of the Indian Tribes," 330.

62.   Brugge, *Navajos in the Catholic Church Records*, 103–104. See also "An Act to Establish a Bureau for the Relief of Freedmen and Refugees," 1865, NARA.

63.   Brugge, *Navajos in the Catholic Church Records*, 103–104. See also "An Act to Establish a Bureau for the Relief of Freedmen and Refugees," 1865, NARA.

64.   Lawrence Murphy, "Reconstruction in New Mexico," *New Mexico Historical Review* 43, no. 2 (April 1, 1968): 101.

65.   "Santa Fe," *Santa Fe Weekly Gazette*, August 21, 1869, Chronicling America, LOC.

66.   Kiser, *Borderlands of Slavery*, 231.

67.   Helen Hunt Jackson, *A Century of Dishonor: A Sketch of the United States Government's Dealings with Some of the Indian Tribes* (Boston: Roberts Brothers, 1888), 331.

68.   Dan L. Thrapp, *The Conquest of Apacheria* (University of Oklahoma Press, 1975), 89–92.

69.   Brugge, *Navajos in the Catholic Church Records*, 104.

70.   Rael-Gálvez, "Identifying Captivity," 340ff.

71.   Rael-Gálvez, "Identifying Captivity," 362.

72.   Vincent Coyler to Columbus Delano, December 12, 1871, Third Annual Report of the Board of Indian Commissioners, in *ARCIA, 1871* (Washington, DC: Government Printing Office, 1872), 434.

73.   Blackmon, *Slavery by Another Name*.

74.   Madley, *American Genocide*, 347.

75.   George M. Hanson to Chas. E. Mix, July 23, 1861, in Heizer, *Destruction of California Indians*, 232.

Chapter 16. The Primer and the Hoe

1.   Helen Sekaquaptewa and Louise Udall, *Me and Mine: The Life Story of Helen Sekaquaptewa* (University of Arizona Press, 1969), 31–32.

2.   "Report on Indian Education: Final Report to the American Indian Policy Review Commission," *Task Force Five: Indian Education* (Government Printing Office, 1976), 32.

3.   Richard Henry Pratt, "The Advantages of Mingling Indians with Whites," in *Proceedings of the National Conference of Charities and Correction . . . June 23–29, 1892*, ed. Isabel C. Barrows (Boston: George H. Ellis, 1892), 48.

4.   Bryan Newland, "Federal Indian Boarding School Initiative Investigative Report" (US Department of the Interior, May 2022); Newland, "List of Federal Indian Boarding Schools, Appendix A and Appendix B of the Federal Indian Boarding School Report" (US Department of the Interior, 2022); Zach Levitt et al., "'War against the Children,'" *New York Times*, August 30, 2023.

5.   "Residential School History," National Centre for Truth and Reconciliation, December 21, 2020; "Indian Residential Schools Settlement Agreement," 2007, Government of Canada, Canada.ca.

6. Jane Griffith, "Of Linguicide and Resistance: Children and English Instruction in Nineteenth-Century Indian Boarding Schools in Canada," *Paedagogica Historica* 53, no. 6 (November 2, 2017): 763–782; "The Survivors Speak: A Report of the Truth and Reconciliation Commission of Canada" (Truth and Reconciliation Commission of Canada, 2015); Sari Horwitz et al., " 'In the Name of God': Native American Children Endured Years of Sexual Abuse at Boarding Schools," *Washington Post*, May 24, 2024.

7. I'm grateful to Kimonee Burke for this last insight.

8. Brenda J. Child, "The Boarding School as Metaphor," *Journal of American Indian Education* 57, no. 1 (2018): 38.

9. "Trigger Points: Current State of Research on History, Impacts, and Healing Related to the United States' Indian Industrial/Boarding School Policy" (Native American Rights Fund, 2019), 33.

10. Linford D. Fisher, "America's First Bible: Native Uses, Abuses, and Reuses of the Indian Bible of 1663," in *The Bible in American Life*, ed. Philip Goff, Arthur E. Farnsley II, and Peter Thuesen, 1st ed. (Oxford University Press, 2017).

11. Governor Spotswood to Lord Dartmouth, November 11, 1711, *Collections of the Virginia Historical Society, New Series*, 11 vols. ([Richmond], 1833), 1:125, 167.

12. Fisher, *Indian Great Awakening*, 140, 145.

13. Edward Deake to Eleazar Wheelock, June 21, 1768, Dartmouth College Archives, Hanover, NH.

14. Joseph A. Parsons, Jr., "Civilizing the Indians of the Old Northwest, 1800–1810," *Indiana Magazine of History* 56, no. 3 (1960): 195–216.

15. Edmund Schwarze, *History of the Moravian Missions among Southern Indian Tribes of the United States* (Times Publishing, 1923), 114–115.

16. Acts Passed at the First Session of the Fifteenth Congress of the United States, in *The Public Statutes at Large of the United States of America*, vol. 3 (Boston: Charles C. Little and James Brown, 1846), 516.

17. "Let All That Is Indian within You Die!" *Native American Rights Fund Legal Review* 38, no. 2 (Summer/Fall 2013): 3.

18. Christina Snyder, *Great Crossings: Indians, Settlers, and Slaves in the Age of Jackson*, 1st ed. (Oxford University Press, 2017), 14.

19. Martha B. Caldwell, *Annals of Shawnee Methodist Mission and Indian Manual Labor School* (Kansas State Historical Society, 1939), 33–34.

20. Caldwell, *Annals*, 37.

21. Caldwell, *Annals*, 30, 33.

22. Kevin J. Abing, "A Fall from Grace: Thomas Johnson and the Shawnee Indian Manual Labor School, 1839–1862" (PhD diss., Marquette University, Milwaukee, WI, 1995), 139–140.

23. Abing, "Fall from Grace," 278–281.

24. Robert Laurence, "Indian Education: Federal Compulsory School Attendance Law Applicable to American Indians—The Treaty-Making Period: 1857–1871," *American Indian Law Review* 5, no. 2 (1977): 401.

25. Jean Pfaelzer, *California, a Slave State* (Yale University Press, 2023), 339.

26. "The End of Treaty Making," in Vine Deloria Jr. and Raymond J. DeMallie, *Documents of American Indian Diplomacy*, vol. 1 (University of Oklahoma Press, 1999), 233.

27. Brad D. Lookingbill, *War Dance at Fort Marion: Plains Indian War Prisoners* (University of Oklahoma Press, 2006), 68–69.

28. Robert A. Trennert, "From Carlisle to Phoenix: The Rise and Fall of the Indian Outing System, 1878–1930," *Pacific Historical Review* 52, no. 3 (1983): 270; David Wallace Adams, *Education for Extinction: American Indians and the Boarding School Experience, 1875–1928*, 2nd ed. (University Press of Kansas, 2020), 47–48.

29. Candace S. Greene, "Being Indian at Fort Marion: Revisiting Three Drawings," *American Indian Quarterly* 37, no. 4 (2013): 289–316.

30. Pratt, "Advantages of Mingling Indians with Whites," 50; Adams, *Education for Extinction*, 49.

31. See the Carlisle Indian School Digital Resource Center, Dickinson College, Carlisle, PA.

32. Zitkala-Ša, *American Indian Stories: Illustrated* (Strelbytskyy Multimedia, 2023), 34.

33. Brenda J. Child, *Boarding School Seasons: American Indian Families, 1900–1940* (University of Nebraska Press, 1998), 1; Trennert, "From Carlisle to Phoenix."

34. Trennert, "From Carlisle to Phoenix," 272–273.

35. Trennert, "From Carlisle to Phoenix," 275.

36. Mrs. Joseph Peck to the Carlisle Indian School Press, December 14, 1909, NARA, RG 75, Series 1327, Box 149, Folder 5812.

37. Trennert, "From Carlisle to Phoenix," 276.

38. Newland, "Federal Indian Boarding School Initiative Investigative Report," 37.

39. Kristin T. Ruppel, *Unearthing Indian Land: Living with the Legacies of Allotment* (University of Arizona Press, 2008), 30.

40. Trennert, "From Carlisle to Phoenix," 278.

41. "The History and Evolution of the Phoenix Indian School Visitor Center," Native American Connections (website).

42. Trennert, "From Carlisle to Phoenix," 280. For comparable national wages, see Lucy Maynard Salmon, *Domestic Service*, 2nd ed. (Macmillan Company, 1901), 88.

43. Trennert, "From Carlisle to Phoenix," 282.

44. Kevin Whalen, "Labored Learning: The Outing System at Sherman Institute, 1902–1930," *American Indian Culture and Research Journal* 36, no. 1 (2012): 154.

45. Whalen, "Labored Learning," 155–156.

46. Pfaelzer, *California, a Slave State*, 349.

47. Adams, *Education for Extinction*, 168.

48. John A. Goodwin, *Without Destroying Ourselves: A Century of Native Intellectual Activism for Higher Education* (University of Nebraska Press, 2022), 26.

49. Simon Johnson student file, Carlisle Indian Industrial School, NARA, RG 75, Series 1327, Box 149, Folder 5812.

50. Jean Pfaelzer, "The 'Outing Programs': Human Trafficking at California's Native American Boarding Schools," Supportive Testimony H.R. 5444/S. 2907, Truth and Healing Commission on Indian Boarding School Policies in the US (US House of Representatives, 2023), 17–18.

51. Adams, *Education for Extinction*, 179.

52. Charles Peters to Commissioner Cato Sells, Indian Affairs Office, December 1, 1913, Charles Peters student file, Carlisle Indian Industrial School, NARA, RG 75, Series 1327, Box 4, Folder 165.

53. "Let All That Is Indian within You Die!" 7.

54. Irene Stewart, *A Voice in Her Tribe: A Navajo Woman's Own Story* (Ballena Press, 1980), 18.

55. Laura Tohe, *No Parole Today* (West End Press, 2005), xiv.

56. "'In the Name of God.'"

57. "'In the Name of God'"; Andrea Smith, "Boarding School Abuses, Human Rights, and Reparations," *Social Justice* 31, no. 4 (98) (2004): 91.

58. Stewart, *Voice in Her Tribe*, 20.

59. Stewart, *Voice in Her Tribe*, 19.

60. "Let All That Is Indian within You Die!," 7.

61. "Treaty with the Yakama, 1855," Governor's Office of Indian Affairs, Washington State; Laurence, "Indian Education," 393–395.

62. Neil Birch, "Helen John: The Beginnings of Indian Placement," *Dialogue: A Journal of Mormon Thought* 18 (Winter 1985): 119.

63. K. Tsianina Lomawaima, *They Called It Prairie Light: The Story of Chilocco Indian School* (University of Nebraska Press, 1995), 129; Child, *Boarding School Seasons*, 69–70.

64. Laurence, "Indian Education," 395.

65. "Report on Indian Education," 60, 325.

66. *"Nothing Servile": Native Resistance at the Santee Normal Training School,* "Maintaining Tribal Identity at Santee," Logan Museum Online Exhibits, Beloit College, Beloit, WI; *The American Missionary* (American Missionary Association, 1912), 104.

67. *Sixty-Third Annual Report of the American Board of Commissioners for Foreign Missions, 1873* (Boston: Riverside Press, 1873), 85.

68. *ARCIA, 1887* (Washington, DC: Government Printing Office, 1887), 18–20.

69. Matthew T. Sakiestewa Gilbert, "'The Hopi Followers': Chief Tawaquaptewa and Hopi Student Advancement at Sherman Institute, 1906–1909," *Journal of American Indian Education* 44, no. 2 (2005): 7.

70. K. Tsianina Lomawaima, "Estelle Reel, Superintendent of Indian Schools, 1898–1910: Politics, Curriculum, and Land," *Journal of American Indian Education* 35, no. 3 (1996): 16.

71. "Indian Servant Girls: Domestic Science Solves the Problem for a Wisconsin Town," *New York Times*, July 14, 1905, 2.

72. "Trigger Points," 12.

73. Whalen, "Labored Learning," 173.

74. Estelle Reel, *Course of Study for the Indian Schools of the United States: Industrial and Literary* (Government Printing Office, 1901).

75. Lomawaima, "Estelle Reel," 12.

76. "Report on Indian Education," 46.

77. *The Problem of Indian Administration*, repr. ed. (New York: Johnson Reprint Corp., 1971), 11, 13, 211–212, 382–392.

78. Blackhawk, *Rediscovery of America*, 401.

79. Vine Deloria, *The Indian Reorganization Act: Congresses and Bills* (University of Oklahoma Press, 2002), xi.

80. Newland, "List of Federal Indian Boarding Schools, Appendix A and Appendix B."

81. "Remains of 9 Lakota Children Who Died at Pennsylvania Boarding School Are Returned to Rosebud," InForum, July 16, 2021.

82. Teresa Evans-Campbell et al., "Indian Boarding School Experience, Substance Use, and Mental Health among Urban Two-Spirit American Indian/Alaska Natives," *American Journal of Drug and Alcohol Abuse* 38, no. 5 (September 2012): 421–427.

83. Matthew Sakiestewa Gilbert, "Revisiting the Hopi Boarding School Experience at Sherman Institute and the Process of Making Research Meaningful to Community," *Journal of American Indian Education* 57, no. 1 (2018): 118.

84. Tohe, *No Parole Today*, xii.

CHAPTER 17. LOST SPARROWS AND SELF-DETERMINATION

1. *Santa Fe New Mexican*, June 4, 1924, 5.

2. Patrick Anderson, "Native American Victims of Sex Abuse at Catholic Boarding Schools Fight for Justice," *Argus Leader* (Sioux Falls, SD), May 16, 2019.

3. Angela Kennecke, "South Dakota's Secret Past," keloland.com (blog), April 6, 2018.

4. Irene Powell and Mark Montgomery, "Transracial Adoption in the Time of Black Lives Matter," Institute for Family Studies, November 25, 2020.

5. Margaret D. Jacobs, "Entangled Histories: The Mormon Church and Indigenous Child Removal from 1850 to 2000," *Journal of Mormon History* 42, no. 2 (2016): 50; *Report on Federal, State, and Tribal Jurisdiction: Task Force Four* (US Government Printing Office, 1976), 79.

6. Margaret D. Jacobs, *A Generation Removed: The Fostering and Adoption of Indigenous Children in the Postwar World* (University of Nebraska Press, 2014), chaps. 6–8.

7. Blackhawk, *Rediscovery of America*, 431.

8. Blackhawk, *Rediscovery of America*, 411.

9. Jacobs, "Entangled Histories," 33; Paul C. Rosier, "The Association on American Indian Affairs and the Struggle for Native American Rights, 1948–1955," *Princeton University Library Chronicle* 67, no. 2 (2006): 369.

10. Blackhawk, *Rediscovery of America*, 412.

11. Margaret D. Jacobs, "Remembering the 'Forgotten Child': The American Indian Child Welfare Crisis of the 1960s and 1970s," *American Indian Quarterly* 37, no. 1–2 (2013): 137–139.

12. Dawn Peterson, *Indians in the Family: Adoption and the Politics of Antebellum Expansion*, 1st ed. (Harvard University Press, 2017).

13. Reel, *Course of Study for the Indian Schools*, 190.

14. *Report on Terminated and Nonfederally Recognized Indians: Task Force Ten Report* (US Government Printing Office, 1976), 104.

15. The details of Helen's life are drawn from Birch, "Helen John."

16. Brandon Morgan, "Educating the Lamanites: A Brief History of the LDS Indian Student Placement Program," *Journal of Mormon History* 35, no. 4 (2009): 195–197.

17. Jacobs, "Entangled Histories," 40; Bruce A. Chadwick and Thomas Garrow, "Native Americans," in *Encyclopedia of Mormonism*, ed. Daniel H. Ludlow, 6 vols. (New York: MacMillan Publishing, 1992; 2007), 3:984–985.

18. "Education: Red and Delightsome," *Time*, September 7, 1959.

19. Jack Ryan Evans, "From Captivity to Placement: Re-examining the Indian Student Placement Program, 1947–2000" (MA thesis, University of Oregon, 2020), 3.

20. Jacobs, "Entangled Histories," 44.

21. Claire Palmiste, "From the Indian Adoption Project to the Indian Child Welfare Act: The Resistance of Native American Communities," 2011, hal-01768178, p. 3.

22. *Report on Federal, State, and Tribal Jurisdiction: Task Force Four*, 79.

23. Trace L. Hentz, *Two Worlds: Lost Children of the Indian Adoption Projects: Vol. 1*, 2nd ed. (Blue Hand Books, 2017), 102–103.

24. Hentz, *Two Worlds*, 63.

25. Trace L. Hentz, *Stolen Generations: Lost Children of the Indian Adoption Projects*, ed. Trace Lara Hentz, 1st ed. (Blue Hand Books, 2016), 133.

26. *Report on Federal, State, and Tribal Jurisdiction: Task Force Four*, 80.

27. Patricia Busbee, Trace L. Hentz, and Suzie Fedorko, *Called Home: The Roadmap* (Blue Hand Books, 2016), 146–150.

28. "SD Expands Indian Adoption Project," *Daily Republic* (Mitchell, SD), March 25, 1967, 8.

29. "Indian Boy, 3, Finds No Prejudice in Hampton," *Des Moines Register*, August 9, 1964, 17.

30. "Adoption of Indian Children 'In Thing' among Well-to-Do," *Current-Argus* (Carlsbad, NM), July 11, 1968, 8.

31. "SD Expands Indian Adoption Project."

32. "Plans Mapped for the Adoption of Indian Children," *Billings Gazette* (Billings, MT), July 27, 1962, 18.

33. P. J. Randhawa, "'Indian Orphan Nobody Wanted Gets Parents': The Dark History of the Indian Adoption Project," king5.com, June 23, 2023.

34. Jacobs, "Remembering the 'Forgotten Child,'" 136.

35. *Report on Federal, State, and Tribal Jurisdiction: Task Force Four*, 82

36. Jacobs, "Entangled Histories," 43–44.

37. Alvin M. Josephy, Joane Nagel, and Troy R. Johnson, *Red Power: The American Indians' Fight for Freedom* (University of Nebraska Press, 1999); Dennis Banks, *Ojibwa Warrior: Dennis Banks and the Rise of the American Indian Movement* (University of Oklahoma Press, 2011).

38. Dennis Banks, "Native American Leader Dennis Banks on the Overlooked Tragedy of Nation's Indian Boarding Schools," *Democracy Now!* October 8, 2012.

39. Dean J. Kotlowski, "Alcatraz, Wounded Knee, and Beyond: The Nixon and Ford Administrations Respond to Native American Protest," *Pacific Historical Review* 72, no. 2 (2003): 202.

40. See for example, the statements listed in the table of contents of "Indian Child Welfare Act of 1977: Hearing Before the United States Senate Select Committee on Indian Affairs," *95th Cong., 1st Sess., on S. 1214* (Government Printing Office, 1977).

41. *Indian Education: A National Tragedy—A National Challenge* (US Government Printing Office, 1969).

42. *Indian Education: A National Tragedy*, 209, 216.

43. Kim Phagan-Hansel, "With Supreme Court Battle over Native American Rights Looming, New Documentary Focuses on Removals of Native Children in Maine," *Imprint*, November 5, 2018; Blackhawk, *Rediscovery of America*, 431. See also the movie *Dawnland*: Adam Mazo and Ben Pender-Cudlip, dir., *Dawnland* (Upstander Project, 2018).

44. "Indian Child Welfare Act of 1977: Hearing," 152.

45. "Indian Child Welfare Statistical Survey," 537–603. See also "Statement of the National Tribal Chairmen's Association before the Select Committee on Indian Affairs," August 4, 1977, "Indian Child Welfare Act of 1977: Hearing," 155.

46. "Indian Child Welfare Statistical Survey," 538. See also Matthew Garrett, *Making Lamanites: Mormons, Native Americans, and the Indian Student Placement Program, 1947–2000*, repr. ed. (University of Utah Press, 2016).

47. *Report on Federal, State, and Tribal Jurisdiction: Task Force Four*, 87.

48. "Indian Child Welfare Act of 1977: Hearing," 9.

49. "Indian Child Welfare Act of 1977: Hearing," 2.

50. "Indian Child Welfare Act of 1978, S. 1214, 95th Congress (1977–1978)," Congress.gov.

51. Chris Billing, dir., *Lost Sparrow* (Independent Lens, 2010); "Independent Lens Presents: *Lost Sparrow*," Getafilm (blog), November 14, 2010.

52. Elise Boxer, "'The Lamanites Shall Blossom as the Rose': The Indian Student Placement Program, Mormon Whiteness, and Indigenous Identity," *Journal of Mormon History* 41, no. 4 (2015): 132–133.

53. John McCain, "Indian Adoption Proposal Offers New Hope," *Bellingham Herald* (Bellingham, WA), August 4, 1996, 12.

54. *Haaland v. Brackeen*, 599 US 255, docket no. 21-376, US Supreme Court, June 15, 2023.

55. Peter Read, *The Stolen Generations: The Removal of Aboriginal Children in New South Wales 1883–1969* (New South Wales Department of Aboriginal Affairs, 2006).

56. *Teresa Bernie v. Blue Cloud Abbey and Catholic Diocese of Sioux Falls*, 2012 SD 64, 821 N.W.2d 224, September 5, 2012.

57. Paula Peters, personal correspondence, April 3, 2024.

Epilogue: Forgetting and Remembering

1. Hentz, *Two Worlds*, 70.

2. Helen Hunt Jackson, *Ramona: A Story* (Boston, 1888 [1884]); John R. Byers, "The Indian Matter of Helen Hunt Jackson's *Ramona*: From Fact to Fiction," *American Indian Quarterly* 2, no. 4 (1975): 332, 345–346.

3. Ray, "Constructing a Discourse," 20.

4. Thomas Jefferson, *Notes on the State of Virginia: With an Appendix*, 9th American ed. (Boston: H. Sprague, 1802), 86.

5. "Slavery in Early Times," *Times-Picayune* (New Orleans, LA), September 13, 1892.

6. Lauber, *Indian Slavery in Colonial Times*.

7. Louis Pelzer, "Review of Indian Slavery in Colonial Times within the Present

Limits of the United States, by Almon Wheeler Lauber," *Mississippi Valley Historical Review* 1, no. 1 (1914): 123.

8. There were some sporadic exceptions, including Sanford Richard Winston, *Indian Slavery in the Carolina Region* (Association for the Study of Negro Life and History, 1934); Marcel Trudel, *L'esclavage au Canada français*, first published in 1960 but only translated into English in 2013; William Robert Snell, "Indian Slavery in Colonial South Carolina, 1671–1795" (PhD diss., University of Alabama, 1972), which remained unpublished; and Barbara Olexer, *Enslavement of the American Indian* (Library Research Associates, 1982).

9. "Indian Slavery," *Galveston Daily News*, March 5, 1911, 11.

10. "Last Indian Slave Dead," *Valdez Prospector* (Valdez, AK), January 10, 1916, 1.

11. "Last Indian Slave Dead," *Rock Rapids Review* (Rock Rapids, IA), August 10, 1916.

12. For another example, see "Alaska Notes," *Nome Daily Nugget* (Nome, AK), March 14, 1916, 2, which reported the death of eighty-year-old "King George," who was "one of the last living slaves of the Alaska Natives."

13. Jean M. O'Brien, *Firsting and Lasting: Writing Indians out of Existence in New England* (University of Minnesota Press, 2010).

14. William Evans Deahl, "A History of Buffalo Bill's Wild West Show, 1883–1913" (PhD diss., Southern Illinois University at Carbondale, 1974).

15. Laura Ingalls Wilder, *Little House on the Prairie* (Harper & Row, 1971), 134, 308–309.

16. Such sentiments have frequently been communicated to me during conversations with tribal collaborators and leaders.

17. "Federally Recognized American Indian Tribes and Alaska Native Entities," usa.gov.

18. "Three Million Acres of Land Returned to Tribes through Interior Department's Land Buy-Back Program for Tribal Nations," press release, US Department of the Interior, December 4, 2023.

19. For some of the primary websites, see Missing and Murdered Indigenous Women USA; "Missing and Murdered Indigenous Women (MMIW)," nativehope.org; "Missing and Murdered Indigenous People Crisis," US Department of the Interior (website). See also Leslie A. Hagen and Benjamin L. Whittemore, "Combatting Trafficking of Native Americans and Alaska Natives," *United States Attorneys' Bulletin* 65, no. 6 (November 2017): 149–167.

20. "Native Incarceration in the U.S.," Prison Policy Initiative website.

21. Megan Korchak, "Decolonization and Prison," in *Decolonization and Justice: An Introductory Overview*, SaskOER (website); Lindsay Whitehurst, "How to Tackle Crime in Indian Country? Empower Tribal Justice, Ex-Justice Department Official Says," Associated Press, April 14, 2024.

22. "About NAISA," Native American and Indigenous Studies Association, naisa.org.

23. Neal Morton, "Native Americans Turn to Charter Schools to Reclaim Their Kids' Education," *Hechinger Report*, May 20, 2024.

24. Morton, "Native Americans Turn to Charter Schools"; Jamesha Begay, "Former Native American Boarding School in Albuquerque Repurposed," KOB .com, May 19, 2022.

25. Dawn Dove, "Narragansett: Introduction," in *Dawnland Voices: An Anthology*

of Indigenous Writing from New England, ed. Siobhan Senier, 1st ed. (University of Nebraska Press, 2014), 496–497.

26. I'm grateful to Chickasaw-enrolled member Chase Bryer for informing me of this motto.

Author's Note

1. DuVal, *Native Nations*; Blackhawk, *Rediscovery of America*; Roxanne Dunbar-Ortiz, *An Indigenous Peoples' History of the United States* (Beacon Press, 2015); David Treuer, *The Heartbeat of Wounded Knee: Native America from 1890 to the Present*, 1st ed. (Riverhead Books, 2019); Hämäläinen, *Indigenous Continent*.

2. Sleeper-Smith et al., eds., *Why You Can't Teach United States History*.

3. Maggie Blackhawk, "Foreword: The Constitution of American Colonialism," *Harvard Law Review* 137, no. 1 (November 2023): 1–152; Smith, *Decolonizing Methodologies*.

INDEX

ABOUT THE AUTHOR

LINFORD D. FISHER is an associate professor of history at Brown University in Providence, Rhode Island. He received his doctorate from Harvard University in 2008, and after teaching for a year at Indiana University, South Bend, moved to Brown. He is the author of *The Indian Great Awakening: Religion and the Shaping of Native Cultures in Early America* (Oxford University Press, 2012), the coauthor of *Decoding Roger Williams: The Lost Essay of Rhode Island's Founding Father* (Baylor University Press, 2014), and the coeditor of *Reading Roger Williams: Rogue Puritans, Indigenous Nations, and the Founding of America—A Documentary History* (Pickwick, 2024). He has also published more than a dozen articles and chapters.

Fisher's work has received support from a wide variety of institutions, including the National Endowment for the Humanities, the American Council of Learned Societies, the Massachusetts Historical Society, the American Antiquarian Society, the Newberry Library, the John Carter Brown Library, and Brown University. Fisher is the principal investigator of *Stolen Relations: Recovering Stories of Indigenous Enslavement in the Americas* (stolenrelations.org), which is a community-centered, tribal-collaborative project that seeks to broaden our understanding of Indigenous experiences of settler colonialism and its legacies through the lens of slavery and servitude.

Fisher loves to run, hike, cook, play music, and travel. But above all, he relishes sailing and feels most alive when he is cruising the Narragansett Bay and the wider New England waters with his family. He lives with his wife, Jo, and their four children (when they are around) in Cranston, Rhode Island.